W9-CQI-174

Human Development

SECOND EDITION

DIANE E. PAPALIA
University of Wisconsin—Madison

SALLY WENDKOS OLDS

McGRAW-HILL BOOK COMPANY

New York | St. Louis | San Francisco | Auckland
Bogotá | Hamburg | Johannesburg | London | Madrid
Mexico | Montreal | New Delhi | Panama | Paris
São Paulo | Singapore | Sydney | Tokyo | Toronto

**HUMAN
DEVELOPMENT**

3 4 5 6 7 8 9 0 VHVH 8 9 8 7 6 5 4 3 2 1

See Acknowledgments on pages 650–651. Copyrights
included on this page by reference.

This book was set in Helvetica by Black Dot, Inc.
The editors were Janis M. Yates and James R. Belser;
the designer was Nicholas Krenitsky;
the production supervisor was Leroy A. Young.
Cover photograph by Larry Tamaccio.
The photo editor was Inge King.
Von Hoffmann Press, Inc., was printer and binder.

Library of Congress Cataloging in Publication Data

Papalia, Diane E
   Human development.

   Includes bibliographies and index.
   1. Developmental psychology. 2. Human biology.
   I. Olds, Sally Wendkos, joint author. II. Title.
   BF713.P35   1981   155   80-19429
   ISBN 0–07–048391–4

To our husbands,
Jonathan L. Finlay
and
David Mark Olds,
our loved and loving partners
in growth and development

CONTENTS

In the preface to the first edition of *Human Development* we spoke of change as a principle that governs all our lives. For as we said then, through every moment of every day, we change, we grow, we develop. The changes in this new edition of this book represent, we feel, growth and development in our thinking, so that we can more effectively present the story of human development from the moment of conception until that moment at the other end of the life cycle when death ends the continuing process.

The goal of this second edition is the same as the first: to emphasize the continuity of development throughout the life span and to understand the influences upon us from our genes, our families, the world we live in. We are still looking at the findings of scientific research and the theories of learned people. We are still applying these to our understanding of ourselves. And we are still asking the same basic questions: What influences have made us the way we are today? What factors are likely to bend us in the future? How much control do we have over our lives? How are we like other people? How are we different? What is normal? What is cause for concern?

We are also asking some new questions and coming up with some new answers. This is partly in response to important new research and important new theories. It is also responsive to those teachers and students who have shared with us their experiences in using the first edition. While we are delighted that almost all those we have heard from have found the book helpful, there is virtually nothing in this world that cannot be improved upon. So we have eagerly sought suggestions for reorganizing or re-presenting material in a way that will make it even more accessible. We want to invite you as the users of this second edition to communicate to us any such suggestions that you have, in anticipation of the continuing development of this book.

CHANGES IN THIS EDITION

You will see an expansion of our coverage of contemporary patterns of living, of working, of rearing children. You will find new discussions of friendship and its importance at every age level throughout life. You will find a greatly expanded analysis of current theories and research findings to help evaluate the different points of view presented here.

You will find three additional chapters in this edition. They allow us to add new material on infant intellectual development; on many aspects of life during middle age, including the much talked about midlife crisis; and on death and dying. This last topic is so rich in thought-provoking material—the ethical dilemmas revolving around the end of life, the new emphasis on dying with dignity, the changing attitudes toward death as people move through the life cycle—that we felt it was imperative to devote an entire chapter to it. This expanded coverage fits in with our firm belief that we continue to develop during our final days on earth. Throughout the book you will find other instances of new topics and new treatments of other topics.

One special feature of this edition, which we think you will enjoy reading as much as we enjoyed seeking them, are the diary excerpts scattered throughout the text. Finding these excerpts from the spoken and written words of people reflecting on their own lives and that of their children took some concerted detective work. When we saw how vividly they portray moments ranging from the highly dramatic to the day to day, we felt that they were worth digging for. We hope you do too.

With this new edition, then, we hope that you will understand yourself and those around you even better. We hope you will be informed and intrigued and inspired by the constantly changing process we are all part of: human development.

SUPPLEMENTARY AIDS

A *Study Guide* is available to aid the student in study and review. The guide contains chapter overviews, integrators, objectives, self-test questions, practice exercises, and vignettes.

A *Test File* containing in excess of 1500 items categorized both by type of question (factual or application) and by major topic being tested is available to all instructors who adopt *Human Development*. Some items have been validated.

An *Instructor's Manual* is also available to all instructors who adopt *Human Development*. The manual contains chapter overviews, key terms, objectives, topics for expansion and demonstration, backup readings, general resources, and a film guide.

ACKNOWLEDGMENTS

We especially wish to acknowledge those who reviewed the published first edition and the manuscript drafts of the second edition, whose evaluations and suggestions helped greatly in the preparation of this new edition. They are Harry J. Berman, Sangamon State University; Doris Capps, Atlantic Christian College; Don C. Charles, Iowa State University; Karen Dinsmore, University of Nebraska at Lincoln; Kenneth Gamble, Gannon College; Anne Godfrey, Case Western Reserve University; Rita Heberer, Belleville Area College; Kathleen Hulbert, University of Lowell; Chadwick Karr, Portland State University; Nancy King, Iowa Central Community College; Eleanor Levine, California State University at Hayward; Rick Mitchell, Hartford Community College; Sue Saxon, University of South Florida; Beverly Slichta, Trocaire College; Sister Mary Constance Stopper, Kent State University; and Douglas Uselding, University of South Dakota.

We are indebted as well to the many friends and colleagues who, through their work and their interest, helped us clarify our thinking about the course of human development. We appreciate the strong support we have had from our publisher and would like especially to recognize the help of Robert Weber and Janis M. Yates, our perceptive and understanding editors for the first and second editions, respectively; of James R. Belser, who shepherded both editions through their many phases of production; and of Brenda J. Gillette, whose consistently cheerful efforts smoothed out many of the bumps along the way to publication. Inge King's sensitivity to issues in human development made her a particularly valuable contributor to this edition, as attested by the high quality of the diary excerpts, quotations, and photographs that she found.

We owe a very special word of gratitude to Nancy Gordon, whose charming and loving record of Elizabeth's day-by-day development inspired us to incorporate such personal reflections throughout the text. Joan Gage's accounts of Christy's growth fit in beautifully with this concept.

We would also like to express special thanks to Stuart Green, M.D., M.R.C.P., Consultant in Developmental Pediatrics and Pediatric Neurology, Birmingham Children's Hospital, Birmingham, England, for his assistance on the chapters on prenatal development and infancy; to Norma M. Deull for her thoughtful review of the chapter on death; to Mary Dellmann, M.S., for her assistance in tracking down research; and to Jane A. Weier for her aid with the bibliography and the typing.

Diane E. Papalia
Sally Wendkos Olds

Introduction

IN THIS CHAPTER
YOU WILL LEARN ABOUT

Why the study of human development is important, and how it has changed throughout history

The main types, periods, principles, models, and theories of human development

How heredity and environment interact to affect human development, and how we can study their relative effects

The methods available for studying people—and some ethical considerations that must be applied in using them

INTRODUCTION

1

ISSUES AND THEORIES

OF

HUMAN DEVELOPMENT

What made you the kind of child you were—and the kind of adult you are now? What made your parents, your friends, your teachers, the leaders of governments around the world the way they are? What factors will influence how your children will turn out? What influences one person to become a mass murderer, and another to become a humanitarian? What made you turn out differently from your next-door neighbors—and even from your own brothers and sisters? The answers to these questions are what we hope to find by studying human development throughout the life span.

By examining how people develop, from the moment of conception throughout old age, we learn more about ourselves and about our fellow inhabitants on this planet. Only by knowing who we are and how we became this way can we hope to create a better world. Only by learning how people respond to influences around them can we meet our own and others' needs, so that more people will be better equipped to fulfill their individual potential and to help society fulfill its potential.

WHAT IS DEVELOPMENT AND WHY SHOULD WE STUDY IT?

The study of *human development* focuses on the *quantitative* and *qualitative* ways people change over time. *Quantitative change* is fairly straightforward and relatively easy to measure. A person's growth in height and weight is a quantitative change. So are the expansion of vocabulary, the increase in physical skills, the number of relationships with other people, and so forth. The study of *qualitative change* is more complex, involving "leaps" in functioning—those changes in kind that distinguish a talking child from a nonverbal baby or a self-absorbed adolescent from a mature

adult. These changes trace the growth of intelligence, creativity, sociability, and morality. But even these leaps result from a series of small steps. No one wakes up on his or her twenty-first birthday suddenly thinking and acting vastly differently from the day before. Quantitatively and qualitatively, human development is a continuous, irreversible, and complex process.

Furthermore, development does not stop at adolescence or young adulthood. It continues throughout life, continually influenced by characteristics we were born with and by those we acquire through our experiences. As we shall see, even very old people continue to develop and often experience personality growth. We will even look at the experience of dying itself as a final attempt to resolve one's identity crisis and come to terms with oneself—in short, to develop.

The modern science of human development is concerned most of all with behavioral changes—things we can see. We emphasize aspects of change that are readily observable in an effort to apply rigorous scientific criteria to our study of the developing individual. Thus, we measure and chart people's physical growth. We follow their progress in emotional expression. We study the development of language from an infant's babbling to more mature, grammatically correct speech.

The field of human development has developed itself, as a scientific discipline. Originally, its focus was on the recording of observable behavior, from which age norms for growth and development could be derived. Today, developmentalists try to explain *why* certain behaviors occur. In keeping with the tradition of scientific investigation, the next step is the prediction of behavior—a challenging and complex task.

What are the practical implications in the study of human development? There are many. By learning about the usual course of development, we can look at the different factors in an individual's life and attempt to *predict* future behavior. If our predictions hint at problems in the future, we can often try to *modify* development, by offering some type of training or therapy.

For example, if Susie seems backward in development, her parents may either be reassured that she is normal, or they may be advised how to help her overcome her deficiencies. If Billy is a perpetual truant, his parents may receive sound psychological advice that enables them to divert him from a path that looks certain to lead to trouble. If educators understand how children of different ages learn best, they can plan better classroom programs.

Understanding adult development and the predictable crises of adulthood helps professionals and lay persons alike to be prepared for life's situations: the mother returning to the world of work when her youngest child marches off to kindergarten, the 50-year-old man who realizes he will never be president, the person about to retire, the widow or widower, the dying patient.

This book is about all people, and it is also about each person. In our study of development we are interested in patterns that govern the development of all individuals of the species *Homo sapiens*. But since each member of the species is unique, we want to know what factors make one person turn out differently from another.

THE HISTORY OF THE STUDY OF HUMAN DEVELOPMENT

The study of human development focused first on children, then on adults, and finally on the entire life span.

THE STUDY OF CHILDREN

How did child development pass from something that just happened (almost unnoticed by anyone except children's mothers) into an academic discipline that grants Ph.D.s, spends millions of dollars on research projects, and affects the rearing of billions of children? Child development is a study that examines how the whole child changes over

time. It is concerned with children's physical, intellectual, emotional, and social growth. In the history of science, it is a child itself.

People have long held various ideas about what children are like and how they should be raised to cause the least amount of trouble to their parents and to society, turning out to be decent, contributing adults. But childhood as we know it and are interested in it is a very recent concept. For centuries children were considered as nothing more than smaller, weaker, dumber versions of adults (Looft, 1971).

Adults did not see children as being qualitatively different from themselves, or as having any special needs, or as making any significant contributions to their own development (Aries, 1962). Even artists seemed unable to see that children *looked* different from adults with different proportions and different facial features. Except for the ancient Greeks, early painters and sculptors portrayed children as shrunken adults. Not until the thirteenth century did artists again show children who actually looked like children. And not until the seventeenth century did the concept of childhood itself become exalted in art as well as in life. Around this time, parents began to notice the "sweet, simple, and amusing" nature of children. They began to dress them differently, instead of just cutting adult-styled garments in small sizes, and they confessed to the joys they received from playing with their children.

The first books of advice for parents had begun to appear during the sixteenth century, most of them written by physicians. These books were distinguished by their almost complete lack of reliance on scientific truth and their almost total dependency on the biases, prejudices, and pet theories of the individual authors, who dispensed such advice to mothers as: not to nurse their babies

Until the seventeenth century, children were viewed as miniature adults. (The Bettmann Archive, Inc.)

right after feeling anger, lest their milk prove fatal; to begin toilet training their infants at the age of three weeks; and to bind their babies' arms for several months after birth to prevent thumbsucking (Ryerson, 1961).

During the eighteenth century, a combination of scientific, religious, economic, and social trends formed the perfect soil for the birth of the new study of child development. Scientists had unraveled the basic mysteries of conception and were now embroiled in the "nature versus nurture" argument about the relative importance of heredity and environment, which we'll discuss later in this chapter. The discovery of germs had opened up a whole new vista to the populace, who now realized that they could stave off the tides of plagues and fevers which had been snatching their children from them at tender ages. Parents could now dare to love and treasure their children.

The rise of Protestantism emphasized self-reliance, independence, and the respon-sibility of each individual. Adults began to feel more responsible for the way children turned out, instead of just accepting misfortune or misbehavior as something brought by fate. With the Industrial Revolution, the family changed from an extended, clanlike group to the nuclear family. In the nuclear family, children are more visible, their individual personalities show up more, and their parents' concentration upon them is more intense.

Another current in this stream was the tendency to provide more education for children. They now had to be kept busy and occupied in school for longer periods of time, and so their teachers needed more understanding of what children were all about. The spirit of democracy was filtering into the household, as parents began to feel uncomfortable with the old autocratic attitudes and sought to bring children up better by understanding them better. Finally, the new science of psychology, the study of human behavior, led people to feel they could better understand themselves by learning what made some children turn out differently from others.

By the nineteenth century, all these currents had come together, and people of science were devising all manner of ways to study children. (See "Methods for Studying People," later in this chapter.)

Historically, children were people who one day became adults. The transitional period of adolescence was not considered as a stage in human development until the twentieth century. Instead, children went through puberty and immediately entered some sort of apprenticeship in the adult world. In 1904, G. Stanley Hall, a pioneer in the child study movement and the first psychologist to formulate a theory of adolescence, published his two-volume work, *Adolescence*. While the book was very popular, it had very little scientific basis. Instead, it served as a forum for Hall's theories, which did stimulate thinking about this period of life. Hall, for example, believed that it was not until adolescence that one could be molded by society.

THE STUDY OF ADULTS

The nineteenth century also ushered in an interest in studying people at the other end of the life span, old age. The history of the study of aging is usually said to begin with the publication in 1835 of a book by Quetelet, a French mathematician with an interest in sociology and psychology, who was particularly interested in the relationship of age to creativity. Influenced by Quetelet, Sir Francis Galton, an English scientist who was a cousin of Charles Darwin, began to investigate individual differences in relation to age and in 1883 published his book, *Inquiries into Human Faculty and Its Development*.

Almost half a century later in the United States, G. Stanley Hall achieved another first. He is generally credited with pioneering the study of the psychology of aging in this country. In 1922 when Hall himself was 78, he published his book, *Senescence: The Last Half of Life*. During these years right after World War I, the scientific study of old people

began. The first major research unit devoted to the study of aging was opened at Stanford University in 1928.

It was not for another generation, though, after World War II, that the study of aging really blossomed. By 1946, a large-scale research unit had been established by the federal government's National Institutes of Health, and specialized organizations and journals were promoting and reporting the newest findings. The initial emphasis was primarily on intelligence, reaction time, ability, and achievement in old age. Later researchers delved into the emotional aspects of growing old.

During most of this time, however, practically no one was showing any appreciation for the continuity of the entire human life span. While researchers were coming up with fascinating blocks of information about children and about the elderly, they were ignoring the vital adult years between adolescence and old age.

LIFE SPAN STUDIES

Today, a growing group of psychologists recognize that human development is an ongoing process that continues throughout life. Each portion of a person's life span is influenced by earlier years, and each affects the years that follow. As these researchers probe the changes that a human being undergoes "from womb to tomb," they describe and explain various age-related behavioral changes.

Life span studies originally grew out of programs that had been designed to follow selected groups of children over a period of years. As these children grew up, the researchers who had been studying them were interested in following them into adulthood. Life span development as a subject for research has since expanded backward in time to the womb and forward to old age. So far, there have been no studies of the *entire* life span, but only of certain segments.

Several major long-term studies have yielded a great deal of information about children as they mature. The Stanford Studies of Gifted Children (begun in 1921 under the direction of Lewis Terman) continue to focus upon the development of people who were identified as unusually intelligent children. The Berkeley Growth Study (begun in 1928) and the Oakland Growth Study (begun in 1932) have provided important information about physical, intellectual, and motor skill development. Then, the Fels Research Institute Study (begun in 1929) has investigated intellectual and personality functioning and parent-child interaction.

Long-term studies focusing on adults were undertaken a little later. Some of the best known of these are the Grant Study of Adult Development, which in 1938 began to follow 18-year-old Harvard University students and has since taken them into middle age; the studies of middle-aged people by Bernice Neugarten and her associates at the University of Chicago, which began in the mid-1950s; and the studies at Yale University by Daniel Levinson and his colleagues, who interviewed men in their middle years and reconstructed their young adult development.

VARIOUS ASPECTS OF DEVELOPMENT

Human development is complex, for growth and change occur in different facets of the self. To simplify the discussion in this book, we talk separately about physical, intellectual, and personality development. But these divisions are often arbitrary and rarely neat, since each type of development affects development in the other spheres.

The physical self, for example, helps to determine both personality and intellect. If a girl is in good health, of normal physical stature, and attractive in appearance by the standards of her culture, her parents and other significant persons in her life will react to her in certain ways right from birth. The degree to which she is accepted—initially, perhaps because of her physical characteristics—helps to determine the level of her self-confidence and self-esteem. If her parents are disappointed in her looks or in the slowness of her physical development, their feelings may affect her psyche adversely. As she grows taller and stronger, as she develops the skills that will enable her to master her environment, she will develop good feelings about herself, even though they may be tempered to some degree by the frustrations she experiences when on the threshold of some new ability. Thus, the combination of her physical self and capabilities, plus the way others react to them, has strong effects on her personality. Abnormal physical development has many emotional consequences.

The physical person also affects the intellectual person, since good physical health is often important for normal intellectual development. Malnutrition can impede brain development, and certain physical disabilities—like Down's syndrome ("mongolism")—impede mental processes as much as or more than they affect physical functioning. If physical health is so poor that lengthy hospitalization is required, it may affect intellectual and personality development. We shall see that among the elderly, those who have been institutionalized—a step often taken because of poor physical health—do more poorly on intellectual measures than do those who live in the community. Furthermore, shortly before people die, they often experience personality disorganization and intellectual decline.

Intellectual capabilities are closely related to both the motor and the emotional aspects of being. In infancy, virtually the only way to measure intelligence is through a

Intellectual capabilities are closely related to both the motor and the emotional aspects of being. (Erika Stone/Peter Arnold, Inc.)

baby's motor development. If a little boy holds his head up, reaches for a toy, and pulls himself to a sitting position at certain ages, he probably is normal both mentally and physically. Slowness in these activities is often the first sign of mental retardation.

The social and emotional aspects of personality affect both the physical and the intellectual aspects of functioning. Emotional deprivation in infancy can have devastating effects on a child's mental and motor development, as well as on personality.

Throughout our discussion of the ways people develop, we will consider physical, intellectual, and personality development separately. In our discussion of personality, we will group together a variety of aspects involving *interpersonal interaction*: Our emotions affect our personalities, which in turn affect the way we act socially. Thus, interpersonal aspects of development tell us a great deal about how and why a certain individual reacts a certain way in certain situations involving certain other people. But while we view people as three beings for convenience and ease of discussion, we always have to

bear in mind that these aspects are inseparable in living people. We do not "know" anyone until we understand her or him in all spheres of functioning.

PERIODS OF THE HUMAN LIFE SPAN

This book is organized along chronological lines, rather than following a topical approach. A topically organized book would discuss the various aspects of development separately. For example, it would present physical development throughout the entire life span, followed by intellectual development, social development, sexual development, and so forth. A chronologically organized discussion looks at the total human being and discusses the various aspects of development that take place at different times in the person's life. Both these methods of organization are valid, although each has its inadequacies. Discussing growth chronologically, for example, means that we have to divide the life cycle into different time periods, or levels of development.

For this discussion, we have divided human beings into the following chronological groups: the prenatal period (from the moment of conception to the moment of birth); infancy and toddlerhood (birth to 3 years); early childhood (ages 3 to 6); middle childhood (6 to 12); adolescence (12 to 18); young adulthood (18 to 40); midlife (40 to 65); and late adulthood (65 and over). All these divisions are somewhat arbitrary, especially in adulthood. With fewer specific physical criteria to signal change from one period to another (such as puberty, for example), and with a bewildering array of social criteria (rather than, say, the simple one of school admission), it is especially difficult to assign definite ages. So we need to remember that all these age ranges are somewhat subjective, that all ages for the beginning and end of a period are only approximate, and that individual people's lives are not marked off so precisely. In our discussions of stage theories such as those of Freud, Erikson, and Piaget, we use the theorists' own age ranges, and the same reservations apply to them.

People are often at one level in one area of development and at another level in another area. For example, a 10-year-old girl may have begun to menstruate—an activity that marks her physical transition from childhood to puberty—before she has outgrown many of her childish feelings and thoughts. Or a 45-year-old man who took several years to find his career direction, who married in his thirties, and who became a father in his forties may—in many important psychological ways—be in the young adulthood period; on the other hand, his 45-year-old neighbor who settled early on a professional direction and into family life may already be a grandfather and may act and feel more like a middle-aged man.

Furthermore, individual differences among people are so great that they enter and leave these age periods at different times of life. Annie, at age 2, may have achieved milestones of physical development that Brian will not reach for another year. Yet Brian may be more advanced socially or intellectually. If Brian spends most of his days with loving, nurturant, stimulating parents and little time with children his own age, he is likely to have a fluent command of language, but little idea of how to approach and play with other children.

Most adults have strong feelings about the time in life when certain activities are considered acceptable (Neugarten, Moore, & Lowe, 1965). People are aware of their own timing and are quick to describe themselves as "early," "late," or "on time" regarding the time they married, settled on a career, had children, or retired from work. While people actually do all these things in response to many different life circumstances, they have a sense of the "best" time for doing them.

These ideal norms for different kinds of behavior vary among different groups of people. The entire life cycle is speeded up for working-class people, who tend to finish their education earlier than middle-class people, to take their first jobs sooner, to marry younger, to have children earlier, to reach the peaks of their career earlier, and to become grandparents earlier (Neugarten, 1968). The unskilled worker considers a man mature and in the prime of life at age 35, middle-aged at 40, and old at 60; whereas the upper-middle-class business executive or professional person considers a man to be in the prime of life at 40, middle-aged at 50, and old at 70 (Neugarten, 1968). These differences are related to financial needs, which make it imperative for working-class people to get paying jobs earlier in life. People from more affluent backgrounds can pursue their educations for a longer time, can use young adulthood to explore options, and can delay becoming financially independent and beginning a family. These socioeconomic differences underscore the importance of not pigeonholing people in rigid age strata, but rather trying to

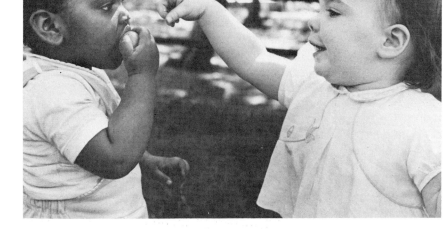

Although people go through developmental stages in the same sequence, there are wide ranges in normal development, with a great deal of individual variation. (© Ed Lettau/Photo Researchers, Inc.)

understand development within the context of total life experiences.

DEVELOPMENTAL PRINCIPLES

Certain principles apply to all developmental change and can guide us in interpreting raw information. As you study the various types of development that occur at different times in human beings, keep the following principles in mind.

INDIVIDUAL DIFFERENCES IN DEVELOPMENT

Although people go through developmental stages in the same sequence and according to the same general chronology, we shall see how wide ranges in normal development allow for a great deal of individual difference. Throughout this book we talk about *average* ages for the occurrence of certain behaviors: the first smile, the first word, the first step. In all cases, these ages are *only* averages. The normal range of behavior includes a wide spectrum of individual differences—with re-

spect to measures of height and weight, walking and talking, understanding various ideas, and so forth. All the average ages we give should be regarded as flexible. Only when someone's deviation from these norms is extreme is there cause for considering her or him exceptionally advanced or retarded. The important point to remember is that virtually all people go through the same general sequence of events, even though the timing varies greatly from person to person.

There is an especially wide range of individual differences among elderly people. Some feel, act, and consider themselves old at 60; others, not till 80 or even later. Some remain active, replacing each lost role (as spouse, parent, employed person) with a new one (as friend, foster grandparent, volunteer worker). Others prefer to disengage from people and events around them and lead a more solitary, inwardly turned life. As you read the later sections of this book, it will be clear that chronological age alone really tells us very little about people, especially as they grow older. It is important to remember that older people are as diverse in their personalities as younger ones.

CRITICAL PERIODS
IN DEVELOPMENT

If a woman undergoes irradiation, ingests certain drugs, or contracts certain diseases at specific times during the first three months of pregnancy, her unborn baby may show specific effects. The amount and kind of damage to the fetus will vary according to the particular insult and its timing. Pregnant mice that have received x-rays 7 or 8 days after conception are likely to have pups with brain hernia, whereas those irradiated 9½ days after conception are more likely to bear pups with spina bifida, a disease of the nervous system (Russell & Russell, 1952). Similar mechanisms operate in human beings.

A *critical period* in development is a period of time when a given event will have its greatest impact. The same event—such as radiation—would not have as great an influence if it took place at a different time in development. This concept of critical periods has been incorporated into a number of theories regarding various aspects of human behavior, including intelligence and emotional attachment between babies and their mothers.

Psychoanalysts, especially, have embraced the concept of critical periods. As we shall see, Freud maintained that certain experiences which a baby or young child undergoes could set that individual's personality for life. Erikson proposed eight ages in life, each of which constitutes a critical period for social and emotional development.

Although some of the supporting evidence for critical periods of development is undeniable (such as that involving the physical development of a fetus), some other theories, while persuasive, still need to be followed further, to be backed up by more research.

DEVELOPMENT IS ORDERLY,
NOT RANDOM

There is nothing haphazard about human development. It follows a well-defined path.

Development always proceeds from the simple to the complex. In the development of language, babies go from crying to babbling, then to words, and finally to more and more complicated sentences.

Development proceeds from the general to the specific. Emotions begin as an overall state of excitement in a newborn babe and gradually differentiate into a wide repertoire of feelings that include love, hate, fear, anger, jealousy, and so forth.

Physical development follows the rules of cephalocaudal *(head-to-toe) development*, by which the upper parts of the body develop earlier than the lower, and *proximodistal* (near-to-far) *development*, by which the central parts of the body develop before the extremities.

Cognitive development (the development of logical thought processes) *proceeds along orderly lines.* Piaget describes the levels of human thought as developing through sensorimotor, preoperational, concrete operational, and formal stages, all of which will be explained later on.

Although the precise timing of all these facets of development varies for each person, their sequence is the same.

DIFFERENT TYPES OF
DEVELOPMENT ARE IMPORTANT
AT DIFFERENT TIMES

Motor and physical development are most rapid in infancy. Language develops most quickly during the preschool years. The development of logical thinking and of sociability speeds up during the elementary school years. The reproductive system develops dramatically in adolescence. The ability to form and sustain intimate relationships (such as spouse or parent) develops in young adulthood. The ability to be introspective and evaluate one's life is particularly relevant in middle age, as is the acceptance of mortality in old age. During any stage, people seem to concentrate intensely on those facets of development that are currently emerging. Earlier abilities may even seem to regress.

MODELS AND THEORIES OF HUMAN DEVELOPMENT

What is the basic nature of human beings? Are we active or passive as we live out our time upon this earth? Do we control our own destiny—or are we simply vessels that react to the stimuli in the world around us? Different philosophers have seen us through different prisms, and their concepts of our fundamental nature have given rise to different explanations, or theories, of why we behave as we do. Each of the following models differs in its view of the nature of people, its assumptions about developmental phenomena, its methods of inquiry, and its explanations of development (Langer, 1969; Thomas, 1979).

Each of the theories mentioned here has its dedicated supporters and its equally impassioned critics. While some developmentalists align themselves strongly with a single body of thought, most thoughtful students of human development can find in each of them enough truth to explain a part of people's behavior over time, without feeling that any one of them has the entire explanation. In a brief overview like this, we cannot, of course, analyze each of the theories we are presenting. We will, though, point out some of the strengths and weaknesses of each. In addition, these theories and the people associated with them will be explained and discussed more fully in pertinent places throughout the book.

THE MECHANISTIC PERSPECTIVE

This view of humanity, also called the *mechanical mirror model*, equates people with machines; it sees us as reacting, rather than initiating. We are what our environments make of us. Thus, if we can break down all the components of a particular environment, we can predict how a person will react.

Mechanistic theorists see change as quantitative and development as continuous. Psychological research spurred by this viewpoint attempts to identify and isolate all the factors in the environment that make certain individuals behave in certain ways. It focuses on how early experiences affect later behavior. It tries to understand the effects of experience by breaking down complex stimuli and complex behaviors into simpler elements. This view is held by social learning theorists and behaviorists.

Behaviorists believe that human beings learn about the world the same way that lower animals do, by reacting to the rewards and punishments of their environments. According to these theorists, conditioning is the basic mechanism determining human behavior. The two kinds of conditioning are *classical*, also known as *respondent*, and *operant*, also called *instrumental*. In classical conditioning, which was first demonstrated by *Ivan Pavlov*, a previously neutral stimulus comes to elicit a response not ordinarily associated with it. Pavlov, a Russian physiologist, taught dogs to salivate upon hearing a bell by offering them food right after the bell sounded. Soon the bell (the neutral stimulus) was able to induce salivation, even without the appearance of food. In operant conditioning, such as that shown by *B. F. Skinner*, a system of rewards and punishments shapes a response. New responses are acquired in this way. Skinner, an American behaviorist, taught pigeons to tell different colored bars apart by rewarding them with food when they pressed the right bar.

Behaviorism emphasizes the role of the environment in producing behavior. Since it sees all change as alteration in the *quantity* of behavior, it denies the possibility of *qualitative* change. It is not a true developmental theory, since it applies the same basic learning laws to explain behavior at all ages. It is, however, a powerful tool for enhancing development along certain lines and has been useful in designing behavior modification programs and programmed learning. By applying behaviorist principles, parents and teachers can shape children's behavior by rewarding the actions they consider desirable and by punishing or ignoring the undesirable ones.

John B. Watson was the first behaviorist to apply stimulus-response theories of learning. We will read in Chapter 4 about the way he conditioned "Little Albert" to fear furry objects.

Social learning theorists such as Jerome Kagan and Albert Bandura share the mechanistic perspective of behaviorists, but disagree that all behavior is reducible to simple principles of conditioning and reinforcement. These theorists maintain that children learn most, if not all, of their behavior by imitating models, like their parents. Children's identification with their parents is the most important element in the way they learn a language, deal with aggression, and develop a sense of morality.

Social learning theory is also clearly defined, has also generated a great deal of research, and has also had many practical applications for child rearing. Since social learning researchers study children rather than rats or pigeons, their conclusions do have a more direct applicability to human behavior. Yet social learning theory is incomplete because of its lack of attention to hereditary influences and to what children are like in various stages of their development. Furthermore, psychoanalysts charge that a major weakness is the theory's failure to consider any underlying problems that cause children to engage in undesirable behaviors, and maintain that eliminating one (such as

stealing) by punishing it will result in the substitution of some other kind of negative behavior (like bed-wetting), leaving the basic problem unresolved.

THE ORGANISMIC PERSPECTIVE

In direct contrast to the mechanistic model, this theory, which is also called the *organic lamp model*, sees people as active organisms who, by their own actions, set in motion their own development. They initiate acts. Change is an inherent part of life. It is internal rather than external. The whole of a human being's behavior is greater than the sum of the parts that go to make it up. Since the whole is greater than the sum of its parts, we cannot break behavior down into separate elements to predict cause-and-effect relationships.

Organicists are more interested in process than in product—in how an individual comes to believe certain things and to act in certain ways, rather than in specifics of the person's thinking or behavior. They are more interested in qualitative change than in quantitative—in the leaps from one stage of development to another. They see life experiences not as the basic cause of development but as factors that can make it proceed more quickly or more slowly. They often describe development as occurring in a set sequence of qualitatively different stages, as discontinuous.

Jean Piaget is the most prominent advocate of the organismic world view. Much of what we know about the way children learn is due to the creative inquiry of this Swiss psychologist. He applied his broad knowledge of biology, philosophy, logic, and psychology to meticulous observations of children, and constructed complex theories about *cognitive*, or knowledge-acquiring, development.

Piaget explains many aspects of children's thought and behavior by considering them as going through definite stages. Each stage represents a qualitative change from one type of thought or behavior to another. Such stage theories have certain characteristic points to make: All individuals go through the same stages in the same order, even though the actual timing will vary from one person to another, making any age demarcation only approximate; each stage builds on the one that went before and constructs the foundation for the one that comes next; and each stage has many facets to it.

According to Piaget, at each stage of development, an individual's personal representation of the world—or, to use the Piagetian term, his or her *schema*—will become more complex, more abstract, and more realistic. This cognitive growth results from a two-step process of taking in new information about the world (*assimilation*) and changing one's ideas to include this new knowledge (*accommodation*). Thus, human cognitive development progresses through four major stages, each of which is characterized by a unique view of the world that results from an interaction between maturation and environment. Since he defines intelligent behavior as the ability to adapt, even preverbal behavior is intelligent. In each stage the organization and structure of a child's thinking differ qualitatively, and the often imperceptible step between stages involves a leap forward in the child's ability to handle new concepts.

The sequence of stages in cognitive development never varies; nor is any stage skipped, since each one rounds out the preceding stage and lays the groundwork for the next. As with all development, individuals reach each stage according to their own unique timetable. For this reason, and also because there is considerable overlapping between the stages and retention of some characteristics from preceding stages in those that follow, all age norms are approximate.

Piaget's four major stages of cognitive development are:

Sensorimotor (birth to 2 years): The infant changes from a creature who responds primarily through reflexes to one who can organize his or her activities in relation to the environment.

Preoperational (2 to 7 years): The child begins to use symbols such as words, imitates the behavior of others, and remains illogical in his or her thought processes, because he or she is highly egocentric.

Concrete operations (7 to 11 years): The child is beginning to understand and use concepts that help him or her deal with the immediate environment.

Formal operations (12 to 15 years through adulthood): The individual can now think in abstract terms and deal with hypothetical situations.

These stages are discussed in detail throughout the chapters dealing with the developing child.

After decades of studying and writing about cognitive development from birth through adolescence, Piaget has become widely recognized as the world's leading expert on how children think. He has put his brilliantly creative mind to work studying children's minds and has come up with an elaborately thought-out scheme of intellectual growth. He has opened the door to a novel way of evaluating the development of logical thinking; he has inspired more research than has any other theorist in the last decade; and he has stimulated many practical innovations in the education of young children.

Yet Piaget is faulted on several counts by thoughtful critics. He speaks primarily of the "average" child's abilities and takes little notice of such influences as education and culture as they affect performance. He says little about emotional and personality development, except as these aspects are related to cognitive growth. He has also been criticized because so many of his ideas emerged from his highly personal observations of his own three children and from his own idiosyncratic handling of the clinical method.

Inspired by Piaget, psychologist *Lawrence Kohlberg* developed a stage theory of children's moral development. Children go from a *premoral* stage, when they observe the standards of others only to reap rewards or to avoid punishment; through a *conventional* stage, when they operate from the standards of others and think about what they can do so someone else will consider them "good"; to the highest level of moral reasoning, the *postconventional* one of self-accepted moral principles, in which people act according to their own internal standards of right and wrong.

Kohlberg's theory is the most comprehensive and the most exciting effort to build on Piaget's concept that moral development is related to cognitive development and that it proceeds in a definite sequential pattern. By investigating children's reasons for their choices, Kohlberg has uncovered a great deal about the thinking that underlies moral judgment. He has also spurred research by others and inspired many classroom programs on morality.

Kohlberg's scheme has several limitations. It concerns itself only with moral thinking, as opposed to behavior, leading to the contradiction that a person may think one way about a moral issue but behave completely opposite. Furthermore, Kohlberg's view of moral judgment is narrow in the sense that it is based only on the development of a sense of justice, while it omits other aspects of morality such as compassion and integrity. Other problems revolve around the difficulty in determining which stage an individual is in. Since scoring is subjective, despite the existence of supposedly standardized scales, it is difficult for other researchers to confirm Kohlberg's findings. Another problem has been the occasional regression of an individual to a lower level of moral reasoning, a step that negates the stage principle of development as an invariable sequence from lower to higher levels of moral thought.

THE PSYCHOANALYTIC PERSPECTIVE

The view of people first developed by *Sigmund Freud*, the Viennese physician who originated psychoanalysis, does not fit neatly into either of the above models. It holds that people are neither active nor passive but always in flux between the two states, always in conflict between their natural instincts and the constraints imposed upon them by society. The nature of these conflicts depends upon the stage of development that a person is in at any one time.

To the psychoanalysts, a child is a reactive organism whose development proceeds through stages.

In Freudian thought the human organism goes through several different stages of psychosexual development (oral, anal, and genital) named for those parts of the body that are primary sources of gratification in each phase.

The order of the shifts of instinctual energy from one body zone to another is always the same, but the level of a child's maturation determines when the shifts will take place, as follows:

Oral stage (birth to 12–18 months[1]): The child receives gratification through the mouth; sucking is important.

Anal stage (12–18 months to 3 years): The child receives gratification at the anus, primarily in defecation; toilet training is important.

Phallic stage (3 to 5–6 years): Gratification is through genital stimulation, and the Oedipus/Electra complexes are critical.

Latency stage (5–6 years to puberty): The child is sexually quiescent, at the resolution of the Oedipus and Electra complexes.

[1]Here, too, ages are only approximate.

Genital stage (from puberty on): The hormonal changes in the body give rise to mature adult sexuality. Sexual urges reawaken, to be directed toward heterosexual relations with people outside the family.

The experiences during these stages determine adjustment patterns and personality traits people will have as adults. Individuals may be *fixated* at a particular stage if their needs are not met or if they are overindulged. *Fixation* implies an immature attachment that remains in a neurotic way and interferes with normal development. Freud is vague about how fixation occurs; he, too, could only theorize about what happens in a baby's mind.

Freud also conceptualized the human personality as being made up of three aspects: the id, the ego, and the superego. The *id* is the unconscious source of motives and desires which operates on the "pleasure principle"; it strives for immediate gratification. The *ego*, which represents reason or common sense, mediates between the id and, eventually, the superego. The ego develops when gratification is delayed; it operates on the "reality principle" and seeks an acceptable way to obtain gratification. The *superego*, or conscience, incorporates the morals of society, largely through identification with the parent of the same sex.

The id is present at birth. Infants are egocentric in that they do not differentiate themselves from the outside world. All is there for gratification, and only when it is delayed (as when they have to wait for food), do they develop their ego and begin to differentiate themselves from the surroundings. Thus the ego develops soon after birth. The superego does not develop until the age of 4 or 5.

Freud's original and creative thinking has made immense contributions to our beliefs about children and adults, and has had a major impact on the child-rearing practices of the Western world. He made us aware of infantile sexuality, the nature of our unconscious thoughts and emotions, our defense mechanisms, the significance of dreams, the importance of parent-child relationships in the early years and the ambivalence in those relationships, and many other aspects of emotional functioning.

Yet in many ways Freud's theory grew out of his own place in history and in society. For example, much of his theory seems patronizing or demeaning toward women, no doubt because of its roots in the social system of a Victorian culture convinced of the superiority of the male. Also, the source of the data, on which Freud based his theories about normal development, was not a population of average children, but a highly selective clientele of upper-middle-class neurotic adults in therapy. His concentration on the resolution of psychosexual conflict as the key to healthy development seems too narrow, and the subjective way in which he enunciated his theories has made them resistant to being tested with research studies.

Erik H. Erikson, a psychoanalyst who extended the Freudian concept of ego, is interested in society's influence on the developing personality. Erikson outlined eight stages of psychosocial development, each of which depends upon the successful revolution of a turning point, or crisis. In the above list of Erikson's eight crises, the approximate ages given represent the sensitive period for the development of the characteristics involved.

In the psychoanalytic world view, the child undergoes a different major conflict at each stage. The way each stage is or is *not* resolved influences the individual's ultimate personality development.

Erikson's theory gives credit to social and cultural influences on development, whereas Freud's focuses on biological and maturational factors. Another strength of Erikson's theory is that it covers the entire life span, while Freud's stops at adolescence. Erikson, how-

TABLE 1-1
Erikson's Eight
Stages of
Development

CRISIS	AGE	IMPORTANT EVENT
Basic trust vs. basic mistrust	Birth to 12-18 months	Feeding
Autonomy vs. shame and doubt	18 months to 3 years	Toileting
Initiative vs. guilt	3 to 6 years	Locomoting
Industry vs. inferiority	6 to 12 years	School
Identity vs. role confusion	Adolescence	Peer relationship
Intimacy vs. isolation	Young adult	Love relationship
Generativity vs. stagnation	Maturity	Parenting and creating
Ego integrity vs. despair	Old age	Reflecting on and accepting one's life

ever, has also been criticized for an antifemale bias that emerges from his failure to take into account the social and cultural factors that influence the attitudes and behaviors of the sexes. Furthermore, some of his terms are difficult to assess objectively as the basis for follow-up research.

THE HUMANISTIC PERSPECTIVE

In 1962 a group of psychologists founded the Association of Humanistic Psychology as a reaction against what they considered the mechanistic and essentially negative beliefs underlying behaviorist and psychoanalytic theories. The humanists, like the organicists, see people as having within them the ability to take charge of their lives and to foster their own development. Furthermore, these theorists emphasize the individual's abilities to do this in healthy, positive ways through the distinctively human qualities of choice, creativity, valuation, and self-realization. This theory stems from a belief that basic human nature is either neutral or good, and that any bad characteristics are the result of damage that has been inflicted on the developing self.

Humanism, the philosophy behind humanistic psychology, presents a less developmental perspective than the organismic and psychoanalytic views, since its proponents do not clearly distinguish stages of the life span, but make a broad distinction only between the periods before and after adolescence. However, humanism's two principal leaders. Abraham Maslow and Charlotte Bühler, do talk about sequential stages in the development of the individual. In that sense, the theory does describe the psychological growth of the person.

Abraham Maslow (1954) identified a hierarchy of needs which motivate human behavior. When a person has fulfilled the most elemental needs, she or he strives to meet those on the next level, and so forth, until the highest order of needs is reached. The person who fulfills the loftiest needs is Maslow's ideal, the "self-actualized person," an achievement attained by possibly 1 percent of the population (Thomas, 1979).

In ascending order, these needs are:

1 *Physiological:* for air, food, drink, and rest, to achieve balance within the body

2 *Safety:* for security; stability; and freedom from fear, anxiety, and chaos, achieved with the help of a structure made up of laws and limits

3 *Belongingness and love:* for affection and intimacy, to be provided by family, friends, and lover

4 *Esteem:* for self-respect and the respect of others

5 *Self-actualization:* the sense that one is doing what one is individually suited for and capable of, to be "true to one's own nature"

Maslow's fully developed, self-actualized person displays high levels of all the following characteristics: perception of reality; acceptance of self, of others, and of nature; spontaneity; problem-solving ability; self-direction; detachment and the desire for privacy; freshness of appreciation and richness of emotional reaction; frequency of peak experiences; identification with other human beings; satisfying and changing relationships with other people; a democratic character structure; creativity; and a sense of values (Maslow, 1968). No one ever becomes completely self-actualized, but the person developing in a healthy way is always moving up to more self-fulfilling levels.

Charlotte Bühler analyzed more than 200 biographical studies and conducted intensive, in-depth psychotherapeutic interviews over a period of years to come up with her five-phase theory of human development, which focuses on setting and attaining a personal goal.

She maintains that *self-fulfillment* is the key to healthy development, and that unhappy or maladjusted people are unfulfilled in some way. She emphasizes the intentionality of human nature, with special attention to those activities that people do on their own initiative. She points to some sort of lifelong orientation toward a goal among those people who lead fulfilling lives—even though in the early years some individuals are not conscious of these goals. Sometimes only in looking back over their lives can people see them as a total unit, recognize expectations that they held throughout the years, and evaluate the degree to which those expectations have been met.

In Bühler's concept, originally delineated in 1933 and expanded upon in 1968, there are five phases in the attainment of a personal goal, described below.

1 *Childhood* (till age 15): People have not yet determined life goals; they think about the future in vague ways.

2 *Adolescence and young adulthood* (15 to 25): People first grasp the idea that their lives are their own, analyze their experiences so

far, and think about their needs and their potential.

3 *Young and middle adulthood* (25 to 45–50): People adopt more specific, definite goals.

4 *Mature adulthood* (45–65): People take stock of their past and revise their planning for the future.

5 *Old age* (after 65 or 70): People rest from their concentration on achieving goals.

Humanistic theories have made a valuable contribution in promoting child-rearing approaches that respect the child's uniqueness. Humanism is an optimistic, positive model of humankind, as opposed to the more negative Freudian viewpoint. It goes deeper than behaviorism in its consideration of internals such as feelings, values, and hopes, as opposed to limiting itself to observable behavior. Its limitations as a scientific theory rest largely on its subjectiveness. Since terms are not clearly defined, they are difficult to communicate and to use as the basis for research designs.

THE INFLUENCES OF HEREDITY AND ENVIRONMENT

Is our future laid out at birth by the many traits we inherit? Or is each of us a *tabula rasa*, a "clean slate" that awaits being written on by the stylus that our life becomes? The history of the science of human development is a history of the shifting views regarding the relative strengths of heredity and environment. This nature versus nurture controversy has bounced back and forth between those who felt that *nature* (or inborn hereditary factors) explained all development and those who believed that *nurture* (or environment) was the

Language develops most quickly during the preschool years. (David Strickler/Monkmeyer)

sole determinant of the way we are. Today we realize that both these major factors act together. We also realize that individuals themselves react differently to the same hereditary legacy (as in the case of identical twins) and to the same kinds of environments, to write their own life scripts. So nature, nurture, and the individual interact to influence development.

A girl's intelligence, for example, may be determined partly by her heredity; but the kind of home she grows up in, the degree to which she is encouraged to pursue intellectual interests, her physical health, the kind of education she receives, and her own decisions in life will all have an effect on the eventual expression of her intelligence. Or a boy whose hereditary endowment predisposes him to shortness may never grow up to be a six-footer; but if he is well cared for and makes sound health decisions, he will grow taller than he would have if he were kept in cramped quarters and got too little food, too little exercise, and too little love.

Throughout this book we will be discussing the many factors that influence human growth and development. These elements are an integral part of the various subcultures all people belong to. Race, sex, ethnic background, and socioeconomic status all influence development, just as heredity does. Not to know the environmental factors that influence a particular individual leaves large gaps in our understanding of that person and limits our means to help him or her develop to full potential.

No one grows up in a vacuum. When we talk about normal development for individuals in favored circumstances, we cannot generalize our conclusions to persons who are born to a malnourished teenager, are raised in a rural shack, do not know both their parents, do not get enough to eat, fend for themselves much of the time, are rarely spoken to at any length, receive a deficient education, and are unemployed or underemployed much of their lives. These persons are living in a world light-years away from that of the "typical" person most likely to be studied by developmentalists. What we say about one often does not apply to the other. We will never have the total story of human development because

Nature, nurture, and the individual interact to influence development. (Erika Stone/Peter Arnold, Inc.)

there are too many interacting factors ever to be able to draw neat, precise conclusions. We have, however, learned a great deal about certain aspects of development and can draw certain conclusions, which are stated throughout this book. Most of the studies of human development have focused on the white middle class, although an increasing amount of research attention is being paid to development among members of minority groups.

NATURE VERSUS NURTURE

What do we know about the relative influences of heredity and environment? We know, for example, that motor behaviors such as creeping, crawling, walking, and running unfold in age-related sequence, showing the importance of maturation. Environmental forces interfere with this hereditary timetable only when they take extreme forms, such as long-term deprivation. This was seen in infants in an Iranian orphanage who received little attention and no exercise. These babies sat up and walked quite late, compared with Iranian children who were well cared for (Dennis,

1960). Those behaviors that depend largely on maturation tend to appear whenever the organism is ready, but not before, and, except under extreme deprivation, not afterward.

Regarding the development of intellect and personality, the mixture of nature and nurture is much more important. Let's consider talking. Maturation is required for language development. Before children can talk they have to reach a certain level of neurological and muscular development. No matter how enriched their home life might be, they could not speak, read, or write this sentence at the age of a year. But environment plays a larger part in language development. If parents encourage their children's first efforts to make sounds by babbling back to them, children will start to speak earlier than if the early vocalizing is ignored. Maturation, then, lays the foundation, and the environment helps to build the structure.

HOW HEREDITY AND ENVIRONMENT INTERACT

The influences of nature and nurture can be arranged on a continuum as in Figure 1-1,

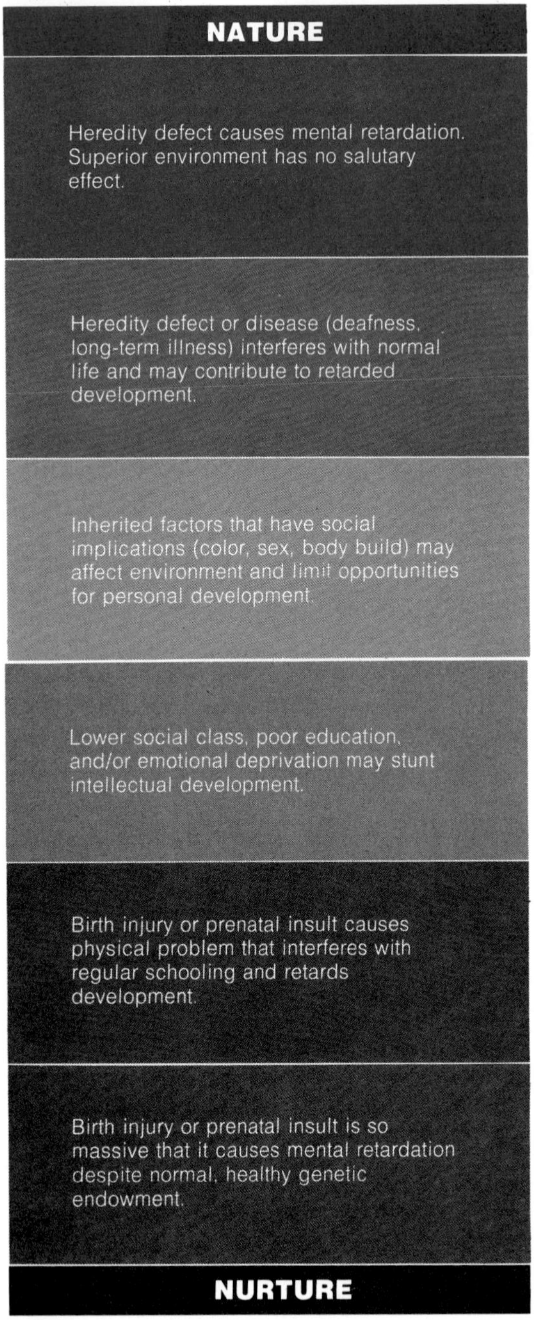

NATURE

Heredity defect causes mental retardation. Superior environment has no salutary effect.

Heredity defect or disease (deafness, long-term illness) interferes with normal life and may contribute to retarded development.

Inherited factors that have social implications (color, sex, body build) may affect environment and limit opportunities for personal development.

Lower social class, poor education, and/or emotional deprivation may stunt intellectual development.

Birth injury or prenatal insult causes physical problem that interferes with regular schooling and retards development.

Birth injury or prenatal insult is so massive that it causes mental retardation despite normal, healthy genetic endowment.

NURTURE

Fig. 1-1
Nature-Nurture Continuum Related to Intellectual Retardation (After Anastasi, 1957)

which illustrates how these two forces can cause intellectual retardation. Eye color and blood type are relatively simple inherited characteristics. But more complex traits such as health, intelligence, and personality are subject to an interplay between heredity and environment. How much is inherited? How much is environmentally influenced?

Why do these questions matter? If we discover that a trait such as high intelligence can be influenced by environment, we can try to make the environment as favorable as possible. On the other hand, if we find that a child's activity level is mostly inherited, we can be realistic in our efforts to raise this child. If we find that a certain birth defect is hereditary, we can better counsel prospective parents.

WAYS TO STUDY THE RELATIVE EFFECTS OF HEREDITY AND ENVIRONMENT

We can study the effects of heredity and environment in several ways. We can study *twins*. When twins reared together are more alike than those reared apart, we see the importance of environment. When identical twins are more alike than fraternal twins, we see the importance of heredity. We can also study *adopted children*. When they are more like their biological parents, we see the influence of heredity; when they resemble their adoptive parents more, we see the influence of environment. Similarly, we can compare *full* and *half siblings*. We can also conduct *consanguinity* (blood relationship) studies, examining as many members of a family as possible to discover whether certain characteristics are shared and whether the closeness of the relationship affects the degree of similarity for specific traits. Through *selective breeding*, researchers working with animals mate them to bring about *strains*, or family lines, that will be particularly strong or weak in the traits being studied. If such strains can be produced, this may be considered evidence that the trait is strongly influenced by genetics. Investigating relationships between various conditions of children and their mothers' experiences during pregnancy points up the importance of the *prenatal environment*. This kind of medical detective work pinpointed the dangers of taking thalidomide and other drugs during early pregnancy. *Manipulating the environment* of young laboratory animals by changing diet, diminishing opportunities for exercise, and causing sensory deprivation affects various aspects of behavior, which then can be related to comparable human experiences in early childhood. And *studies comparing parental practices* can look at the relationship between various child-rearing practices and outcomes (intellectual, emotional) in the child. We will study examples of all these effects of heredity and environment as we move through our discussion of development.

CHARACTERISTICS INFLUENCED BY HEREDITY AND ENVIRONMENT

Physiological Traits

On September 28, 1962, 24-year-old Roger Brooks was drinking a cup of coffee in a Miami pancake house. A busboy walked over to ask him, "Aren't you Tony Milasi?" In this way, Roger and Tony, identical twins who had been separated at birth, found each other again (Lindeman, 1969).

The many instances of mistaken identity among identical twins attest to their carbon-copy physical appearance. Identical twins also have a number of other physiological traits in common, supporting a belief that these characteristics are genetically determined. For example, identical twins are more *concordant*, that is, like each other, than fraternal twins in their rates of breathing, perspiration, and pulse and in their blood pressure (Jost & Sontag, 1944).

When both identical and fraternal twins were measured on galvanic skin response (GSR), which records the rate of electrical changes of the skin, identical twins showed greater concordance than did fraternals (Lehtovaara, Saarinin, & Jarvinen, 1965). Identical twin girls are likely to begin to menstruate

within a couple of months of each other, while fraternal twin sisters show a mean difference of a year for the age of *menarche*, or first menstruation (Petri, 1934).

Height and weight can both be environmentally influenced, but seem to be determined primarily by heredity, since identical twins reared together or apart are more similar in both these measures than are fraternal twins reared together. The correlation is not quite so strong for weight as it is for height (Newman, Freeman, & Holzingen, 1937; Mittler, 1969). Visual sensory and perceptual functions are highly influenced by heredity (Mittler, 1971). Our days on earth may even by numbered by our genes, since senescence and death occur at more similar ages for identical twins than for fraternals (Jarvik, Kallmann, & Klaber, 1957).

Intelligence

Performance on intelligence tests, especially in infancy, appears to be greatly influenced by genetic factors. The closer the biological relationship between two people, the closer their scores on intelligence tests are (Newman, Freeman, & Holzinger, 1937). As the child matures, however, the environment becomes much more influential in intellectual development.

Several types of research bring out the importance of the environment in shaping intellectual development. One line of inquiry looks at the ways caregivers interact with children. When caregivers talk to and play with children in a way that helps them make sense of their world, the children show enhanced intellectual development. (Elardo, Bradley, & Caldwell, 1975; Bradley & Caldwell, 1976). Another line of study shows how the effects of an impoverished environment can be overcome. Researchers have raised children's intelligence scores by working with

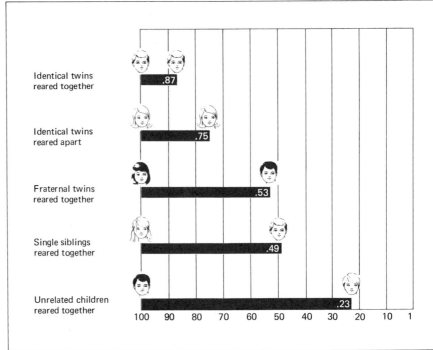

Fig. 1-2
IQ Correlations for
Twins, Siblings, and
Unrelated Children
(*Source*: Scheinfeld, A.
*Your heredity and
environment*.
Philadelphia: Lippincott,
1965)

parents (Karnes, Teska, Hodgins, & Badger, 1970) or directly with children (Blank & Solomon, 1968). These areas of research will be discussed more fully in Chapters 4, 6, and 8.

Our definition of intelligence influences our conclusions. Ordinarily, it is construed as an inborn, general cognitive factor, or a basic potential for learning. It is virtually impossible, however, to test for this innnate capacity without also measuring the actual learning a person has absorbed, much of which is dependent on what she or he has been taught in the home, in school, or in the community. So it is difficult to measure the elusive characteristic of basic intelligence. It is likely that what we describe as intelligence—how well a person performs in school and in life—is a product of genetic and environmental factors that interact in proportions as yet unknown. With this consideration in mind, let's take a look at some of the research on the heritability of intelligence.

Newman, Freeman, and Holzinger (1937) studied mental and physical variables in identical twins who had been reared together, in identicals who had been reared apart, and in fraternal twins reared together. They found that physical traits of identical twins were very similar whether the twins had been reared together or apart, and that IQ scores were affected more than the physical variables when identical twins had been reared apart, but that they were still generally more closely related for identical twins reared apart than for fraternal twins reared together. Achievement scores, however, were more closely related for both identical and fraternal twins who had been reared together than for identical twins who had been reared apart. The more the home environments differed, the more they were likely to have affected any measures of intelligence or achievement.

A smaller number of studies (Vandenberg, 1966) have isolated specific cognitive skills and found genetic determinants for verbal, space, number, and word-frequency tasks.

In 1976, Fisch, Bilek, Deinard, and Chang compared 144 adopted children, matched (for gestational age, birthweight, sex, and their biologic mothers' socioeconomic levels) with a control group of 288 children who were reared by their biologic parents. The adoptees were raised in a higher socioeconomic status than they had been born into or than their matched controls grew up in.

At the age of 7, all the children took IQ tests (The Wechsler Intelligence Scale for Children) and achievement tests in reading, spelling, and arithmetic. An IQ test is supposed to show a person's innate capacity to learn, while an achievement test measures what the individual has already learned. The adopted children showed the effects of their more advantaged surroundings by doing better than the controls in reading and spelling. Furthermore, they were less likely to have repeated kindergarten or first grade. On the IQ tests, though, there was no difference between the two groups, suggesting that elevated socioeconomic status in the adoptive families' homes did not serve to raise these children's IQ scores.

What does this study tell us? Possibly that the unknown construct that we call "innate intelligence" (see the discussion of intelligence on pages 132–134) may be determined largely by heredity, but that children's environments influence the way they *use* that intelligence. After saying that the adoptees were more highly motivated and interested in learning, Fisch et al. state, "Children from lower socioeconomic environments fall behind in academic achievement because of the lack of some of these essential learning prerequisites" (p. 499).

For several years the Louisville (Kentucky) Twin Study has conducted a longitudinal study of growth and development of twins, testing them periodically up to the age of 2 with the research version of the Bayley Scales of Mental and Motor Development. On the degree of *developmental maturity* that persists across several ages, and also on the *spurt-lag factor* (the age-to-age changes in

precocity), this study found that identical twins were more alike than fraternals, indicating a significant genetic influence on both these aspects of infant mental development. Although differences between homes did affect the babies, these investigators found that it took an unusual disparity in environmental conditions to impose a major change in the normal course of infant development (Wilson, 1972).

Intelligence is affected by maturation, and maturation is affected by heredity. The mental functions measurable in infancy change rapidly as new capabilities emerge and become fully developed, producing sharp spurts and lags in development. Every child seems to have his or her own rate of development. Jason, for example, may be precocious on some measures of development at 6 months of age, but may gain slowly for the next 6 months, and will have fallen behind the average child by the time he is 1 year old. Vicky, on the other hand, may be a slow starter, but at 2 years of age she may be far ahead of the average baby.

Most studies on intelligence have been done on people from relatively advantaged social environments. The differences among these individuals may result more from genes, whereas in a disadvantaged community the environment may become more important. We can see how this would work in a comparison of people's height. Under the best conditions, our genes determine how tall we grow. But illness, malnutrition, or neglect can counteract the power of the genes and keep a person from growing to her full potential. The same mechanism may well operate in the case of intelligence.

Scarr and Weinberg (1978) found, for example, that, given a basically favorable environment, minor differences in social class and in child-rearing practices are not as important as genes in determining intelligence. They compared 16- to 22-year-olds who had been adopted in infancy with adolescents who had been raised by their biologic parents. Even though the families ranged from working class to upper middle class, the researchers found that the differences in IQ among the young people seemed to be more closely related to the IQs of their natural parents than to the ways they had been raised. It seems unwarranted, therefore, to promote the child-rearing practices of the professional class as surefire ways to raise children's IQs. It doesn't seem to make much difference whether parents take their children to plays (as professionals are likely to do) or to baseball games (as working-class parents do more often), so far as the child's intelligence is concerned. Perhaps the important thing is the interest shown in the child, whatever form it takes.

Scarr and Weinberg take pains to point out that their research has no applicability to children who grow up in poverty, who are abused or neglected by their parents, or who suffer other traumatic experiences early in life. They emphasize that *the average level of our environment is the most important determinant of the level of behavioral development*" (p. 690). If you agree with this statement—as do the authors of this book—you will recognize the importance of our society's continuing to make massive efforts to improve the levels of schooling, mental and physical health, and living conditions for all elements of the population. Our society can only come out ahead as a result.

Personality

If we define personality as "the pattern of collective character, behavioral, temperamental, emotional and mental traits of an individual" (*American Heritage Dictionary*, 1971), we realize that we are talking about something so complicated that it would be impossible to ascribe it all to one major influence, either hereditary or environmental. But if we separate out specific aspects of personality, we can find many grounds for assuming that some individual factors are inherited. We have already, for example, looked at some of the evidence pointing to a genetic basis for the development of intelligence.

In 1956, two psychiatrists and a pediatrician (Thomas, Chess, & Birch, 1968) launched the New York Longitudinal Study to determine those aspects of personality that babies seem to be born with and that remain consistent through the years. By closely following 231 children from infancy through adolescence and examining them in regard to several traits, the researchers concluded that temperament, or the basic behavioral style of an individual, appears to be inborn.

They looked at such characteristics as a baby's activity level; regularity in biological functioning (for hunger, sleep, and bowel movements); readiness to accept new people and new situations; adaptability to changes in routine; sensitivity to noise, bright lights, and other sensory stimuli; whether a child's mood tended toward cheerfulness or unhappiness most of the time; intensity of responses; distractibility; and degree of persistence.

They found that babies vary enormously in all these characteristics, almost from birth, and that they tend to continue to behave according to this initial behavioral style. They also found, however, that many children show changes in behavioral style, apparently reacting to special experiences or to parental handling.

Using the twin study method, other researchers have established closer *concordance*, or similarity, between identical twins than between fraternals on a wide range of personality traits, and, therefore, evidence for genetic influences on such characteristics as extroversion-introversion, emotionality, and activity (Vandenberg, 1967); depression, psychopathic behaviors, and social introversion

Temperament, or the basic behavioral style of an individual, appears to be inborn. (Erika Stone/Peter Arnold, Inc.)

(Gottesman, 1963, 1965); anxiety, depression, and obsession (Gottesman, 1962; Inouye, 1965); and neuroticism (Eysenck & Prell, 1951; Slater, 1953, 1958). And identical twins have been found to show more similar responses than fraternal twins to the Rorschach test, an inkblot test used as a measure of personality (Basit, 1972).

The *hyperactive child syndrome* is a complex of behavioral characteristics, including impulsivity, restlessness, inability to concentrate, a high activity level, and emotional swings from one extreme to another. Two recent studies point to genetic transmission of these traits. A twin study in which mothers rated their children on their activity level in a variety of situations found a much higher concordance in identical twins than in fraternals (Willerman, 1973).

Morrison and Stewart (1973) compared hyperactive children living with their biologic parents, adopted hyperactives who had had no contact since birth with their natural parents, and children who had not been diagnosed as hyperactive. When the families of the three groups of children were compared, the researchers found a higher rate of alcoholism, sociopathy, and hysteria in the first group than in the other two groups. Also, more relatives of the biologic hyperactive group had been hyperactive themselves as children than was true for either of the other two groups. The authors suggest a multifactorial transmission of the syndrome, by which genetic, environmental, and hormonal elements interact. They also theorize that a number of genes, rather than one single gene, transmit various facets of the syndrome.

BEHAVIOR TRAITS   John walks in his sleep; David doesn't. Gina bites her nails; Dora doesn't. Both Stephen and Alan wet the bed practically every night. John and David, Gina and Dora, and Stephen and Alan are among 338 pairs of same-sex, school-age twins whose physical, mental, and behavioral attributes were measured in a twin study that sought genetic causes for various aspects of children's behavior.

The pediatrician who conducted this study (himself the father of twin daughters) found that many behavior characteristics appear to have a genetic basis. In this study, identical twins were twice as likely as fraternal twins to be concordant for bed-wetting and nail-biting, 2½ times for car sickness, 4 times for constipation, and 6 times for sleepwalking (Bakwin, 1970, 1971a,b,c,d).

Cadoret, Cunningham, Loftus, and Edwards (1975a) compared two groups of adopted adolescents, with an average age of 17. All had been separated at birth from their biologic parents. The biologic parents of the first group had been emotionally disturbed; those of the second group were normal. These researchers found evidence that a tendency toward behavior problems may be inherited. For one thing, 37 percent of the offspring of disturbed parents had received professional treatment for a behavior disorder, compared to only 14 percent of the controls. More of the boys in the first group had been considered "difficult" children (as defined by Thomas, Chess, & Birch, 1968), and more were hyperactive (1975b). No such differences showed up among the girls, however. Certain behavior patterns may, then, be partly hereditary.

SCHIZOPHRENIA Schizophrenia is a blanket term for a complex of mental disorders marked by an escape from reality and characterized by such symptoms as hallucinations, delusions, feelings of passivity, and other types of thought disorder. This form of psychosis appears all over the world and has been the basis for many studies seeking to determine its causes. The findings point to some degree of genetic transmission.

One twin study found that 86.2 percent of identical co-twins of schizophrenic patients were schizophrenic or had once been, compared with only 14.5 percent of fraternal co-twins (Kallman, 1953). Another study found that the identical twin of a schizophrenic is at least forty-two times as likely to be schizophrenic as someone from the general population, and a fraternal twin of the same sex, nine times as likely (Gottesman & Shields, 1966).

Still another study compared a group of forty-seven adults born to schizophrenic mothers, but separated from them by birth, with a control group of fifty adults who had no history of parental psychopathology. This study bore out the findings of the twin studies. Schizophrenia was diagnosed *only* in the offspring of schizophrenic mothers, and about one-half of the adults in this group exhibited major psychosocial disabilities, such as police records, neuroses, and so forth, as compared with only nine of the fifty in the control group. Although only one of the seventeen control males who had served in the military was discharged for psychiatric or behavioral reasons, eight out of twenty-one in the experimental group received such discharges (Heston, 1966).

Two other types of studies have given rise to the belief that schizophrenia has a hereditary component: consanguinity studies, which show that the risk of schizophrenia rises in direct proportion to the closeness of the genetic relationship with an affected relative, and the exploration of schizophrenia in different societies, which shows surprisingly small variations from society to society (Mittler, 1971).

Although there is, then, strong evidence of biological transmission of schizophrenia, we have to ask why all identical twins are not concordant for this trait. One answer may lie in tendencies and environmental situations. In other words, what appears to be transmitted is not the illness itself, but the predisposition toward the illness. If certain environmental stresses occur in the life of someone who is so genetically predisposed, that individual may respond to these stresses with schizophrenia. At this time, we do not know either the actual genetic mechanisms involved in transmitting such a predilection or the precise stresses that act as its trigger.

Naturalistic studies depend on observation.
(© Alice Kandell/Photo Researchers, Inc.)

METHODS FOR STUDYING PEOPLE

How do we know what people are like at various stages of development? Developmentalists use a variety of research approaches to observe people either as they go about their daily lives or as they act in planned experimental situations. Researchers are constantly coming up with new techniques for finding out about people and recording their findings.

NATURALISTIC STUDIES

Naturalistic studies depend on observation, pure and simple. Researchers look at people in their natural habitats, making no effort to alter behavior. Naturalistic studies generally provide us with *normative* information, or information about the average times for vari-

ous behavior to occur among normal people. These data may be based on averages of groups of people or may be derived from individual case histories. The major types of naturalistic studies are *baby biographies*, *naturalistic observations*, and *time-sampling*.

Baby Biographies

Our earliest information about infant development comes from journals kept to record the progress of a single baby. The first such diary that we know about is that of Heroard, who in 1601 began to keep such a record about the heir of France, the child of Henry IV, who was born in that year. Almost two centuries later, in 1787 in Germany, Dietrich Tiedemann published his observations about the first 2½ years of his son's sensorimotor, language, and intellectual development. His work, laced with comments, included passages like this:

On the day after his birth, when the nurse placed her finger in the boy's mouth, he sucked at it, but not continuously, only in a smacking fashion. When, however, a sweet, tied in a cloth, was placed in his mouth, he sucked continuously; a proof, I think, that sucking is not instinctive but acquired [Murchison & Langer, 1927, p. 206].

The earliest baby biography to be published in English was by an American educator, Emma Willard, who in 1835 brought out her observations about her son's first year of development. Baby biographies didn't gain scientific respectability until 1877, when the evolutionist Charles Darwin published notes about his son's early development and put forth the view that we could better understand the descent of our species by carefully studying infants and children. About thirty such studies were published over the next thirty years (Dennis, 1936). As recently as the twentieth century, Piaget based his highly original theories about the ways children learn on his meticulous, day-by-day observations of his own three children (1952).

Baby biographies give us much useful, in-depth information, especially about normative development. They allow us to glimpse a single child's personality, as we could in no other way, as is shown by this excerpt from a contemporary journal:

On Thanksgiving, [Debbie] spied the turkey all stuffed and ready for the oven, and somehow or other recognized this bald, headless, footless object lying on its back as "Bird, oh dear, *poor* birdie." At dinner she was so concerned for "Poor birdie, oh dear, oh dear," so insistent on patting and trying to reassure it that eating was of no importance whatsoever [Church, 1966].

But baby biographies have several shortcomings from a scientific point of view. Often, they only record behavior; they don't explain it. Since they tend to be written by fond parents, they may suffer from "observer bias," in which the recorder emphasizes the positive aspects of a child's development and gives short shrift to the negative. Furthermore, isolated biographies tell us a great deal about an individual child, but because of the uniqueness of each individual, we cannot apply such information to children in general.

Naturalistic Observations

In making *naturalistic observations*, researchers observe large numbers of children and record information about their development at various ages to derive average ages for the appearance of various skills, behaviors, or growth measures. Bridge's studies on emotional development (1932), Shirley's on motor development (1933), and Gesell's on motor

and behavioral development (1929) all fall into this category. In these studies, researchers neither make experimental manipulations nor attempt to explain behavior.

Time-Sampling

In *time-sampling*, researchers record the occurrence of a certain type of behavior—such as aggression, babbling, or crying—during a given time period. Rebelsky and Hanks (1972), for example, went into ten homes on six different occasions to make twenty-four-hour tapes. They analyzed the tapes to count the number of minutes in each twenty-four-hour period that a father spent talking to his baby. From studying these tapes, the investigators drew various conclusions about father-infant relationships.

CLINICAL STUDIES

There are two kinds of clinical studies: the *clinical method* and the *interview method*.

The Clinical Method

Piaget began his work with children by asking them all sorts of questions so that he could determine which questions children of various ages should be able to answer, for the purpose of standardizing an intelligence test. He became more interested in the wrong answers he heard than in the right ones, since he felt that the wrong answers held clues to the ways children reason. When he decided to study the content of children's thought, Piaget developed the *clinical method* of examination, which combines observation with careful, individualized questioning. This is a flexible way of assessing thought by tailor-making the test situation to the individual being questioned so that no two persons are questioned in exactly the same fashion. This open-ended, individualized method is quite different from the standardized testing technique, which aims to make the testing situation as similar as possible for all subjects. With the clinical method, an experimenter can probe further into responses that seem especially interesting, can use language that a particular individual understands, and can even change to the language that a child is using spontaneously.

Although each subject is asked the same basic questions, the clinical experimenter remains flexible in responding to each individual's unique answers. The replies determine the next question asked by the experimenter. In this way the experimenter can probe for the underlying meaning behind what a subject says. Examples of the clinical method as used with children can be found in Chapter 8.

There are drawbacks to the clinical method. Its flexibility means that we have to have a great deal of confidence in the interviewer's ability to ask the right questions and to draw the right conclusions. The only check on the method is to provide it to a great number of investigators who have varying points of view and then see whether their results corroborate each other.

The Interview Method

By interviewing a large number of people about one or more aspects of their lives, investigators get a broad picture—at least, of what the interviewees say they believe or do or did. Interview studies have focused on parent-child relationships, on sexual activities, on occupational aspirations, and on life in general. Very often interviews are combined with physical examinations, intellectual tests, and personality measures. A problem with relying on interviews alone for information is that the memory and accuracy of interviewees are often faulty. Some subjects forget when and how certain events actually took place, and others distort their replies to make them more acceptable to the interviewers or to themselves.

EXPERIMENTAL STUDIES

In an *experimental study*, researchers look at one factor in a person's life to determine its effect on another factor. For instance, if we wanted to examine the influence of socioeconomic status on language development, we could compare two groups of children: a group of 4-year-olds from homes that have been rated as lower class (based on a standardized rating system that assigns socioeconomic status on the basis of the parents' occupations) and a group of 4-year-olds from middle-class homes. Then we could devise a way to measure the size of the children's vocabularies.

In such a study we call the factor of socioeconomic status the *independent variable* and the factor of vocabulary size the *dependent variable*. We assume that socioeconomic status exerts some influence on vocabulary size, or, in other words, that differences in vocabulary size *depend*, at least partially, on socioeconomic status. The reverse could not be true: A child's vocabulary size could not influence his or her socioeconomic status (although an *adult's* might).

The two groups of subjects in an experimental study must be chosen carefully to ensure their similarity on every other independent variable. That is, the groups should be comparable in terms of age, of male-female ratios, of schooling, and so forth. We wouldn't compare a group of nursery school children with a group that does not attend school, or boys with girls, or 3-year-olds with 4-year-olds—unless these variables are the ones we want to test.

Another type of experimental study manipulates the independent variable even more. Suppose researchers want to study the value of an enrichment program for underprivileged preschool children. They will draw up two groups of children comparable in virtually every respect—age, sex, race, socioeconomic status, school attendance, IQ, and so forth. Then they offer the enrichment program to the children in only one group. After a certain time, the investigators will try to measure the effects of the enrichment program by giving both groups of children a test, say an IQ test.

If the group that received the enrichment program (called the *experimental group*) has a higher average score than the group that did not receive it (called the *control group*), then the researchers may conclude that this particular program does raise the IQ level of children. If there is no difference between the groups, the investigators conclude that the program is not effective in raising IQ levels, and they usually try to determine why the program did not work. Was it begun at too late an age? Was it administered for too short a time? Were the teachers inadequately trained? Then the researchers may put together a different sort of program and test it in a similar fashion.

Comparing Experimental and Naturalistic Approaches

Experimental studies have several advantages over naturalistic ones. Naturalistic studies, being *correlational*, cannot make statements about cause-and-effect situations. Correlational studies can only tell us about the *direction* and *magnitude* of a relationship between variables [that is, are two variables related in a positive direction (both increase and decrease together) or negative direction (as one increases, the other decreases)?]. Magnitude refers to the *degree* of a relationship. Correlations are reported as numbers ranging from -1.0 [a perfect negative (inverse) relationship] to $+1.0$ [a perfect positive (or direct) relationship]. The higher the number (whether $+$ or $-$), the stronger the relationship (either positive or negative).

If we find that there is a positive correlation between the amount of TV violence watched and the amount of aggressive behavior during free play, we cannot conclude that watching TV violence *causes* aggressive play. We can conclude only that the two variables are related in a positive way. An *experimental* study, which manipulates exposure to TV violence, is needed before we can come to a conclusion about cause and effect.

Experimental studies are so highly regimented and carefully described that the study can be *replicated*, that is, carried out by other researchers in exactly the same way. By repeating studies with different groups of subjects, the reliability of results can be checked. However, many experimental studies can look at only one or two facets of development at a time. By zeroing in so narrowly, they sometimes miss some larger, more general knowledge about people's lives. We have to be careful in designing and analyzing such studies not to miss the forest for the trees.

Some developmentalists criticize the great emphasis in recent years on the use of experimental studies and the relative lack of contemporary interest in naturalistic description. McCall (1977, p. 5) cites Bronfenbrenner (1974) as charging that developmental psychology has become "the science of the influence of one strange environmental factor or one strange person on one isolated behavior of a single child placed in a largely artificial context." He contends, therefore, that "the process of development as it naturally transpires in children growing up in actual life circumstances has been largely ignored" (p. 5).

While, as we said, the correlations observed in naturalistic observations cannot be shown to have a cause-and-effect relationship, the problem with conclusions drawn from experimental studies is that we cannot necessarily generalize from the laboratory to real life. Experimental manipulation shows what *can* happen if certain conditions are present: that is, children who watch violent TV shows in the lab *can* become more aggressive in the lab. It does not tell us what actually *does* happen in the real world: Do children who watch a lot of "shoot-'em-ups" hit their little brothers more than children who watch a different kind of show?

The route to greater understanding of human development may well lie in combining the naturalistic and experimental approaches. Researchers can first observe people as they go about their everyday lives, determine the correlations that exist, and then, armed with this information, go on to design experimental studies that will zero in on some of these apparent relationships.

METHODS OF DATA COLLECTION

Information about development can be obtained by *longitudinal, cross-sectional,* or *sequential* studies.

Longitudinal Design

Under the *longitudinal design*, we measure the same people more than once to see changes with age. We may measure stability or change with regard to one specific characteristic, such as vocabulary size, IQ, height, or aggressiveness. Or we may look at people in toto, measuring as many aspects of their lives as possible, with an eye to assessing interrelationships among various factors. This design provides a more accurate picture of the *process* of development, rather than its status at any given time.

Cross-Sectional Design

The *cross-sectional design* allows us to compare groups of people who differ from other groups of people on a particular dependent variable by observing, at a single time of measurement, many people who differ in a known way with regard to one or more independent variables. Suppose we want to measure the effect of various independent variables on one dependent variable, such as vocabulary size. We can look at different people of various ages, of both sexes, of different socioeconomic status, of different IQ levels, and so forth. We may find that girls with high IQs from middle-class homes have the largest vocabularies. Or we can get a picture of the size of the average California 2-year-old as compared with the average California 3-year-old, or the average 2-year-old in New York City as compared with the average 2-year-old in Tanzania.

Comparing Longitudinal and Cross-Sectional Designs

Longitudinal studies assess changes undergone by one or more individuals at more than one time, and cross-sectional studies look at differences among groups of individuals. Each design has strengths and weaknesses. Because of their different approaches, developmental trends derived from the two different methods are sometimes contradictory.

Longitudinal studies are more sensitive to individual patterns of behavior and to the changes that people undergo. They're also more difficult to run. It's hard to keep track of a large group of subjects over a period of twenty to thirty years, to keep records, and to keep the study unified despite inevitable changeovers in research personnel. One methodological shortcoming of these studies is a probable bias in the sample. People who volunteer for them tend to be of higher than average socioeconomic status and intelligence. Those who drop out or become lost to the study may not be random members of the sample. Then there is the effect of repeated testing. People tend to do better upon subsequent administration of certain tests simply because of the "practice effect." How might this affect test scores in a study like the Berekley Growth Study, which tested most of its subjects at least thirty-eight times over a period of eighteen years (Bayley, 1949)?

The cross-sectional method has its drawbacks, too. It masks individual differences by yielding average measures for the various subgroups in the study; and it tends to give a misleading picture of specific individuals' changes over time. The major disadvantage of this method is that it cannot eliminate the generational influence that shows up when we measure people who were born at different times.

The different *cohorts*, or age groups, in a study have been subjected to different influences at critical times in their lives. Even when we find that a group of 60-year-olds and a group of 30-year-olds differ in certain ways, we cannot necessarily attribute their physical, intellectual, or personality differences to the effects of age. The 60-year-olds, for example, may not do as well as the 30-year-olds on a science test. Our first thought may be that this is because the older people have suffered some memory loss. An equally likely explanation, though, is that the 30-year-olds received a much more extensive scientific education than did the older group, who went to school at a time when the humanities held sway in the schools. Or on a personality test a group of people in their fifties may show up as much more concerned with financial security than people in their twenties. This may be because older people have more responsibilities. It also may be because the older subjects were teenagers during a major economic depression, while the younger people never knew hunger or want.

Cross-Sequential Design

In an attempt to overcome some of the drawbacks of both the longitudinal and cross-sectional designs, the *cross-sequential design* was developed. This method is a combination of the other two: people in a cross-sectional sample are tested more than once, and the results are analyzed to determine the differences that show up over time for the different groups of subjects. Some recent work on intellectual functioning in adulthood employs sequential techniques. These techniques seem to provide a more realistic assessment, since the cross-sectional method tends to overestimate a drop in intellectual functioning in the later years, while the longitudinal method tends to

underestimate it (since factors such as selective dropout make the sample at the end of the study different and more able than the original sample). This is discussed in more detail in our discussion of intellectual functioning in old age, in Chapter 16.

Alas, the cross-sequential design is not the perfect solution, either, because it is complicated and expensive. If the sequential method had been used in the Berkeley Growth Study, which began in 1928 and examined a total of 74 people at yearly intervals, from the age of 1 year to the age of 36, more than 5500 subjects with no dropouts would have been required, according to McCall (1977). Furthermore, he contends, the study, which actually ended in 1964, would not be finished until the year 2008.

Analysis of several longitudinal studies shows that researchers may have been worrying too much about two concerns, says McCall (1977): first, the effect of repeated testing. While it is strongest between the first and second testings, there does not seem to be much effect beyond this point. Second, there is the concern of the blurring of individual differences among the subjects. This does not seem to take place, since the same kinds of correlations keep showing up across age levels.

Researchers need to be sensitive to those topics of inquiry in which cohort membership (the year in which subjects were born and their different life circumstances because of their place in history) is likely to have an effect. When this does not seem to be significant, the simpler longitudinal strategy may serve better than the more complex sequential one.

ETHICAL CONSIDERATIONS IN STUDYING PEOPLE

With the proliferation of projects involving research on human beings, a bewildering array of ethical questions has arisen. The basic issue involves balancing the quest for

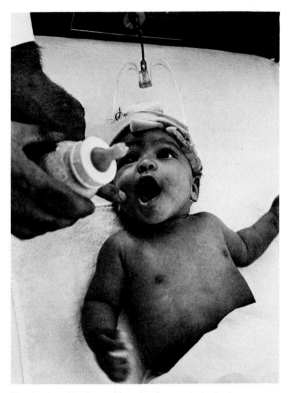

The basic ethical consideration in psychological research involves balancing the quest for knowledge about people in general while retaining intact the intellectual, emotional, and physical integrity of the individual.

At the Lipsitt Lab at Brown University, this infant is being tested for the sucking reflex. (© Jason Laurè/Woodfin Camp and Associates)

knowledge about people in general while retaining intact the intellectual, emotional, and physical integrity of individual persons. In all research, a risk-benefit ratio must be weighed: are the possible benefits of the research (either to individuals directly involved or to humanity in general) great enough to justify posing some risk to research subjects? If so, how great a risk to the subjects is justifiable?

We have learned the dangers of some kinds of experimentation. In the thirteenth century, Frederick II wanted to find out whether there was a universal language that babies would speak if they did not hear the language of their own culture:

So he bade foster mothers and nurses to suckle the children, to bathe and wash them, but in no way to prattle with them, or to speak to them, for he wanted to learn whether they would speak the Hebrew language, which was the oldest, or Greek, or Latin, or Arabic, or perhaps the language of their parents, of whom they had been born. But he labored in vain because the children all died. For they could not live without the petting and joyful faces and loving words of their foster mothers [Ross & McLaughlin, 1949, p. 366].

Today we would not dream of depriving children of the loving care they need in infancy. Nor would we do to people so many of the things that scientists do in studying animals. Because of what we have learned about the long-term effects of children's early experiences, we would not perform today many of the experiments that have been carried out in the past.

To help resolve some of these difficult questions, many research institutes have set up their own review boards to determine whether proposed research projects meet ethical criteria. Two of the most prestigious bodies that have published guidelines are the federally supported National Commission for the Protection of Human Subjects of Biomedical and Behavioral Research and the American Psychological Association's Committee on Ethical Standards in Psychological Research.

SOME BASIC ETHICAL ISSUES

Right to Privacy

A few years ago a doctor made the front pages of newspapers around the country when he recommended giving psychological tests to young underprivileged children, with the aim of predicting which ones showed signs of someday becoming delinquent. These children could be watched and given extra social help to try to forestall their criminal tendencies. The doctor's proposal was justifiably attacked by many who felt that labeling children as potential delinquents would have detrimental effects. The principle of the *self-fulfilling prophecy* might operate: These children might be treated differently and might actually become delinquent because of the predictions. This is one potentially harmful way that research information can be used. Similar concerns have been voiced with regard to research subjects' results on intelligence and other psychological tests. Such material has the potential for being used against the individual.

One-way mirrors and hidden cameras and tape recorders enable psychologists to observe and record behavior without the subjects' awareness. Furthermore, much private information surfaces through personal interviews—information about income, education, child-rearing techniques, and parent-child relationships. What is the experimenter's obligation with regard to the collection and maintenance of such information? Smith (1967) answers:

Information collected from children for research should never be used to their disadvantage. When the nature of the research permits data to be collected and stored anonymously, the interests of the individual child can be readily protected. When, on the other hand, identification of individual persons is essential to the research—as in "longitudinal" studies that follow the same persons over a period of time—elaborate precautions are essential to safeguard *confidentiality*. In such research, protecting the anonymity of the persons studied is an absolute about which there can be no compromise [p. 55].

The same strictures must be applied to adult subjects, as well, to protect their privacy.

In general, people doing research are not protected by the laws establishing categories of "privileged communication." Under these laws, a doctor, a lawyer, or a priest—and sometimes a therapist—can usually refuse legally to divulge a confidence. But someone who admits on a questionnaire or in an interview conducted for purposes of research that she or he has committed a crime (like selling marijuana or shoplifting, for example) could get into legal hot water.

Says Etzioni (1978):

All people who admit to a researcher that they have participated in a crime must realize that they are taking a calculated risk. Researchers have gone to jail rather than divulge their sources, and many do go to great lengths to protect their sources' identities. Other researchers, however, are not so scrupulous— or careful. (It is easy, for example, to walk into most code rooms, where questionnaires are processed, and get the results.) [p. 14].

Right to the Truth

Some experiments depend on deception of the subjects. Children are told that they are testing out a new game, when they are actually being tested on their reactions to success or failure. Adults are told they are participating in a study on learning when they are really being tested on their willingness to inflict pain on another person. Is it legitimate to deceive subjects about the real purpose of an experiment? If such deception is practiced, how can people's right to the truth and to their own integrity be protected? Does telling the subjects the truth *after* the experiment undo the lie?

Right to Informed Consent

Children do not give their consent to be part of scientific experiments, and even if they did, we could not accept their ability to make mature judgments. We have to rely on parents' regard for the well-being of their children or on school personnel's judgment in cases where students are permitted to participate in research programs. How is a child affected by all of this? Since investigators do not have to justify their procedures to the children, how can we be sure that their judgment takes into account the best interests of the individual child, as well as the best interests of the study of children in general? When (if ever) and under what conditions and with what restrictions is the guardian of an incompetent adult morally justified in giving permission for the individual to participate in a research project? This question is particularly pertinent in view of the increasing amount of research performed with old people. How much do *any* adults have to know about an experiment before the consent they give can be considered "informed"? Can lay people ever give truly informed consent? When the true purpose of an experiment is withheld from a subject, can the consent he or she gives be considered informed?

The National Commission for the Protection of Human Subjects of Biomedical and Behavioral Research (1978) recommends that parents and investigators seek a child's assent to take part in research, from the time the child is 7 years old, and that the child's objection should be overruled only if the research promises a direct benefit to the child, such as the use of a new, still experimental drug.

Right to Self-Esteem

Many researchers try to discover at what point people become capable of certain skills or certain types of reasoning. They study children who are known to be too young to achieve the ability under study. Other investigators want to find out the limits of a child's abilities, and so they continue to pose problems until she or he is unable to answer. Built into the design of all such studies is the certainty of failure. How do these feelings of failure affect individual children? Even if the

experimenter takes special pains to see that a child experiences a feeling of success by the end of the experimental session, does this make up for artificially induced failures? What are the long-term effects of such failures? Is the quest for scientific truth worth the possibility of damaging the self-concept of a single child?

If a subject is troubled by his or her own behavior in an experiment—if he finds, for example, that he is more aggressive than he had thought, more timid, or more willing to inflict pain on another—is the experimenter obliged to provide the subject with an opportunity to explore these feelings with a psychotherapist?

Fetal Research

With the legalization of abortion, research on fetuses has expanded enormously, along with a host of perplexing ethical questions, including the elemental decision about the basic nature of the fetus. Is it a part of the mother's body, like her gall bladder? If so, she can give permission for it to be used for research purposes. Is it an animal, with no more humanity than a guinea pig? If so, it can be treated like a laboratory animal. Or is it a dying person? If this is so, then much more stringent restrictions must apply to any research involving aborted fetuses.

Some fetal experiments involve injecting a drug into a pregnant woman who has already decided to have an abortion, to determine the drug's effect on the fetus. Other experiments measure fetal patterns of swallowing, breathing, eliminating, and sleeping —measures that may indicate fetal maturity and viability. Other experiments try novel ways to save a threatened miscarriage. Some of these experiments are conducted to try to save the life of the fetus that is the subject of the experiments. Others are performed with an eye toward saving the lives of other babies.

Scarf (1975) has summed up some of the very difficult problems of the morality of fetal research:

We are now moving into a time in which critical choices are going to have to be faced and made. We do, on the one hand, share a strong presumption that experimentation on dying people is wrong, and that human life is not to be treated casually. On the other hand, many of us also do have doubts regarding the "personhood" of the fetus and realize that we may be balancing its welfare against that of untold numbers of babies who will live to enter the human community, and can be benefited vastly from this research. On the one side are our concerns about permitting medical researchers to make use of something human; on the other, the promise of great scientific good to be obtained. There is an element of ultimate conflict in this whole, peculiar situation [p. 102].

Research with the Elderly

Disturbing ethical questions arise at the other end of the life span, as well. At a time in life when people's greatest wish may be not to be bothered, are old people disproportionately sought out by researchers because they suffer from the conditions that the researchers want to learn about? If a sick old man's physician asks him to take part in a research project, is the patient under pressure to agree for fear of antagonizing his doctor and jeopardizing his medical care? The 5 percent of the elderly who are in nursing homes account for a disproportionately large share of subjects in old-age research. Do these institutionalized persons feel pressured to take part to please the doctors and staff or to get privileges in the institution?

Reich (1978) proposes a number of policies to protect the elderly from being exploited. They include such safeguards as including on research review boards one or more old people who have no institutional commitments to the research; some way of making sure that people serving as research subjects are competent to give their assent; and placing the burden of proof on investigators to show why they have to use institutionalized people rather than volunteers living on their own.

Social Concerns

The vast amount of research that has been carried out among children of minority groups and among socially disadvantaged children involves a different kind of danger. If we consistently find that children from certain subcultures do not achieve intellectually as well as other children—and if this research is published—what is the ultimate result?

It has been said that the cumulative, if unintentional, effect of years of sociological research in the black community has been to damage the self-esteem of black youngsters [Reinhold, 1973, p. E13].

This damage may come about as a result of published findings showing middle-class children to be academically superior to poor youngsters. It may result from teachers' expectations. If they "know" from published reports that inner-city children are not likely to do so well in school as suburban youngsters, they may gear their teaching to diminished expectations. By so doing, they ensure that their pupils will, indeed, live down to their expectations.

Another major issue for our society is life-extension research, which tries to extend the human life span (Reich, 1978). Our society already has a growing population of people who live longer than they would have before recent medical advances. In many cases, however, medicine prolongs life without restoring health and vigor. So many of our aged are ill and infirm, cannot support themselves, and cannot even take care of themselves. Their plight has many implications, not only for their own lives, but for the society as a whole. What are the political and economic ramifications? What is the role of government in housing, feeding, and caring for them? How are the young and the middle-aged affected by their obligations to aged parents and grandparents? These questions are hard ones, but they must be considered by anyone engaged in research with such far-reaching ramifications.

All these issues are very real ones for researchers. Developmentalists do not want to harm the subjects who help them learn. Yet, severe restrictions would put a halt to many current studies and would limit our understanding of people. Where does the answer lie? In the integrity of each researcher, in the imposition of professional standards that protect individual rights, and in the awareness and sensitivity of every citizen. It is up to everyone in the field of human development to accept the responsibility to try to do good— and, at the very least, to do no harm.

A WORD TO STUDENTS

Our final word in this introductory chapter is that this entire book is far from the final word. We are still learning about people. Some of our research findings have put old ideas to rest forever. Others are still ambiguous and must be pursued vigorously. Some theories seem to make sense but are hard to test.

As you read this book, you will no doubt consider many issues that will raise questions of value judgments in your mind. If you can pursue your questions through research and thought, it is possible that you yourself, now just embarking upon the study of human development, may in future years advance this study to the benefit of all.

SUMMARY

1 The study of human development focuses on the quantitative and qualitative ways people change over time; it is concerned primarily with the examination of overt, observable behavioral changes.   **2** The concept of childhood is relatively recent. Attitudes toward children were quite different in the past, and they affected how children were studied. As researchers became interested in following children's development over a longer period, into adulthood, life span development expanded as a subject for study.   **3** Although we can look at various types of development (for example, physical, socioemotional, or intellectual) and at various periods of the human life span, we must remember that these do not occur in isolation. Each affects the others.   **4** Certain principles of development apply to all individuals and provide useful guidelines in interpreting behaviors. These include individual differences, critical periods, and orderly development. Different types of development are important at different times in life.   **5** The models and theories of human development fit fairly neatly into four perspectives of humankind: the mechanistic, the organismic, the psychoanalytic, and the humanistic.   **6** In determining various types of development, it is difficult to disentangle the relative contributions of heredity and environment and how they interact. Certain aspects of our development are influenced more heavily by our heredity; others, by the environment in which we are raised and live.   **7**   There are many ways to obtain information about people, including naturalistic, clinical, and experimental studies. Each approach has strengths and weaknesses that should be considered in interpreting studies of human development.   **8**   The two major data-collection techniques are the longitudinal design and the cross-sectional method. Each has advantages and disadvantages. The cross-sequential approach attempts to overcome the drawbacks of the other two designs.   **9**   The study of people must reflect certain ethical considerations. A carefully designed study considers its effects on the subjects as well as its potential benefits to the field of human development.

SUGGESTED READINGS

Aries, P.   *Centuries of childhood.* New York: Vintage Books, Random House, 1962. This historical text presents the evolution of the modern family and the nature of modern children. It includes a well-presented discussion of the discovery of childhood as a distinct phase of life.

Carew, J., Chan, I., & Halfar, C.   *Observing intelligence in young children: Eight case studies.* Englewood Cliffs, NJ: Prentice-Hall, 1976. The daily experiences of children from 1 to 3 years of age in their everyday environment. Many observations of children, with commentary by the authors, are included.

Erikson, E. H.   *Childhood and society.* New York: Norton, 1963. This text is a collection of writings by Erik Erikson which includes the "eight ages of man," in which he outlines his theory of psychosocial development from infancy to old age.

Gross, B., & Gross, R.   *The children's rights movement.* Garden City, NY: Anchor Press/Doubleday, 1977. A compendium of timely articles by respected, outspoken advocates of children and young people who protest many forms of oppression of the young.

Maier, H.   *Three theories of child development.* New York: Harper & Row, 1978, 2d edition. This text presents a discussion of each of the following: the psychoanalytical theory of Erik H. Erikson, the cognitive theory of Jean Piaget, and the learning theory of Robert R. Sears. Remaining chapters compare the three theories, discuss the "helping process," and note the implications of the three theories.

Milgram, J. I., & Sciarra, D. J.   *Childhood revisited.* New York: Macmillan, 1974. A fascinating selection of autobiographical excerpts by prominent people whose childhood recollections underscore the personal ways that issues in child development affect real people.

Peterson, C. C.   *A child grows up.* New York: Alfred Publishing Co., 1974. A baby biography of the author, now a psychologist herself, interspersed with a text that interprets the father's original diary entries in the light of recent research in child development.

Thomas, R.   *Comparing theories of child development.* California: Wadsworth, 1979. A critical analysis of the major theories and issues in child development today.

Beginnings

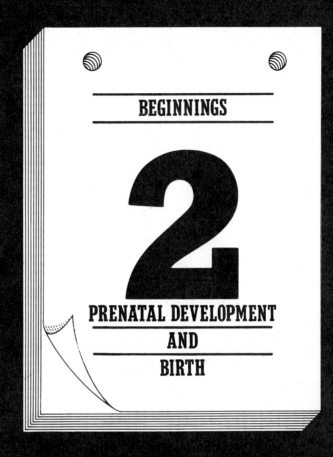

BEGINNINGS

2

PRENATAL DEVELOPMENT

AND

BIRTH

IN THIS CHAPTER
YOU WILL LEARN ABOUT

The process of human reproduction and how it affects—for better or worse—a new individual's sex, appearance, health, and personality

The things that can go wrong in human reproduction, with what effects, and how the effects may be anticipated and minimized

How babies develop inside their mothers' bodies—and how the world outside influences their development

The birth process and how its complications can influence a newborn child's adjustment

CHAPTER OVERVIEW

Fertilization
The Mechanisms of Heredity | Patterns of Genetic Transmission | Chromosomal Abnormalities | Genetic Counseling | Prenatal Diagnosis of Birth Defects

Prenatal Development: Three Stages
Germinal Stage | Embryonic Stage | Fetal Stage | Spontaneous Abortion | Induced Abortion | Prenatal Activities and Abilities | The Prenatal Environment

The Birth Process
Methods of Childbirth | Birth Complications

During the seventeenth and eighteenth centuries, a long debate raged between two opposing schools of biological thought about the origins of human life. The Ovists were convinced that a female's ovaries contained tiny embryos that were somehow activated by the male sperm. The Homunculists held an opposite, if equally incorrect, view—that preformed embryos were contained in the head of the sperm and were enabled to grow only when deposited in the nurturing environment of the womb.

Both these schools of thought were, of course, incorrect. Their mistaken thinking reflected the lack of appreciation and understanding of the fundamental discoveries of two scientists from the Netherlands: Regnier de Graaf, who first viewed some embryonic cells removed from the reproductive tubes of a female rabbit, and Anton van Leeuwenhoek, who, in 1677, noticed live sperm cells in a drop of semen viewed under the newly invented microscope. By the middle of the eighteenth century the work of the German-born anatomist Kaspar Friedrich Wolff had clearly demonstrated to the scientific world that both parents contribute equally to the beginning of a new life and that this new being is not preformed but grows from single cells, one male and one female in origin.

The beginning of life for all of us came long before that first lusty yell when, as newborn babies, we left our mother's womb. Instead, the beginning is a split-second event when a sperm (*spermatozoon*) joins an egg (*ovum*) to start a new life. The question of which sperm joins which egg has tremendous implications for the kind of person that new being will become: what sex it will be, what it will look like, which diseases it will be susceptible to, even—to a hotly disputed extent—what kind of personality it may possess. Let us now see how this important union takes place

and what then occurs during the nine months of life inside the womb.

FERTILIZATION

About fourteen days after the beginning of the menstrual period, fertilization may occur. This takes place when a sperm cell from a male unites with an egg from a female to form a single cell. This cell is called a *zygote* until it begins to grow through cell division. The eggs and sperms are known as *gametes*, or sex cells.

A newborn girl has about 400,000 immature eggs (*ova*) in her *ovaries*, each one in its own small sac called a *follicle*. The ovum, about one-fourth the size of the period that ends this sentence, is the largest cell in the human body. *Ovulation* occurs about once every twenty-eight days in a sexually mature female; that is, one mature follicle in one of her two ovaries ruptures and expels an ovum. This travels toward the *uterus* (the womb) through the *Fallopian tube*, where fertilization normally occurs.

The tadpolelike sperm, at 1/600 inch from head to tail, is one of the smallest cells in the body and is much more active than the ovum. Spermatozoa are produced in the testicles (*testes*) of a mature male at a rate of several hundred million a day and are ejected in his semen at sexual climax. An ejaculation carries about 500 million sperm cells; for fertilization to occur, at least 20 million sperm cells must enter a woman's body at one time. They enter the vagina and try to swim through the *cervix* (the opening to the uterus) and into the fallopian tube. Only a tiny fraction of those millions of sperm cells make it this far. More than one may penetrate the ovum, but only one can fertilize it to create a new human being.

Spermatozoa maintain their ability to fertilize an egg for a span of from twenty-four to forty-eight hours; ova can be fertilized for about twenty-four hours. Thus there are about forty-eight hours during each menstrual cycle when conception can take place (Patten,

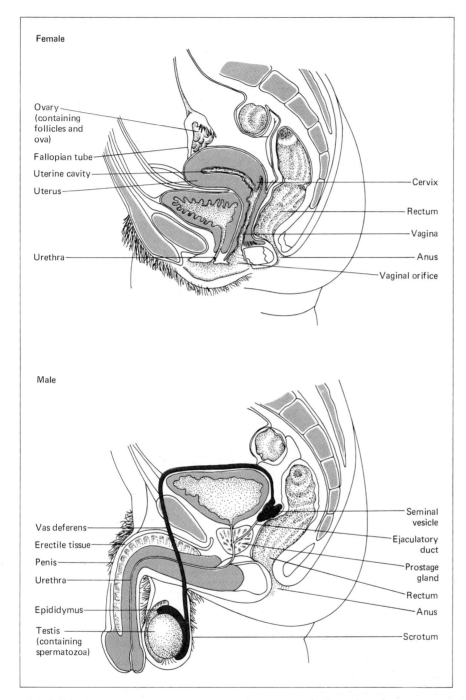

Female

Ovary (containing follicles and ova)

Fallopian tube

Uterine cavity

Uterus

Urethra

Cervix

Rectum

Vagina

Anus

Vaginal orifice

Male

Vas deferens

Erectile tissue

Penis

Urethra

Epididymus

Testis (containing spermatozoa)

Seminal vesicle

Ejaculatory duct

Prostage gland

Rectum

Anus

Scrotum

Fig. 2-1
Human Reproductive Systems

1968). If it does not occur, the sperm cells and the egg die. The sperm cells are devoured by white blood cells in the woman's body, and the egg passes through the uterus and exits through the vagina.

THE MECHANISMS OF HEREDITY

When sperm and egg unite to form the first one-celled organism (the zygote), they endow the new life with a rich legacy. Sperm and egg each contain twenty-three rod-shaped parti-

The body cells of women and men each contain 23 pairs of chromosomes.

At maturity, each germ cell has only 23 single chromosomes. Through meiosis, a member is taken randomly from each original pair of chromosomes.

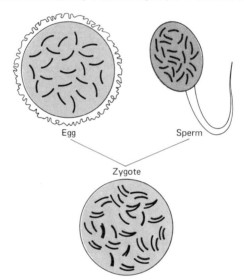

Egg   Sperm

Zygote

At fertilization, the chromosomes from each parent pair up so that the zygote contains 23 pairs of chromosomes — half from the mother and half from the father.

Fig. 2-2
Early Development
of Human Egg
and Embryo

cles called *chromosomes*, so that the zygote will have forty-six chromosomes, like every other cell in the human body except the mature gametes, which (as a result of meiosis) contain only twenty-three each (see Figure 2-2). As the fertilized egg develops into a complex human being, it gradually differentiates into billions of cells specializing in hundreds of different functions. Every one of these cells has the same hereditary information. Every one has forty-six chromosomes, each of which contains about 20,000 seg-

ments strung out on it lengthwise like beads. These segments are the *genes*. Various genes appear to be located according to their functions in definite positions on particular chromosomes.

All genes are made up of DNA (*deoxyribonucleic acid*). The DNA molecules possess the information that determines the makeup of every cell in our bodies—information that this is a human cell, that it will perform specific functions, and that it will perform these functions in a way unique to the individual. The

Multiple births have become more frequent in recent years due to the administration of certain fertility drugs that spur ovulation and often cause the release of more than one egg. (Erika Stone Peter Arnold, Inc.)

thousands of genes play a major part in determining all our hereditary characteristics. Genes on the *autosomes* (nonsex chromosomes) can be transmitted equally to males or females, but those of the *sex chromosomes* are transmitted differently to males and females.

Determination of Sex

King Henry VIII divorced Catherine of Aragon because she bore him a daughter rather than the son he so desperately wanted. It's ironic that this basis for divorce has been valid in so many different societies, since we now know that it is the *father* who determines the child's sex.

As we have noted, at the moment of conception, every human being receives a total of forty-six *chromosomes*—twenty-three from the sperm and twenty-three from the

egg. These chromosomes from the father and the mother align themselves in pairs. Twenty-two pairs are *autosomes*; the twenty-third pair, the sex chromosomes, determines the child's sex. The sex chromosome of every ovum is an X chromosome, but the sperm may carry either an X or a smaller-sized Y chromosome. When an ovum (X) meets an X-carrying sperm, called a *gynosoperm*, the zygote is XX, a female. When an ovum is fertilized by a Y-carrying sperm, called an *androsperm*, the zygote is XY, a male.

Multiple Births

Occasionally two ova are released within a short time of each other; if both are fertilized, *fraternal* (also called *dizygotic*, or two-egg) twins will be born. Created by different eggs and different sperm cells, they are no more alike in their genetic makeup than any other siblings. They may be of the same or different sex. If the ovum divides in two *after* it has been fertilized, *identical* (*monozygotic*, or one-egg) twins will be born. They have exactly the same genetic heritage, and any differences they will later exhibit must be due to the influences of environment, either before or after birth. Identical twins are, of course, always of the same sex. Other multiple births—triplets, quadruplets, and so forth—result from either one or a combination of these two processes.

Multiple births have become more frequent in recent years due to the administration of certain fertility drugs that spur ovulation and often cause the release of more than one egg. The tendency to bear twins appears to be inherited and to be more common in some ethnic groups than in others. In Nigeria, twins account for 1 birth in 22; in Britain, for 1 in 80; and in Japan, for only 1 in 160 (Gedda, 1961). More than half of all twins are of low birthweight, and thus at greater risk. In 1 out of 6 twin pregnancies, one or both of the twins die, with the second-born twin particularly vulnerable (Dunn, 1965).

PATTERNS OF GENETIC TRANSMISSION

The science of genetics owes a large debt to Gregor Mendel, a once-obscure Austrian monk who, in the 1860s, conducted experiments on plants that laid the basis for modern theories of inheritance.

Understanding how hereditary traits are transmitted helps us to understand how birth defects and inherited illnesses occur.

Autosomal Dominant Inheritance

Mendel crossbred one strain of pea plants that produced only yellow seeds with another purebred strain that produced only green seeds. The offspring of these plants all had yellow seeds. The trait for yellow seeds is the *dominant* trait, and the one for green seeds, which is suppressed in the first generation, is the *recessive* trait.

When Mendel crossbred two yellow-seeded first-generation plants, 75 percent of the second-generation plants had yellow seeds (showing the dominant trait), while the other 25 percent had green seeds. This 3:1 ratio is the pattern of *autosomal dominant inheritance*.

The 3:1 ratio of dominant to recessive genes turned out to be the same for other traits, like smooth or wrinkled seeds and tall or short plants. This ratio holds true throughout nature. It affects, for example, eye color (brown is dominant over blue); hair shape (kinky is dominant over straight); and certain diseases carried by either dominant or recessive genes and described below.

Genetic transmission is based upon the fact that a gene can often take two or more forms. For example, a gene for eye color may have a form for brown and an alternate form for blue eyes. A gene for blood type may have several different forms, such as for types O, A, B, or AB. These different forms of a gene are called *alleles*. During fertilization a child receives two alleles of each gene, one from the mother and one from the father. The makeup of these allele pairs will determine many of the child's characteristics. The observable traits (like eye or skin color or blood type) represent the *phenotype* for the individual, while the underlying genetic pattern is called the *genotype* (see Figures 2-3 and 2-4).

People with identical phenotypes do not necessarily have the same genotype, since identical observable traits may come from several different genetic patterns. For example, Frank received identical alleles from both parents for brown eyes; he has brown eyes himself and is considered *homozygous* for eye color. Eleanor, however, inherited two different alleles—one for brown eyes and one for blue. She is said to be *heterozygous* for this trait. In a case like this, one allele is *dominant*, and the other is *recessive*. The dominant allele—in this case, for brown eye color—will override or suppress the phenotypic expression of the recessive allele (the one for blue). Heterozygous Eleanor still has brown eyes, but her genotype is quite different from Frank's.

This difference in their genotypes means that homozygous Frank can pass on only brown-eyed genes to his children, while heterozygous Eleanor can pass on genes for either brown or blue eyes. The recessive gene—in this case, blue eyes—*can* be passed on. It will be expressed in future generations *only* if a child receives the same recessive allele from the other parent as well. Genotypes are sometimes modified by experience—that is, a person with a genotype that would make him tall might suffer from illness or malnutrition and end up being shorter than the blueprint on his genotype.

The method of inheritance for some characteristics is quite complex. A heterozygous child can possess a trait intermediate be-

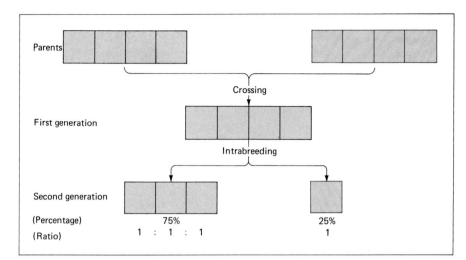

Fig. 2-3
Genotype: The
Genetic Composition
of a Trait

Parents

Crossing

First generation

Intrabreeding

Second generation

(Percentage)   75%   25%

(Ratio)   1 : 1 : 1   1

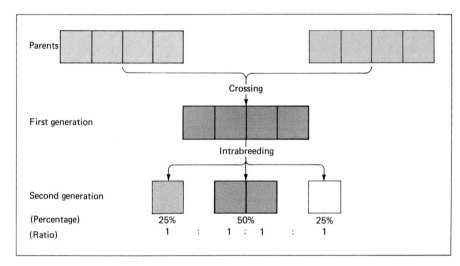

Fig. 2-4
How Autosomal
Dominant Inheritance
Works

Parents

Crossing

First generation

Intrabreeding

Second generation

(Percentage)   25%   50%   25%

(Ratio)   1   :   1 : 1   :   1

tween her parents, as in height or skin color, indicating that these traits are the result of several genes. Or sometimes a trait will combine the attributes of both alleles, as with some chemical substances in the blood. Some genes, such as blood groupings, exist in three or more allelic states and are known as *multiple alleles* (Boston Children's Medical Center, 1972). Hetherington and Parke (1979) point out, "There are about 3.8 billion people alive today, but there are about 70 trillion potential human genotypes" (p. 29).

What happens when an abnormal trait is carried by a dominant gene? When one parent, say the mother, has one normal gene

(recessive) and one abnormal gene (dominant), and the other parent, the father, has two normal genes, each of their children will have a 50-50 chance of inheriting the abnormal gene from the mother and of having the same defect she has. (See Figure 2-5.) Every individual who has this abnormal gene has the defect. The defect cannot be one that kills a person before the age of reproduction: if it did, the defect could not be passed on to the next generation. Among the diseases passed on this way are achondroplasia (a type of dwarfism) and Huntington's chorea (a progressive degeneration of the nervous system).

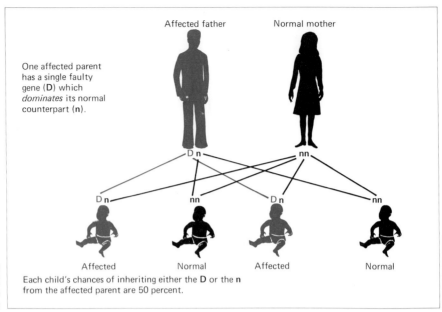

One affected parent has a single faulty gene (**D**) which *dominates* its normal counterpart (**n**).

Affected father

Normal mother

D n

nn

D n

nn

D n

nn

Affected

Normal

Affected

Normal

Fig. 2-5
How Autosomai Dominant Inheritance Works

Each child's chances of inheriting either the **D** or the **n** from the affected parent are 50 percent.

The well-know folk singer Woody Guthrie died of Huntington's Chorea. His son, singer Arlo Guthrie, still does not know whether or not he inherited the disease from his father, since its symptoms do not show up till a person is in his thirties or forties. If Arlo was lucky, he inherited one of his mother's two normal genes for this trait and a normal one from his father, rather than the father's abnormal dominant gene, which would doom the son to the same fate as the father.

Autosomal Recessive Inheritance

Blue-eyed people and green-seeded plants demonstrate the pattern of *autosomal recessive inheritance*. Recessive traits show up only if a child has received the same recessive gene from each parent.

When one parent, for instance, the mother, has two dominant genes, say, for brown eyes, and the other parent, the father, has one gene for brown eyes (dominant) and one gene for blue eyes (recessive), none of their children will have blue eyes. Each child, though, has a 50-50 chance of being a *carrier* for blue eyes, like the father, and of passing the recessive gene on to his or her children.

When one carrier marries another carrier of the same recessive gene, each of their children has a 50-50 chance of inheriting one dominant (brown-eyed) gene and one recessive (blue-eyed) gene and being a carrier himself. And each child has 1 chance in 4 of inheriting one dominant (brown-eyed) gene from each parent, so he not only does not have blue eyes himself, but he cannot pass them on to his children. But each child also has 1 chance in 4 of receiving one recessive (blue-eyed) gene from each parent. This is the only way that blue eyes can show up.

Blue eyes are welcome recessive traits, but the more than 700 illnesses or other types of birth defects that are carried by recessive genes are not. One reason marriage between relatives is discouraged is to diminish the chance of children's inheriting a disease passed on by recessive genes that both parents may have inherited from a common ancestor.

Diseases transmitted by recessive genes are often killers in infancy. Examples are sickle-cell anemia, a blood disorder seen most often among black people, and Tay-Sachs disease, a deteriorative disease of the

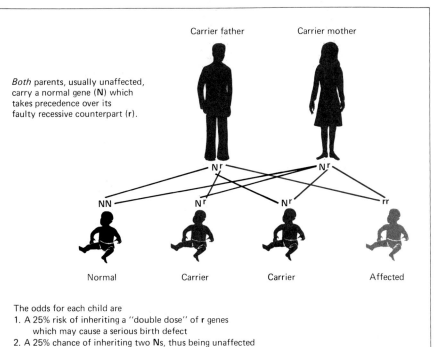

Both parents, usually unaffected, carry a normal gene (**N**) which takes precedence over its faulty recessive counterpart (**r**).

Carrier father   Carrier mother

N r   N r

NN   N r   N r   rr

Normal   Carrier   Carrier   Affected

The odds for each child are
1. A 25% risk of inheriting a "double dose" of **r** genes which may cause a serious birth defect
2. A 25% chance of inheriting two **N**s, thus being unaffected
3. A 50% chance of being a carrier as both parents are

Fig. 2-6
How Autosomal
Recessive Inheritance
Works

central nervous system that occurs mainly among Jews of Eastern European ancestry.

Sex-Linked Inheritance

Red-green color blindness is one of about 150 known conditions that may be transmitted by recessive genes. Carried on the X chromosome of an unaffected mother, these sex-linked recessive traits are almost always expressed only in male children. The blood-clotting disorder called hemophilia is passed on in this way and used to be known as the "royal" disease because it affected so many members of the ruling family of England. The sons of a normal man and a woman with one abnormal gene will have a 50 percent chance of inheriting the abnormal X chromosome and the disorder, and a 50 percent chance of inheriting the mother's normal X chromosome and being unaffected. Daughters will have a 50 percent chance of being *carriers*. (See Figure 2-7.) An affected father can never pass on such a gene to his sons, since he contrib-

utes a Y chromosome to them; but he can pass the gene on to his daughters, who then become carriers.

In rare instances a female can inherit one of these sex-linked conditions. The daughter of a hemophiliac man and a woman who is a carrier for the disease has a 50 percent chance of inheriting the abnormal X chromosome from each of her parents. Should this happen, she will suffer from the disease.

Independent Segregation

Mendel also experimented with two traits at once, crossing one seed in which yellow was dominant with another in which a round shape was dominant. He found that color and shape were transmitted *separately*. Most of the offspring were yellow and round; about the same number were either yellow and wrinkled or green and round; and the smallest number were green and wrinkled (Timiras, 1972). Thus he showed that every hereditary trait is transmitted as a separate unit.

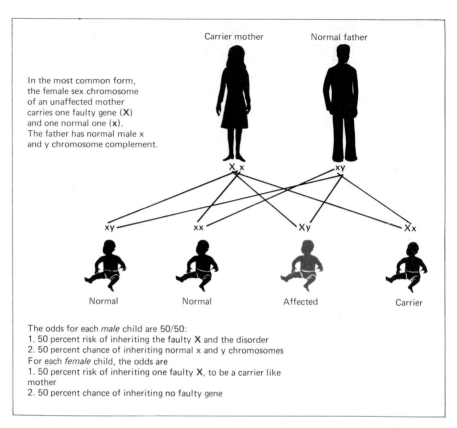

In the most common form, the female sex chromosome of an unaffected mother carries one faulty gene (**X**) and one normal one (**x**). The father has normal male x and y chromosome complement.

Carrier mother   Normal father

X x   xy

xy   xx   Xy   Xx

Normal   Normal   Affected   Carrier

The odds for each *male* child are 50/50:
1. 50 percent risk of inheriting the faulty **X** and the disorder
2. 50 percent chance of inheriting normal x and y chromosomes
For each *female* child, the odds are
1. 50 percent risk of inheriting one faulty **X**, to be a carrier like mother
2. 50 percent chance of inheriting no faulty gene

Fig. 2-7
How Sex-Linked
Inheritance Works

Multifactorial Inheritance

Many normal traits and a number of abnormal ones appear to be inherited in a much more complicated way, either through certain combinations of genes, or through the interaction of environmental factors and genetic predispositions. Height, weight, some elements of intelligence, and other general traits are probably determined by many genes, rather than by one or two. Some human defects thought to be passed on through the interaction of factors include spina bifida (a defect in the closure of the vertebral canal) and cleft palate (incomplete fusion of the roof of the mouth or upper lip). The mental illness schizophrenia and the behavior disorder hyperactivity also may be transmitted multifactorially.

CHROMOSOMAL ABNORMALITIES

Every cell in the human body carries all our chromosomes. Each one, then, reflects the genetic makeup we are born with. Once determined, the chromosomes are stable over a lifetime. When something goes wrong with chromosomal development, serious abnormalities are likely to develop. Some chromosomal defects are inherited, while others result from accidents that occur during the development of an individual organism. Accidental abnormalities are not likely to recur in the same family.

Down's Syndrome

Down's syndrome, the most common chromosomal defect, is also called "mongolism" because affected persons have an Oriental-looking skin fold at the inner corners of the eyes. Other signs of Down's syndrome are a small head; flat nose; protruding tongue; defective heart, eyes, and ears; and mental and motor retardation.

This disorder, which is caused by an extra twenty-first chromosome, or the translocation of part of the twenty-first chromosome

Down's syndrome children tend to be cheerful and sociable. (©Bruce Roberts/ Rapho/Photo Researchers, Inc.)

onto another chromosome, occurs once in every 700 live births. The risk rises sharply with the age of the parents. Among 25-year-old mothers, the incidence is 1 in 2000 births; for 40-year-olds, it is 1 in 100; and among mothers 45 and older, the risk is 1 in 40. Incidence also rises with the age of the father: slowly up to age 49, sharply among fathers 55 and over (Abroms & Bennett, 1979). Recent analyses of the karyotypes of Down's syndrome parents have shown that more than 1 case in 4 may be traceable to the father (Abroms & Bennett, 1979).

This disorder is hereditary only about 3 percent of the time and is more likely when the affected child is born to younger parents; when the parents are older, the defect is more likely a chromosomal accident. The mistake in chromosome distribution may occur during development of the ovum, the sperm, or the zygote (Smith & Wilson, 1973).

So far almost all research into the causes of the syndrome has concentrated on the mother's role. Researchers have suggested that the eggs of some women deteriorate with advancing age, that younger mothers of Down's syndrome babies may be characterized by acceleration of biological aging, and that seasonal variations in the births of these babies may be related to seasonal fluctuation in women's hormonal levels (Emanuel, Sever, Milham, & Thuline, 1972; Robinson et al., 1974; Janerick & Jacobson, 1977; Holmes, 1978). Now that newer techniques for identifying parental chromosomes have shown a greater paternal involvement in the syndrome, more attention will no doubt be paid to the possible mechanism behind the father's contribution.

Children with Down's syndrome have a limited intellectual potential, with most ranging from moderately retarded to dull normal. While most professionals used to recommend institutionalization for these children, the trend today is toward home care. A growing number of families are even choosing to adopt children with the syndrome whose own families do not feel they can care for them at home (Oelsner, 1979). The children, who tend to be cheerful and sociable, with a gift for mimicry, are often pleasant companions who enjoy their day-to-day life. Many learn simple skills and, as teenagers and adults, can help to support themselves.

In recent years, educators have instituted programs to help these children improve their skills on many levels. One of the most comprehensive intervention programs was established in 1971 at the experimental education unit at the Child Development and Mental Retardation Center of the University of Washington (Hayden & Haring, 1976). This program admits children from the age of 2 weeks to 6 years and works with parents on a variety of exercises and activities to help the children develop motor, language, social, cognitive, and self-help skills. The program's goals, for example, for an 18-month-old baby are that he or she will be able, with 80 to 100 percent accuracy:

. . . to sit without support and to stand for 5 minutes with support; to make eye contact with people and objects and respond to auditory stimuli; to reach, grasp, hold, and release objects on cue; point to pictures in a book; and perform at least three manipulative tasks, such as placing six rings on a stick, without adult help [Hayden & Haring, 1976, p. 593].

Many of the children in this program have shown remarkable early gains, making the educators involved revise their expectations of Down's syndrome children upward, but long-term studies are needed to determine whether the children will maintain these gains over time.

The mortality rate for Down's syndrome children is very high early in life—especially for females—with 40 to 55 percent of Down's syndrome babies dying in the first year. Once they come through the early years, these individuals have longer life expectancies than they used to because of the increased use of antibiotics. Many live until middle age (Scully, 1973).

Other Chromosomal Disorders

About twenty years ago officials of the Olympic Games became concerned that some of the athletes participating in the women's events may have originally been males, who had undergone sex change operations and/or received large amounts of female hormones to change some of their physical attributes, while retaining advantages of masculine strength and basic body build. To set a measure of "femininity control," women Olympic athletes have in recent years been required to take the Barr body test.

The test is simple and quick, consisting of scraping the insides of both cheeks with a tongue depressor. The scrapings are then analyzed to determine whether a *Barr body* is present. This material, discovered in 1949 by Dr. M. L. Barr, is found in the nucleus of the female cell but not in that of the male. The presence of this substance is generally considered proof that the individual is indeed female.

However, there are certain chromosomal disorders, such as Klinefelter's syndrome, in which a person who appears to be a male has the Barr body, and Turner's syndrome, in which a person who appears to be a female does not. In either of these cases, sexual underdevelopment and sterility are present.

KLINEFELTER'S SYNDROME Affecting males only, this syndrome occurs in 1 in 800 live male births, more frequently in sons of older women (Kennedy, 1971). Instead of the normal male chromosome arrangement (XY), Klinefelter males have an extra X chromosome (XXY), and they show the Barr body in their cells. This syndrome includes mental retardation; small testes; sterility; pubertal development of female secondary sex characteristics, such as breast enlargement; and the possibility of effeminacy, homosexuality, transvestism, and transsexualism (Money & Pollett, 1964). The administration of the male sex hormone *testosterone* to Klinefelter adolescent males gives them more masculine body contours and sexual characteristics, makes them more assertive, and heightens their sexual drive (Johnson et al., 1970).

XYY SYNDROME Some males have an extra Y chromosome. The full significance of this condition is not known, although there has been some speculation about it in recent years. The incidence of XYY in the general population of tall men—5 feet 11 inches or taller—is 1 in 80. Telfer and his associates (1968), however, found that 1 in 11 tall men found in a criminal population of imprisoned men had marked chromosomal abnormalities. This finding gave rise to the theory that the single Y chromosome found in most men contributes to male aggression, and an extra Y causes excessive aggression.

However, Witkin et al.'s 1976 study of XYY, XXY, and XY men disproves this rationale. This study did find a larger proportion of XYY and XXY men in prison than their numbers in the general population would lead us to expect. However, the crimes both groups had been convicted of were more likely to be those of property rather than of aggression against another person. They were no more likely to commit violent crimes than were XY men.

Both the XYY and XXY men did differ from XYs in another way, though—intelligence. Their mean scores on army intelligence tests were lower. So the explanation for these men's greater presence in jail may simply be that people of lower intelligence are no more adept at committing crimes without getting caught than they would be in carrying out legal activities.

TURNER'S SYNDROME This syndrome affects females only. It occurs in 1 of every 3000 female births (Kennedy, 1971) and results in a female's having only forty-five chromosomes—twenty-two pairs of autosomes and one X. The other X is missing, and the Barr body is lacking or minimized. The chromosome picture is XO. An affected individual is dwarfed with webbing of the neck. She may be mentally retarded (most often in spatial ability) and sexually underdeveloped, with the ovary almost entirely atrophied. Estrogen therapy at puberty induces sexual maturation (Timiras, 1972), although the girl remains sterile.

XXX SYNDROME Characterized by three X chromosomes and two Barr bodies, this syndrome occurs three times as often as Turner's. Even though the individual appears as a normal female, her sexual characteristics are often poorly developed and the incidence of mental disturbances and psychotic behaviors is higher than in the general population (Timiras, 1972).

GENETIC COUNSELING

Five years after their marriage, Bill and Mary Brown decided that they were ready to start their family. Mary became pregnant right away; the couple turned their study into a nursery; and they eagerly looked forward to bringing the baby home. But Bill and Mary's first baby never set foot in that brightly decorated nursery. She was born dead, a victim of *anencephaly*, a birth defect in which the baby's skull is missing and some of the internal organs are malformed.

The young couple were heartbroken over the loss of the baby they had both wanted. More than that, they were afraid to try again. They were afraid that they might not be able to conceive a normal child. They still wanted to have a baby but felt they could not go through another crushing disappointment.

Each year in the United States, from 100,000 to 150,000 infants with a significant genetic disorder or malformation are born. These babies account for 3 to 5 percent of the total of 3 million births and for at least 20 percent of infant deaths (Clinical Pediatrics, 1979) Nearly half of the serious malformations involve the central nervous system. Eight out of ten babies with congenital abnormalities who survive the first year of life do reach adulthood (Vuillamy, 1973).

The relatively new service of *genetic counseling* has been developed to help couples—like Mary and Bill—who have some reason for believing that they may be at high risk for bearing a child with a birth defect. People who have already borne one handicapped child, who have a family history of hereditary illness, or who suffer from a condition known or suspected to be inherited can get information that will help them determine their chances for producing future afflicted children. Genetic counseling aims to discover the cause of a specific defect in a specific child, to establish patterns for inheritance, and to determine an individual couple's chances of producing normal children.

The genetic counselor may be a pediatrician, an obstetrician, a family doctor, or a genetic specialist. He or she takes a thorough family history, including information relating to diseases and causes of death of siblings, parents, blood-related aunts and uncles, and grandparents; any marriages between relatives; previous abortions or stillbirths; and other relevant material. Then each parent and any children in the family receive a physical examination, since a person's physical appearance often gives a clue to the presence of certain genetic abnormalities.

Sophisticated laboratory investigations of a patient's blood, skin, urine, or fingerprints may also be indicated. Chromosomes prepared from a patient's tissue are analyzed, then photographed. The photographs of the chromosomes will then be cut out and arranged according to size and structure on a chart called a *karyotype* to demonstrate any chromosomal abnormalities that may exist. Improved techniques for examining karyotypes make it possible to determine whether an individual who appears normal could possibly transmit genetic defects to his or her children.

Based on all these tests, the counselor determines the mathematical odds for this couple's having an afflicted child. If a couple feels that the risks are too high, the husband or wife sometimes chooses to be sterilized or the couple may consider artificial donor insemination or adoption.

A genetic counselor does not give a couple advice on whether to take the risks indicated for the condition in question. Rather, the counselor can only try to find out and help a couple understand the mathematical risks and the implications of particular diseases and to make them aware of alternative courses of action.

Some people think that a 25 percent risk of inheriting a recessive disease, for example, means that if the first child is affected, then the next three children will not be similarly affected. But the saying "chance has no memory" applies here. A 25 percent risk means that the odds are 1 out of 4 for every child born of the union to inherit the disease. If a disorder is not particularly disabling or is amenable to treatment, a couple may choose to take a chance. In other cases, counseling will enable a couple to realize that the risk they feared so much is actually quite slight or even nonexistent. In the future, geneticists hope to be able to do much more to help parents; they even hope to be able to modify abnormal genetic structure to cure inherited genetic defects.

The National Clearinghouse for Human Genetic Diseases of the Department of Health, Education, and Welfare can answer questions relating to genetics and genetic diseases. It has a library on the topic and offers a directory of places that offer genetic counseling. The Clearinghouse is at 1776 West Jefferson St., Rockville, MD 20852.

PRENATAL DIAGNOSIS OF BIRTH DEFECTS

In recent years medical technology has offered a growing array of revolutionary tools to assess the health of children even before birth. These new techniques, coupled with the legalization of abortion, have encouraged many couples with troubling family or personal medical histories to take a chance on conception.

Many couples who would never have dared risk a pregnancy have been reassured by in utero examinations that their babies would not be born with the defects they have feared, and have gone on to bear and rear them. In other cases, expectant parents who received the sad news that their babies would be born with disabling medical conditions have chosen to terminate these pregnancies and have embarked on new conceptions with a more fortunate blending of genes. And those parents who have chosen to continue a pregnancy even though they were aware of the handicaps their children would be born with, have, through prenatal diagnosis, had more time to adjust to their children's conditions and to plan for special care for them. Let us look at some of these new techniques.

Amniocentesis

Under this procedure, a sample of the *amniotic fluid* (in which the fetus floats within the uterus) is withdrawn and analyzed. Amniocentesis can detect a growing number of birth defects and can alert doctors to the need for special treatment even before birth, as in Rh disease, for which blood transfusions in utero may be needed.

Amniocentesis is indicated for women who are over 35, who are of East European Jewish ancestry (and thus at higher than average risk for Tay-Sachs disease), or who have a family history of such other conditions as Down's syndrome, spina bifida, sickle-cell anemia, Rh disease, or muscular dystrophy. Currently, only 10 percent of women at risk in these areas undergo amniocentesis (Clinical Pediatrics, 1979).

A survey of 3000 women who received amniocentesis between 1970 and 1978 at the University of California in San Francisco yielded results that indicated that the procedure is "safe, highly reliable and extremely accurate"

(Golbus, Loughman, Epstein, Halbasch, Stephens, & Hall, 1979, p. 157). In this series, there were only fourteen errors in analyzing and reporting test findings, only six of which influenced the course of pregnancy. Two women aborted fetuses that turned out to be normal, and four serious abnormalities were not detected.

Maternal Blood Test

Between the fourteenth and twentieth weeks of pregnancy, a woman's blood can be tested for the amount it contains of a substance called alpha fetoprotein (AFP). The test is not indicated for routine use in all pregnant women—only for those considered to be at risk for bearing a child with neural tube defects. These are major structural defects in the formation of the brain and spinal cord such as spina bifida and anencephaly.

An unduly high AFP level may point to the possibility of these disorders. The tests do not, however, detect all of them, and in about 1 case in 1000 they produce a false positive result. Therefore, when a high AFP level is found, ultrasound and amniocentesis (which can enable the measurement of AFP in the amniotic fluid) are called for to confirm or contradict the diagnosis (Ferguson-Smith et al. 1978; Clinical Pediatrics, 1979). If the amniotic AFP level is high, fetoscopy can be used to examine the fetus.

Ultrasound

High-frequency sound waves directed into the abdomen of the pregnant woman yield an "echo-visual" picture of inner structures such as the uterus, the fetus, and the placenta. Ultrasound is considered a "noninvasive" technology since direct entry is not made into the patient's body. Doctors use it to measure the size of the baby's head and thus determine its gestational age; to detect the presence of twins and other multiple births; to make amniocentesis easier by locating the fetal structures, the umbilical cord, and the placenta; to evaluate uterine abnormalities that might complicate the birth; and to find out whether the fetus has died in the uterus. In a few centers around the country, ultrasound is used to diagnose abnormalities of the fetal skeleton or other major organ systems, but in most places this diagnostic use is still in the research stage (Clinical Pediatrics, 1979).

While ultrasound has not been shown to have ill effects on human development, it is so new that its long-range effects won't be known for years. For the time being, then, it seems prudent to use it only when medically indicated, and not routinely in all pregnancies.

Fetoscopy

Guided by ultrasound, which helps them scan the womb and detect the fetal outline, doctors can insert a tiny telescope directly into the uterus. Equipped with a light, the scope permits direct visual examinations of a limited surface of fetal anatomy and has made it possible to detect such abnormal conditions as anencephaly, spina bifida, or placenta previa. (In this last disorder, the baby's exit from the womb is blocked, causing major problems during delivery if not recognized in time.)

Fetoscopy also makes it possible to use a small needle to draw a fetal blood sample, which can be used to diagnose such disorders as sickle-cell anemia, "classical" hemophilia, Duchenne's muscular dystrophy, and possibly Tay-Sachs disease (Rodeck & Campbell, 1978; Clinical Pediatrics, 1979; Mennut, 1977; Perry, Hechtman, & Chow, 1979).

While fetoscopy is 98 percent accurate, it carries a greater risk to the fetus than does amniocentesis. Miscarriages occur in some 5 percent of pregnancies in which fetoscopy

has been used, and one major medical center noted a 9 to 10 percent prematurity rate, compared with 7 percent in a control group (Clinical Pediatrics, 1979). Because of these risks, fetoscopy is in the "applied research stage," not ready for general use (Check, 1979).

Electronic Fetal Monitoring

Machines that monitor the fetal heartbeat throughout labor and delivery first came into general use in the 1960s. In 1978, they were used in an estimated 7 out of 10 births (Check, 1979). With the soaring popularity of fetal monitoring, many criticisms are being raised about its use.

Banta and Thacker (1979), who evaluated nearly 300 medical reports on the procedure and its effects, claim that routine monitoring is unduly costly, that it results in more babies being born by the riskier cesarean delivery than the vaginal route, and that it occasionally causes injury to mother or child. These researchers, as well as the American College of Obstetricians and Gynecologists (1979) recommend that monitoring be reserved only for high-risk pregnancies, including premature and small-for-date babies.

PRENATAL DEVELOPMENT: THREE STAGES

The new life in the womb, the *conceptus*, goes through three stages of development: *germinal*, *embryonic*, and *fetal*. It is hard to establish exact prenatal age because no one knows the exact moment of fertilization. Physicians generally date a pregnancy from either the last menstrual period (*menstrual age*, or 280 days) or two weeks after the last period (*fertilization age*, or 266 days). Ovulation usually occurs midway in the menstrual cycle, but its timing varies somewhat from woman to woman, and even from cycle to cycle in the same woman. So although the following sequence of development is true for all embryos, it is hard to be precise in the actual timing. However, upon birth there are ways to esti-

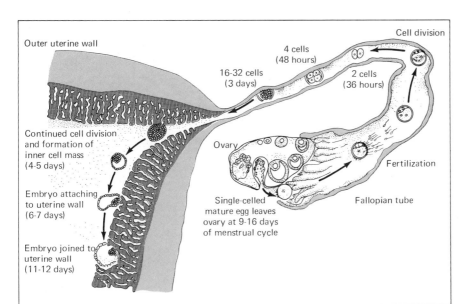

Outer uterine wall

Cell division

4 cells
(48 hours)

16-32 cells
(3 days)

2 cells
(36 hours)

Continued cell division
and formation of
inner cell mass
(4-5 days)

Ovary

Embryo attaching
to uterine wall
(6-7 days)

Single-celled
mature egg leaves
ovary at 9-16 days
of menstrual cycle

Fertilization

Fallopian tube

Embryo joined to
uterine wall
(11-12 days)

Fig. 2-8
Early Development of
Human Egg and
Embryo

mate an infant's gestational age. These include assessing neurological signs such as reflexes and assessing the baby's physical development (skin color, body hair, nipple formation, ear formation, and so forth).

A month-by-month description of prenatal development is given in Table 2-1.

GERMINAL STAGE (FERTILIZATION TO TWO WEEKS)

During the *germinal stage* the organism divides, becomes more complex, and is implanted in the wall of the uterus.

Within thirty-six hours after fertilization, the single-celled zygote (created by sperm and ovum) enters a period of rapid cell division. Seventy-two hours after fertilization, it has divided into thirty-two cells; a day later it has seventy cells. This division continues, until the original single cell develops the 800 billion or more specialized cells each of us is made of.

While the fertilized egg is dividing, it is also making its way down the fallopian tube to the uterus, which it reaches in three or four days. By the time it gets there, its form has changed into a fluid-filled sphere called a *blastocyst*, which then floats freely in the uterus for a day or two. Some cells around the edge of the blastocyst cluster on one side to form the *embryonic disk*, a thickened cell mass from which the baby will develop. This mass is already differentiating into two layers. The upper layer, the *ectoderm*, will eventually become the outer layer of skin, the nails, hair, teeth, sensory organs, and nervous system, including the brain and spinal cord. The lower layer, the *endoderm*, will develop into the digestive system, liver, pancreas, salivary glands, and respiratory system. Later, a middle layer, the *mesoderm*, will develop and differentiate into the inner layer of skin, muscles, skeleton, and excretory and circulatory systems.

With my first child I missed a period and my breasts hurt. With Jesse, I knew the moment I conceived him. There's no way of pinning that down, no way of explaining how I felt. I just knew.

from *Our Bodies, Ourselves,* p. 258.

During the germinal stage other parts of the blastocyst develop into the nurturing and protective organs: the *placenta*, the *umbilical cord*, and the *amniotic sac*. The miraculous multipurpose placenta is connected to the embryo by the umbilical cord, through which it delivers oxygen and nourishment to the fetus and removes its body wastes. The placenta also helps to combat internal infection, makes the unborn child immune to various diseases, and produces the hormones that support pregnancy, prepare the mother's breasts for lactation, and eventually stimulate the uterine contractions that will expel the baby from her body. The amniotic sac is a fluid-filled membrane that encases the developing baby, protecting it and giving it room to move.

The *trophoblast*, the outer cell layer of the blastocyst, produces tiny threadlike structures that penetrate the lining of the uterine wall. In this way, the blastocyst burrows in until it is implanted in a warm, nurturing nesting place. Upon implantation, the blastocyst has about 150 cells; when this cell mass is fully implanted in the uterus, it is called an *embryo*.

EMBRYONIC STAGE (TWO TO EIGHT WEEKS)

During the embryonic stage, the major body systems (respiratory, alimentary, nervous) and organs develop. Because of rapid growth and development in this stage, the embryo is most vulnerable to prenatal environmental influences. Almost all developmental birth defects (cleft palate, incomplete or missing limbs, blindness, deafness) occur during the critical first *trimester* (three-month period) of

Table 2-1
The Development of Embryo and Fetus

1 MONTH

During the first month, the new life has grown more quickly than it will at any other time during its lifetime, achieving a size 10,000 times greater than the zygote. It now measures from ¼ to ½ inch in length.

Blood is flowing through its tiny veins and arteries. Its minuscule heart beats sixty-five times a minute. It already has the beginnings of a brain, kidney, liver, and digestive tract. The umbilical cord, its lifeline to its mother, is working. By looking very closely through a microscope, it is possible to see the swellings on the head that will eventually become its eyes, ears, mouth, and nose. Its sex cannot yet be distinguished.

2 MONTHS

The embryo now looks like a well-proportioned, small-scale baby. It is less than 1 inch long and weighs only ⅟₁₃ ounce. Its head is one-half its total body length. Facial parts are clearly developed, with tongue and teeth buds. The arms have hands, fingers, and thumbs, and the legs have knees, ankles, and toes. It has a thin covering of skin and can even make hand and foot prints.

The embryo's brain impulses coordinate the function of its organ systems. Sex organs are developing; the heartbeat is steady. The stomach produces digestive juices; the liver, blood cells. The kidney removes uric acid from the blood. The skin is now sensitive enough to react to tactile stimulation. If an aborted 8-week-old embryo is stroked, it reacts by flexing its trunk, extending its head, and moving back its arms.

3 MONTHS

Now a fetus, the developing person weighs 1 ounce and measures about 3 inches in length. It has fingernails, toenails, eyelids (still closed), vocal cords, lips, and a prominent nose. Its head is still large—about one-third its total length—and its forehead is high. Its sex can be easily determined.

The organ systems are functioning, so that the fetus may now breathe, swallow amniotic fluid in and out of the lungs, and occasionally urinate. Its ribs and vertebrae have turned to cartilage, and its internal reproductive organs have primitive egg or sperm cells.

The fetus can now make a variety of specialized responses: It can move its legs, feet, thumbs, and head; its mouth can open and close and swallow. If its eyelids are touched, it squints; if its palm is touched, it makes a partial fist; if its lip is touched, it will suck; and if the sole of the foot is stroked, the toes will fan out. These reflex behaviors will be present at birth but will disappear during the first months of life.

4 MONTHS

The body is catching up to the head, which is now only one-fourth the total body length, the same proportion it will be at birth. The fetus now measures 8 to 10 inches and weighs about 6 ounces. The umbilical cord is as long as the fetus and will continue to grow with it. The placenta is now fully developed.

The mother may be able to feel the fetus kicking, a movement known as *quickening*, which some societies and religious groups consider the beginning of human life. The reflex activities that appeared in the third month are now brisker, because of increased muscular development.

5 MONTHS

Now weighing about 12 ounces to 1 pound and measuring about 1 foot, the fetus begins to show signs of an individual personality. It has definite sleep-wake patterns, has a favorite position in the uterus (called its *lie*), and becomes more active—kicking, stretching, squirming, and even hiccuping. By putting an ear to the mother's abdomen, it is possible to hear the fetal heartbeat. The sweat and sebaceous glands are functioning. The respiratory system is not yet adequate to sustain life outside the womb; a baby born at this time has no hope of survival.

Coarse hair has begun to grow on the eyebrows and eyelashes, fine hair is on the head, and a woolly hair called *lanugo* covers the body but will disappear at birth or soon thereafter.

6 MONTHS

The rate of fetal growth has slowed down a little—the fetus is now about 14 inches long and 1¼ pounds. It is getting fat pads under the skin; the eyes are complete, opening and closing and looking in all directions. It can maintain regular breathing for twenty-four hours; it cries; and it can make a fist with a strong grip.

If the fetus were to be born now, it would have an extremely slim chance of survival because its breathing apparatus is still very immature. There have been instances, however, when a fetus of this age has survived outside the womb.

7 MONTHS

The 16-inch fetus, weighing 3 to 5 pounds, now has fully developed reflex patterns. It cries, breathes, and swallows and may suck its thumb. The lanugo may disappear at about this time, or it may remain until shortly after birth. Head hair may continue to grow. Survival chances for a fetus weighing at least 3½ pounds are fairly good, provided it receives intensive medical attention. It will probably have to live in an incubator until a weight of 5 pounds is attained.

8 MONTHS

The 18- to 20-inch fetus now weighs between 5 and 7 pounds and is fast outgrowing its living quarters. Its movements are curtailed because of cramped conditions. During this month and the next, a layer of fat is developing over the fetus's entire body, to enable it to adjust to varying temperatures outside the womb.

9 MONTHS

About a week before birth, the baby stops growing, having reached an average weight of just over 7 pounds and a length of about 20 inches, with boys tending to be a little longer and heavier than girls. Fat pads continue to form, the organ system is operating more efficiently, the heart rate increases, and more wastes are expelled. The reddish color of the skin is fading. On its birthday, the fetus will have been in the womb for approximately 266 days, although gestation age is usually estimated at 280 days since doctors date the pregnancy from the mother's last menstrual period.

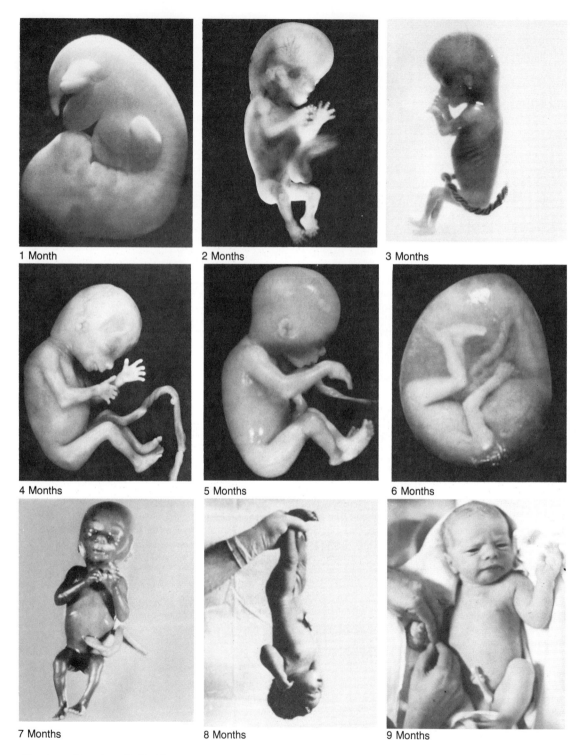

1 Month

2 Months

3 Months

4 Months

5 Months

6 Months

7 Months

8 Months

9 Months

(Courtesy of Landrum B. Shettles, M.D.)

pregnancy. The most severely defective embryos usually do not survive beyond this time and are aborted spontaneously (Garn, 1966).

FETAL STAGE (EIGHT WEEKS TO BIRTH)

With the appearance of the first bone cells at about eight weeks, the embryo becomes a *fetus*. During the long period until birth, the finishing touches are put on the various body parts, and the form of the body changes and grows about twenty times in length.

SPONTANEOUS ABORTION

A miscarriage, or a *spontaneous abortion*, is the expulsion from the uterus of a conceptus that could not survive outside the womb. Three out of four miscarriages occur within the first trimester, affecting an estimated 30 to 50 percent of all pregnancies (Gordon, 1975; Garn, 1966).

In ancient times, people believed that a woman could be frightened into miscarrying by a clap of thunder or jostled into it if her chariot hit a rut in the street. But today we realize that the conceptus is well protected from almost all jolts. Guttmacher (1962) has said, "You cannot shake loose a good human egg any more than you can shake a good unripe apple from the apple tree." Most miscarriages result from abnormal pregnancies.

Ash, Vennart, and Carter (1977) estimate that chromosomal abnormalities are present in about half of all spontaneous abortions. A defective ovum or sperm, an unfavorable location for implantation, a breakdown in supplies of oxygen or nourishment caused by abnormal development of the umbilical cord, and some physiological abnormality of the mother are all possible causes of spontaneous abortion.

INDUCED ABORTION

The deliberate termination of pregnancy is an issue with many medical, psychological, and social ramifcations. A woman may choose abortion if carrying a pregnancy to term could affect her health, if she learns she is at risk of bearing a defective child, if her pregnancy resulted from rape or incest, or if, for other reasons, she does not want to bear this child. Perhaps she is not married; perhaps she wants to continue her education; perhaps she is poor; or perhaps she is in a collapsing marriage.

Abortion has been used as a backstop to birth control through the ages. Under English common law before 1803 and in the American colonies, abortion was legal if it took place before "quickening," or the first sign of fetal movement. It did not become a sin under Catholic doctrine until 1869 if it was performed before the soul of the fetus was thought to become rational (forty days after conception for a male and eighty or ninety days for a female) (Pilpel, Zuckerman, & Ogg, 1975).

Abortion is again legal in the United States. In 1973 the Supreme Court decided that during the first three months of pregnancy the state cannot prohibit any woman from obtaining an abortion from a licensed physician; that after the first trimester the state can regulate abortion when such regulations reasonably relate to the preservation or protection of the woman's health; and that after the fetus is considered viable (usually twenty-four to twenty-eight weeks), the state can regulate or even bar all abortions except those necessary to protect the mother's health.

When abortions were illegal, they were extremely dangerous, injuring, rendering sterile, and even killing many women. Legal abortion, however, is a very safe, simple procedure, especially when performed early in the pregnancy (Tietze & Lewit, 1977).

In any unwanted pregnancy there is a certain amount of psychological pain no matter how the woman resolves her problem. None of the alternatives—terminating the pregnancy, giving the child up for adoption, or keeping the child despite whatever problems are attendant in raising it—is without stress. A review of the literature indicates that:

. . . the mild depression or guilt feelings experienced by some women after an abortion appear to be only temporary, although for women with a previous psychiatric history, abortion may be more upsetting and stressful [Institute of Medicine, 1975, p. 98].

PRENATAL ACTIVITIES AND ABILITIES

The fetus is far from a passive passenger in its mother's womb. It kicks, turns, flexes its body, turns somersaults, squints, swallows, makes a fist, hiccups, and sucks its thumb. It responds to both sound and vibrations, indicating that it can hear and feel (Grimwade, Walker, & Word, 1970; Sontag & Wallace, 1934, 1936).

I have felt my child quicken in me. A curious stir, a faint throb like a pulse; and my belly moved in a strange undulation. I was elated.

Evelyn Scott (b. 1893) in *Revelations*, p. 101.

I was lying on my stomach and felt— something, like someone lightly touching my deep insides. Then I just sat very still and for an alive moment felt the hugeness of having something living growing in me. Then I said, 'No, it's not possible, it's too early yet, and then I started to cry . . . . that one moment was my first body awareness of another living thing inside me.

Our Bodies, Ourselves, p. 262.

Even within the womb, each of us is unique. Fetuses vary in the amount of their activity, in the kind of moving they do, and in the regularity and speed of their heart rates. Some of these patterns seem to persist into adulthood, supporting the notion of inborn temperament.

THE PRENATAL ENVIRONMENT

From the moment of conception throughout our lives, we are shaped by our environment. Even before birth, we are subjected to a myriad of environmental influences. The food a mother eats, the drugs she takes, the illnesses she suffers, the radiation she receives—even the emotions she feels—can all affect the baby in her womb.

Maternal Nutrition

At one time an unusually large number of *cretins* (persons with a thyroid disorder that produces physical and mental deficiency) were being born in several Swiss areas where the soil lacked iodine. Supplementary iodine was prescribed for all pregnant women in these regions, and the result was "magical." "In the course of one generation, cretinism all but vanished" (Montagu, 1964).

This is a dramatic example of the relationship between maternal nutrition and the health of the child. Many studies have been conducted on this relationship, but results are contradictory. Some show that when an expectant mother eats well, her child will benefit, and when she eats poorly, her child will suffer. Others, surprisingly, indicate that the pregnant woman's diet doesn't affect her offspring much one way or the other. There is also disagreement about which period of pregnancy is most important for fetal nourishment.

Some studies show the fetus suffers more when the mother is malnourished early in pregnancy (Vore, 1971), while others find the effects of maternal malnutrition more extreme in the last trimester (Naeye, Blanc, & Paul, 1973). Stein and Susser (1976, in Lloyd-Still, 1976) feel the second trimester is critical. During these middle three months, neurons, specialized nerve cells that control impulses, are increasing in number. These cells, which underlie the integrity of brain function, are irreplaceable. Therefore, any damage done to them at this time may well be irreversible.

Many studies have found that mothers who eat well have fewer complications of pregnancy and childbirth and bear healthier babies, and that mothers with inadequate diets are more likely to bear premature or low-birthweight infants, or babies who are born dead or die soon after birth (Burke, Beal, Kirkwood, & Stuart, 1943; Read, Habicht, Lechtig, & Klein, 1973).

A study of poor Guatemalan women has demonstrated that nutritional supplements given to pregnant women increased their chances of having healthy babies. As the mothers consumed more calories, the babies' birthweights rose and their general health improved. Furthermore, the better nourished women breast-fed their babies for a longer time, possibly because they were better able to produce high-protein milk (Read et al., 1973).

One team of researchers examined fetuses obtained from therapeutic abortions on malnourished women, and infants who had died accidentally or of severe malnutrition in the first year of life. Their data indicated that the number of cells in the human brain increases in a linear fashion until birth, and then more slowly until 6 months of age. After that, there is no increase in the number of brain cells, only in weight. Since the brains of the malnourished infants contained fewer cells than normal (at times only 60 percent of the expected number), it seemed that these infants had suffered malnutrition in utero (Winick, Brasel, & Rosso, 1972).

Research with malnourished rats indicates that fetal malnutrition produces apparently permanent deficits in brain cell number (Winick, 1969; Winick & Noble, 1966). Rats are not people, of course, and it is not always possible to draw conclusions about human beings from animal work. But a number of investigators believe it is possible that the same irreversible results of poor prenatal nutrition may occur in humans.

Children's intellectual development also may be related to prenatal nutrition. One-half of one group of malnourished pregnant women received dietary supplements, while the others got placebos (inactive substances). At ages 3 and 4, the children whose mothers had received supplements had a higher average IQ score (Harrell, Woodyard, & Gates, 1955). Yet these findings seem to be contradicted by a 1972 study that found no relationship between a mother's starvation during pregnancy and the child's mental performance at age 19 (Stein, Susser, Saenger, & Marolla, 1972). In connection with routine army examinations, 125,000 Dutch men took IQ tests. When the scores of those who had been conceived or were gestating during a severe famine were compared with those who had not been exposed to famine conditions, no detectable differences showed up. There was a strong association, though, with social class. This study isolated malnutrition from other environmental factors, which studies of poor women cannot do.

Prenatal starvation may have an all-or-none effect. Affected fetuses may die; the others may survive unaffected. Possibly because these women were well-nourished before, the famine did not have devastating effects. Good long-term nutrition may be critical. In any case, the contradictory evidence points to a need for more research on this topic.

As long as there is any possibility that maternal nutrition does affect fetal development, on both physical and intellectual levels, it behooves us as a society to improve the nutrition of pregnant and nursing women, especially in low-income neighborhoods where other environmental factors aggravate the effects of poor nutrition. If we wait for conclusive research on this topic, it may be too late for generations of children.

Maternal Drug Intake

In 1960 they began to appear—babies born with *phocomelia*. These infants came into the world with no arms and legs, or with small, pitiful, useless limbs. Many had defects of sight and hearing; some lacked ears and eyes; others had fallen victim to a monstrous assortment of other abnormalities. Horror-struck investigators finally linked these infants' birth defects to an innocent-seeming tranquilizer, *thalidomide*, that had been taken by the children's mothers early in pregnancy (Lenz, 1966).

The hundreds of thalidomide babies who are now adolescents and young adults bear tragic witness to the potent effects on the fetus of drugs taken by the pregnant mother. At one time it was believed that the placenta protected the developing baby from injurious elements in the mother's body. We now know that virtually everything the mother takes in makes its way in some form and to some degree to the new life in her uterus. Drugs may cross the placenta, just as oxygen, carbon dioxide, sodium chloride, water, and urea do. They have their strongest effects if taken early in pregnancy. As we have seen, the fetus develops most rapidly in its first few months. It is not surprising, then, that the fetus is especially vulnerable to disease and accident during this period.

Drugs known to be harmful are the antibiotics streptomycin and tetracycline; the sulfanomides; excessive amounts of vitamins A, B_6, C, D, and K; certain barbiturates, opiates, and other central nervous system depressants; and several hormones, including progestin, diethylstilbestrol, androgen, and synthetic estrogen. Aspirin, phenobarbital, the tranquilizer chlorpromazine, and several anti-nausea drugs are known to cause fetal abnormalities in animals (Brody, 1973). Tetracyclines administered during pregnancy may cause retardation of bone growth in premature infants (Drage et al., 1966); taken late in pregnancy, they can cause staining of the infant's teeth (Mull, 1966). The tranquilizers Miltown and Librium, especially when taken during the first six weeks of pregnancy, have been related to mental retardation, deafness, and defects of heart, joints, and limbs (Milkovich & Van den Berg, 1974). Cardiac defects and delayed growth and development have been noted in the offspring of women who took anticonvulsants during pregnancy (Anderson, 1976; Rosen & Lightner, 1978). And some studies have pointed to the possibility of a relationship between hexachlorophene and birth defects. Nurses, doctors, and other health care personnel who are or may become pregnant have been advised to avoid hexachlorophene antibacterial scrubs (FDA Drug Bulletin, 1978).

A few drugs are known to be safe to take during pregnancy, such as the commonly prescribed antibiotics ampicillin and penicillin (McDougall, 1971). The most prudent course for a woman who might possibly be pregnant is the ingestion of as few drugs as possible. She should avoid over-the-counter drugs and should question her doctor about the safety during pregnancy of any prescribed medication. The annoyance of minor discomforts should be weighed against the dangers of long-term effects on a developing fetus.

HORMONES Taking oral contraceptives either just before pregnancy or after a woman has unknowingly become pregnant may harm the developing fetus. Of 34 fetuses that had been spontaneously aborted within six months after the mother stopped taking The Pill, 16, or 48 percent, had chromosomal abnormalities, compared with only 50, or 22 percent, of 227 spontaneously aborted fetuses whose mothers had not been taking oral contraceptives (Carr, 1970).

More benign results were obtained when

Rothman and Louik (1978) reviewed the hospital records of 7723 babies whose mothers had used The Pill. The overall frequency of malformation was 4.3 percent for infants whose mothers used birth control pills till shortly before conception, compared to 3.3 percent for infants whose mothers had not taken them for three years before conception.

When they broke the figure down further, they found that the frequency of malformations was essentially the same for all infants except those whose mothers had taken oral contraceptives within one month of conception. Since the researchers approximated the time of conception by the infants' birthdates, it is possible that some of these mothers had continued to take The Pill after they had become pregnant. Therefore, Rothman and Louik conclude that while the Pill presents no major *teratogenic*, or deformity-causing, risk when taken *before* pregnancy, it may produce defects if taken *during* pregnancy.

A well-controlled 1977 study (Heinonen et al.) found more cardiovascular defects in the children of women who had received female hormones early in pregnancy, compared to a control group whose mothers had not taken the hormones while pregnant. However, a 1979 study of 390 infants born with congenital heart disease who were compared to 1254 children with no heart problems found no clear relationship between pill use during pregnancy and heart defects (Rothman, Fyler, Goldblatt, & Kreidberg). They found no substantial increase in congenital heart malformations among The Pill babies but were not able to totally rule out a small increase.

A delayed consequence of hormone ingestion during pregnancy can be seen in the cases of the ninety-one adolescent girls and young women who, as of December 1972, had developed either vaginal or cervical cancer, which had been fatal to some of them (Herbst, Kurman, Scully, & Poskanzer, 1972). Doctors at Vincent Memorial Hospital in Massachusetts had previously found that 7 out of the 8 mothers of such patients treated there had received diethylstilbestrol (DES) during the first trimester of pregnancy, a drug thought to prevent miscarriage. In a control group of patients without vaginal cancer, no mother had taken DES. Since there was no significant difference between the two groups of mothers on such variables as age, smoking, x-ray exposure, or breast feeding (Herbst, Ulfelder, & Poskanzer, 1971), the DES appeared the cause of these young women's vaginal cancers.

Another study of 528 women and girls, aged 11 to 25, found that 90 percent of those whose mothers had taken DES while pregnant now had either gross or microscopic abnormalities of the vaginal tract, while the 41 unexposed controls exhibited no such abnormal conditions (Sherman et al., 1974).

On the other hand, a recent study commissioned by the National Cancer Institute found no cancers among a group of 1275 DES daughters identified through prenatal records, although 34 percent of these young women did show changes in vaginal tissue or in vaginal or cervical structure (O'Brien, Noller, Robboy, Barnes, Kaufman, Tilley, & Townsend, 1979). In another group of 2064 DES daughters, 59 percent of whom had vaginal abnormalities, 4 had cancer of the genital tract. So while the risk of genital cancer does not seem to be so great as originally feared, the DES Task Force of the United States Department of Health, Education, and Welfare still recommends that the daughters of women who took the drug during pregnancy should be examined regularly (Elliott, 1979).

Evidence has also begun to mount that maternal ingestion of DES during pregnancy can cause sterility and testicular abnormalities in male offspring (Bibbo et al., 1977). And a recent study (Banes et al., 1980) indicates increased risk of unfavorable outcomes of pregnancy in women who were themselves exposed to DES in utero.

Other hormones administered in cases of treatened abortion have been known to bring about partial sex reversal. Progesterone, for example, overmasculinizes male infants, causing hypertrophy (overdevelopment) of penis and scrotum, exceptional muscularity, accelerated neuromuscular development, hyperkinesis, gastrointestinal difficulties, tension, and irritability in the infant. Progesterone can also pseudomasculinize females, causing an enlarged clitoris and increased neuromuscular development (Russell, 1969; Erhardt & Baker, 1973). *Androgens* and *synthetic estrogens* can also masculinize the female fetus (Bongiovanni et al., 1959; Grumbach et al., 1960). Early surgery and/or cortisone treatment are often successful in helping to establish sexuality and helping such children to live a normal life.

SMOKING The pregnant woman enjoying her after-dinner cigarette may not think of herself as ingesting a potent drug. But the nicotine in her cigarette goes through her system. Smokers tend to have more spontaneous abortions, more stillbirths, and more babies who die soon after birth (U.S. Department of Health, Education, and Welfare, 1973).

The clearest finding related to smoking is the tendency of pregnant smokers to bear smaller babies. On the average, the smoker is twice as likely to deliver a low-birthweight baby, a baby whose weight is low for its gestation age, as a nonsmoker (U.S. Department of Health, Education, and Welfare, 1973). This appears to be due to an insufficient supply of oxygen to the fetus, which is probably caused by the direct effect of some ingredient of tobacco smoke, most likely carbon monoxide (*Lancet*, 1979). It is not, as some have believed, related to any tendency of smokers to eat less or to different personali-

(American Cancer Society)

ty traits in the smoker. It is encouraging to learn that the woman who gives up smoking by her fourth month of pregnancy cuts her risk of delivering a low-birthweight infant to that of a nonsmoker (Butler et al., 1972).

ALCOHOL About 1 million American women of childbearing age are alcoholics; that is, they cannot function without alcohol (National Foundation/March of Dimes, 1973a). Many more are "social drinkers." Doctors have long been concerned about the effects of alcohol on the human fetus, since animal research has shown that alcohol does cross the placenta and remains highly concentrated for long periods of time in the body of the unborn baby.

In 1973 Jones, Smith, Ulleland, and Streissguth identified a "fetal alcohol syndrome" (FAS) that affects children of women who drink excessively during pregnancy. A 1978 review by Clarren and Smith indicates that FAS is widespread: it includes dysfunction of the central nervous system, retarded growth and motor development, facial abnormalities, subnormal intelligence, and variable malformations. Some ⅓ to ½ of children of alcoholic women are affected to some degree, and it's possible that heavy paternal drinking may also be a factor (Corrigan, 1976).

Even moderate "social" drinking can affect a fetus, especially early in pregnancy. Hanson, Streissguth, and Smith (1978) found lesser defects in the offspring of mothers who reported drinking an average of 1 ounce or less of absolute alcohol per day in the month before they realized they were pregnant. These authors offer the following "crude estimates" of risk related to alcohol consumption:

less than 1 ounce per day
. . . . low risk of abnormality

1 to 2 ounces per day . . . . 10% risk

2 or more ounces per day . . . . 19% risk

chronic alcoholic . . . . about 40% risk.

The prudent woman will, therefore, want to reduce—and preferably stop—drinking before pregnancy.

MARIJUANA Investigation into the possible effects on the fetus of marijuana smoking by the mother has not yielded any relationship. But animal research has shown that fetal malformations can be produced experimentally. The 1972 report on marijuana by the National Institute of Mental Health recommended that women of childbearing age should not use marijuana since its potential for producing birth defects is unknown.

The Director of the National Institute on Drug Abuse (DuPont, 1977) refers to recent research findings that suggest possible hormonal effects in chronic marijuana users. The levels of growth hormone and serum testosterone may be lowered, which in turn may cause feminization of the male fetus and/or adversely affect growth and development in early adolescence for both sexes. While there is no clinical evidence that either of these consequences follow heavy marijuana use, their possibility indicates caution in the use of this, as any other "recreational" drug.

LYSERGIC ACID DIETHYLAMIDE (LSD) This hallucinogenic compound has been implicated as a possible cause of chromosomal defects in the user, with an unknown effect on the next generation (Berlin, 1969; Jacobson & Berlin, 1972). One study showed that seventy-five pregnant LSD users had more spontaneous abortions, more major abnormalities in these aborted fetuses, and more chromosomal abnormalities in the mother and surviving infants than would be expected in such a group (Jacobson, cited in Brazelton, 1970). But these findings are complicated by the fact that many of these mothers used other drugs as well, suffered from various infectious diseases, and were marginally nourished, making it impossible to ascribe to LSD alone their high rate of fetal complications. Another study of forty-seven infants whose parents had used LSD before and during pregnancy found no statistically significant difference in the incidence of chromosomal breakage or rearrangement among these infants, compared to a control group of babies whose parents were not users of illicit drugs (Dumars, 1971).

ADDICTIVE DRUGS Women who are addicted to such drugs as morphine, heroin, and codeine are more likely to have premature babies. These babies become addicted to the drugs within the womb. When born, they show such withdrawal symptoms as restlessness, irritability, sleeplessness, yawning, sneezing, tremors, convulsions, fever, and vomiting. Sometimes the withdrawal symptoms are severe enough to cause death (Cobrinik, Hood, & Chused, 1959; Henly & Fitch, 1966). The child can be cured of its addiction by administering certain other drugs in gradually decreasing amounts, although it is often difficult.

Even though infants may be cured of addiction, some of its results may have long-term consequences. Strauss, Lessen-Firestone, Starr, and Ostrea (1975) found that addicted infants are less alert and less responsive to stimuli they can see or hear than are nonaddicted babies. They cry more often but are less likely to cuddle when they are held, probably because withdrawal from the drug involves their motor abilities. Their crying and irritability, their lack of alertness, and their resistance to cuddling are all characteristics that can interefere with the relationship between these babies and the people who take care of them, usually their parents. Normal babies actively contribute to the bond between their parents and themselves; addicted babies may suffer emotionally from their deficiencies in reaching out, in addition to the physical suffering caused by the drug.

In an effort to look at even more long-term effects of prenatal drug exposure, Wilson, McCreary, Kean, and Baxter (1979) examined seventy-seven 3- to 6-year old children. Twenty-two children whose mothers had used heroin during pregnancy were compared with three other groups: twenty whose mothers had not used heroin during pregnancy but were involved in the "drug culture," either living with narcotics addicts or using heroin after the birth; fifteen who had been considered "high-risk" infants on the basis of medical factors, whose mothers used no psychotropic drugs; and twenty children of the same socioeconomic level whose births had been normal and whose mothers used no drugs during or after pregnancy.

The overall performance of the heroin-exposed children on a variety of tests was within the normal range, but these children weighed less, were shorter, were less well adjusted, and scored lower on perceptual and learning tests than did those in all three of the other groups. The fourth group made the best showing, indicating that cultural and perinatal risk factors also affect children's development. The heroin-exposed children differed from the others in one more way: They had less contact with their natural mothers, a factor that may also have influenced their development. The authors conclude that children exposed to heroin in utero "must be considered more vulnerable to suboptimal social and environmental conditions" (p. 141).

Maternal Illness and Blood Type

Pregnant women who have rubella (German measles), toxoplasmosis, diabetes, syphilis, gonorrhea, and certain other illnesses are more likely to bear children with birth defects, including vision and hearing defects, mental retardation, brain damage, and growth retardation.

A problem caused by the interaction of the prenatal environment with heredity is *incompatibility of blood type* between mother and baby, most commonly because of the Rh factor. When a fetus's blood contains this protein substance but its mother's blood does not, antibodies in the mother's blood may attack the fetus and possibly bring about spontaneous abortion, stillbirth, jaundice, anemia, heart defects, mental retardation, or death. Usually the first Rh-positive baby is not affected, but with each succeeding pregnancy the risk becomes greater. A vaccine can now be given to an Rh-negative mother which, when given within three days of childbirth or abortion, will prevent her body from making antibodies. Babies already affected with Rh disease can be treated by repeated blood transfusions, sometimes even before birth.

Other Influences in the Prenatal Environment

The rate of miscarriages for the month of June over the past six years was 130 per 1000 live births in Alsea, Oregon, compared to 45 per 1000 in a nearby area. Blaming the high rate of miscarriage on the annual spring sprayings in Alsea of two herbicides used to kill weeds and trees, the Federal Environmental Protection Agency banned most uses of 2,4,5-T and Silvex (McFadden, 1979).

After finding unusually high rates of birth defects, miscarriages, and underweight children in the Love Canal neighborhood of Niagara Falls, near a site where a local manufacturer had dumped large quantitites of toxic chemicals, the New York State Health Commissioner recommended that no families with pregnant women or children under 2 years of age remain within a 20-square-block area around the canal (McNeil, 1979).

When an accident occurred at the nuclear reactor at Three Mile Island in Pennsylvania, the first people to be evacuated from the area were pregnant women and young children, in recognition that the developing embryo, fetus, and child are most vulnerable to the dangers of radiation (Altman, 1979).

An increasingly sophisticated awareness of the teratogenic nature of many chemicals, sources of radiation, extremes of heat and humidity, and other hazards in modern industrial life has led to new efforts by scientists to protect the health of pregnant women and their unborn babies. Studies of work conditions in factories, plants, and offices are leading to new standards and recommendations for working women.

We have known for more than fifty years, for example, that radiation can cause gene *mutations*, minute changes that alter a gene to produce some new, often harmful, characteristic (Murphy, 1929). X-rays can also cause chromosome breakage. Critical periods seem to exist for radiation damage, with certain specific defects likely to result from radiation received during certain times during the pregnancy. Most damage is done before the sixth week of conception, at the time of major organ development.

We do not know how much radiation will produce abnormalities in the fetus of an irradiated pregnant woman, so caution in this area is indicated.

The recent recommendations of the American College of Radiology (ACR) that pregnant women should not forgo important diagnostic x-rays have engendered a great deal of controversy, especially among obstetricians and pediatricians (Marano, 1977). The ACR maintains that pregnant women should not postpone abdominal x-rays until after birth and that termination of a pregnancy is not justified because of radiation risk from diagnostic x-rays. On the other hand, the National Council on Radiation Protection and Measurements recommends the scheduling of diagnostic x-rays only for the first ten to fourteen days of the menstrual cycle in women of childbearing age to avoid risk to the embryo when it is most vulnerable.

The Committee on Radiology of the American Academy of Pediatrics (AAP) supports the position of the ACR. Scheduling is not useful, says the AAP (1978), since there is no "safe" period, and postponement of needed examinations might jeopardize the health of the mother. The committee recommends finally that doctors should be familiar with the appropriate radiologic information, should take a woman's potential or actual pregnancy into account, and should carefully consider the need for radiologic examinations.

Birth Defects
Transmitted by the Father

We have already seen how the genes of both mother and father and how various aspects of the prenatal maternal environment can cause birth defects. In recent years, further study has been made of the male's role in transmitting defects. Genetic mutations in sperm occur very rarely, in fewer than 1 percent of the population. They may be caused by irradiation, infection, drugs, and chemicals (Evans, 1976). These mutations occur more frequently as a man ages and may be responsible for the occurrence of some inborn disorders. Advanced paternal age is associated with increases in several rare conditions, including achondroplastic dwarfism, Marfan's syndrome (causing extreme height, thinness, and heart abnormalities), Apert's syndrome (deformities of the head and limbs), and fibrodysplasia ossificans progressiva (bone malformations). In studies on each of these conditions, the mean paternal age was in the late thirties.

So we see the swirling mass of influences, both hereditary and environmental, that affect the life of each of us well before the time when we first see the world beyond the womb.

THE BIRTH PROCESS

The young woman woke up feeling rather strange. She felt some unfamiliar sensations in her belly, heavy with child. According to the doctor, the baby wasn't due for another couple of weeks. But these certainly felt like the birth contractions she had heard and read so much about. Was she in labor?

No one knows why this specific woman's uterus began to contract at that precise moment with the express purpose of expelling from her womb the life that had been there for some 266 days. The fetus's maturational level may signal its readiness to begin independent life. The placenta may be genetically programmed. Changes in fetal and uterine size are a definite factor, since twin births are usually about three weeks early and other multiple births are even earlier. Changes in hormonal levels may set off labor. And outside physiological and psychological influences may also play a part.

Childbirth takes place in three overlapping phases.

The *first stage of labor* is the longest, lasting an average of twelve to twenty-four

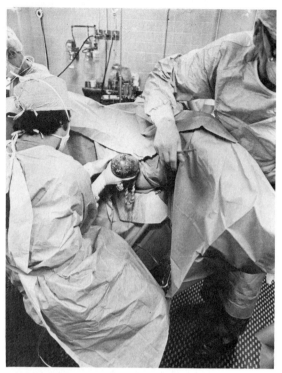
At the end of the second stage of labor, the baby is born but is still attached to the mother by the umbilical cord. (© Geissinger/Photo Researchers, Inc.)

hours for the woman having her first child. During this stage, uterine contractions cause the cervix, the opening of the uterus, to widen until it becomes large enough for the baby's head to pass through. At the beginning of this stage, the contractions tend to be fairly mild. Toward the end of this stage they become more severe and more uncomfortable. The more quickly the cervix dilates, the less pain the mother will feel (Timiras, 1972). Women who have been prepared for childbirth through a special class learn breathing techniques that help them overcome the discomfort of these stronger contractions.

The *second stage*, which typically lasts about 1½ hours, begins when the baby's head begins to move through the cervix and the vaginal canal, and ends when the baby emerges completely from the mother's body. During the second stage, the prepared mother bears down hard with her abdominal muscles at each contraction, helping the baby in its efforts to leave her body. At the end of this stage, the baby is born, but is still attached by its umbilical cord to the placenta, which is still inside the mother's body.

During the *third stage*, which lasts only a few minutes, the umbilical cord and the placenta are expelled.

The tiny, wrinkled creature who first forsakes the womb for the unknown excitements of the larger world hardly looks like the adorable, dimpled infants we see smiling at us from the pages of magazines. A baby is the ultimate emigrant to an unknown land, having struggled through a difficult passage to be faced with the overwhelming mission of learning the language and customs. In Chapters 3 and 4 we will see how newborn babies rally to the challenges of infancy. But first let us look at the methods and possible complications of childbirth.

METHODS OF CHILDBIRTH

Medicated Childbirth

Did God tell Eve "In travail shalt thou bring forth children" or "In sorrow shalt thou bring forth children"? Whichever it may have been, most societies have evolved techniques to hasten delivery, make the mother's work easier, and lessen her discomfort. Some type of pain relief during labor and delivery is taken for granted among most Western middle-class women. In 1974, anesthesia was used in 95 percent of all deliveries performed in eighteen teaching hospitals, a percentage that represents a general increase in obstetric medication over the previous decade (Brackbill & Broman, 1979).

Some women receive general anesthesia, which renders them completely unconscious; others get a regional anesthetic (such as a spinal or caudal block), which blocks the nerve pathways that would carry the sensation of pain to the brain; still others receive analgesics, which relax the mother.

All these drugs pass through the placenta and enter the fetal blood supply and tissues.

Critics attribute the relatively high rate of infant mortality in the United States to our routine use of obstetric medication (Haire, 1972).

In the first week of life, childbirth drugs decrease newborn babies' initial weight gain, diminish their ability to nurse, and lower their performance on early learning tasks (Brazelton, 1970). In the first month, they have negative effects on babies' muscle tension, vision, maturation, and psychomotor and mental development (Conway & Brackbill, 1970). Now a major new study reveals that many of the effects of childbirth medication persist through the first *year* of life—and possibly longer. In a study of 3500 healthy full-term babies, Brackbill and Broman (1979) found that children whose mothers had received no obstetric medication showed the most progress in sitting, standing, and moving around, followed by those whose mothers had received regional anesthetic, with those whose mothers had received general anesthetic doing the most poorly.

The American Academy of Pediatrics' Committee on Drugs (1978) has expressed its concern with the negative consequences of drugs given during labor and delivery by issuing a statement recommending the avoidance of drugs or drug dosages known to produce significant changes in neurobehavior of the infant.

This statement does not mean that the patient in labor should be denied reasonable relief of pain by analgesic or anesthetic agents, but rather that the minimum effective dose of these agents should be administered when indicated. Moreover, the committees recommend that the physician discuss with the patient, whenever possible before the onset of labor, the potential benefits and side effects of maternal analgesia and anesthesia on both the mother and infant [p. 403].

This statement is particularly significant in view of Brackbill and Broman's (1979) conclusions that "women have little voice in deciding which if any drugs they will consume" (p. 48). In view of the fact that the woman is the only person who can gauge the degree of her pain and that she is most personally concerned about the well-being of her child, she should have a strong voice in making decisions about obstetric medication.

Obstetric medication has another effect. There is no such thing in human beings as "maternal instinct." Much of a woman's motherly feeling comes about because of the positive responses she receives from the baby. An infant who nurses eagerly and who acts alert sets up positive feelings in the mother. What, then, are the long-range psychological implications for the mother-child relationship when a drugged mother is interacting with a drugged infant? As a society we need to examine the routine use of these drugs. There *is* an alternative.

Childbirth without Drugs

In 1914 Dr. Grantly Dick-Read questioned the inevitability of pain in childbirth and propounded the theory of "natural childbirth." To eliminate fear, which he felt caused most childbirth pain, he educated women in the physiology of reproduction and delivery and trained them in breathing, relaxation, and physical fitness. By midcentury Dr. Fernand Lamaze was using the psychoprophylactic, or "prepared childbirth," method of obstetrics. This method substituted new breathing and muscular responses to the sensations of uterine contractions for the old responses of fear and pain.

The rapid spread in recent years of drugless childbirth can be attributed to two factors. First, the psychological benefits for the parents—for the awake mother who can actively participate in the birth and for the involved father who can assist throughout labor and delivery and also know the joy of participating in his child's birth. The other compelling reason, of course, is the benefit to the babies themselves.

"Birth without Violence"

A controversial new childbirth technique involves delivering babies in barely lit delivery rooms, refraining from slapping them to initiate breathing, bathing them immediately in warm water, and calmly placing them on their mother's bellies right after birth. LeBoyer (1975) maintains that such gentle practices eliminate much of the trauma of birth and produce happier people. Critics maintain that the dim lighting used may cause doctors to miss vital signs of distress and that the technique exposes babies to infections from the water or the mother's body (Cohn, 1975). Recent research suggests that the LeBoyer approach has no advantage over a gentle, conventional delivery on morbidity, infant behavior, and maternal perception of the birth experience. Also, the LeBoyer method did not increase danger to infant or mother (Nelson et al., 1980).

BIRTH COMPLICATIONS

Cesarean Delivery

About 5 percent of all deliveries in this country do not take place vaginally, but through abdominal surgery which allows the baby to be lifted out of the uterus (Boston Children's Medical Center, 1972). A cesarean section is indicated in certain situations. The most common are when labor does not progress as quickly as it should, when the baby is so positioned in the uterus that its legs or buttocks would emerge before its head, when the baby's head is too big to pass through the mother's pelvis, when the baby appears to be in trouble, or when the mother is bleeding vaginally.

A cesarean section, considered major surgery, takes a longer time for the mother to recover from than a vaginal delivery does. It also poses somewhat more risk to the mother, and since it always requires some form of anesthesia, may pose more to the infant, as well. While a "C-section" has often saved the life of a mother and baby who could not have managed a traditional delivery, many critics of current American childbirth practices claim that the rapidly increasing rate of cesarean deliveries in this country represents an unnecessarily high incidence, that too many cesareans are performed when they are not strictly necessary.

Low-Birthweight Babies

All very small infants used to be considered *premature*, that is, born before the full term of a normal pregnancy. In recent years, though, doctors have classified these babies as being very small for one of two reasons. *Premature* babies, sometimes called *preterm*, are those born before the thirty-seventh gestational week as dated from the first day of the mother's last menstrual period. *Small-for-date* babies weigh less than 90 percent of all babies of the same gestational age; abnormally small, they may or may not be premature (Robinson, 1972).

Since the distinction between preterm and small-for-date infants has evolved only within the past decade or so, it has not been considered in most studies on the effects of "prematurity." So we don't actually know whether those studies on low-birthweight babies yield information about babies who were born early or those who were small for their age.

Babies born after a gestation period of thirty-six weeks generally have few problems. Those born at thirty-three weeks or less and/or weighing less than 4½ pounds are in a high-risk group, with a mortality rate of 1 in 10 (Behrman, Babson, & Lessel, 1971). These infants are vulnerable to infection, have trouble maintaining body temperature, and often succumb to respiratory failure or cerebral hemorrhage (Robinson, 1972).

Miller, Hassanein, Chin, and Hensleight (1976) compared mothers from four levels of socioeconomic status and found that those mothers who smoked, used drugs, had no prenatal care, and gained very little weight during pregnancy were most likely to have low-birthweight babies. More of these mothers were in the lowest socioeconomic level, but it was the practices themselves and/or medical problems of the mothers that were associated with the babies' low birthweight, and not the socioeconomic status itself.

Many researchers have looked at the long-range effects of prematurity, and some studies show that low-birthweight babies who survive are often at a disadvantage. The more severely premature they are, the more marked their long-term deficits. In one study of 2-year-olds who had been extremely small at birth—less than 1000 grams (about 2 pounds, 4 ounces)—Pape, Buncic, Ashby, and Fitzhardinge (1978) found that on the average these youngsters still were shorter and weighed less than most other children their age. There was a high (35 percent) incidence of respiratory tract infections; of the eye disorder retrolental fibroplasia (16 percent), and of severe developmental delays (21 percent). The encouraging aspect of this study, however, lies in its comparison with former years. Before 1970, about 75 percent of such tiny newborns died and only 15 percent survived as normal children. In this study, only 53 percent died and 33 percent survived with no handicaps. So the proportion of surviving normal children has doubled.

Many premature infants do catch up in later years. Taub, Goldstein, and Caputo (1977) looked at thirty-eight 7- to 9½-year-olds who had been born prematurely and at a control group of twenty-six children who had been full-term babies. They found no significant difference in verbal IQ, or in scholastic and social functioning between the two groups. And even though the prematures scored lower than the full-term children in performance IQ, their scores were still within the "average" range for the tests.

The cause of an early onset of labor is unknown. Different theories ascribe it to cervical incompetence, multiple pregnancies, internal hemorrhage, or premature rupture of the membranes. Small-for-date babies may grow extremely slowly within the womb because of maternal problems such as undernutrition, severe toxemia (hypertension of pregnancy), or multiple pregnancies, or because of fetal problems caused by chromosomal defects or intrauterine infection (Robinson, 1972).

Because of low-birthweight infants' vulnerability to infection and their inability to maintain body temperature, they usually spend their first weeks in an antiseptic, temperature-controlled incubator. Until recently, medical practice indicated a "hands-off" policy in the belief that the less these fragile little beings were disturbed, the better their chances for the future. But now it seems that this very isolation, and the sensory impoverishment which results, may contribute to some infants' difficulties. Enriching the environment of low-birthweight babies is beneficial (Stewart & Reynolds, 1974). When they are picked up, fondled, rocked, and generally paid attention to, these babies seem to thrive better than when they are left alone in incubators (Scarr-Salapatek & Williams, 1973; Solkoff, Yaffe, & Weintraub, 1967).

When low-birthweight babies have to stay in the hospital after their mothers go home, their parents may have more trouble being effective later on. Leifer, Leiderman, Barnett, & Williams (1972) found that mothers of full-term infants—who had had many opportunities to hold their babies in the hospital—smiled at their babies more and held them close more often than did the mothers of preterm infants,

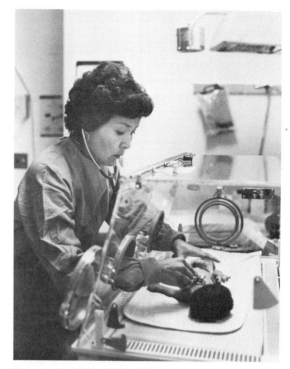

Because low-birthweight babies are vulnerable to infection and unable to maintain body temperature, they usually spend their first weeks in an antiseptic, temperature-controlled incubator. (Mimi Forsyth/Monkmeyer)

even though some of the latter had visited their babies regularly and handled them through the incubator portholes. These differences in maternal behavior held true just before hospital discharge and up to four weeks later.

Why this difference? The mothers of the preterm infants may have been frightened by their babies' fragility. Or there could be a deeper disruption of the parent-infant bond. Parents often deliberately stay aloof from a sick, weak baby, trying to protect their own emotional vulnerability if the baby should die. Said one mother: "I don't want to get that close. I don't want to touch her. . . . She isn't really a part of our family, but she will be when she comes home" (Barnett, Leiderman, Grobstein, & Klaus, 1970, p. 202). When such babies survive, the parents have to overcome this distance and take up where they left off. It is not always easy. And it may be harder for white mothers than for black: Although only about 7 percent of white babies are premature, 39 percent of those abused by their parents are. This compares with a 16 percent rate of prematurity among black battered babies, the same as their incidence in the general black population (Elmer & Gregg, 1967).

While we are seeking new and better ways to save the lives and health of premature babies, then, we also have to pay attention to improving their emotional environments once they get home.

Birth Trauma

For a small minority of babies, the passage through the birth canal is the most difficult journey of their lives and may leave lasting marks in the form of brain injury. In Rubin's 1977 study of 15,435 births over six years "at an outstanding medical school," 1 infant in every 133, or less than 1 percent, suffered some type of injury at birth. He found birth injuries the second most common cause of neonatal death, after suffocation and the failure of the infant's lungs to expand.

Some infants who have suffered from *anoxia* (oxygen deprivation) at birth, mechanical birth injury, or neonatal diseases or infections are left with permanent brain injury, causing mental retardation or behavior problems. Relationships have been found between birth trauma and childhood reading retardation; impairment in verbal abstract ability, perceptual skills, and social competence; and a variety of neurological and psychological problems (Lyle, 1970; Bishop, Israel, & Briscol, 1965; Corah, Anthony, Parnter, Stern, & Thurston, 1965).

Birth trauma is not always so debilitating. Almost 900 children born on the island of Kauai, Hawaii, in 1955 and 1956 were examined ten years later (Werner, Bierman, French, Simonian, Connor, Smith, & Campbell, 1968). A few had survived severe birth complications

and still bore scars in the form of major physical handicaps or retardation. But most of those who had been premature, or had had difficult births, or had been sick when newborn were now doing well. They were no more likely to get poor grades or have language, perceptual, or emotional problems than were the other children—unless they had been affected so severely that they had had to be institutionalized.

The kinds of homes the children lived in had a much greater effect. Most of the 10-year-olds with problems had suffered no stress at birth but had grown up in poor homes where they received little educational stimulation or emotional support. They may be said to have suffered "environmental trauma."

Zarin-Ackerman, Lewis, and Driscoll (1975), however, did find a relationship between birth trauma and impaired language development at age 2, even when they controlled for socioeconomic differences by matching thirty-six children who had suffered birth injury or neonatal illness with thirty-six children from comparable social levels who had normal birth histories. By the age of 2, the children who had experienced birth trauma had smaller vocabularies and poorer comprehension of relationships between contrasting adjectives. In other language tests, though, there was little or no difference between the two groups of children.

It is possible that at the age of 2 these children are still being affected by the original trauma. It is also possible that their problems at birth interfered with the parent-child relationship that we will see, in Chapter 5, as being so vital to children's language development. It is also possible that with the right kind of environmental support, the birth trauma group will catch up with the other children over the next few years.

78

SUMMARY

1   At conception, each normal human being receives twenty-three chromosomes from the mother and twenty-three from the father. These align into twenty-three pairs of chromosomes—twenty-two pairs of autosomes and one pair of sex chromosomes. A child who receives an X chromosome from each parent will be female. But if the child receives a Y chromosome from the father, a male will be born.   **2**   The patterns of genetic transmission are (a) autosomal dominant inheritance, (b) autosomal recessive inheritance, (c) sex-linked (X-linked) inheritance, and (d) multifactorial inheritance. Various birth defects and diseases can be transmitted through each of these patterns. Chromosomal abnormalities may also result in birth defects, most notably, Down's syndrome. Genetic mutations in the father's sperm have been implicated in certain types of birth defects.   **3**   Through genetic counseling, expectant parents can obtain information about the mathematical odds of having children who are afflicted with specific birth defects. Amniocentesis, maternal blood testing, and ultrasound are three procedures used to determine whether a fetus is afflicted with certain conditions or is developing normally.

4   Prenatal development occurs in three stages: (a) the germinal stage is characterized by rapid cell division and increased complexity of the organism; (b) the embryonic stage is characterized by rapid growth and differentiation of major body systems and organs; and (c) the fetal stage is characterized by rapid growth and changes in body form.

5   Although conception usually results in a single birth, multiple births can occur. When two ova are fertilized, fraternal (dizygotic) twins will be born with different genetic makeups. When a single fertilized ovum divides in two, identical (monozygotic) twins will be born with the same genetic makeup.   **6**   Nearly all birth defects and three-fourths of all spontaneous abortions occur during the critical first trimester of pregnancy.   **7**   The developing organism is affected greatly by its prenatal environment. We have considered the effects of maternal nutrition, drug intake, illness, and irradiation.   **8**   The birth process begins some 266 days after conception and occurs in three stages: (a) during the first stage, uterine contractions cause the cervix to dilate; (b) during the second stage, the baby descends from the uterus and emerges from the mother's body; and (c) during the third stage, the umbilical cord and the placenta are expelled.   **9**   Obstetric medicine can have harmful effects on the newborn. "Natural" or "prepared" childbirth methods can offer both psychological and physical benefits. "Birth without violence" is a new childbirth technique designed to minimize the trauma of birth.   **10**   Birth trauma and low birthweight can influence a child's early adjustment to life outside the womb and may even exert an influence on later development.

SUGGESTED READINGS

Apgar, V., & Beck, J.   *Is my baby all right?* New York: Trident, 1973. An explanation, for lay readers, of birth defects—what they are, how they are caused, how they may be prevented, and when to seek genetic counseling. It includes many good illustrations.

Arms, S.   *A season to be born*. New York: Harper/Colophon, 1973. A record of one woman's pregnancy, told through text and photographs.

Arms, S.   *Immaculate deception*. Boston: Houghton Mifflin, 1975. A controversial case is presented for bringing childbirth out of the hospital and into the home.

The Boston Children's Medical Center.   *Pregnancy, birth and the newborn baby*. Boston: Delacorte Presse/Seymour Lawrence, 1972. A comprehensive guide to pregnancy, childbirth, and the first six weeks of life. Includes discussions of problems such as infertility, abortion, and disorders of the newborn.

Feldman, S.   *Choices in childbirth*. New York: Grosset & Dunlap, 1978. A practical guide through all the choices and decisions that a pregnant woman faces: giving birth at home or in the hospital, "natural" or "managed" childbirth, vaginal or cesarean delivery, obstetric medication, breast or bottle feeding, and so forth, as described by a knowledgeable and sympathetic psychotherapist.

Flanagan, G. L.   *The first nine months of life*. New York: Simon & Schuster, 1962. A lucid, well-illustrated, and scientific account of prenatal development.

Guttmacher, A.   *Pregnancy, birth, and family planning*. New York: New American Library, 1973. This revised version of the classic book on prenatal development and birth is very practical.

LeBoyer, F.   *Birth without violence*. New York: Knopf, 1975. Presents LeBoyer's controversial procedures to minimize the trauma of birth; includes beautiful photographs.

Milinaire, C.   *Birth*. New York: Harmony Books, 1974. A well-written, nicely illustrated book about pregnancy, birth customs and techniques, and infant care; has a very practical orientation.

Nyhan, W.   *The heredity factor*. New York: Grosset & Dunlap, 1976. A fascinating, comprehensive account of genetics, genetic defects, genetic counseling, and the effects of the prenatal environment on development. Written for the layperson.

Parfitt, R. R.   *The birth primer*. Philadelphia: Running Press, 1977. A sourcebook about various methods of childbirth. Includes an extensive annotated bibliography of popular childbirth books.

Rugh, R., & Shettles, L. B.   *From conception to birth*. New York: Harper & Row, 1971. This text presents a complete and clear description of conception and prenatal development and includes beautiful color photographs.

Infancy and Toddlerhood

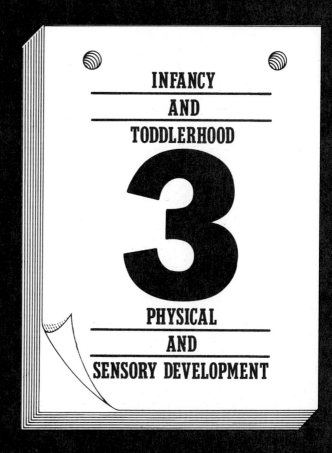

INFANCY
AND
TODDLERHOOD

3

PHYSICAL
AND
SENSORY DEVELOPMENT

IN THIS CHAPTER
YOU WILL LEARN ABOUT

How newborn infants adjust to life outside the womb, and how we can tell whether or not they are making a satisfactory adjustment

The stages of physical development that newborn infants go through, and how heredity and environment affect their physical growth and development

What infants can and cannot do at birth—and how they acquire the physical and sensory abilities we all take for granted

CHAPTER OVERVIEW

Who Is the Neonate?
Medical Assessment of Neonates | How the Body Systems Help Neonates Adjust | The States of Newborn Infants | Early Sensory Capabilities of Infants

Physical Development of Infants
Growth: Height and Weight | Infant Feeding | Motor Development | Sudden Infant Death Syndrome (SIDS)

WHO IS THE NEONATE?

The first two to four weeks of life mark the *neonatal period*, a time of transition from intrauterine life—when the fetus was supported entirely by its mother—to an independent existence. This transition period generally takes longer for low-birthweight babies, since they enter the world with less fully developed body systems.

After two years of wanting a baby and not being able to get pregnant, followed by nine months of knowing you were in there but not knowing if you were a girl or a boy, if you were healthy or not, it was an incredible experience to watch you being born and then to have you lying there on my belly instead of in it. You were round and healthy looking and covered with dark fuzz. Even your ears were fuzzy.

Nancy Gordon

An average newborn, or *neonate*, is about 20 inches long and weighs about 7 pounds. At birth, 95 percent of full-term babies weigh between 5½ and 10 pounds and measure between 18 and 22 inches in length (Nelson, Vaughan, & McKay, 1975). Birth size is related to such factors as parent size, race, sex, maternal nutrition, and maternal health (Vulliamy, 1973). Males tend to be a little longer and heavier than females, and a first-born child is likely to weigh less at birth than will later-born siblings. Size at birth is related to size during childhood (Vulliamy, 1973).

In their first few days, neonates lose as much as 10 percent of body weight, primarily because of a loss of fluids. On about the fifth day they begin to gain and are back to birthweight by the tenth to fourteenth day. Light full-term infants lose less weight than heavy ones, and first-borns lose less than later-borns (Timiras, 1972).

Newborns are quite pale—even black babies who later will be very dark. They have a pinkish cast because of the thinness of their skin, which barely covers the blood flowing through tiny capillaries. Some neonates are very hairy, since some of the *lanugo*, that fuzzy prenatal body hair, has not yet dropped off. It will, in a few days. All new babies are covered with the *vernix caseosa* ("cheesy varnish"), an oily protection against infection that dries over a few days' time.

During the Middle Ages special healing powers were attributed to "witch's milk," a secretion that sometimes issues from the swollen breasts of newborn boys and girls. Like the blood-tinged vaginal discharge of some baby girls, this results from high levels of the hormone estrogen, which is secreted by the placenta just before birth.

The neonate's head is one-fourth of body length and may be long and misshapen because of the "molding" that eased its passage through the mother's pelvis. This temporary molding was possible because the baby's skull bones are not yet fused; they will not be completely joined for eighteen months. The places on the head where the bones have not yet grown together—the soft spots, or *fontanels*—are covered by a tough membrane. Since the cartilage in the baby's nose is also malleable, the trip through the birth canal leaves that looking squashed for a few days.

MEDICAL ASSESSMENT OF NEONATES

One minute after delivery, and then again five minutes after, the *Apgar Scale* (see Table 3-1) is administered routinely to all infants. The five subtests devised by Dr. Virginia Apgar (1953) yield measures of Appearance (color), Pulse (heart rate), Grimace (reflex irritability), Activity (muscle tone), and Respiration (breathing).

SIGN*	0	1	2	**TABLE 3-1**
				Apgar Scale
Heart rate	absent	slow (below 100)	rapid (over 100)	
Respiratory effort	absent	irregular, slow	good, crying	
Muscle tone	flaccid, limp	weak, inactive	strong, active	
Color	blue, pale	body pink, extremities blue	entirely pink	
Reflex irritability	no response	grimace	coughing, sneezing, crying	

*Each sign is rated in terms of absence or presence from 0 to 2; highest overall score is 10.

The infant receives a rating of 0, 1, or 2 on each measure, for a maximum total of 10.

Ninety percent of normal infants score 7 or better; a score of 4 or less calls for immediate treatment. The risk of perinatal death is greatest for the first-born child, lowest for the second. It rises from the third- to the fifth-born, until the risk for the fifth child is as high as for the first (Vulliamy, 1973). The Apgar scores bear a relationship to fetal life and later development.

Serunian and Broman (1975) found that Apgar scores taken one minute after delivery were related to measures on the Bayley Mental and Motor Scores at the age of 8 months. Eight-month-old babies whose infant Apgar scores had been very low (0 to 3) scored lower on mental and motor tests than those whose infant Apgars had been high (7 to 10). The Apgar scores predicted abnormalities in neurological status, motor development, muscle tone, and grasping ability. Those children classified as "abnormal" at 8 months had had lower Apgar scores as infants than did those who were considered either "normal" or "suspect."

HOW THE BODY SYSTEMS HELP NEONATES ADJUST

The Circulatory System

Before birth, mother and baby had independent circulatory systems and separate heartbeats; but the fetus's blood was cleansed through the umbilical cord, which carried used blood to the placenta and clean blood back. Upon birth, the baby's own system must take over to circulate blood through the body. The neonatal heartbeat is still accelerated and irregular, and blood pressure does not stabilize until about the tenth day.

The Respiratory System

The umbilical cord also brought oxygen to the fetus and carried back carbon dioxide. The newborn needs much more oxygen and must now get it all alone. More babies die from respiratory problems than from any other single cause. Most start to breathe as soon as they hit the air; a few need a little slap; and one who is not breathing within two minutes after birth is in trouble. If breathing has not begun within five minutes, the baby may suffer to a greater or lesser degree the results of permanent brain injury caused by *anoxia*, or a lack of oxygen.

The Gastrointestinal System

In the uterus, the fetus also relied on the umbilical cord to bring food from the mother and to carry body wastes away. Upon birth, the infant has a strong sucking reflex to take in milk. It also has the gastrointestinal secretions to digest it. *Meconium* (a stringy, greenish-black waste matter formed in the fetal intestinal tract) is excreted during the first couple of days after birth. When the neonate's bowels and bladder are full, the sphincter muscles open automatically. Many months will pass before the baby can exert control over these muscles.

Three or four days after birth, about half of all babies develop physiological jaundice:

TABLE 3-2
A Comparison of Prenatal and Postnatal Life

CHARACTERISTIC	PRENATAL LIFE	POSTNATAL LIFE
Environment	amniotic fluid	air
Temperature	relatively constant	flutuates with atmosphere
Stimulation	minimal	all senses stimulated by various stimuli
Nutrition	dependent on mother's blood	dependent on external food and functioning of digestive system
Oxygen supply	passed from maternal bloodstream via placenta	passed from neonate's lungs to pulmonary blood vessels
Metabolic elimination	passed into maternal bloodstream via placenta	discharged by skin, kidneys, lungs, and gastrointestinal tract

SOURCE: P. S. Timiras. *Developmental physiology and aging* New York. MacMillan, 1972, p. 174.

Their skin and eyeballs look yellow. This kind of jaundice is caused by the immaturity of the liver; it usually is not serious, has no long-term effects, and occurs most often in premature babies.

Temperature Regulation

The layers of fat that developed during the last couple of months of fetal life enable healthy, full-term infants to keep their body temperature constant despite changes in air temperature. It is especially important to keep low-birthweight babies warm while they are still quite small, because they lack the fat that enables them to generate heat and thus maintain body temperature (Vulliamy, 1973). Babies also maintain body temperature by increasing their activity in response to a drop in air temperature (Hey, 1972; Mestyan & Varga, 1960; Pratt, Nelson, & Sun, 1930).

THE STATES OF NEWBORN INFANTS

Our bodies are governed to a great degree by inner "clocks" that control our cycles of eating, sleeping, elimination, and possibly even mood. These biological clocks seem inborn, since they contribute to the various *states* in infancy, the variations in arousal and activity in a baby's day.

Let's look at a typical day in a newborn baby's life (Hutt, Lenard, & Prechtl, 1969). Of the seventeen to twenty hours a day that a baby sleeps, 75 percent is spent in irregular sleep. She or he is awake and quiet for two to three hours every day, is awake and active for one to two hours, and cries and fusses the rest of the time awake—anywhere from one to four hours. A baby's sleep cycles range from forty-five minutes to two hours, divided into ten- to twenty-minute periods of regular sleep and twenty- to forty-minute periods of irregular sleep. Other perfectly normal babies have very different schedules, because of individual temperaments and differences in environments.

The following description combines two separate but similar classifications of state (Wolff, 1966; Prechtl & Beintema, 1964):

1 *Regular sleep*—eyes closed; breathing regular; no movements except for sudden generalized startles; unable to be aroused by mild stimuli

2 *Irregular sleep*—eyes closed; breathing irregular; muscles twitch, but no major movements; sounds or light bring smiles or grimaces in sleep

3 *Drowsiness*—eyes open or closed; body somewhat active; breathing irregular; may smile, startle, suck, or have erections in response to stimuli

4 *Alert inactivity*—eyes open; quiet; may move head, limbs, and trunk while looking around

5 *Walking activity and crying*—eyes open; much motor activity; reacts to external stimuli

by increasing activity, which may begin with soft whimpering and gentle movements and turn into a rhythmic crescendo of crying or kicking, or may begin and remain as uncoordinated thrashing and spasmodic screeching; activity may be caused by hunger, cold, pain, being restrained, or put down

Babies' states give us clues to how they are responding to the environment. A state influences physiological characteristics and determines how the baby will respond to stimulation. It can be affected by environment. Parents try to change state all the time when they pick up, feed, rock, or swaddle a crying baby. Constant stimulation—a rhythmic sound, a sweetened pacifier, immersing a foot in warm water, being put in a warmer place, and being clothed rather than unclothed—also soothes irritable infants. Determining how to quiet an unhappy baby has particularly important implications for the premature, since quiet babies maintain their weight better. If we want to understand how the body of a newborn baby works, we always have to be conscious of the particular state the baby is in. A baby in a state of deep sleep will respond quite differently from either an alert baby or a drowsy one.

The usual state of a particular infant can have a great effect on how the parents treat that child, which itself has major consequences for the kind of person the baby will turn out to be. Just as parents react differently to babies who respond differently to stimulation, they also are influenced by their babies' states—by whether a baby is awake and crying much of the time; or is spending a great deal of time in a state of interested, quiet wakefulness; or is almost always drowsy or asleep.

Individual Differences among Neonates

Babies behave uniquely right from birth. Jenny sticks her tongue in and out of her mouth; Davey makes rhythmic sucking movements; Nancy does neither. Some infant boys

The nurses knew you because you started each cry with a high-pitched squeak!

Nancy Gordon

AT 4 WEEKS

You are on much more of a schedule than you were. You nearly always sleep for four-hour stretches at night — occasionally a little longer — and you take at least two long naps during the day. Now if your father and I could only take two long naps during the day as you do, we'd all be in good shape.

Nancy Gordon

have frequent erections; others never do. Some smile often; others don't. Neonatal responsivity may hold important clues for later psychological functioning. Parents respond very differently to a placid baby than to an excitable one, to a baby they can quiet than to one who's inconsolable, to a baby aware of his environment than to one "in a world of her own."

EARLY SENSORY CAPACITIES OF INFANTS

In 1890, the psychologist William James said, "The baby, assailed by eyes, ears, nose, skin, and entrails at once, feels that all is one great blooming, buzzing, confusion." We now know that this is far from true. Right from birth, all the senses operate—and make sense—to some degree.

Seeing

The eyes of neonates differ from those of adults. They are smaller, the retinal structures are incomplete, and the optic nerve is underdeveloped. But upon birth, babies' eyes blink

All the senses operate to some degree from birth on. (Lew Merrim/Monkmeyer)

...he brought him to me. I felt the child's still eyes upon me and was astonished by the movement of his lids. His body had a faint odor that enchanted and disturbed me. I wanted to hide my face against him.... My senses were marvelously, voluptuously agitated.

Evelyn Scott (b. 1893) in *Revelations*, p. 108.

at bright lights (Lightwood, Brimblecombe, & Barltrop, 1971); they shift gaze to follow a moving light (Lightwood et al., 1971); and they can follow a moving target (Nelson, Vaughan, & McKay, 1975; Rosenblith, 1961). New babies see best at a distance of about 7½ inches (Haynes, White & Held, 1965).

Newborn babies often look cross-eyed. Sometimes this is because the skin around the eyes tends to obscure some of the eyeball; at other times it is because the newborn's eyes are indeed oriented in different directions. Within a few months this is usually no longer apparent. (When a baby still does not seem to be focusing both eyes together by the age of 6 months, it is time to consult an opthalmologist.)

DEPTH PERCEPTION Very young babies seem to have some idea of depth, which may be innate or learned during the first couple of months. Walk and Gibson (1961) constructed a "visual cliff," consisting of a flat, glass-covered board on one side of which a checkerboard pattern creates an illusion of depth. Six-month-old babies crawl readily on the side without the illusion but refuse to crawl on the side that looks deep, even to reach their mothers. Two- to three-month-old babies placed on their stomachs on the "deep" side

Very young babies seem to have some idea of depth, which may be innate or learned during the first couple of months. (Photo courtesy of William Vandivert and *Scientific American*)

have slower heart rates than those on the shallow side, which is probably a sign that they respond to the illusion of depth (Campos, Langer, & Krowitz, 1970).

VISUAL PREFERENCE Babies seem to be born with some preference for looking at a human face, but since they are just as interested in looking at faces with scrambled, missing, or distorted features, it is possible that they like faces at first simply because of their visual complexity and for no other reason.

Maurer and Salapatek (1976) showed 1- and 2-month-old babies three different faces: their mother's, a strange woman's, and a strange man's. All the adults remained still and without expression. The 1-month-olds tended to look away from these faces, particularly from their mothers'. This may have been because these expressionless faces seemed

so incongruous. The fact that they looked away more from their mothers' faces indicates that by the age of 1 month, babies can recognize their mothers. Corneal photography showed that the 1-month-olds' eyes focused on the borders of the faces, indicating that their recognition was probably based on differences in their mothers' chins or hairlines.

The 2-month-olds gazed longer at the faces, especially at the eyes. (Other studies have shown that by this age babies look longer at a face if the eyes are open and smile at it only if it has two eyes.) The 2-month-olds may have looked longer at these expressionless faces because they had become more familiar with faces in a variety of expressions.

Leahy (1976) noted that young infants (4 to 6 weeks old) limit their fixations to smaller areas of the visual stimulus than do older infants (10 to 12 weeks old); that is, they tend to focus on one small part of a stimulus.

Salapatek and Kessen (1966) observed that newborns looked at a single feature of a geometric figure rather than at the whole figure. These studies indicate that infants appear to respond to part of a visual stimulus (such as individual lines) rather than to the entire figure (such as a triangle).

Visual preferences tell us that the neonate's world is far from chaotic. Certain inborn mechanisms predispose us from a few hours after birth to gaze at others of our kind, and these mechanisms help us to become social beings.

Neonatal pattern vision may even be used as a predictive measure of future development. Thirty-three neonates who were considered to be at high risk for subsequent neurologic-intellectual handicap were tested on their ability to discriminate patterns. Based on the babies' performance in fixating several pairs of patterns, they were designated "normal," "suspect," or "abnormal." A few days later the infants' reflexes and neuromuscular maturation were examined in a neurological test. Then, at the age of 3 or 4 years, nineteen of the children took the Stanford-Binet IQ test.

The authors (Miranda et al., 1977) found that the visual fixation test ratings were better predictors of the children's IQ scores than were the neurological ratings. Although these results are tentative, they do suggest the feasibility of assessing future intellectual performance by looking at neonatal visual performance.

Whoever put the mirrors in the nursery knew how to please a baby. You are delighted with the kid who always lies next to you when you're being changed, and the two of you carry on very involved conversations.

Nancy Gordon

COLOR VISION By the age of 4 months, infants can see colors: They see the physically continuous spectrum as divided into blue, green, yellow, and red (Bornstein, Kessen, & Weiskopf, 1976).

Hearing

Within a few hours after birth, neonates can differentiate between distinctive sounds. When presented with sounds of varying intensity, their heart rates and body movements increase as the intensity of sound increases (Lipton, Steinschneider, & Richmond, 1963). New babies react in two ways to unusual sounds: They turn their heads toward the sound, and they stop anything else they are doing (such as sucking).

Smelling

Newborns also are able to discriminate among distinctive odors. For example, they can distinguish between the onionlike asafoetida smell and licorice-smelling anise oil. When they smell the asafoetida solution, they breathe faster and move around more than when they are presented with an odorless solution (Lipsitt, Engen, & Kaye, 1963).

When presented with small amounts of ammonium chloride, infants ranging from 16 hours to 5 days of age turned away from the odor, demonstrating that they could locate it in space (Rieser, Yonas, & Wikner, 1976).

Tasting

Infants have a relatively insensitive palate, but they can distinguish among various strong-tasting solutions (Pratt, Nelson, & Sun, 1930). Newborns can also distinguish between pure water and a sweet glucose solution (Weiffenbach & Thach, 1975). When either substance is placed on the tongue, the babies move their tongues to the side. The experimenters found that the higher the concentration of glucose, the more the babies responded.

Feeling Pain

Babies feel pain more with each day of life. Lipsitt and Levy (1959) gave a series of

They are doing blood tests on you every day or two because you are badly jaundiced and the pediatrician is concerned. So they poke your toes but you hate to bleed so they have to squeeze your toes hard. You scream and I perspire and we are both miserable.

Nancy Gordon

two-second electric shocks to 1-day-old babies, continuing for four days. They increased the voltage in 5-volt increments until the baby immediately pulled back the affected leg. The infants were much more sensitive to pain on the fourth day. This study reminds us of some of the ethical issues that were raised in Chapter 1. There *are* useful, practical applications in knowing just when an infant reacts most strongly to pain—for example, in setting the date for such operations as circumcision, and in weighing the dangers of anesthesia against the infant's degree of discomfort. But since an infant's life experiences may well influence his or her future emotional development, few experimenters are willing to risk subjecting young children to repeated painful experiences. We don't know what such a child's initial view of the world would be—or what far-reaching effects such experiences might have.

PHYSICAL DEVELOPMENT OF INFANTS

An infant is primarily a motor creature who learns about the world by manipulating the things in it. Physical gestures accompany a baby's first attempts at language: As she says "Bye-bye," she opens and closes her hand; as he says "Up," he raises his arms. Babies do not tell themselves apart from their physical surroundings. They have to learn where their bodies stop and the world begins. As they drop toys, splash water, and hurl sand, they learn how their bodies can affect their world.

Normal physical development follows an apparently preordained course, even though the time when individual babies perform specific activities varies widely. There is no "right" age when a child should be a certain height or weight or should be performing specific activities. The range of normality is broad, but all of us follow basic patterns. Almost all children progress in a definite order from certain activities to others. Only with specific kinds of stimulation—such as is sometimes found in mother-child interactions in certain non-Western cultures—is the sequence altered noticeably. Even though Dorri is able to sit up at 6 months and Jason not until 11 months, both babies hold up their chins before they raise their chests, both sit with support before they sit alone, and both stand before they walk. Children learn to perform simple movements before complicated ones.

GROWTH: HEIGHT AND WEIGHT

Not only do babies grow rapidly in total body size during their first three years, but the very proportions of their bodies change markedly. They gain about twice as much in height during their first year of life as during the second, and most triple their birthweight during the first year and then gain only about one-fourth of that during the second. During the third year, increments in both height and

AT 14 WEEKS

We took you in for a check-up this morning. You're not as heavy as we thought (although I know you gain a pound a minute when I'm carrying you). You weigh 13 lbs., 1 oz. You're now 25 inches long and your head circumference is larger by an inch since last time -- 15 inches now.

Nancy Gordon

TABLE 3-3
Physical Growth,
Birth to Age Three
(Fiftieth Percentile)

AGE	LENGTH (INCHES)		WEIGHT (POUNDS)	
	BOYS	GIRLS	BOYS	GIRLS
Birth	20	19¾	7½	7½
1 month	21¼	21	10	9¾
6 months	26	25¾	16¾	15¾
12 months	29½	29¼	22¼	21
18 months	32¼	31¾	25¼	24¼
24 months	34½	34	27¾	27
30 months	36¼	36	30	29½
36 months	38	37¾	32¼	31¾

SOURCE: From *growth and development of children*, 5th edition, by Ernest H. Watson and George H. Lowrey. Copyright © 1967, Year Book Medical Publishers, Inc., Chicago. Used by permission of Year Book Medical Publishers.

weight are smaller, and the 3-year-old is slender, compared to the chubby 1-year-old (see Table 3-3). A baby's brain reaches about two-thirds of its eventual adult size during the first year, and four-fifths by the end of the second (Nelson et al., 1975).

AT 10½ MONTHS

We took you for a check-up. You are quite healthy and big. You weigh 21 lbs. 4 oz., which is the 75th percentile for girls and you are 30½ inches long, the 99th percentile.

Nancy Gordon

Influences on Growth

The genes we inherit have the biggest say in molding our basic body—whether we will be tall and thin, short and stocky, or just in between (Mittler, 1971). Height and weight are also affected by such environmental factors as nutrition, living conditions, and general health.

Well-fed, well-cared-for children grow taller and heavier than their counterparts in poor homes; they mature sexually and attain maximum height earlier, and their teeth erupt sooner. These differences usually show up by the first year and remain consistent throughout life (American Academy of Pediatrics, 1973). Children are growing taller and achieving maturity sooner than they did a century ago, probably because of better nutrition, the decrease in child labor, and the elimination of early marriage. Better medical care, and especially the use of immunizations and antibiotic drugs, also play a part. Congenital heart disease, nephritis, inborn metabolic disorders, and certain other illnesses can have grave effects on growth. Children who are ill for a long time may never achieve their genetically programmed normal stature be-

cause they may never be able to make up for the growth time lost while they were sick.

Boys are slightly longer and heavier than girls at birth and remain larger through adulthood, except for a brief time during puberty when the girls' growth spurts make them overtake the boys. The bones of black children harden earlier, their permanent teeth appear sooner, they mature earlier, and they tend to be larger than white children (American Academy of Pediatrics, 1973). Infants who suffer emotional deprivation may fail to gain weight normally, even when nutrition and medical care are adequate (Whipple, 1966).

INFANT FEEDING

As long as doctors, philosophers, psychotherapists, and other experts have been advising parents on the best way to raise healthy children, they have based their recommendations on a combination of research findings, impressions gained from their professional and personal daily lives, and on what in one person may be termed "wisdom," in another "superstition." We do not always *know* what is best for children. So the best we can do is go by whatever scientific evidence is available, whatever recommendations come from people who seem knowledgeable in the field, and whatever intuitive feelings parents have about their own children.

A recent comprehensive article on infant feeding by a group of eminent pediatric

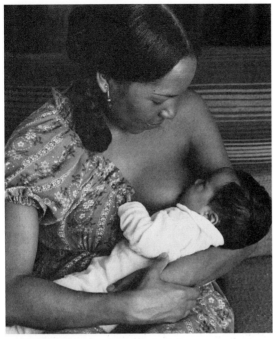

The best food for newborn infants is breast milk, unless the mother or child has a physical condition that makes nursing impossible. (Erika Stone/Peter Arnold, Inc.)

nutritionists sums up some of the dilemmas of making recommendations in this area:

In technically developed countries, most infants seem to grow normally and to remain healthy in spite of wide differences in feeding practices. One infant may be fed a formula for three months and then be fed whole milk, receiving a wide variety of other foods beginning at 3 or 4 weeks of age. A second infant may receive only infant formula, and a third infant may be fully breast-fed to age 6 months. The infants may or may not receive supplements of various vitamins and minerals. If we detect no differences in health as a result of such divergent feeding practices, it does not necessarily mean that the choice of feeding practice is inconsequential. Rather, the consequences may be too subtle to be detected by casual observation or may be of long-term rather than short-term nature. Little is known

about long-term consequences of infant feeding practices [Fomon, Filer, Anderson, & Ziegler, 1979, p. 52].

Still, as these same doctors point out, "infants must be fed and decisions must be made about how this should be done" (p. 52). So let us see what they and other experts on children's well-being have found and recommend in regard to several infant feeding issues.

Breast Feeding

After a fifty-year decline in the popularity of breast feeding, this natural means of nurture is returning to favor, especially among better-educated, higher-income women. In 1976, more than half of all American infants and almost half of Canadian babies were breast-fed at time of hospital discharge (American Academy of Pediatrics, 1978).

Even in a society where technological advances have provided excellent infant formulas that approximate breast milk, the American Academy of Pediatrics recently stated that the best food for every newborn infant is breast milk, unless mother or child has some specific physical condition that makes nursing impossible (American Academy of Pediatrics, 1978).

Breast milk has been termed the "ultimate health food" (Olds & Eiger, 1973) because it offers so many benefits to babies. Breast-fed children are protected in varying degrees against diarrhea, respiratory infections, allergy, colds, bronchitis, pneumonia, German measles, scarlet fever, and polio (Cunningham, 1977; Jelliffe & Jelliffe, 1977; Baum, 1971; Hodes, 1964). They are more likely to have healthy teeth and less likely to be obese or to suffer from premature atherosclerosis (Fomany, 1971; Fomon, 1971; Tank, 1965).

Since the mother's health, emotional

state, and attitudes toward breast feeding affect her ability to nurse her baby, the academy recommends a number of measures that can provide her with information and support: education about nutrition and, specifically, lactation to school children, expectant parents, doctors, and nurses; establishment in the hospital and at home of "demand" feeding schedules rather than rigid three- to four-hour feeding times; and day nurseries adjacent to workplaces so that working women may nurse their infants.

Although breast feeding is generally preferable, it is not, of course, the only way to nourish a baby. A tiny proportion of women are physically unable to nurse, and others have strong feelings against it or are prevented by factors such as work or travel needs. While Fomon and his colleagues (1979) recommend breast feeding for as long as eighteen to twenty-four months, with other foods being introduced to the baby at 5 or 6 months, they add:

We do not believe that strong social pressures should be exerted to coerce women into breast-feeding, nor do we believe that any woman should be made to feel guilty because she elects not to breast-feed [Fomon et al., 1979, p. 52].

Babies fed with formula and raised with love also grow up healthy and well adjusted. Long-term studies that have compared breast-fed and bottle-fed children have found no significant differences (Schmitt, 1970). The quality of the relationship between mother and child is probably more important than the feeding method:

A baby raised in a loving home can grow up to be a healthy, psychologically secure individual no matter how he receives his nourishment.

While successful nursing is a beautiful, happy experience for both mother and child, the woman who nurses grudgingly because she feels she *should* will probably do more harm to her baby by communicating her feelings of resentment and unhappiness, than she would if she were a relaxed, loving, bottle-feeding mother [Olds & Eiger, 1973, p. 18].

Bottle Feeding

Most bottle-fed babies receive a commercially prepared formula based on either cow's milk or soy protein. These formulas are manufactured to resemble mother's milk as closely as possible (although they will never be *exactly* identical), with the exception that they contain supplements of vitamins and minerals that breast milk does not have. Like breast milk, formula feedings are the only food most babies need till about 5 or 6 months of age.

One common infant feeding practice—letting a baby take a bottle of milk, juice, or other sweetened liquid to bed—has been indicted as a major cause of cavities in babies. In "nursing-bottle mouth," the sugar from the drink causes decay to the teeth in a pattern that corresponds to the area where the liquid comes out of the bottle. Dentists recommend that children who nurse for a long time between meals or while they're sleeping receive only water in their bottles. Other ways to avoid this include teaching a baby to drink from a cup before the first birthday, always offering juice from a cup, and not using milk in a bottle to help a baby fall asleep (American Academy of Pediatrics, 1978).

Solid Foods and Cow's Milk

Because some infants fed plain cow's milk in the early months of life have been found to develop gastrointestinal bleeding (Wilson, Lahey, & Heiner, 1974), babies should receive breast milk or formula until they are over 6 months of age and eating the equivalent of 1½ jars of baby food a day (Fomon et al., 1979). The milk they drink then should be homogenized, vitamin D–fortified whole milk, as opposed to skim milk, since babies need the

Feeding solid food to Nancy is a gooey mess because of her hand-to-mouth reflex. The minute the spoon leaves her mouth, in pop her middle two fingers, which she happily sucks on until the next spoonful arrives.

S. O.

AT 7 MONTHS

Tonight while I was feeding you, you collected a large mouthful of cereal and carrots and then, without swallowing, proceeded to tell me a rather involved joke (of which I understood nothing, of course), at the end of which you went into gales of laughter. It was a very colorful mess, but irresistible.

Nancy Gordon

calories in whole milk for proper growth (Fomon et al., 1979).

Most infants in the United States are fed some solid foods—usually cereal or strained fruits—by the age of 2 months, mainly due to their parents' desires not to let other babies get ahead of them, to aggressive marketing by the baby food industry, and to the belief that the solid food will help the baby sleep through the night (Fomon et al., 1979). Yet many pediatric nutritionists deplore this pattern:

If an infant is to be encouraged to discontinue eating at the earliest sign of satisfaction, it must be possible for him to communicate in some way with the individual who is feeding him. At 5 or 6 months of age, the infant will be able to sit with support and will have good neuromuscular control of the head and neck. He or she will be able to indicate desire for food by opening the mouth and leaning forward, and to indicate disinterest or satiety by leaning back and turning away. Until the infant can express these feelings, feeding of beikost [foods other than milk or formula fed to infants] will probably represent a type of forced feeding [Fomon et al, 1979, p. 54].

Obesity

A major nutritional problem among modern American children is obesity. Some people may be fat because they have inherited more subcutaneous fat or a more sluggish metabolism. But it seems that most fat people eat too much food for the energy they expend.

There appears to be a relationship between obesity and income, but it is not yet fully understood. Stunkard and associates (1972) compared children from different social classes and found that obesity was more prevalent among lower-class children by the age of 6, apparently reflecting poor eating habits. The American Academy of Pediatrics' ten-state nutrition survey found a different and more complex relationship. Basically, this study found that from infancy through adolescence, obesity increases directly with income. Poor children are leaner and smaller in general. This relationship is reversed, though, for females at adolescence. By the midteens, poorer girls become fatter and stay fatter as women than their leaner, higher-income counterparts (Garn & Clark, 1976).

The different findings between these two studies may be related to the ways the researchers measured obesity. Stunkard used weight, while the ten-state researchers measured fat folds (Weil, 1977).

Many nutritionists believe that people may become obese in later life from being overfed in infancy. Feeding infant rats too many calories causes them to develop an abundance of fat cells, and it is possible that overfed infants also develop extra fat cells that persist through life (Jelliffe, 1974; Mayer, 1973; Hirsh, 1972).

One recent study questions this concept that obese infants become obese children

Motor development proceeds from good control of the hands to good control of the fingers in infancy to use of the entire body in a coordinated manner in toddlerhood. (Photos by Erika Stone/Peter Arnold, Inc.)

(Dine, Gartside, Glueck, Rheines, Greene, & Khoury, 1979). When researchers followed 582 children in a suburban private pediatrics practice from birth to age 5, they found no differences between breast-fed and bottle-fed infants at any age point. Furthermore, only 30 percent of the fattest 5-year-olds (those in the top 10 percent) had been among the fattest 6-month-olds, and only 30 to 40 percent had been among the fattest 10 percent at 1 year of age. Dine and his colleagues found that about 70 percent of the variance in fatness measures at age 5 did not seem to be related to these measures during the first year of life. More research along these lines needs to be carried out. In any case, whether or not parents can prevent obesity by proper feeding habits in the first year of life, it is clear that proper nutrition is an important element and an ongoing concern throughout the life span. In fact, it is possible that cutting down on the amounts of salt and sugar a baby eats may prevent hypertension, heart attacks, and diabetes in adulthood, as well as obesity (Piscano, Lichter, Ritter, & Siegal, 1978).

MOTOR DEVELOPMENT

There is a definite order for the acquisition of motor skills, proceeding from the simple to the complex.

With age, babies' motor development shows more control and a specificity of function. Their control of body parts is *differentiating*. They proceed from good control of their hands to good control of their fingers. After they have gained control over various differentiated movements, they integrate the movements into complex behavior patterns. So they integrate control over leg, foot, and arm movements to manage walking.

Fetuses move about a great deal, turning somersaults, kicking, and thumb sucking. Newborn babies turn their heads, kick their legs, flail about with their arms, and display an array of reflex behaviors. These prenatal and early postnatal movements represent a generalized type of activity under subcortical control; that is, the brain stem, lying under the cortex, is responsible for the involuntary, primitive reflexes of infants. By about the fourth month, voluntary, cortex-controlled movements take over.

TABLE 3-4
Human Reflex
Behaviors

NAME OF REFLEX	STIMULATION	BEHAVIOR	AGE OF DROPPING OUT
ROOTING	Cheek stroked with finger or nipple	Head turns; mouth opens, sucking movements begin	9 months
MORO (STARTLE)	Sudden stimulus such as gun shot or being dropped	Extends legs, arms, and fingers; arches back, draws back head	3 months
DARWINIAN (GRASPING)	Palm of hand stroked	Makes such a strong fist that can be raised to standing position if both fists are closed around a stick	2-3 months
SWIMMING	Put in water face down	Well-coordinated swimming movements	6 months
TONIC NECK	Laid down on back	Head turns to one side; assumes "fencer" position; extends arms and legs on preferred side, flexes opposite limbs	
BABINSKI	Sole of foot stroked	Toes fan out, foot twists in	6-9 months
WALKING	Held under arm, with bare feet touching flat surface	Makes steplike motions that look like well-coordinated walking	8 weeks
PLACING	Backs of feet drawn against edge of flat surface	Withdraws foot	1 month

Reflex Behaviors

When we blink at a bright light, we are not acting deliberately. We are reacting involuntarily through a *reflex* behavior. Human beings have an arsenal of reflexes, many of which are present before birth (see Table 3-4). Some reflexes help us survive; others seem to offer protection. The presence or absence of reflexes is a guide to evaluating neurological development, since there is a definite timetable for the development and dropping out of most reflexes.

The primitive reflexes are present at birth or shortly after. Many can be elicited even before birth. In a neurologically healthy baby, these primitive reflexes tend to drop out at different times during the first year or so (for example, the Moro reflex drops out at 2 to 3 months; the rooting, at 9 months; and the Babinski, at 6 to 9 months). The brief appearance of the primitive reflexes reflects the subcortical control of the infant nervous system, since the maturation of the cerebral cortex inhibits their expression. Those reflexes that are clearly protective—such as the pupillary, the eye-blink, yawning, coughing, gagging, and sneezing—do not drop out.

Milestones in Motor Development

When babies' central nervous systems, muscles, and bones have matured enough and they are in an appropriate position with freedom to move, they will lift their heads. They do not have to be taught to do this, and the more they practice it, the better they become at it. Each newly mastered activity prepares a baby to tackle the next in the preordained sequence of motor skills (see Table 3-5).[1]

HEAD CONTROL   At birth most babies can turn their heads from side to side while supine (lying on their backs) and can lift their heads enough to turn them while prone (on their stomachs). First they master lifting the head while prone, then holding it erect while sitting, and then lifting it while supine.

AT 14 WEEKS

I've been putting you on a clean sheet on the rug most afternoons and you have a great time swimming. You move quite fast over to the edge of the sheet so you can taste the green rug.

AT 8 MONTHS

Yesterday you decided it was silly to scoot on your stomach when you could just as well crawl on your hands and knees, so now you crawl. The first thing you went after was your orange plastic bathtub. You seem to think it's a teething toy.

Nancy Gordon

[1]The ages given here and in Table 3-5 are averages. About half of all normal babies master these skills before the ages given, and about half afterward. There is no "average" baby, and normality includes a wide age range.

SITTING   Babies learn to sit either by getting up from a lying position or by getting down from a standing one. The average baby sits with support at 4 months, in a high chair at 6 months, and alone at 7 months (Shirley, 1933).

ROLLING OVER   At 5 to 7 months the average baby rolls from stomach to back, and later from back to stomach (Nelson, Vaughan, & McKay, 1975).

PREWALKING LOCOMOTION   Before they walk, babies get around in a variety of ways. They *crawl* by wriggling on their bellies and pulling their bodies along with their arms, dragging their feet behind. They *hitch* or *scoot*, moving along in a sitting position, pushing forward with arms and legs. They *bear-walk*, with hands and feet touching the ground. And they *creep*, crawling on hands and knees with trunk above the floor. Most babies creep and crawl at about 9 to 10 months (Nelson et al., 1975).

STANDING   With a helping hand, the average baby can stand at 8 months, stand holding onto furniture a month later, pull to a standing position at about a year, and stand alone at 13 to 14 months (Shirley, 1933).

WALKING   Less than a month after first standing alone, babies take their first step, tumble to the floor, go back to creeping, and then try another step. Within a few days, they are walking regularly, if shakily. The average baby can walk with help at 9 to 11 months, walk alone at 15 months, run stiffly at 18 months, climb stairs with one hand held at 18 months, and jump at 20 months (Nelson et al., 1975).

MANIPULATION   Neonates show the grasping reflex: When the palm is stimulated, they grasp a cube. Babies 5 months old don't grasp firmly, but they do touch objects. At 7 months, grasping doesn't include the thumb; at 9 months it does. Early grasping involves the entire arm, but the 15-month-old shows

TABLE 3-5

Normal Development in Infancy and Childhood

AGE IN MONTHS*	MOTOR	SOCIAL	HEARING AND SPEECH	EYE AND HAND
1	Head erect for few seconds	Quieted when picked up	Startled by sounds	Follows light with eyes
2	Head up when prone (chin clear)	Smiles	Listens to bell or rattle	Follows ring up, down, and sideways
3	Kicks well	Follows person with eyes	Searches for sound with eyes	Glances from one object to another
4	Lifts head and chest prone	Returns examiner's smile	Laughs	Clasps and retains cube
5	Holds head erect with no lag	Frolics when played with	Turns head to sound	Pulls paper away from face
6	Rises on to wrists	Turns head to person talking	Babbles or coos to voice or music	Takes cube from table
7	Rolls from front to back	Drinks from a cup	Makes four different sounds	Looks for fallen objects
8	Sits without support	Looks at mirror image	Understands "No" and "Bye-bye"	Passes toy from hand to hand
9	Turns around on floor	Helps to hold cup for drinking	Says "Mama" or "Dada"	Manipulates two objects together
10	Stands when held up	Smiles at mirror image	Imitates playful sounds	Clicks two objects together in imitation
11	Pulls up to stand	Finger feeds	Two words with meaning	Pincer grip
12	Walks or sidesteps around pen	Plays pat-a-cake on request	Three words with meaning	Finds toy hidden under cup
13	Stands alone	Holds cup for drinking	Looks at pictures	Preference for one hand
14	Walks alone	Uses spoon	Recognizes own name	Makes marks with pencil
15	Climbs up stairs	Shows shoes	Four to five clear words	Places one object upon another
16	Pushes pram, toy horse, etc.	Tries to turn doorknob	Six to seven clear words	Scribbles freely
17	Picks up toy from floor without falling	Manages cup well	Babbled conversation	Pulls (table) cloth to get toy
18	Climbs on to chair	Takes off shoes and socks	Enjoys rhymes and tries to join in	Constructive play with toys
19	Climbs stairs up and down	Knows one part of the body	Nine words	Tower of three bricks
20	Jumps	Bowel control	Twelve words	Tower of four bricks
21	Runs	Bladder control by day	Two-word sentences	Circular scribble
22	Walks up stairs	Tries to tell experiences	Listens to stories	Tower of five or more bricks
23	Seats self at table	Knows two parts of body	Twenty words or more	Copies perpendicular stroke
24	Walks up and down stairs	Knows four parts of body	Names four toys	Copies horizontal stroke

SOURCE: From Wood, 1974.

*Conceptual rather than chronological age.

mature prehension using fingers and thumb together (Halverson, 1931). The use of thumb and fingers to manipulate tools doesn't come till much later. Even the 2-year-old is awkward handling a fork (Corbin, 1973).

AT 7½ MONTHS

You sit up quite well, although you can't quite get yourself into a sitting position. You have just learned to creep (knees, one hand and one elbow, usually), although you've been able to go backward for a couple of weeks. You can stand up holding on for a couple of minutes.

AT 8 MONTHS

You've been very busy the past two days. Yesterday you finally discovered how to sit yourself up without leaning on one arm, and within an hour of that discovery, you pulled yourself up onto your feet for the first time. You sit like crazy, but you're still a bit wobbly on your feet.

AT 10½ MONTHS

You love to climb stairs, which is fine except that you aren't quite sure about how to come down again. I hope you learn soon, since you tend to stand up and wobble when you want to get down.... You still don't really walk and you still don't really talk. You still only take a step or two alone and you use a word for a few days and then drop it. It's frustrating, but I expect there will be a sudden developmental burst and you'll do both.

AT 11½ MONTHS

You enjoy walking holding onto the back of Rafferty (your wheeled giraffe chair). If there's anything to hold onto, you prefer to walk rather than crawl -- unless you are in a hurry.

ONE WEEK BEFORE THE FIRST BIRTHDAY

You took five steps on your own today. You could be fairly proficient if you wouldn't lunge at your target when you are halfway there.

ONE WEEK AFTER THE FIRST BIRTHDAY

I can't get over how much you've changed since last week .... The day before your birthday you were still at the walking-from-one-person-to-another stage, with the first person getting you balanced and started and the other person catching you. Two days later you were taking off across the room on your own and even stopping to pick something up along the way.

Nancy Gordon

DEVELOPMENT OF EYE-HAND COORDINATION During the first year of life, the basic operations develop in the coordination between what Jason sees and how he moves his hands. Over the next few years, he will be refining and extending the use of these basic operations as he explores and achieves an increasing degree of mastery over his world.

Corbin (1973) has delineated four major stages in eye-hand coordination:

1 *Static visual exploration:* From birth to 16 weeks, Jason spends much of his time looking at his hands. He looks at a toy in the corner of his crib and then immediately looks back at his hands, while waving his arms and legs around at random.

2 *Active and repeated visual exploration:* Between 17 and 28 weeks, Jason seems to manipulate objects with his eyes in "a kind of ocular grasping" that seems like a preparation for actual manual grasping. So at about 20 weeks, Jason seems to "pick up" an object (say, a dangling ring) with his eyes, "drop" it (look at his hands), and then "pick it up" again (look back at the ring). While he is looking at the ring, the rest of his body stops moving until he flings his arms outward in a crude attempt to catch the ring as it swings near his hands. If he happens to grasp the ring, he takes it right to his mouth, where he still tries to look at it. He seems to be trying to coordinate seeing the ring with feeling it.

3 *Initiation of grasping and/or manipulation:* Between 28 and 40 weeks, Jason intensifies his visual activity to correct his reaching and grasping abilities. First he locates a toy with his eyes; then as he starts to reach out for it, he relaxes his visual fixation—and often misses the toy. When he does, he fixates more intensely on the toy and adjusts his reaching response and finally touches the toy. As he holds it, he continues to look at it. He seems to be going through a step-by-step process of interrelating what he sees with what he feels, and vice versa. He is learning how to use his eyes to guide his actions, which is what eye-hand coordination is all about.

4 *Refinement and extension:* From about 40 weeks throughout middle childhood, Jason will continue to explore and manipulate objects in a refinement and extension of these behaviors. He'll be able to pick up blocks and put them in a box, to feed himself fairly efficiently, to draw on paper, to use silverware, to master more and more skills.

Repetitive Processes in Motor Development

As we have said, development is a continuous process. As children grow older, they get progressively better at all sorts of tasks. Bower (1976), however, has pointed out a few specific instances in which children display a

particular ability at a very early age, after which they seem to lose it until a later time. This shows up in walking, for example, as indicated by the walking reflex. From the age of 4 to 8 weeks, Vicky will make steplike motions that look like well-coordinated walking if she is held under the arm, with her bare feet touching a flat surface. After 8 weeks, though, she loses this ability and will not walk at all for about a year. The same thing seems to happen with regard to reaching out for objects that she has seen or heard. In the first few weeks of life, she will reach out, but at about the age of 4 weeks, eye-hand coordination disappears, not to reappear till the age of 20 weeks, and at the age of 5 or 6 months, ear-hand coordination disappears—that is, the ability to reach out and grasp objects that can be heard but not seen.

Bower feels that the various phases of development are related, and that the early appearance of some of these abilities is important in the child's ability to use them later on. He says:

It has been suggested that the acquisition of certain concepts in infancy is necessary for the *permanent emergence of those concepts later in life*, and that a child who does not acquire normal concepts during infancy may be permanently unable to acquire them [Bower, 1976, p. 39; *emphasis added*].

He also feels that the reason such abilities disappear is that they are not exercised. To test this hypothesis, he provided practice for some infants in some abilities, and got mixed results. Those babies who received practice in eye-hand coordination in their first four weeks showed an earlier reappearance of the ability later on, and indeed some of the practiced babies never lost their reaching abilities. On the other hand, ear-hand coordi-

nation seemed to disappear more quickly with practice, and its reappearance was retarded. (A different experiment, which concentrated on giving 1- to 8-week-old infants practice in walking, found that the practiced babies walked unassisted earlier than a control group who did not have practice sessions [Zelazo, Zelazo, & Kolb, 1972]. This experiment will be discussed later in this chapter.)

Experiments like these raise ethical questions about providing artificial types of practice, especially since normal development seems to be retarded in some of the cases and also since we don't know the long-term effects of artificially induced precocious development. The concepts are intriguing, but their practical effects questionable.

Environmental Influences on Motor Development

In Chapter 1 we examined the relative effects of heredity and environment on many aspects of development. Motor development is a good example of the interaction of these two influences. Human beings appear to be genetically programmed to perform many different activities such as sitting, standing, and walking. All these skills unfold in a regular, largely preordained pattern. Children have to reach a certain level of physiological maturity before they can exercise them.

The environment also plays a role, even though in most cases it is rather limited. Motor development does not appear to be affected by sex, geographical residence, or level of parental education (Bayley, 1965). At some ages, first-born children score slightly better than later-borns on motor development measures (Bayley, 1965). This may be because parents might be spending more time with their first children and stimulating them to greater activity. In any case, these small differences are probably temporary. When children get good nutrition and good health care, physical freedom, and the opportunity to practice motor skills, their motor development will be normal (Clarke-Stewart, 1977). But when the environment is grossly deficient in any of these areas, development suffers.

HOW ENVIRONMENT CAN RETARD DEVELOPMENT In two Iranian institutions for children, the children were hardly ever handled by the overworked attendants. The younger babies spent practically all their time on their backs in cribs. They drank from propped bottles. They were never put in a sitting position nor placed on their stomachs. They had no toys and were not taken out of bed until they could sit unsupported (often not till 2 years of age, as compared with 9 months for the average American child). And once a sitting child did reach the floor, there was no child-sized furniture or play equipment. These children were retarded in their motor development because of the deficient environment which kept them from moving around.

The children in a third home were fed in the arms of trained attendants, were placed on their stomachs and propped up sitting, were in playpens at 4 months, and had many toys. These children showed normal levels of motor development.

When the children in the first two groups did start to get about, they scooted (moved around in a sitting position, pushing their bodies forward with arms and feet), rather than creeping on hands and knees. Since they had never been placed on their stomachs, they had had no opportunity to practice raising their heads or pulling their arms and legs beneath their bodies—the movements needed for creeping. Also, since they had never been propped in a sitting position, they had not been raising their heads and shoulders to learn how to sit at the usual age. Surprisingly, this retardation appeared to be temporary: school-aged children at the second institution, who presumably had also been retarded as toddlers, now worked and played normally (Dennis, 1960).

Such severe levels of environmental deprivation are fortunately rare. Environment can play a part in motor development and the more it departs from the typical, the greater its effect will be.

Can Motor Development Be Accelerated?

Gesell (1929) examined one set of twins to study the effects of training babies to perform developmental activities. T, one of a pair of identical twins, was trained in stair-climbing, block-building, and manual coordination; twin C was not so trained. With age, C became just as expert as T, leading Gesell to conclude that "the powerful influence of maturation of infant behavior pattern is made clear."

However, a 1972 study (Zelazo, Zelazo, & Kolb) indicates that training infants in walking—starting at 1 week of age—may indeed lead to early walking. Twenty-four babies were assigned to four groups, from the beginning of their second week through the end of their eighth. Those in the *active-exercise* group had four 3-minute exercise sessions every day; they were held under the arms while the soles of their feet touched a flat surface. The legs and arms of those in the *passive-exercise* group were pumped gently while they lay in their cribs, in infant seats, or on laps. Those in the *no-exercise* group were tested weekly, and a fourth group was tested only once at the end, to be sure the weekly testing had no effect.

The babies in the active-exercise group walked at an average age of 10.12 months, while the average control child began later—as late as 12.35 months for the fourth group. All the babies walked earlier than the Gesell-Thompson 1934 norm of 14 months, probably because of heightened parental interest. This study suggests that there is a critical period during which the walking response can be transformed intact from a reflex to a voluntary action. This reflex may have a definite function in helping infants become more mobile, and perhaps it should be stimulated rather than allowed to fade through disuse.

Toilet Training

Initially, in human beings, elimination of body waste is involuntary. When an infant's bladder or bowels are full, the appropriate sphincter muscles open automatically. Before children can control elimination, they have to learn a lot. They have to know what is expected of them: that there is a proper time and place to eliminate. They have to become familiar with the feelings that indicate the need to eliminate, and they have to learn to tighten the sphincters to inhibit elimination and to loosen them to permit it.

McGraw (1940) measured the effects of very early training. One twin was put on the toilet every hour of every day from 2 months of

AT 20 MONTHS

We bought you a potty chair about a month ago and you love to sit on it since that guarantees you a parent's undivided attention and look reading for as long as you stay put, but you don't know what it's for at all. You've only produced twice in what must have been 60 sittings.

AT 22 MONTHS

You're getting pretty good about the potty. If we take your diaper off and let you go potty when you want to (instead of sitting and waiting), you don't make mistakes. You've been going about three times a day on your own so we bought you some training pants and we'll let you proceed from here. You do not, however, want to move your bowels without the security of a diaper.

Nancy Gordon

age. Eighteen months later he started to show some control, and by about 23 months of age he had achieved almost perfect success. His twin, never put on the toilet till 23 months of age, quickly caught up. A certain level of maturation has to exist for training to be effective.

Generally, the later toilet training is begun, the faster a child learns. Sears, Maccoby, and Levin (1957) found that most parents begin their child's bowel training at about 11 months of age, achieving success some seven months later. Training begun before 5 months of age usually takes ten months to complete; but when begun later than 20 months of age, success comes after only about five months. Babies whose training begins between 5 and 14 months, or after 20 months, seem to take it all with the most equanimity. Parents who scold and punish a lot do not complete training any sooner than more easygoing parents, and they often produce emotional upset in their children.

According to a study of 859 children in Baltimore (Oppel, Harper, & Rider, 1968), only 8 percent of 1-year-olds had achieved daytime dryness. By age 2, 55 percent were dry; by 3 years, 84 percent; and by 5 years, 95 percent. Nighttime dryness came later. Only 7 percent of 1-year-olds ever stayed dry through the night, compared with 41 percent of 2-year-olds, 66 percent of 3-year-olds, 90 percent of 7-year-olds, and 97 percent of 12-year-olds. One child out of four relapsed at some point, accounting for most of those wetting the bed after the age of 6. Girls became dry day and night earlier than boys, probably because of earlier maturation. Children who were low-birthweight infants had more trouble attaining bladder control than those who were full-term babies, possibly because of neurological deficits.

Generally, the later toilet training is begun, the faster a child learns. (Erika Stone/Peter Arnold, Inc.)

Cross-Cultural Perspectives on Motor Development

What is normal and typical for children in one culture may not be so in another. The Arapesh in New Guinea, for example, hold their babies a great deal, "often in a standing position so that they can push with their feet against the arms or legs of the person who holds them. As a result infants can stand, steadied by their two hands, before they can sit alone" (Mead, 1935, p. 57). Differences in motor development have been demonstrated between black and white American children (Bayley, 1965); between African, European, and Indian children (Geber & Dean, 1957); and between African and American babies (Tronick, Koslowski, & Brazelton, 1971).

African newborns seem precocious in motor development. Geber and Dean (1957) assessed Ugandan, European, and Indian children born in Africa and found that the African babies had superior muscle tone and could turn their heads from side to side, pursue moving objects with their eyes, and raise their heads earlier. The African babies seemed to have been born at a more advanced stage of development, since many of their activities at less than a week corresponded to those of European children aged 4 to 8 weeks.

Some genetic differences may be responsible, since American black babies are also advanced in both gross and fine motor development during the first year (Bayley, 1965). On eleven of sixty items on the Bayley Infant Scale of Motor Development, black babies did better by at least 0.7 month, while white babies did not do better on any by as much as half a month. The skills are well distributed throughout the first year and show no particular pattern of superiority by age or by any one kind of coordination.

Some differences probably result from how babies are handled. Zambian mothers rouse their babies by picking them up and tossing them up and down. Twenty-four hours after delivery, a mother begins to carry her baby in a dashiki, a length of cloth worn on the body and arranged to form a sling. Since it provides no head support, Zambian babies quickly learn to keep their heads steady. Tronick, Koslowski, and Brazelton (1971) tested Zambian and American infants on days one, five, and ten. On the first day, the Zambian infants reacted less than the Americans, showing the effects of a poor prenatal environment. But by the fifth day they had caught up, and by the tenth they had become much more attentive, presumably because of more vigorous, socially stimulating child-care practices.

Before African children are weaned, their mothers sleep with them, breast-feed on demand, continually stimulate them by activities and conversation, and never leave them. After weaning, the mother not only stops

giving the breast but may also stop giving of herself, seeming to make a deliberate effort to separate herself from her child. When weaning causes such a sudden change in a child's way of life, the child usually becomes less lively. Children weaned more gradually generally remain vigorous. European-reared African children, who spend a lot of time in their cribs and are fed on schedule rather than on demand, are not precocious in motor development after the first month (Geber, 1958).

The study mentioned above that stimulated the walking reflex (Zelazo, Zelazo, & Kolb, 1972) incorporated some types of parental treatment common in African cultures. One psychologist who studied Bushmen infants says: "In many infant care contexts the newborn reflex repertoire in general has functions [that] may have survival value" (Konner, 1973). But survival value in the African bush may be very different from optimum development in an urban or suburban setting. Before we counsel parents to try to accelerate their babies' motor development, we have to weigh the potential benefits and risks.

Even though the above studies seem to demonstrate motor precocity in African infants, there is a possibility that this is not an established fact, but is instead a conclusion reached because of methodological problems in the studies. Warren (1972) has criticized many of the studies, claiming that the African precocity shows up in studies where the behaviors of the African babies are compared, not to control groups of Western babies, but to test norms. He feels that more and better research is called for to resolve the controversy over whether African babies are indeed precocious in their motor development.

As we have seen, child-rearing practices may produce both precocity and retardation

in motor development. A recent cross-sectional study of 288 normal, full-term babies from the Yucatan, Mexico, underscores this (Solomons, 1978). These babies, from 2 weeks to just over a year old, from three different social backgrounds (rural, urban working-class, and urban middle- to upper-class) were ahead of United States babies in their motor skills at the age of 3 months but had fallen behind by 11 months.

The decline was so striking that, were this pattern evident in a single child, any pediatrician or psychologist reviewing the results would be concerned about progressive neurologic disease [Solomons, 1978, pp. 836–37].

With a plea for establishing different norms for different cultural groups for the times at which babies acquire various skills, Solomons points out some child-rearing practices that may account for her findings. The more advanced manipulative abilities of Yucatecan babies may arise from their not having toys to play with: As a result, they discover and play with their fingers at earlier ages. Their delayed skills in moving about are probably related to several conditions in their lives: As infants, they are swaddled, which restricts their freedom of movement; as older children, they continue to be restrained by being held more in the arms or on the hips of their parents and older brothers and sisters, by sleeping in hammocks (which become net "cages" compared to the open space of a firm-mattressed crib), and by not being put on the ground to play (partly because of the presence of tropical insects and partly because of local folk beliefs about the dangers of cold floors).

We see, then, that there is no universal standard of what is best for children, and that the children in every culture are encouraged to—and, in fact, do—develop along somewhat different lines. So before we adopt or condemn another culture's child-rearing attitudes and practices, we have to ask ourselves, "What is best for *our* babies in this time and place?"

SUDDEN INFANT DEATH SYNDROME (SIDS)

The scenario is tragically similar from case to case. An apparently healthy baby goes to sleep at the usual naptime or at nighttime. When the parents come in, the baby is dead. *Sudden Infant Death Syndrome*, or "crib death" strikes some 8000 to 10,000 babies a year, making it the leading cause of death in infants aged 1 month to 1 year (Arnon, Midura, Damos, Wood, & Chin, 1978).

No one knows the cause of SIDS, which apparently has existed from the beginnings of recorded history, but a number of factors seem to be related to it. In a major prospective study, which started out with 19,047 infants and followed almost all of them through the first year of life, eight risk factors showed up (Lewak, Van den Berg, & Beckwith, 1979). Those babies who succumbed to SIDS (2.3 per 1000) were more likely to be premature, or low birthweight, and male. Their mothers were more likely to be poor, to smoke, to be under 25 years old, to have received little or no prenatal care, and to have had another baby less than a year before this one. There seemed to be no relationship between SIDS and race, blood type, maternal hemoglobin level, placental abnormality, a low Apgar score, or twinship. Of the fifty-six infants in this group who had all eight risk factors, six died of SIDS (an incidence of 107 per 1000). However, 90 percent of the babies who were considered at high risk for SIDS did not die.

Many other possible causes of this disease have been proposed and discounted, including suffocation from bedding, bottle feeding, bacterial infection, and enlarged thymus glands (Consumer Reports, 1975).

Several other theories are currently under investigation. Because SIDS is more apt to strike babies with colds, who live in over-crowded conditions, and during the winter months, many researchers feel that a virus is to blame. Suspicion has recently been cast on the infant's exposure to cigarette smoke, either prenatally or postnatally. Bergman and Wiesner (1976) found that SIDS infants were more likely to have mothers who smoked during pregnancy (61 percent of fifty-six mothers, compared to 42 percent of eighty-six mothers of non-SIDS infants), as well as after birth (59 percent versus 37 percent). "Passive smoking" (exposure to cigarette smoking) has also been linked to lower respiratory tract disease during infancy, giving rise to the speculation that there may be a relationship between difficulties in respiration and SIDS.

Researchers exploring this dreaded baby-killer are investigating many other possible causes, and new ideas are being published almost weekly (Beckwith, 1975). Finding that 4.3 percent of SIDS cases had botulism poisons or organisms in their systems, Arnon et al. (1978) suggest that infant botulism may be a cause. Shannon, Kelly, and O'Connell (1977) propose a generalized neurological dysfunction that causes an impaired response to breathing carbon dioxide during quiet sleep. Kravitz and Scherz (1978) suspect an airway obstruction that interferes with breathing and suggest a semireclining sleep position rather than a horizontal one.

While these and many other researchers continue to ask why this disease strikes, other investigators ask what happens to the bereaved families. Of course, they suffer greatly. Each one of the thirty-two Nebraska parents who filled out a thirteen-page questionnaire for researchers DeFrain and Ernst (1978) rated SIDS as the most severe family crisis they had ever experienced. More than 2 out of 3 felt guilty, even though no one really knows

what causes these deaths. More than 3 out of 4 reported that their other children reacted to the baby's death with such problems as nightmares, bed-wetting, school and discipline difficulties, excessive crying, blackout spells, and extreme quietness. The parents said that it took an average of 8.3 months for their families to regain the level of family organization they had had before the infant death, and almost 16 months to regain pre-death happiness levels.

A major problem for most of these parents was the disapproval they felt from society—being treated as criminals by the police, being ignored by friends and relatives, or worse yet, being criticized for negligence. Sixty-nine percent of these parents felt that they could have weathered the crisis better if the general public had been better informed. It's possible that many parents move to a different community to avoid this sense of societal disapproval: Sixty percent of parents who had lost a baby through SIDS during the time this study focused on had moved out of town within 2½ years of the death, a very high rate of mobility for this particular county.

So far, none of the research has shown us how to prevent SIDS. Subscribers to the virus theory do advise parents to avoid taking young babies into crowded places. Monitoring machines have been developed that sound an alarm during a period of *apnea*, or cessation of breathing, but the American Academy of Pediatrics advises against their use in the home, since they are expensive, hard to operate, and likely to cause psychological stress to parents who try to use them.

WE PROPOSE . . .

1. . . . a standardized procedure in every community for handling cases of infants who die suddenly and unexpectedly that is both compassionate and medically sound. Autopsies must be performed and parents promptly informed of the results.

**SUDDEN INFANT
DEATH
SYNDROME—A
PROPOSAL BY
PARENTS**

2. . . . that the criteria for the diagnosis of SIDS be disseminated to coroners and medical examiners throughout the United States, and that the term, "Sudden Infant Death Syndrome," be utilized on death certificates.

3. . . . that every SIDS family receive authoritative information about SIDS from a physician, nurse, or other health professional who is both knowledgeable about the disease and skilled in dealing with characteristic grief reactions.

4. . . . that a major effort be undertaken to increase the amount of research being conducted on SIDS through solicitation of the scientific community by the National Institute of Child Health and Human Development.

5. . . . that parent volunteer groups be available in every state or large community to promote the aims of the Foundation on a local level. Close ties should be maintained with local physicians, particularly pediatricians and pathologists.

From a prospectus on the National Foundation for Sudden Death, Inc., 1971, in A. Bergman and J. Choate, *"Why did my baby die?"* New York: The Third Press, Joseph Okpaku Publishing Co., Inc., 1975, pp. 84–85.

SUMMARY

1 The neonatal period, from birth to about 4 weeks of age, is a time of transition from intrauterine to extrauterine life. At birth, the neonate's circulatory, respiratory, gastrointestinal, and temperature regulation systems become independent from the mother's. **2** Shortly after birth the neonate is assessed medically by the Apgar scale, which measures five factors (heart rate, respiration, color, muscle tone, and reflex irritability) that indicate how well the newborn is adjusting to the extrauterine environment. **3** An infant's nervous system; sensitivity to temperature and pain; and senses of sight, hearing, smell, and taste are all operational to some extent at birth, and then they improve. When assessing these abilities, we must take an infant's *state* into account. **4** Normal physical and motor development proceed in a preordained sequence, and there is a wide range of individual differences in the ages at which various milestones of development are attained. Physical development is influenced by heredity as well as by environmental factors such as income, nutrition, race, and sex. **5** Breast feeding seems to offer physiological benefits to an infant and facilitates the formation of the mother-infant bond. However, the quality of the relationship between mother and infant is more important than the feeding method in promoting healthy development. There seems to be a relationship between overfeeding in infancy and obesity in later life. **6** Early motor development occurs when an infant is maturationally ready to engage in certain activities, although environmental factors may influence the expression of specific behaviors. Some studies indicate that black babies are more advanced motorically than white babies, which may result in part from genetic factors but also may be influenced by how infants are handled. Children raised in isolated, impoverished conditions may show motoric retardation, but powerful environmental influences are needed to accelerate or retard motor development markedly. Short-term experiments aimed at accelerating specific kinds of development such as stair-climbing and toilet training generally have had little effect. **7** Sudden Infant Death

Syndrome (SIDS) is the leading cause of death in infants between the ages of 1 month and 1 year. There are many theories about the causes of SIDS, but no theory is accepted universally.

SUGGESTED READINGS

Bergman, A., & Choate, J. *Why did my baby die?* New York: The Third Press, Joseph Okpaku Publishing Company, Inc., 1975. An in-depth study of Sudden Infant Death Syndrome, including a historical account of the phenomenon, coverage of current research, and suggestions for parents on coping with this painful experience.

Bower, T. G. R. *A primer of infant development.* San Francisco: Freeman, 1977. An analysis of physical/motor, cognitive, and social development in infancy.

Bower, T. G. R. *The perceptual world of the child.* Cambridge: Howard University Press, 1977. A fascinating discussion of the remarkable sensory and perceptual abilities of infants.

Caplan, F. *The first 12 months of life.* New York: Grosset & Dunlap, 1973. A detailed description of physical, emotional, and behavioral development during the first year; well illustrated with photographs and charts.

Caplan, F. *The second 12 months of life.* New York: Grosset & Dunlap, 1977. A detailed description of development during toddlerhood. Well illustrated.

Olds, S. W., & Eiger, M. S. *Complete book of breastfeeding.* New York: Bantam, 1973. A comprehensive guide that pays particular attention to the benefits of breast feeding for mother and baby, and how it fits into family life. It includes beautiful photographs.

Osofsky, J. *Handbook of infant development.* New York: Wiley, 1979. A comprehensive collection of articles about the major issues and developments in the study of infants today, written by experts in each area.

Tanner, J. M. *Education and physical growth.* New York: International Universities Press, 1971. A brief and easily read text that summarizes the basic principles of physical and mental development. Tanner discusses growth from birth to maturity, developmental versus chronological age, growth gradients, critical periods, stage concepts, brain development, and the influence of heredity.

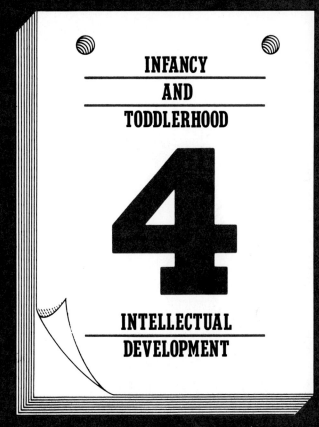

INFANCY
AND
TODDLERHOOD

4

INTELLECTUAL
DEVELOPMENT

IN THIS CHAPTER
YOU WILL LEARN ABOUT

The methods and difficulties of measuring the intelligence of infants, and the factors that influence intelligence even at this early age

The contributions of Jean Piaget to our understanding of cognitive processes in infancy

The rapid expansion of learning and language ability in early life

CHAPTER OVERVIEW

Piaget's Theory of Cognitive Development
Some Definitions | Sensorimotor Stage (Birth to about 2 Years) | Research Based on Piaget's Theories

Learning in Infancy
Instinct | Habituation | Imitation |
Classical (Conditioned) Learning |
Instrumental (Operant) Conditioning |
Complex Learning: Combined Classical
and Operant Conditioning

Learning the Language
Understanding Language | Prelinguistic Speech | Linguistic Speech | Research into Influences on Early Language Development | Theories of Language Acquisition

Measuring Intelligence of Infants
What Is Intelligence | Intelligence Testing | Difficulties in Measuring Intelligence of Preverbal Children | Infant Intelligence Tests

Influences on Intelligence
Heredity versus Socioeconomic Status | Nutrition | Child-Rearing Approaches | Importance of Stimulation | Family Size and Birth Order | Societal Supports for Parents

From the time they are born, infants show by their behavior that they are of the highest order of animal life, possessed of a functioning brain that helps them begin to make sense of the world they live in (Bower, 1977). On the very first day of life, they can determine the direction from which a sound comes and look toward that sound—thereby showing that they expect to see whoever or whatever is making that sound. Babies not yet a week old will imitate other people—open and close their mouths, stick out their tongues, flutter their eyelashes—when an adult performs any of these actions in front of them.

And by the age of 2 weeks, babies show that they know not only what their mothers look like but also what they sound like. In an experiment that lets them see their mother's face or a stranger's face through a porthole over their cribs, they look at their mothers much more often than at the stranger, and they look away whenever the mother's face is accompanied by the stranger's voice rather than her own.

This, of course, is only the beginning. Infants begin to learn from the time they are born, and possibly even within the womb, going on to increasingly complex thought processes. The way they learn and the way their intellectual capacities develop have fired an explosion of research projects in recent years.

PIAGET'S THEORY OF COGNITIVE DEVELOPMENT

Much of the research in this area was born in the mind of one man—Jean Piaget, the Swiss psychologist whom you met briefly in Chapter 1. Piaget took a totally new approach to the entire issue of children's *cognitive* development, or the way in which they get and process information about the world. *Cogni-*

tion includes the way people perceive, learn, think, and remember. To learn about the way children learn, Piaget posed questions that no one had ever thought to ask before. He spurred huge quantities of research in the areas he opened up. Some researchers have confirmed Piaget's theories, while others have modified them.

SOME DEFINITIONS

A few definitions are crucial for understanding Piaget's theories. The *schema* (plural, *schemata*) is the basic cognitive unit. This complex concept involves both mental organization, or a child's conceptualization of a specific situation, and behavior that can be seen. A schema is known by the behavior it involves: We have schemata of sight, of sucking, of shaking, and so forth. The schema of sucking implies that a baby recognizes hunger, knows how to get food, and therefore sucks. This schema develops from a simple reflex action to a controlled activity.

Two general principles, organization and adaptation, influence cognitive development through all stages and are known as *functional invariants* because they operate at all stages. *Organization* involves the integration of all processes into one overall system. Initially an infant's schema of looking and of grasping are quite different, resulting in faulty hand-eye coordination. Eventually the baby organizes these schemata in order to hold and look at the object at the same time.

Adaptation is a twofold process through which children create new structures to deal effectively with their surroundings. It involves both assimilation and accommodation, which are the essence of intelligent behavior. *Assimilation* is the "taking in," or incorporation, of a new object, experience, or concept into an existing set of schemata. At any age babies have a stock of mechanisms they know how to use. When they use them to respond to a new stimulus, they are assimilating, as when they assimilate the rubber nipple on a bottle into their schema of sucking. *Accommodation* is the process by which children change their

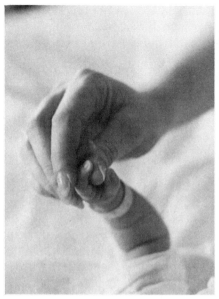

Through actively manipulating objects, babies progress from reflex behavior to trial-and-error learning to solving simple problems. (Suzanne Szasz; Erika Stone/Peter Arnold, Inc.)

actions to manage new objects and situations. The mouth movements used in drinking from a bottle are somewhat different from those used in nursing from the breast. When babies realize that different tongue and jaw motions result in more efficient intake of milk, they accommodate to the rubber nipple and develop a new schema of sucking.

Assimilation and accommodation are constantly working together to produce changes in a child's conceptualization of the world and reactions to it. The state of balance between assimilation and accommodation is called *equilibrium*. This necessary state protects children from being overwhelmed by new experiences and new information and from overreaching themselves in an attempt to accommodate to a rapidly changing environment (Pulaski, 1971).

SENSORIMOTOR STAGE (BIRTH TO ABOUT 2 YEARS)

In the *sensorimotor stage*, an infant changes from a creature who responds primarily through reflexes to one who can organize activities in relation to the environment. Babies' activities are no longer random. Through actively manipulating objects, they progress

from reflexes to trial-and-error learning to solving simple problems. They become more goal-oriented and differentiate themselves from their surroundings—all before the age of 2.

Baldwin (1968) has described the major abilities of the sensorimotor period as:

1 Understanding that information received from different senses relates to the same object rather than to different unrelated ones (Children do not at first associate the tinkling music they hear with the music box on the table; they consider these two completely unrelated aspects of their environment. They have to learn that they can see, hear, and touch the same object.)

2 Recognizing that the world is a permanent place whose existence does not depend on the child's perceiving it (This is the schema of the permanent object discussed below.)

3 Exhibiting goal-directed behavior (To get something, a baby performs several different actions and constructs new actions never before attempted. Since these actions are very concrete, a baby's ability to plan ahead is limited.)

The *schema of the permanent object* (Piaget, 1952) is the most important acquisition of the sensorimotor period. The permanent object is one that exists even though the child cannot see, feel, hear, taste, or smell it. If an object is taken away and if the child begins to search for it even after it can no longer be perceived, she has a schema of the permanent object. If the child does not seem to remember the object's existence, this schema has not been attained. It is basic to understanding such vital concepts as space, time, and causality. Until children understand that objects are separate from themselves, they cannot grasp reality.

Substages of Sensorimotor Stage

Stage 1: Use of reflexes (birth to 1 month) Reflexes are *adaptive*: They enable infants to survive and learn. Intelligent reflex behavior forms the basis for later intelligent activity as children change from passive recipients of stimulation that elicits the reflex to active seekers of stimulation.

Stage 2: Primary circular reactions/the first acquired adaptations (from 1 to 4 months) The baby blissfully sucking a thumb demonstrates a *primary circular reaction*, an active effort to reproduce something first achieved by chance. The content of the behavior, the ability to suck, is inborn. One day she put her thumb in her mouth, exercised her reflex by sucking it, and liked it. Then she made acquired adaptations: deliberate efforts to put her thumb in her mouth, keep it there, and keep sucking it—not for food, just for the fun of sucking.

The baby now starts to coordinate sensory information. He looks at, listens to, and touches his sister. He coordinates vision and grasping. When he hears her speak, however, he does not try to look at her unless he has just seen her face in motion (Beard, 1969).

Object permanence: In stages 1 and 2 a baby is constantly encountering, losing contact with, and reencountering objects—a pacifier, father's finger, mother's blouse. But when something disappears, the baby does not look for it. It has ceased to exist when it cannot be seen, felt, heard, smelled, or tasted. There is no object permanence.

Stage 3: Secondary circular reactions (4 to 8 months) This is the beginning of intentional action. An infant who used to repeat primary circular reactions for the joy of the actions themselves now wants results. New patterns of behavior continue to occur accidentally during random movement; babies learn the patterns and then repeat them to see what results they will bring. Infants no longer focus only on their own bodies but are concerned with external objects and events. They now shake a rattle—not just for the movement, but to hear the noise it makes. They babble—not just for fun, but to get a response from their parents.

Object permanence: Babies still do not have the schema of the permanent object. They will look for a bottle—or will kick and scream for it—*if* they see any part of it. If it is hidden entirely, they will forget about it and act as though the bottle no longer exists.

Stage 4: Coordination of secondary schemata and their application to new situations (8 to 12 months) Infants can now solve simple problems by using previously mastered responses. Their actions are increasingly goal-directed. Piaget (1952, p. 219) shows his daughter overcoming the obstacle of his hand:

At 0;8(8) [8 months, 8 days] Jacqueline tries to grasp her celluloid duck but I also grasp it at the same time she does. Then she firmly holds the toy in her right hand and pushes my hand away with her left. I repeat the experiment by grasping only the end of the duck's tail; she again pushes my hand away.

*It's interesting to watch you general-
ize from one situation to another.
You learned that some things come
apart if both ends are pulled -- pens
and their caps, for instance. So you
tried to pull a cracker in half. You
learned to turn the knobs on your
"Busy Box" toy and the radio. Then
you tried to turn the light switch.*

Object permanence: Infants are beginning to develop the schema of the permanent
object. At 9 to 10 months, they look for an
object behind a screen if they have seen it
being hidden. But if the object is moved from
one hiding place to another while the baby
watches, he looks for it in the *first* hiding
place.

Stage 5: Tertiary circular reactions/the discovery of new means through active experimentation (12 to 18 months)   This is the last cognitive stage that does *not* include mental representations of external events, or *thought*, and
the first stage that includes trying out new
activities. Infants still make accidental discoveries of actions that produce pleasing results,
but they no longer repeat them exactly. They
vary their actions, experimenting to find out
how an object, event, or situation is new.

For the first time babies intentionally
accommodate to find new solutions for new
problems. They try out new behavior patterns
to reach some goal, and they learn by trial and
error. As they vary their actions and cause
new results, they are led to new complete acts
of intelligence. Piaget (1952, p. 272) describes his daughter:

At 1;2(8) Jacqueline holds in her hands an
object which is new to her: a round, flat box
which she turns all over, shakes, rubs against
the bassinet, etc. She lets it go and tries to pick
it up. But she only succeeds in touching it with
her index finger, without grasping it. She

nevertheless makes an attempt and presses
on the edge. The box then tilts up and falls
again.   Jacqueline . . . immediately applies
herself to studying it. . . .

[She] rests the box on the ground and
pushes it as far as possible. . . . Afterward
Jacqueline puts her finger on the box and
presses it. But as she places her finger on the
center of the box she simply displaces it and
makes it slide instead of tilting it up. She
amuses herself with this game and kept it
up . . . for several minutes. Then, changing
the point of contact, she finally again places
her finger on the edge of the box, which tilts it
up. She repeats this many times, varying the
conditions, but keeping track of her discovery:
now she only presses on the edge!

Object permanence: Although infants
now have a schema of the permanent object
and can follow a sequence of object displacements, they still cannot imagine movement
that they do not see. If you were to put a toy in
your hand, put your hand behind a pillow,
leave the toy there, and bring out your closed
hand, the baby would look for the toy in your
hand. It would not occur to her that the toy
might be behind the pillow, because she did
not see you putting it there (Baldwin, 1968).

Stage 6: The invention of new means through
mental combinations (18 to 24 months)   Babies can now picture events in their minds
and follow them through to some degree.
They can think. This is a great breakthrough,
since infants no longer have to go through the
laborious process of trial and error in solving
new problems. They can now "try out" solutions in their minds and discard those that
won't work. They also can imitate actions even
after whatever they are copying is no longer in
front of them.

Object permanence: This schema is now

TABLE 4-1

Multidimensional View of Development during the Sensorimotor Period

STAGE	DEVELOPMENTAL UNIT	INTENTION AND MEANS-END RELATIONS	MEANING	OBJECT PERMANENCE
1	Use of reflexes (0–1 months)			
2	Primary circular reactions (1–4 months)		Different responses to different objects	
3	Secondary circular reactions (4–8) months	Acts upon objects	"Motor meaning"	Brief single-modality search for absent object
4	Coordination of secondary schemes (8–12 months)	Attacks barrier to reach goal	Symbolic meaning	Prolonged multi-modality search
5	Tertiary circular reactions (12–18) months	"Experiments in order to see"; discovery of new means through "groping accommodation"	Elaboration through action and feedback	Follows sequential displacements if object in sight
6	Invention of new means through mental combinations (18–24 months)	Invention of new means through reciprocal assimilation of schemes	Further elaboration; symbols increasingly covert	Follows sequential displacement with object hidden; symbolic representation of object, mostly internal

fully developed. Babies can see a series of displacements, look for an object in the last hiding place, and search for objects they have not actually witnessed being hidden.

RESEARCH BASED ON PIAGET'S THEORIES

Since Piaget first proposed his theories of cognitive development, they have moved in and out of favor among educational, psychological, and scientific communities. Yet interest in Piaget's theories has continued to mount over the years, especially since the 1960s. Not all the theories are accepted at face value. On the contrary, they have spurred a growing body of research as other workers try to determine whether, being based largely on Piaget's observations of his own children, they apply to children in general. So far his constructs have held up quite well under standardized testing programs, although some recent research, such as that by Bower (1976), raises questions.

Uzgiris (1972) observed infants from 4 weeks of age to about 2 years and confirmed Piaget's invariant order for the progressive stages of the sensorimotor period.

The translation of Piaget's complex theories into concrete, standardized testing situations provides researchers with an additional tool for measuring intellectual development in very young, preverbal children. The scales of sensorimotor development developed by Corman and Escalona (1969) and by Uzgiris and Hunt (1975) are in wide use.

Wachs (1975) tested twenty-three babies on the Uzgiris and Hunt Infant Psychological Development Scales (IPDS), which measure the development of sensorimotor abilities. The babies were tested every three months from the age of 1 to 2 years. Then at 31 months, they all were given the Stanford-Binet intelligence test (see page 212). A positive relationship showed up between each of the eight subscales of the IPDS and later Stanford-Binet performance, with object permanence serv-

TABLE 4-1
(Continued)

SPACE	TIME	CAUSALITY	IMITATION	PLAY
			Pseudo-imitation begins	Apparent functional autonomy of some acts
All modalities focus on single object	Brief search for absent object	Acts; then waits for effect to occur	Pseudo-imitation quicker, more precise; true imitation of acts already in repertoire and visible on own body	More acts done for their own sake
Turns bottle to reach nipple	Prolonged search for absent object	Attacks barrier to reach goal; waits for adults to serve him	True imitation of novel acts not visible on own body	Means often become ends; ritualization begins
Follows sequential displacements if object in sight	Follows sequential displacements if object in sight	Discovers new means; solicits help from adults	True imitation quicker, more precise	Quicker conversion of means to end; elaboration of ritualization
Solves detour problem; symbolic representation of spatial relationships, mostly internal	Both anticipation and memory	Infers causes from observing effects; predicts effects from observing causes	Imitates (1) complex (2) nonhuman (3) absent models	Treats inadequate stimuli as if adequate to imitate an enactment—i.e., symbolic ritualization or "pretending"

SOURCE: From Phillips, J. *The origins of intellect: Piaget's theory.* San Francisco, Freeman, 1975.

ing as the strongest predictor of later intelligence scores. Wachs concluded that the development of this concept constitutes a major developmental trend, providing a good basis for predicting a child's later performance on intelligence tests. Since it is extremely difficult to assess infant intelligence, as we shall see in our discussion of intelligence testing later in this chapter, this is an important finding.

Gottfried and Brody (1975) also found positive relationships when babies aged about 11 months were tested on Piagetian scales and on the Bayley mental scales, indicating that both kinds of tests seem to be measuring some of the same basic abilities.

Kramer, Hill, and Cohen (1975) adminis-tered six tasks to children aged 5 to 32 months—finding partially and completely hidden objects, finding objects that had been moved and hidden several times, finding objects hidden under three layers of cloth, and so forth. This study found that babies develop the concept of object permanence in the same order outlined by Piaget.

Bower (1976), however, has found that cognitive development does not always proceed in the orderly sequence described by Piaget. Instead, certain abilities show up at an early age (sometimes earlier than in Piaget's framework), only to disappear and then be relearned later. Besides the physical abilities of walking and reaching, which we discussed on page 101, the same repetitive process

Bower found evidence of such concepts as object permanence in very young infants. (Courtesy of T.G.R. Bower)

seems to occur with regard to some cognitive concepts.

Piaget and other researchers have found that children generally do not grasp the concept of weight *conservation* (discussed in detail in Chapter 8) until about the age of 9. Briefly, conservation can be summed up as the awareness that matter does not change in quantity if it is rearranged. A ball of clay, for example, that is then rolled into the shape of a sausage still contains the same amount of clay and weighs the same. Bower found that 18-month-old babies move their arms in picking up the two different shapes of clay in such a way that shows that they know the weight remains the same. When he tested the same children two years later, however, he found that they no longer acted as if they understood this principle. They seemed to reacquire it at the age of 7 or 8, lose it again, and not have a stable grasp of it until they turn 13 or 14.

Bower also found evidence of other concepts at an early age, such as object permanence and number conservation (when objects are rearranged into different patterns,

the number of items remains constant). Suggesting that children lose these concepts because they don't practice them, Bower provided practice—and got some unexpected results.

When babies who had achieved object permanence received practice in locating an object going into one end of a tunnel and reappearing after several seconds at the other end, they became expert at tracking the object. However, infants who had a great deal of tracking practice did not do so well in a similar task of locating a toy under a cup as did children who had had a little tracking experience but less than the first group. The highly practiced infants seemed to repeat a developmental phase and failed to understand for a second time the relationship between two objects when one is inside the other.

Bower (1976) suggests that this repetition is caused by the fact:

. . . that with so much practice at tracking an object going through the tunnel the infant has evolved such specific rules in dealing with the tracking task that he is actually hampered by them when he is faced with a similar but not identical situation [pp. 46–47].

A similar kind of regression has shown up among older children who give incorrect answers to a problem that younger children answer correctly. In such cases, the older children, who may have acquired the original concept in a very specific way, have not been able to apply their discoveries to other similar situations, and must then "dredge the initial discovery from their memory, erring until they do, and seem to repeat an earlier phase of their cognitive development" (Bower, 1976, p. 47). These apparent reversals and repetitions are difficult to explain by Piagetian interpretation, even though, in the final analysis, they do not contradict Piaget's basic claim that cognitive growth is a continuous process that builds on what has gone before.

Even if Piaget's theories are eventually modified in response to the work of other psychologists, his enormous contributions to the entire field of developmental psychology will continue to hold a prominent place in the history of science. If it had not been for the highly creative, prolific body of work he had produced, many of the experiments that question his theses would never have been conceived, let alone carried out.

LEARNING IN INFANCY

As a newborn, Angela started to make sucking movements with her mouth whenever the nipple was in it. Within weeks she started to make the movements as soon as she saw her mother. She had learned that her mother's presence presaged good things.

As an infant, Brad was not afraid of animals. At 11 months he was happily sitting on the lawn when a large, friendly St. Bernard loped over and licked his face. Brad howled and would then cry whenever he saw a dog. He had learned to fear dogs.

What *is* learning? In psychological terms it is the establishment of new relationships or the strengthening of weak ones between two events, actions, or things. The child responds differently, resulting in a relatively permanent change in behavior. Learning can be extremely complex, since a stimulus can cause a new response and the new response itself can cause still another, establishing a learning chain.

One good definition of learning deems it "a change in behavior as a result of experience—excluding changes due to heredity, growth, or temporary conditions such as the effects of drugs or fatigue" (Sherrod, Vietze, & Friedman, 1978, p. 51).

INSTINCT

Among lower animals, much complex activity is based on *instinct*, an inborn ability to perform certain functions such as the food collecting of ants, the nest building of birds, and the nursing of cubs. Human beings, however, have no abilities we could properly call instincts. We come into this world with a handful of reflexes, a maturational timetable,. and a capacity for infinite learning.

HABITUATION

This process of becoming accustomed to a sound, a sight, or some other stimulus is a kind of learning. The existence of this process in very young children has enabled researchers to determine their sensory abilities. In one study (Bronstein & Petrova, 1952), forty-three infants—thirty-three aged from 2 hours to 8 days, and ten from 1 to 5 months of age—were presented with a variety of sounds: the playing of organ pipes and harmonica, the blowing of a whistle, and the tapping of a pencil. The first time they heard a sound, they usually stopped sucking and did not begin again until it stopped. After the same sound had been presented again and again, however, it lost its novelty and had no further effect

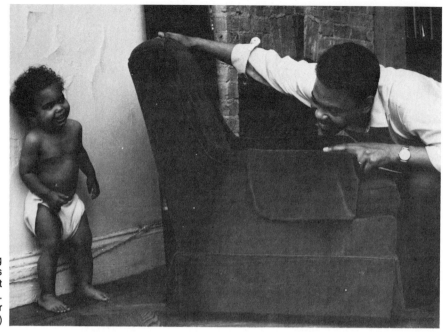

Observing and copying other people are forms of learning that originate in infancy. (Erika Stone/Peter Arnold, Inc.)

on sucking activities. The infants habituated, or adapted to, the stimulus.

Habituation is related to neurological development. A rare study of an anencephalic infant who lived long enough to be tested found that the baby (who had no cortex) was unable to habituate to auditory stimulation (Brackbill, 1971). Another study yielded a relationship between rapid habituation and high performance on a neurological measure (Sigman, Kapp, Parmelee, & Jeffrey, 1973). And without drawing any conclusion, it's interesting to note that female infants habituate faster than males (Sherrod et al., 1978).

IMITATION

When Vicky's mother smiles at her, Vicky smiles back. When Jason's father talks "baby talk," Jason babbles back. Observing and copying other people is a form of learning that originates in infancy.

Uzgiris (1971) observed twelve babies between 8 and 24 months. The experimenter visited the babies' homes regularly, presented different acts, and watched. The experimenter cooed, babbled, made novel sounds that do not occur in English, spoke words the infant was familiar with, and spoke new words the infant had not yet used. The experimenter also performed actions the infant had already done, complex actions that required the baby to combine actions in a new way, unfamiliar actions the baby could easily see, and unfamiliar actions involving subtle facial gestures. The babies responded in a definite sequence, first copying actions they already were doing, then copying part of the experimenter's performance, then trying to copy the whole performance but recognizing their limitations, and then doing the whole thing.

Recent research shows that within the first few weeks of life babies can imitate facial and hand gestures. Moore and Meltzoff (1975) found that 2-week-old babies will imitate adults in sticking out their tongues, making their lips protrude, opening their mouths, and moving their fingers.

Findings like these contradict Piaget's (1951) developmental theory of imitation, in which he states that "invisible" imitation (that is, imitation with parts of the body that babies cannot see for themselves, such as the

This morning you woke up hungry at about 5 a.m. so we took you into our bed and I nursed you. When you were through nursing, we lay quietly -- me hoping against hope for more sleep, you not quite sure how awake you were.... Dan started to snore. As soon as he started you became very still. The snores got louder and louder and then stopped. As soon as Dan stopped, you started! You were imitating him and doing a very good job of it! Naturally I couldn't help laughing and woke us all up.

AT 14 MONTHS

It's funny to see you sitting in your high chair solemnly scraping the meat from an artichoke leaf with your teeth just like an adult. No one ever taught you how; you must have learned from watching us.

Nancy Gordon

mouth) does not begin until about 9 months of age, after a period of "visible" imitation (when infants can see their own actions, such as with hands and feet, as well as those of the models they are imitating). Conditioning (as explained in the following sections) cannot account for this early imitative ability, since these 2-week-old infants were not rewarded in any way for their imitative acts, unless the acts themselves were self-reinforcing.

Moore and Meltzoff consider this very early imitation as evidence of inborn sensori-motor coordination, that infants are born with "the competence to match their own motor behavior to a seen model with some sort of knowledge about that match" (p. 7).

Bower (1976) points out the social aspects of infant imitation, the way in which adults and babies become "raptly involved with each other as they play games of imitation" (p. 38). He also points out the way that imitative ability fades away after its very early appearance, reappearing later (when Piaget notes it, at about the ninth month). Bower maintains that the reason this ability, like a number of others, disappears is that it is not exercised.

CLASSICAL (CONDITIONED) LEARNING

In the 1890s, Pavlov (1927) conducted experiments in conditioning. When he fed his dogs, he rang a bell. When the dogs saw and smelled the food, they salivated. After repeated feedings just after the bell had been rung,

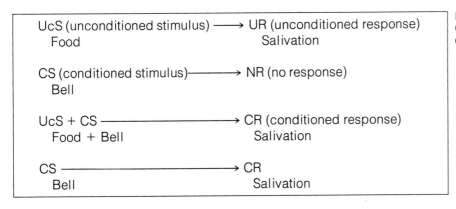

UcS (unconditioned stimulus) ⟶ UR (unconditioned response)
Food   Salivation

CS (conditioned stimulus) ⟶ NR (no response)
Bell

UcS + CS ⟶ CR (conditioned response)
Food + Bell   Salivation

CS ⟶ CR
Bell   Salivation

Fig. 4-1
Classical,
or Conditioned, Learning

the dogs eventually salivated upon hearing the bell, even when no food was presented. The dogs' salivary reflexes had been conditioned to respond to the bell as they did to food.

Pavlov's dogs represent a classic example of classical conditioning. Let us use them to explain this type of learning. In Pavlov's experiment, the *bell* is a neutral stimulus, which becomes a *conditioned stimulus* (CS). Under ordinary circumstances, of course, a bell does not cause salivation. The experiment conditions the stimulus to make the dogs salivate. How does it do this? By pairing the neutral stimulus, the bell, with an *unconditioned stimulus* (US), the food. The US does not *have* to be conditioned; under ordinary circumstances it causes a reflex response, or an *unconditioned response* (UR). In this experiment the US is *food* and the UR is *salivation*. After pairing the CS with the US for enough trials, eventually the CS (the bell) will cause a *conditioned response* (salivation) without the food's even being present.

The equation for classical conditioning is shown in Fig 4-1.

Extinction occurs after repeated presentation of CS without US.

Classical Conditioning of the Newborn

Can newborns be conditioned classically? This is a complex and controversial issue. Some studies have seemed to show that it is possible to teach newborns to suck when they hear a buzzer or a tone (Marquis, 1931; Lipsitt & Kaye, 1964), but contemporary critics point to flaws in the way these experiments were conducted. Sameroff (1971) claims that no research has clearly established the possibility of teaching the newborn infant by means of classical conditioning techniques.

Maybe newborns cannot learn this way because they haven't had the chance to interact long enough with their environment. Before babies can respond to a sound like a bell or a buzzer, they need to have had enough experience in hearing sounds to identify them. In some preverbal way, they have to be able to say to themselves, "Hey, that's a bell!" If they can't tell a particular neutral stimulus from the other stimuli around them, they can't respond to it (Sameroff, 1971).

But what about the conditioning of *autonomic* responses, those we do not consciously control, like our heart rate? Researchers have been able to effect changes in heart rate by classical conditioning, both in adults and children. Crowell et al. (1976) reported that they were able to do this for newborn infants, but Stamps (1977) found that the newborns' conditioned heart rate responses were not as stable as those of older subjects.

In sum, then, recent research on classical conditioning in infancy—much of which is being done in the Soviet Union—indicates that conditioning involving motor behaviors does not occur in newborn infants. Conditioning of autonomic responses, such as heart rate, appears to hold more promise as an area in which to demonstrate newborn learning ability (Sherrod et al, 1978).

Classical Conditioning in Infancy beyond the Neonatal Period

The classic story about a classically conditioned baby is that of little Albert (Watson & Rayner, 1920). When Albert was 9 months old, he loved furry animals. When he was 11 months old, behaviorist John B. Watson brought him into the laboratory. Just as Albert was beginning to grasp a white rat, Watson sounded a noise. Frightened, Albert jumped, fell forward, and cried. A week later, Albert again saw the rat. Again, the loud noise. Again, frightened tears. Eventually, as soon as Albert saw the rat, he whimpered with fear. He also became afraid of rabbits, dogs, and furry objects. This experiment demonstrated that young children can be classically conditioned, that an emotional reaction such as fear can be conditioned, and that such conditioned fear can be *generalized*; that is, stimuli similar to those on which the original learning occurred can elicit the same learned reaction.

Since Watson ruined the category of furry objects for little Albert, many other researchers have been exploring many other aspects of classical conditioning in babies, and have come up with some answers—and many questions. The subject is extremely complex, and the research so far has shown that it is not always possible to apply to babies those principles of learning based upon research with adults and animals.

What have we learned? In reviewing the literature, Fitzgerald and Blackbill (1976) found that there does seem to be a relationship between the *orienting response* and the ability of an infant to be classically conditioned. The orienting response (OR) is an alerting response; it indicates that the baby is paying attention to some stimulus. The infant can show the OR motorically by stopping some activity that she or he has been engaging in, such as sucking. Or we can measure the OR by observing changes in an infant's heartbeat or rate of breathing. The evidence shows that the greater an infant's OR, the more likely the child will "take to" classical conditioning.

State is another important influence. Babies appear to be conditioned more easily when they are sleeping quietly than when they are restless. Conditionability does not seem to be related to a baby's age, except for one way: Younger babies need longer times between the presentation of the CS and US than do older ones. Other factors that affect conditioning are the intensity of the stimulus (the loudness of a sound or the brightness of a light), the length of time it is presented, and its nature (electric shock, for example, is not a good teaching tool).

INSTRUMENTAL (OPERANT) CONDITIONING

Skinner (1938) experimented with rats and pigeons. When they pecked on a particular bar, they received a food pellet. They quickly learned to press the bar to get food. Further experiments rewarded the animals with food when they pecked on a green bar and punished them with a mild electric shock when they pecked on a red bar. They soon learned to distinguish the colors.

In this kind of learning, an individual makes a response—sometimes accidentally—which is then rewarded. When it is rewarded (*reinforced*), the individual repeats it. When it is not rewarded, it will eventually stop (be *extinguished*). Punishment, or following a behavior with an unpleasant stimulus such as electric shock (known as an *aversive event*), is used to reduce responses. Reinforcement can be either *positive* or *negative*. Positive reinforcement consists of rewarding the organism—giving a pigeon a pellet of food or giving a child a token that can be redeemed for a toy, for example. Negative reinforcement involves removing an aversive event, such as shutting off an electric shock after a rat has gone down the proper tunnel. *Immediate* reinforcement is typically more effective than *delayed* reinforcement in causing behaviors.

A response that stops being reinforced or punished will return to, or near, its *baseline*, the initial level at which it appeared. *Intermittent reinforcement*, that is, rewarding the

| AR (accidental response)→ R (reinforcement) ⟶ DR (deliberate response) |
| Animal pecks at bar. Animal gets food. Animal pecks at bar. |

Fig. 4-2
Operant, or Instrumental, Learning

response on some occasions and ignoring it on others, causes a response to appear more consistently and to be more durable (more resistant to extinction) than rewarding it on every occasion. This is because it takes longer for the subject to become aware that reinforcement has ended when it has been occurring at irregular intervals rather than after every response.

Shaping is used to bring about new responses. When the subject shows a response that is somewhat similar, or "on the right track," as the response that is ultimately desired, the person shaping the behavior reinforces the response. When that reinforcement has taken hold, the shaper continues to reward responses that are closer and closer to the desired behavior. For example, the parent of a child who refuses to talk might first give him candy after he makes any sound at all. Then the parent would give the candy only after the child said a word, and then only after a sentence.

Shaping is often used in *behavioral modification*, a form of operant conditioning that is increasingly used to eliminate undesirable behavior in children. This practical application of the principles of this type of learning is used to teach a variety of behaviors besides speaking, including toilet training and behaving well in school. It is used most often for children with special needs, such as retarded or emotionally disturbed youngsters, but its techniques (discussed in Chapter 9) are also used effectively in the day-to-day management of normal children.

Operant Conditioning in Newborns
Newborn babies like music. How do we know this? Partly from one study of instrumental learning in which two-day-old infants were rewarded by the playing of music for as long

as they sucked on a nipple (which did not provide milk). The babies would suck longer when the music continued, but they would not increase the amount of time they sucked when the sucking turned the music off (Butterfield & Siperstein, 1972). This study and others that have succeeded in changing babies' behaviors by rewarding them in various ways seem to provide evidence that operant conditioning is possible in the neonatal period (Sherrod et al., 1978).

When conditioning is based on a preexisting behavior pattern that is biologically important (such as sucking), operant conditioning "works" for the newborn infant. It is more difficult to apply when based on behavior that the baby would not ordinarily perform.

Operant Conditioning in Older Infants
During a study of smiling in infants (Brackbill, 1958), eight 3½- to 4½-month-old babies were picked up every time they smiled, and then were returned to their cribs. When all the babies were smiling more, four were reinforced *intermittently* (reward or punishment after *some* trials), and four were reinforced *continuously* (after *every* trial). During the extinction phase, smiling was never rewarded. Picking up the babies made them smile more, all the babies smiled less during extinction, and those who had been reinforced intermittently continued to smile more than those who had been reinforced continuously.

Three-month-old infants babble more if, after babbling, adults smile, make "tsk" sounds, and touch them lightly on the abdomen (Rheingold, Gewirtz, & Ross, 1959). But what comes first? Is adult attention a stimulus that causes babbling? Or do babies babble more because they are rewarded for it? Weisberg (1963) divided 3-month-old infants into six groups to look at all relevant factors. Group 1 received *contingent* reinforcement (the experimenters smiled, made an approving sound, and rubbed the babies' chins every time they babbled). Group 2 received the same type and amount of adult attention on a *noncontingent* basis (adults paid attention to the infants at times not directly related to their babbling). Group 3 received *contingent nonsocial* reinforcement (door chimes sounded after babbling). Group 4 heard door chimes at times unrelated to babbling. Groups 5 and 6 were control groups that had no contact with the experimenters.

The door chimes produced no change in babbling and are an ineffective means of reinforcement. Adult smiles, sounds, and touch increased infant babbling only when contingent. When noncontingent, the reinforcement produced no changes. When the social reinforcer was withdrawn during extinction, the rate of infant babbling fell off. If the babies were babbling because adult attention elicits babbling, then those who received the noncontingent social reinforcement would have increased their babbling as much as the babies in the contingent group. They did not. The babies were learning to babble because the adult responses rewarded babbling.

Watson and Ramey (1972) used operant conditioning to teach 10-week-old infants to move their heads to make a crib mobile move. They put forty 8-week-old infants into three groups. For fourteen days every mother hung a mobile about 18 inches over her baby's head for ten minutes daily. In the experimental group, the mobile moved in response to the baby's head movements; in one control group, the mobile moved randomly; and the other control groups had nonmoving mobiles. The mothers recorded their babies' head movements. The experimental babies increased their head movements; the rates of movement for babies in the control groups didn't change at all.

COMPLEX LEARNING: COMBINED CLASSICAL AND OPERANT CONDITIONING

Classical and operant learning differ: Classical conditioning requires a *reactive* organism, while operant conditioning demands an *active* one. If the organism never makes the desired response, it cannot be reinforced. Classical conditioning is *involuntary*; operant conditioning involves actions that are under the organism's control. In both types, intermittent reinforcement causes more durable learning than continuous reinforcement.

The two kinds of conditioning can be combined to produce increasingly complex activities. Papousek (1961, 1960a, 1960b, 1959) exposed infants from 1 to 20 weeks old to complex learning situations. In the operant phase, the babies learned to turn their heads left at the sound of a bell to receive milk. The ones who did not learn this were classically conditioned. When the bell sounded, the left corner of the baby's mouth was stimulated; the baby then would turn his or her head and would get the milk. At ages of 4 to 6 weeks, the babies learned to turn their heads when hearing the bell. Once they learned to turn their heads for milk, the infants were trained to differentiate the bell from a buzzer. They were fed on the left when the bell rang and on the right when the buzzer sounded. At about 3 months, the babies had learned to turn to the appropriate side. Infants 4 months old even learned to reverse the response to bell and buzzer, demonstrating the remarkable complexity of babies' learning capacities.

LEARNING THE LANGUAGE

At 3 months, Elise laughs out loud. At 4 months she coos when someone talks to her or when she wakes up. At 11 months she says "dada," at 12 months, "mama." At 13 months she introduces her own word, "hadja," which her parents take to mean, "I want that." At 17 months she says 'ma' for more, 'me' for give it to me, 'ha' for hot, 'ca' for cracker. At 22 months she knows the rhyming words for "Hey Diddle-Diddle" and loves to shout them out on cue.

All children in all countries go through the same basic well-defined stages in the aquisition of language. (© Marc & Evelyne Bernheim/Woodfin Camp & Assoc.)

At 26 months Elise says her first four-word sentence. She holds her pajamas out to her father, commanding, "Daddy—on my jamans," and he realizes she wants him to help her. This first "long" sentence is not conventionally grammatical. But it is of relative high order of linguistic communication.

All children in all countries go through the same basic, well-defined stages in the acquisition of language. What are these stages?

UNDERSTANDING LANGUAGE

Children learn to understand language before they can speak it. Eleanor and George Kaplan (1971) have distinguished five stages in the development of this understanding:

1   Only a few minutes after birth, infants can determine where sounds are coming from. Neonates also can tell the difference between sounds, based on frequency, intensity, duration, and tempo.

2   Infants 2 weeks old recognize the difference between voices and other sounds.

3   When about 2 months old, babies pick up emotional cues, withdrawing from angry voices and smiling and cooing at friendly ones. They can tell the difference between familiar and unfamiliar voices and between male and female.

4   At about 6 months, babies are conscious of intonation and rhythm and respond intelligently to phrases in a strange language that have a familiar overall intonation pattern.

5   Toward the end of the first year, babies can distinguish among the *phonemes*, or individual sounds, of their language. They can tell the difference between pairs of words that differ only in initial sound (like *cat* and *bat*).

AT 14 WEEKS

While the pediatrician was trying to listen to your heart, you were talking constantly (mostly about how cold the stethoscope was, I think), and he said it was very unusual for a baby of your age to vocalize so much.

AT 10 MONTHS

You do some new vocalizing now--most

of it loud. You still wisper to yourself sometimes, but most often you speak in a loud voice with lots of expression and your words all have lots of consonants -- your speech is quite guttural. You say quite a few words, but I think they are mostly accidents.

AT 1 YEAR

You say about ten words that we can understand: "mama," "bird" (for bird), "kaka" (cracker), "hi," "kitty," "mao" (mouse), and words for Daddy, Snoopy and Elizabeth, but I can't reproduce them. There are others, and you understand hundreds.

Usually when we ask, "Where's the ___" you usually point to it. Today I asked you where your chair was. You hadn't seen it in over a month. So you went straight to your bear and picked him up.

AT 12½ MONTHS

Your speech seems to have regressed a bit. You understand a great deal, but you no longer use more than two or three understandable words. Are you saving up for something?

AT 15 MONTHS

You're talking more again. When you want to be carried you say "up" (without the "p"). You often answer "yes" ("eth"). You identify cars, ducks, trucks and juice quite often.

AT 15 ½ MONTHS

Your vocabulary is in another slump. You are only saying, "Hi," "meow," "arf arf," "yeah" and "mama" now. Otherwise you say "ga" for everything. It's very frustrating.

AT 19 MONTHS

You are finally really talking -- and a blue streak .... You use many two- and three-word sentences ("Dan shower," "pig not lion") and you understand everything. You also can point to anything that has previously been identified for you.

Nancy Gordon

PRELINGUISTIC SPEECH

The following stages of speech precede the first real word (Lenneberg, 1967; Eisenson, Auer, & Irwin, 1963):

1 UNDIFFERENTIATED CRYING   Early crying is a reflexive reaction produced by the expiration of breath. It is a form of communication, the only way infants can signal their needs. In this crying, babies emit vowel sounds, like the short *a* (as in "fat").

2 DIFFERENTIATED CRYING   After the first month, a close listener can often tell by the different patterns, intensities, and pitches of a baby's cries whether she or he is hungry, sleepy, angry, or in pain. Crying is becoming a more precise means of communication.

3 COOING   At about 6 weeks chance movements of the vocal mechanisms produce simple sounds called *cooing*. These squeals, gurgles, and bleats are usually emitted when the baby is happy and contented. The first sounds are vowels; the first consonant is *h*. Cooing has been elicited by visual matter by the fifteenth day (Stechler, Bradford, & Levy, 1965), but this generally comes later.

4 BABBLING *Babbling* involves "vocal gymnastics" that begin at about 3 or 4 months, as babies playfully repeat a variety of

simple consonant and vowel sounds: "ma-ma-ma-ma," "da-da-da-da," "bi-bi-bi-bi." They are most likely to babble when contented and alone. Deaf children babble normally at first but lose interest when they cannot hear themselves (Clifton, 1970). In Piagetian terms, first a baby babbles for the joy of it (primary circular reaction), and then for its effect on the environment (secondary circular reaction).

5 LALLATION, OR IMPERFECT IMITATION During the second half of the first year, babies become more aware of the sounds around them. They become quiet while listening, and when the sound stops, they babble in excitement, accidentally repeating what they have heard. Then they imitate their own sounds.

6 ECHOLALIA, OR IMITATION OF THE SOUNDS OF OTHERS At about 9 or 10 months, babies consciously imitate other people's sounds even though they do not understand them. Since middle-class babies vocalize more during this stage than babies from working-class homes (Rheingold, Gewirtz, & Ross, 1959), it is probable that parental vocalizing encourages infant vocalizing.

During stages 4, 5, and 6, babies acquire their basic repertoire of sounds. Once they can make them and invest them with meaning, they are ready to learn their language.

7 EXPRESSIVE JARGON During the second year many children use a string of utterances that sound like sentences, with pauses, inflections, and rhythms; but the "words" in such utterances are no more than meaningless gibberish. Speech is not yet communicative.

LINGUISTIC SPEECH
When babies do begin to utter meaningful

speech, they again go through distinct stages (Eisenson et al., 1963):

1 ONE-WORD SENTENCE (HOLOPHRASE) One-year-old Frank points to the door and says "out." Depending on the situation, he may mean, "I want to go out" or "Mommy went out." His single word thus expresses a complete thought.

2 MULTIWORD SENTENCE At about 2, Gwen strings together two or more words to make a sentence. When she sees her father putting on his coat, she says "Me go." The earliest of these sentences are combinations of nouns and verbs, without any articles, prepositions, or adjectives. This *telegraphic speech* contains only words that carry meaning.

3 GRAMMATICALLY CORRECT VERBAL UTTERANCES Three-year-olds have an impressive command of the language. They have a vocabulary of some 900 words; they speak in longer sentences that include all parts of speech; and they have a good grasp of grammatical principles. They make little allowance for exceptions to linguistic rules ("We goed to the store"). Their vocabulary and the complexity of their sentences are increasing rapidly and constantly.

When he was 13 months old he first put two words together: when the ball rolled out of his reach, for instance, he would say "Ball all gone."

His use of the word "block" is interesting. First he used it when I bought him a set of small, wooden square blocks. Then he applied it to a set of large plastic pop-it beads. Then, one day when I brought home a large bunch of grapes and showed it to him, he promptly dubbed it "blocks." Even after I showed him it was something to eat and put some grapes in

his mouth, he still called them "blocks."
He must use the word to mean "a
series of identical objects."

(Christy's) first real word was "car,"
around a year. It started out as an
unrecognizable "guff" but soon developed into a respectable imitation of
car. We would sit on the balcony...
and watch the buses, motorcycles,
trucks, bicycles and cars go by, and
though I identified each one Christy
would point and always say "car."

Joan Gage

RESEARCH INTO INFLUENCES ON EARLY LANGUAGE DEVELOPMENT

Studies of very early language development have focused largely on aspects of the mother-infant relationship. The basic issue is the kind of verbal interaction that goes on between the baby and the baby's principal caretaker. What have these studies found?

For one thing, mothers talk differently to very young children than they do to other adults. They use shorter sentences, fewer words, simpler grammar, slower speech, and a lot of repetition (Benedict, 1975). All these speech characteristics help children learn the language. Benedict (1975) looked specifically at repetition in the language comprehension of babies between the ages of 9 and 16 months. When mothers repeated simple commands to their babies, the children paid more attention and were more likely to carry out the command than when the mothers gave the order only once. The importance of repetition is underscored by the author's comment:

When I asked mothers not to repeat, they became frustrated and even angry and most, including myself when I tried it, were unable to completely inhibit repeating with children this age. It seemed likely that a behavior so frequent and compelling plays a functional role in language comprehension [Benedict, 1975, p. 2].

For another thing, babies are more likely to talk to their mothers when their mothers are talking to them—and the mothers are more likely to talk to their babies when the babies start cooing and babbling (Strain & Vietze, 1975). There is a "joining in" pattern that indicates a symmetrical relationship. Both mother and child are likely to talk at the same time twice as often as when only the baby is making sounds. In some ways, mothers' talking patterns are influenced even more by their babies than the babies' patterns are by the mothers. The mother is less likely to stop talking when the infant is making sounds, but the infant is just as likely to fall silent whether the mother is talking or not. Also, the baby makes more sounds and talks to inanimate objects more often when the mother is out of the room than when she is present. Vocalizing seems to help babies make sense of their environment, as well as provide a means of communication with other people.

Cohen and Beckwith (1976) examined the ways mothers talk to their babies and found large differences between verbal patterns, mostly based on the mother's level of education and the baby's place in the family. They observed forty-six babies in their homes at one, three, and eight months past their expected delivery dates (thirty-six had been preterm, ten full-term).

Individual mothers were consistent in their language behaviors at the different ages, although the frequency and style of their talking changed as the babies matured. At 3 months, for example, face-to-face talking peaked, possibly because babies smile a lot at this age and mothers like to look at smiling babies. By 8 months the mothers were talking less but were giving more orders as the babies were getting around more.

The more highly educated mothers talked more to their babies, were more likely to

praise them, and gave more specific communications at 8 months. The mothers of first-borns talked to them more, and more positively, at 3 and 8 months than did the mothers of later-born children. There were no differences in the ways the mothers spoke to boys as compared to girls or to full-term babies as opposed to those who had been born early.

Social-class differences show up at a very early age in the way mothers talk to children. The differences that surfaced between working-class and middle-class mothers of 10-month-old baby girls provide clues to the greater verbal facility among middle-class children (Tulkin & Kagan, 1972). Both groups of mothers seemed to care for their children with equal devotion. There were few differences in the amount of physical contact between mother and child, in the number of times a mother kept her baby from doing things, and in such nonverbal interactions as picking up, touching, or tickling the baby.

The middle-class mothers, though, talked much more to their babies, largely because of different beliefs about the nature of infancy. Some working-class mothers felt that it was a waste of time to try to talk to young babies who couldn't really communicate or understand what they were saying. Some thought it was important to speak to babies only after the children themselves had begun to talk. Some felt silly talking to a baby. Furthermore, many working-class mothers believe that they have little influence on their children's development, that children are born a certain way, and that there's not much anyone can do to change them.

These findings have important implications for programs that try to encourage verbal interaction between mothers and babies. Professionals running such programs need to understand and respect the feelings of people in low socioeconomic circumstances and should not attempt to impose middle-class behaviors on them. A goal might be, though, to help parents recognize how early babies do respond to their parents' involvement with them, to help the parents recognize how much influence they do have over their children's development, and to realize that the way they act toward their children right from infancy can have far-reaching effects.

To learn how to speak, children need practice. Moskowitz (1978) tells about a boy with normal hearing whose parents were deaf and communicated in sign language. The child was confined to his home because he was asthmatic. Even though he watched television every day, he neither understood nor spoke English by the time he was three, although he was fluent in sign language, which his parents and their visitors all used. "It appears that in order to learn a language a child must also be able to interact with real people in that language" (p. 94B).

The best kind of interaction comes from adults who speak to children at a complexity of speech only slightly in advance of their current level of skill, who talk about the children's immediate day-to-day concerns, and who answer their questions somewhat elaborately and informatively (Clarke-Stewart, 1977).

THEORIES OF LANGUAGE ACQUISITION

Like so many other issues in the study of human development, the mechanism for the ways in which children learn how to speak and understand language is hotly debated. No wonder! Even the simplest human languages are so complex that:

Ten linguists working full time for 10 years to analyze the structure of the English language could not program a computer with the ability for language acquired by an average child in the first 10 or even five years of life [Moskowitz, 1978, p. 92].

The major theories about why and how

children learn language range along a continuum on the relative influences of environment
and heredity. Those most wedded to a belief
in the strength of environmental interests are
the *behaviorists*. These are followed by the
cultural relativists, the *interactionists*, and,
finally, by those most convinced of an innate
capacity for learning language, the *preformationists* (Houston, 1971). Let us see how these
different theories offer explanations for the
uniquely human capacity for an extremely
complex system of language.

Behaviorism

Behaviorists are environmentalists who believe that language is learned through operant
conditioning. Since parents and teachers
selectively reinforce infant vocalizations, they
shape language behavior. Parents usually
respond with delight to their babies' babbling,
talking back and thus reinforcing it. Gradually,
adult reinforcement goes more and more to
those sounds that approximate adult language. In this way babies proceed from
meaningless babbling to meaningful speech.
Thorndike (1943) calls this the "babble-luck"
theory, because infants randomly emit sounds
and are reinforced for those that sound like
meaningful language.

Various studies show the effect of reinforcement. Babies in institutions (where babbling is less likely to be noticed and reinforced) vocalize less often and make fewer
kinds of sounds than babies reared at home
(Brodbeck & Irwin, 1946). And there is the
increased vocalizing by middle-class babies,
probably because their parents talk to them
more.

Mowrer (1960) claims that children learn
language by imitating a model (parents) and
by having their own utterances reinforced.
Infants associate the human voice with need
gratification, since the adults they hear are the
ones who meet their needs. Because of this
association, an infant's own voice—
particularly when it makes sounds that imitate
the parents—is reinforcing.

Cultural Relativism
and Cultural Determinism

Both these anthropological approaches are
somewhat less environmentalist, but they still
emphasize the role of culture and minimize
the importance of individual differences and
heredity. Children have innate predispositions
for learning language, but it is learned because it is a social necessity. From field
observations of cultures where children are
not specifically taught to use language, these
theorists conclude that children learn it naturally.

These theories emphasize the differences among languages. Sapir (1921) feels that
each linguistic system is unique and that it is
hard to express the dominant cultural themes
of one linguistic group in another language.
The Whorfian hypothesis (Whorf, 1956) says
that the specific language we learn influences
our mental processes, so that people who
speak different languages perceive the world
differently and also think differently. Thus, as
Eskimo children learn many different words for
"snow" to describe it in its various conditions
(such as powdery, wet, icy, and so forth), they
learn to perceive snow with greater accuracy
than do children whose vocabulary for it is
more limited.

Interactionism

This Piagetian approach maintains that language develops through the interaction
among heredity, maturation, and encounters
with the environment. Children learn language
not because of reinforcement, but because
they are born with the capacity and the need
to acquire it. Language is an essential part of
human development.

At about 2 years old, children begin to
connect sounds with actual events, persons,
and situations. They develop a representational, or symbol, system by which certain

words represent certain people or objects. Such a system is essential for further cognitive development, since language and thought are parallel, interconnected processes. Houston (1971) says, "Language develops along with the child's capacities for logical thought, judgment, and reasoning, and reflects these capacities at each stage" (p. 267).

Preformationism/Predeterminism

These two theories, popular among contemporary linguists (the most renowned of whom is Noam Chomsky), hold that human beings have an inborn biological predisposition for language. It occurs naturally just as walking does. Chomsky (1968) maintains that the experiences children have activate their innate language capacity and that this is the function of early experience. The fact that language develops so rapidly provides strong support for this position.

All normal children learn their native language, no matter how complex, and they all master the basics some time between 4 and 6 years of age. In all cultures children follow the same stages for prelinguistic and linguistic speech. They use the same kinds of one- and two-word sentences, in the same kind of telegraphic speech. Since there are aspects of acquisition and linguistic structure common to *all* languages, there must be inborn mental structures that enable children to build systems of rules. These structures have been termed the *Language Acquisition Device* (LAD).

These theorists challenge behaviorism. They claim that the knowledge of language is infinite, in the sense that we can always create new and longer sentences; it would be impossible to have learned all the language we are capable of expressing by simple operant conditioning. Also, small children do not imitate adult speech. When they try to, they typically repeat only some of the words and omit parts of speech. And they often express themselves in such original ways that it is virtually impossible for them to have learned from others the precise way they put words together. The preformationists also point to the universality of language: It exists in every known human society, and even Stone Age speech is astronomically more complex than the rudimentary systems of communication systems worked out among some nonhuman animals. All of this seems to point to the heritability of the neurological mechanism for language, if not language itself.

MEASURING INTELLIGENCE OF INFANTS

An adoption agency is trying to decide which of several prospective homes a baby would best fit into. A psychologist has to answer the worried parents who ask, "Our baby isn't doing the things our other children did at his age. Is he normal?" A school district needs to find out how many children will need special teaching.

In just such a practical situation was the concept of intelligence testing born. At the beginning of the twentieth century, school administrators in Paris wanted to relieve overcrowding by removing youngsters who did not have the capacity to benefit from an academic education. They called in psychologist Alfred Binet and asked him to devise a test to identify those children. Binet's IQ test, still being used in amended forms, was the precursor for a wide variety of tests that try to measure intelligence.

WHAT IS INTELLIGENCE?

The countless concepts of what intelligence is range from (1) a genetically endowed, inborn, general capacity to develop a number of intellectual abilities; to (2) the ability to do a variety of specific things and to engage in rational, productive behavior; to (3) "whatever intelligence tests measure." Terman (1921) described intelligence as the ability to think

TABLE 4-2
Overview of Theoretical Positions
on Language Development:
General Characteristics

BEHAVIORIST	CULTURAL RELATIVIST/ DETERMINIST	INTERACTIONIST	PREFORMATIONIST/ PREDETERMINIST
1. Environmental orientation.	1. Environmental orientation—less emphatic than behaviorists.	1. Developmental orientation	1. Hereditary orientation.
2. All learning is based on a few basic principles.	2. Theory and methods borrowed from anthropology.	2. Rooted in European psychological and developmental thought.	2. Concern with generative linguistics Distinction between deep and surface structure. Determination of ways sentences are formed and related to one another. Analysis of linguistic transformation.
3. Language development is part of a universal learning system. Anything that learns, learns the same way. Anything that anyone learns, is learned the same way.	3. Influence of culture on language and influence of language on thought.	3. Concern with development of perceptions and relation between language and cognition. Growth and development take place through organism's adaptation to environment and organization of conceptual schemes. Language part of general scheme of human development.	3. Emphasis on similarity of languages.
4. Language mechanisms are simple. Stimulus-response. Operant behavior.	4. Different cultures, languages, and societies are unique. Kinds of verbal responses that compose language differ for each linguistic system.	4. Continuous interaction between hereditary structure of organism and input from environment.	4. Goal of language study is development of language theory.
5. Language is an acquired function. Only innate aspect is ability to deal with stimulus-response. Shared with all other creatures.	5. Individual contributes little to his own linguistic and perceptual development.	5. Concern with linguistic ontogeny. Language develops as child passes through endogenously motivated stages. Language develops along with capacity for logical thought.	5. Linguistic structuring and acquisition are innate.
6. Interest in language as an observable behavior.	6. No biological predisposition for language acquisition.	6. Belief that language and thought influence and reflect each other.	6. Concern with question of internalized competence. Syntactic structures. Biological foundations.

SOURCE: I. Shigaki and V. Zorn. *Leadership program in the care of infants and toddlers: A training model.* NIH, August 1978.

abstractly. This definition, however, precludes the existence of intelligence in young children, and most contemporary psychologists are more likely to agree with Piaget (1952), who finds evidence of intelligence in the newborn infant's first adaptive behaviors, or with Wechsler (1944), who defines it as the ability "to act purposefully, to think rationally, and to deal effectively with the environment" (p. 3).

Some early theorists (Binet, Simon, Goddard, and Terman) believed that intelligence was an all-encompassing factor (the more intelligent you were, the better you were at everything); they considered it to be determined genetically, stable throughout life, and modifiable only within limits. Spearman (1927) proposed the two-factor theory: the *g* factor (general intelligence) influences all-round performance, and the *s* factor (specific abilities) accounts for differences between an individual's scores on different tasks—that is, the situation in which someone's verbal scores are much higher than math scores. Thurstone and Thurstone (1941) identified seven separate factors that combine to make up intelligence: memory, reasoning, number, perceptual speed, space, verbal comprehension, and word fluency. They devised tests to measure these primary mental abilities.

Guilford (1959) proposed a three-dimensional model of intelligence (see Figure 4-3). Intelligence is made up of 120 different intellectual abilities, the result of interaction by three major dimensions: *operations* (the ways we think), *contents* (what we think about), and *products* (the results of the application of a certain operation to a certain content, or our thinking a certain way about a certain issue). For example, to test the cognition of figural units, a person is asked to recognize pictures of familiar objects when parts of their silhouettes are blocked out. To test the ability to make transformations of meaning in semantic

relations, the testee is asked to state several ways in which two objects, say an apple and an orange, are alike. To test the ability of divergent production of symbolic units, the examinee may be asked to list as many words as possible beginning with the letter *s*.

When we use the term *intelligence* in this book, we will consider it to be a constantly active interaction between inherited ability and environmental experience, which results in an individual's being able to acquire, remember, and use knowledge; to understand both concrete and abstract concepts; to understand the relationships among objects, events, and ideas and to apply this understanding; and to use all the above in daily functioning.

INTELLIGENCE TESTING

The widespread administration of intelligence tests has become a highly controversial political issue. The tests are used by some to demonstrate supposed superiority of certain ethnic or racial groups and are castigated by others as racist instruments designed to keep minority groups from attaining full equality. Just how and why are intelligence tests used, and how much information can or cannot be obtained from them?

The *intelligence quotient*, or *IQ*, is the "sitting duck" of psychological testing. It is nothing more than a mathematical score computed according to a formula derived by Binet, but a great mystique has grown up around it. IQ is expressed by a number that is the ratio of a person's mental age to chronological age multiplied by 100, or IQ = MA/CA × 100. The DQ (development quotient) is computed similarly to gauge the developmental level of infants. The score is derived from a test in which tasks are set up in order of increasing difficulty. Each task is given a numerical value, and the final score is the child's mental age. When mental age is the same as chronological age, the child has an IQ of 100, which is average; when mental age exceeds chronological age, the IQ is over 100; and when mental age is less than chro-

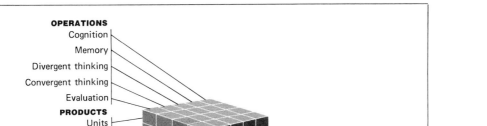

OPERATIONS
Cognition
Memory
Divergent thinking
Convergent thinking
Evaluation
PRODUCTS
Units
Classes
Relations
Systems
Transformations
Implications
CONTENTS
Figural
Symbolic
Semantic
Behavioral

Cognition
Units
Semantic

Operations are the *ways* we think:
1 Cognition (discovery or recognition)
2 Memory (retention)
3 Divergent thinking (seeking new answers by exploring different avenues of thought)
4 Convergent thinking (leading to one right, or best, answer)
5 Evaluation (deciding about adequacy of knowledge)

The *contents* of our intellectual functioning—*what* we think about—may be:
1 Figural (concrete information perceived through the senses)
2 Symbolic (words and numbers)
3 Semantic (verbal meanings or ideas)
4 Behavioral (social intelligence)

Products are the *results* of our thinking a certain way about certain issues. In other words, a *product* is the result of the application of a specific *operation* to a kind of *content*.
1 Units (a single word, number, or idea)
2 Classes (a set of related units)
3 Relations (relationships between units or classes)
4 Systems (ideas organized in a logical way)
5 Transformations (changes, including modifications in arrangements, organization, or meaning)
6 Implications (seeing certain consequences from the information given)

Fig. 4-3
A Three-Dimensional Model of Intellect (Guilford, 1959)

nological age, the IQ is under 100. No one is likely to get exactly the same IQ score on different tests, because of the different character of each test.

Standardization of a Test

The constructors of a test must decide what it is supposed to evaluate and predict. They choose items that seem to fit, and then they try the test on a group of subjects like those for whom the test is being devised. If the test is supposed to predict the ability of ghetto children to benefit from an educational program, it would be standardized on a sample of poor children, not those from a prosperous suburb. Test constructors determine the ages by which most children master the various tasks, retaining items that discriminate between children of different ages and abilities and discarding items that don't. Then they

administer the refined test to a *standardization sample*, a different group of children. An individual child's score is assessed in relation to the scores of the standardization sample.

Reliability of a Test

A test is *reliable* when a person who takes it several times obtains consistent scores. The reliability of the IQ as a *group* measure is good: If one group of children is retested, there will be about the same number of 100s, of 85s, and of 115s as at the original time of testing. The IQ of an individual, though, fluctuates because of fatigue, distractions, and poor administration and scoring (Reese & Lipsitt, 1970).

The closer the scores at two times of testing, the higher is the reliability of the test. Generally, the older the child and the shorter the time lapse between tests, the more stable the IQ will be. There is very poor reliability on IQs obtained by testing a child under 5, and virtually none on those obtained under the age of 3 (Honzik et al., 1948; Anderson, 1939). The important thing to remember about the IQ is that it is not a score which we are born with, which we carry around unchanged for the rest of our lives. A better emotional and cultural climate can bear fruit in better IQ scores, and a poorer one can bring them down. It is unwarranted to pigeonhole children from an early age because of IQ scores.

Validity of a Test

A test is *valid* if it measures what it is supposed to measure, as judged by how well the scores correlate with other measures. The intelligence tests in use today correlate very well with success in school. The Stanford-Binet is especially good at predicting success in such heavily verbal courses as English and history, and less good with arithmetic. IQ tests are moderately successful in predicting some types of vocational success—those that depend on "book-learning"—but are virtually useless in predicting success in any career that depends on social maturity, creativity, drive, or some special talent, like music or art. Predictive values of IQ tests are valid only when we apply them to people who are like the children on whom the tests were standardized, namely, white middle-class children.

Binet's original test was designed to help predict achievement in school, and today's intelligence tests still do this quite well. While claims are sometimes made for their ability to measure *aptitude*, or what an individual might learn from an optimal learning environment, a large element of the score rests on *achievement*, or what someone has already learned. A child who comes from a more favored setting will do better than one who has not had the same opportunities for learning. The basic skills and attitudes picked up in the early years help later learning; and so the more one has learned, the more one is able to learn. Compensatory programs like Head Start operate on this principle and try to reach children early to try to improve later learning.

DIFFICULTIES IN MEASURING INTELLIGENCE OF PREVERBAL CHILDREN

Intelligence is an elusive quality to define, much less measure. And the intelligence level of infants is most elusive of all.

Infants do not have a command of language. An examiner cannot ask babies questions, and babies cannot show by spoken or written answers how they reason. The only way to test infants' intelligence is to observe their behavior. But infants have a limited range of behaviors; they just don't do much. A third obstacle to measuring intelligence accurately is inability to control infants' motivation. If a 6-month-old baby does not pick up a block, we don't know whether the baby doesn't know how to pick it up or just doesn't feel like doing so.

Goodenough (1949) has said, "Attempting to measure infantile intelligence may be like trying to measure a boy's beard at the age of three" (p. 310). There is an almost complete lack of predictability between babies' intelligence test scores and their scores in adulthood or even later in childhood. There is almost no basis for predicting the intellectual functioning of normal children from their scores as infants. This may be because early intelligence tests, which measure motor activity, are so different from the heavily verbal tests for older children. The tests may be measuring two different things.

The only predictive value in testing infants is in general terms. Scores can sometimes tell us whether a baby is mentally retarded, normal, or unusually superior, and we can predict the future performance for deficient children more often than we can for average or superior ones. When psychologists and pediatricians add their assessments of a baby's level of development to the test score, we can obtain a more accurate prediction of that child's future school achievement level (Werner, Honzik, & Smith, 1968; Knobloch & Pasamanick, 1963).

At 20 months of age, 639 children were tested on the Cattell Infant Intelligence Scale and were examined by pediatricians and evaluated by psychologists. At 10 years, these same children were tested for intelligence and rated for school achievement. Those who had an IQ of 72 or less on the Cattell at 20 months had problems in school at age 10. Three children who, at 20 months, had been rated defective by the psychologists and three-fourths of 96 children rated below average had school problems at age 10, as did three-fourths of those who had been labeled "low normal" or "retarded" by pediatricians (Werner, Honzik, & Smith, 1968). When both the pediatrician and the psychologist had agreed on the status of an infant, they were better able to predict the child's future status.

A child's home environment is so important that Werner, Honzik, and Smith say, "The combination of retarded development and a deprived environment in infancy is more predictive of serious achievement problems at

school age than either infant or family variables alone" (p. 1074). Anastasi (1968) maintains that when there is no marked physical defect, we can predict childhood IQ better from knowing the educational levels of a baby's parents than from knowing the baby's test scores.

However, Cameron, Livson, and Bayley (1967) found that specific items on infant intelligence tests may be predictive of IQ scores in adulthood. The age at which girls first passed certain verbal skills on the Bayley Scales of Mental and Motor Development predicted their verbal IQ at the age of 26. There was no such relationship for males. Precocious verbal ability may be a predictor of later intellectual prowess, at least for females.

INFANT INTELLIGENCE TESTS

At 2.3 months, Hank can follow a moving pencil with his eyes; at 6.5 months he can reach for a block with one hand; at 13.1 months he can dangle a ring on a string; and at 17.2 months he can put two round blocks in two round holes (Bayley, 1935). These skills are test items on the Bayley Scales of Mental and Motor Development. These scales, the Gesell Development Schedules, and the Cattell Infant Intelligence Scale are the tests used most often to measure infants' mental development. They all work on the same principle and are quite similar. Through careful observation of a large number of babies, researchers determine what things most infants can do at particular ages. The researchers then develop a standardized scale, assigning a developmental age for each specific activity.

The Gesell Developmental Schedules (Gesell & Amatruda, 1947)

These schedules measure four major areas of development and cover an age range from 4

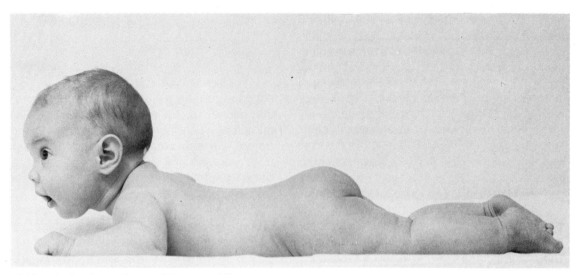

Holding the head erect is one of the motor skills measured on the Gesell Developmental Schedule. (Suzanne Szasz)

weeks to 6 years. They emphasize *motor behavior*: holding the head erect, sitting, standing, creeping, walking, jumping, and hopping. They also measure certain forms of *adaptive behavior*: eye-hand coordination in reaching for and handling things; solving problems, such as putting round and square forms into the appropriate holes; and exploration of new objects and surroundings. As children develop, *language behavior* is assessed: how well they seem to understand people and how they react through facial expressions, gestures, body movements, babbling, and speech. Finally *personal social behavior* is evaluated: How does a child respond to other people and to the culture? Is she toilet-trained? Does he feed himself? When does the child smile and at whom?

Based on a sample of only 107 infants in 1927, the Gesell schedules are considered less standardized and more subjective than many other psychological tests. This, plus the fact that some of the items seem to have been put in somewhat arbitrarily, is balanced by "the wealth of thorough observations and the careful delineation of each of these behaviors" (Brooks & Weinraub, 1976, p. 31).

The Cattell Infant Intelligence Scale (Cattell, 1947)

This is a downward extension of the Stanford-Binet test that covers ages from 2 to 30 months. It uses items from the Stanford-Binet, the Gesell, and other tests, as well as new ones. It tests perception (paying attention to a voice or a bell, or following movement with the eyes) and motor abilities (lifting the head or using the fingers). It has no time limits for any tasks.

This test, too, has standardization problems: Based on a middle-income group, the sample did not include infants from either well-to-do or poor families. Also, since the test was standardized at 3-month intervals, item placements for ages 2, 4, 5, 7, 8, 10, and 11 months are interpo'ated, making transitions less smooth than would occur if standardization had been done at monthly intervals. While the total number of items is less than in other tests and there are no social items, the ones that are included are interesting to children. Another plus is the clarity of instructions for administration and scoring.

The Bayley Scales (Bayley, 1933; revised 1969)

These scales cover babies from birth to 15

months, and also use items from several other tests, as well as new ones. Measures include grasping a piece of paper and a cube, turning the head to follow an object, imitating simple actions and words, and drinking from a cup.

Originally assembled on a group representing children from all socioeconomic backgrounds but overrepresenting those whose fathers were students or professionals, this test has largely adaptive or language items with a few personal-social and motor items (Honzik, 1976).

The Brazelton Behavioral Assessment Scale (Brazelton, 1973)

This scale is a neurological and behavioral assessment used to measure interactive behavior in newborn infants. It measures an infant's "available responses to his environ-

ment and so, indirectly, his effect on the environment" (p. 4). Scores are based on an infant's *best* performance rather than an average. The testers make every effort to determine that the neonates are giving their best performances, sometimes repeating tests later in the examination and sometimes using the mother to alert the infant. The test, which takes twenty to thirty minutes, involves about thirty different tasks such as noting response decrement to a rattle, a bell, and a pinprick; eliciting reflexes; checking orientation toward various stimuli; general tonus, alertness, and motor maturity.

TABLE 4-3
Comparison of Gesell, Cattell, and Bayley Tests

GESELL AND AMATRUDA (1941; YIELDS DQ)	CATTELL (1940; YIELDS IQ)	BAYLEY (1933; YIELDS IQ)
(Key age, 28 weeks)	(Key age, 6 months)	5.8 mo. Exploitive paper play. Present a piece of paper to child so he may grasp edge of it.
Lifts head.	Secures cube on sight. When child is sitting in upright position before table, a 1-inch cube is placed within easy reach.	
Sits erect momentarily.		5.8 mo. Accepts second cube. When child is holding one cube, place a second in easy reach.
Radial palmar grasp of cube.		
Whole hand rakes pellet.	Lifts cup. Place straight-sided aluminum cup upside down within easy reach of child as he is sitting at table.	5.9 mo. Vocalizes pleasure.
Holds two cubes more than momentarily.		5.9 mo. Vocalizes displeasure.
Retains bell.		6.0 mo. Reaches persistently. Place cube just far enough away from child so he cannot reach it. Credit if he reaches persistently.
Vocalizes *m-m-m* and polysyllabic vowel sounds.	Fingers reflection in mirror. While child is in sitting position, a framed mirror is held before him in such a manner that he can see his reflection but not that of his mother or other persons.	
Takes solid food well.		
Brings feet to mouth.		6.1 mo. Turns head after spoon. Hold spoon so that it protrudes over edge of table by child's side, and when he is interested, suddenly drop it to floor.
Pats mirror image.	Reaches unilaterally. Child sits with shoulders square to front and both hands an equal distance from examiner. A 2-to-3 inch door key or peg is presented in perpendicular position.	

TABLE 4-3
(continued)

GESELL AND AMATRUDA (1941; YIELDS DQ)	CATTELL (1940; YIELDS IQ)	BAYLEY (1933; YIELDS IQ)
		6.1 mo. Mirror image approach. Hold mirror before child, bringing it close enough so that he may reach it easily.
	Reaches persistently. One-inch cube is placed on table just out of child's reach. Credit if child reaches several times.	6.2 mo. Picks up cube deftly.
	Approaches second cube. Child is presented with one cube, and as soon as he has taken it a second is held before him in such a position as to favor his grasping, but is not actually placed in his hand.	6.3 mo. Says several syllables.
(Key age, 52 weeks)	(Key age, 12 months)	11.5 mo. Inhibits on command. When child puts an object in mouth or on some other pretext, say "no, no." Credit if he inhibits.
Walks with one hand held.	Beats two spoons together. Two spoons are taken, one in each hand, and beaten gently together while child watches, then they are presented to child, one in each hand.	
Tries to build tower of cubes, fairly.		11.6 mo. Repeats performance that elicited laughter.
Dangles ring by string.		
Tries to insert pellet in bottle.	Places cube in cup. Aluminum cup and 1-inch cube are placed before child, and he is asked to put "block" in cup. If no response, placing cube in cup is demonstrated and request repeated.	11.6 mo. Strikes doll. Place small rubber whistle doll on table. Hit it smartly to produce whistle, encourage child to do the same. Credit if he imitates the hitting motion.
Two words besides "mama" and "dada."		
Gives toy on request.		
Cooperates in dressing.		
Releases ball towards adult (56 weeks).	Marks with pencil. Piece of paper and pencil are placed before child with request, "_____write." If no response, writing is demonstrated and request repeated. Credit if child makes any marks on paper.	11.7 mo. Imitates words. Say several words, as mama, dada, baby, etc., and credit attempts to imitate.
	Rattles spoon in cup. Aluminum cup is placed before child, and spoon is moved back and fourth in it, hitting edges; then spoon is placed beside cup with handle toward child.	12.1 mo. Spoon imitation. Rattle spoon in cup with stirring motion. Credit if child succeeds in making a noise in cup by a similar motion with spoon.
	Speaking vocabulary—two	12.2 mo. Holds cup to drink. Hand cup to child saying, "Take a drink."

	CATTELL (1940; YIELDS IQ)	BAYLEY (1933; YIELDS IQ)
	words. "Ma-ma" and "da-da" are not credited.	Credit if he takes it in his hands, and holds it adaptively to drink.
	Hits doll. Rubber doll with whistle is put face up on table before child, and hit gently with open hand several times. Credit if child makes a definite attempt to hit doll.	12.6 mo. Adjusts round block. Three-hole (Gesell) form board is laid on table before child with round hole at child's right. Give round block to him with no directions. Credit if child puts block in round hole.

SOURCE: W. Kessen, M. Haith, and P. Salapatek. Infancy. In P. H. Mussen (Ed.), *Carmichael's manual of child psychology*, Vol. I (3d ed.). New York: Wiley, 1970.

INFLUENCES ON INTELLIGENCE

HEREDITY VERSUS SOCIOECONOMIC STATUS

Social class and parental education levels seem to influence infant development less than they affect later intellectual development. The Louisville Twin Study used the Bayley Scales to test 261 pairs of identical and fraternal twins at 3, 6, 9, 12, 18, and 24 months. The twins were from homes that represent "nearly the full spectrum of conditions under which urban families live, ranging from the welfare case to the wealthy professional family" (Wilson & Harpring, 1972, p. 286). There was *no* correlation between socioeconomic status and development. There *was* a high degree of concordance between identical twins in both mental and motor development at every age tested—much higher than between fraternal twins. Differences between unrelated children may, then, be due largely to the genetic blueprint. In extreme cases of serious prematurity, an impoverished environment, or brain injury, this genetic factor is outweighed by the strong environmental influence.

As children grow, facility with language becomes more important, and their home environments assume a more important rule. But in infancy, the genes seem to be the important determinants of development. More than 1000 babies aged 1 to 15 months, from different socioeconomic backgrounds, were tested on the Bayley Scales to uncover relationships between infant development and other factors (Bayley, 1965). No relationships were found on either the mental or the motor scale for sex, birth order, education of either parent, or geographic residence. No racial differences were found on the mental scale, although black babies scored higher than white babies on the motor scale.

Socioeconomic status is a good predictor of the *direction* of DQ change from infancy to preschool age. Test scores of children in middle-class and superior working-class homes increase after infancy; children from average working-class homes stay pretty much the same; and children from deprived working-class homes show a decline (Knobloch & Pasamanick, 1963). As children grow, then, their home environment assumes more and more importance.

This increasing importance of the home is underscored by a 1979 study by Rubin and Balow. Using the Bayley Scales, they measured the IQs of 1382 eight-month-old babies whose families represented a range of socio-

economic levels. Then the researchers followed up with the children, to measure their intelligence and academic achievement at ages 4 through 9. The Bayley scores predicted future performance better for the low-IQ children than those with high scores, but as a single predictor for later intelligence, socioeconomic status was more accurate than early test scores.

An interesting interaction between family background and IQ showed up in this study. The children with low Bayley scores who came from poor homes did the most poorly later on, while children from more prosperous homes who had also scored poorly at 8 months of age eventually performed at a level considered average for the general population. The environmental advantages did much to overcome their developmental impairment.

Comment Brody and Brody (1976):

A large number of studies have reported significant correlations between social class background and intelligence scores in school age and adult populations. These findings clearly indicate that the variables that relate to performance on infant tests are quite different from those that influence performance on tests given in later life [p. 77].

NUTRITION

Severe early malnutrition may retard mental development. Infants who died of the protein deficiency disease marasmus had fewer brain cells than did normal babies of the same age (Winick & Rosso, 1969), and the brains of children who were malnourished in early childhood weighed less than those of normal children (Stoch & Smythe, 1963). Children who had pyloric stenosis (a condition of early infancy in which an obstruction of the small intestine causes vomiting and short-term starvation until correction by surgery) suffered

impaired learning ability, especially in short-term memory and attention (Klein, Forbes, & Nader, 1975).

Malnutrition seems to affect children's abilities to pay attention, and since attentional deficits interfere with learning, this can affect their intellectual development. Lester (1975) found that well-nourished Guatemalan 1-year-olds showed an orienting response to a sound, followed by rapid habituation, while malnourished babies showed a diminished or completely absent orienting response. Brody and Brody (1976) report that 1-year-olds whose mothers had received protein supplements during pregnancy showed faster habituation to a visual stimulus and maintained their attention span longer in playing with a toy than did children whose mothers had received either no supplement or one consisting of calories with little protein.

However, the damaging effects of malnutrition seem to be contradicted by other research, such as that of Stein, Susser, Saenger, and Marolla (1972), who found no differences in intelligence test scores of 19-year-old Dutch men whose mothers had lived under famine conditions while they were pregnant, as compared to the sons of mothers whose nutrition had been adequate.

It is possible that the contradictory findings about the effects of malnutrition on intelligence can be explained by the fact that the severity and duration of the malnutrition are crucial factors. A physiological factor such as malnutrition may assume greater importance when it occurs in conjunction with unfavorable social conditions or during certain fairly specific periods of physical development.

A 1974 study (Lloyd-Still, Hurwitz, Wolff, & Schwachmar) found that the effects of severe malnutrition during the first six months of life are potentially reversible under conditions of "adequate nutrition, stimulation, and a stable socioeconomic environment" (p. 309). When 2- to 5-year-old children were given intelligence tests, those who had been severely

The way parents treat children can determine much of the basic quality of the entire life of an individual. (Erika Stone/Peter Arnold, Inc.)

malnourished during their first six months performed less well than a sibling control group, but after the age of 5 they did just as well as their well-fed siblings.

Brody and Brody (1976) refer to the intellectually debilitating malnutrition that is a way of life for millions of children in developing countries, but discount its effect in depressing the intelligence test scores of American children. They say:

Severe malnutrition in childhood occurring under the most adverse conditions and perhaps combined with the occurrence of chronic undernourishment might depress intelligence test scores. However, there is little available evidence at present that suggests that nutritional factors will account for any, or for any appreciable, variance in intelligence test scores in a representative sample of the U.S. population. And, there is little evidence to suggest that variations in intelligence test scores among different social groups are attributable to variations in nutritional status [p. 157].

CHILD-REARING APPROACHES

When something gets in Ilene's way, she figures out a way around it, while Jackie bursts into tears and gives up. Ilene knows where to look for her mother's keys, but Jackie stares vacantly when asked to get them. The Harvard Pre-School Project set out to determine what makes preschoolers competent. Researchers tested and observed some 400 preschoolers and rated them for competence (White, 1971).

The "A" children knew how to get and hold the attention of adults in socially acceptable ways, how to use them as resources, and how to show both affection and hostility. They got along well with other children, were proud of accomplishments, and showed a desire to act in grown-up ways. They used language well, showed a range of intellectual abilities, could plan and carry out complicated activities, and were able to "dual-focus" (pay attention to one task while being aware of what else is going on). The "B" children were less able in these skills, and the "C" children

were markedly deficient. Follow-up studies two years later showed a notable stability in the classifications (Pines, 1969).

The researchers identified A's and C's who had younger siblings and then sent observers into their homes to find differences in early environments. They found an enormous difference in parenting, and they concluded that the way parents treat children 1 to 3 years old can determine "much of the basic quality of the entire life of an individual" (White, 1971, p. 100). (This study focused on mothers, since it was felt that few fathers spent enough time to be influential with children of this age.)

How the A and C Mothers Differed
At first, most mothers seemed to treat their babies similarly. But when the children were about 8 months old, differences became apparent. At this time, children start to understand language, and the way their parents talk to them is important. They begin to crawl, and some parents react with pleasure, some with annoyance. They become attached to the person they spend most time with, making that person's personality more important.

Mothers from all socioeconomic levels were in both groups, with some welfare mothers raising A children and some middle-class women raising C's. But by and large, the A mothers were more likely to be middle class. Middle-class children spent much less time than poor children did sitting around and doing nothing, and they spent much more time playing make-believe games, making things, or practicing new skills (Pines, 1969).

The C mothers were a diverse group. Some were overwhelmed by life, ran chaotic homes, and were too absorbed by daily struggles to spend time with their children. Others spent too much time: hovering, being overprotective, pushing their babies to learn,

making them dependent. Some were physically present but rarely made real contact, apparently because they really didn't enjoy the company of babies and toddlers. These mothers provided for their children but confined them in cribs or playpens.

The A mothers served as "designers" and "consultants." They designed a physical environment full of interesting things to see and touch, although these things were common household objects as often as expensive toys. They were pretty much "on call" to their babies, but did not devote their entire lives to them. A number had part-time jobs, and those who did stay home generally spent less than 10 percent of their time interacting with their infants. They went about their daily routines but made themselves available for a few seconds or minutes when needed to answer a question, label some object, or help the toddler climb stairs. These women generally had positive attitudes toward life, enjoyed being with young children, and generously gave themselves. They were energetic, patient, tolerant of mess, and relatively casual about minor risks.

IMPORTANCE OF STIMULATION
Holding and handling babies and being a consistent and skillful caregiver are good for their emotional well-being, but do not seem to influence their cognitive development (Clarke-Stewart, 1977). For this, they apparently need certain specific kinds of active interaction. They need to be looked at, they need to be talked to, and they need to be played with. And they need an extremely important kind of stimulation—that provided by caregivers in response to the infants' own behavior.

If babies are to develop intellectually, they have to be willing to explore new places, new people, and new objects in their world. To gain the self-confidence that will enable them to investigate the unfamiliar, they need to know that they are somewhat in control of their environment. To get this feeling of control, they need feedback. When babies' cries bring solace or their babbling brings interest, they learn that what they do matters. Armed with this assurance that they can exert control over their lives, they can go out to conquer new worlds increasingly farther from home.

You just finished having a very engrossing time. I finally gave in and let you open the bottom drawer in the kitchen which holds measuring cups, potato mashers, cake decorators and other utensils. You spent 45 minutes quietly unloading the drawer, examining each item, putting some back and taking them out again.

Twice today you brought one of your books for me to read to you and you sat on my lap quite quietly while I read. You turn on the radio when one of us suggests it and you go get a book on request. Yesterday you walked outside with us a little . . . and you were captivated by each fallen leaf and rock that we passed.

Nancy Gordon

Recent research confirms the importance of the home environment in influencing intellectual development. Elardo, Bradley, and Caldwell (1975) and Bradley and Caldwell (1976) looked at various aspects of the home settings of seventy-seven normal children, and administered intelligence tests to them at 6 months, 1 year, and 3 years of age. The children who showed a progressive increase in test scores tended to have mothers who were closely involved with them, encouraged and challenged them to develop new skills, and gave them the kinds of play materials that enhance development. The parents of the children whose performances declined were less successful at organizing their children's environment.

While most research has been done with mothers and children, Clarke-Stewart (1977) says, "One point that does seem clear is that at this age the stimulation need not come from the permanent mother-figure. Nurses, research assistants, and principal investigators can all apparently effect changes in infants' performance" (p. 16).

The ability of caretakers outside the family to help children develop intellectually has been acknowledged by a landmark study by Kagan, Kearsley, and Zelazo (1978). They compared children who had been raised at home with those who had been attending a high-quality day-care center from infancy (3½ to 5½ months of age at time of enrollment) to 29 months of age (when the study ended). At periodic intervals the children were tested on attentiveness, excitability, reactivity to others, attachment, and cognitive functioning. To evaluate the children's cognitive development, the researchers used measures of vocabulary, of the ability to solve test problems involving embedded figures, and of memory for the location of familiar objects, as well as selected items from the Bayley Scales. Their conclusion: "The day care and home-reared children developed similarly with respect to cognitive, social, and affective qualities during the first three years of life" (p. 259).

FAMILY SIZE AND BIRTH ORDER

If you were your parents' first child, you may be more likely than your younger brothers and sisters to want company in times of stress, to be enrolled in an elite college, to make it into *Who's Who*, and to become an astronaut (Irwin, 1969; Helmreich, 1968; Schachter, 1959). A definite birth order relationship showed up among 400,000 Dutch men aged 19 years who were tested for intelligence; first-borns scored better than second-borns, who in turn scored better than third-borns, and so forth (Belmont & Marolla, 1973). The

birth order effect was most consistent in families with two to four siblings. Birth order also seemed to have an effect on the emotional adjustment of these Dutch men, with firstborns the healthiest and lastborns at greatest risk of developing a psychiatric disorder (Belmont, 1977). Family size has its effects, too, since the men who grew up in smaller families were taller and had better IQ scores. While the Dutch findings were for men only, having been analyzed from data from Dutch military preinduction examinations, other researchers have come up with similar findings on intellectual competence for both sexes (Breland, 1974; Glass et al., 1974).

Social class appears to be one ingredient in this somewhat confusing stew, since the findings of Glass and his associates (1974) that first and only children were better readers and had higher educational goals held true only for children of higher socioeconomic status. Middle-class parents may be more likely than poorer parents to treat first-born children differently from the others.

The effects of birth order on intellectual functioning may be more complex than the research has so far indicated. Zajonc (1976) feels that it is the family configuration, rather than birth order per se, which affects intellectual growth. How many brothers and sisters are there—and how close in age are they? Zajonc suggests that the negative effects of late birth order could be reduced if there is a large age gap between a child and the next older sibling. The crucial factor might well be the time that parents have available to give to each individual child, which is affected by the number of other children close in age who demand their attention.

In a study testing Zajonc's theory that the combined influences of birth order, child spacing, and family size shape intellectual development, Grotevant, Scarr, and Weinberg (1977) looked at the 176 adopted children and the 143 biological children in 101 middle- to upper-middle-class adoptive families. They found that while Zajonc's generalizations fit large groups of people and can be used to predict population trends, they don't hold up when applied to individual families.

> Just as the birth rate cannot predict whether the Joneses or Smiths will reproduce, [this] model cannot predict whether first- or fourth borns in smaller or larger families will be brighter, when both genetic and environmental variables within and between families contribute heavily to their IQ differences [Grotevant et al., 1977, p. 1703].

These authors found that the IQs of the biological children were closer to the parents' IQs than were those of the adopted children, pointing to a genetic factor in intelligence. In fact, they reported that:

> Genetic variance has been shown to account for approximately *25 times* as much of the variance in children's IQ scores as the combination of birth order, family size, and childspacing variables [Grotevant et al., 1977, p. 1702; emphasis in original].

SOCIETAL SUPPORTS FOR PARENTS

Under what Keniston (1978) calls the "myth of the self-sufficient family," the belief has arisen that the ideal nuclear family in America brings up its children with no help from other forces in society and that "for a family to need help—or at least to admit it publicly—is to confess failure" (p. 12). Yet families at every socioeconomic level have always received help from others—from members of the extended family, from governmental institutions such as schools and hospitals, from friends and neighbors, and from paid servants and services.

Today, with the vast changes that have taken place in society, families turn more than ever to outside forces. Parents, say Keniston, have had to become executives, to choose, meet, talk with and coordinate the experts, the technology, and the institutions that help bring up their children. At the same time, with the proliferation of research on child development and the abundance of (often conflicting) advice from experts, parents have taken more and more seriously their role in helping their children meet the demands of today's complex modern society.

As a result, parents sign up by droves for prenatal classes that will enhance their experience of childbirth and aid them in caring for their new babies; for Parent Effectiveness Training courses that will help them help their children navigate the crises of growing up; and for innumerable lectures and workshops in school, church, and community. For a variety of reasons, this push toward parent education has been largely a middle-class phenomenon. Yet when programs have been offered to low-income parents that hold promise of helping their children improve their verbal, academic, and general coping skills, they often embrace them eagerly. When middle-class professionals run these programs, they need to be extremely careful to avoid imposing middle-class values in an arbitrary way and they need to be exquisitely sensitive to the parents' feelings about themselves and their children.

One example of a program that seems to have embodied this philosophy concentrated on developing children's language abilities—not by making a frontal attack on parental language patterns but by trying to change certain aspects of parent-child interaction. Karnes, Teska, Hodgins, and Badger (1970) recruited twenty poor mothers of 1- and 2-year-old children to attend a weekly two-hour meeting for fifteen months to learn how to teach their children. The emphasis was on the need for the mothers to respect their children, to maintain a positive approach that focused on success, to teach a task by breaking it into separate components, and to keep learning fun. These mothers' children and a control group whose mothers received no training were tested on the Stanford-Binet intelligence test and the Illinois Test of Psycholinguistic Abilities (ITPA). On both tests the experimental children scored much higher than the control children did in language and intellectual functioning.

Although we don't know how well the experimental children's advantages will hold up over time, this study and similar ones indicate that professionals can work successfully with parents to help children develop their cognitive and linguistic abilities.

A worthwhile goal for those who care about children—and society—would be to incorporate into the environment of all children those experiences that would enable them to reach their intellectual potential, while at the same time preserving the self-esteem of their parents and the integrity of the family bond.

SUMMARY

1 According to Piaget's interactionist theory of cognitive development, a child progresses through four sequential stages of cognitive development: *sensorimotor* (birth to age 2), *preoperational* (2 to 7), *concrete operational* (7 to 11), and *formal operational* (after 12). Each stage is attained through an interaction of maturational and environmental factors, and each is qualitatively different from the other stages. In this chapter we have described the six substages of the sensorimotor stage. **2** During the sensorimotor stage of cognitive development, an infant—though still a preverbal creature—exhibits intelligent (adaptive) behaviors. During this period, an infant develops from a primarily reflexive individual to one who shows rudimentary foresight. One significant development during this stage is the concept of object permanence, through which the child comes to understand the implications of visible and invisible displacements.   **3**   Through learning, a change in behavior occurs as a result of experience. The type and extent of learning in infants have been the subject of much controversy. There is evidence that infants are capable of several types of learning, including habituation, imitation, classical conditioning, and operant conditioning.   **4**   During the second year of life, an infant begins to speak the language, though certain verbal utterances have been understood even earlier. There is little agreement about how to account theoretically for language acquisition; theories range from those stressing environmental and cultural factors (behaviorism, cultural determinism, cultural relativism) to those stressing innate, maturational explanations (preformationism, predeterminism).   **5**   There are a variety of definitions of intelligence; none is universally accepted.   **6**   It is difficult to assess the intelligence of infants because (a) they have not acquired language and cannot be tested verbally, (b) they have a limited range of behavioral capacities that can be assessed, and (c) motivation cannot be controlled in the testing situation to ensure that infants will perform "their best." An infant's scores on intelligence tests are poor predictors of later intellectual ability, as this is influenced greatly by heredity, socioeconomic factors, child-rearing techniques, and nutrition.

SUGGESTED READINGS

Evans, R. I.   *Jean Piaget: The man and his ideas*. New York: Dutton and Co., 1973. A fascinating dialogue with Jean Piaget. Includes Piaget's discussion of his theory and his reactions to the viewpoints of Freud, Erikson, gestalt psychology, and learning theory.

Ginsburg, H., & Opper, S.   *Piaget's theory of intellectual development*. Englewood Cliffs, NJ: Prentice-Hall, 1979/second edition. A clear, readable discussion of Jean Piaget's research on intellectual development. It includes outlines of Piaget's basic ideas, his early research and theory, his use of logic as a model for the adolescent's thinking, and a discussion of the implications of his work.

Keniston, K., and The Carnegie Council on Children.   *All our children: The American family under pressure*. New York: Harcourt Brace Jovanovich, 1977. A strong indictment of the lack of support modern families receive from society, a searching analysis of the plight of the contemporary American family, and a prescription of sweeping reforms that add up to a national family policy.

Lewis, M. (Ed.)   *Origins of intelligence: Infancy and early childhood*. New York: Plenum, 1976. A collection of advanced-level articles on the history and issues of intelligence testing in the early years of life examines the impact of factors such as social class, cultural differences, and environmental risks in measuring intelligence.

Piaget, J.   *The origins of intelligence in children*. New York: International Universities Press, Inc., 1952. Piaget's now classic presentation of the six sequential stages of the sensorimotor period. Abundantly illustrated with observations of his own children.

Pulaski, M. A. S. *Understanding Piaget: An introduction to children's cognitive development*. New York: Harper & Row, 1971. A clear, easy-to-understand interpretation of Piaget's research and theories, with examples, simple illustrations, and practical application.

Pulaski, M. A. S. *Your baby's mind and how it grows: Piaget's theory for parents*. New York: Harper & Row, 1978. A clearly written, interesting explanation of Piagetian theories in terms that lay readers can grasp, illustrated by many examples and anecdotes from the personal experiences of the author, a psychologist, mother, and grandmother.

Reese, H. W. *Basic learning processes in childhood*. New York: Holt, 1976. An introduction to the psychological study of learning in children by an outstanding researcher. Focuses on conditioning and discriminative and verbal learning.

White, B. L. *The first three years of life*. Englewood Cliffs, NJ: Prentice-Hall, 1976. A descriptive account of behavioral development during the first three years, along with practical suggestions to parents about their infants' capabilities.

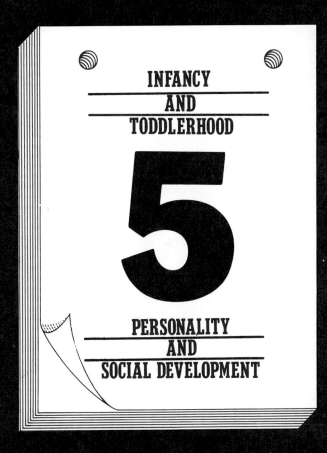

INFANCY
AND
TODDLERHOOD

5

PERSONALITY
AND
SOCIAL DEVELOPMENT

IN THIS CHAPTER
YOU WILL LEARN ABOUT

The meanings behind babies' tears, smiles, and laughter

Sigmund Freud's and Erik Erikson's theories about what causes babies to become unique individuals

How a baby's family life—or lack of it—helps shape personality and social adjustment

CHAPTER OVERVIEW

What Emotions Do Babies Have?
Crying | Smiling | Laughing

Personality Development in Infants
The Psychosexual Theories of Sigmund Freud: The Oral and Anal Stages | The Psychosocial Theories of Erik H. Erikson: The First Two Crises

The Infant in the Family
Family Constellation | Sex Differences in Infancy | Sex Differences in Parent-Infant Interaction

The Family's Role in Personality Development
Imprinting | Attachment Between Mother and Child | Stranger Anxiety | Maternal Deprivation | Father-Infant Interaction

Friendship in Infancy

Childhood is joy and laughter and innocent moments of delight. It is also, of course, fear and worry, uncertainty, pain, rage, and frustration. The range of emotions in our early years—and the people and experiences that evoke them—have far-reaching effects in determining our personalities.

AT 6 WEEKS

You are becoming more and more fun. You smile quite a bit and chuckle occasionally. You lie in your crib and gurgle and coo at your animals. When I pick you up you put your arms around my neck and nuzzle my ear which naturally causes me to forgive you immediately for wanting to be fed when I'm in the middle of a project.

Nancy Gordon

Emotional development is a major part of our personality development. We begin to show our emotions right from birth. In the first month of life, babies are already manifesting their own unique temperaments; they are gaining a sense of the world—whether it is friendly and caring or cold and hostile; and they are responding to and evoking responses from the people around them.

Much of what we believe about emotional development in infancy is just that—belief. It is difficult, if not impossible, to know and prove what is happening in a baby's mind. Based on what we can see, though—the crying and the smiling and the laughing and the way babies respond to people around them—we can try to explain what we think is going on.

WHAT EMOTIONS DO BABIES HAVE?

It is easy to tell when infants are unhappy: They emit a piercing cry in an ever-rising crescendo; they flail their arms and legs about; and they stiffen their bodies until they are rigid. It is harder to tell when babies are happy. During the first month they quiet at the sound of a human voice or when they are picked up, and they smile when their hands are moved together pat-a-cake style (Wolff, 1963; Griffiths, 1954; Bayley, 1933). With every passing day they respond more to people—smiling, cooing, reaching out, and eventually going to them. But are these early moments of quiet really expressions of happiness, or do they tell us only that a baby is not *un*happy? It is hard to say whether infants are truly happy or just neutral until about the third month, when their more frequent smiles and delighted coos signal their times of joy.

The study of emotion—especially in infancy—poses a mighty challenge. It is very hard to determine exactly what a baby is feeling, and it is often difficult to pinpoint the cause of feelings. Yet this has been the traditional line of study of infant emotion—identifying specific expressions of feeling. In 1919 John B. Watson, the behaviorist, claimed that infants are born with three major emotions—*love*, *rage*, and *fear*—which are unconditioned responses to stimuli. But investigators who tried to confirm these theories had trouble identifying babies' emotional states. Someone who had seen an infant girl being dropped would identify her subsequent crying as fear, but if observers simply saw a film of the same crying infant, they could not pinpoint the emotion being expressed. Sherman (1927) concluded that emotional states are generalized in infants and not nearly so specific as behaviorists had believed. By 1932, Bridges made the point that newborns show only one emotion, an undifferentiated excitement (later termed "distress") and that babies' emotions *differentiate* as they grow older, proceeding from the general to the specific. In short, babies may, from an early age, have a wide range of emotions that they cannot express specifically or that we cannot identify with certainty.

The newest thinking on the study of

emotional development emphasizes the inter-relationships between different expressions of feeling. As Yarrow (1979) says:

Although emotion is evidenced in many different kinds of behaviors, it seems to have a dynamic unity. Emotions appear to be so interrelated dynamically that to isolate them might limit or distort our understanding [pp. 951-2].

Emotions are interrelated in several ways. From infancy on, for example, people use anger or even laughter (ostensibly an expression of joy) to deal with underlying feelings of hurt or fear. People often feel a range of conflicting feelings at the same time: They cry when they are happy, or laugh so hard that tears flow. Sometimes it's hard to tell whether someone is laughing or crying. A baby may react to a stranger with a combination of smiles and tears, coming closer and backing off, thus showing both interest and curiosity in a new person, as well as fear of the potential threat posed by this person (Yarrow, 1979).

Furthermore, the same physical signals can be present in widely differing emotional states. The heartbeat may quicken in fear or in delighted anticipation; or one's stomach may quiver with "butterflies" at the sight of a loved one, or at the thought of speaking before a large audience.

Infants' physiological signals, therefore, cannot be interpreted as indicating any one emotional state, even though mechanical evaluations of heart rate, electrogalvanic responses of the skin, and changes in glandular systems are useful in assessing emotional change. Other techniques for studying emotion are parents' reports and ratings of their children, and the children's own reports in interviews or on questionnaires. So far, attempts to find correlations between these various measures have yielded contradictory results, with some studies, for example, finding relationships between a faster heartbeat and facial expressions of distress, and others finding no clear relationships. Yarrow (1979) suggests combining some of these tech-niques, starting by observing children in their everyday lives at home or in day care, and then testing them in the laboratory.

The exact time when emotions first appear in human beings has long been a controversial topic. It still is. Investigators such as Lewis and Brooks (1978) feel that children are not aware of their own emotional states until about a year of age, while others, like Sroufe (1979) feel that 2- to 3-month-old infants are actively involved with their environment, and thus able to feel real emotion. Yarrow (1979) feels that the infant must have at least a rudimentary self-concept before being conscious of his or her feelings.

Another line of research has sought to find out at what age babies can recognize the emotions of other people. LaBarbera, Izard, Vietze, and Parisi (1976) showed slides of three facial expressions—joy, anger, and neutrality—to twelve 4-month-old and twelve 6-month-old babies. At both ages, the infants looked longer at the joyful facial expressions, indicating that babies as young as 4 months old can pick up another person's happiness. The researchers suggest that an infant learns to recognize joy because this recognition can produce rewarding experiences for the baby. They feel that such young babies may not respond differently to anger than to the absence of emotion because they still do not have the coping mechanisms to deal with another person's anger.

Using a new experimental procedure, which involved determining when an infant "got used" to seeing a particular expression, Young-Browne, Rosenfeld, and Horowitz (1977) found that infants as young as 3 months could tell the difference between expressions of happiness and surprise, and sometimes between sadness and surprise.

The same emotional response can have different meanings at different times. In early infancy, crying usually signals physical discomfort; later on it is more apt to indicate psychological distress. The early smile often comes spontaneously as an expression of internal well-being, while smiles after a couple of months of age are more often social signals, in which the baby expresses pleasure in other people.

The complexity of emotion becomes even more obvious when we think about the variety of its expression. For example, the context of an event—how it is presented and how we see it—influence the way we react to it. What we bring to an event determines in large measure the way we will react to it. What are our expectations? How do our past experiences affect the way we interpret what we perceive? The baby who sees a mask over his mother's face as part of a game she is playing with him will chortle with delight, while the one who sees the mask as an incomprehensible threat will cry in terror at the same sight. Here we see, too, how an infant's emotional state is tied to his or her cognitive development. The baby who cannot understand why his mother is wearing that mask may be more afraid of it than the one who realizes that underneath, she is still the same loving mother. "Getting the joke" may enable an infant to smile rather than cry.

There are many individual differences in people's emotional responses right from infancy—in the kinds of events they react to, the intensity of their reactions, and their tendencies to react positively or negatively. Some of these differences seem to stem from inborn differences in temperament. Some babies seem to be born with a cheerful nature, display a sense of humor from a very early age, and generally have a more positive outlook on life. Other individuals, from shortly after birth on, become angry or sad more easily and take less joy in living.

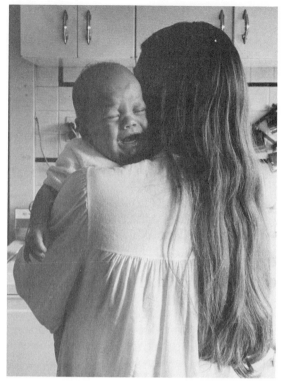

Babies whose caregivers respond promptly to their crying with tender, soothing care cry less often. (Suzanne Szasz)

The prenatal environment, the baby's experiences soon after birth, and the present environment undoubtedly all play their roles in shaping these differences in emotional expression. Extreme emotional deprivation— rejection, lack of stimulation, and lack of positive emotional response—can lead to emotional disturbance in infants and young children (Rutter, 1974; Yarrow, 1961). There is evidence, though, that such deprivation can sometimes be overcome by positive later experiences.

Continued research can help us learn about the ways different factors affect emotional development and can provide clues for encouraging emotional health and preventing and treating emotional disorders.

CRYING

Why do babies cry? From the first week of life they cry because of hunger, cold, pain, being undressed, and having their sleep interrupted. Over the next few weeks, they also cry when their feedings are interrupted, when stimulated in a fussy state, and when left alone in a room (Wolff, 1969). Wolff (1969) found different patterns between infants' basic rhythmical cries and their cries of anger, pain, and frustration. He recorded four examples: the *basic rhythmical cry* (often called the "hunger cry," but not always associated with hunger); the *angry cry* (a variation of the basic cry in which a baby forces excess air through the vocal cords); the *pain cry* (distinguished by a sudden onset of loud crying, without preliminary moaning, and an initial long cry followed by an extended period of breath-holding); and the *cry of frustration* (starting from silence, with no long breath-holding, and the first two or three cries long and drawn out).

Oswald and Peltzman (1974) recorded the cries of babies undergoing routine medical procedures (like the taking of blood samples) and minor surgery (like circumcision), and found that babies in distress cry louder, longer, more noisily, and more irregularly than hungry babies. Also, distressed babies are more likely to gag and to interrupt their crying.

Babies' cries give physical as well as emotional clues. A pediatrician and an engineer used a computer to analyze tape-recordings of babies' cries in an effort to diagnose various illnesses on the basis of the distinctive crying patterns associated with them. Corwin and Golub (1979) recorded the cries of fifty-five healthy infants who were pricked in the heel for a routine blood test at the age of 2 to 4 days. They then compared these cries to those of forty-three babies with known or suspected abnormalities. The researchers were able to identify nineteen of twenty-one babies known to have jaundice and nine of ten babies known to have respiratory illness. Since the test missed some abnormal children and showed abnormalities in some apparently healthy ones, it is not yet ready for general use. But should its accuracy be improved, it may help us to detect and treat a number of serious illnesses.

Crying is the most powerful way—and sometimes the only way—that babies can signal to the outside world when they need something. It is, therefore, a vital means of communication and a way for infants to establish some kind of control over their lives. Those babies whose cries of distress do bring relief apparently gain a measure of self-confidence in the knowledge that they can affect their own lives. This can be inferred from the findings that by the end of the first year, babies whose mothers respond promptly to their crying with tender, soothing care cry less. The more the mother ignores, scolds, hits, commands, and restricts the baby, the more the baby cries, frets, and acts aggressively (Clarke-Stewart, 1977).

SMILING

A baby's smile is a basic means of communication that sets in motion a beautiful cycle. Gewirtz and Gewirtz (1968) proved the power of the smile when they found a probability of from 0.46 to 0.88 that an infant's smile would elicit a smile from an adult.

The smile appears early. Babies 1 week old smile spontaneously and fleetingly when their stomachs are full or when they hear soft sounds. At about 1 month, these smiles become more frequent and are directed more toward people. Babies 4 to 5 weeks old smile at having both hands clapped together (Wolff, 1963), or when they can hear a familiar voice (Kreutzer & Charlesworth, 1973). Not till 3½ months will babies smile more to a familiar face than an unfamiliar one.

Infants vary considerably in their smiling (Tautermannova, 1973), and the differences are significant. The happy, cheerful baby who rewards her parents' caretaking efforts with smiles and gurgles is almost certain to form a more positive relationship with them than will her brother, who smiles less readily.

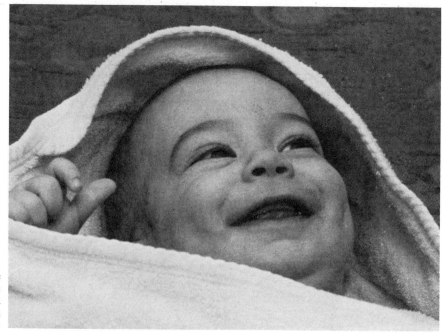

A baby's smile is a basic means of communication which sets in motion a beautiful cycle. (Erika Stone/Peter Arnold, Inc.)

LAUGHING

At about the fourth month of life, babies start to laugh out loud. They chortle at all sorts of things—being kissed on the stomach, hearing various sounds, and seeing their parents do unusual things. As babies grow older, they laugh at more and more different situations, apparently because their cognitive development enables them to recognize what is expected and to be aware of incongruity when it appears. Sroufe and Wunsch (1972), who studied the development of laughter in the first year of life, conclude that it marks an important transaction between infants and their environment, that it helps babies to discharge tension in situations which otherwise might be upsetting, and that there is "an important tie between cognitive development and emotional growth and expression" (p. 1341).

AT 1 YEAR

You played a trick on me today! You enjoy watching the birds at the bird feeder, but when a squirrel comes you laugh and chatter so much that I usually come to see it and I talk to you about the squirrel. The other day you were in your playpen, seemingly pretty content, and I was sitting nearby reading.... then you went into your "There's a squirrel!" act, looking out the window and laughing. So I went to see him. You were scooting across the playpen and hugged me and laughed. There was no squirrel!

Nancy Gordon

PERSONALITY DEVELOPMENT IN INFANTS

As Sigmund Freud tried to help turn-of-the-century Viennese adults overcome neuroses, he formulated a broad philosophy to explain how the neuroses had developed, and to explain how children develop emotionally. Erik Erikson, a student and disciple, disagreed with some aspects of Freud's theory and expanded upon others. These two analysts have had a tremendous impact on Western

TABLE 5-1
Stages in Infant
Emotional
Development

APPROXIMATE AGE	STAGE*	CHARACTERISTICS
0–1 mo.	"Absolute stimulus barrier"	Infants are relatively unresponsive, rarely reacting to outside stimulation.
1–3 mo.	"Turning toward the environment"	Infants are open to stimulation. They begin to show interest and curiosity, and they smile readily at people.
3–6 mo.	"Positive affect"	Babies can anticipate what is to happen and experience disappointment when it doesn't. They show this by getting angry or acting wary. They smile, coo, and laugh often. This is a time of social awakening and early reciprocal exchanges between the baby and the caregiver.
7–9 mo.	"Active participation"	Babies play "social games" and try to get responses from people. They "talk" to, touch, and cajole other babies to get them to respond. They express more differentiated emotions, showing joy, fear, anger, and surprise.
9–12 mo.	"Attachment"	Babies are intensely preoccupied with their principal caregiver, become afraid of strangers, and act subdued in new situations. By 1 year, they communicate emotions more clearly, showing moods, ambivalence, and gradations of feeling.
12–18 mo.	"Practicing"	Babies explore their environment, using the person they're most attached to as a secure base. As they master the environment, they become more confident and more eager to assert themselves.
18–36 mo.	"Formation of self-concept and identification"	Children sometimes become anxious because they now realize how much they are separating from their caregiver. They work out their awareness of their limitations in fantasy, in play, and by identifying with adults.

SOURCE: Adapted from Sroufe (1979) in Osofsky, J. (ed.), *Handbook of infant development*. New York: Wiley, 1979.
*Stages here is simply a descriptive term. Sequence and ages may vary.

society. Their ideas have been assimilated as unquestioned truths by so many professionals and parents that there is probably no one under the age of 40 whose upbringing does not owe something to them. Because of the nature of the theses, neither philosophy has generated much research to support it. Many developmentalists now question many aspects of these theories. But because of Freud's and Erikson's great influence on child rearing, it is important to be familiar with their ideas.

THE PSYCHOSEXUAL THEORIES OF SIGMUND FREUD: THE ORAL AND ANAL STAGES

The Oral Stage (Birth to 12–18 Months)[1]

Babies are "all mouth" in the oral stage; they attain most of their gratification from sucking nipples, bottles, fingers, and anything else that can go into the mouth. They *cathect*, or form attachments to, these sources of gratification. During this stage of "primary narcissism," infants are concerned only with their own gratifications. They are all id, as they operate on the pleasure principle.

People with "oral" personalities, says Freud, were fixated during this period. They may derive a disproportionate amount of satisfaction from the mouth—kissing, smoking, nail-biting, overeating, or overdrinking. Or they may develop an "imperious demand for the love object when desire is high together with ignoring it the rest of the time" (just as babies demand feeding when hungry but are not interested in food at other times) or "a passive, unrealistic optimism that someone will appear to solve one's problems" (just as infants wait to be fed; Baldwin, 1968, p. 357).

The Anal Stage (12–18 Months to 3 Years)

Children's greatest pleasure during the anal stage comes from moving their bowels, and the way toilet training is handled determines the resolution of this stage. The "anal" personality may be shaped by two factors: a concern with cleanliness or the view of one's feces as gifts to one's parents. In the first instance, a person may become obsessively clean and neat or defiantly messy. Or one may become pedantic, obsessively precise, and rigidly tied to schedules and routines. Fixation to the

[1]All ages are approximate.

Christy is obsessed with the subject of "ca-ca" (Greek all-purpose word for dirt, garbage, B.M., etc.). When we go to the park he will point to trash containers, saying ca-ca, and he likes to pick up bits of leaves and paper... and deposit them in the trash cans. At home he regards the diaper pail with a combination of fascination and slight fear, and if not watched will stash things in there (including Dorothy's watch).... While eating, he is very fastidious—too much so—although I never taught him this. If any food falls on his table he will point and say "ca-ca" and want me to clean it up. Once I got a dab of jelly on a counter top and he refused to go on eating until I cleaned it up.

Christy, age 1 yr., 3 mos.
Joan Gage

gift-giving aspects of anality may make people hoard their possessions (as they once withheld their feces) or may cause them to identify love with the bestowing of material objects.

THE PSYCHOSOCIAL THEORIES OF ERIK H. ERIKSON

Whereas Freud stresses biological determinants of behavior, Erikson looks to cultural and societal influences. His major concern is with the growth of the ego, especially with the ways society shapes its development. In each of Erikson's "Eight Ages of Man" (1950) crises occur that influence ego development. How these crises are resolved determines the course of ego development.

Crisis I: Basic Trust versus Basic Mistrust (Birth to 12–18 Months)

The creation of trust through sensitive care for an infant's physical and emotional needs is the basis of later identity. Trusting babies sleep deeply, eat well, and enjoy bowel relaxation, showing their secure feelings that the world is a good place to live in. (This theory does not account for temperamental differences in infancy that may prevent some children from showing their trust in these ways.)

THE MOTHER-INFANT RELATIONSHIP

This bond is an important determinant of an infant's sense of trust, with the *quality* of the mother-child tie being more important than its *quantity*. Erikson's period of trust versus mistrust coincides with Freud's oral stage, both in chronology and in the importance of early feeding experiences. Feeding alleviates an infant's generalized sense of discomfort, provides its own sensual satisfaction, establishes the infant's primary contact with the outside world, and has a certain regularity and consistency. According to Maier (1969),

The Mother, or caring person, brings the social world to the infant. The environment expresses itself through the mother's breast, or the bottle substitute. Love and the pleasure of dependency . . . are conveyed to him by the mother's embrace, her comforting warmth, her smile, and the way she talks to him [p. 35].

Trust enables an infant to let the mother out of sight "because she has become an inner certainty as well as an outer predictability" (Erikson, 1950, p. 247).

Crisis II: Autonomy versus Shame and Doubt (18 Months to 3 Years)

Children's sense of trust in their mothers and in the world leads them to a realization of their own sense of self. Realizing they have a will, they assert themselves. Yet they realize the limitations of their abilities, and their continued dependency makes them doubt their ability to be autonomous, or self-directed. If they do not receive enough control from adults, they develop their own "precocious conscience" and with it, a sense of *shame*, or "rage turned against the self." Children who fail to develop

a sense of autonomy, either because of overly controlling or permissive parents, may become compulsive about controlling themselves. Fear of losing self-control may inhibit their self-expression and make them doubt themselves, be ashamed, and, consequently, suffer a loss of self-esteem.

The push toward autonomy is partly maturational, as children try to use developing muscles to do everything themselves—to walk, feed, and dress themselves; to eliminate when they feel like it; and generally to expand their boundaries. Language markedly enhances children's ability to make their wishes understood and, thus, increases their ability to be autonomous. During the first phase (crisis I), a mutual trust grew up between mother and child so that the child accepted doing what the mother wanted. Now, for the sake of the child's growth, this "agreement to agree" must be violated in the relentless quest to do everything without the mother's guidance or help. Parents provide a safe harbor, with safe limits, from which the child can set out and discover the world—and keep coming back to them for support.

The "terrible two's" are a normal manifestation of autonomy. This shift from a docile and agreeable baby to a terrible-tempered two-year-old, known as "negativism," is normal. Babies have to test the new notion that they are individuals, that they can make decisions, and that they have new, hitherto undreamed-of, powers.

THE INFANT IN THE FAMILY

Most developmental theories and research projects have been based on the premise that children grow up in a nuclear family with both mother and father but no other adult relatives; that the mother assumes primary, almost total

care of the child; and that the most important factor is the mother-baby bond. The almost universal implication is that a child's healthy emotional development is fostered almost entirely by good mothering. This emphasis on the mother's importance has been influenced by our societal patterns and, in turn, has reinforced these patterns. The father has been almost ignored by developmentalists. Says Wortis (1971):

It is scientifically unacceptable to advocate the natural superiority of women as child-rearers and socializers of children when there have been so few studies of the effects of male-infant or father-infant interaction on the subsequent development of the child [p. 739].

We also need to know much more about the influence on children of substitute parents. In our discussion of day care in Chapter 6, we will present some findings along these lines. This is an area where much more research needs to be done, in view of today's changing lifestyles. In 1979 about one out of every three mothers of children under 3 were in the labor force. These children are cared for in their mothers' absence by their fathers, other relatives, baby-sitters, day-care workers, and so forth. Children are reared in many ways—in the extended family; communally, as in Israel, Russia, and isolated spots in the United States; in two-parent families in which the father plays as large a role as the mother or a larger one; and in a combination of home and community (in the form of a group nursery). We need to know what constitutes good care in all these situations. In citing research, which usually is based on children in nuclear families, we have to keep an open mind, reevaluate constantly, add new knowledge to old, and be ready to modify former beliefs.

An infant's family life depends on many

factors: whether the pregnancy was planned and welcomed; both parents' personalities, life experiences, health, and ages; the family's financial circumstances; other adults and children in the home; and the infant's own temperament, health, birth order, and sex.

The way children are cared for right from birth depends not only on the parents' personalities, but on their own as well. Soon after birth, they develop their own styles of approaching people and situations, or what we call *temperament*.

In a longitudinal study that closely followed 231 New York children from infancy through adolescence, Thomas, Chess, and Birch (1968) identified nine aspects of temperament that appear to be inborn. These include activity level; regularity in biological functioning (hunger, sleep, elimination); readiness to accept new people and situations; adaptability to change; sensitivity to noise, light, and other sensory stimuli; mood (cheerfulness or unhappiness); intensity of responses; distractibility; and persistence. Babies vary enormously in all these characteristics, almost from birth, and they tend to continue to behave according to this initial behavioral style.

These apparently inborn traits have been found in a number of populations, including a group of Puerto Rican working-class children, a group of premature babies with a high incidence of neurological damage, children with congenital rubella, and children from an Israeli kibbutz. Other investigators have found them in populations studied at other centers in the United States and in foreign countries (Thomas & Chess, 1977).

When fifty-three same-sexed twin pairs were studied at 2 and at 9 months with respect to these nine attributes, identical twins turned out to be more alike than fraternal twins, showing that heredity plays a major role in the development of temperament (Torgersen & Kringlen, 1978).

Thomas and Chess (1977) identify three temperamental types: the easy child, the difficult child, and the slow-to-warm-up child.

The way children are cared for depends not only on their parents' personalities, but on their own as well. (Erika Stone/Peter Arnold, Inc.)

Nancy, for example, is an easy child. She wakes up happy: At a year of age, she wakes occasionally in the middle of the night, but instead of crying, she amuses herself with a musical crib toy. She has a very regular biological time clock and gets hungry and sleepy at preditable times. She usually smiles at strangers, accepts most new foods easily, accepts most frustration with little fuss, and adapts easily to new situations. About 40 percent of the New York Longitudinal Study (NYLS) sample are easy children.

Jason is a difficult child. He wakes up with a howl: His mouth opens to cry before his eyes open to see. His biological functions are irregular: His parents never know when he will wake with hunger, when he will move his bowels, or when he will get sleepy. He laughs loudly—and cries even louder, often bursting into a tantrum at the slightest frustration. He takes a long time adjusting to new routines, people, or situations. Difficult children account for about 10 percent of the NYLS sample.

Cindy is among the 15 percent of NYLS children considered slow-to-warm-up. She is mild in her responses, both positive and negative. She doesn't like most new situations—the first bath, the first taste of a new food, or the first meeting with a stranger—but if she is allowed to reexperience the new situations without pressure, she eventually becomes interested and involved.

Not all children fit neatly into one of these three groups, and even those who do sometimes behave uncharacteristically. Also, many children do show changes in behavioral style over the years, apparently reacting to special experiences or to parental handling.

By identifying a child's basic temperament, parents can adapt their care to the child's characteristics. Thus, the parents of a rhythmic child like Nancy can use a "demand" feeding schedule, letting her set the pace, while the parents of an irregular child like Jason do better to institute a more structured schedule based on both his needs and those of his parents. The parents of a child like Cindy can learn to give her time to adjust to new situations, without feeling embarrassed if she dissolves in tears when Uncle Harry walks into her room.

Thomas and Chess (1977) emphasize that "a constructive approach by the parents to the child's temperament does not mean an acceptance or encouragement of all this youngster's behavior in all situations" (p. 188). Parents can, though, do their best to help children work within the limits of their own temperaments. Instead of expecting a very active, distractible child to concentrate for a long period on his homework, they can encourage him to take a series of breaks until the task is finished. They can teach a mildly expressive child to speak up for what she wants.

Another trait babies seem to be born with is their feeling about close physical contact. Right from birth, some infants love being cuddled; some hate it. The "cuddlers" show that they like to be picked up, held closely, and stroked gently by pressing themselves against whoever picks them up and nestling in the adult's arms. The "noncuddlers" pull away and stiffen when they are picked up.

When Will (1979) looked at thirty-two infants and their mothers, first when the babies were 3 days old and then at 1 month, she found that these infants were sending out clear messages and that mothers tend to respond to their babies' desires. While some mothers, for example, picked up their "low-cuddly" infants a great deal, they were more likely to tickle and bounce them than to hold them gently, as they tried to find ways to be close to their babies in a way that would make the babies happy. These mother were just as attached to their children as were the mothers of the cuddly infants. This study shows how powerful human beings are from their earliest days: They have ways of showing what they want and—when their caretakers are sensitive—they influence the treatment they get.

When parents can recognize that a child behaves in a certain way not out of willfulness, hostility, laziness, or stupidity, but because of inborn temperament, they are less likely to respond with guilty, anxious, and hostile feelings and with impatient, inconsistent, or rigid behavior. Most of all, recognition of children's basic temperament relieves parents of a feeling of omnipotence—that they, and they alone, are responsible for turning them out in a certain mold.

AT 14 MONTHS

You are slowly making friends with Kelly, the 2½-year-old next door. Mostly you just stare at each other, but you do it from closer each day. You say something that sounds very much like ... Kelly .... and we are told that she looks outdoors and asks where you are.

Yesterday Kelly invited you to play in her wading pool. You loved it and played happily for about half an hour. Kelly was glad to have you as long as you didn't touch her toys.

Nancy Gordon

AT 23 MONTHS

Nancy is definitely an "easy" baby. As an infant, she was extremely happy and contented, she smiled readily and rarely fussed. Even though she is still friendly and good-natured, she has become more assertive. She demands company and resents being left alone. When she does not get her way, she hits out at her mother (or any other available object). She is very sensitive to a harsh or impatient tone of voice, which makes her cry bitterly. In one such episode, she looked up at her mother, said "Sassy cwy." (translation: Nancy is crying) and then went back to her tears.

S.O.

Jenny is a much more difficult baby than her older sister was. She cries to be taken out of bed when she's not sleepy, whereas Nancy would play happily with toys in her crib. She refuses coarse-textured food even when she's hungry, whereas Nancy opened her mouth like a baby bird for practically anything.

AT 19 MONTHS

Jenny's definite personality becomes more and more so. She's the proverbial ...little girl with a curl... who can be very playful, very cuddly, very adorable -- and can also be a lump of whining and temper. One trick for effect is throwing herself down on the floor when her feelings are hurt and bawling for as long as it takes to get some sympathy.

S.O.

FAMILY CONSTELLATION

Only Children

About 1 in 10 couples are now choosing to have only one child. What about the only child? How does she or he turn out, compared to children with brothers and sisters? Quite well, according to many different studies reported by Hawke and Knox (1978). Besides being bright and successful, only children tend to be self-confident, self-reliant, and resourceful; popular with other children; and just as likely to grow up to be successful in their jobs, their marriages, and their parenting experiences. A contradictory note is sounded, though, by Belmont (1977), whose analysis of the data on 19-year-old Dutch men showed that only children are less intellectually competent than firstborns and are at greater risk of psychiatric disorders than are children with brothers and sisters. As in so many other child development issues, the findings are far from clear-cut in the matter of the only child.

Sibling Influences

The great majority of children, of course, still do grow up in households that include older or younger brothers and sisters. How do these children influence each other? It's hard to tell, because there have been very few studies of what goes on between siblings in infancy, and studies of older children have yielded contradictory and inconclusive findings (Lamb, 1978). Some of the findings reported from these studies by Clarke-Stewart (1977) do seem logical from a commonsense point of view—that the closer in age siblings are, the more they influence each other; that a two- to four-year age spacing is the most stimulating as well as the most stressful; and that children with opposite sex siblings show more of the characteristics associated with that other sex.

SEX DIFFERENCES IN INFANCY

There are many differences between the sexes aside from the anatomical, and some begin to appear at the moment of conception. Some 120 to 170 males are conceived for every 100 females (Shettles & Rugh, 1971), but since males are more likely to be aborted or stillborn, only 106 are actually born for every 100 females (Hutt, 1972). More males die during the first few years (*Health United States 1975*, U.S. Department of Health, Education, and Welfare, 1976); and males remain more susceptible to many disorders (such as ulcers and viral infections) throughout life (Hutt, 1972). There are now only 95 males for every 100 females in the United States (U.S. Department of Health, Education, and Welfare, 1976).

Furthermore, the male develops more slowly from early fetal life into adulthood. At 20 weeks after conception, he is two weeks behind the female; at 40 weeks he is four weeks behind; and he continues to lag behind till maturity (Hutt, 1972).

Why are males more vulnerable? No one really knows. The X chromosome may contain certain genes that protect females against life stresses. If so, females (who have two X's, one from each parent) benefit from their more varied active genetic material. Or the Y chromosome may contain genes that are actually harmful. Since the female has no Y's, she cannot be hurt by them. Perhaps the difference lies in the different hormones secreted by male and female. The possibility has even been raised that some women become "allergic" to male fetuses (Renkonnen & Makela, 1962, from Singer et al., 1968). Whatever the basic cause of this male vulnerability, poverty makes it worse, with the sons in low-income families suffering the most (Birns, 1976).

Many studies have sought to detect other physiological and behavioral differences between baby boys and girls, but their findings have turned out to be contradictory and controversial. Research has been done on infants' activity levels, their responses to things they see as opposed to those they hear, how irritable they are, and how interested they are in exploring their surroundings versus staying close to a parent. A number of these studies have found some differences between the sexes, but the problem is that these findings have rarely held up when the studies have been repeated by the same or other investigators (Birns, 1976). After a careful literature review, Birns (1976) concludes that sex differences cannot be described clearly until after age 2:

At this time it seems safe to conclude that given a room full of infants, under 2 years of age, all dressed in yellow, it would be difficult if not impossible to identify males and females on the basis of activity level.

Clearly neither the presence or absence of early sex differences can be claimed with great conviction . . . it appears that behavioral sex differences, like beauty, might exist primarily in the eye of the beholder [p. 238].

Another set of studies has focused on the ways adults act toward infants. These findings are much clearer: A baby, even a newborn, who is identified as a female will be treated differently from one who is identified as a male. When strangers think a crying baby is a male, they are likely to see "him" as crying from anger; when they think the baby is female, they think "she" is afraid (Condry & Condry, 1974). Parents' reactions toward their babies are complicated by the parents' own sex, the age of the infant, and the personality of the infant, but there do seem to be some consistent findings. Baby boys get more attention in infancy, but the attention baby girls get is designed to make them smile more and be more social creatures (Birns, 1976).

SEX DIFFERENCES IN PARENT-INFANT INTERACTION

As soon as a new baby is born, the parents' first question is, "Is the baby normal and healthy?" In the same breath, they ask, "What is it?" Once they know whether it is a boy or a girl, they know a basic fact of the infant's identity that will have a major effect on the child's development. First, this fact of sex may determine the degree of pleasure with which the baby is welcomed into the family. Then, in virtually every society, boys and girls are apt to develop considerably differently in social roles and personality.

Within twenty-four hours after birth, parents—and especially fathers—tend to describe their baby daughters as little, beautiful, pretty, and cute and their baby sons as firm, strong, and alert—even when the male and female infants do not differ in height, weight, or Apgar scores (Rubin, Provenzano, & Luria, 1974). Parents apparently wrap their newborn infants in the cloaks of sex-role stereotypes carried to the delivery room.

Thinking differently of sons and daughters leads to treating them differently. After three months, mothers are more likely to babble back to baby daughters than to sons, thus reinforcing verbalization and perhaps paving the way for verbal superiority in females (Moss, 1967). Fathers talk to baby sons in "a sort of hail-baby-well-met style," saying things like, "Come here, you little nut," while talking to and treating daughters much more gently (Shenker, 1971). And mothers are more indulgent and warmer toward baby daughters than toward sons (Sears, Maccoby, & Levin, 1957).

Even in these "liberated" times adults treat baby girls and boys very differently. An interesting study was set up in which twenty-four 14-month-old children, half boys and half girls, were introduced to adults who did not know them, sometimes according to the sex they actually belonged to, sometimes as belonging to the other sex. When the adults were asked to play with the children (without knowing the real purpose of the study), they were more likely to encourage the "boys" in active play and more likely to choose a ball rather than a doll for the two of them to play with. The adults tended to talk more to the "girls," and to pick a doll or a bottle to play with. Interestingly, though, these children did not show sex differences themselves; the boys and girls played in very similar ways, even though they were treated differently by the adults (Frisch, 1977).

Thus, it appears that although sex differences may not be present at birth, environmental shaping does occur very early in life. The sex of the infant seems to be more important than behavioral and physiological differences in bringing about parental behaviors.

THE FAMILY'S ROLE IN PERSONALITY DEVELOPMENT

Traditionally, developmentalists have concentrated on studying the ways by which mothers affect their children's personality develop-

ment. Recently, however, our views of early socialization have been revolutionized as more and more observers recognize that babies grow up in a complex family system, which includes their fathers, their brothers and sisters, their grandparents, and other significant people as well. Lamb (1978, in Lerner & Spanier, 1978) concludes that it is impossible to explain infant sociopersonality development without including a discussion of the infant's family.

In most societies, mothers have been the primary caretakers of children, and most research on early bonds between children and their closest caregivers have focused on the mother-baby tie. Until more research considers other important relationships in babies' lives, we will have to discuss emotional development largely in terms of what we know about the bonds between mothers and children. We need to remember, though, that the relationship between a child and his or her primary caregiver, which plays a vital role in the child's emotional and social development, could also be formed with another significant person in the child's life. The "mother" could be a father, a grandparent, or a loving parent substitute.

In recent years, more attention has been paid to the ties between fathers and their children, and Lamb (1978) emphasizes the probability that both parents make important contributions to the baby's personality development. He has found that the infant seems to form attachments with both parents at about the same time, but at the end of the first year prefers the mother. This may be because in most families the mother is likely to be much more involved with the baby.

The influence that siblings exert on an infant's development has hardly been looked at. In one of the few observations of this relationship, Lamb (1978) found that even

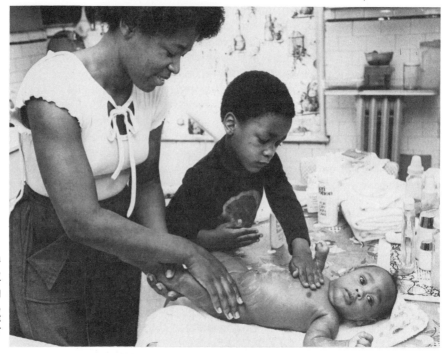

Babies grow up in a complex family system, which includes their parents, their brothers and sisters, their grandparents, and other significant people. (Erika Stone/Peter Arnold, Inc.)

though 18-month-old babies do not have much direct interaction with their preschool brothers and sisters, they watch them closely and imitate what they do. The way an older child adjusts to a new baby depends on many factors, one of them being the time and attention devoted by the father to make up for the mother's sudden involvement with the new baby (Lamb, 1978, in Lerner & Spanier, 1978). The more secure the older child feels, the less likely he or she is to resent the newcomer.

Let us see how babies affect and are affected by the people in their intimate worlds.

IMPRINTING

Newly hatched chicks will follow the first moving objects they see, whether this object is a member of their own species or not, and they become increasingly attached to these objects. Lorenz (1957) describes this behavior as *imprinting*, an innate, instinctual, rapid form of early learning that takes place during a critical period in an animal's life. Usually this first attachment is to the mother; but if the natural sequence is altered, other (often bi-

zarre) attachments can occur. In conducting his study, Lorenz waddled, honked, and flapped his arms—and got newborn ducklings to "love him like a mother."

Among higher animals such as goats and cows, certain standardized rituals occur right after birth. If these rituals are prevented or interrupted, neither mother nor baby will recognize each other, and no mother-child attachment will take place. The results for the baby are devastating—physical withering and death or abnormal, neurotic development (Moore, 1960; Scott, 1958; Blauvelt, 1955).

Can we extrapolate these findings to human beings? Since we do not rely on instinct as the lower animals do, we can usually overcome early adverse experiences. While the human mother-baby bond appears to be formed during the second half of the first year, its absence then may be overcome by later compensatory care. Children who are institutionalized at this time but adopted before the age of 2 recover both physically and mentally (Dennis, 1973). Most adopted children form close, loving ties with their adoptive parents and grow up well adjusted. The significance of animal studies on imprinting may be to determine just what behaviors do take place that help to form the mother-infant bond and, thus, to understand it better.

Harry and Margaret Harlow's studies among rhesus monkeys point to several important factors affecting the mother-baby bond. In one famous study, monkeys were separated from their mothers six to twelve hours after birth and were raised in the laboratory. The infants were put in cages with one of two surrogate "mothers"—one a plain cylindrical form of wire mesh, the other covered with terry cloth. Some monkeys were fed from bottles connected to the wire "mother"; others were "nursed" by the warm, cuddly, cloth ones.

When the monkeys were allowed to spend time with either "mother," they all spent more time clinging to the cloth surrogates—even if they were being fed totally by the wire ones. In an unfamiliar room, the babies of cloth surrogates showed more natural interest in exploring than did those raised by the wire substitutes, even when the appropriate "mothers" were there (Harlow & Zimmerman, 1959). The monkeys remembered the cloth surrogates better, too. After a year's separation, the cloth-raised monkeys eagerly ran to embrace the terry-cloth forms, whereas the wire-raised monkeys showed no interest in the wire forms (Harlow & Zimmerman, 1959).

The essential feature of the mother-infant relationship is not, then, the mere provision of nutrients; it includes the comfort provided by close bodily contact and, in monkeys, the satisfaction of an innate need to cling. But even the cloth-raised monkeys did not grow up normally. At maturity they turned out to be sexually inadequate and unable to mate normally (Harlow & Harlow, 1962). It is not surprising that a cloth dummy should not provide the same kind of stimulation as a normal live mother. One of the most important thrusts in modern psychology is to find out just what parents do to achieve normal emotional development in their children.

ATTACHMENT BETWEEN MOTHER AND CHILD

When Andrew's mother is in the room, he looks at her, smiles at her, talks to her, and crawls after her. When she leaves, he cries; when she comes back, he squeals with joy. When he is frightened or unhappy, he clings to her. Andrew has formed his first attachment to another person.

Attachment is an active, affectionate, reciprocal relationship specifically between two individuals, as distinguished from all other persons. The interaction between the two parties continues to reinforce and strengthen their bond.

Paradoxically, the stronger a child's attachment to the nurturing adult, the easier it is for him to leave her. Children who are secure in their attachments do not need to stay close to their mothers. Knowing that they have a safe base to return to, they are free to explore, returning periodically for reassurance. These initial attachments are the most intense between 7 and 16 months of age (Clarke-Stewart, 1977).

The ability to form intimate relationships later in life may well depend on the quality of the attachments that people forge in their infancy. Let us look, then, at some of the factors that influence the development of early attachment.

AT 14 MONTHS

It's lovely to go out on the lawn with you. I sit under the apple tree while you pick dandelions (heads only) and bring them to me to wear in my buttonholes. You wander about eight feet away from me, and then come running back and fling yourself into my arms. I love it.

Nancy Gordon

What the Mother Does

Attachment thrives when the mother is affectionate, attentive, and responsive to the baby's signals. The *quality* of care determines the strength of the attachment, rather than the amount of time spent with the infant. The intensity of a baby's attachment:

. . . does not seem to depend solely on how much [the mother] is available or even around, or if there are other people involved in the child's physical care; it does not matter how much time she spends in caretaking activities or how skillful she is at them. *It is the amount of time the mother spends in positive interaction with the child* [Clarke-Stewart, 1977, p. 30; emphasis added].

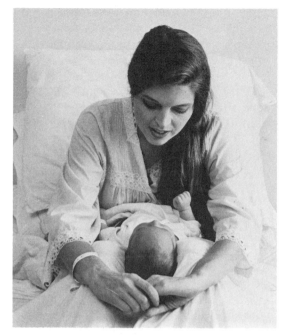

Maternal love is not an instinct; it takes time to develop. (Suzanne Szasz)

A mother's personality, her general attitudes toward children, and her present circumstances (including the kind of marriage she has and whether her husband is nurturant both to her and their baby) are all significant in the awakening of mother love. The sum total of her life experiences affect her ability to relate to others, including her own children. Many new mothers are guilt-ridden to realize that they feel no great surge of love when they first see their babies. But maternal love is not an instinct; it takes time to develop. Robson and Moss (1970) found that only about half of fifty-four new mothers said they had had positive feelings when they first saw their babies; only 13 percent identified those feelings as love; and 34 percent had no feelings at all. It took most mothers about three weeks to begin to love their babies. This love was strenghtened by the babies' behavior. As they smiled and looked at their mothers, their mothers' love grew. By the end of the third month, most of the mothers were strongly attached to their infants.

Experiences centering around parenthood itself may have special significance. Special advance preparation for labor and delivery, for example, seems to help mothers react more positively to their newborn infants. Doering and Enwistle (1975) found that prepared mothers are more likely to choose rooming-in, to breast-feed rather than bottle-feed, and to nurse for a longer period of time.

The nature of the hospital experience right after delivery also seems important. Of a group of twenty-eight mothers of full-term infants, half followed normal hospital routine. They saw their babies only briefly right after birth, then once again six to twelve hours later, and then for twenty- to thirty-minute feeding periods every four hours. The other half spent a total of sixteen hours more with their babies during the first three days. For one hour within three hours after birth, the mother had her naked baby in bed with her, and for each of the three first days, mother and baby spent an extra five hours together.

Researchers followed up the mother-baby pairs at the ages of 1 month, 1 year, and

2 years, and found differences large enough to indicate that early extended contact may help mother and child to forge a closer bond (Kennell, Jerauld, Wolfe, Chesler, Kreger, McAlpine, Steffa, & Klaus, 1974; Ringler, Kennell, Jarvella, Navojosky, & Klaus, 1975).

At 1 month, the extended-contact mothers fondled their babies more and engaged in more eye-to-eye contact. They said that they picked up their babies more often when they cried and that they were more likely to stay home with their infants. At 1 year, besides these same differences, the extended-contact mothers kissed their babies more and spent more time soothing them when they cried. At 2 years, a follow-up of ten of the original pairs showed that the extended-contact mothers seemed more sensitive to their children's needs to learn about the world. They asked their children twice as many questions as the other mothers did, taught them more, issued fewer commands, and spoke in a more mature and grammatical way (although the control mothers were more fluent with the adult interviewer).

Is it possible that the critical period for attachment that exists right after birth among cattle, sheep, and goats also applies to human beings? Rutter (1979) feels that the evidence for a critical period for mother-infant bonding is not fully supported by the data. "If the early hours are critical," he asks, "how is it that fathers or adoptive parents develop close ties to their children, which they do?" (p. 152). He suggests that *forced* separation because of hospital practices may be a crucial element in disturbing affectional ties on a short-term basis, and that this may also produce long-term effects in certain vulnerable individuals.

Even though all the evidence may not be in, it seems fairly certain that those few hours and days after delivery *are* important, even if any damage done during this time can be undone later on. What we have learned so far points to the need to reevaluate infant-care practices, particularly in the case of preterm and sick infants, who are often separated from their parents for long periods of time.

What the Baby Does

Far from considering infants the passive recipients of child-rearing practices, we now realize that they influence the people who take care of them. Virtually any activity on the baby's part that leads to a response from the adult is an attachment behavior: sucking, crying, smiling, clinging, choking, hiccupping, moving the body, changing the rhythm of breathing, sneezing, burping, looking into the mother's eyes, and even, soiling the diapers (Richards, 1971; Robson, 1967; Bowlby, 1958).

As early as the eighth week, babies initiate some of these behaviors more toward their mothers than toward anyone else. Their overtures are successful when their mothers respond warmly with frequent physical contact, freedom to explore, and delight (Ainsworth, 1969). The babies gain a sense of consequence for their own actions and a feeling of power and self-confidence in their ability to bring about results.

Ainsworth (1964), who studied attachment in 2- to 15-month-old African babies, noted four overlapping stages of attachment behavior during the first year:

1 Infants respond indiscriminately to anyone.

2 At about 8 to 12 weeks, babies cry, smile, and babble more to the mother than to anyone else, but they continue to respond to others.

3 At 6 or 7 months, babies show a sharply defined attachment to the mother, with a waning of friendliness to others.

4 Overlapping stage 3, babies develop an attachment to one or more familiar figures like the father or siblings. Fear of strangers usually appears between 6 to 8 months.

The baby's level of cognitive develop-

ment seems related to the ability to form attachments. Roe (1978) found that 3-month-old babies who babbled much more to their mothers than to a stranger (indicating that they could tell the difference between the two and acted differently toward them) did better on intelligence tests at 3 years and at 5 years of age than did other children who had not "talked" more at the age of 3 months.

HOW A BABY'S PERSONALITY AFFECTS ATTACHMENT

The parent-child relationship is like the marital tie. Yet parents can't choose their infants as they choose their mates. Brian's lively, exuberant parents, for example, consider their quiet, shy son somewhat mamby-pamby, while Polly's quiet parents are driven to distraction by their bouncy daughter. Parents react differently to their different children, depending on the youngster's personalities and how well they mesh with their own.

Schaffer and Emerson (1964) studied "cuddlers" (babies who enjoy physical contact) and "noncuddlers" (who usually try to break free). Nineteen of thirty-four infants were cuddlers, nine were noncuddlers, and nine were in the middle. The noncuddlers sought visual rather than physical contact with their mothers. They liked being swung, kissed, and tickled, but they did not want their movements restrained by close physical contact. The babies' attachments were judged by their reactions to being left alone or with other people, or being put down. At 12 months the noncuddlers had formed less intense attachments, but by 18 months there were no differences between noncuddlers and the other infants. Visual contact may be at the root of human sociability, along with physical contact.

SEX DIFFERENCES IN ATTACHMENT

Sex differences showed up in the attachment behavior of seventeen pairs of opposite-sex twins aged 11.8 to 15 months (Brooks & Lewis, 1974). The girls looked at and stayed near their mothers more often than did their brothers. Such differences may result from differential reinforcement of sex-stereotyped behaviors. Mothers may encourage their daughters to be closer to them while encouraging independence in their sons.

STRANGER ANXIETY

What has happened to Vicky? She used to be such a friendly baby, smiling at and going to strangers, continuing to coo happily as long as someone—anyone—was around. At 8 months, she seems like a different baby. She howls when a new person approaches her or when her parents try to leave her with a sitter. She has simply become astute enough to recognize the difference between people she

AT 15 MONTHS

You say "hi" to everyone, especially when they aren't listening.

Last night we had dinner on our front lawn with our next-door neighbors. You took a real liking to Rick, Kelly's father, and finally asked him to pick you up. You stayed happily in his arms for 45 minutes! Then we went into their house, where you made yourself at home, turning on their dishwasher, wandering in and out of their bedrooms and eating other people's food.

You are suddenly extremely independent, and it makes dealing with you much more difficult. You used to stay within ten feet of a parent at all times when we were outside. Now you just take off, especially if there are other children to watch.

Nancy Gordon

Most babies become somewhat wary of
strangers once they have learned to tell
them apart from familiar people.
(Suzanne Szasz)

knows and those she doesn't know. After a
few months, she will go back to being the
basically friendly person she had been. Some
feel that stranger anxiety is a signal that
attachment has occurred and that it is a
normal aspect of development.

Stranger anxiety may be normal, but it is
not universal. The number of adults a baby is
familiar with influences the degree of stranger
anxiety. Babies who are raised around few
adults show more anxiety than those raised
around a greater number (Schaffer & Emerson, 1964); and those raised by many adults,
as on a kibbutz, don't show stranger anxiety at
all (Spiro, 1958). Parents' behavior is important, too. The more suppressive and critical a
mother is of her baby, the less responsive the
baby will be to her. And the more the baby
responds to the mother, the less he or she will
respond to strangers (Beckwith, 1972).

While most babies become somewhat
wary of strangers once they have learned to

tell them apart from the people in their lives,
they are not necessarily afraid of new people.
They tend to be more afraid when their
attachments to their own caregivers are insecure, probably because they feel they have no
one to turn to for protection if the new people
prove dangerous (Lamb, 1978).

Babies who sit in front of television sets in
the first 3 months, who are close to radios and
music boxes, and who have toys shaken in
front of them are less likely to fear strangers
later on, probably because they are used to
new situations (Moss, Robson, & Pederson,
1969).

Not all infants fear strangers—even after
they have reached the age when stranger
anxiety is common. Sometimes a child will be
afraid of a stranger in one context but not in
another. A great deal of this fear seems to be
situational. For example, what is the baby
doing at the time? While 40 percent of a group
of 1-year-olds reacted negatively when
picked up by a stranger, so did 25 percent
when picked up by their mothers (Klein &
Durfee, 1975). Babies may react against
being disturbed in whatever they are doing.
Then, too, how does the stranger approach?
Does he or she try to attract the baby's
attention from a distance or swoop down on
the unsuspecting child? Children react more
negatively to the second kind of approach,
when they are taken by surprise. The presence or absence of the baby's parents also
affects the child's response. Children generally accept the approach of a stranger more
easily when the company of a parent makes
them feel secure.

Thomas and Chess (1977) found that
stranger anxiety at or after 6 months of age is
highly variable. Some children get very upset
for a long time, some only mildly and briefly,
and some don't react at all negatively to
strangers. Much depends on the baby's own

temperament. Easy children show little or no negative reaction, while difficult and slow-to-warm-up children become more disturbed and stay that way for a longer time.

Who the stranger is has an effect. Very young babies often show a delighted interest in somewhat older children. This recognition of a "soul mate" in another child has been confirmed by Lewis and Brooks (1974) and Brooks and Lewis (1976). In two different experiments, they presented infants from 7 months to 2 years with a variety of strangers, one at a time; a 5-year-old girl, a 5-year-old boy, a female and a male adult of the same size, a male adult (5 feet 6 inches) and a female adult (5 feet 3 inches), and a female adult who, as a midget, was the same size as the 5-year-old children.

Infants as young as 7 months of age smiled at the children, whereas they frowned and moved away from the adults. They exhibited the same reaction toward the midget as toward the full-size adults except that they stared more at the midget, indicating that babies must get cues as to age other than size. In these studies the babies reacted the same toward both children and adults of both sexes. Other studies, which have shown that infants fear strange men more than strange women, have used taller men. So in this regard, height may be more relevant than sex. Like most other phenomena involving people's reaction to one another, stranger anxiety is complex and cannot be explained in a simplistic way.

Kagan (1979) notes that usually attachment occurs and separation anxiety emerges sometime between 8 and 12 months of age—at just about the same time babies understand the concept of the permanent object. He suggests that it is the cognitive ability to recall stored information that enables these emotional events to take place. In other words, Robin becomes attached to her father because—even in his absence—she remembers the warmth and good feelings she experiences when he is with her. She cries when her father leaves the room because she remembers what it was like when he was there—but cannot yet predict what it will be like when he is *not* there. She is at a stage of cognitive development when she tries to anticipate her future—but is not yet able to.

This cognitive interpretation of separation anxiety helps to explain why it is rare for babies in many different cultures studied to show distress upon being left with an unfamiliar person or in an unfamiliar place before the age of 7 months; why the likelihood of their being disturbed rises to a peak at 13 to 15 months; and why it declines after that until it becomes quite rare by the age of 3 years (Kagan, 1979).

MATERNAL DEPRIVATION

What happens to infants who are deprived of their mothers early in life? It all depends. It depends on the reason the child and the mother are apart, on the kind of care the child receives from other people, on the child's age and maturity, and on what the child's family relationships are like both before and after the separation.

For the past thirty-five years or so, much of the child-care literature has been influenced by the writings of a handful of investigators who pointed out the devastating effects that institutionalization can have for children's physical, intellectual, and emotional development. These observations did a great deal to cut down on the use of large institutions and to increase foster family care for children who had to be away from their parents. Yet these same findings have formed the basis for many unwarranted assumptions about briefer separations between mothers and their children, such as those undergone every day by the children of working parents.

What, then, do we know about the results of separating children from their mothers? Let us look at several different kinds of separation.

Institutionalization

When orphanages were the most popular way of taking care of children whose parents were dead or unable to care for them, 31.7 to 90 percent of the babies in them died in the first year (Spitz, 1945). We know that children who were institutionalized for long periods of time often showed drops in intellectual functioning and also suffered from major psychiatric problems.

The devastating effect of institutionalizing healthy children for long periods of time is termed *hospitalism*, as opposed to *hospitalization*, which refers to the hospital care of an ill child (Spitz, 1945). Spitz (1946, 1945) compared 134 institutionalized babies under age 1 with 34 home-reared children. At the end of the first year, the control children and those in one institution (labeled "Nursery") were well-developed and normal. Those in "Foundling Home" had "spectacularly deteriorated."

How did these institutions differ? The babies in Nursery were the offspring of delinquent girls, many of whom were emotionally disturbed or retarded. Those in Foundling Home came from a variety of backgrounds, many quite favorable. The most significant difference between the homes revolved around the amount of personal attention the babies got. In Nursery they all received full-time care from their own mothers or from individual full-time substitutes. In Foundling Home eight children shared one nurse. The Foundling Home children were retarded in height and weight and much more susceptible to disease, often fatally so. Their developmental quotients, which had started out at 124, sank to 75 by the end of the first year and plummeted to 45 by the end of the second. Spitz's studies pointed out the urgency of providing foster care that approached "good mothering" as closely as possible:

Spitz's work hastened the trends toward use of foster homes rather than institutions and toward much earlier adoptions; it obviously made no sense to follow the common practice

of the 1930's and 1940's of delaying adoption until a better IQ determination could be made (for purposes of matching infant and adoptive parents) if the delay itself resulted in severe damage to the very IQ that was to be studied [Stone et al., 1973, p. 754].

The quality of care within an institution can make a world of difference to the children in it. Other studies have confirmed Spitz's findings that "children in well run children's homes have no impairment of general intelligence" (Rutter, 1979, p. 151). The crucial factor appears to be a variety of active, meaningful experiences offered to the children, which include a great deal of conversation.

There is, however, another major problem associated with institutional care. Children admitted to institutions—even good ones—in the first two years of life, who are not adopted till after the age of 4, are likely to have trouble making friends and forming close relationships. This does not happen so often to children institutionalized later in childhood. Separation from the parents does not seem to be the cause, since children placed in foster homes are less likely to have this problem. Rutter (1979) suggests that:

The lack of opportunity to form early emotional bonds to particular individuals constitutes the damaging factor. Children can cope with several caretakers, but they seem to suffer if they experience a large number of changing caretakers. If institutions could ensure personal caretaking from a limited number of adults who remained responsible for the same individual children over the first few years of life, perhaps the social damage could be avoided. In practice this has proved difficult to arrange, and institution-reared children continue to remain at risk [p. 151].

Enriching the Environment of Maternally Deprived Children

Infants who are hospitalized or placed in some other kind of institution usually show a drop in responsiveness until they return home. Clarke-Stewart (1977) suggests that this seeming decline in intellectual ability may not be a real decrease, but a reflection of the fact that babies are less motivated to perform for strangers than for their parents. They may not be stimulated enough in the institution, or they may be reacting to the unfamiliar people and place. Yet when substitute caregivers give babies a great deal of attention, they can overcome this effect. Children over 6 months of age respond best to a particular individual to whom they can become attached as a "substitute mother" (Clarke-Stewart, 1977).

In one study of institutionalized babies, the psychologist herself served as substitute mother. For 7½ hours a day, 5 days a week, for 8 weeks, Rheingold (1956) played with, fed, diapered and otherwise mothered a group of eight 6-month-old infants. Eight control infants got the usual institutional care—adequate attention to physical needs from a variety of caretakers. After two months. the mothered babies differed dramatically from the control children and were much more likely to smile and babble to the experimenter and other adults. A year and a half later, the experimental babies still vocalized more than the control infants, but there were no other differences between them. All were now in foster or adoptive homes. The period of enrichment might have been too brief to bring about lasting changes, or the individual care all the babies eventually received in their new homes may have made up for the institutionalization.

A classic study of enrichment yielded striking long-term results (Skeels, (1966; Skeels & Dye, 1939). Thirteen apparently retarded 2-year-olds were moved from an orphanage to an institution for mentally retarded young adults who doted on the babies and spent a lot of time playing with, talking to, and training "their" children. As adults, all thirteen were functioning in the community and were married, with normal children of their own. Four had attended college. By contrast, a control group of twelve youngsters who had stayed in the orphanage until later placement had a much lower average IQ, and four were still in institutions.

Old people in a foster grandparent program (Saltz, 1973) rocked, fed, walked, and talked to a group of eighty-one institutionalized babies for four hours a day, five days a week. The adults read stories, played games, talked with, and taught skills to older children. After four years of foster grandparenting, the children had gained considerably in IQ and social competence, compared with a control group. Thus, individual attention from a warm, affectionate person can compensate considerably for the absence of a close mother-child relationship.

Hospitalization

Even short-term hospital stays can, of course, be disturbing to small children. Bowlby (1960) found that hospitalized 15- to 30-month-old infants went through three fairly well-defined stages of what Bowlby termed *separation anxiety*. In the *protest stage*, infants actively try to get their mothers back by crying, shaking the crib, and throwing themselves about; they continually expect their mothers to return. In the *despair stage*, infants diminish active movements, cry monotonously or intermittently, and become withdrawn and inactive; because they are so quiet, it is often assumed that they have accepted the situation positively. In the *detachment stage*, children accept care from a succession of nurses and are willing to eat, play with toys, smile, and be sociable; when their mothers visit, the children remain apathetic and even turn away. Children between 6 months and 4 years are most likely to react this way, but even within this age range not all children show this degree of disturbance (Rutter, 1979).

When a child needs to be hospitalized, a number of steps can be taken to reduce the stress of separation from family and home. The policy in many hospitals of allowing a parent to stay with the child, even sleeping overnight, helps diminish a child's fear of a strange place and frightening procedures (Olds, 1975). Daily visiting from other family members, having the same few people care for the child in the hospital, and keeping to the child's familiar routines as much as possible all help to allay the strangeness in the situation (Rutter, 1979).

Providing happy separations ahead of time can take some of the sting out of a hospital visit, too. Children who are used to being left with grandparents or sitters, or who have stayed overnight at friends' houses, are less likely than other children to be upset by having to go to the hospital (Stacey, Dearden, Pill, & Robinson, 1970).

Temporary separations

Many studies have focused on brief separations between mothers and infants. In general, when a mother walks out of a room where her baby is playing happily and shuts the door behind her, the baby will begin to cry and stop playing (Ainsworth & Bell, 1970). Other experiments, in which the mother leaves without shutting a door, have found that young children often continue to play contentedly after their mothers have walked away (Corter, Rheingold, & Eckerman, 1972; Anderson, 1972). And when it's the baby who wanders away from the mother, he or she usually does so cheerfully (Rheingold & Eckerman, 1970).

Corter (1976) examined brief separations in forty 10-month-old babies. He found that the babies accepted separation from the mother very well, whether she walked away from the baby or the baby crawled away from her. In fact, these infants left their mothers' sides to play with an assortment of appealing toys much sooner than they left the toys to go to their mothers. Babies who could see their

mothers sitting in another room stayed away from them to play with the toys almost twice as long as those whose mothers were not visible. in either case, though, distress was rare. It's possible that the babies in the study accepted the mother's departure so well because of the way she left—without any worried good-byes and without closing a door.

Total replacement of a child's primary caretakers and familiar environment in an institutional setting can produce severe emotional disturbance, at least on a short-term basis. But Rutter (1971) concluded, after studying children who had experienced various types and lengths of parental separation, that "children can be separated from their parents for quite long periods in early childhood with surprisingly little in the way of long-term ill effects" (p. 238).

Children who are separated from *one* parent for at least four consecutive weeks are no more likely to develop any kind of psychiatric or behavioral disorder than are those who have never been separated (Rutter, 1971). It does not matter how old a child was when the separation occurred nor which parent is absent. Children who are separated from *both* parents are more likely to be disturbed, but it is not only the *fact* of separation that's important but the *reason* behind it. When the separation results from family discord or deviance, children are four times as likely to show antisocial behavior than when the separation results from vacation or physical illness. Children who are separated from both parents are more likely to become disturbed when the parents' marriage is rated "very poor" than when it is rated "good" or "fair." Some separation experience may actually be beneficial, since "children used to brief separations of a happy kind are less distressed by *unhappy* separations such as hospital admission" (Rutter, 1971, p. 237).

WORKING MOTHERS In general, the children of mothers who work outside the home turn out just as well as those whose work is homemaking and child care. Good day care does not seem to interfere with babies' attachments to their parents nor with adjustment in other areas of life. For more detailed discussions of day care and the effects of parental employment, see the discussions in Chapters 6 and 9.

Death and divorce

We know very little about the effects of death and divorce on infant personality development. Most of the research that exists in this area pertains to older children, and so we will consider these topics at greater length in Chapters 9 and 18.

FATHER-INFANT INTERACTION

Most of the psychological literature about babies' emotional development has focused on the bond between babies and their mothers. The father has been a shadowy figure in the background. In recent years, however, the father-baby bond has received more attention.

Greenberg and Morris (1974) interviewed a group of new fathers and found that almost all of them had formed a close attachment with their babies by the third day after birth. Both members of the pair contributed to this attachment. These authors call the father's attachment to his child *engrossment*, a term that includes more than the father's involvement with his baby; it also includes a sense of the infant's assuming large proportions for the father and the father's sense of self-esteem that grows from this bond.

Soon after their babies' births, these fathers enjoyed looking at their babies and considered them attractive. They felt drawn to pick up and feel their infants, and they perceived their children as distinctly unique and perfect. The babies contribute to this bond simply by doing the things all normal babies do. As they open their eyes in the father's presence, grasp his fingers, or move in his arms, they transmit a sense of their own vitality and inspire responsiveness in the father. Pedersen and Robson (1968) rated forty-five young middle-class fathers on time, care, playing, attitudes, emotional investment, and other aspects of their relationships with their babies. The infants' attachment to their fathers was judged by the babies' smiling, babbling, and general excitement upon seeing the father. These fathers were greatly involved with their infants. Three-fourths of the babies, at 8 months and again at 9½ months, showed real attachment to their fathers. The boys' attachment seemed related to the fathers' involvement, but not the girls'.

Not all fathers, of course, become *engrossed* with their babies, especially in early infancy. Rebelsky and Hanks (1972) went into homes and made six 24-hour tapes of father-baby interaction for each of a group of ten lower-middle-class to upper-middle-class fathers of 2-week-old to 3-month-old babies. These fathers spoke very little to their infants: The average father spent only 37.7 seconds in

AT 1 YEAR

You love riding on Daddy's shoulders. When he goes fast you let go and flap your hands as you speed around the house. Lately he has held your feet and turned you upside down. It delights you much more when he does it than when I do. It's a Daddy game.

AT 21 MONTHS

Yesterday your father was taking a shower. You were playing in the bedroom, waiting for him to finish. Daddy called out, "Is there an Elizabeth out there?" You calmly answered, "No."

Nancy Gordon

Today, the trend is for fathers to become more involved with their children right from the start. (Photos by Erika Stone/Peter Arnold, Inc.)

a day doing things with or for his baby, and the most devoted spent less than 10.5 minutes a day. At first, these men spent more time talking to their baby daughters, but by 3 months the sons were getting more attention. By the end of the study, the fathers were spending less time talking to their babies than they had at the beginning.

So there are still many fathers who act as if parenting is "woman's work." The trend in society today, however, is for fathers to become more closely involved with their children, right from the start. We would think that those men who devote the most amount of time to their children would have the closest relationships with them, but, surprisingly, research shows that this is not always so.

Kotelchuck (1973), for example, studied the strength of babies' ties to their fathers. He observed 144 boys and girls at ages 6, 9, 12,

15, 18, and 21 months. Each child sat in an unfamiliar playroom surrounded by toys as his or her mother and father and a stranger took turns leaving the room. The 6- and 9-month-old babies did not protest anyone's departure; infants 12 months and older protested the departure of both parents but not of the stranger. Their responses to both parents were very similar. Just over half were more likely to go to their mothers when both parents were present, a quarter preferred the father, and the others showed no preference. The extent of the fathers' involvement in caretaking did not seem related to their children's behavior, suggesting that neither "quantity of interaction nor specific caretaking practices are the critical issues in the formation of a relationship" (Kotelchuck, 1973, p. 8).

What, then, determines the strength of father-child attachment? The simple truth is that we do not yet know, but that time is probably not the crucial element. Lamb (1978) points out that babies have very different kinds of experiences with their fathers than with their mothers. Whereas the mothers are gentler in their play, concentrating on games like pat-a-cake and peek-a-boo, fathers are more likely to toss their babies up in the air and play more unusual games. Furthermore, when mothers hold their babies, they are likely to be taking care of them; when fathers pick them up, it is usually to play with them.

The difference between mother-infant and father-infant interactions is important, for it implies that an infant shares different experiences with each parent and consequently (if we presume that different experiences are causally related to different outcomes) that mothers and fathers have independent influences on their children's development [Lamb, 1978, p. 39].

The nature of relationships between human beings is so complex, with so many different facets in different situations, that it is extremely difficult to draw clear-cut conclusions about them. Nowhere is this truer than in the father-infant relationship. While it is very clear that babies do form strong attachments to their fathers, it is not always so clear why—and just how the strength of this attachment compares with that to the mother.

Cohen and Campos (1974) found that babies aged 10, 13, and 16 months were more attached to their mothers than to their fathers, but more attached to their fathers than to strangers. When both parents were present, the children were twice as likely to go to their mothers as to their fathers; they took less time to get to their mothers; and they spent more time close to their mothers. A few of the children, though, seemed closer to their fathers. When only one parent was present, the children responded similarly to either one, staying close to the mother 82 percent of the time, close to the father 80 percent, and acting similarly to both: clinging, asking to be picked up, crying at their absence.

On the other hand, Lamb (1977) found that babies in the second year of life preferred their fathers over their mothers at home, but in a laboratory setting showed no preference for either parent. They were more likely to touch, reach out to, fuss to, and ask to be picked up by their parents than by a strange visitor, but, surprisingly, they were more likely to smile, talk, look, laugh, and offer toys to the visitor than to either parent! When babies were alone with either parent, there was more interaction than when both parents were present. This finding would seem to suggest to parents that both mother and father should plan to spend time alone with their babies if they want to form closer attachments to them.

How does a father's presence or absence affect his baby's development? Pedersen, Rubenstein, and Yarrow (1973) studied fifty-four poor and lower-middle-class black babies and found that the more attention a father pays to his baby son, the brighter, more alert,

To study friendship in infancy, researchers measure the frequency with which infants approach, touch, talk to, look at, or give things to other babies. (Ron Siguyama/Editorial Photocolor Archives)

more inquisitive, and happier that baby is likely to be at 5 or 6 months. No similar results were found for girls.

We see, then, that babies form an active and close relationship with their fathers, and fathers are much more important to their infants than was realized previously. Our new awareness of a father's importance comes at a time when more men are assuming larger roles in caring for their children. Burgeoning interest in the father's role will probably bring about new theoretical perspectives on father-child relationships as theorists reckon with the presence of a baritone voice in the nursery.

FRIENDSHIP IN INFANCY

It seems fanciful to talk about friendship at a time when people can't even speak to confide their troubles or share their joys, can't take up hobbies, can't borrow money, or do most of the other things we associate with friends. And yet human beings are social animals, whose friends become significant factors in their lives throughout the life span. A growing number of researchers have begun to explore the impact of friends on our lives, and some of them are reaching into the cradle to look at the very beginnings of friendship.

The study of friendship falls in the field of *social cognition*, or the consideration of social relations and events. This area of study also includes role-taking ability, moral judgment, intentionality, and the child's conception of other people. Studies in social cognition represent an area in which two schools of thought come together: the Piagetian perspective of children as active participants and determiners of their own development, and social learning theories that see children as people who respond to social experiences and other aspects of their environments.

AT 13 MONTHS

WE spent four days of last week at your grandparents' house, where you ran them ragged. They seemed to love it. You learned to play to an audience more than ever. If anyone appears to let their attention wander from you, you certainly remind them of your presence. You now yell at people you can't see but can hear in another room.

You even developed a phony grin and a phony laugh for your grandparents. I wish you didn't feel they were necessary.

Nancy Gordon

To study friendships, researchers use a number of techniques for learning about relationships and group structures known by the general term of *sociometry*. For example, they measure the frequency with which infants approach, touch, talk to, look at, or give things to other babies.

What have we learned about friendship in infancy? For one thing, we are finding that young babies are fascinated by others like themselves. Eckerman and Whatley (1977) brought together forty-four pairs of babies who had never met before—either 10 to 12 months of age or 22 to 24 months. The babies playfully reached out toward each other—poking, patting, rubbing, and hitting in the same way that they played with their mothers. They did more of this when there were no toys around, but when there were toys, the babies handed them back and forth to each other and played with them more or less together.

Some people, of course, are more sociable than others. And this shows up from a very early age. Among a group of five 8- to 10-month-old babies in a day-care center,

Lee (1973) was able to identify a most and a least popular child. The baby whom the others approached most consistently was nonassertive; she responded to the other babies in a way that reciprocated the attentions they paid her. The baby whom the others avoided most consistently was described as "almost asocial in his behavior." He acted very differently toward the other children, depending on whether or not he had initiated the contacts with them.

Young children vary in their interest in being with other people, and their patterns of friendliness hold up to some degree over time. Children who at the age of 2½ are friendly, involved with other children, and able to cope with aggressive youngsters are sociable at the age of 7½. At 7½, patterns of sociability vary across sex lines, with sociable girls usually playing with one other girl and sociable boys playing with groups of boys (Waldrop & Halverson, 1975).

What makes some babies friendlier than others? Some aspects of sociability, such as the readiness to accept new people, the adaptability to change, and a baby's usual mood, appear to be inherited traits of temperament (Thomas, Chess, & Birch, 1968). Babies are also influenced by the attitudes of those around them. When Stevenson and Lamb (1979) looked at forty middle-class 1-year-olds and their mothers, they found that sociable infants had sociable mothers. They also found that sociable infants scored higher on intelligence tests than did less sociable babies, indicating that a baby who feels comfortable with a strange tester may perform better than a baby who may have the same basic level of intelligence but is uncomfortable with an unfamiliar person. Once more, we see the interrelationship between our emotional and intellectual functioning.

One measure of friendship is comfort given to someone in distress. Even very young children commonly reach out to someone else: Between 10 and 12 months of age, babies often cry when they see another child in tears; by 13 or 14 months, they pat or hug the crying child; and by 18 months, they offer specific kinds of help like holding out a toy to replace a broken one or giving a Band-Aid to someone with a cut finger (Yarrow, 1978). This desire to reach out to other people is one more measure of the child's development toward emotional maturity.

AT 2 YEARS

This morning when I picked you up, my elbow joint cracked and I said, "Ouch, my elbow cracked." You said, "We'll fix it with tape after a while."

Nancy Gordon

When Mueller and Lucas (1975) looked at the development of very early friendship, they noted three stages in the way young children relate to each other. In the *first stage*, children's contacts are usually *object-centered*. Rachel, 14 months old, will show interest in a toy train, say, and Daniel, 16 months old, will come over to play—not with Rachel—but with the train. This can be the beginning of a beautiful friendship, because even though the children are not interacting with each other, they are close enough so that they can learn a little bit about another child. They often imitate each other in this stage. After Daniel hears Rachel sounding the train's whistle, he does it, too, without looking at Rachel at all.

In stage 2, children *try to get responses from each other*. So Rachel may offer a toy to Daniel, and Daniel laughs. She keeps offering the toy, and he keeps laughing. They both keep doing what they're doing to get the same reaction from the other.

By the time Rachel and Daniel are in the *third stage*, they are now *capable of switching*

roles, so after Daniel has received a toy from Rachel, he may now offer it back to her. Or after Rachel has been chasing Daniel, she may suddenly turn and expect him to chase her. They can reverse roles in their play, indicating their ability to assume the viewpoint of another person.

Despite their early overtures toward other children, infants and toddlers still do most of their socializing with adults—their parents and other people who care for them. Not until they reach the age of 3 or 4 are they interacting as much with other children as they are with adults, as Finkelstein, Dent, Gallagher, and Ramey (1978) found in a sample of children who attended a day-care center.

One reason why children don't form such close relationships before this time may be because many families don't provide opportunities for children under 12 to 18 months to spend much time with other children of the same age. Both researchers and parents alike may underestimate their ability to form such relations (Lewis, Young, Brooks, & Michalson, 1975). If we expect very young children to be egocentric and incapable of forming relationships with other children, we may put such constraints on their "social lives" that they meet our expectations. Yet Mueller and Lucas's (1975) findings that children who are still in the sensorimotor stage are capable of complex interactions with each other may lead us to take a new look at the friendship potential in very young children.

SUMMARY

1 Considerable disagreement exists over the nature of emotions and emotional development in infants. Behaviorist James B. Watson believed that infants are born with three emotions (love, rage, and fear) and that emotional development is a conditioning procedure. K. M. B. Bridges, another early researcher, claimed that infants have only one emotion—excitement—which gradually differentiates into a wide range of emotional manifestations. Today, both theories are regarded as limited interpretations of infants' emotions. Recent research indicates that differentiation between crying and smiling responses begins early in life.   **2**   Two major theories of personality development are the psychosexual theory of Sigmund Freud (which stresses biological and maturational factors) and the psychosocial theory of Erik Erikson (which emphasizes cultural and societal influences).   **3**   According to Freud's psychosexual theory of personality development, an infant (birth to 1½ years) in the *oral stage* receives pleasure and gratification through oral stimulation. From 1½ to 3 years, a child in the *anal stage* receives pleasurable stimulation from movement of the bowels. During early infancy, a baby's *id* operates on the pleasure principle, striving for immediate gratification. When gratification is delayed, the *ego* develops and operates on the reality principle, striving to find acceptable ways to obtain gratification. Events during these and later periods are thought to influence adult personality.   **4**   According to Erikson's psychosocial theory, an infant (birth to 1½ years) experiences the first in a series of eight crises that influence personality development throughout life. The first critical alternative focuses on *basic trust versus basic mistrust*. Like the Freudian oral stage, the resolution of this crisis is influenced greatly by events surrounding the feeding situation and by the quality of the mother-child relationship. From 1½ to 3 years, an infant faces the second crisis: *autonomy versus shame and doubt*. Parental methods of dealing with children greatly affect the resolution of this crisis.   **5**   Individual personality differences among infants result in part from their sex, their temperament, and their family size and birth order.   **6**   The mother-infant relationship and factors that affect it have received theoretical and empirical attention that focuses on *attachment* and *stranger anxiety*.   **7**   Studies of maternal deprivation—generally conducted among institutionalized orphans—point to the need for consistent parenting in a stimulating environment. Attempts at enriching orphan's environments have resulted in remarkable gains for the children's emotional and intellectual development.   **8**   Although the father's role has received less empirical attention than the mother's, studies indicate that a father-child attachment also develops early in life.   **9**   Recent research indicates that infants are remarkably social creatures who react to others like themselves.

SUGGESTED READINGS

Chess, S., Thomas A., & Birch, H. G.   *Your child is a person: a psychological approach to parenthood without guilt.* New York: Viking, 1965. A very readable book that translates the findings of the New York Longitudinal Study into practical words of wisdom and reassurance for parents. The major premise is that children differ temperamentally from birth and that parents will be most successful if they take these differences into account.

Evans, R. I.   *Dialogue with Erik Erikson.* New York: Dutton, 1967. An intriguing discussion with Erik Erikson, including his comments on his theory of psychosocial development.

Fraiberg, S. H. *The magic years*. New York: Scribner's, 1959. A delightful classic written by a psychoanalyst that describes in warm, insightful terms how children mature from birth to age 6.

Klaus, M., & Kennell, J. *Maternal-infant bonding*. St. Louis: Mosby, 1976. A review of research on the formation of the mother-infant bond by leading researchers in that area.

Lamb, M. (Ed.) *The role of the father in child development*. New York: Wiley, 1976. A collection of articles by leading researchers in the area of father-child interaction. Includes discussion of the role of the father in the child's moral, cognitive, social, and personality development.

Lewis, M., & Rosenblum, L. (Eds.) *The origins of fear*. New York: Wiley, 1974. A collection of papers dealing with the development of fear in human beings and animals; for advanced students.

Rutter, M. *Maternal deprivation reassessed*. New York: Penguin, 1972. A review of evidence about the effects of different types of maternal deprivation (e.g., short- or long-term).

Schaffer, R. *Mothering*. Cambridge: Harvard University Press, 1977. An analysis of "mothering" which emphasizes the infant's role as an active participant in mother-infant interchanges and the importance of sensitivity by the mother when she interacts with her infant.

Spock, B. *Baby and child care*. New York: Pocket Books, 1976. The "Bible" for millions of parents and still the most complete easy-to-read guide to all aspects of children's day-by-day development. From this guide you can get a picture of what children are like from infancy to adolescence. It includes the behavioral problems and physical disorders that are common to children.

Stern, D. *The first relationship: Infant and mother*. Cambridge: Harvard University Press, 1977. A look at how mothers' interactions with infants influence what the infant learns about the nature of the social world.

Thomas, A., Chess, S., & Birch, H. G. *Temperament and behavior disorders in children*. New York: New York University Press, 1968. A report of the ten-year-old New York Longitudinal Study. It emphasizes the different temperamental characteristics that show up right from birth and the ways these characteristics combine with certain methods of child rearing to create problems for children.

Early Childhood

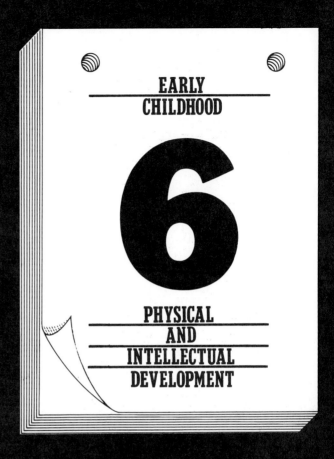

EARLY
CHILDHOOD

6

PHYSICAL
AND
INTELLECTUAL
DEVELOPMENT

IN THIS CHAPTER
YOU WILL LEARN ABOUT

Physical growth and development during the preschool years, and how children's homes and family life can affect their physical well-being

How children come to think abstractly by learning to deal with symbols

Children's language and schooling—and the purpose they serve

What "intelligence" is, and how preschool children are tested for it

CHAPTER OVERVIEW

Physical Growth and Motor Development
Dental Problems | Abnormal Growth | Motor Development

Abused and Neglected Children
Helping Abused Children and Their Families

Intellectual Development
Piaget's Preoperational Stage (2 to 7 Years) | Cognitive Concepts in Early Childhood | School in Early Childhood | Language in Early Childhood | Measuring Intelligence of Young Children | Influences on Intellectual Achievement

PHYSICAL GROWTH AND MOTOR DEVELOPMENT

Children's height no longer increases so rapidly as during infancy, although typical 3-year-olds have grown almost 4 inches during the past year. They will continue to grow a steady 2 to 3 inches per year until they reach the growth spurt that occurs during puberty.

The potbellies of 3-year-olds will slim down over the next two years as their trunks get longer, along with their arms and legs. Their heads are still relatively large, but the rest of their bodies are catching up, and their proportions are steadily becoming more like those of adults. Other changes are also taking place in the bodies of 3-year-olds. Nervous and muscular systems are maturing, as is skeletal growth. Cartilage is turning to bone at a faster rate, and bones are becoming harder. All the primary teeth are in now, and they can chew anything.

Nutrition has a strong influence on the growth, thickness, and shape of bones in the body. Malnourished children show retarded bone development and smaller head circumference (Scrimshaw, 1976).

DENTAL PROBLEMS

Nutrition also affects tooth development. One of the greatest health problems of Americans is tooth decay, a problem that generally begins shortly after tooth eruption, increases until the late teens, and then levels out during the decade of the twenties. Some 5 percent of 1-year-olds have cavities, as do 10 percent of 2-year-olds and 40 percent of 3-year-olds (Thomas et al., 1976).

Infante and Russell, writing in 1974, found dental problems more common among poor children, a finding that could be laid at the door of faulty diet and inadequate dental care. However, the Ten-State Nutrition Survey of 1968–1970 found exactly the reverse. Dentist Nathaniel H. Rowe and other members on the American Academy of Pediatrics' committee to review the survey reported in 1976 after analyzing the survey data that poor children have *fewer* cavities than those from higher-income families. This may be because children in higher economic groups eat more frequently or eat more sucrose, or refined sugar. The Ten-State Survey also found that black children are less cavity-prone than white children, even when factors such as income, developmental status, and other possibly influential elements are taken into account. Why this should be so no one knows.

Another habit—this one child-initiated—that can affect tooth development is thumb-sucking. This is common among babies, with almost half of all American children under 4 sucking their thumbs or fingers (Traisman & Traisman, 1958). It probably will have little or no effect on tooth development unless it persists past the age of 5. For a young infant, Curzon (1974) recommends giving the baby a pacifier to help fill sucking needs, since babies usually give up their pacifiers much more easily than they give up putting their own thumbs or fingers into their mouths. Otherwise, parents are advised to ignore the habit in children under 3 or 4 years of age.

Prolonged sucking seems to be more of a habit than the result of any emotional disturbance, and it responds better to treatment designed to break the habit, like a dental appliance, than to psychologic counseling, which has little or no effect. Children over 4 who still suck their fingers are sometimes fitted with a dental appliance that corrects any existing malformation of teeth and also discourages the sucking. Success rates with these appliances have been high, with 81 percent of treated children giving up their sucking habits (Haryett, Hansen, & Davidson, 1970).

ABNORMAL GROWTH

Parents of an unusually small child often worry that some abnormal condition is interfering

	HEIGHT (INCHES)		WEIGHT (POUNDS)	
AGE	BOYS	GIRLS	BOYS	GIRLS
3	38	37¾	32¼	31¾
3½	39¼	39¼	34¼	34
4	40¾	40½	36½	36¼
4½	42	42	38½	38½
5	43¼	43	41½	41
5½	45	44½	45½	44
6	46	46	48	47

TABLE 6-1
Physical Growth,
Ages 3 to 6 (*Fiftieth
Percentile*)

189

SOURCE: From *Growth and development of children,* 5th edition, by Ernest H. Lowrey. Copyright © 1967, Year Book Medical Publishers, Inc., Chicago. Used by permission of Year Book Medical Publishers.

with normal growth. The child's small size may reflect nothing more than a family tendency to shortness. But sometimes lack of growth is caused by illness or malfunction of the *pituitary gland*. Located at the base of the brain, this gland secretes the hormone that ensures normal growth. When growth retardation is caused by hormonal deficiency, injections of human growth hormone can often increase the rate of growth dramatically.

Emotional Factors in Growth Retardation

Doctors were puzzled when a 5-year-old girl whose small size had been diagnosed as growth-hormone deficiency failed to respond to administration of the hormone. Suspecting that a poor home situation was interfering with the course of treatment and the child's growth, they stopped the hormone treatment and sent the little girl to live with an aunt. During the time she lived away from home *without* the hormone treatment, the child grew at about twice the rate as when she had been getting the treatment but living at home (Frasier & Rallison, 1972). This case is one striking example of many that seem to point to the conclusion that growth is affected by other than physical factors.

One group of thirteen very short children between the ages of 3 and 11 were originally thought to have a condition called *idiopathic hypopituitarism*, a type of growth-hormone deficiency, until investigation into the chil-

dren's family constellations revealed abnormal home environments and emotional disturbances. The children were suffering hostility and abuse at the hands of ill-tempered parents, when the parents bothered to spend time with them at all. Although the youngsters were abnormally small, many had huge appetites. Several were retarded in IQ, speech, and social maturity. These children gained in height and weight when hospitalized and given good nutrition and good all-round care (Powell, Brasel, & Blizzard, 1967).

Children who are abnormally small— below the third percentile in height and weight for their age—for no apparent reason are often called "failure-to-thrive" children. In 1975, Pollitt, Erchler, and Chan compared a group of mothers of normal children, aged 1 to 5, with mothers of failure-to-thrive children of the same ages. After visiting the homes on a weekly basis and interviewing the mothers, the researchers found no obvious psychopathology in the failure-to-thrive mothers. These mothers, though, were less affectionate with their children and more likely to spank them. It wasn't clear, however, whether the more distant parent-child relationship was responsible for the child's failure to thrive, or whether the child's own personality and behavior (such as poor eating habits) may have set up barriers to intimacy with the parents.

MOTOR DEVELOPMENT

When we see what 3-year-olds can do, we realize how rapid physical development has been during the past months. One minute Alicia puts on her ballet tutu and walks on her tiptoes; the next, she's back in overalls, whipping around corners or riding her tricycle. At age 4, Dana is skipping and hopping on one foot and reliably catching the ball her father tosses. On his fifth birthday, Derek is skipping on alternate feet, jumping rope on the sidewalk, and starting to skate and swim.

Boys are a little stronger than girls and have a little more muscle even at this age (Garai & Scheinfeld, 1968), and they are better at throwing a ball, jumping, and going up and down ladders (McCaskill & Wellman, 1938). But girls outshine boys at several other tasks involving limb coordination. Five-year-old girls, for example, do better than boys at "jumping jacks," foot tapping, balancing on one foot, hopping, and catching a ball (Cratty, 1979). And when it comes to small-muscle coordination, girls are always one step ahead. These different proficiency levels may be a result of skeletal differences, but it just as possible that they reflect different societal attitudes that encourage different types of activities for boys and girls.

(Nora) could dress and undress herself with a minimum of help, even to unbuttoning. When given a stool to stand on, she could turn on faucets after she had been shown how.

from *Observing and Recording
the Behavior of Young Children,* 2/e., p. 39

Three-year-olds have made big gains in eye-hand and small-muscle coordination. Bobbie can sit down with a crayon and a big sheet of newsprint and draw a circle. She can pour her own milk into her cereal bowl, and she can button and unbutton well enough to dress herself and tend to her own toilet needs. At 4, Chris can cut on a line with scissors, draw a person, make designs and crude letters, and fold paper into a double triangle. At 5, Ellen can string beads well, control a pencil, copy a square, and show a preference for using one hand more than the other. About 1 child in 10 is left-handed, and this child is more likely to be a boy.

TABLE 6-2
Motor
Characteristics of
Perceptual-Motor
Development

MOTOR PATTERN	SKILL CHARACTERISTICS		
	THE 3-YEAR-OLD	THE 4-YEAR-OLD	THE 5-YEAR-OLD
Walking, running	Run is smoother and stride is more even than at 2	Run is improved in form and power	Has effected adult manner of running
	Cannot turn or stop suddenly or quickly	More effective control over stopping, starting, and turning	Can use this effectively in games
	Can take walking and running steps on the toes	In general: greater mobility than at 3	Runs 35-yard dash in less than 10 seconds
	Can walk a straight line		
	Can walk backward long distances	Coordinates body parts better in independent activities	
	Walks path (1 inch wide, 10 feet long) without stepping off	Walks 6 centimeter board part way before stepping off	
	Cannot walk circular path (1 inch wide, 4 feet in circumference)	Walks circle (1 inch wide, 4 feet in circumference) without stepping off	

MOTOR PATTERN	SKILL CHARACTERISTICS		
	THE 3-YEAR-OLD	THE 4-YEAR-OLD	THE 5-YEAR-OLD
Jumping	Jumps distance of 36–60 centimeters	Jumps distance of 60–85 centimeters	80% have mastered the skill of jumping
	42% rated as jumping well	72% skilled in jumping	More adept at jumping over barriers
	Clears rope less than 20 centimeters high	Most show difficulty in executing jump over a barrier	Makes running broad jump of 28–35 inches
	Can jump down from an 8-inch elevation	Jumps down from 28-inch height with feet together	Makes vertical jump and reach of 2½ inches
	Leaps off floor with both feet	Crouches for a high jump of 2 inches	
	Jumps down from heights of 8, 12, and 18 inches alone, feet together (preceded at early ages by stages of jumping with help followed by jumping alone, one foot in front of the other)	Makes standing broad jump of 8–10 inches	
		Makes running broad jump up to 23–33 inches	
		Jumps down from 28-inch height, alone with feet together	
	Jumps down from a 28-inch height with help		
	Ascends stairway unaided, alternating feet	Descends long stairway by alternating feet, if supported	Descends long stairway alternating feet
	Ascends short stairway unaided, alternating feet; 31 months	With no support: marks time	Descends long stairway alternating feet, unaided
	Ascends long stairway unaided, alternating feet; 41 months	Ascending skills mastered (stairways)	Ascending skills mastered (ladder)
	Descends both short and long stairways, marking time: not supported	Descends long stairway, alternating feet if supported	Descends large ladder, alternating feet
	Ascends small ladder, alternating feet	Descends short stairway, alternating feet unaided	
		Ascends large ladder, alternating feet	
		Descends small ladder, alternating feet	
Throwing	Frequently engaged in ball throwing, but does not throw well	20% are proficient throwers	74% are good throwers—great variation at each age level
	Throws without losing balance	Beginning to assume adult stance in throwing	Assumes adult posture in throwing
	Throws approximately 3 feet: uses two-hand throw	Can toss ring successfully at peg 4 feet 10½ inches away	Some throw distances of 17 feet: uses primarily unilateral throw
	Anteroposterior movement dominant in throwing	Distance of throw increases	Introduction of weight transfer: right-foot–step-forward-throw
	Body remains fixed during throw	Horizontal plane movements dominate	At 6–6½ years: mature throw: left-foot–step-forward; trunk

TABLE 6-2 (*continued*)

MOTOR PATTERN	SKILL CHARACTERISTICS		
	THE 3-YEAR-OLD	THE 4-YEAR-OLD	THE 5-YEAR-OLD
	Arm is initiating factor	Whole body rotates right, then left Feet remain together in place Arm is the initiating factor	rotation, and horizontal adduction of arm in forward swing
Catching	Attempts to stop rolling ball with hands or corrals it with legs Gradually synchronized movements with speed of rolling ball and hands reach around object Aerial ball: first attempts—hands and arms work as a single unit in an attempt to corral the ball against the body Catches large ball with arms extended forward stiffly Makes little or no adjustment of arms to receive ball Catches large and small ball: arms straight	29% are proficient in catching Catches large ball tossed from 5 feet away with arms flexed at elbows Moves arms in accordance with direction, definite efforts to judge position at which ball will land Depends more on arms than hands in receiving ball Catches both large and small balls: elbows in front of body	56% are skilled at catching; 6–63% Catches small ball: uses hands more than arms Judges trajectory better than at 4: not always successful Attempts one-hand catches Catches both large and small balls: elbows at side of body
Striking			Kicks soccer ball through air: 8–11½ feet
Bouncing	Bounces small ball distance of 1–5 feet: uses one hand Cannot perform this task with a large ball	Bounces large ball distance of 4–5 feet: uses two hands	Bounces large ball 6–7 feet: uses two hands One-hand bounce: large ball attempted at 72 months
Hopping, galloping, skipping	Some attempt at hopping by 29 months Hopping is largely an irregular series of jumps with some variations added Executes 1–3 consecutive hops on both feet: 38 months Executes 10 or more hops on both feet: 42 months (rapid skill development) Executes 1–3 consecutive hops: 1 foot; 43 months Performs a shuffle skip	Hops 2 meters on right foot Only 14% skip well 43% are learning to gallop Hops 4–6 steps on one foot Skips on one foot Executes 1–10 hops consecutively: one foot	22% skip well at end of fifth year 78% gallop but are not rated as skilled Hops distance of 16 feet easily Ten or more consecutive hops: one foot Alternates feet in skipping
Climbing	50% rated as proficient in climbing on jungle gyms, packing boxes, inclined planks, etc.	Further increase in proficiency	Still further increase in proficiency

SOURCE: Corbin, Charles B. *A textbook of motor development.* Dubuque: William C. Brown, 1973.

(Leo De Wys, Inc., George Roos/Peter Arnold, Inc., Suzanne Szasz)

ABUSED AND NEGLECTED CHILDREN

Children known as "battered babies" are kicked, beaten, burned, thrown against walls and radiators, strangled, suffocated, and even buried alive. Their bones are broken, their teeth are knocked out, their eyesight is destroyed, and their internal organs are injured. Many battered children who live suffer mental, physical, and emotional damage that can never be fully repaired (Solomon, 1973). Child abuse affects 360 children out of a million, and neglect usually is estimated at 90 percent more than abuse (Schmidt, 1975).

Physical abuse is a greater killer of infants 6 to 12 months old than is any specific cancer, malformation, or infectious disease. From 1 to 6 months, it is second to SIDS as a baby-killer. And after 1 year, it is second only to true accidents (Lloyd-Sills, 1976). While children of any age may be abused or neglected, most victims are under the age of 3; worst of all, half the battered children who are returned to their homes eventually die of abuse or neglect (Fontana, 1976).

Abused children are often different from their nonabused siblings, as well as from children in other families. They tend to be "difficult" babies—premature, low birth-weight, and sickly (George & Main, 1979). George and Main (1979) compared ten 1- to 3-year-olds who had been abused in various ways ranging from severe punishment to skull fractures, broken collar bones, and severe burns, with ten children from equally stressed families who had not been so ill-treated. There were a number of differences in the abused children's behavior toward adults and toward their ego-mates in the day-care center.

The abused children hit other children more often, and also tended to avoid them, even when the other children made friendly overtures. They also hit, harassed, threatened, and avoided the adult caregivers, *especially* when the adults approached them in a friendly way. When the abused children did approach either an adult or a child, they tended to do so indirectly—to the side or the rear, by turning around and backstepping, or by moving the body in one direction while moving the head in the other. It seems as if they could not decide whether or not to make the approach. These children resembled their parents both in their difficulty with controlling aggression and in their tendency to withdraw from people who could offer them comfort and help.

Why do they act this way? One logical conclusion would be that they have learned—from painful lessons—not to trust people, especially the adults who are taking care of them. Feeling that adults are dangerous, the children may be inclined to strike first. They may also be expressing a generalized anger, they may be looking for attention—even negative attention—or they may be imitating the treatment they themselves have too often received. Another reasonable explanation might be that children are abused, in part, as a consequence of their own personalities. Those who are difficult from birth, more aggressive or more withdrawn, may bring out the worst in their parents. Some parents may be especially maddened when they see their own worst traits reflected in their children.

Our society's high rate of child abuse may be partly an outgrowth of our general acceptance of physical force in child rearing. One common justification given for spanking children is that "it makes the parents feel better," thus favoring the parent's needs over the child's needs. Abusing parents carry societal values just one step further. Their pathology lies in the inappropriateness of their expectations and the severity of their punishments. Abusing a child is different in degree, but not very different in kind, from any parent's striking any child in anger. In cultures that have strong taboos against striking children, such as among American Indians, abuse is extremely rare (Gil, 1970).

Abusing parents come from all income levels, all ranges of intelligence, and all cultural, religious, and racial groups; yet, reported abuse occurs most often in large, poor families (Gil, 1970). The poor suffer more of life's stresses: They cannot take vacations, cannot hire baby-sitters, cannot fill their lives with other pleasures. "It is the poor . . . who are expected to be perfect mothers seven days a week" (Kempe, 1973). Children mistreated by more prosperous parents are also more likely to be seen by private physicians, who are less likely to report abuse than representatives of public clinics.

Often beaten themselves as children, abusing parents were emotionally deprived in other ways as well. They have low self-images and have felt like failures for many years. They generally feel isolated, have no one whom they can depend upon to help them in times of distress, are unhappily married, and have unrealistic expectations of their children (Schmidt, 1975).

On the increase is sexual abuse of children. In such cases an adult—sometimes a member of the child's own family—fondles, engages in sexual intercourse with, or rapes a child. In 1972, the Children's Division of the American Humane Society reported 5000 cases of sexual abuse, but the true prevalence may well be closer to 50,000 cases per year (Kempe, 1978).

Although neglecting parents are usually equally indifferent to all their children, abusing parents sometimes pick a scapegoat. This child may have the misfortune to resemble a hated relative, may have been the cause of a forced marriage, may have "caused" the mother a difficult pregnancy, may have been born prematurely or with a birth defect, or may simply have a personality that one or both parents cannot stand. Usually only one parent inflicts the injuries, but by allowing the mistreatment, the other parent demonstrates his or her own inadequacy (Steele & Pollack, 1968).

Since abused children often grow up to be abusing parents, the cycle can be broken only by preventing the abuse altogether. We need to find ways to help infants at risk. George and Main (1979) suggest the establishment of specially staffed day-care centers. Here, abused and nonabused children could

It shouldn't hurt to be a child.

🌣 **prevent child abuse.** write: Box 2866, Chi., Ill. 60690

National Committee for Prevention of Child Abuse

A Public Service of Traffic Advertising and The Advertising Council

(The Advertising Council)

be cared for together by caregivers who are especially sensitive to and trained to deal with problem infants and their parents.

HELPING ABUSED CHILDREN AND THEIR FAMILIES

Abusing parents are often prosecuted in the courts, but they are not always convicted; and when they return home, they may be harsher than ever. Authorities often remove a child from an abusing home, and the parents sometimes transfer their brutality to another child. Since abusing parents are at times kind and loving, their children may genuinely grieve to be taken from them. The ideal solution is to help the entire family.

Traditional psychotherapy is often ineffective in dealing with the "battered child" syndrome, since abusing parents tend to deny reality, blaming the child for the injuries. They often respond well, though, to warm, compassionate "mother surrogates"—lay persons who visit them, help with day-to-day living, and show sympathy for their problems and interest in them as people (Fontana & Robinson, 1976; Kempe, 1973).

What can concerned citizens do to pre-vent child abuse in their communities? In some places task forces have developed comprehensive child-protection services, which include the encouragement of reporting cases of child abuse by neighbors and friends, as well as doctors, teachers, and other professionals; the establishment of tele-phone hot lines that parents can call when they are afraid of losing control; group pro-grams for abusing parents similar to those sponsored for drinkers by Alcoholics Anony-mous; and the education of school children for family life (Helfer, 1973; Johnston, 1973; Nemy, 1972; Kempe & Kempe, 1978). Vital to the success of any of these programs is the realization by the public—and by abusing parents themselves—that they *can* be rehabil-itated.

INTELLECTUAL DEVELOPMENT

During the ages of 3 to 6, children become more competent in cognition, intelligence, language, and learning. They develop the ability to use symbols in thought and action, and they are more able to handle concepts of

195

age, time, space, and morality. Yet they still do not completely separate real from unreal, and much of their thinking is egocentric.

PIAGET'S PREOPERATIONAL STAGE (2 TO 7 YEARS)

Children enter Piaget's second major stage of cognitive development, the *preoperational stage*, at about age 2, as they come out of the sensorimotor stage (see Chapter 4); and they emerge from it at about age 7, as it overlaps the concrete operations stage (Chapter 8).

The preoperational stage ushers in the *symbolic function*. Children's thought processes used to be chained to the actual, the present, the concrete. Now that they can use symbols to represent objects, places, and people, their thinking can dart back to past events, surge forward to anticipate the future, and dwell on what might be happening elsewhere in the present. Mental processes are active, but they are also, for the first time, reflective. Once children enter the preoperational stage, their ability to represent things with symbols enables them to share a symbol system with others.

Before the preoperational stage, children could not yet evoke for themselves—without external clues—symbols of persons or events. Now they can. They can think of the mother's voice without actually hearing it or conjure up in the mind the sight of an ice-cream cone upon hearing the word for it. These mental representations are called *signifiers*, and the objects or events that they represent (mother, cone) are called *significates*. Signifiers may be *symbols* (very personal representations that involve visual, auditory, or kinesthetic images which bear some resemblance to the object). Or they may be *signs*, like words or numerals. Young children think first in symbols and continue to think in them even after they become proficient with language.

We can see that children have the symbolic function when they demonstrate deferred imitation, symbolic play, and language. *Deferred imitation* explains the process whereby children see something, form a mental symbol of it (probably a visual image), and later—when they no longer see it—imitate the activity. David, age 3, sees his father shaving. When he goes to nursery school that afternoon, he heads for the housekeeping corner and begins to "shave." He obviously has a mental picture of his father's shaving behavior, or he would not be able to copy it.

In *symbolic play*, children make one object stand for something else. At 15 months, Jacqueline found a cloth with fringed edges that reminded her of her pillow. She treated it as she would her pillow, but laughed unreservedly. Her laughter is our clue that she knows this piece of cloth is not the pillow (Ginsburg & Opper, 1979).

Preoperational children use *language* to stand for absent things or events. They therefore have invested words with a symbolic character.

Characteristics of Preoperational Thought

Preoperational children have made such a leap forward from the sensorimotor stage that it comes as a shock to realize how elementary their thinking still is, as demonstrated by the following characteristics identified by Flavell (1963, pp. 156–162).

EGOCENTRISM   Preoperational children cannot take the role of another person. When Sarah is asked to describe what a three-dimensional model would look like to someone on the other side of the model, she persistently describes it only from her own point of view. She cannot imagine that someone else would have a different viewpoint. This, then, is *egocentrism*: the awareness of self without recognizing the different perspectives, needs, and interests of other people. Egocentrism is especially noticeable in the use of language. Listening to a preoperational

A four-year-old was told the birds were migrating because the seasons were changing, agreed heartily: "Yes," he said. "The birds will fly north in the summer and south in the winter, and time will fly."

from *Observing and Recording the Behavior of Young Children,* 2/e., p. 135

conversation is like being in the Theater of the Absurd. Children may politely wait for each other to finish; they may alternate sentences; and they may stay remotely within the same subject area. But each child speaks without knowing or caring whether the others are interested or even listening. The following conversation between two 4-year-olds is typical of such dual monologues:

Jason: What will we have for supper tonight?

Vicky: Christmas is coming.

Jason: Cake and coffee would be good.

Vicky: I have to do my shopping soon.

Jason: I really like chocolate cake.

Vicky: I think I will buy some slippers and candy.

CENTRATION Preoperational children tend to *centrate;* they focus on one aspect of a situation and neglect others, leading to illogical reasoning. They cannot *decenter,* or consider more than one dimension. In one of Piaget's most famous experiments, Eric is shown two identical glasses, each one short and wide, each one holding the same amount of water. When asked which has more water, Eric, age 5, says, "They're both the same." While he watches, the experimenter pours water from one of the wide glasses into a tall, thin one, and asks, "Now which one has more water?" Eric points to the short glass. The experimenter pours the water back and forth several more times, and Eric continues to say the short, wide glass has more water. When asked why, he says, "This one is bigger this way," pointing to the width. Other children say the tall glass contains more water. Children this age cannot consider both height and width at the same time. They center on one or the other and cannot solve the problem. Because one glass *looks* larger, they think it *is* larger; their faulty perception inhibits logical thinking.

IRREVERSIBILITY Preoperational children fail to understand that the pouring operation can go both ways. If Eric could imagine the possibility of restoring the original state by pouring the water back into the other glass, he would realize that the amount of water in both glasses is the same. He does not realize this.

THE PRACTICAL APPLICATION OF THESE INSIGHTS The theories developed by Piaget have vast implications for education. While Piaget himself never applied his theories to education, his followers have.

Educational principles rest largely on the way we see children. Piaget sees them as active, as constantly building an understanding of themselves and their world, as increasingly more organized, more objective, and more able to handle abstractions. With this view we can shape an educational program that will help children develop (Furth & Wachs, 1975).

The Piaget-inspired changes in preschool education in recent years rest on our new understanding of children and of the way intelligence develops. An understanding of Piaget's work helps teachers to decide when and how to present various concepts to children. Teachers can adapt Piagetian tasks for classroom use to teach concepts and to assess students' levels of reasoning ability. Those who recognize children's motivation to learn can provide materials and time to help students learn at their own pace. Such teachers make it easier for children to pursue individual interests and do not feel that they have to direct all the interests the children should pursue.

Understanding how children think has ramifications that extend into all corners of their lives. Resnick (1975) has identified some aspects of preoperational thinking in children's thoughts about illness, hospitalization, and surgery. Egocentric preschoolers cannot accept logical explanations for why dinner is late ("I am hungry; so my dinner should be here when I want it") or for why they cannot have a drink ("I am thirsty; so what do I care if the doctor ordered 'nothing by mouth' ") or for why the nurse cannot stay ("If I need her, what difference does it make if she has five other patients to take care of?"). Children this age may center upon the length of a needle or the size of an x-ray machine to the exclusion of other properties, including their functions. They cannot understand the reversibility of mending a broken leg and, therefore, see traction not as a healing process but simply as an annoying and uncomfortable procedure. Adults who care for children will be better able to communicate with them and understand them if they remember that children think differently from adults.

COGNITIVE CONCEPTS IN EARLY CHILDHOOD

Children learn how to deal with time, space, causation, judgment of age, and morality. Other concepts Piaget has studied are *seriation* (the ability to arrange stimuli according to one or more dimensions, such as shortest to tallest or lightest to heaviest) and *classification* (sorting stimuli into categories of characteristics, such as color or shape). Piaget found that such concepts come naturally to children at certain points in their development. Let us look at *classification*: When children can sort

Children can be taught such concepts as seriation, classification, and conservation. (Suzanne Szasz/Photo Researcher, Inc.)

Laura walks by and accidentally bumps into the table. "Oops, sorry," she says as half of Bryant's (block) creation crumbles and falls. A long drawn out "Ooooo" pierces the air as Bryant's shoulders go up and his hands make an ineffective attempt to catch the pieces. His face is red and crumpled with anger but slowly turns pink as he begins once more to rebuild. Eventually his face regains its natural color and composure.

from *Observing and Recording the Behavior of Young Children*, 2/e., p. 127

objects into categories according to particular attributes, they show that they can see color, shape, and size, and that they understand the concept of categorization. Verbal ability enters in as they label what they perceive.

Children of various ages were given

plastic pieces of different colors and shapes and told to "put together those that are alike" (Piaget & Inhelder, 1959). From the ages of 2½ to 4½ years, the children made *figural* collections: They did not sort out shapes but instead used the plastic circles, triangles, and squares to make their own shapes—usually a line or a circle. From the ages of 4½ to 6 or 7 years, children made quasi-classifications, jumping capriciously from one basis of classification to another. Typically, they would sort some materials by color and others by shape, ending up with one pile of red triangles and circles and another pile of red, blue, and yellow squares. By the end of this age level, the children would sort by one dimension at a time, but only one.

Children 7 or 8 years old and older classified exhaustively. They now were able to deal with several dimensions, or classes, at once, ending up with piles of large red circles, small red circles, large blue circles, small blue circles, large yellow triangles, small yellow squares, and so on.

Accelerating the Piagetian Concepts

Can children be taught such concepts as seriation, classification, and conservation? Apparently so, if they are ready and if the training is specific. Children who respond to such training are generally those on the verge of discovering a specific concept. A structured learning experience may push them into acquiring the concept earlier.

In one study (Bingham-Newman & Hooper, 1974), sixty 3- to 5-year-old urban middle-class children were trained in seriation, classification, or a combination of the two. The seriation-trained children did better than those trained in classification, probably because children grasp the former concept at an earlier age. The older children did better at seriation than the younger ones, showing the importance of maturation.

Piaget himself has reservations about programs to train children in Piagetian concepts:

This is not true learning in his view; it is an artificial, verbally acquired, "deformed" response, a rote memorization of responses to a specific situation only. It is neither stable nor permanent; children will revert quickly to the usual errors, nor can they generalize to similar situations. The logical structure can be acquired only through internal equilibrium, Piaget insists [Pulaski, 1971, pp. 33–34].

Children may be better off spending their time making mudpies, playing with blocks, or going to the park than engaging in "accelerating" activities.

SCHOOL IN EARLY CHILDHOOD

Public nursery schools were first established in 1919 and began to flourish within the decade. Today, about half of all 3- to 5-year-olds go to nursery school or kindergarten, compared to the 1 in 3 children of this age who were enrolled in preschools in 1966. Between 1966 and 1976, the percentage of children 3 to 4 years old who went to nursery school more than doubled, from 14 to 31 percent (*Wall Street Journal*, 1978).

The children of both employed and at-home mothers are about twice as likely to go to nursery school today than they were a decade ago, although mothers who work full-time are less likely to use them than are mothers who work part-time. This is undoubtedly because most nursery schools operate on only a half-day schedule. In fact, the major difference between "nursery schools" and "day-care centers" is more of a difference in hours than in program (U.S. Department of Health, Education, and Welfare, 1976).

Nursery schools cover a wide range. They may be commercial or nonprofit enterprises or parent-run cooperatives. Teachers may be accredited and certified or completely untrained. Some schools operate two or three

Nursery school activities foster both motor and social development. (Erika Stone/Peter Arnold, Inc.)

half-days a week, others five full days. They are located on campuses, in churches, in apartment buildings, and at shopping centers. Very few are run by public school systems. Some are models of what early childhood education should be, while others are no more than glorified baby-sitting services. And sometimes even the baby-sitting is inadequate.

A Typical Day at Nursery School

When Laura arrives at school at 8:50 A.M., she hangs up her jacket on the hook labeled with her name. She greets her teacher with a kiss, and hoots at her best friend, Bobby. She and Bobby scamper over to the dress-up corner, where they don hard hats and play at being construction workers. When she tires of this, Laura wanders over to the easel to paint and then goes into the washroom (shared by both sexes) and chats while washing off the paint. When she comes out, she finds a spot in the circle the children have formed around Tom, their new student teacher, who is about to lead some simple, catchy songs. Then it's time for juice and crackers. No one scolds

Laura when she spills juice on the floor. As the children munch and sip, conversation goes on at a brisk pace about baby brothers who spit up their dinner, Sunday visits to the zoo, overflowing toilets, new shoes, and all sorts of other important experiences. At rest time, Laura sits quietly, putting together wooden puzzles. Later, she and Bobby take turns being babies and pushing each other around in a sturdy wooden carriage. Thumb in mouth, Laura listens to her teacher read a story, the last indoor event of the morning. The class dashes out to the playground where, with whoops and hollers, yowls and squabbles, they climb on the jungle gym, go up and down on the seesaw, pedal furiously on tricycles, crawl in corners, or stand around deciding what to do. Just before noon, Laura's father picks her up, and another day at school is over.

How Nursery School Fosters Development

Nursery school activities foster both large- and small-motor coordination. They also foster social skills. Through play, children have opportunities to cooperate toward common goals and to begin to understand other people's perspectives and feelings. When cooperation turns into conflict, they learn how to deal with frustration, anger, and hurt feelings. Preschool experiences help children from small families to learn how to get along with others.

How does the kind of nursery school children attend influence them? O'Connor (1975) compared forty-eight 3½- to 5-year-olds from two different schools. The schools were similar in many ways but differed in their teacher-child ratios and in their age-grading policies. Twenty-nine of the children were in the school that put children of different ages in the same classroom; in this school there were 3.5 preschoolers to every adult. Nineteen were in the other school, which placed the 3-year-olds in one classroom and the older children in another; in this school there were 7 children to every teacher.

The age grading made no difference in the children's behaviors, but the adult-child ratio did have some effects. In the school with the higher adult-child ratio, the children interacted more with the adults and less with the other children. The ratio of adults to children did not seem to affect the children's degree of independence. However, children who did show dependency behaviors (such as seeking physical contact or reassurance, asking for unnecessary help, or showing off) were more likely to go to adults rather than to other children when they were in a classroom that had more adults per child.

Those schools based on the theories of Piaget or the Italian educator Maria Montessori have a strong cognitive bent. Some schools place heavy emphasis on teaching the alphabet and numbers; others feel this can wait for kindergarten. Teachers in a good nursery usually try to advance children's cognitive development in many other ways. They provide a variety of experiences so that children learn by doing. They stimulate the children's senses through art, music, and tactile materials such as clay, water, and wood. They

encourage powers of observation, curiosity, creativity, and language proficiency. They encourage children to solve social, practical, and intellectual problems. Throughout everything, they encourage the children to talk. Nursery school's most important contribution may well be the feeling that children get there that school is fun, that learning is satisfying, and that they are competent in the school situation.

The Montessori Method

This system for educating young children, originally designed to teach retarded and poor Italian children, has become extremely popular in this country, where Montessori-inspired nursery schools abound, catering to the normal children of the affluent, who can afford the costs of private nursery schools.

The first woman in Italy to earn a medical degree, Dr. Maria Montessori achieved remarkable success with the method she developed, based on the *prepared environment*, a carefully planned arrangement of surroundings, equipment, and materials. The objective of the Montessori method is to help children realize their full potential. The method has three main components; motor, sensory, and language education.

Motor education is basic, since motor activity is considered essential for mental development. The emphasis is on the development of life skills, so that children can learn how to care for themselves and the property they deal with in their everyday lives. They receive precise instruction in carrying out the activities of daily life, even down to the ways they walk, sit, and carry objects. They do exercises in opening and shutting drawers, pouring water from a pitcher to a basin, using scissors, and buttoning. They learn such occupational skills as sweeping, washing, and caring for plants and animals. They do gymnastics and rhythmic movement exercises.

Sensory education is furthered by the use of elaborate materials, including specially designed blocks of various colors and sizes, different-textured touchboards, thermic bottles, and sound boxes. These and other materials are used to teach concepts of form, size, color, weight, temperature, taste, smell, and sound. Children learn to recognize and match identical stimuli as well as contrasts and extremes, and to discriminate among similar items.

Education for language follows specific guidelines for teaching children to name objects, recognize concepts, and pronounce words. Evans (1975) points out an example of the concern for precise language provided in Montessori's 1914 handbook:

After the directress had ruled a blackboard with extremely fine lines a child claimed spontaneously, "What small lines." They are not small," reminded a second child, "they are thin!" [Evans, 1975, p. 262].

By the age of 4, the Montessori child is ready for academic learning—writing and reading (which are taught together) and arithmetic, all of which are seen as a natural extension of the previous activities. Here, too, the children use special materials such as sandpaper letters, which let them feel the shapes of the letters as they see them and hear their sounds, and sets of red and blue rods and golden beads based upon the decimal system, which help children learn numbers.

The Montessori method is a child-centered curriculum, "fueled in principle by love for the child and respect for his natural capabilities" (Evans, 1975, p. 264). Learning is seen as something that children do for themselves, while teachers are expected to be resource people who provide emotional support and help, along with their skilled observations that help them determine when children are ready to advance to the next phase of the program.

Some of the principles basic to the method include grouping children of different ages together, encouraging their active involvement, letting them select their own materials within the teaching framework and then use them in such a way that they themselves can tell whether they are using them correctly, and holding to a carefully planned, graduated sequence of learning from simple to complex. The method fosters moral development, too, emphasizing cooperation, self-control, order, responsibility, patience, and the common good.

Preschools for Deprived Children

Michael, the only child of middle-class parents, is about to begin his first day of kindergarten. The first five years of his life have prepared him for this day. From infancy his parents have engaged him in conversation, taught him nursery rhymes, and answered his questions. Today he is fluent with words, adept with crayons and scissors, and familiar with many of the places he will read about in his first readers.

Wendell, the oldest of four children in a poor family trying to escape an overcrowded apartment, is also going to kindergarten. For him it is like going to a strange world where the teacher will have trouble understanding him—and he, her. He will not realize it when she calls him by name, because at home he is always called "Junior." As a matter of fact, he is spoken to very little at home, by any name. Caught up in the daily struggle for survival, Wendell's mother and father have little time or inclination for answering questions, telling stories, or teaching rhymes. Wendell has never seen a book at home; has had few toys; has never colored with a crayon nor cut with scissors. He has rarely been out of his immediate neighborhood, and when he has, the trips were not for his benefit. (These descriptions of Michael and Wendell were based on Crow, Murray, & Smythe, 1966, pp. 205–208.)

For more than fifty years, educators have recognized that children with deprived socioeconomic backgrounds enter school with a considerable handicap. Not until the last decade, though, have large-scale programs been developed to help the Wendells of our society *before* they reach the age of formal schooling. Such programs try to compensate for the experiences that these children miss out on—with language, materials, and opportunities to learn.

The best-known compensatory preschool program is *Operation Head Start*, the federally funded program launched in the mid-1960s by the Office of Economic Opportunity. Head Start tried to give deprived children a boost early in life by tending to their physical health, their social welfare, and their educational needs. Millions have received medical checkups and follow-up care, an enriched school curriculum, and special attention in learning how to speak and listen, overcoming shyness, and developing motor coordination.

Head Start became a political issue, with supporters claiming great gains in children's IQs and opponents calling it a waste of public funds. Follow-up studies (Westinghouse Learning Corporation, 1969) have shown that the IQ rises of Head Start children did not persist through later school years. Instead of being an indictment of Head Start, this probably means that intensely individualized education should be started earlier and continued for at least some elementary grades.

Home Start, another program for young children, was begun in 1972 by Head Start to move early childhood education into the home. It tries to bring comprehensive developmental services to children who cannot go to a center. It relies principally on home visitors—paraprofessional workers who come from the same community as the families they serve—and also offers group meetings for parents, special television programs, and mobile classrooms (Almy, 1975).

In an effort to respond to criticisms of Head Start as being too little and too late, other programs have been instituted at both earlier and later ages. Infant programs try to enrich the early experiences of children under 3. The *Brookline Early Education Project* (BEEP) was the first such program to be launched by a public school system (Pines, 1975). This program enrolls children at birth and provides extensive medical, psychological, and educational services to raise levels of competence. The founders of BEEP, which is based on the findings of the Harvard Preschool Project (White, 1971) (see Chapter 4), consider the span between 8 and 18 months of age to be a most critical period for learning.

Other programs, some of which are described by Almy (1975), try to provide enrichment either in or out of the home to toddlers between the ages of 18 months and 3 years, largely because testing generally does not pick up differences among children of different socioeconomic status until about 18 months.

Day-Care Centers

More than 700,000 children under 6 spend their days in licensed day-care centers, usually because their parents are working outside the home (Olds, 1978). The quality of day care varies enormously, with the best happy, wholesome, and development-enhancing and the worst unsafe, unsanitary, and injurious to body and soul. Much hovers in the realm of mediocrity.

What constitutes good group care? The Office of Child Development of the U.S. Department of Health, Education, and Welfare has defined three types of child care (Stocker, 1973):

1 *Comprehensive child development programs*, which embrace all or nearly all the

needs of growing children and their families—educational, nutritional, and health—plus involvement of parents through instruction in child development and family counseling.

2 *Developmental day care* provides young children with opportunities for social and educational development. Trained people work with them, books and toys are available, meals meet nutritional requirements, and medical care is offered.

3 *Custodial child care* involves little more than ensuring the supervision and physical safety of children. Caretakers usually have little or no training; there are few books or educational toys; and the children usually spend much of their day watching television.

The first type of day care is very expensive and is unnecessary for middle-class children, though desirable for disadvantaged youngsters. The third type is inexpensive and common, but inadequate. The second type, developmental day care, is the most realistic goal. A good day-care center has many of the same activities as a good nursery school. It runs longer—possibly from 7:30 A.M. till 6:00 P.M.—and thus must provide more of what a good home provides.

A government-sponsored, four-year study of center-based preschool day care (Abt Associates, 1978) found some interesting patterns in the quality of day care. One major finding is that children do best in small groups: The best care exists in schools where small numbers of children interact with small numbers of adults. When groups are too large, adding more adults to the staff does not help.

It does not seem to matter how many years of formal education adult caregivers have had. What does matter is how much they have specialized in a child-related field, whether they took specialized courses in high school, college, or a special post-high school training course. Those caregivers who had specialized in fields like developmental psychology, early childhood education, or special education gave better care, and the children in their care did better on tests of school readiness skills.

The study also found that centers that are either partially or totally funded by the government are different from private centers that are supported only by parent fees. Centers that serve federally subsidized children have more adults per child and offer more extra services, such as health and developmental examinations, transportation, nutrition advice, counseling, and other social services.

THE EFFECTS OF DAY CARE ON CHILDREN Many studies have asked whether and how children develop differently in day-care centers than at home. Yet because the research has been narrow in scope, we still know relatively little about the way care by people other than a child's parents affects the child. In a comprehensive review and analysis of the research on day care, Bronfenbrenner, Belsky, and Steinberg (1977) summarize the findings from over forty studies, which, in turn, had been selected from a much larger number on the basis of their scientific quality.

What do we know about the effects of day care on children? Almost all of what we know is about children cared for in high-quality, well-funded, university-based centers. In the cognitive sphere, the average child in a good program seems to be unaffected for either better or worse. Children from disadvantaged backgrounds, however, who go to a good day-care center, are less likely to show declines in their IQ scores when they get to school than are children from similar backgrounds who have not had the educational experiences that good day care seems to provide.

In the emotional sphere, most studies

Early day care probably has some
effect on children's development, but it
is not yet clear what that effect is.
(Erika Stone/Peter Arnold, Inc.)

focus on the mother-child relationship and
show few if any differences in children's
attachment to their mothers, whether the
children have been in day care or not. And on
the social level, day-care children seem to
interact more with other children—both positively and negatively—than do home-reared
children, an effect that lasts at least through
early elementary school. Children who have
been in day care a long time are sometimes
less cooperative, less involved with schoolwork, and more aggressive than home-reared
children. This result is more characteristic of
group care in the United States than in other
countries, possibly indicating transmission of
cultural values rather than the effects of group
care itself.

These findings need to be tempered with
an understanding of the limitations of the
present research on day care, as pointed out
by Bronfenbrenner and his coauthors. First of
all, while most children in this country are
cared for in their own or other people's homes,
by relatives, neighbors, or paid caretakers,
almost all the research is about group care in
day-care centers. In addition, most of the
center care that children receive is run-of-
the-mill or worse; yet almost all the research
has been carried out in exceptionally high-
quality centers. The studies we do have yield
only short-term effects of day care since they
typically do not include follow-ups of the
children. And larger issues, such as the
significance and effects of day care for parents, for the family as a whole (with consideration for different kinds of families), and for
society in general, have been virtually ignored.

So we know very little about day care,
compared to what we should know. Early day
care probably has some effect on children's
development, but it is not clear what that
effect is. Much, of course, depends on the
particular day-care program and, even more,
on the particular people who actually care for
the children. At this time there is no way to
draw any conclusion about the ultimate benefits or harm of day care in general.

Kindergarten

The kindergarten experience is a year of
transition between the relative freedom of
nursery school and the relative structure of
formal schooling. In 1972, more than 2½
million 5-year-olds were attending kindergarten (Stocker, 1973), almost all in programs run
by local public schools. In many ways, kindergarten is an extension of nursery school, but
there are differences. Kindergarten teachers
usually have to be certified by the state, while
nursery school teachers sometimes do not.
Kindergarten is usually located in a neighbor-

hood public school and thus marks the beginnings of "real" school. There is usually a fair amount of emphasis on preparing children for first grade, by teaching them letters and numbers. Children who attend kindergarten generally do better later on with such reading skills as word recognition, word comprehension, and reading rate (Evans, 1975). Though this is not true of all children nor all kindergartens, the value of this experience appears to be well accepted by both educators and the public.

LANGUAGE IN EARLY CHILDHOOD

Between 3 and 4 years of age, children use three- to four-word "telegraphic" sentences that include only the most essential words. They ask many questions and can give and follow simple commands. They name familiar things like animals, body parts, and important people. They use plurals and the past tense, and they use I, you, and me correctly. Their vocabulary includes about 900 to 1200 words.

Between the ages of 4 and 5, children's sentences average four to five words. They now can deal with prepositions like "over," "under," "in," "on," and "behind." They use verbs more than nouns, and they now understand and speak a total of some 1500 to 2000 words.

Between ages 5 and 6, children begin to use sentences of six to eight words. They can define simple words, and they know some opposites. They use more conjunctions, prepositions, and articles in everyday speech. Speech is fairly grammatical, although children still neglect the exceptions to rules. Language is becoming less egocentric and more socialized, and vocabulary ranges from 2000 to 2500 words.

Between 6 and 7 years of age, children's speech becomes quite sophisticated. They

In response to the question while looking at the (jobs) chart, "What is your job today, Marya?" she replied, reading the chart incorrectly intentionally, "Marya is Today." Teacher: What is your job? It starts with the sound Ch (airs). Marya: Cheese. My job today is cheese. Smiling, very pleased with herself, she announced to the other teacher that she was doing her cheese.

Marya, age 5,
observed by Francesca Elms, her teacher

now speak in compound, complex, and grammatically correct sentences; they use all parts of speech; and they have a vocabulary of 3000 to 4000 words.

The relationship between language and thought is controversial, with Piaget (1926) feeling that thought comes first—that language does not structure thought but is the vehicle for communicating it. To Vygotsky (1962), speech regulates cognitive behavior and guides one's actions. Children's speech does not always guide their actions, of course, as David's mother found out when she walked into his room to see him crayoning huge circles on the wallpaper and saying, "Mommy said I must not write on the walls."

The Development of Social Speech

Not only does the form of speech change as children mature, but its functions often become different, as well. The kind of early

INTERCHANGE BETWEEN TWO 5-YEAR-OLDS
IN NURSERY SCHOOL:

M: Know what I'm going to do for Holloween? Know what I'm going to do for Holloween? I'm going to be a mouse
Marya: Know what I'm going to be for Holloween? A cat.

Observed by Francesca Elms, teacher

speech that Piaget classified as *egocentric* serves many purposes, even though it is not designed for communication. Just as infants babble for sheer pleasure, preoperational children repeat words and phrases to exercise their verbal schemata. Children talk to themselves partly because they do not yet fully differentiate words from what the words represent. Speech becomes another kind of activity.

Another purpose served by the *monologue*, in which one talks to oneself, is wish fulfillment. When children cannot attain their goals, they may still speak as if they can. Thus, afraid of the thunder, Carla scolds it and says, "Be quiet, thunder. You bother me." Small children often speak in *collective monologues*: They talk *at* each other but remain wrapped up in their own thoughts.

Social, or *socialized*, speech is for communication. Garvey and Hogan (1973) define it as "speech that is strictly adapted to the speech or behavior of the partner" (p. 563). It may involve an exchange of information, with or without questions and answers; criticism; or commands, requests, and threats (Piaget, 1955).

While Piaget and other social scientists have characterized most preschool speech as egocentric, recent research seems to show that children's speech is quite social from a very early age, that it may indeed make sense to regard children as "sociocentric" right from birth (Garvey & Hogan, 1973).

Children can and often do take into account the needs of other people when they speak, and they use speech from a very early age to establish and keep up contact with other people. The reason they often do not tailor their speech to the requirements of a specific situation is not so much because they don't recognize the need for doing it, but because they don't know how. We see this in adult life, for example, when a tourist in a foreign country asks a question in his own language, receives an uncomprehending stare, and then repeats his question more

loudly. If he knew the language of the listener, he would use it. Frustrated by his inability to communicate, he ignores the obvious truth that raising the decibel level is not a substitute for translating the words.

What research evidence do we have for assuming early social speech? Wellman and Lempers (1977) videotaped 2-year-olds in a toddler play group, concentrating on those times when the children pointed out or showed various objects to each other or to adults. They found that 79 percent of these toddlers' messages met with an adequate response from their listeners, indicating that the speakers had been able to capture their attention. The children adapted their messages to the demands of the situation and the people involved, and they reacted to the feedback they received, responding differently when the listener understood what they were saying, when the listener responded in some way but didn't understand, and when the listener ignored the message totally. Interestingly, the children spoke more often to adults, addressing other tots only when it was easier to do so.

Garvey and Hogan (1973) videotaped eighteen pairs of 3½- to 5-year-olds in fifteen-minute periods of free play and found the children using a great deal of social speech. The majority of the children's utterances (62 percent) received a definite response, 23 percent attracted the listener's attention, and only 15 percent drew no response at all. These children often used speech to achieve and maintain contact with each other. In one common pattern, a child would say, "You know what?"; a second child would say, "What?"; and the first would come back with some "reason" for having opened the conversation, like "Sometime you can come to my house."

The 3- to 5-year-olds asked by Maratsos (1973) to communicate their choice of a toy—either to a person who *could* see or to one who could *not*—behaved quite differently in the two conditions. They were likely to *point to* a toy in the seeing-person situation, whereas they *described* the toy to the person who could not see.

When Krauss and Glucksberg (1977) tried to find out when children learn to consider the listener in communicating, they came up with some surprising findings. They set up a "stack-the-blocks" game in which a child had to describe unusual block designs to another child, who had a matching set of blocks but was behind a barrier so he or she could not see the particular block the first child had picked up.

Four- and five-year-old children were unable to describe the designs on the blocks in a way that enabled other children to know which ones they were talking about. It was evident that the children's descriptions were meaningful to them, since they rarely changed the original description during the course of a game. But the descriptions were so personal that they didn't transmit useful information to the other person.

The researchers were not surprised that these nursery school children could not transmit the necessary information. They were surprised, though, when they found that children up to the fifth grade did little better, and that even ninth-graders failed to perform at adult levels. As Krauss and Glucksberg (1977) point out, "By the age of eight most children should be beyond the point where egocentrism is an important factor in their behavior and yet 13- and 14-year-olds did not perform with adult competence in our task" (p. 104).

What, then, accounts for the poor showing of even older children? In this experiment it may have been the difficulty of the task. The designs on the blocks were unusual and quite abstract, posing problems in describing them. When Dickson (1979) tested 4- to 8-year-olds on their ability to describe a variety of pictured objects, ranging from simple nameable pictures to abstract figures. When the children were faced with pictures they could name (most of which depicted monkeys or people), they did much better than when they had to describe abstract figures. Even 4½-year-olds communicated better than chance, suggesting that their poorer performance on the Krauss and Glucksberg block-sorting task reflects the difficulty of that test. Or, as Krauss and Glucksberg themselves concluded (1977), "The social use of language depends as much on . . . knowledge as it does on knowledge of language itself" (p. 105).

Apparently, then, when children are not sure what to do—how to perform a task or what the needs of the listener is—they do not go beyond egocentric speech. When a task is simple, though, and when children can quickly assess the needs of the other person in a specific situation, they are capable of social speech from an early age.

How Children Learn Language

Preschoolers say many things that have never been said exactly the same way before. They obviously know a limited set of rules from which they can generate an infinite number of sentences. The way they learn how to use these rules is termed *language acquisition*. Children probably do not learn to speak through imitation, even when reinforced. For one thing, their early grammatical mistakes do not reflect anything they have heard adults say. And even hearing the correct way does not ensure accurate imitation, as we see here (Gleason, 1967; cited in Cazden, 1971):

She said, "My teacher holded the baby rabbits and we patted them."

I asked, "Did you say the teacher held the baby rabbits?"

She answered, "Yes."

I then asked, "What did you say she did?"

She answered again, "She holded the baby rabbits and we patted them."

"Did you say she held them tightly?" I asked.

"No," she answered, "She holded them loosely."

Also, parents rarely bother to correct their small children's grammar, intuitively realizing this is unnecessary. As long as children hear well-formed sentences and take part in conversations, they will learn their native tongue.

Twins take longer to learn language than do single-born children (Mittler, 1970). Language retardation among twins probably results in part from their general developmental immaturity, but there seems to be other reasons as well. Twins 2½ years old are able to make up phrases as well as singletons, but they speak in shorter phrases and use sentences less often (Conway & Lytton, 1975).

What does it mean to be a twin? According to Lytton, Conway, and Sauve (1977), who compared ninety-two twin and forty-four singleton 2½-year-old boys, it means that you get less attention from your parents. The mothers and fathers of the single-born children spoke to them more and gave them more commands and suggestions, more explanations, more praise and approval, more threats and refusals, and more overt expressions of affection than the parents of twins. They also showed more consistency in following through rules and prohibitions. This study found that being a twin was more influential than the families' socioeconomic status in determining the way the parents acted toward their children. Apparently, the doubled demands on parents' time and energy with the need to take care of two children with similar if not identical demands takes its toll on the parent-child relationship.

Children acquire language largely through interaction with adults. When this is diminished—for whatever reason—language skills take longer to develop.

Language and Social Class

Hess and Shipman (1965) sum up one of the most pressing problems in our society:

Children from deprived backgrounds score well below middle-class children on standard individual and group measures of intelligence (a gap that increases with age); they come to school without the skills necessary for coping with first grade curricula; their language development, both written and spoken, is relatively poor; auditory and visual discrimination skills are not well developed; in scholastic achievement they are retarded an average of 2 years by grade 6 and almost 3 years by grade 8; they are more likely to drop out of school before completing a secondary education; and even when they have adequate ability are less likely to go to college [p. 870].

Children who come from lower-class homes acquire language more slowly, retain immature pronunciations longer, know fewer words, and speak shorter sentences than middle-class children (Cazden, 1968). In our highly verbal society, this is a crippling handicap. Through *sociolinguistics*, the study of the interaction between language and social setting, researchers are trying to discover what causes these different speech patterns. Lower-class children are not simply less mature linguistically; their language is different in kind.

Basil Bernstein, an English sociologist, has identified two speech patterns, the restricted code and the elaborated code (1961). The *restricted code* is used among lower social classes; it uses short, simple sentences and offers little detail or precision of concepts and information. The *elaborated code*, used by the middle class, has more complex, more individualized, and more specific messages. Since language is a form of social behavior, the way it is used in the home influences the way children relate to their parents and the world.

PARENT-CHILD INTERACTION AND LANGUAGE
Bernstein (1964) also distinguishes two types of family control, pointing up the social significance of language. Families who use elaborated codes are more likely to be person-oriented and to consider the unique characteristics of an individual child, rather than the demands of a role for that child ("smart boy," "good girl"). Users of restricted codes are more status-oriented and expect children to obey the more powerful parent and fulfill particular roles. In these families, "there is little opportunity for the unique characteristics of the child to influence the decision-making process or the interaction between parent and child" (Hess & Shipman, 1965, p. 871).

Hess and Shipman (1965) interviewed 163 black mothers from professional, skilled blue-collar, semiskilled, or unskilled and public assistance families. They taught the mothers three simple tasks to pass along to their 4-year-olds. There was very little difference among the groups in mother-child emotional attachment, but great differences in verbal and cognitive styles.

The middle-class mothers were much better teachers—more likely to offer explanations and specific information, to define the tasks clearly, and to offer various kinds of support and help. They criticized their children as much as the lower-class mothers did, but they praised them much more. The lower-class mothers had little success. They had trouble getting ideas across because they were vague in instructions and expectations. Furthermore, instead of encouraging their children to solve the problems, they stressed compliance and passivity, implying that the children were supposed to follow orders unquestioningly, to do what they said just because they said it. Hess and Shipman (1965) conclude:

The picture that is beginning to emerge is that the meaning of deprivation is a deprivation of meaning—a cognitive environment in which behavior is controlled by status rules rather than by attention to the individual characteristics of a specific situation and one in which behavior is not mediated by verbal cues or by teaching that relates events to one another and the present to the future. This environment produces a child who relates to authority rather than to rationale, who, although often compliant, is not reflective in his behavior, and for whom the consequences of an act are largely considered in terms of immediate punishment or reward rather than future effects and long-range goals [p. 885].

When Zegiob and Forehand (1975) looked at the influences of race, socioeconomic status, and children's sex on the way mothers act toward 4- to 6-year-olds, they found that middle-class mothers were less critical and more talkative with their children than lower-class mothers were. When commands had to be given, middle-class mothers used questions or indirect commands, while lower-class mothers were more directive and controlling. The child's sex had no effect, and race had practically none, except that white mothers were somewhat more cooperative with their children. The big difference revolved around social class.

IMPROVING CHILDREN'S LANGUAGE BY WORKING WITH PARENTS
A great deal of sensitivity is required in any program that attempts to alter families' basic styles of living and interrelating. But the justification for stepping in lies in the reality that success in our society comes more easily to people who have verbal and academic skills. Some programs have succeeded in improving children's language and intellectual abilities by

Once children have acquired facility with language, tests gain in predictive value. (Nancy Hays/Monkmeyer)

changing certain aspects of parent-child interaction. An example is the one conducted by Karnes et al. (1970), described on p. 147.

WORKING DIRECTLY WITH CHILDREN To develop such abstract concepts as time, space, direction, and comparison, children need feedback from an articulate older person who can help them clarify their ideas. Such feedback is often missing in lower-class homes.

To teach urban slum children how to think abstractly, Blank and Solomon (1968) developed a specialized language tutoring program for 3- and 4-year-olds. They encouraged the youngsters to look for the meanings of words, to reason, and to speak. After drawing a circle, for instance, a child was asked to draw something "other than a circle." The question "Where would the doll be if it fell from the table?" was used to increase the child's capacity to imagine future events. And to strengthen cause-and-effect reasoning, the children were asked, "What is the weather outside?" followed by, "Why can't we go out to play?" After four months of such individual tutoring, children showed IQ increases and changes in behavior and attitudes, including "an apparent joy in learning and the feeling of mastery" (p. 388).

MEASURING INTELLIGENCE OF YOUNG CHILDREN

For children under the age of 3, there is virtually no correlation between the scores on intelligence tests and those they will make later on, because of the nonverbal nature of infant intelligence tests. But with the arrival of language, the tests can include verbal items. Facility with language differentiates the baby from the child. From about the age of 3, there is a relatively steady correlation between children's intelligence scores now and those they will achieve later in life (Honzik, Macfarland, & Allen, 1948).

Preschoolers are generally tested one at a time. Anastasi (1968) describes a typical preschool test-taker:

[T]he subject can walk, sit at a table, use his hands in manipulating test objects, and communicate by language. At these ages, the child is also much more responsive to the examiner as a person, whereas for the infant the examiner serves chiefly as a means of providing stimulus objects [p. 457].

The Stanford-Binet
This test is generally given to children between the ages of 3 and 8. It is an individual test that takes thirty to forty minutes to administer. The child is asked to give the meanings of words, to string beads, to build with blocks, to identify the missing parts of a picture, to trace mazes, and to show an understanding of numbers. The IQ yielded by the Stanford-Binet is supposed to be a measure of practical judgment in real-life situations, memory, and spatial orientation.

The Wechsler Preschool and Primary Scale of Intelligence (WPPSI)
This test is used with children aged 4 to 6½, takes about an hour, and is sometimes given in two separate sessions, since children of this age are distracted easily and soon tire out. It is divided into eleven subtests that are grouped into two separate scales, verbal and performance. This test yields a Verbal IQ, a Performance IQ, and a Full Scale IQ. The subjects are similar to those in the Wechsler Intelligence Scale for Children (see Chapter 8).

INFLUENCES ON INTELLECTUAL ACHIEVEMENT
As a typical college student, you probably have taken many intelligence tests, from nursery school through high school. Your scores were influenced by many factors: your personality, your cognitive style, your socioeconomic status, your ethnic background, your ease in the testing situation, your social and emotional adjustment, and the interaction between you and your parents. Let's look more closely at these factors.

Social and Emotional Development
Intellectual functioning is closely related to emotional functioning. It is also related to temperament. An active child who is assertive, curious, and likely to use initiative does well on IQ tests and in school. Children's social and emotional functioning during the preschool years appears to influence how well they will do in first and second grades.

A group of 323 three-year-olds attending public day-care centers in New York City were rated on socioemotional functioning and then were followed up in first and second grades. Test scores and teachers' academic ratings were compared with preschool socioemotional ratings. There was a strong relationship between preschool social and emotional functioning and later intellectual achievement. Report Kohn and Rosman (1972):

These findings suggest that the child who is curious, alert, and assertive will learn from his environment and that the child who is passive, apathetic, and withdrawn will, at the very least, learn less about his environment because of his diminished contact; he may even actively avoid contact [p. 450].

Parent-Child Interaction and Intelligence
What kinds of parents have bright children? Warm and loving ones? Pushy ones? How are they different from the parents of other children? What do they do?

Radin (1972, 1971) defined warm, nurturant parents as those who commend their children with either words or gestures, who consult with their children and ask them to share in decisions, and who are sensitive in anticipating their children's requests or feelings. When she rated fifty-two lower-class black and white mothers, she found that, in general, the 4-year-old children of warm mothers scored higher on intelligence tests and made greater gains during the preschool years than the children of less nurturant mothers. An exception was a group of white boys, who may have been responding more to their fathers (Radin, 1971).

She then looked at fathers of 4-year-old boys and found that the nurturant fathers had sons with higher IQs. The more restrictive fathers—the ones who threatened, gave orders without explanations, and scolded or spanked—had sons with lower IQs. This held true, however, only for middle-class fathers and sons. There was no such relationship among the lower classes. In both class levels, a father's tendency to ask information of his child showed a positive relationship to the boy's IQ (Radin, 1972). Maybe boys whose fathers ask them questions are encouraged to learn and express themselves well. On the other hand, maybe fathers are more likely to ask questions of bright children.

In another study, this one of 4-year-old girls and boys from middle-, working-, and lower-class families, Radin and Epstein (1975) found that boys' intellectual development was more advanced when they had warm fathers, but girls were not affected by their fathers' behavior. Could this be because fathers have ambivalent attitudes toward assertiveness in girls and give their daughters "mixed" messages, strengthening the girls' tendencies to model themselves after their mothers?

What about "pushiness"? When mothers are so concerned with growth, achievement, and development during their children's first three years that they prod them and show off their skills, what happens? Apparently, not much in the long run. Moss and Kagan (1958) rated forty-four middle-class mothers for acceleration, or "pushiness." They found that at the age of 3 the sons (but not the daughters) of the accelerated mothers had higher IQs than other children, but by the age of 6 there was no difference for either sex. It seems, then, that the "stage-mother" doesn't necessarily write the script.

Based on the results of many studies (Clarke-Stewart, 1977), we can draw a picture of the parents of young children who score high on intelligence tests and whose IQs *increase* during the preschool period. These

parents are sensitive, warm, and loving. They are very accepting of their children's behavior, letting them explore and express themselves. When they do want to change certain aspects of the child's behavior, they use reasoning or appeals to feelings rather than rigid rules. They use relatively sophisticated language and teaching strategies, and they encourage their children's independence, creativity, and growth by reading, teaching, and playing. The children respond to these actions by expressing curiosity, being creative, exploring new situations, and doing well in school.

Most of the studies on parental influences on children's intellectual development have concentrated on the mother's role. The father is important, too. Children who do not have fathers living with them, or whose fathers are physically present but uninvolved with their lives, do less well on intelligence tests, especially in the mathematical portions (Shinn, 1978). Children seem to suffer more severely when their fathers are away during the children's early years than when the absence occurs later. They may need the early interaction with this important person in their lives to stretch their intellectual abilities. Children do, of course, form strong emotional ties with their fathers: a child seems to suffer more when his or her father's absence stirs up anxiety and feelings of abandonment, as in divorce, than when the father has died. Another fact that cannot be ignored is the financial hardship suffered by many families when a widowed or separated mother has to support the family herself. So the situation is complex. It isn't hopeless, though. When mothers go out of their way to compensate for the absence of the fathers—by spending more time with their children, by encouraging them to be independent and to take risks, and by bringing other men into their lives to act as father substitutes (relatives, friends, Big Brothers, and so forth)—the children do better.

Socioeconomic Status

During the preschool years, the gap in intellectual skills between children from low-income homes and those from more financially comfortable ones continues to widen. One important reason is undoubtedly the difference in their parents. Parents at higher income and social levels are more likely to act in ways that meet children's needs for companionship, affection, and intellectual stimulation. Says Clarke-Stewart (1977), "they are more likely to request, consult, explain rather than coax, command, threaten, and punish" (p. 33).

Upper-income parents don't love their children any more than do poor parents, and, in fact, the social behaviors of low-income children, like cooperating with others and helping, are no different from their more affluent age-mates. So what accounts for the differences in parental behavior—and the differences in children's responses? The parents may be different because of varying cultural traditions or because better-educated parents have learned more about the kind of care that children need. Or they may be different simply because they have more money. Freed from the necessity of spending most of their energy on satisfying basic needs (as in Maslow's hierarchy), more affluent parents can relax more with their children and turn their attention to aspects of their development that go beyond mere survival. There are still many unanswered questions, and additional research is needed that focuses on specific parental behaviors rather than on broad socioeconomic categories.

Educational Television

What influence does TV have on children's intelligence development? A number of studies have assessed the effects of Sesame Street, the most far-reaching effort to date to teach over the tube. This show was specifically designed to teach preschoolers definite cognitive skills, such as the ability to use letters and numbers, to solve problems, to reason, and to understand their physical and social environment. How well has the show succeeded?

When Stein and Friedrich (1975) reviewed several studies comparing children who watched the show with those who did not, they found a certain measure of success. Children who often view it tend to improve more on the skills taught than those who watch seldom or never. Furthermore, this learning often carries over to a wider range of verbal skills, which are not specifically taught. Although improvements showed up for all the groups of children tested, there were some variations. Younger children (3-year-olds) make more gains than 5-year-olds. Disadvantaged youngsters who watch often gain as much as advantaged children who watch often, but when it comes to infrequent viewing, the advantaged children gain more than the disadvantaged. Apparently a little viewing builds on other sources of learning, which the advantaged children have access to while the disadvantaged children don't. So even though Sesame Street does not close the gap in achievement between advantaged and disadvantaged children, it may be able to help prevent that gap from increasing.

While some educators have been afraid that Sesame Street's fast pace and slapstick approach would make school seem boring by comparison, children who watch the show often like school more and do better than those who watch rarely (Bogatz & Ball, 1971). Other critics are concerned that the program's fast pace will discourage children from developing a long enough attention span for work that requires a sustained effort. However, there's no evidence that children become impulsive when they see impulsive or fast-moving models.

Another area for concern is attitudinal. *Sesame Street* portrays a great deal of physical aggression (in slapstick sequences), verbal aggression (in name-calling), and sex stereotypes (females tend to be underrepresented and passive). The voicing of these criticisms has brought about some

changes in the show, especially with regard to sex-role steretyping.

SUMMARY

1 Physical development increases rapidly during the preschool years, with no significant differences in growth between boys and girls. The muscular, nervous, and skeletal systems are maturing, and all primary teeth are present. Motor development improves vastly. **2** Factors such as nutrition and emotional deprivation can affect physical growth and development. Malnourished children show retardation in bone development and smaller head circumferences than well-nourished children. Some children in conditions of extreme emotional deprivation are abnormally small, but height and weight increase upon removal from a hostile environment. Abused and neglected children have received widespread social attention and medical documentation; family therapy is recommended. **3** According to Piaget's *preoperational* stage of cognitive development (ages 2 to 7), the *symbolic function* develops and enables children to represent and reflect upon people, places, and events. Thought is more flexible than during the sensorimotor stage but still is not mature in the adult sense, since children cannot yet deal with abstractions. The presence of the symbolic function is manifest through *language*, *deferred imitation*, and *symbolic play*. However, preoperational children are still burdened with cognitive limitations such as *egocentrism* and *irreversibility*. Some evidence indicates that carefully designed "training studies" can accelerate cognitive development. **4** Many children from 3 to 6 years of age attend preschools and kindergartens. These preparations for formal schooling are of many types and focus on children's cognitive, emotional, and physical growth. **5** Preschooler's speech is of two main types: egocentric and socialized. *Egocentric speech*, which fails to take into account the listener's needs, may be used to guide behavior rather than to communicate. *Socialized speech* is intended to communicate. The meaning of egocentric speech has been debated by theoreticians such as Piaget and Vygotsky. Generally, the younger a child is, the greater the proportion of egocentric speech. **6** During the preschool period, the environment to some extent influences children's facility with language. *Sociolinguistics* is the study of interaction between language and social setting. Through sociolinguistics we learn that the language of lower-class children is different from that of middle-class children, largely as a result of parent-child interaction. Children's language has been improved by instructing parents in how to teach their children effectively. **7** Intelligence is influenced by an individual's inherited potential, home life, relationships with parents, and personality. Intelligence tests for preschool children tend to be verbal rather than motoric. All intelligence tests must be assessed in terms of validity and reliability.

SUGGESTED READINGS

Anastasi, A. *Psychological testing* (4th ed.). New York: Macmillan, 1976. Intended as a college text, this is a comprehensive view of current psychological tests and testing problems. It provides material dealing with individual intelligence tests, measurement of intellectual impairment, projective techniques, and other personality tests, as well as a description of the principles of test construction and a discussion of problems with psychological testing.

Berland, T., & Seyler, A. E. *Your children's teeth*. New York: Hawthorn, 1968. A guidebook for parents, which discusses all aspects of dental health from the prenatal period through adolescence. Written by a dentist and a medical writer, the book has the seal of approval from the American Dental Association.

Evans, E. *Contemporary influences in early childhood education* (2d ed.). New York: Holt, 1975. Discusses relevant topics in early childhood education—Piaget, Montessori, behavioral analysis, open education.

Flavell, J. H. *The development of role-taking and communication skills in children*. New York: Wiley, 1968. Flavell's experimental background provides a basis for discussion of children's ability to discriminate role attributes in other persons. This text is particularly valuable to behavioral scientists and students of the research process.

Fontana, V. *Somewhere a child is crying*. New York: Mentor, 1976. A discussion of causes and treatment of child abuse.

Galinsky, E., & Hooks, W. H. *The new extended family: Day care that works*. Boston: Houghton Mifflin, 1977. An inspiring book that reports on some of the best day care to be found in the United States and explains what makes it good.

Kempe, R., & Kempe, C. H. *Child abuse*. Cambridge: Harvard University Press, 1978. A discussion of the nature of child abuse which emphasizes various treatment approaches.

Piaget, J., & Inhelder, B. *The psychology of the child*. New York: Basic Books, 1969. Piaget's own synthesis of his theory of cognitive development. With the assistance of his long-time collaborator Barbel Inhelder, he traces the stages of cognitive development over the entire period of childhood, from infancy to adolescence.

Roby, P. (Ed.) *Child care—who cares?* (student ed.). New York: Basic Books, 1973. A collection of articles about various aspects of day care in this country and abroad.

EARLY CHILDHOOD

7

PERSONALITY AND SOCIAL DEVELOPMENT

IN THIS CHAPTER YOU WILL LEARN ABOUT

The personality development of preschool children—how girls and boys come to identify with appropriate adult models and develop sex-appropriate behaviors

How a child's heredity, environment, culture, and parents influence sexual identification

Children's fears and ways to overcome them

Child-rearing practices that influence aggression, passivity, dependence, independence, and achievement

Children's play and friendship patterns and their effects on development

CHAPTER OVERVIEW

Some parents, who find it burdensome caring for a tiny infant or running after an active toddler, suddenly look at their 3-year-old and exclaim, "Hey, he's a real person!" While, as we have seen, emotional and social development begins right from birth, it is during the next few years from about 3 on that personality development seems to come into full flower.

During this time, children emerge more fully as individuals. We find them good company, with a cheerful disposition and a lively sense of humor—or, sometimes, difficult to be with, because they are whiny or aggressive. Their feelings about themselves come through, with their beginning sense of self-esteem coloring the characteristic ways they relate to other people. They begin to develop a conscience, to make moral judgments of right and wrong, and to act according to (or in spite of) those judgments. They show how they identify with their parents and with others of their same sex. They form friendships with other children, who now occupy a more important place in their lives.

THEORETICAL PERSPECTIVES ON PERSONALITY IN EARLY CHILDHOOD

FREUD'S THEORY: THE PHALLIC (EARLY GENITAL) STAGE

According to Freud, the primary zone of psychosexual pleasure changes at about the age of 3 or 4, when interest and pleasure become concentrated in the genital area. This stage gets its name from *phallus*, another term for the penis. Preschoolers are fascinated by anatomical differences between girls and boys and adults and children; they want to find out where babies come from and learn about the adult sex act. Their conversation is

full of "dirty" jokes, although more of these still seem to be centered on the bathroom than on the bedroom.

According to the theory of the *Oedipus complex*, a 3- to 6-year-old boy lavishes love and affection with decidedly sexual overtones on his mother, thus competing with his father for the mother's love and affection. Unconsciously, the little boy wants to take his father's place, but he recognizes his father's power. The child is caught up by conflicting feelings—genuine affection for his father, tempered by hostility, rivalry, and fear. Noticing that little girls don't have penises, he wonders what happened to them, and his guilt over his feelings for his mother and father makes him worry that he will be castrated by his father. This is the *castration complex*. Fearful, he represses his sexual strivings toward his mother, stops trying to rival his father, and begins to identify with him.

The *Electra complex* is similar to the Oedipus: A little girl desires her father, fears her mother, represses these feelings, and eventually identifies with the same-sex parent.

Freud was specific about penis envy in little girls, saying:

The first step in the phallic phase . . . is a momentous discovery which little girls are destined to make. They notice the penis of a brother or playmate, strikingly visible and of large proportions, at once recognize it as the superior counterpart of their own small and inconspicuous organ, and from that time forward fall a victim to envy for the penis [1905, quoted in Schaeffer, p. 16].

According to Freud, a little girl just can't win. If she succumbs to *penis envy*, she hopes to get one for herself and become a man; if not, she is denying her envy, which could cause adult neurosis. Either way, she develops a sense of her own inferiority, and is likely to become a jealous person and turn against her mother, who is responsible for her lack of a penis. Eventually, if the girl develops normally (for a female), she:

... gives up her wish for a penis and puts in place of it a wish for a child: and *with this purpose in view* she takes her father as a love-object. Her mother becomes the object of her jealousy. The girl has turned into a little woman [quoted in Schaeffer, p. 19].

The very desire for motherhood, then, is the result of penis envy. Freud claims that a woman's procreative urge is most fully satisfied by the birth of a son, "who brings the longed-for penis with him."

Development of the Superego

By identifying with the parent of the same sex, children actually take the parent's personality into their own. In psychoanalytic terms, this is called *introjection*:

When the boy introjects his father, or the girl her mother, either child constantly then carries around a conscience, representing the parent's wishes, values and standards. When the child transgresses, this inner voice reprimands him and makes him feel guilty; it is part of the child's own wishes and values [Baldwin, 1968, p. 367].

Freud's *superego* is comparable to the conscience. At this stage a child's conscience is rigid. The daughter of parents who value cleanliness may become so compulsive that she will want to change clothing six times a day. Or a little boy may be tormented by guilt because he fought with a friend, even though his parents do not disapprove of harmless tussling. With maturity, the superego, or conscience, becomes more realistic and flexible, allowing an individual to function according to higher principles while also considering self-interest.

ERIKSON'S THEORY: CRISIS III: INITIATIVE VERSUS GUILT

Young children are still trying to gain and maintain a sense of autonomy. Parental guidance and their new ability to express themselves in words help them. At this stage

children are energetic and are eager to try new things and work cooperatively. They turn from a total *attachment* to their parents to an *identification* with them, which comes about partly as a result of Oedipal rivalry and guilt, but more from "a spirit of equality experienced in doing things together" (Erikson, 1950, p. 258).

The basic conflict at this time is between *initiative*, which enables children to plan and carry out activities, and *guilt* over what they want to do. This conflict is a split between that part of the personality that remains a *child*, full of exuberance and a desire to try new things and test new powers, and the part that is becoming an *adult*, constantly examining the child's motives and actions for propriety. Children have to learn how to regulate these aspects of their personalities so that they will develop a sense of responsibility but still be able to enjoy life.

If the superego becomes too strict and leaves too much guilt, children may overcontrol and overconstrict themselves until their personality has been obliterated. Adults who did not develop initiative during these years may suffer from repression: They may develop

The memory of my early years seems to consist of a continuous series of crimes which brought in their wake an equally monotonous succession of punishments and disgraces. Though it was impossible to know beforehand whether an action constituted a crime or not, there never was any doubt in my mind about my guilt. One acquired guilt automatically, in the same way one's hands grew dirty as the day wore on, and to be in disgrace was the natural outcome of this process.

Arthur Koestler, in *Arrow in the Blue*

psychosomatic illness, paralysis, inhibition, or impotence; they may overcompensate by showing off; or they may become self-righteous and intolerant, concerned more with negative aspects of prohibiting their own and others' impulses than with positive tasks of guiding initiative.

Detachment from Parents

With the development of autonomy and initiative, children detach themselves from their parents. Rheingold and Eckerman (1970) found that children's readiness to leave their mothers increases regularly with age. For each added month, forty-eight 1- to 5-year-old children went about one-third meter farther away from their mothers. After the second year, the children varied considerably in the distance they were willing to go away.

Where do children go when they leave their parents? They explore new territory, learn new games, and form new relationships. The most significant type of new relationship among preschoolers is between peers. Real friendships with other children and peer influences continue to grow until, by middle childhood, friends are as important as parents, if not more so.

IDENTIFICATION

Timmy went to the library with his grandfather, who took care of him every day while his parents were at work. The librarian asked Timmy, "Can you read?" and handed him a book which he opened. With a motion he had seen his grandfather perform many times, Timmy felt in all his pockets. He then looked up and said, "I must have left my glasses at home."

The process of *identification*, by which a child not only imitates the actions of another person but actually acquires many of that person's characteristics, is explained in several different ways. Both Freud and Erikson turn to psychoanalytic theory to explain a child's identification with the parent of the same sex. Kagan (1971) defines identification in learning-theory terms, also seeing it as an important development in early childhood.

Identification is, in part, the belief of a person that some attributes of a model (for example, parents, siblings, relatives, peers, and fictional figures) are also possessed by the person. A boy who realizes that he and his father share the same name, notes that they have similar facial features, and is told by relatives that they both have lively tempers, develops a belief that he is similar to his father. *When this belief in similarity is accompanied by vicarious emotional experiences in the child that are appropriate to the model, we say that the child has an identification with the model* [Kagan, 1971, p. 57; italics in the original].

According to Kagan (1971), four interrelated processes establish and then strengthen identification: Children believe that they share particular physical or psychological attributes with the model; they experience vicarious emotions similar to those the model is feeling; they want to be like the model; and they behave like the model and adopt the model's opinions and mannerisms.

SEX TYPING

Wendy, at age 5, is playing house with Michael. "I'm the mommy," she says as she cooks and cleans and takes care of her dolls, while Michael puts on a hat and "goes to work." A minute later, Michael "comes home," sits at the table, and says, "I'm hungry. Where's dinner?"

These children exemplify the results of *sex typing*, the process by which children acquire the behavior and attitudes regarded by their culture as characteristically masculine or feminine. Sex typing goes much deeper than this anecdote indicates. It involves the motives, emotions, and values that help us direct our lives from infancy to the grave. Most of us grow up with strongly defined notions of the behavior, opinions, and emotions that are appropriate for males and females. Children develop these notions very early, and their sex-role patterns remain remarkably stable throughout life (Hetherington, 1970).

As we noted in Chapter 5, the evidence on sex differences in infancy is so confusing and contradictory that it is difficult to see any clear patterns. By the age of 2 or 3, though, consistent differences do show up between the sexes. Little boys are more aggressive and more likely to explore their surroundings; run, jump, and climb; and manipulate toys. Little girls sit still longer, are more persistent, and pay attention for a longer time (Birns, 1976).

One interesting example of a trait that shows up differently over time is that of *field independence*. Tests that measure this ability ask a person to find geometric figures embedded in larger figures. People who find the correct figures easily are thought to rely more upon themselves for information than upon the environment. Field independence is said to be related to analytic thinking. At the ages of 2 and 3, boys and girls do not differ on this trait; at ages 4 and 5, girls do better; and by the age of 6, boys are more field-independent (Birns, 1976).

HOW SEX TYPING COMES ABOUT

Are differences between males and females biological or cultural? Some researchers who have found differences between male and female infants—in hormonal levels or in activity levels, for example—pursue their studies with an eye to determining innate differences to account for the greater aggression levels in boys and men or the more nurturant behavior of girls and women. Other researchers feel that even if such predispositions do exist, their eventual flowering or withering depends in large part on the ways children perceive the sex-oriented values of their culture.

If male and female behavior were unalter-

ably established by nature, we could not have deviant patterns such as those reported by Margaret Mead (1935) in three New Guinea tribes. Among the Arapesh, both men and women are "placid and contented, unaggressive and non-initiatory, non-competitive, and responsive, warm, docile, and trusting" (p. 56), and nurturant toward children. Among the cannibalistic Mundugumor, "both men and women are expected to be violent, competitive, aggressively sexed, jealous and ready to see and avenge insult, delighting in display, in action, in fighting" (p. 213). The occasional mild man and nurturant woman are social misfits. The Tchambuli tribe has different expectations for males and females, directly opposite to those in most societies: The woman is dominant, impersonal, and hard-working while the man is less responsible, more concerned about personal appearance, and more dependent emotionally.

Other evidence against wholly biological sex typing is drawn from research on persons with genital anomalies. Occasionally a child is born with sex organs that are not obviously of one sex or the other. At birth the doctor assigns the child a sex to the best of his or her ability. Then later chromosomal or hormonal evidence sometimes indicates that the sex assignment was wrong and that "she," say, is more properly "he." If the child is less than 2 years old, the child can be reassigned to the other sex without severe psychological stress. After the age of 2, sexual orientation—even when contradictory to biological sex—will be too strongly entrenched to change (Money, 1963). This testifies to the strong reinforcement children receive for thinking of themselves as members of one sex or the other.

Probably, characteristically male or female behavior is determined by some combination of hormones and upbringing.

Female guinea pigs whose mothers had

received testosterone while pregnant exhibited masculine behavior when they reached maturity (Dantchakoff, 1938); the administration of testosterone to young female rats made them act in typically masculine patterns (Gray, Lean, & Keynes, 1969); and female rhesus monkeys masculinized in utero acted more like males in initiating play, engaging in more rough-and-tumble play, and other activities (Phoenix, 1966).

Animals are not people, of course, and the behavior of human beings is determined socially to an infinitely greater extent than that of any animal. Furthermore, we cannot confirm animal studies with human beings. We can, though, observe and draw inferences from those occasional individuals in whom sex assignment is not clear-cut. Of particular interest are two studies involving a total of twenty individuals.

Ehrhardt and Money (1967) saw ten girls, aged 3 to 14, who had been born to women who had received synthetic progestins during pregnancy. Nine of the girls were born with abnormal external sexual organs, which had to be surgically corrected to make the girls look normal and enable them eventually to participate in sexual intercourse. Internally, they were females capable of normal reproduction. All were raised as girls from birth and generally looked forward to the role of wife and mother. As children, though, they were closer to the male stereotype. Nine were called "tomboys": They liked to compete with boys in active sports and liked playing with trucks, guns, and other "boys' toys" better than with dolls and other "girls' toys." Tomboyishness *is* common among middle-class girls, and there is nothing pathological about it. But while acknowledging that tomboyishness does not preclude eventual romance, marriage, child bearing and full-time home and family care" (p. 96), the authors still raise the

The child assimilates the attitudes and behavior of the same-sex parent, many of which are related to sex-role expectations. (Photos by Erika Stone/Peter Arnold, Inc.)

possibility that there might be something in fetal masculinization which affects that part of the central nervous system that controls energy-expending behavior. From an early age, boys are more active than girls. How much of this is hormonal and how much cultural? We don't know.

The ten people, aged 13 to 30, in the other study (Money, Ehrhardt, & Masica, 1968) looked like females but were chromosomally male. They had testes instead of ovaries and they were unable to bear children since they could not ovulate. Their condition appeared to have been inherited; the particular mechanism may have involved an inability to utilize androgen prenatally. Since they looked like normal girls, they had been brought up as females. All were "typically female" in behavior and outlook. They all considered marriage and raising a family to be very important, and all had had repeated dreams and fantasies about bringing up children. Eight had played primarily with dolls and other "girls' toys," and the seven who reported having played "house" in childhood had always played the mother. There was no ambiguity in their psychological sex role. Their experiences and attitudes show the strong influence of environment on sex typing.

In most cultures men are more aggressive and have more authority than women, and they usually do the dangerous, physically strenuous jobs, while the women generally perform routine jobs closer to home. These patterns grew up because of anatomical differences. The average man is taller, heavier, and more muscular than the average woman, and the woman bears and nurses the babies. Today, however, most work in an industrial society can be performed as well by a 90-pound woman as by a 200-pound man, and women are bearing fewer children and nursing them more briefly, if at all. The old bases for assigning work along sex lines do not seem so relevant.

THEORETICAL EXPLANATIONS OF SEX TYPING

As with so many other issues in human development, there is a wide range of conflicting opinion to explain why and how sex typing comes about. The major theories are presented here:

1 *Biological theory:* Biological factors such as sex hormones or brain lateralization cause sex differences. Much research in this area was done on lower animals; the results were extrapolated to humans.

2 *Psychoanalytic theory:* According to Freud, sex typing is the indirect result of anatomical differences, an integral part of the identification process, and an upshot of the Oedipus complex. The child assimilates the attitudes and behavior of the same-sex parent, many of which are related to sex-role expectations.

3 *Social learning theory:* Social learning can take place in one or more of these ways, as described by Lamb and Urberg (1978):

- *Socialization:* Children are rewarded for sex-role behavior their parents think is appropriate and punished for inappropriate behavior.
- *Observation:* The child identifies with and imitates the parent of the same sex. Observational-learning theorists and psychoanalysts suggest that boys and girls both originally imitate their mothers when the mother is the primary caretaker; later the boys switch over to identify with their fathers. The more nurturant and competent the father, the more likely his son is to identify with him.
- *Reciprocal role:* The cross-sex parent influences the child's sex typing, a finding that shows up especially strongly with girls. While several studies have found that the daughter of a feminine woman is not necessarily feminine herself, the daughter of a strongly masculine man who approves of femininity does tend to be feminine.

4 *Cognitive developmental theory:* In the cognitive developmental theory proposed by Kohlberg, sex typing comes about as a natur-

al corollary of cognitive development. First, babies hear and learn the words "boy" and "girl"; then they are labeled as one or the other; and by the age of 2 or 3, they know the appropriate labels for themselves and begin to organize their lives around these labels. While children are learning what they are, they are also learning what to do. They learn what activities, opinions, and emotions are considered masculine or feminine, and they incorporate the appropriate ones into their daily lives. Sometime between the ages of 5 and 7, children achieve what Kohlberg calls "gender conservation," when they realize that they will always be male or female.

As cognitive development progresses, children think in terms of cross-cultural stereotypes, which "are not derived from parental behavior or direct tuition, but rather, stem from universal perceived sex differences in bodily structure and capacities" (Mussen, 1969, p. 411). When they notice the differences in male and female body structure and capacities, they consider dominance and aggression as male characteristics and nurturance as a female trait. They try to live up to these stereotypes, as well as trying to copy directly the attitudes and activities of individual adults of the same sex.

Once children consider themselves male or female, they seek out models of their sex to copy. They don't confine themselves to identifying with their own same-sex parent, but look toward teachers, neighbors, friends, sports heroes, and television personalities. This casting wide the net for models explains why daughters are often so different from their mothers; sons, from their fathers.

Young children have very rigid views of authority, as we will see in our discussion of moral development in Chapter 8. Until they enter early adolescence, they are likely to view moral laws as inviolable, never able to be modified for any reason. The same thing seems to happen with sex-role stereotypes. Young children tend to follow slavishly the sex-typing customs of their society, not recognizing, for example, that a boy can retain his maleness without doing or being everything that his society identifies as male.

Critique of Theories of Sex Differences

None of these theories fully explains why the sexes turn out differently from each other in so many respects, while retaining so many other traits in common. As with other developmental phenomena, it is probable that many of the forces described in the different theories interact with each other.

Biological factors have been implicated most clearly in the areas of aggression and visual-spatial ability. It's possible, for example, that masculine hormonal levels provide boys with a greater readiness to learn aggression. Mead's work and Money's work, referred to above, cast doubt, however, on strict biological explanations for sex typing.

There are also a number of problems with the "identification with the same sex parent" that is the key to both the psychoanalytic and social learning approaches. For one thing, there is no good explanation for the way a boy's switch to identifying with his father takes place. And while identification theorists suggest that a girl's sex-role learning is easier because she has continuous identification with the mother, there is no real evidence for this statement. If the father's power in the family is the major reason why his son identifies with him, why doesn't his daughter take on his characteristics, too, to get that power? And why does the reciprocal role theory apply to girls but not boys? A major limitation of the socialization model of social learning theory is the fact that boys and girls may not be treated so differently by their parents. (See the section "Parental Influences on Sex Typing.") Yes, parents dress their children differently and buy them different kinds of toys, but, as Lamb and Urberg (1978) point out, parents don't punish girls more than boys for being aggressive. And yet girls are less aggressive.

The cognitive developmental model is the one most favored by contemporary students of sex typing. While its biggest weakness is Kohlberg's setting of gender identity at an age some three to five years later than most data suggest, this theory does answer many of the questions raised by the other theories, such as the problems with the psychoanalytic and social learning approaches raised by Maccoby and Jacklin (1974):

Children have not been shown to resemble closely the same-sex parent in their behavior. In fact, the rather meager evidence suggests that a boy resembles other children's fathers as much as he does his own, at least with respect to most of the behaviors and attributes measured so far. The same applies to girls' resemblance to their mothers [p. 363].

A second problem is that when offered an opportunity to imitate either a male or female model, children (at least those under age 6 or 7) do not characteristically select the model whose sex matches their own; their choices are fairly random in this regard . . . A final problem is that children's sex-typed behavior does not closely resemble that of adult models. Boys select an all-male play group, but they do not observe their fathers avoiding the company of females [p. 363].

SEX TYPING IN THE UNITED STATES

Our society is less rigid in its sex-role definitions than many others, but sex typing is still very much with us. Furthermore, our society consistently undervalues abilities that fall within "feminine competence." While women in other cultures are proud of their skills in caring for children, our girls learn from an early age to devalue these tasks and yet to associate them with femininity. The little girl is in a double bind. She identifies with her mother's skills in caring for children and keeping the home, but at the same time she picks up all the cultural nuances that let her know that

"woman's work" is not nearly so important as "man's work."

These attitudes crystallize very early. Greenberg and Peck (1974) asked 120 children, aged 3 to 6, to look at photos of boys and girls and say which ones would grow up to be doctors, dentists, teachers, and so on. With adult photos, the children were asked: "All of these people are scientists (or artists, or teachers, etc.). Who is the best?" The children also were tested for intelligence. All the children tended to give highly stereotyped answers, with the brightest ones giving the most traditional responses. They were most likely to see boys growing up to be doctors and dentists, girls being teachers, and men being the smartest scientists. Even at this early age, girls expect that their adult roles will be more limited than those of boys. They are more likely to see themselves in adult life as a mother, a nurse, or a teacher, whereas boys look forward to a wide range of active, exciting, non-family-oriented careers (Papalia & Tennent, 1975).

There is much more pressure for boys to adopt "male" behaviors. Most parents look with mild amusement at the antics of a tomboy, whereas they react strongly and negatively to "sissyish" behavior in boys—crying, passivity, and an interest in the arts, playing with dolls, and helping around the house. As the tomboy approaches adolescence, she too is expected to shed her childish interests in active sports and "boyish" games and to become feminine.

Socioeconomic Differences

The pressure on children to conform to sex-role expectations is more marked in the lower socioeconomic groups. Lower-class boys show a strong preference for so-called boys' toys at the age of 4 or 5, lower-class girls and middle-class boys prefer "sex-appropriate" toys at about 7, and middle-class girls do not show a preference for girls' toys until they are about 9 (Rabban, 1950). Lower-class adults tend to offer more rigidly stereotyped models. The fathers are more likely to work in traditionally masculine occupations involving heavy labor, and the mothers in such traditionally feminine, service-oriented occupations as cleaning and cooking. The fathers help around the house and care for children less often than middle-class fathers, who are more likely to change diapers, shop for groceries, or dry dishes. Middle-class mothers are usually more assertive and more likely to participate in a variety of activities or in a profession not generally regarded as feminine.

PARENTAL INFLUENCES ON SEX TYPING

Do fathers and mothers treat their sons and daughters differently? Are the differences based on the sex of the child *and* parent? How influential are these differences?

Young children of both sexes usually see their fathers as the parent more likely to punish them. Both boys and girls report being kissed more by the parent of the opposite sex, and they tend to see the same-sex parent as "less benevolent and more frustrating" (Rothbart & Maccoby, 1966). Kagan and Lemkin (1960) interviewed sixty-seven 3- to 8-year-olds and found that children see their mothers as more nurturant and their fathers as more punitive, competent, and powerful. The girls saw their fathers as both more affectionate and more punitive, implying more power both positively and negatively. These children may have been influenced as much by the way books, mass media, and other children portray masculine and feminine roles as by what their parents are actually like.

Other studies have looked at the parents themselves. Fathers report different expecta-

tions for, and different participation in, activities with their sons and daughters; mothers tend to treat both sexes similarly. However, mothers do permit more aggressiveness from boys when directed toward parents and children outside the family. (They are no more likely than their husbands to let their sons beat up siblings.) Fathers are more concerned about sex typing (Rothbart & Maccoby, 1966).

Rothbart and Maccoby (1966) studied ninety-eight upper-middle-class mothers and thirty-two fathers of nursery school children. They played the recorded voice of the same child in a variety of hypothetical situations, telling some parents that the child was a boy, and others that it was a girl. The parents were asked to imagine they were at home reading while a 4-year-old daughter or son was playing with a puzzle in the next room. A year-old baby was with the preschooler. The parents were asked to write down what they would say or do in response to such statements as "Come help me"; "Tell the baby he can't play with my puzzle"; and (to the baby) "Leave my puzzle alone or I'll hit you in the head!" Parents also were questioned on their feelings about the degree to which boys and girls should and actually do differ on selected characteristics.

Mothers turned out to be more permissive toward their sons—and fathers toward daughters—on comfort-seeking, dependency, allowing the child to stop the game, and siding with the older child against the baby. Fathers allowed more aggression toward themselves from girls, as mothers did from boys. Fathers allowed both sexes to be more autonomous than did mothers. Parents who felt sex roles should be highly differentiated showed larger differences in the way they treated boys and girls, but not by promoting dependency in girls and assertiveness in boys. Rather, they were more permissive to the opposite-sex child on both traits. The authors concluded:

Rather than consistent reinforcement of sex-typed behavior by both parents, inconsistency

The warmth that parents show exerts a strong influence on whether their children will want to be like them. (Erika Stone/Peter Arnold, Inc.)

between parents seems to be the rule, and while a parent may treat his child in a manner consistent with the cultural stereotype in one area of behavior, in another he may not [p. 242].

Other societal factors may have more influence than parents in developing sex roles, and parents may shift their encouragement toward sex typing as children grow older. This study brings out the great difficulty in trying to ascribe single causes for the very complex behaviors of human beings.

Parental Warmth

The warmth that parents show exerts a strong influence on whether their children will copy them. Boys rated highly masculine see their fathers as more rewarding and nurturant than

do low-masculine boys, and the warmth of both parents appears positively related to high levels of femininity in girls (Hetherington, 1970). The influence of the father seems especially important in sex typing, since fathers usually respond differently to sons and daughters, while mothers treat their children more similarly (Hetherington, 1970).

The Father's Role

Psychoanalytic theory emphasizes the *negative* forces underlying a little boy's identification with his father—the resentment and fear that make him "identify with the aggressor." Learning theory stresses the positive forces:

If the father is an important source of nurturance, reward, and satisfaction, his responses and characteristics acquire secondary reward value and the boy imitates his father's behavior in order to "reproduce bits of the beloved and longed for parent" [Mussen & Distler, 1959, p. 350].

As we pointed out earlier, the father also exerts a major influence on his daughter's sex typing. A masculine father who disciplines consistently, gets along well with his wife, and encourages his daughter to participate in female activities is more likely to produce a feminine daughter (Clarke-Stewart, 1977).

What happens when the father is not in the home? In many cases, especially if a boy is 5 or younger when his father leaves or dies, his masculine identity does seem to falter. But a mother can compensate for a father's absence by encouraging assertive, independent behavior; by making a boy aware of the value of the masculine role; and by taking special steps to bring other men into her son's life— friends, relatives, teachers, scout leaders, and so forth (Biller & Bahm, 1971).

TWO CHILDREN IN NURSERY SCHOOL PLAYING AT "DRESS-UP":

Aaron gets an apron and puts it on. Jan turns to him and says to him reprovingly, "No. That's a girl's suit." Aaron takes it off and Jan puts it on over the long skirt. He gets another apron, a full-sized one with a bib. He asks, looking for approval, "Is this a boys?" Jan nods.

from *Observing and Recording the Behavior of Young Children*, 2/e., p. 86

OTHER INFLUENCES

Children's views of sex-appropriate behavior are also influenced by what they observe at school, in the neighborhood, on television, in the homes of friends, and in the activities of siblings. Children with older siblings of the same sex are more likely to behave in ways culturally associated with that sex than children with opposite-sex older siblings (Koch, 1956); and teachers of children from two-child families are more likely to rate boys as masculine and girls as feminine when they have same-sex older siblings (Brim, 1958).

Television shows perpetuate outdated stereotypes, showing males to be aggressive and constructive, while females more often are portrayed as dependent and inactive. Not surprisingly, boys and girls who watch a lot of television develop more traditional sex-role attitudes than those who watch little (Frueh & McGhee, 1975). Recent studies of children's books have also found the same patterns (Weitzman, Eifler, Hokada, & Ross, 1972).

Playmates encourage sex typing in each other. Lamb and Roopnarine (1978) looked at thirty-two 3- to 5-year-olds in nursery school and found that the children reacted to different kinds of play. They reinforced each other by praising, imitating, or joining each other in play, and they punished by criticizing, showing disapproval, or walking away. When children were reinforced, they kept at that kind of play longer, and they were especially sensitive to the encouragement of sex-typed behavior. That is, if a girl was joined by another child while she was playing in the kitchen, she would stay there longer than if she was joined by another child while she was playing with blocks. It seems that young children already know society's rules about the ways boys and girls should play, and they keep reminding each other of those rules. Boys are especially conscious of sex-appropriateness: In this study, the boys were more likely to encourage sex-typed play in both sexes.

For many years, nursery school teachers have been influenced by psychoanalytic theories that teach that children's healthy sexual identification depends on distinct differentiation between male and female roles. As a result, many conscientious teachers have tried to help children by emphasizing the differences between the sexes. More recent thinking, however, has shifted to the view that strongly differentiated sex roles *impede* the intellectual and psychological development of children (Maccoby & Jacklin, 1974).

Many teachers and school administrators are now making strong efforts to overcome old ideas. They are recruiting male teachers to let children know that men, too, can enjoy being with, teaching, and caring for children. They are renaming the "doll corner" the "family corner" and are stocking it with tools as well as dishes. They are emphasizing not what *boys* can do or what *girls* can do, but what *children* can do.

CHILDREN'S FEARS

People of every age are afraid of some things. Many fears—of fire, deep water, and fast cars—are essential for self-preservation. Babies just starting to crawl will not cross what looks like a deep cliff (Walk & Gibson, 1961). Infants under a year are frightened by loud noises or people or things associated with

The years from 2 to 6 seem to harbor the greatest number of new fears for children. (David Strickler/ Monkmeyer)

them, as well as by the sensation of falling, sudden movements, flashes of light, people or objects associated with pain, and strange people, things, or situations (Jersild, 1946). With time, some of these fears diminish, and new ones take their place. Not until the second year are children afraid of the dark or of being left alone.

The years from 2 to 6 seem to harbor the greatest number of new fears. Children may have had some frightening experiences, such as being lost, being bitten, or being injured. They've also heard of scary things that have happened to others, either in real life, in stories, or on television. They *know* so much more now, and one of the things they know is that there are a lot of things to be afraid of. Then, too, their imaginations go wild, and they worry about being attacked by a lion,

I was only two and Mommy was reading me a book, so when she came to the word "snake," I thought maybe there might be a real snake in the book. From then on I was always wondering. I looked everywhere and I'd always made sure that there wasn't a snake. Every time I went to bed, I always used to check under the covers.

Julia, 7
from *Listen to Us!*, p. 211

being in the dark, being abandoned, or going up to high places (Jersild & Holmes, 1935).

CAUSES OF CHILDREN'S FEARS
Some fears are linked to actual events. A boy who had been hit by a car became afraid of

crossing the street, and also of being alone in a dark room (Jersild & Holmes, 1935; in Jersild, 1946). Parents sometimes instill fear: Children are more likely to be afraid of thunder and lightning, dogs, and insects when their mothers are also (Hagman, 1932). Overprotective parents make their children feel the world is a dangerous place. Freudian thinkers believe that the upsurge of fears during the preschool years results from children's anxiety about being injured (the castration complex) and their guilt feelings toward their parents (the Oedipus complex), which makes them feel as though they deserve punishment.

As children grow older, bigger, and more competent, some of the things that used to seem so menacing lose their fangs. In a study of fifty-four children, almost 75 percent of the kindergartners expressed fear of ghosts and monsters, while only 50 percent of the second-graders and 5 percent of the sixth-graders interviewed described similar fears (Bauer, 1976). Kindergartners were also more likely than either second- or sixth-graders to be afraid of animals, although second-graders were even more likely than the kindergartners to have fears at bedtime and to have scary dreams. By the sixth grade, all these fears had lessened.

The older children had different kinds of fears. More than 50 percent of the 10- to 12-year-olds expressed fears of bodily injury and physical danger, compared to only 11 percent of the 4- to 6-year-olds. This shift coincides with the child's changing perception of reality and to the ability of the older child to recognize cause-and-effect relations. No longer is the child afraid of someone because of his looks ("His face looks ugly"); the second- and sixth-graders are more concerned about what the feared person or animal might do ("Guess he would have choked me or something").

Girls express more fears than boys (Bauer, 1976; Croake, 1973; Jersild & Holmes, 1935). This may be because more dependent children are more fearful and girls are encouraged to be more dependent, because parents accept girls' fears and discourage those of boys, or because boys do not admit to having fears.

Poor children are afraid of more things than those from more comfortable circumstances (Croake, 1969; Jersild & Holmes, 1935), maybe because poor children are less secure about life in general. Fear is also related to society. School-aged American children used to fear supernatural beings and events the most, but are now more worried about war and Communists (Croake, 1973). This change probably results at least in part from the influence of television, which brings war and politics into our living rooms. Television and movies themselves are often frightening, and some children have nightmares after every "cops and robbers" show. The shows themselves may not make children fearful, but they provide frightening images in which to cloak their anxieties.

HELPING CHILDREN OVERCOME FEARS

As children grow older and lose their sense of powerlessness, many fears evaporate. When they don't, parents may try to get rid of fears through ridicule ("Don't be such a baby!"); coercion ("Pat the nice doggie—it won't hurt you."); logical persuasion ("The closest bear is 20 miles away, locked up in a zoo!"); or ignoring the fears. None of these approaches works (Jersild & Holmes, 1935), and some may even aggravate a child's fearfulness.

The best ways to help children overcome fears—which they are usually eager to shed—involve activity by the children themselves. Children are most successful when they find their own practical methods to deal with what they fear, and when they are helped to gradually experience the frightening situations. Explanations can help when combined with active conditioning. Holmes (1936) helped children who were afraid of the dark, by repeatedly setting up situations in which they were encouraged to go into a dark room to retrieve a ball. The investigator reassured them of the room's safety and went in with them. After three to seven exposures, thirteen of the fourteen children entered the dark room alone.

Murphy and Bootzin (1973) worked with sixty-seven first-, second-, and third-grade children who were so afraid of snakes they couldn't touch one for ten seconds. The children were divided into two groups, and those in the experimental group were gradually induced to have closer and more frequent contact with snakes. Ten days after the experiment ended, thirty-nine of the forty-five children in the experimental group held a snake in their laps for fifteen seconds, but only five of the twenty-two control children were able to do this. The treatment time was brief: an *average* of fifteen minutes per child, in 1.9 sessions, and a maximum of thirty-two minutes (four sessions of eight minutes each).

Modeling, or showing fearlessness in others, is also useful. Nursery school children who were afraid of dogs took part in eight brief sessions in which they observed an unafraid child playing happily with a dog. Later, two-thirds of the fearful children climbed into a playpen with the dog (Bandura, Grusec, & Menlove, 1967).

HOW CHILD-REARING PRACTICES AFFECT PERSONALITY DEVELOPMENT

Why does Nicole hit and bite the nearest person when she can't complete a jigsaw puzzle? What makes David sit with that puzzle for hours, until he solves it? Why does Michele walk away from it, after a minute's trial? What makes children turn out the way they do? We are light-years away from having all the answers, though we do have some partial clues. Children are born with varying degrees of biological hardiness, intellectual capability,

and temperamental leanings. Yet in each of these areas, a child's environment during the first few years exerts a strong influence on development.

The most important facet of children's emotional environment involves the ways their parents raise them. When parents get their children to do what they want by reasoning, by playing on their sense of guilt, or by withdrawing approval and affection, the children are much more likely to develop a strong conscience and suffer from guilt feelings— and much less likely to become aggressive— than children who are disciplined by spanking, threats, or the withdrawal of privileges. Since parents are more likely to use the former methods with girls and the latter with boys, this may be why girls show more guilt and boys more aggression (Sears, Maccoby, & Levin, 1957).

In an effort to find out the effects on children of various parental behaviors, a team of social scientists at Columbia University's School of Public Health conducted a ten-year study of some 2000 New York City children and parents (Trotter, 1976). They found that parents who punish their children often by hitting them with strap or stick and by withdrawing privileges and parents who show little affection to their children are likely to produce anxious youngsters who fight a lot, don't get along with the parents, and become delinquent. Parents who are excitable, rejecting, nervous, and/or ill also produce children with more than their share of behavioral problems. Chief investigator Thomas S. Langner came up with some recommendations based on these findings: Parents should not hit their children, they should kiss and hug them to create warmer relationships, and they should have an opportunity to talk about parental behavior and its origins in PTA meetings and pregnancy classes.

These are some examples of specific child-rearing practices that are associated with specific behaviors in children. Let us look more closely at the relationship between parental behavior and the appearance of aggression, dependency, independence, prosocial behavior, and maturity in children.

AGGRESSION

What makes some children so ready to hit, bite, scream, be cruel, and destroy property, all elements of aggressive behavior? One newspaper article offers "A Sure Formula for Raising a Violent Child":

This is how you raise a violent child:

Ignore, humiliate, and tease him. Yell a lot. Show your disapproval for everything he does. Encourage him to fight with his brothers and sisters. Fight a lot, especially physically, with your spouse. Hit him a lot.

And if all that doesn't do the trick, plop him down in front of a television set and give him carte blanche to watch every violent show that's available [Kramer, 1973].

This reporter based her "advice" on sound theoretical ground, for each of the above directives reflects the findings of numerous studies that have explored the origins of aggression.

Frustration—often brought about by punishment, insults, and fears—does not necessarily lead to aggression, but a frustrated child is more likely to act aggressively than a contented one (Bandura, Ross, & Ross, 1961). Hitting children provides a double incentive to make them violent: Aside from suffering the pain and humiliation, the children see an example of an adult with whom they identify acting aggressively. Parents who spank provide a "living example of the use of aggression at the very moment they are trying to teach the child not to be aggressive" (Sears, Maccoby, & Levin, 1957, p. 266).

Bandura, Ross, and Ross (1961) divided seventy-two 3- to 6-year-olds into three groups. One by one, each of the children in the first group went into a playroom. An adult model (male for half the children, female for the other half) quietly played in a corner with some toys. The model for the second group began to assemble Tinker Toys, but after a minute, spent the rest of the ten-minute session punching, throwing, and kicking a 5-foot inflated doll. The children in the third group saw no model.

After the sessions, all the children were subjected to mild frustration and then were taken into another playroom. The children who had seen the aggressive model were much more aggressive than those in the other groups. They said and did many of the same things they had seen the model do. Both boys and girls who had seen an aggressive male model were more strongly influenced than those who had seen the aggressive female model, apparently because the children were responding in terms of behavior considered appropriate only for males. Both sexes approved of male aggression, and boys were more aggressive than girls. The subjects who had been with the quiet models were less aggressive than the controls, showing how adult models can influence children's behavior in more than one direction.

What kinds of rewards exist for aggressiveness? Sometimes the reward is negative attention like scolding or spanking—which some children seem to prefer to being ignored! Nursery school teachers have decreased the amount of aggression exhibited by 3- and 4-year-old boys by ignoring aggressive behavior and rewarding cooperative activities (Brown & Elliott, 1965). On the other hand, one cannot always ignore aggression. Indeed, permitting it by not interfering with it can communicate implicit approval. Some parents actively reward and encourage aggression toward other children, while discouraging it toward themselves: The children learn not to hit their parents, but they become aggressive toward other children (Bandura, 1960).

Smith and Green (1975) surveyed incidents in fifteen English nursery schools, play groups, and day nurseries, and they found that boys were more aggressive than girls in thirteen of the groups. Most fights occurred when one child tried to take another's toy. Of 239 aggressive incidents, 114 were between boys only; 93 were between boys and girls; and 32 were between girls only. While Serbin, O'Leary, Kent, and Tonick (1973) found that teachers interfered more in boys' fights, this study found no difference. It did find that when an adult did *not* intervene, the child who had started the fight was more than twice as likely to get what he or she wanted than when a teacher stepped in. This supports another finding that when teachers ignore hitting, pushing, fighting, or other similar behavior, other children are more likely to reinforce the aggressive behavior than when an adult becomes involved (Patterson, Littman, & Bricker, 1967).

Does Television Cause Aggressive Behavior?

Yes, say Singer and Singer (1979), after a year-long study of a hundred forty-one 3- and 4-year-olds who were observed at play in nursery school while their parents logged the TV programs the children watched and were then interviewed themselves. The programs that seemed to make children the most aggressive were the detective-action shows— and also, especially for girls, "the frenetic situation comedies and the game shows where there's all that yelling and jumping around," according to Jerome L. Singer (Locke, 1979). This study brings out the interrelationship between parental child-rearing attitudes and other aspects of a child's environment, since it found that the most aggressive children came from homes where the parents did not monitor their children's TV viewing.

This study is the most recent of several that have demonstrated a relationship between viewing violence and putting it into action.

Of 136 boys and girls aged 5 to 9, an experimental group watched a 3½-minute segment from a popular television series. In these 3½-minutes were a chase, two fistfights, two shootings, and a knifing. A control group watched 3½ minutes of athletic competition. After the televiewing, the children were asked to take part in a "game" that involved pushing either a *help* button (which would help an unseen child win a game) or a *hurt* button (which would make a handle touched by that child so hot that it would hurt). Of course, there was no such mysterious child; the only child in the experiment was the one pushing the buttons. Children who had watched the violent programming were more willing to hurt the unseen child and more willing to inflict more severe pain than were those who had watched the neutral sports program (Liebert, 1972).

Bandura, Ross, and Ross (1963) divided ninety-six preschool boys and girls into four groups. Group 1 observed real-life aggressive models; group 2 saw films of these same models acting aggressively; group 3 saw a film featuring an aggressive cartoon character; and the control group saw no models. Each child then was brought into a playroom, was frustrated slightly, and then was taken into another room that contained both aggressive and nonaggressive toys.

The children who had seen the real-life aggressive models, or the filmed aggressive models, or the cartoon aggressive model all showed much more aggression than did children who had seen none of these. Of this group of normal children, 88 percent who saw real-life or filmed human models and 79 percent who saw an aggressive cartoon

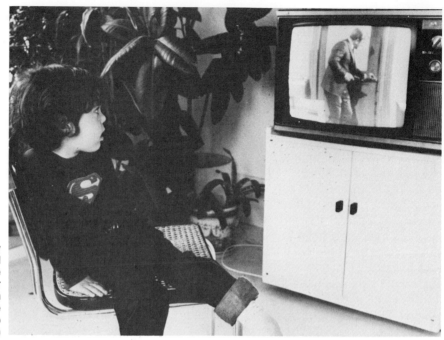

Some studies clearly show that normal children will act more aggressively after viewing violence on television. (© Alice Kandell/Photo Researchers, Inc.)

model imitated in some way the aggression they had just witnessed. The children who had seen the filmed people seemed to have been influenced the most, a finding with implications for violent television shows and movies.

These and other studies clearly show that some normal children will act more aggressively after viewing media violence.

This tendency for children to act more aggressively themselves is not, however, the only effect of televised violence. Liebert and Poulos (1976, in Lickona, 1976) have described several other effects of a steady diet of video violence. Children who see TV characters—both heroes and villains—accomplishing their aims through violence, lawbreaking, and other antisocial behaviors come to accept these means. Children who see their heroes breaking established rules are more willing to break rules themselves. Children used to seeing violence on TV may become less sensitive to aggression when they see it in real life. This can have practical results, such as failing to protect the victim of a bully. Aggression on TV also discourages children from cooperating to resolve their

differences, since it offers an example of using violence to solve problems.

Interestingly, children retain the aggressive acts enacted before their eyes much more vividly than any negative outcome for the aggressor. Thus the fact that the "bad guy" gets punished does not seem to outweigh the effects of whatever violence he has committed.

INDEPENDENCE AND DEPENDENCE

At 3 years old, Amy is independent and capable. She has a strong, intense personality and is stubborn. At 5, she is a successful leader who can organize a group on a hike, directing them and arranging things. She consistently shows a strong drive for achievement—and for doing everything herself, with a minimum of help. At age 3, Barbie is timid and tense. She follows meekly behind a particular friend or the teacher. At 4, she stays close to the teacher, and when she wants a turn on the slide, she asks the teacher to get it for her instead of asserting herself.

At 21, Amy is a strong-minded college senior who has an intense drive for achievement, is trying to be independent of her mother, and hates to appear weak. At 23, Barbie is working and living with her parents. She depends on her friends for advice, likes being close to her family, accepts her dependency on people she considers authority figures, and sees herself as inadequate when faced with problems.

"Amy" and "Barbie" are among twenty-seven women in a group of fifty-four adults observed for passivity and dependence by Kagan and Moss (1960). Passivity is more than inactivity: It is the state of being done to, rather than doing; it is the failure to initiate behavior. Dependency is the opposite of self-sufficiency: it can involve a wide variety of behaviors that demonstrate the individual's need for reassurance, love, approval, and help from others (Hetherington, 1970). Dependency as a lifelong character trait does not develop until the school years, and often not till past the age of 10. The passive and dependent preschooler often emerges as an independent adult. What differences can we see between the early environments of children who will eventually be dependent or independent?

Hartup (1970) claims that dependent, passive, clinging persons were frustrated in infancy, rejected and punished severely during the preschool years, scolded when they clung to their parents or wanted to sit in their laps (but allowed to do so anyway), and, in general, treated inconsistently. Hetherington (1970) attributes dependency in children to overprotective, excessively controlling, and dominating parental practices.

Right from infancy, children differ in their inborn drives to persist in overcoming obstacles to achieve some goal (Thomas et al., 1963). By the preschool years, these differences become much more evident, but so much so that we wonder whether inborn personality is the only factor that accounts for the difference. Why does Gina keep trying to scale the jungle gym, day after day, until she makes it to the top—while Barry gives up after one unsuccessful effort? One factor is the

different ways their parents treat them. When Gina tries something new, her parents encourage her; and when she succeeds, they praise her and show their approval. They are slow to respond to pleas for help or emotional support in little problems, and as a result Gina does more on her own. Barry's parents show less approval for his achievements, but they come to his aid more often. He does not try as hard as Gina, and when he runs into trouble, he is more likely to go to his mother's knees rather than keep trying.

PROSOCIAL BEHAVIOR: CARING FOR OTHER PEOPLE

Kelly, B.J., and Kate are sisters and brother. Kelly, 9, was in a park one day, about to eat a tuna sandwich—her favorite food—when she saw a raggedly dressed man going through a garbage can. Without hesitation she went over and gave him her lunch. B.J., 8, cuts the grass regularly for an elderly neighbor and refuses to accept money from him. And Kate, 11, was recently late for school because she stopped to pick up a woman who had fallen in the street and stayed with her until an adult came along.

Obviously, a value held by the children in this family is concern for other people. What makes some people reach out to others like this? What makes them generous, compassionate, and sensitive to other people's needs? In recent years, a number of researchers have delved into the origins of what psychologists call *prosocial* behavior, what we know generally as *altruism* and what has been defined as "actions that are intended to aid or benefit another person or group of people without the actor's anticipation of external rewards. Such actions often entail some cost, self-sacrifice, or risk on the part of the actor" (Mussen & Eisenberg-Berg, 1977).

From the many studies on this important

topic that have been conducted over the past fifteen years or so, we have learned a little about the origins of caring behavior. Socio-economic status, for example, is *not* a factor: The amount of money or social standing in a child's home makes no difference in how that youngster will behave toward others.

In the great majority of studies, no sex differences have turned up either. Some research, though, has found more generosity, helpfulness, and considerateness in girls than boys. This may be because nurturance is generally considered a more feminine trait, so girls are encouraged more often to help others; it may also be related to the fact that girls receive less physical punishment, more affection from their parents, and more explanations of the consequences of their actions.

Age is a factor in altruism. While even toddlers of 18 months will show sympathy toward someone who is hurt or unhappy and may make efforts to help, not until about the age of 4 do children display a significant amount of altruism. The level increases steadily to the age of 13, apparently in relation to the child's growing ability to burst through egocentric thinking and to put himself in another person's place.

Altruistic children tend to be advanced in mental reasoning and able to take the role of others; they are also relatively active and self-confident. How do they get this way? The results of many studies point to the home. John and Mary, for example, parents of the three children described above, are typical in several ways of the parents of prosocial children.

First, they set an example. For years, two elderly people who have no family of their own have been celebrating holidays with their family. When John takes out his snow blower to clear his own driveway, he does his neighbors' as well. For two weeks while Mary was nursing her own baby, she took in and breast-fed the infant of a sick friend.

When their children misbehave, Mary and John reason with them and encourage them to reflect on their own and others' feelings. When Kelly, at age 4, took a package of barrettes from a store, Mary didn't tell her how bad she had been, but did point out that the man in the store had to pay for them himself and then took Kelly with her to return them. A frequent question is, "How do you think —— feels? How would you feel if you were ——?"

They maintain high standards for their children and are explicit about their expectations for honesty and helpfulness. With six children in the family, they assigned responsibility for others early on, a necessity that turned out to have good results for all.

John and Mary also enlist an ally—television. They encourage their children to watch shows that encourage prosocial behavior, like *Mister Rogers' Neighborhood*, which shows cooperation, sharing, and understanding the feelings of others, and they discourage their viewing of aggressive cartoons. This attitude toward TV builds on the results of a number of studies that show that prosocial programs can encourage children to be more sympathetic, generous, and helpful (Mussen & Eisenberg-Berg, 1977). In today's complex society, it is more important than ever to encourage people to be their "brothers' keepers." As research in this area continues, we will look to it for answers in our continuing quest for a richer quality of life.

SOCIAL AND MORAL MATURITY

In the long run, how important are the specific ways parents deal with a variety of child-rearing issues in their children's first five years? According to one team of researchers, not very. In a major follow-up study of the children whose mothers had been interviewed about their child-rearing techniques by Sears, Maccoby, and Levin (1957), seventy-eight of these "children," now 31 years old, were interviewed themselves (McClelland, Constantian, Regalado, & Stone, 1978).

The major finding from this follow-up is that what parents *do* in those first five years is less important than the overall way parents *feel* about their children. The way these adults had turned out seemed to bear little or no relation to the length of time they had been breast-fed, whether they had had early or late bedtimes, or whether they had been spanked or reasoned with when they misbehaved. The most important influence in these people's lives—dwarfing all others—was how much their parents, especially their mothers, had really loved them and had shown their affection for and enjoyment of them.

The most beloved children grew up to be the most tolerant of other people, the most understanding, and the most likely to show active concern for others. (These standards for psychosocial maturity were based on both Erikson's and Kohlberg's theories.) The least mature adults had grown up in homes where they were considered a nuisance and an interference with adult-centered standards. Their parents had tolerated no noise, mess, or roughhousing in the home and had reacted unkindly to the children's aggressiveness toward them, sex play, or expressions of dependency needs.

Pointing out that the children of "easygoing, loving parents" often seemed to show less moral behavior as they were growing up than the children of stricter parents, the authors emphasize that this is often a necessary step on the way to moving away from wholesale adoption of parental values and to developing one's own value system. They conclude with a word to parents:

Parents also need faith—faith that loving and believing in their children will promote maturity in the long run, even though some of their offsprings' behavior seems outrageous in the short run as they learn to make their own decisions. There are no shortcuts to perfection. Children have to explore some detours if they are to reach the heights. The best we parents can do to help is to love them, and not stand in the way of their groping attempts to

grow up or force them at all times to conform to adult-centered codes of moral behavior [McClelland et al., 1978, p. 114].

SHIFTING STYLES OF CHILD REARING

Through the years we have had fashions in child rearing. For much of our country's early history, the "father knows best" school, in which the parents know everything and the child nothing, held sway. Parents made their will known to their children and enforced it strictly. About a third of the way into the twentieth century, psychoanalytic theories presaged a shift to permissiveness, or a belief that the child knows everything and the parent knows nothing. Since parents and professionals alike were convinced of the harm done when children were not satisfied in the oral, anal, and genital stages of psychosexual development, children set their own pace for feeding, weaning, toilet training, and so forth. Now we are in the middle of the democratic way of bringing up children—that parents probably know best in many things, but children know something, too. Therefore, the parents should guide their progeny, with respect, through childhood.

Most children seem to have thrived equally well throughout these shifting ideas, although with each method, a few children have been unable to adapt.

The small proportion of children who fail to adapt and thrive with one type of child care practice may be totally different from those who fail to thrive with another type of practice. During the centuries when infants were fed whenever they were hungry, most children apparently adapted to this approach. When feeding by the clock according to a predetermined schedule became the advocated pattern, most children adapted to this. When once

We are now in an era of bringing up children democratically; parents probably know best in many things, but children know something, too. (Erika Stone/ Peter Arnold, Inc.)

again it was decided to feed children when they were hungry—now called "self-demand feeding"—in response to the awareness that a small group of children did not adapt to clock feeding, again most, but not all, children adapted to this method. . . .

The enormous variety of child care practices which have succeeded in maintaining the race does not, however, attest to the equality of excellence. With the understanding that no general rule of child care practice will be appropriate for every child, it nevertheless can be argued that some general rules will be optimal for a higher percentage of children than other modes of practice. Defining such optimal practices still remains a goal, even though it will always be necessary to deviate from such general rules with some children [Thomas et al., 1963, p. 151].

One such rule, for example, is that noted by Clarke-Stewart (1977):

At least in the area of social relations, and possibly for achievement as well, the key to optimal development for boys and girls seems to be a *balance* between the roles and behav-

iors of mother and father. If either parent, but particularly the opposite sex parent, is markedly more affectionate, dominant, or demanding than the other, the child's development may suffer. Extreme domination by either parent has been related to lower intellectual achievement for both boys and girls, and extreme domination or excessive affection by the opposite-sexed parent to problems in children's development of sex-role identity [pp. 44–45].

Here again, we see that even a rule like this, which is backed up by research and which also seems sensible, is not infallible. Many children grow up in one-parent families, or in families with one weak and one strong parent, and turn into models of well-adjusted, achieving individuals. However, by and large, it is important to be aware of the kinds of child-rearing practices that can lead to trouble and of those that more often achieve happy results.

Current Styles of Parenting

Baumrind has defined three kinds of parental practices—the *authoritarian*, the *permissive*, and the *authoritative*—and has examined pre-school children with reference to their parents' styles (Baumrind, 1971; Baumrind & Black, 1967).

Authoritarian parents try to control their children's behavior and attitudes and make them conform to a set and usually absolute standard of conduct. They value unquestioning obedience and punish their children forcefully for acting contrary to parental standards. They are more detached, more controlling, and less warm than other parents; their children are more discontent, withdrawn, and distrustful.

Permissive parents make few demands, allowing their children to regulate their own activities as much as possible. They consider themselves resources, but not standard-bearers or ideal models. They explain to their children the reasons underlying the few family rules that do exist, consult with them about policy decisions, and hardly ever punish. They are noncontrolling, nondemanding, and relatively warm, and their children as preschoolers are immature—the least self-reliant, the least self-controlled and the least exploratory.

Authoritative parents try to direct their children's activities rationally, with attention to the issues rather than the children's fear of punishment or loss of love. They exert firm control when necessary, but they explain the reasoning behind their stands and encourage verbal give-and-take. While they have confidence in their ability to guide their children, they respect the children's interest, opinions, and unique personalities. They are loving, consistent, demanding, and respectful of their children's independent decisions, but they are firm in maintaining standards and willing to impose limited punishment. They combine control with encouragement. Their children apparently feel secure in knowing they are loved, and also in knowing what is demanded of them. As preschoolers, these children are the most self-reliant, self-controlled, self-assertive, exploratory, and content.

Children from authoritarian homes are so strictly controlled, either by punishment or guilt, that they are often prevented from making a conscious choice about the merit of a particular behavior because they are overly concerned about what their parents will do. Those from permissive homes receive so little guidance that they often become uncertain and anxious about whether they are doing the right thing. But in authoritative homes, children know when they are meeting expectations, learn how to judge those expectations, and are able to decide when it is worth risking parental displeasure or other unpleasant consequences in the pursuit of some goal. Children whose parents expect them to perform well, to fulfill commitments, and to participate actively in family duties as well as family fun learn how to formulate goals. They also experience the satisfaction that comes from meeting responsibilities and achieving success. The essential factor appears to be the parents' reasonable expectations and realistic standards.

CONTEMPORARY VOICES IN PARENT EDUCATION

The first sentence in Dr. Benjamin Spock's book *Baby and Child Care* (1976) is "You know more than you think you do." This seems ironic, because parents have probably become more dependent on Spock than on any other person in their lives. His book, which appeared in its first version in 1946, filled a crying need. It came at a time when young families, many of whom had been uprooted by World War II, were living far from their parents. The generation gap seemed to be widening. Even those young people who did live near their families felt that they were a new generation that didn't want to keep doing the same old things. Psychoanalytic thinking had become popular and Freudian terms were on everyone's lips. Spock, a pediatrician who had almost become a psychoanalyst, combined a comprehensive collection of advice about medical care of children with a Freudian-influenced understanding of children's emotional development.

Spock was—and still is, in the latest, newly revised version of his book—generally in favor of firmness, encouraging parents to stand up for what they feel is important. He combines this support to parents with a plea that they understand why children feel and act as they do—why, for example, contrariness is to be expected of a 2-year-old; why preschoolers develop all sorts of new fears; why a child is jealous of the new baby.

Even with Spock's manual, parents were finding it harder and harder to get along with their children. Along came Haim Ginott, a psychologist who had been influenced by the psychotherapist Carl Rogers (1951) and had found that the Rogerian approach of "active listening" was effective in communicating with children. Ginott wrote a book, *Between Parent and Child* (1965), urging parents to embody many of the principles he believed in; he used case histories to underscore his basic points, which focused largely on communication between parents and children. These points include respecting a child's self-esteem by refraining from using sarcasm or calling names, stating rules impersonally, avoiding accusations, encouraging children to draw their own conclusions and make their own decisions when possible, and accepting children's perceptions and feelings.

Another Rogers-influenced psychologist, Thomas Gordon, has influenced thousands of parents through his book *P.E.T.: Parent Effectiveness Training* (1970) and in courses given by specially trained instructors in communities all over the country. This approach also embodies "active listening." It encourages parents to express their honest feelings to

their children and to encourage their children to express their feelings to them. It also urges parents to draw their children into the active process of making decisions and solving problems. It discourages the use of rewards and punishment in favor of teaching children to consider the needs of others.

All three of these parental approaches can be considered in the authoritative mold as described by Baumrind. Their wide popular appeal rests on two bases. First, this is the general approach that most sophisticated contemporary parents seem most interested in trying to achieve. Second, the books written by these three authorities are all extremely specific in their advice. Parenthood seems to be more complicated than ever. Contemporary parents recognize the influence that they have over their children's development, take their responsibility seriously, and look eagerly for help in doing the job well. Parents do need education. They do need to be sensitive to children's needs. But they also need to gain enough self-confidence in their own parenting abilities that they don't have to raise their children "by the book," but can instead evaluate the opinions of experts, use what seems helpful, and disregard the rest.

A most encouraging movement in modern parent education is the offering of classes in parenthood to high school students. These courses give young people an inkling of what parenthood involves, helps them decide whether they want to have children, and—if they do decide to—aids them in giving some thought ahead of time to the issues that are likely to arise.

PLAY IN EARLY CHILDHOOD

Vicky wakes up to see her clothes for the day laid out for her. She tries putting her overalls on backward, her shoes on opposite feet, her socks on her hands, and her shirt inside out. When she finally comes down to breakfast, she pretends that the little pieces of cereal in her bowl are "fishies" swimming around in the milk, and, spoonful by spoonful, she goes fishing. After breakfast, she hops on a little stool by the kitchen sink, plunges her arms in soapsuds up to the elbows, and "washes" the dishes.

Throughout the long, busy morning, she plays. She puts on an old hat of her mother's, picks up the discarded briefcase she has given her, and is the "mommy" going to work. Next, she becomes the doctor. "There, there, dolly, this'll hurt a little but then you won't get sick," she says in a soothing voice as she administers a "shot" to her doll. She runs outside to splash in the puddles, comes in for an imaginary telephone conversation, turns a wooden block into a truck and makes the appropriate sound effects, and so on, and on, and on. Vicky's day is one round of play after another. She makes a game of everything— and nearly all becomes play.

An adult might be tempted to smile indulgently at Vicky, envy her, and dismiss her activities as a pleasant, trivial way to pass the time. Such a judgment would be grievously in

error. For play is characteristic of all young mammals and is the work of the young.

Through play, children grow. They learn how to use their muscles; they coordinate what they see with what they do; and they gain mastery over their bodies. They find out what the world is like and what they are like. They acquire new skills and learn when to use them. They try out different aspects of life. They cope with complex and conflicting emotions by reenacting real life. Play is so much a part of children's lives that they do not completely differentiate reality from fantasy. Jason, for example, may play that one wooden block is a rabbit and that another block is a carrot the rabbit is eating. The blocks actually become the rabbit and carrot to him, and he treats them as such.

Preschoolers engage in many types of play. They tickle their senses by playing with water, sand, and mud. They master a new skill like riding a tricycle. They pretend to be all kinds of things, as well as other people. By the end of the preschool years, they delight in formal games that have routines and rules. Children progress from playing alone, to playing alongside other children but not with them, and finally to cooperative play, when they interact with others.

HOW CHILDREN PLAY

In the 1920s, Mildred B. Parten observed thirty-four 2- to 5-year-olds during free play periods in nursery school. In her 1932 report, she distinguished six types of play (see Table 7-1), determined the proportion of time spent in each type, and charted the activities of the children. Some forty years later, Barnes set up a similar study with forty-four children and reported in 1971 that these 3- and 4-year-olds played quite differently. The group played much less socially than Parten's group of forty years before. This could be because

With her left hand, Marya picked up a wide brush and made one wide yellow stripe on the right side of the page. She then picked up the sponge in her right hand, and blotched the line with her sponge. She began stirring with her brush in the water, singing, "I'm stirring up the pudding, ymmm, I'm making pudding, I'm stirring pudding." She continued singing and humming to herself, seemingly just as interested in playing with the sponge and brush as she was in painting. The painting itself spongey, blotted texture, with spreading of the shapes of color. When I wandered over to look at her picture, she volunteered, "This is a worm down here, a catapitter, and I will paint a butterfly up here."

Marya, age 5,
observed by Francesca Elms, her teacher

children of the seventies have spent more time watching television and less time playing with other children, because elaborate modern toys encourage solitary play more than simpler ones had, and because children now grow up with fewer brothers and sisters.

The differences between the two groups may have arisen not only because of cultural differences over the years, however, but also because of social-class differences that may have existed between Barnes's and Parten's subjects. Social class does make a difference in the way children play, as Rubin, Maioni, and Hornung discovered in their 1976 study. They found more parallel play among preschoolers from lower socioeconomic strata and more associative and cooperative play among middle-class children. There were no differences between the two groups in unoccupied, onlooker, and solitary play.

If Barnes and Parten had looked at children in laboratory settings instead of in nursery school, they might both have found different results. In a 1978 study Roopnarine and Johnson compared 3- to 6-year-old children of the same age (within four months) and of different ages (fourteen months or more apart) during a morning free play hour at nursery school and then again in a laboratory room supplied with child-size furniture and toys. The children played with each other more in the lab and were more likely to engage in *functional* play—that is, simple repetitive play like bouncing a ball. *Constructive* play, defined as being goal-directed, was more common in the nursery school. In both settings, the children, who all knew each other, were just as likely to play with others of either the same or different ages.

Why did the children play differently in the lab and in nursery school? For one thing, nursery school teachers usually encourage constructive play, whereas the lab teacher stayed strictly neutral. Second, constructive play takes a longer time to develop, and the children were observed in the lab right after they began to play for only ten minutes at a time. The puzzling finding in this study is the children's greater sociability in the lab, as compared to the more familiar nursery school. It is possible that they turned to other children in the lab to alleviate the strangeness of the unfamiliar setting.

This study emphasizes the importance of considering the setting in which we observe children before we draw any conclusions about their activities.

Parents and teachers need to be alert to the levels of play that children exhibit so that they will have realistic expectations for them and can help them get the most out of a group play situation.

Fantasy play, or make-believe, in which children pretend to be other things or other people, is often a coping strategy through which they work through their fears, deal with emotional conflicts, and satisfy their needs for mastery over life situations. Psychologist James E. Johnson wrote in 1975:

Since play involves the use of images and representations, and representations are needed for thinking and reasoning, play can be said to be a vehicle for accelerating development of cognitive capabilities [p. 1].

Johnson looked at the relationship between fantasy play, creativity, and intelligence in 3- to 5-year-olds. He found that there was a relationship among measures of all three, and concluded that there seems to be a cycle operating whereby cognitive skill and play feed into one another. Before children can pretend to be something that they are not, they need to have reached a certain minimal level of cognitive development. That is, Jason needs to know the difference between *being* something and *pretending* to be something, and then he needs to have some ideas in his head of what a lion is and does before he can begin to roar like one. Then the cycle contin-

TABLE 7-1
Types of Play in
Early Childhood

UNOCCUPIED BEHAVIOR

The child apparently is not playing, but occupies himself with watching anything that
happens to be of momentary interest. When there is nothing exciting taking place, he
plays with his own body, gets on and off chairs, just stands around, follows the teacher,
or sits in one spot glancing around the room (p. 249).

ONLOOKER

The child spends most of his time watching the other children play. He often talks to the
children whom he is observing, asks questions, or gives suggestions, but does not
overtly enter into the play himself. This type differs from the unoccupied in that the
onlooker is definitely observing particular groups of children rather than anything that
happens to be exciting. The child stands or sits within speaking distance of the group so
that he can see and hear everything that takes place (p. 249).

SOLITARY INDEPENDENT PLAY

The child plays alone and independently with toys that are different from those used by the
children within speaking distance and makes no effort to get close to other children. He
pursues his own activity without reference to what others are doing (p. 250).

PARALLEL ACTIVITY

The child plays independently, but the activity he chooses naturally brings him among the
other children. He plays with toys that are like those which the children around him are
using, but he plays with the toy as he sees fit, and does not try to influence or modify the
activity of the children near him. He plays *beside* rather than *with* the other children.
There is no attempt to control the coming or going of children in the group (p. 250).

ASSOCIATIVE PLAY

The child plays with other children. The conversation concerns the common activity; there
is a borrowing and loaning of play material; following one another with trains or wagons;
mild attempts to control which children may or may not play in the group. All the
members engage in similar if not identical activity; there is no division of labor, and no
organization of the activity of several individuals around any material goal or product.
The children do not subordinate their individual interests to that of the group; instead
each child acts as he wishes. By his conversation with the other children one can tell
that his interest is primarily in his associations, not in his activity. Occasionally, two or
three children are engaged in no activity of any duration, but are merely doing whatever
happens to draw the attention of any of them (p. 251).

COOPERATIVE OR ORGANIZED SUPPLEMENTARY PLAY

The child plays in a group that is organized for the purpose of making some material
product, or of striving to attain some competitive goal, or of dramatizing situations of
adult and group life, or of playing formal games. There is a marked sense of belonging
or of not belonging to the group. The control of the group situation is in the hands of one
or two of the members who direct the activity of the others. The goal as well as the
method of attaining it necessitates a division of labor, taking of different roles by the
various group members and the organization of activity so that the efforts of one child are
supplemented by those of another (p. 251).

SOURCE: From Parten, 1932.

ues, because the more children play out their
fantasies with each other, the more they will
continue to develop cognitively. The interaction during fantasy play seems to be an
important aspect of the relationship of play
with development.

Thus, pretending to be "the big bad wolf"
can help children in their intellectual development. Recent research shows that children
who don't ordinarily play in this way—

disadvantaged preschoolers—can be encouraged to do so and can make real intellectual gains. Saltz, Dixon, and Johnson (1977)
assigned 3- to 5-year-olds to one of four
groups. In the *fantasy play* group, the children
acted out simple fairy tales like *The Three Billy
Goats Gruff* and *The Three Pigs*. In the *fantasy
discussion* group, they heard and talked
about the same stories. In the *sociodramatic
play* group, children acted out experiences in

everyday life, like visits to the doctor and school outings to the zoo. And in the *control* group, they did standard preschool activities like cutting and pasting.

After six or seven months, all the children were tested on several measures. Those youngsters in the two play groups—and especially in the fantasy play group—scored higher on IQ tests and were better able to distinguish reality from fantasy, to recognize an orderly sequence of events, to delay impulsive behavior, and to put themselves in the place of other children.

While young children tend to become friendly with others of the same age, youngsters are often exposed to younger and older children—brothers and sisters, cousins, neighbors, the children of their parents' friends. Are there differences in the ways they play with children of the same and of different ages?

Lougee, Grueneich, and Hartup (1977) looked at the different ways fifty-four 3- to 5-year-old children played with children within two months of their own age and with children who were at least sixteen months older or younger. They found the least amount of interaction and talk between the youngest same-age pairs, a middling amount in the mixed-age pairs, and the most among the oldest same-age pairs, reflecting the developing social competence of the children.

In mixed-age pairings, younger children were more sociable than they were with children their own age, and the 5-year-olds were less sociable than they were with other 5-year-olds, in apparent response to the differing social competences of their playmates. Most children were able to "fine tune" their styles of speech and play based on their playmates' social abilities. Many questions remain about the significance of play among children of different ages. The important find-

ing to emerge from this study is that playing with an older or younger child is not the same as playing with one of the same age, and studies of children's sociability need to take into account the age of the playmates as well as that of the primary targets of the study.

Imaginary Playmates

As Stephen's aunt starts to sit down next to him, Stephen cries out, "You can't sit there!" The chair is taken by "Schultzie," Stephen's invisible friend. When Stephen spills his milk, he blames Schultzie. Though Stephen is afraid to climb, he is proud that Schultzie got to the top of the jungle gym. Schultzie is a normal manifestation of childhood. Some 15 to 30 percent of children between the ages of 3 and 10 have imaginary companions (Schaeffer, 1969). They come into the child's life after the age of 2½ and drop out when the child goes to school (Ames & Learned, 1946). The imagined person or animal seems real to the child, who talks to it and about it and plays with it. First-born and only children have imaginary companions more often than do children with older siblings, using them to overcome loneliness (Manosevitz, Prentice, & Wilson, 1973); and bright, creative children are especially likely to have them (Schaeffer, 1969; Jersild, 1968).

THEORIES OF PLAY

Play transcends all levels of a child's life. It engages the emotions, the intellect, the culture, the behavior. Different theorists explain its function in different ways.

Cognitive Theory

Piaget (1951) sees play as a way to learn about new and complex objects and events, a way to consolidate and enlarge concepts and skills, and a way to integrate thinking with actions. The way children play at any given time depends upon their stage of cognitive development. Sensorimotor children play in a concrete fashion, moving their bodies and manipulating tangible objects. When they develop the symbolic function, they can pre-

TABLE 7-2
Stages in Play in
Early Childhood

TYPE	AGE	EXAMPLE
Functional play	To 2 years (sensorimotor period)	Any simple repetitive action with or without objects, such as rolling a ball or pulling a pull-toy
Symbolic play	2 to 6 years (preoperational period)	Pretending to be someone or something (doctor, nurse, Superman), beginning with fairly simple activities but going on to develop more elaborate plots
Games with rules	Over 7 years (concrete operations period)	Any activity with rules, structure, and a goal (such as winning), like tag, hopscotch, marbles

SOURCE: From Piaget, 1951.

tend that something exists when it does not; they can play in their minds, so to speak, rather than with their entire bodies.

When children can integrate symbols into their thought processes, they can, as a consequence, play games that have well-defined rules and goals.

Psychoanalytic Theory

As explained by Freud (1924) and Erikson (1950), play helps children to develop ego-strength. Through play they can work out conflicts between the id and the superego. Motivated by the pleasure principle, play is a source of gratification. It is also a cathartic response that lessens psychic tension and gives a child mastery over overwhelming experiences. (When Aaron gives his doll a shot, it helps him to work out the feelings of fear and helplessness he himself felt the last time he received an injection.)

Learning Theory

According to Thorndike (in Kimble, 1961), play is learned behavior. Each culture or subculture values and rewards different types of behavior, and children's play reflects these differences. Roberts and Sutton-Smith (1962) studied differences in child-rearing patterns and in the games played by children in three separate societies. Children raised in cultures that emphasize responsibility and doing what one is told tend to play games of chance. These games respond to the players' passive

roles in life and hold the promise of lifting them out of their lives of humdrum responsibility. Children in societies that value achievement or performance like to play games of physical skill. They can compete in these games in a relaxed way, since the outcome is less critical than it is in their pressured performances of daily life. And children raised to be obedient tend to play games of strategy. By controlling others in the game, they can displace their aggressive tendencies.

Testing the Theories

Gilmore (1966) tested the relative influences of the cognitive aspects of play (children want to play with novel toys) and the psychoanalytic aspects (children want to use toys to relieve their anxieties). He offered different types of toys to two groups of children, aged 4 to 11. Those in one group were hospitalized for tonsillectomy, and the others were a matched group of schoolchildren. Some of the toys, like a toy stethoscope, syringe, thermometer, and scissors, were relevant to the hospital experience, whereas others were not; some were novel, others familiar.

All the children in this study preferred novel toys to familiar ones; the hospitalized children were more likely to prefer the hospital-relevant toys than were the control children, but they were also more likely to prefer the novel toys. Therefore, in this case, the children's toy choices could be explained by both the cognitive and the psychoanalytic theories, with the cognitive influences apparently the more important. In other words, the anxiety of the hospitalized children affected their toy choices to some degree, but it was not so strong an influence as the relative novelty of the toys.

This study illustrates the intertwining of cognitive and emotional factors, an intertwining, as we said, that runs through the entire fabric of a child's life.

FRIENDSHIP IN EARLY CHILDHOOD

Three-year-olds Nancy and Janie have become fast friends. They have worn a path between their backyards, they ask for each other as soon as they wake up in the morning, and neither is so happy as when she is in the company of her friend. In these years from 3 to 6 many children form their first true friendships, relationships that last beyond a brief play period to become an important element in their lives.

Most friendships between children of this age tend to be at a relatively primitive level compared to the form they will take in later years. The distinctive ways children of different ages think about friendship emerge dramatically from a major new study about the ways people's ideas about friendship develop over the life span. Selman and Selman (1979) interviewed more than 250 people between the ages of 3 and 45 to get a developmental perspective on this important factor in our lives.

These researchers call the first in five separate stages in children's thinking about friendship *Stage 0, or the stage of Momentary Playmateship*. Most children between 3 and 7 years of age, they say, have trouble making a distinction between a physical action and the psychological intention behind

Seven little girls sit busily drawing at a round table.... Koko has been displaying the contents of a plastic doctor's bag that she has brought to school. She hovers about the circle speaking and gesticulating importantly. Calling out in a stentorian voice meant to arrest all activity, she offers, "Who wants some gum?" Eva asks politely and cajolingly, "Can I have some?" Koko answers in a stern, firm manner, "Only my best friends." Instantly, a chorus of voices pledge in unison eternal friendship with Koko, Eva among them with her lisping, "I'm your best friend."

from *Observing and Recording
the Behavior of Young Children, 2/e., p. 66*

the action. (A 4-year-old said he trusted his friend because "if I give him my toy, he won't break it. He isn't strong enough.") They are still unable, for the most part, to consider the viewpoint of another person, and they think only about what *they* want from the friendship. They define their friends by how close they live ("She's my friend—she lives on my street") and value them for their material and physical attributes ("He's my friend. He has a giant Superman doll and a real swing set.").

Sometime in early childhood, often at about the age of 4, many children cross over into Stage 1, *One-Way Assistance*, which lasts until about age 9. There is a great deal of overlap between Stage 0 and Stage 1, in which children *can* tell the difference between their own perspectives and those of other people. Still, in Stage 1, which we'll discuss more fully in Chapter 9, a "good" friendship is one in which your friend does what you want him to do.

Gamer, Thomas, and Kendall (in Rebelsky, 1975) reviewed articles on determinants of friendship across the life span and found that nursery school youngsters tend to be friendly with other children who are of the same age

In the years between 3 and 6 many children form their first true friendships. (David Strickler/Monkmeyer; Erika Stone/Peter Arnold, Inc.)

and sex, who have similar energy and activity levels, and who engage in like activities. They do not seem to consider such traits as mental age, IQ, height, outgoingness, laughter, or even attractiveness of personality.

Friendships begin, of course, with two children having access to each other. What determines the way they approach or respond to each other's approaches? Where does social competence begin? Possibly in the early attachments children form to their parents.

Lieberman (1977) looked at forty 3-year-old girls and boys to see relationships between how well they got along with other children and such factors as the security of their attachments with their mothers and their experiences with other children. She found that both attachment and previous social experiences were related in different ways to the social competence of 3-year-olds.

Observers judged the degree of mother-child attachment by looking at forty children in their homes with their mothers, and then by seeing the way both mother and child acted in the laboratory. They got reports from the mothers on the children's contacts with other tots over the past several weeks. Then they set up free play sessions in the lab, pairing two same-sex youngsters who were close in age and did not know each other. After they videotaped them through a one-way mirror, they analyzed the tapes to see how able and willing each child was to interact with the other (how often a child made an approach, responded to the other's approach, talked, showed something, and shared); how positive or negative the child's behaviors were (how often they laughed, cried, tried to leave the room, hit each other, threw toys around, threatened each other, and fought over toys); and how often they refrained from any interaction (by just staring or standing around).

What did Lieberman find? First, children who were attached to their mothers were more likely to have had more experience playing with other children. Perhaps warm, loving mothers like people in general and are more likely to encourage their children to be sociable, too. Or perhaps children who feel good about being with their mothers feel good about being with other people as well, and their mothers, realizing this, are more likely to set up play sessions with other children.

These two factors in children's lives seem to affect them differently. The securely attached youngsters were more likely to act positively with other children, especially through actions rather than words (maybe

because nonverbal behaviors continue to closely reflect emotional attitudes even after children learn to talk), while the children who had played with others a great deal were more likely to talk to other children (maybe because they are more used to conversation).

An important element in friendship is reciprocity, or give-and-take. Selman and Selman (1979) found that children are not able to see relationships as reciprocal, taking into account other people's perspective, until Stage 2, which begins at about the age of 6. There *are* forerunners to this stage, though. How do reciprocal relationships originate in the first place and what keeps them up?

To find answers to these questions, Leitner (1977) looked at a range of social interactions between pairs of 4½-year-old children. He identified two boys and two girls in each of the following categories: assertive; passive and whiny; friendly leader; and friendly follower. He and his colleagues observed them for twenty 15-minute periods each (five hours per child) during free play times. How did they approach others? Were they friendly, demanding, or whiny? What kinds of responses did they receive—friendly agreement, joking laughter, a counterproposal, a refusal, a shove, an argument, tears, or being ignored, walked away from, or tattled on?

In this study, children who approached others with a friendly smile and a noncoercive suggestion were more likely to get a response of agreement. Those who commanded, shoved, or took away a toy got back in kind: The second child was likely to hit, yell, shove, threaten, command, or take away something from them. Children who whined, begged, cried, or just stood close to another child without doing anything were more likely to be ignored. The children who approached others most often were themselves approached more often by others. And children who responded agreeably themselves to other children's approaches got more agreeable responses when they began an encounter than did children who gave fewer agreeable responses.

This study shows then that reciprocity actually begins quite early, even if young children are not always aware of its existence. A child's way of approaching other people strongly influences the way they will respond to her and helps to etch the pattern of her future relationships.

Studies of children's ideas about friendship fall into the relatively new branch of developmental study called *social cognition*.

This approach refers to thinking about social relations and events. As such, it includes role-taking ability, moral judgment, understanding of intentionality, and conceptions of other people and their role in one's life.

SUMMARY

1 According to Sigmund Freud, the preschool child is in the *phallic stage* of psychosexual development and receives pleasure from genital stimulation. This sexuality is not like the mature adult's; however, Freud postulated the male *Oedipus complex* and its female counterpart, the *Electra complex*, to account for a child's feelings toward the opposite-sex parents. Because of the conflict a child feels, he or she eventually represses sexual urges, identifies with the same-sex parent, and enters latency. The *superego* (or conscience) develops when the complex is resolved.   **2** Erik Erikson maintains that the chief developmental crisis of the preschool period focuses on the development of a sense of *initiative* or *guilt*. The successful resolution of this conflict enables the child to undertake, plan, and carry out activities. Success or failure is strongly influenced by parents' dealings with their children.   **3** During the preschool period, the child identifies with adult models and develops sex-typed behaviors. There are many theoretical interpretations of identification and sex typing. In psychoanalytic terms, the child identifies with the same-sex parent at the resolution of the Oedipus/Electra complex. According to social learning theory, the child adopts the behaviors and attitudes of a model in order to possess the desirable attributes of that model.   **4** Theoretical explanations of sex typing (the acquisition of sex-appropriate behaviors, values, motives, and emotions) range from those which focus on biological-hormonal differences between the sexes, psychosexual factors, learning (primarily through parental rewards and punishments for "appropriate" or "inappropriate" behaviors), or cognitive development. Sex typing is influenced by one's particular cultural membership (different cultures regard different behaviors as sex appropriate); the attitudes of one's parents; one's socioeconomic status; and factors such as television programming, schools, textbooks, and children's books.   **5** Preschool children may have a great number of fears, both real and imaginary, that may be overcome through conditioning procedures.   **6** Child-rearing techniques influence children's personalities. Traits such as aggression, dependence, independence, and prosocial behavior are molded by the particular way parents deal with their children. Baumrind has identified three types of parenting styles: *authoritarian*, *permissive*, and *authoritative*. Each encourages certain personality traits in children.   **7** There are many types of play and various theories to explain play's purpose. Through play, children grow and exercise their physical capabilities, learn about their world, and cope with conflicting emotions. **8** Studies of children's friendships highlight the importance of social interaction between peers.

SUGGESTED READINGS

Clarke-Stewart, A. *Child care in the family: A review of research and some propositions for policy.* New York: Academic, 1977, A review of recent research on the effects of various child-care practices on children's development. After a thorough review of research findings, comments on child-care policies are offered.

Ellis, M. J. *Why people play.* Englewood Cliffs, NJ: Prentice-Hall, 1973. A scientific approach to what play is and why people play, including classical, recent, and modern theories of play.

Fricke, I. *Beginning the human story: A new baby in the family.* Glenview, IL: Scott, Foresman, 1967. Twelve large color charts are designed to instruct children 4 to 8 years of age on sex education within the framework of family living. Each card has information on the back to aid in use of the card and discussion.

Garvey, C. *Play.* Cambridge: Harvard University Press, 1977. A look at the development of play from the infant's game of peek-a-boo to play with objects, language, and social materials and finally to play with rules.

Ginott, H. G. *Between parent and child.* New York: Avon, 1965. Many case histories underscore this communication-focused approach to parenting.

Gordon, T. *P.E.T.: Parent effectiveness training.* New York: New American Library, 1970. A program of training for parenting, based upon the "active listening" method. A practical guide for raising mature, healthy, happy, loving children.

Greenberg, S. *Right from the start: A guide to nonsexist child rearing.* Boston: Houghton Mifflin, 1978. An indictment of the ways in which society locks children into sex-stereotyped roles, with suggestions for parents who want to raise "liberated" children, by a professor of early childhood education.

Maccoby, E., & Jacklin, C. *The psychology of sex differences.* Stanford, CA: Stanford, 1974. An authoritative review of findings of sex differences (or similarities) in intellect, achievement, social behavior, and socialization. Extensive annotated bibliography.

Mussen, P., & Eisenberg-Berg, N. *Roots of caring, sharing, and helping.* San Francisco: Freeman, 1977. A report on the current status of research in the area of prosocial behavior. Considers the influence of biology, culture, and individual and family variables on the development of prosocial behavior.

Middle Childhood

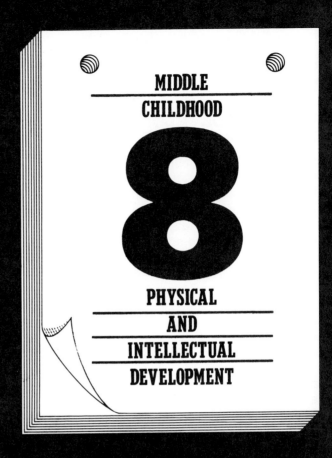

MIDDLE
CHILDHOOD

8

PHYSICAL
AND
INTELLECTUAL
DEVELOPMENT

IN THIS CHAPTER
YOU WILL LEARN ABOUT

The gains schoolchildren make in growth and motor development, and some health hazards that they face

Schoolchildren's thinking: their ideas about reality and morality and how their viewpoints affect communicative abilities

Measuring the intelligence of schoolchildren (including some issues) and factors that affect intellectual achievement

The special needs of gifted children and disadvantaged children

Children and the school experience: the ideal and some problems

CHAPTER OVERVIEW

PHYSICAL DEVELOPMENT OF SCHOOLCHILDREN

Schoolchildren between the ages of 6 and 12 look very different from their preschool brothers and sisters. They're much taller and thinner; most are fairly wiry, although girls generally retain more fatty tissue than boys and will continue to do so throughout adulthood. Black children are slightly larger than white. There is very little difference in weight and height between younger boys and girls, though boys are generally slightly heavier and taller. But the girls reach their pubescent growth spurt before boys, and now tend to be larger. Normal children of the same age show a wide range in height, reflecting the wide variations among individuals in all aspects of development (see Table 8-1). This range is so wide "that if a child who was of exactly average height at his seventh birthday grew not at all for two years, he would still be just within the normal limits of height attained at age nine" (Tanner, 1973, p. 35). Children from more affluent families are somewhat larger and more mature than those from lower socioeconomic groups. The fat children—the overnourished—mature earliest of all.

Meredith (1969) found a range of about 9 inches between mean heights of the shortest 8-year-old children in various parts of the world (from Southeast Asia, Oceania, and South America) and the tallest (mostly from northern and central Europe, eastern Australia, and the United States). While genetic differences probably account for some of this diversity, environmental influences also play a part. The tallest children come from parts of the world "where nutritious food is abundant and where the infectious diseases are well controlled or largely eliminated" (Meredith, 1969).

Children this age have much keener vision and sight than they did earlier, because organ systems are more mature. Children under 6 tend to be farsighted, since their eyes have not fully matured and are different in shape from adults'. By 6 years, their binocular coordination is well developed, enabling them to focus their eyes better. Brain development is virtually complete.

HEIGHT PREDICTION

There are several ways of predicting adult stature and treating abnormal growth. Often, height can be predicted within a range of about 2 inches in either direction. When the human skeleton first begins to form (during the second month of prenatal life), it starts out as cartilage, a tough elastic tissue that gradually changes to hard bone. This process of bone formation is called *ossification*, and it continues until an individual achieves full growth at about age 18. Bone shows up in an x-ray; cartilage does not. The rate of ossification is an important measure of growth. We can make much more accurate predictions of final height if we have access to skeletal age, rather than chronological age.

A child's skeletal age, or bone age, is derived by looking at an x-ray, usually of the hand and wrist, to determine how much of the cartilage has turned into bone and how closely fused the ends of one bone are to the one next to it. The closer the bones are fused together, the more advanced the skeletal age. By comparing a particular child's x-ray to those standardized for age, we can determine that child's bone age and predict ultimate height more accurately. People destined to be tall usually reach their full growth sooner than average, and short people take a longer time to reach full growth. Prophecies of height are somewhat closer than a guess, but they are still not completely accurate for many reasons, including differences in growth rates.

If hormonal tests show that a child is not growing normally because of a malfunctioning pituitary gland, it is sometimes possible to accelerate development by injecting human growth hormone, a precious commodity pres-

TABLE 8-1
Physical Growth,
Ages 6 to 10 (Fiftieth
Percentile)

	HEIGHT (INCHES)				WEIGHT (POUNDS)			
AGE	WHITE MALES	NONWHITE MALES	WHITE FEMALES	NONWHITE FEMALES	WHITE MALES	NONWHITE MALES	WHITE FEMALES	NONWHITE FEMALES
6	46	47	46	47	48	49	47	46
7	49	49	49	49	53	55	52	51
8	51	52	50	51	61	61	57	58
9	53	53	53	53	66	66	63	65
10	55	55	55	57	73	72	70	78
11	57	58	58	59	81	80	87	90
12	59	60	60	61	91	93	95	99

SOURCE: Adapted from J. L. Rauh, D. A. Schumsky, and M. T. Witt, "Heights, Weights, and Obesity in Urban School Children," *Child Development, 38*, 515–530. Copyright © The Society for Research in Child Development, Inc.

ently in very short supply. It must be injected regularly before puberty, when growth slows down markedly.

HEALTH PROBLEMS OF CHILDREN

Vicky, 10, is home in bed with a cold, her second of the year. She sneezes, snoozes, watches a lot of TV, pulls out her old coloring book, and, in general, enjoys being sick. Vicky is lucky. She has had no other illnesses this year other than the two colds. Her good health reflects medical progress over the past several decades.

Children born in the 1920s and 1930s—of all social classes—were prone to many diseases whose rates have dropped sharply over the years. They were likely to contract whooping cough, mumps, chickenpox, and measles; scarlet fever, diphtheria, and polio were also common dangers (Bayer & Snyder, 1950). These diseases were often serious and sometimes fatal.

Over the years we have made great strides in safeguarding children's health, so great that mortality rates during early childhood have shown a greater decline than those for any other age group since the beginning of the century (U.S. Department of Health, Education, and Welfare, 1976). The death rates from all causes for 5- to 14-year-olds were in 1973 only one-fifth of what they had been in 1925, and the years from 1 to 14 have the lowest mortality of any stage in the life span (U.S. Department of Health, Education and Welfare, 1976).

Illness

Jason has received a full program of inoculations, which have protected him from such classic childhood illnesses as measles, whooping cough, mumps, and others. The incidence and death rate from many childhood diseases—most notably diphtheria, polio, measles, and whooping cough—have decreased, due to immunization, improved diet, improved sanitation, and the development and use of antibiotics (Profiles of Children, 1970). Cholera, plague, typhus, smallpox, and yellow fever have been extremely rare since the first quarter of this century.

Some of these medical advances have been fairly recent. In 1950, for example, tuberculosis, diphtheria, polio, and measles combined claimed the lives of 2729 American children; in 1973, only 43 died of these causes. In 1930, 14,000 children succumbed to influenza and pneumonia; in 1950, 3245 died; and by 1973, the death toll had dropped to 1345 (U.S. Department of Health, Education, and Welfare, 1976).

Yet too many children are still suffering from too many preventable illnesses. Tuberculosis, gonorrhea, and syphilis are a major health problem among children under 14. Low-income minority-group children have disproportionately high levels of influenza and pneumonia.

Chronic conditions, especially those of the respiratory tract, are low during childhood. One disturbing trend, however, has been the increase since 1925 in fatal childhood malignancies. It remains to be seen whether this is a function of improved diagnosis or whether cancer is in fact afflicting more children today than it did half a century ago.

Many children have problems with vision. By the age of 6, 7 percent have defective binocular distant vision (20/40 or less), and 10 percent have defective near vision. By 11 years of age, 17 percent have defective distant vision, and 10 percent have poor near vision. Yet many of these children have either no eyeglasses or inadequate ones (U.S. Department of Health, Education, and Welfare, 1976).

Teeth also present problems during childhood. At the age of 6, 1 child in 8 has one or more decayed permanent teeth. By the age of 11, 3 out of 4 have one or more decayed teeth. And by age 17, 19 out of 20 have either decayed, missing, or filled teeth, averaging about 9 per person (U.S. Department of Health, Education, and Welfare, 1976).

Researchers who compared a group of ill

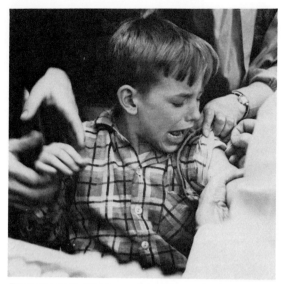

Extensive immunization programs have wiped out many diseases that used to take children's lives. (APF/Photo Trends)

children with a group of healthy ones found that two or three times as many of the sick children had experienced more frequent and/or more severe stressful life events during the previous year (Heisel, Ream, Raitz, Rappaport, & Coddington, 1973). This was true in both physical and emotional illness, pointing to a strong psychosomatic element in children's health.

Accidents

The leading cause of death among children is accidents. Some 15,000 American children under age 15 die each year, and another 19 million are injured severely enough to seek medical care or restrict their usual activity (White House Conference on Children, 1970). Most of these accidents occur in or around the home. Children are killed by automobiles; they drown in pools, lakes, rivers, and oceans; they are fatally burned in fires and explosions; they drink poisonous substances; they fall from heights; they get caught in mechanical contrivances.

Children are naturally venturesome, and naively ignorant of the dangers that surround

February 21 and I am nine years old today it is my Birthday that's why, and tomorrow is George Washington's Birthday only he is not living and I am. He died of laryngitis and I have had it twice and never died yet.

Mary Scarborough Paxson, age 9,
from *Small Voices*, p. 14

them. Their innocence puts a large burden on parents and other adult caretakers, who must tread a delicate line between supervising children adequately or smothering them with oversolicitousness. The greatest burden, though, should be on society at large. Federal laws have already been passed, to require "child-proof" caps on medicine bottles, and to require minimum spaces between the bars on babies' cribs, so that babies cannot get their heads caught and strangle.

Concerned citizens need to be eternally vigilant to protect children as much as possible. One ironic development occurred in the wake of a national law requiring manufacturers of children's sleepwear to make them flame-retardant. Further research brought out the possibility that the chemicals used in fireproofing the sleepwear might be carcinogenic, posing a different hazard.

Poverty

Poverty is the most serious health problem among American children today. Some 20 percent of our total population do not have enough money to maintain an adequate standard of living. They live in substandard, crowded, unsanitary housing; they don't eat enough of the right kinds of foods; they don't go to doctors and dentists often enough; and parents are too busy keeping body and soul together to provide adequate supervision for their children. Poverty is unhealthy.

The problems of poor children begin long before birth. Poor mothers don't eat well themselves and don't get adequate prenatal care. They are more likely to have premature and low-birthweight babies and babies who are born dead or who die soon after birth. More poor children are born with venereal disease, drug addiction, and hepatitis than middle-class children.

As poor children grow older, they are more likely to contract diseases like tuberculosis. They have a higher rate of untreated dental cavities, and are more likely to suffer from lead poisoning and rat bites. Poor children are less likely than middle-class children

to be fully protected by immunization. American Indian children are still suffering from typhoid, dysentery, tuberculosis, hepatitis, diphtheria, and trachoma (White House Conference on Children, 1970).

In view of the overwhelming health problems among the poor—which have far-reaching effects on their intellectual and emotional development—it is imperative to make massive efforts to serve them. Some progress has been made in providing health services to the poor; much more is needed. Free or low-cost health clinics have been set up in many low-income areas, and such clinics have reduced the rate of infant mortality in city slums. But there is a great need for many more preventive health services to poor children and their families. Such programs should include immunization schedules, along with parent education on the need for such immunization and help in getting the children to the clinics. The clinics should emphasize dental care, an often neglected service. More extensive prenatal care is needed. Concurrently, society has to work on the social conditions of poverty that breed disease. We have to help more low-income people get better housing, free from the rats that bite their babies and the lead paint that poisons their toddlers. We have to help people break out of the cycle of poverty, illiteracy, unemployment, and despair, if we are going to make the promise of medical progress become a reality for all our citizens.

MOTOR DEVELOPMENT

Back in that school yard at 3 P.M., we see the grade school children running pell-mell on their way out of the building. Were we to follow them home, we'd see them as they leap up onto narrow ledges and walk along, balancing themselves, and as they jump off, trying to break distance records but occasionally breaking a bone instead. After dashing into the house to drop their books, go to the bathroom, and get a snack, they'll be out on the street again. They'll be jumping rope, playing sandlot baseball, roller skating, bicycling, sledding, throwing snowballs, or jumping into the old swimming hole, depending on the season, the community, and the child. A few may be learning how to ride a horse, skate on ice, dance ballet, or contort their bodies on gymnastics apparatus. It's astonishing how far these children have come in terms of getting their bodies to do what they want them to do. They keep getting stronger, faster, and better coordinated, and they derive great pleasure from testing their bodies and achieving new skills.

Since running, jumping, and throwing are common elements of many childhood games, Espenschade (1960) based her study of age changes and sex differences on these three activities. By examining a large number of reports in the literature of child development, giving measures of children's abilities in running, in doing a standard broad jump, in jump-and-reach, and in throwing, she found wide individual differences and some sex differences. At all ages, she found, ability is closely related to size and build. The effect of maturation can be seen in the improvement, with age, of balance and coordination, which have little relationship to physique or strength. Children's abilities in one activity correlate with their skills in another, so the good runners tend to be good at throwing and jumping too.

Differences showed up between boys' and girls' abilities: Boys improved in performance from ages 5 to 17, while girls improved through their early school years, hit a peak performance at about 13, and then declined or stayed the same. While boys do somewhat better than girls on all skills, their superiority is

Maturation seems to play an important part in the development of motor skills, but culture influences their maintenance. (Suzanne Szasz)

very slight until puberty, when they show sharp increases and the girls either decline or level off. Since girls also continue to grow taller and stronger after 13, it is hard to explain their poorer showings thereafter on the basis of physical maturity, or the development of secondary sex characteristics. A social explanation seems more valid: After this age there is less motivation for girls to excel in physical activities. Traditionally, this has been the age when girls have been encouraged to put aside their "tomboyish" ways.

To determine the relationship between gross motor skills and children's developmental status, Govatos (1959) examined 101 children 6 to 11 years old, measuring height, weight, bone structure, strength, IQ, and the number of permanent teeth. Running, jumping, throwing, and kicking abilities were assessed. Both sexes increased their performances as they matured, getting better at different skills at different age levels. Boys and girls of similar size tended to do equally well in running and jumping, but the boys generally outdid the girls in throwing and kicking. Do girls play tag and jump rope because they're good at running and jumping, or does playing tag and jumping rope improve these abilities? Do boys play football and soccer because they're good throwers and kickers, or do they become good at throwing and kicking from playing football and soccer?

It seems that maturation plays an important part in the development of motor skills, but culture influences their maintenance. The fact that boys and girls are so nearly equal in most physical measures, and particularly running and jumping, means that there is no reason to separate them for physical education, at least in grade school. The fact that girls' physical skills deteriorate or fail to improve after puberty points to the need for greater encouragement of adolescent girls' physical activities. The importance of maturation in the development of various motor skills indicates the problem of putting boys of the same chronological age, but of widely differing maturational levels, on opposing teams.

INTELLECTUAL DEVELOPMENT OF SCHOOLCHILDREN

It is hardly coincidental that the usual starting age for school, at least in the Western world, coincides with a number of qualitative jumps in children's thinking abilities. It also coincides with a new Piagetian stage of cognitive development: concrete operations.

PIAGET'S STAGE OF CONCRETE OPERATIONS (ABOUT 6 TO 11 YEARS)

Sometime between 5 and 7 years of age, children become what Piaget calls *operational*; that is, they become able to use symbols to carry out *operations*, or mental activities, as opposed to the physical activities that were the basis for their earlier thinking. Their use of

I am now going to tell you about the horrible and wretched plaege that my multiplication gives me you can't concieve it — the most Devilish thing is 8 times 8 and 7 times 7 it is what nature itselfe cant endure.

Marjorie Fleming, age about 6,
from *Small Voices*, p. 95

mental representations of things and events allows them to become proficient at classifying, dealing with numbers, and understanding the principles of conservation. They can consider more than one aspect of a situation when drawing conclusions, instead of getting stuck on one aspect. And they understand the reversible characteristic of most physical operations. Their egocentrism is diminishing, and they are beginning to understand other people's points of view. The ability to put themselves in the place of another improves their ability to communicate. It also enhances their ability to make moral judgments, which are becoming more flexible.

The thinking of school-age children is markedly more mature than that of younger children; yet it is clearly not as sophisticated or complex as that of adolescents. We can see this immaturity in children's beliefs about reality, causation, and conservation.

Children's Ideas of Reality

When we look closely at children's jumbled notions of what is real and what is unreal, of what is the product of their own minds and what exists in tangible form, of what has life and what is inanimate, and of their explanations for the existence of many natural phenomena, we cannot help being struck by the similarity between the reasoning of children and the elaborate belief systems of many primitive people (Pulaski, 1971).

REALISM When children confuse psychological events with objective reality, and see names, pictures, thoughts, and feelings as actual entities, they are in the throes of what Piaget calls *realism*. He has brought this out most clearly in his investigations of children's ideas about their own dreams, and has characterized their thought into three stages.

First Stage (Beginning at Age 5 or 6) Children consider the names of things as real and immutable as the things themselves. For children in this stage, "a rose by any other name" would not only not smell as sweet—it could not even exist. Their immature thinking in this regard is illustrated by Diana's experience in first grade, upon meeting a classmate, also named Diana. Since the second Diana is a shy, quiet child, the first Diana feels that, sharing the same name, she has to become shy and quiet, too. Not understanding exactly what a name signifies, Diana invests it with a strange power that creates an almost magical bond with this other Diana.

Children in this stage believe that their dreams come from outside and take place within the room. They dream with their eyes and are able to "see" what they dream. Because of their confusion between moral laws and physical laws, they believe that bad dreams come as a punishment for misbehavior (see the section "Moral Development in Schoolchildren" later in this chapter).

Second Stage (Beginning at Age 7 or 8) Children now think that dreams originate in the head, in thought, or in the voice, but that the dreams are in the room, in front of them. They recognize that dreams are unreal and not true, but still see them as images outside the person, which are seen with the eyes.

Third Stage (Beginning at about 9 or 10) Children now recognize that names have been given to objects by people and that dreams are the products of thought, which take place inside the head.

ANIMISM Young children's egocentric tendency to endow inanimate objects with life, consciousness, and will—like themselves—is known as *animism*. As they mature, children are less and less likely to attribute life to inanimate objects. Eventually they reach a point where they consider animals and plants the only live things in the universe.

First Stage (Until about Age 6 or 7) Children regard everything that has a use of any sort as alive (including a dish, which people eat from).

Second Stage (Until about 8 or 9) Anything that moves or can be moved is alive (like a car or a bicycle).

Third Stage (Until 11 or 12) Things that move spontaneously are alive (like the sun, the wind, or a river); those that require an outside agent to move them (like a motor) are not.

Fourth Stage (At about 12) By now, according to Piaget, people consider only biologically living organisms (plants and animals) to be alive. Recent research, however, has found that many adolescents and adults attribute life to things other than plants and animals (Sheehan & Papalia, 1974; Papalia-Finlay, 1978). They often consider such elements of nature as the sun or the mountains as alive, sometimes using the term poetically. Further investigations are needed to determine whether this is a sign of immature thought structure or a conscious decision to broaden the concept of life.

ARTIFICIALISM Egocentric children consider themselves the center of the universe. They

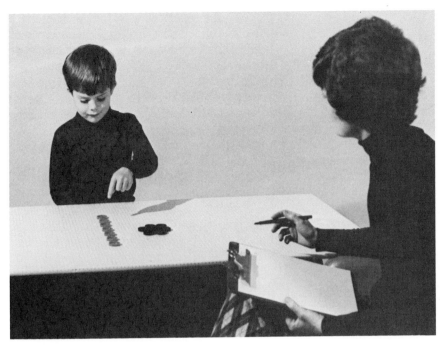

Conservation is the ability to recognize that two equal quantities of matter remain equal even if the matter is rearranged, as long as nothing is added or taken away. (Mimi Forsyth/Monkmeyer)

feel that they, or other human beings, have created everything in the world. People have made the sun, the moon, and the stars and put them in the sky. Only by stages, with adult instruction, do children achieve the realization that human activity is not involved in the creation of natural phenomena. We see vestiges of artificialism in the Old Testament, which describes God creating the world; in the ancient Greek myths, which attribute to the gods the creation of such natural phenomena as the Milky Way, the seasons of the year, and the presence of mountains, flowers, and trees; and, in fact, in the creation stories of religions around the world.

First Stage (Until 7 or 8 Years)   In this stage of complete artificialism, the child explains the presence of the sun and moon as the creation of human or divine agents.

Second Stage (Begins at about 8 Years)   In this transitional stage, the child gives the origin of the solar system as half natural, half artificial.

Third Stage (Begins at about 9 to 11 Years) By this time, the child, with the help of adult instruction, realizes human activity was not involved in the creation of the solar system.

Conservation

Probably the most well known of Piaget's work is his study of *conservation*, or the ability to recognize that two equal quantities of matter remain equal (in substance, weight, length, number, volume, or space) even if the matter is rearranged, as long as nothing is added or taken away. In the conservation of *substance*, a child is shown two equal balls of clay. He agrees they are equal. The child is said to conserve substance if he then recognizes that even after one of the balls has been rolled into the shape of a worm, both lumps of clay have equal amounts of matter. In *weight* conservation, the child is asked whether the ball and the worm weigh the same. And in conservation of *volume*, the child is asked to judge whether both the ball and the worm displace an equal amount of liquid when placed in glasses of water. Children develop different types of conservation at different times. At age 6 or 7, they are able to conserve substance; at 9 or 10, weight; and at 11 or 12, volume.

Horizontal decalage is the term Piaget uses to describe this phenomenon of the child's inability to transfer what he has learned about one type of conservation to a different type, for which the underlying principle is identical.

Before children master any type of conservation problem, they go through three stages. In the first, they fail to conserve: They center on one aspect, are fooled by looks, and cannot recognize the reversible nature of the operation. The second stage in conservation is transitional, during which children vacillate, sometimes passing and sometimes failing. Children in this stage tend to concentrate on more than one aspect but do not realize interrelationships between such dimensions as height and width or length and thickness. They fail more often than they pass. In the third and final stage in conservation, children conserve and give logical justifications for their answers. These justifications may take the form of *reversibility* ("If the clay worm were shaped into a ball, it would be the same as the other ball"); *identity* ("It's the same clay; you haven't added any or taken any away"); or *compensation* ("The ball is shorter than the worm, but the worm is longer than the ball—so they both have the same amount of clay"). Operational children show a *qualitative* cognitive advancement over preoperational preschoolers. Their thinking is reversible, they decenter, and they are aware that transformations are only perceptual alterations.

Children can be trained in *reversibility*, the awareness that a given operation can be reversed to bring back the original situation. One group of 6- and 7-year-olds had all failed number-conservation tasks. The experimenter showed each child some dolls in doll beds and then took the dolls from the beds and placed them sometimes close together, sometimes far apart, occasionally adding or removing a bed. After each manipulation, the experimenter asked, "Can you put a doll in every bed now?" The children learned that the number of dolls and beds remained the same regardless of spacing, as long as no beds were added or removed. They then were able to transfer their number abilities to checkers and cards. In an untrained group, none of the children developed number conservation (Wallach & Sprott, 1964).

Closely related to conservation is *transitivity*, the ability to recognize a relationship between two objects by knowing the relationship between each of them and a third. A child is shown a yellow stick, which is longer than a green one, which itself is longer than a blue one. She is then asked about the relationship between the yellow and blue sticks, based on her knowledge of the relationship each holds to the green stick.

Piaget stresses the maturational components of conservation, saying that children will learn this concept when their cognitive structures are mature enough and that it is only minimally subject to training. Factors other than maturation also affect conservation. We assume this, since children who learn conservation skills earliest have high grades, high IQs, high verbal ability, and nondominating mothers (Goldschmid & Bentler, 1968; Almy, Chittenden, & Miller, 1966). Children from various countries—Switzerland, the United States, Great Britain, and others—achieve conservation at different ages, which points to a cultural, or learned, aspect to this ability instead of maturation alone.

MORAL DEVELOPMENT IN SCHOOLCHILDREN

Why are we discussing morality in a chapter about intellectual development? Isn't moral thinking an outgrowth of personality, emotional attitudes, and cultural influences? A growing number of psychologists and educators are adopting the views of Piaget and Kohlberg—that the development of moral

TABLE 8-2
Piaget's Stages of
Moral Development

Piaget's theory of moral development in children can be summarized by broadly dividing children's moral thinking into two major sequential stages. *(Adapted partly from Kohlberg, in Hoffman & Hoffman 1964; Hoffman, 1970.)*

	STAGE I	STAGE II
MORAL CONCEPTS	Morality of constraint (heteronomous morality).	Morality of cooperation (autonomous morality).
POINT OF VIEW	Child views an act as either totally right or totally wrong, and thinks everyone sees it the same way. Cannot put self in place of others.	Child can put self in place of others. Not absolutistic in judgments; sees possibility of more than one point of view.
INTENTIONALITY	Child tends to judge an act in terms of actual physical consequences, not the motivation behind it.	Child judges acts by intentions, not consequences.
RULES	Child obeys rules because they are sacred and unalterable.	Child recognizes that rules were made by people and can be changed by people. Considers self just as capable of changing rules as anyone else.
RESPECT FOR AUTHORITY	Unilateral respect leads to feeling of obligation to conform to adult standards and obey adult rules.	Mutual respect for authority and peers allows child to value own opinion and ability more highly and to judge other people more realistically.
PUNISHMENT	Child favors severe, expiatory punishment. Feels that punishment itself defines the wrongness of an act; an act is bad if it will elicit punishment.	Child favors milder, reciprocal punishment that leads to restitution of the victim and helps the culprit recognize why an act was wrong, thus leading to reform.
"IMMANENT JUSTICE"	Child confuses moral law with physical law and believes that any physical accident or misfortune that occurs after a misdeed is a punishment willed by God or some other supernatural force.	Child does not confuse natural misfortune with punishment.

values is a rational process which coincides with cognitive development. Children cannot make moral judgments until they achieve a certain level of cognitive maturity and can shed egocentric thinking.

Piaget's theory

According to Piaget, children go through two stages in their conception of morality. He calls these stages the *morality of constraint* (or *heteronomous morality*) and the *morality of cooperation* (or *autonomous morality*). In the first stage a child deals with moral concepts in

a rigid way, while the second stage is characterized by moral flexibility (see Table 8-2).

We can follow the course of moral development by examining children's conceptions of rules, intentionality, punishment, and justice. In regard to all these concepts, children move from rigid to flexible thinking. This change is a sign of cognitive development: True morality is consonant with true cognitive maturity.

As children mature and as they interact more with other children and with adults, they think in a less egocentric manner. They gradu-

Children's increasing interaction with people outside their immediate family helps them to be less egocentric in their thinking and more socially competent. (Nancy Hays/ Monkmeyer)

ally learn to make their own decisions and see themselves as the equals of older people, whom they once accepted as absolute authorities. They have ever-increasing contact with a wide range of viewpoints, many of which contradict what they have learned at home. In an effort to reconcile their home teachings and what other people believe, children conclude that there is not one unchangeable, absolute standard of morality, but that individuals can formulate their own codes of right and wrong. They decide which rules they are going to follow, and are on the way to formulating their own moral codes (see Table 8-3).

People go through definite, distinct, qualitatively different stages of moral development. Different persons go through different stages at different times, but the sequence is always the same. Piaget's theory is that "all morality consists in a system of rules, and . . . the essence of all morality is to be sought for in the respect which the individual acquires for these rules" (1965, p. 13). It is especially

difficult to study the reasoning behind people's adherence to the larger rules that regulate how they relate to each other and to society. But by finding out how children think and act in reference to child-propagated rules, such as those that govern games like marbles, he analyzed children's thinking about rules. What children do does not always corrrespond to what they believe, so the evolution of the way children practice rules goes through stages different, at somewhat different times, from those of the progression of their thinking. Eventually, practice and thinking converge.

Piaget (1932) told children this story: Once upon a time there were two little boys, Augustus and Julian. Augustus noticed one day that his father's inkpot was empty, and he decided to help his father by filling it. But in opening the bottle, he spilled the ink and made a large stain on the tablecloth. Julian played with his father's inkpot and made a small stain on the tablecloth. Piaget then asked, "Which boy is naughtier and why?"

TABLE 8-3
Children's Practice of Rules and Their Thinking about Rules

CHILDREN'S PRACTICE OF RULES	CHILDREN'S THINKING ABOUT RULES
Stage I: Motor Activity Children handle marbles in an individual way to see what they can do with them.	*Stage I:* Absolutism (from 4 to 7) Rules are considered as interesting examples, not obligatory realities. Children consider rules sacred and untouchable, although in practice they are willing to accept changes, possibly because they don't recognize them as changes.
Stage II: Egocentrism (beginning anywhere from 2 to 5 years) Children have a general idea of what rules are, and they like to think they're playing by the rules. Actually, though, they play by their idiosyncratic systems and change the rules about when it suits their purpose.	*Stage II:* Morality of Constraint (from 7 to 10) Children are constrained by their respect for adults and older children. Whatever these authorities say must be so. They refuse to accept any change in rules.
Stage III: Incipient Cooperation (begins about 7 to 8) Each player tries to win and wants to play by a set of rules. But children's ideas are still vague, and three children playing together will give three different explanations of the rules.	*Stage III:* Morality of Cooperation (from 10 on) Children see rules as laws due to mutual consent. Most children have by now cast aside their belief in the infallibility of parents and other authority figures. They see themselves as equals of others and believe that since people made the rules, people can change them. And they see themselves as just as able to change them as is anyone else. They no longer accept adult authority without question.
Stage IV: Codification (begins about 11 or 12) Children know every detail of procedure. All children in a group know and play by the same rules.	

SOURCE: Adapted from Piaget, 1932.

Most adults and older children consider Julian guiltier, since the small stain he made was caused by his doing something he should not have been doing, while Augustus's larger stain was an accidental by-product of a praiseworthy intention. But the child under 7 is more likely to consider Augustus the greater offender since he made the larger stain. Children under 7 make immature moral judgments, since they are more concerned with the magnitude of an offense than with the intention behind the act.

Younger children are also more in favor of punishment that is unrelated to a particular misdeed, while older ones favor making the punishment "fit the crime." As children mature, they judge the value of a punishment not by its severity but as much as possible by the direct material consequences of the misdeed, feeling that appropriate punishments will make misbehavers appreciate the results of their own actions.

Kohlberg's theory

Inspired by Piaget, Kohlberg embarked on his own studies of moral development in children from a variety of cultures—United States, Great Britain, Canada, Taiwan, Mexico, and Turkey. Kohlberg's interest was not in what children actually do about moral issues, but with the way they think about them. Since moral decisions, or actions, do not necessarily progress at the same rate as moral reasoning, he decided to focus only on the thinking level of morality—how people arrive at moral judgments.

To find out how children of different ages think about morality, Kohlberg (1968) told them a number of stories that center on the concept of justice and delve into twenty-five basic moral concepts, such as the value of human life, the motives for moral action, concepts of rights, the basis of respect for social authority, and so forth. The most famous one raises the question of whether Heinz should steal a drug that could save his wife's life if the only druggist who has it demands an exorbitant price, totally out of Heinz's reach. Another poses the dilemma of Sharon, who is stopped by a department store security officer because Sharon's best friend has just walked out of the store wearing a stolen sweater.

Based on the responses he received to such stories, Kohlberg confirmed Piaget's findings that the level of children's moral reasoning depends on their age and maturity. He then developed six levels of moral reasoning, the last of which he has since discarded (see Table 8-4). By paying close attention to the reasoning behind the children's answers, Kohlberg concluded that children arrive at moral judgments in an independent fashion, rather than merely "internalizing" the standards of parents, teachers, or peers.

RECENT RESEARCH ON COGNITIVE THEORIES

There have been many attempts to follow up these theories, and a great deal of research confirms them, relating moral development to cognitive development. Moir (1974) found a positive relationship between the ability of 11-year-old girls to take the roles of others and their level of moral development. Tomlinson-Keasey and Keasey (1974) found that female college students were better able to apply intellectual abilities to moral issues

than were sixth-grade girls. Age, social class, and IQ all correlate positively with moral judgment (Hoffman, 1970).

But not all research findings bear out these theories. Even intelligent adults sometimes confuse intentionality with consequence: College students were more likely to judge someone responsible for causing an accident with severe consequences than one with minor results, even though the hypothetical person was said to have taken identical safety precautions in both cases (Walster, 1966; cited in Hoffman, 1970). Utech's (1972) finding that children's responses can be modified in either a forward or regressive direction by being exposed to a model who espouses the opposite point of view casts question upon the "invariant sequence" notion of moral reasoning. Another finding that contradicts Piagetian thought emerged from a study that set up four different groups to train children to give more mature responses to moral dilemmas (Lickona, 1973). The training techniques included focusing on the issues, exposing the subject to another child who gave a more mature response, exposure to two adults with conflicting points of view (each of whom used reasoning to support the stand taken), and just telling the child the "right" answer. All the training conditions brought about more mature moral reasoning, and the greatest increase showed up in those children who had just been *told* the right answer. This finding contradicts Piaget's and Kohlberg's convictions that children actively work out their own moral systems, and that moral reasoning is consonant with cognitive maturity.

Social Learning Theory

Another way to explain the development of conscience is to say that children learn the moral values of their culture principally by identifying with or modeling themselves after their own parents (see Table 8-5). Children are rewarded by parents for making the right decisions and punished for the wrong ones. When they fail to comply with parental standards, they feel guilty, even when their par-

TABLE 8-4
Kohlberg's Six
Stages of Moral
Reasoning

LEVEL I *Premoral (ages 4 to 10).* Emphasis in this level is on external control. The standards are those of others, and they are observed either to avoid punishment or to reap rewards.

Type 1. Punishment and obedience orientation. "What will happen to me?" Children obey the rules of others to avoid punishment.

Type 2. Naive instrumental hedonism. "You scratch my back, I'll scratch yours." They conform to rules out of self-interest and consideration for what others can do for them in return.

LEVEL II *Morality of conventional role conformity (ages 10 to 13).* Children now want to please other people. They still observe the standards of others, but they have internalized these standards to some extent. Now they want to be considered "good" by those persons whose opinions count. They are now able to take the roles of authority figures well enough to decide whether some action is "good" by their standards.

Type 3. Maintaining good relations, approval of others. "Am I a good girl [boy]?" Children want to please and help others, can judge the intentions of others, and develop their own ideas of what a good person is.

Type 4. Authority-maintaining morality. "We need law and order." People are concerned with doing their duty, showing respect for higher authority, and maintaining the social order.

LEVEL III *Morality of self-accepted moral principles (age 13 or not until young adulthood, or never).* This level marks the attainment of true morality. For the first time, the individual acknowledges the possibility of conflict between two socially accepted standards, and tries to decide between them. The control of conduct is now internal, both in the standards observed and in the reasoning about right and wrong. Types 5 and 6 may be alternate methods of the highest level of reasoning.

Type 5. Morality of contract, of individual rights, and of democratically accepted law. People think in rational terms, valuing the will of the majority and the welfare of society. They generally see these values best supported by adherence to the law. While they recognize that there are times when there is a conflict between human need and the law, they believe that it is better for society in the long run if they obey the law.

Type 6. Morality of individual principles of conscience.* People do what they as individuals think right, regardless of legal restrictions or the opinions of others. They act in accordance with internalized standards, knowing that they would condemn themselves if they did not. Examples are Gandhi and Martin Luther King.

SOURCE: Adapted from Kohlberg, 1968.
*Kohlberg recently dropped Stage 6 from his newly revised scoring manual, partly because it seemed to be culturally based, partly because none of his longitudinal subjects had achieved it by 1976, and also, perhaps, because it has been widely criticized as "elitist" and "merely a scientific justification for libertarian values" (Muson, 1979, p. 57).

ents don't even know what they have done. When this happens, learning theorists say that the child has internalized parental standards and achieved a certain level of morality.

Research does not, however, confirm the generalization of moral standards from the home to other situations. Hartshorne and May's (1928–1930) series of experiments to assess children's moral behavior found that children apply situational morality, acting differently in different situations, even when the same principle is involved. Hartshorne and May could not divide children into groups of "cheaters" and "noncheaters," but found a normal distribution of cheating in experimental situations. "Almost all of the children cheated, but they varied in how much risk and effort they would take to cheat" (Kohlberg, 1963, p. 284). Furthermore, children who cheated were just as likely to say that cheating was wrong as were those who did not cheat. So there was a big difference between moral judgment and moral behavior. Is it morality that is learned, then, or is it the practicality of being moral in certain situations?

This is not to say that children do not learn moral values from their parents. There is a relationship between what parents say and do, and how children act. Sears, Maccoby,

TABLE 8-5
Two Explanations
of Morality

COGNITIVE DEVELOPMENTAL THEORY	SOCIAL LEARNING THEORY
Moral development has a basic cognitive-structural moral judgmental component.	Moral development is growth of behavioral and affective conformity to moral rules rather than cognitive-structural change.
The basic motivation for morality is generalized motivation for acceptance, competence, self-esteem, or self-realization, rather than for meeting biological needs and reducing anxiety or fear.	The basic motivation for morality at every point of moral development is rooted in biological needs or the pursuit of social reward and avoidance of social punishment.
Major aspects of moral development are culturally universal, because all cultures have common sources of social interaction, role-taking, and social conflict which require moral integration.	Moral development or morality is culturally relative.
Basic moral norms and principles are structures arising through experience of social interaction, rather than through internalization of rules that exist as external structures; moral stages are not defined by internalized rules, but by structures of interaction between the self and others.	Basic moral norms are the internalization of external cultural rules.
Environmental influences in moral development are defined by the general quality and extent of cognitive and social stimulation throughout the child's development, rather than by specific experiences with parents or experiences of discipline, punishment, and reward.	Environmental influences on normal moral development are defined by quantitative variations in strength of reward, punishment, prohibitions, and modeling of conforming behavior by parents and other socializing agents.

SOURCE: Adapted from Kohlberg, in Lickona, 1976, p. 48.

and Levin (1957) noted that children who are praised frequently for good behavior and isolated or deprived of love for bad behavior are more likely to develop strong consciences than those who are disciplined by spanking. Psychological techniques are most efficient in homes with a loving atmosphere: If there is no love to withdraw, this cannot be an effective means of discipline.

Children learn by example, too. Stein (1967) asked fourth-grade boys to perform a boring task while an interesting movie was being shown. To see the movie, they would have to disobey instructions. The boys in the first experimental group saw an adult leave his own boring job to peek at the movie; those in the next two groups saw models who resisted the temptation to look at the movie, either by performing their own tasks or by doing nothing; and those in the fourth group saw no

March 8. Mama had some ladies over for tea and I got into trouble.... I decided to play dress-up. I put on Mama's high heal shoes and put my hair up in a pompadour and then put on one of Mama's long dresses. I tried on the visiting ladies hats that were on the bed. I saw one that was just right.... It was big and floppy with black velvet top and fussy veils and a stuffed bird sitting on top. Then the most awful thing happened -- I took it off and the bird fell on the floor. And just then the ladies were leaving so I hid under the bed. I was so scared. But they thought my poor Maggie did it. I wonder if I should tell.

March 19. I told and I'm glad I did. Mama said you'd better call the lady and apologize. So I did and she said, "Never you mind, I'll glue it right back on." So now my conscience is clear.

Margaret O'Brien, age 10,
from *Small Voices*, pp. 78–79

model. The children who saw the model yield to temptation were more likely to do so themselves than were boys in any of the other groups. The boys' attitudes and feelings about disobeying rules had less to do with whether they actually resisted temptation than with whether or not they saw the model. In real life, of course, parents are strong models for their children's moral behaviors.

Psychoanalytic Theory

Freud's theory of moral development rests on the influence of the Oedipus and Electra complexes in helping the child to develop a superego. (See discussion on pp. 220–221.) After children identify with the parent of the same sex, they internalize the parent's moral standards, which then become their own consciences. Research has not been able to confirm the specific details of Freud's theory, mostly because its central concepts, such as castration anxiety, are hard to measure. However, several studies have borne out certain broad implications of Freudian theory (Hogan & Emler, 1978).

Research has found, for example, that the parents of delinquent youths tend to be either lax and erratic in their discipline, or too strict; that psychological, love-oriented discipline ("Mother doesn't love you when you do that") is more likely to produce people who are prone to guilt than is physical discipline; that this relationship shows up on a society-wide basis among different cultures around the world; and that moral development parallels the development of personality.

So there is some backup for such basic Freudian beliefs as the necessity of identification for the development of moral conduct and the capacity for guilt; the relationship of certain child-rearing practices to the development of conscience; and the close tie between moral development and personality development in general (Hogan & Emler, 1978).

Social Role-Taking Skills and Moral Reasoning

A basic component to the development of moral reasoning is, as we have noted, an individual's ability to understand another's point of view. Robert L. Selman, who worked with Kohlberg at Harvard, defines role-taking ability as a "mature conception of the complexity of human relations," encompassing "the developing understanding of just what is a social being, i.e., another's capabilities, attributes, expectations, feelings, motives, potential reactions, and social judgments" (1973, p. 5). Selman has classified the development of role-taking ability in stages that he links to Piaget's cognitive stages and Kohlberg's stages in moral reasoning (see Table 8-6).

How do answers to moral dilemmas change according to the stage of children's role-taking skills? As a young child, Vicky considers the situation of Holly, an 8-year-old girl who has promised her father not to climb trees, then comes upon a kitten caught in a tree, and is torn between wanting to save the kitten by climbing the tree and wanting to keep her promise to her father.

Between the approximate ages of 4 to 6, when Vicky is in Selman's *stage 0*, she thinks that her way of viewing a situation is the only way. When asked, "Do you think Holly's father will get angry if he finds out that Holly climbed the tree," she replies, "No, he will be happy. He likes kittens." Asked, "Why will that make him happy?" Vicky says, "I like kittens."

The *stage 1* Vicky, aged about 6 to 8,

TABLE 8-6 Major Milestones in Social Cognition	DIMENSIONS (YEARS)	COGNITIVE STAGE	MORAL STAGE	SOCIAL ROLE-TAKING	SPATIAL ROLE-TAKING
	Ages 3–5/6	Preoperational	Premoral	Egocentric role-taking. Can't anticipate thoughts of others.	Has rudimentary idea of what another is viewing but not of other's perspective. Can consider some listener's needs but still has relatively egocentric perspective.
	5–7/8	Preoperational/ Early concrete operations	Punishment/ Obedience orientation	Social-informational role-taking. Understands another person can have different thoughts from own. Can distinguish accidental from intended actions and some ability to distinguish good and bad intent. Has trouble inferring if another's actions are intended or accidental when consequence is negative.	Recognizes others can have another visual perspective if they look at an object from a different location.
	8–10	Advanced concrete operations	Instrumental hedonism	Self-reflective role-taking. Has reciprocal awareness: Others can see things differently from her/him. Others can think about *her* intent, feelings, thoughts.	More accurate spatial and communicative perspective. Can consider another point of view.
	10–12	Early formal operations	"Golden rule orientation"	Mutual role-taking. Understands that two people can consider each other's viewpoints simultaneously; can view these two perspectives from a third person's perspective.	
	12–15+	Formal operations	Conventional morality/ Perhaps beginning of self-accepted moral principles	Social and conventional role-taking. Realizes that recognition of different perspectives of others does not guarantee complete understanding. Sees need for social conventions to resolve differences.	Continued development and accuracy of role-taking ability.

SOURCE: Adapted from Shantz, 1975; Selman, 1973; Kohlberg, 1968; and Piaget and Inhelder, 1969.

FEELINGS OF OTHERS	PERSON PERCEPTION
Can identify simple emotions of others by looking at their facial expressions or by seeing another in a familiar situation. By 4 years, can identify situations causing happiness.	Describes others in terms of physical appearance, child's interaction with self ("plays with me") and is very evaluative.
Can identify situations eliciting fear, sad-ness, anger, with increased accuracy.	Often describes people in terms of appear-ance, possessions, and simple evaluative traits (nice, good).
Can figure out feelings of others—even in an unfamiliar situation.	Describes others in terms of attributes—attitudes, interests, skills.
Much more accurate in identifying feelings of others . . . even in an unfamiliar situation when the "other" is not similar to the child (an adult).	Refinement of under-standing of traits in others. Realizes there can be contradictory tendencies within an individual.

realizes that other people may interpret a situation the same way she does or differently, and that other people can consider the inten-tions behind actions. She now answers the question about Holly's father by saying, "If he didn't know why she climbed the tree, he would be angry. But if he knows why Holly did it, he will realize she had a good reason."

When Vicky reaches *stage 2*, sometime between 8 and 10 years of age, she now has a reciprocal awareness. She now knows that what she knew in stage 1—that others can see things differently from her—is also known to others. Thus they can scrutinize her actions, thoughts, and feelings. She says about Holly's father, "He knows that Holly will think about how he would feel. He knows that Holly would realize that he would think it is all right. And so he will think it's okay for her to climb the tree." But if Holly didn't think about what her father thinks is right, Vicky says, "Then he will be angry."

In *stage 3*, Vicky, now aged about 10 to 12, realizes that she and another person can look at each other's point of view at the same time and can even step outside this twosome and view it from a third person's perspective. She now considers the dilemma of Heinz. When asked whether the judge would think Heinz was right to steal the drug, she says, "I think the judge would have thought that it wasn't right for Heinz to steal, but now that he had done it and the judge had heard his side of the story, the judge would feel that Heinz was doing what he thought was right. Heinz realizes that the judge will consider how he felt."

In *stage 4*, which Vicky reaches some-time between the ages of 12 and 15 or later, she realizes that mutual perspective-taking doesn't always produce complete under-standing. She now recognizes that social conventions are needed, so that she can communicate her reactions to other people and understand their behavior. To the question, "What do you think the judge would do?" she answers, "I'm afraid he'd have to convict him. When Heinz stole the drug, he knew it was wrong from society's point of view. He also knew that if he were caught, he'd be convicted because he'd realize the judge would have to uphold the law. The judge has to think about the way it would look to everybody else. If they see Heinz getting no punishment, they might think they can get away with stealing. Even if the judge thought Heinz was morally right, from the legal point of view the judge has to consider the law of the people."

PRACTICAL IMPLICATIONS What are the practical implications for the ability to assume the viewpoint of another person? Only by understanding how someone else would be affected by our actions can we temper what we want to do with what the effects of our actions on others would be. It's possible that an inability to put oneself in another person's place might be responsible for much antisocial behavior. Two studies involving delinquent and disturbed youngsters underscore the importance of role-taking ability.

In one study, forty-five 11- to 13-year-old chronic delinquents and forty-five boys who had never been in serious trouble were shown cartoon sequences that told a story. They were then asked to relate the stories from the point of view of a late-arriving person who had not seen all the events the boys knew about. Chandler (1973) found that the delinquent boys were less able to put themselves in the place of the late arriver.

The delinquent boys were divided into three groups. Those in the first group were enrolled in a ten-week summer program at a storefront where staff members helped them to develop their role-taking skills by making up and filming skits about people their own age. The storefront staff helped the boys in the second group to film cartoons and documentaries that did not portray the boys themselves. And the third group did not attend the program at all. At the end of the summer, all the boys were retested on role-taking ability. Only those who had received the role-taking training had improved. A year and a half later, Chandler reviewed police and court records and found that the boys who had received role-taking training had committed far fewer reported antisocial acts.

This approach, then, offers a new way to look at young offenders, to see their delinquency as the result of a developmental lag, and to try some new approaches to help them act in more appropriate ways. Chandler, though, conscientiously offers several disclaimers, which are good models that point up the need for extreme caution in evaluating all experimental data. In any study, we need to determine exactly what it is we are studying, to be extremely careful in seeing cause-and-effect relationships in correlations, and to look at our findings with a healthy grain of skepticism.

In this study, we need to remember that this was a special subgroup of antisocial youths—those who had been caught. Chandler says:

The possibility exists that the persistent egocentrism which characterized this group was an index of their ineptitude rather than their antisocial orientation. If such were the case, the apparent reduction in delinquent behavior . . . might only reflect an improved ability to avoid detection and what looked like a promising intervention technique might prove only to be a "school for scoundrels" [p. 15].

Chandler, Greenspan, and Barenboim (1974) tested a group of 125 institutionalized emotionally disturbed children, aged 8 to 15, and found that most of them were retarded on measures of both role-taking and *referential communication*, or the ability to transmit specific visual information to someone else so that the second person could duplicate a design he or she could not see. They assigned forty-eight of these children randomly to three groups, training one group in role-taking, training the second in referential communication, and giving the third group no training.

Graduate students helped the role-taking training group to develop and videotape brief skits about people their own age. Those in the referential communication group played games that depended for their success on the players ability to communicate with each other. The experimenters would interrupt from time to time to ask the players to judge their success in verbally cooperating with each other. If unsuccessful, the children were urged to see why they weren't getting the information across.

The children in both the training groups improved in role-taking skills, and also showed a slightly better social adjustment a year later. The small level of improvement, though, emphasizes the fact that not all emotional disorders are related to retarded role-taking abilities and that training in these skills is no panacea. Yet this, like the previous study, points in a promising direction for future research.

Values Clarification

Within the past few years many teachers, parents, and other adult leaders have been implementing an approach called "values clarification," which has been designed to help children make moral judgments by giving them a set of skills that help them to analyze the values they say they hold and the values they actually live by (Raths, Harmin, & Simon, 1966). These skills are:

. . . (1) seeking alternatives when faced with a choice, (2) looking ahead to probable consequences before choosing, (3) making choices on one's own, without depending on others, (4) being aware of one's own preferences and valuations, (5) being willing to affirm one's choices and preferences publicly, (6) acting in

ways that are consistent with choices and preferences, and (7) acting in those ways repeatedly, with a pattern to one's life [Harmin & Simon, 1973, p. 13].

Values clarification uses gamelike exercises called "strategies" that pose provocative questions and ask children to make judgments. The object is not to teach a prescribed set of values, but rather to teach children how to form their own values. The following strategies, from Simon and Olds (1976), are typical:

Provocative questions: Children are asked to respond to questions like "Are there ever times when lying is justified?"; "What would the world be like without cars?"; "What are some things that take courage?" *Are you someone who . . . ?:* Children are asked to answer questions like the following with "Yes," "no," "Sometimes," or "I don't know," and then to discuss their answers: "Are you someone who . . . would take part in a protest demonstration . . . would ever smoke pot with your children . . . throws candy wrappers on the sidewalk . . . says what you think even when it gets you in trouble?"

Values spectrum: Children are asked to place themselves somewhere on a continuum between two extremes:

TEETOTALER TERESA→DRINKING DORIS

believes no one	loves to drink
of any age should	herself and gives
ever drink any	her 5-year-old
alcohol because	child a drink
it's the devil's	every day so
potion.	she'll learn how
	to handle alcohol.

This approach seems to hold promise as

a practical extension of the theories of Piaget and Kohlberg, by encouraging children to reflect upon values and get practice in making moral judgments.

THE DEVELOPMENT OF SCHOOLCHILDREN'S ABILITY TO COMMUNICATE

Language

Let us imagine that you are looking out the window at a snow-covered driveway and you ask how you are going to get the family car out of the garage. If you don't receive a not-too-gentle suggestion that an able-bodied young adult should be able to figure that one out without any help, you might get either one of the following answers:

"John promised Mary to shovel the driveway," or

"John told Mary to shovel the driveway."

Depending on which answer you received, you know whether that bundled-up figure just coming into view, shovel in hand, is John or Mary. But many children under 5 or 6 years of age do not understand the syntactic differences between these two sentences, and think that they both mean that Mary is to do the shoveling (Chomsky, 1969). Their confusion is understandable since almost all English verbs that might replace *told* in the second sentence (such as *ordered, wanted, persuaded, advised, allowed, expected*) would put the shovel in Mary's hand.

Most 6-year-olds have not yet learned how to deal with the exception to the grammatical rule exemplified by the word *promise* in the first sentence above, even though they know what a promise is and are able to use and understand the word correctly in other sentences. By the age of 8, most children can interpret the first sentence correctly. They know the concept attached to the word *promise*, and they know how the word can be used.

Even though most 6-year-olds speak on a rather sophisticated level, using complex grammar and a vocabulary of some 2500 words, they still have not yet completely mastered certain syntactic niceties. (Suzanne Szasz)

The above example shows us that even though 6-year-olds speak on a rather sophisticated level, using complex grammar and a vocabulary of some 2500 words (Lenneberg, 1967), they still have a way to go before they master syntactic niceties. During the early school years, they rarely use passive sentences, verbs that include the form *have*, and conditional sentences ("If you were to do this, I could do that").

Children develop increasingly complex understanding of syntax up to and possibly after the age of 9 (Chomsky, 1969). By testing the understanding of various syntactic structures by forty 5- to 10-year-old children, Carol Chomsky found considerable variation in the ages of children who knew them and those who did not (see Table 8-7).

Is an ice-cream cone food? Is a hat an article of clothing? Many 5- and 6-year-olds would say no to both questions, which tells us something about the way they understand

STRUCTURE	DIFFICULT CONCEPT	AGE OF ACQUISITION	**TABLE 8-7**
John is easy to see.	Who's doing the seeing?	5.6 to 9 years.*	Acquisition of
John promised Bill to go.	Who's going?	5.6 to 9 years.*	Complex Syntactic
John asked Bill what to do.	Who's doing it?	Some 10-year-olds still haven't learned this.	Structures
He knew that John was going to win the race.	Does the "he" refer to John?	5.6 years	

SOURCE: Chomsky, 1969.
*All children 9 and over know this.

I think spelling is very funny I spelt infancy infantsy and they said it was wrong but I don't see why because if my seven little cousins died when they were infants they must have died in their infantsy, but infancy makes it seem as if they hadn't really died but we just make believe.

Catherine Elizabeth Havens, age 9,
from *Small Voices*, p. 210

and use language. In their study of the development of natural language concepts, Saltz and Soller (1972) asked children aged 5 to 12 to classify seventy-two pictures into six concepts: food, animal, transportation, clothes, toy, and furniture.

The youngest children consistently included the smallest number of items in each concept, were least flexible in multiple classification of items, and held narrowly fragmented concepts. That is, they used the concept names in very limited ways that suggested meanings more narrowly circumscribed than in standard adult usage. For example, many of the little children thought that only garments worn between the shoulders and knees could be clothing, leaving out gloves and shoes as well as hats. They were also less likely than the older children to think of snacks as food. The youngest children also depended more heavily on the way things looked. Therefore, they were more likely to classify the stuffed animals as actual animals, even though the stuffed animals were not alive, whereas the older children had a broader sense of abstract concepts.

Egocentrism

Once upon a time there was a lady who had twelve boys and twelve girls, and then a fairy a boy and a girl. And then Niobe wanted to have some more sons. Then she was angry. She fastened her to a stone. He turned into a rock and then his tears made a stream which is still running today [Piaget, 1926, p. 102].

Anyone listening to 8-year-old Gio tell this story would be hopelessly confused about the persons that all those "he's" and "she's" refer to. The story was Gio's rendering of the following, which Piaget told to children 6 to 8 years old to see how well they could retell it:

Once upon a time, there was a lady who was called Niobe, who had 12 sons and 12 daughters. She met a fairy who had only one son and no daughter. Then the lady laughed at the fairy because the fairy only had one boy. Then the fairy was very angry and fastened the lady to a rock. The lady cried for ten years. In the end she turned into a rock, and her tears made a stream which still runs to-day [Piaget, 1926, p. 82].

While most of the children understood the story, their ability to retell it was limited by their egocentrism. Unable to take the viewpoint of the listener, young children omit much crucial information. The older the children, the better their ability to communicate, which reflects children's diminishing egocentrism, brought about by social pressure from peers and adults.

In one test of communication skills, experimenters taught a simple competitive game to children by playing the game with them and using gestures. No words were spoken. Then the children were asked to teach the game to an adult who had not seen it being played. The children were not allowed to touch the game materials, and the adults did not give the children any feedback about the adequacy of their instructions. Half the children at each age level from second to eleventh grades had to teach a blindfolded experimenter. Some of the youngest children "blithely spoke of picking up 'this' and putting it 'over there,' and the like, when trying to explain the game to the unsighted adult" (Flavell, 1966, p. 173). But the older the children, the more useful information they gave to the adults, and the better they took into account the special circumstances of the blindfolded adults.

Children's viewpoints have a great effect on their ability to communicate. As they recognize other perspectives, they can predict other people's responses. The inability to take the role of another explains much of children's thoughtless, seemingly cruel behavior.

MEASURING INTELLIGENCE IN SCHOOLCHILDREN

In many schools all children receive group intelligence tests every few years, partly to determine individual ability and partly to assess the school's standards. Youngsters often are tested individually, too, either for admission to a selective school or because of school problems. Intelligence testing sometimes yields results which indicate that Johnny has specific learning disabilities, that Jenny should be in a less demanding classroom, that Joey is getting into trouble because he's bored, or that Janie needs special help.

Tests for Schoolchildren

THE STANFORD-BINET This individual test is sometimes still used during school years,

but since it emphasizes verbal skills so heavily, it penalizes the child who has a specific language problem and masks the problems of the highly verbal child with perceptual or motor deficits.

THE WECHSLER INTELLIGENCE SCALE FOR CHILDREN (WISC) This individual test was designed to be used with children aged 5 to 15 and is used mostly for youngsters between 7 and 13. It measures verbal and performance abilities separately, yielding separate scores for each, as well as a total score. When the verbal score is significantly lower than the performance score, there may be problems with language development. When the verbal IQ is high but the performance IQ low, perceptual and/or motor development may be retarded. The WISC verbal subtests are Information, Comprehension, Arithmetic, Similarities, Vocabulary, and Digit Span. The performance subtests are Picture Completion, Picture Arrangement, Block Design, Object Assembly, Coding, and Mazes.

THE OTIS-LENNON MENTAL ABILITY TEST, PRIMARY LEVEL This group test is meant for kindergartners and first-graders, who are tested in small groups of ten to fifteen subjects. Each child receives a booklet that consists of pictures and diagrams; no reading is required. The teacher gives instructions orally. The test takes about half an hour to administer and is given in two parts, with an intermission. It asks children to classify items, to show understanding of verbal and number concepts, to display general information, and to follow directions.

THE LORGE-THORNDIKE MULTI-LEVEL BATTERY This group test is designed for children from fourth grade through high school and is divided into several levels, suitable for different age groups. It asks children to give the meanings of words, to complete sentences, to classify words, to do arithmetic problems that require reasoning, and to show an understanding of verbal analogies. On the fourth-grade level, the test takes about an hour.

Cross-Cultural Testing

As far back as 1910, researchers recognized the difficulty of devising tests to measure the intelligence of diverse cultural groups (Anastasi, 1968). Since then, they have tried in vain to devise tests that can measure innate intelligence without introducing cultural bias. It has been possible to design tests that do not require language: Testers use gestures, pantomime, and demonstrations for tasks such as tracing mazes, finding absurdities in pictures, putting the right shapes in the right holes, and completing pictures. But it has not been possible to eliminate all cultural content. If a person is finding absurdities in a picture, the picture has to be something with which the test-taker is familiar. The conventionalities of art will affect the way the test-taker views the picture: A group of Oriental immigrant children in Israel, asked to provide the missing detail for a picture of a face with no mouth, said that the *body* was missing. They were not used to considering a drawing of a head as a complete picture and "regarded the absence of a body as more important than the omission of a mere detail like the mouth" (Anastasi, 1968, p. 252).

Recognizing the impossibility of designing a *culture-free* test, test-makers have tried to produce *culture-fair* tests that deal with experiences common to various cultures. But it is almost impossible to screen for culturally determined values and attitudes. Anastasi (1968) lists some conditions that differ among cultures: "the intrinsic interest of the test content, rapport with the examiner, drive to do well on a test, desire to excel others, and past habits of solving problems individually or cooperatively" (p. 251). There are other cultural attitudes, too. A child from a society that stresses slow, deliberate, painstaking work is handicapped in a test that stresses finishing a task within a set time. One from a culture that stresses sociability and cooperation will be handicapped doing a task alone.

The difficulty of devising culture-fair tests can be seen in the discrepancies on the so-called performance, or nonverbal, tests between black and white children. Many studies "have found larger group differences in performance and other nonverbal tests than in verbal tests" (Anastasi, 1968, p. 252). These nonlanguage tests must be heavily loaded with cultural baggage that, being largely invisible, is hard to allow for. Even if we could devise a test that had no relevance to culture, what would we be measuring? Doesn't intelligence have something to do with how well a person perceives and adapts to the culture? Isn't culture so pervasive that it is bound to affect every aspect of a person's intelligent functioning?

Intelligence Testing of Black and White Children

Black children tend to test lower than whites on intelligence tests (Brody & Brody, 1976). The mean IQ for black samples is usually about 85, or about 15 points below the mean for whites, and rural southern blacks test lower than urban northern whites (Baughman, 1971). There is some overlap: Some blacks score higher than almost all whites, and many blacks score higher than most whites (Pettigrew, 1964). The range of scores within any ethnic or racial group goes from very low to very high, indicating that the differences among individuals of the same group are much greater than the differences in average scores between groups.

During the first two years of life, the only significant difference in motor or intellectual development between black and white babies is the motor precocity of the blacks (Bayley, 1965; Geber, 1962, 1956; Geber & Dean, 1957). But starting at about 2 or 3 years of age, black children begin to lag behind in intelligence scores, and this gap widens as the children grow older (Golden, Birns, & Bridger, 1973).

How can this widening gap be explained? One explanation is that infant tests of development do not measure intelligence. Another is that the older children become, the more verbal ability the tests call for, the more influential environment becomes, and the more tests tap already-learned stores of knowledge. The same pattern that exists between American blacks and whites also holds true between middle-class children and deprived rural and mountain youngsters, and between middle-class English children and those from canal-boat and gypsy families (Pettigrew, 1964). In our society, black children are more likely than white children to come from backgrounds of poverty. Many of the studies comparing black and white children have drawn their subjects from different socioeconomic levels, confounding the effects of socioeconomic status with the effects of race.

The assumption behind intelligence testing is that if two people have grown up in identical environments and if one does much better on the test than the other, then that one is smarter. In some nonreal world this might be true. But in our world, no two children—even identical twins—ever grow up in *exactly* the same environment. If this is true for two children in the same family, how much truer it is for children from very different subcultures!

A California professor of education (Jensen, 1969) referred to a body of evidence which suggests that genetic factors determine most of the differences in measured intelligence among white Europeans and Americans. He then said that the average 15-point difference in IQ scores between blacks and whites in our society also must be hereditary. This argument, "jensenism," has given rise to a debate more political than academic and

has raised an urgent practical question. If intelligence is determined by genes, compensatory education is a waste of time, effort, and money. But if environmental factors play a large role, society has to make ever greater efforts to overcome disparities.

The classic studies of intelligence favor genetic influences, if we define intelligence as an innate general cognitive factor, or a basic potential for learning. The actual learning that occurs—the educational attainments as evidenced in the ability to read, spell, and calculate—are more subject to environmental influences of family and schooling. Newman, Freeman, and Holzinger's classic work from the 1930s, described on p. 24, found that IQ scores seemed to be related to heredity, while measures of achievement reflected differences in environment.

Almost forty years later, Scarr and Weinberg (1976) looked at 130 black and interracial children who had been adopted by 101 white families in Minnesota. These families were advantaged in many ways: They were highly educated and above average in occupational status, income, and IQ. These are the kinds of homes that generally rear children who perform well on IQ tests and in school. The children's biologic parents were at a slightly lower social echelon, with their educational level averaging four to five years less than the adoptive parents. While IQ scores were not available for the biologic parents, in view of their lower-educational levels, they were assumed to be closer to the average than to the superior range of the adoptive parents.

All the children aged 4 and older, including both adoptees and biologic children of the adoptive parents, were tested. The adoptees' IQ scores, which averaged 106, were lower than those of their adoptive parents or than the biologic children of those parents, but higher than the average IQ of 90 usually achieved by black children reared in their own homes in this geographic region. Furthermore, the adopted black children were performing slightly above the national norms on standard scholastic achievement tests. So it seems that adoption into an upper-middle-class white family can have a salutary effect on the IQ score of a black child.

It is hard to draw a clear-cut conclusion about the relative importance of hereditary and environmental factors, because the variables are so intertwined. For example, children with one black and one white parent had higher scores than did those with two black parents. But the all-black children had been older at adoption, had had more placements before being adopted, had biologic parents with lower-educational levels, and had been in their adoptive homes for a shorter time. All these factors correlated with IQ. Furthermore, the adoptive fathers of the all-black children had less education and their adoptive mothers had lower IQs than the adoptive parents of the interracial children. Obviously, social variables are playing a part. The authors conclude:

If all black children had environments such as those provided by the adoptive families in this study, we would predict that their IQ scores would be 10–20 points higher than the scores are under current rearing conditions [p. 738].

Scarr and Weinberg do not endorse adoption of black children by white families as a matter of social policy. They do, though, state:

If higher IQ scores are considered important for educational and occupational success, then there is need for social action that will provide black children with home environments that facilitate the acquisition of intellectual skills tapped by IQ measures [p. 738].

Even more recently and even more surprisingly, Jensen, the same California professor who had argued so strongly for a hereditary basis for the difference in black and white IQ scores, in 1977 reported data pointing to an environmental basis for lower IQs among blacks. He studied black and white children

aged 6 to 16 from one rural area in Georgia, where blacks "are probably as severely disadvantaged, educationally and economically, as can be found anywhere in the United States today" (p. 185).

Comparing the IQs of siblings, Jensen found a substantial drop in verbal and nonverbal scores between kindergarten and grade twelve for blacks, but not for whites. He feels that this drop is environmental rather than racial in cause, however, because a parallel study of California blacks in more favorable environmental circumstances showed only a slight drop in verbal IQ and none in nonverbal IQ. He concludes:

Thus it appears that a cumulative deficit due to poor environment has contributed, at least in part, to the relatively low average IQ in the present sample of blacks in rural Georgia [p. 191].

Other studies have isolated specific cognitive skills and found genetic determinants for verbal, space, number, and word-frequency tasks (Vandenberg, 1966). In evaluating these studies we must take several points into account. First, we have to define intelligence. Then we have to decide whether IQ tests measure it. And finally we have to evaluate our data.

One attempt to take environmental factors into account when measuring intelligence is SOMPA, or the "System of Multicultural Pluralistic Assessment" (Rice, 1979), now being used in some states to place students in special-education programs. This battery of measures for 5- to 11-year-old children includes a complete medical exam, which pays special attention to vision and hearing abilities; a Wechsler IQ test; and a one-hour interview with the child's parent. The interview yields two major areas of information: environmental influences (how many people live in the home, their levels of education, etc.) and the child's own level of social competence (how many classmates she knows by name, whether he prepares his own lunch, etc.). Let us see how SOMPA is used:

Nine-year-old Bernice is a black child who ranks at the bottom of her school population in academic performance. Her score of only 68 on the Wechsler IQ test would make her eligible for placement in a class for the mentally retarded. But her scores on the SOMPA sociocultural scale reflect her impoverished cultural background in a family living on welfare in an urban ghetto. Compared with other children from similar backgrounds, her IQ score of 68 is only 9 points below the mean for that group—not a significant difference. Her scores on the adaptive-behavior inventory show that for her age, she is unusually capable of taking care of herself and getting along in her community. Her estimated learning potential, or "adjusted IQ," of 89 means she belongs not in a class for the retarded but in a regular class that takes her background into account [Rice, 1979, p. 34].

There continue to be major problems in comparing intelligence scores of children from different racial and ethnic groups. Even if we do determine that differences within a subgroup result from genetic differences, we do not know that differences between groups have the same basis—unless we can demonstrate without question that the biological and social environments of the two groups are identical. This is certainly not the case now. Until we can provide all children with the advantages now enjoyed by some children, we have to do our best to compensate for their lack.

How can such compensation be offered?

Free prenatal clinics with first-class maternity care can be set up in poor neighborhoods. Ways of enriching babies' environments can be explored. Programs of compensatory education beginning in early childhood and running through secondary school can be instituted.

There will still, of course, be differences in intelligence among individuals. Pettigrew (1964) likens intelligence to longevity. The tendency to live a long life seems to run in certain families; it probably has something to do with genes. But life span is also affected by environment, a fact borne out by the doubling of the average American's life expectancy over the past century. We have not shrugged and said certain groups of people are bound to live longer than others; we have concentrated on finding out and implementing those factors that will lengthen the life span for everyone. Rather than trying to identify intellectual superiority with race, we must continually seek ways by which all people can fulfill their true intellectual potential. Not until all children can grow up free from the debilitating effects of poverty, racial prejudice, and intellectual deprivation can we attempt to compare group levels of intelligence.

CORRELATES OF COGNITIVE FUNCTIONING

Temperament

Jose moves around so much that he often misses the teacher's instructions. Nancy, slow to warm up to any new situation, usually lags behind the rest of the class in any new task, but—with time, help, and understanding—she eventually catches up. Carl is so distractible that the slightest noise or movement in the corridor takes his attention away from his math. Temperamental characteristics like these, many of which seem inborn, play a major part in the ways children function. They affect how children approach learning tasks, how they relate to teachers and peers, and how they get along in school generally (Stewart & Olds, 1973; Chess, 1968). When parents

283

Temperamental characteristics, many of which seem to be inborn, influence cognitive functioning. (Mimi Forsyth/ Monkmeyer)

and teachers recognize children's unique temperaments and can adapt their own tempo to those of the children, such traits need not be a bar to learning.

Impulsivity versus Reflectivity

Sara is impulsive: She blurts out the first answer that comes to mind, rarely taking time to think of alternate solutions. Rose is reflective: Before she answers, she takes time to consider a variety of possible answers and to choose the best one. Sara makes more mistakes. Impulsive children have more problems with reading; they mispronounce, substitute wrong words, add words not in the text, omit words, and skip entire lines (Kagan, 1965). Reflective children also do better at reasoning tasks and with most school work. They also seem to be more creative, since creativity depends on being able to systematically explore various possibilities in order to come up with new solutions (Fuqua, Bartsch, & Phye, 1975).

During the preschool and primary years, children who later will be judged impulsive behave differently from those who will turn out to be reflective. Impulsive children seek quick success, and reflective ones try to avoid failure. Impulsives like to take risks and enjoy active social participation in new situations, while reflectives avoid physically dangerous activities such as walking a narrow plank, peer-group interaction, and strange social situations. While reflective children seem more worried about making mistakes, they choose harder tasks to work on, and they stick with the tasks longer (Kagan, 1965).

The tendency to be impulsive or reflective may be partly inborn, but it also may be a function of upbringing, since children from lower social classes tend to be more impulsive than those of the middle class (Kagan, 1965). Their lower IQ scores may reflect their impulsiveness in answering questions more than their innate capacities. Impulsivity *is* subject to training; for children whose school failure is linked with it, special training techniques can be effective (Stewart & Olds, 1973; Kagan & Kogan, 1970).

Sex Differences

After reviewing more than 2000 books and

articles on intellectual, social, and emotional differences between the sexes, Maccoby and Jacklin (1974) identified only three intellectual areas where real differences show up. Females excel in verbal ability: They score higher on tests of reading comprehension, writing, spelling, and verbal analogies. Boys do better at math, and their good showing here may be related to their other consistent superiority in visual-spatial ability. This ability is commonly measured by asking the test-taker to match a drawing of an object with another drawing of the same object as it would look if it were seen from another angle.

Why should these differences exist? One biological difference—maturation—may exert some influence. Maturation affects the organization of higher cortical functioning, and boys and girls mature at different rates. Waber (1977) found that late-maturing individuals of both sexes perform better on tests of spatial abilities. Since boys mature later than girls, their slower rate may help them to develop their spatial abilities in a more efficient way. Waber did not find, however, that earlier maturers do better on verbal abilities, an interesting finding in light of the fact that the superiority of females on verbal abilities is less consistent than the superiority of males on spatial abilities.

Since these differences between the sexes generally do not show up until adolescence, and widen thereafter, another explanation for them may be rooted in differences in the ways the two sexes are treated, from early childhood on.

Parental Influences

Parents who value intellectual achievement, who respect their children and show them warmth, are likely to have verbal, intelligent offspring. The same parent, though, often treats sons and daughters differently, such as encouraging independence in a boy and dependence in a girl. Such differential treatment may spur dissimilar abilities.

Bing (1963), for example, found that 10-year-olds whose verbal abilities are much higher than their abilities in numbers or spatial relations tend to have mothers who reinforce dependent behavior. These mothers talk to their youngsters much more during infancy and early childhood, buy them more story-books, let them participate more in conversations, remember more of their early accomplishments, punish them less for poor speech but criticize them more for poor academic achievement, are more restrictive and less permissive, and train for caution by arousing anxiety. They are much more emotionally involved with their children. Their babies get more attention and stimulation; as they grow older, they are more highly pressured, restricted, and controlled.

Mothers of children who do better in spatial and numerical abilities allowed their children more freedom to experiment on their own. This may be a crucial factor in developing these skills, since spatial ability requires interaction with the physical environment, and number facility requires the ability to concentrate and carry through a task by oneself. A greater degree of independence would foster both skills. This study may offer clues to explain girls' general verbal superiority and boys' superiority in spatial and numerical tasks. Different parental attitudes may foster different proficiencies.

Even when parents treat all their children similarly, boys and girls often respond differently. The intellectual development of boys, for example, is associated with a close mother-son relationship during childhood. On the other hand, superior intellectual skills in girls are related to a progressively more distant mother-daughter relationship (Moss & Kagan, 1958).

In the past when this research was conducted, in an era when mothers were not likely to be working, a very close mother-daughter rela-

In the school years, the father's influence on intellectual development moves toward center stage, with both boys and girls responding to him. (Erika Stone/Peter Arnold, Inc.)

tionship could lead, through the daughter's strong identification with the nonworking mother, to a sex-stereotyped, domestic role for the girl—a role that might discourage exploration of the physical environment and manipulation of intellectual ideas. Thus the daughter who was close to, and like, her mother would not do as well in tests of intellectual achievement [Clarke-Stewart, 1977, p. 49].

In the school years, the father's influence on intellectual development moves toward center stage, with both boys and girls responding to him. A boy's ability for flexible thinking is more closely related to his father's love, verbal stimulation, and power than to any attributes of his mother. And a girl's school achievement is closely related to her father's friendliness toward her and her mother (Clarke-Stewart, 1977). Both parents are important to their children's intellectual growth.

GIFTED CHILDREN: INTELLIGENCE AND CREATIVITY

Some years ago the twelve-member admissions committee of a prestigious prep school voted unanimously not to accept a 13-year-old boy whose record contained failing or barely passing marks in almost every subject, and whose teachers' negative comments ranged from "lazy" to "rebellious." The committee then learned that it had just judged the school record of the young Winston Churchill (Fleming & Fleming, 1970). This, then, is the dilemma: How can we recognize children of exceptional ability and how can we nurture their talents?

Identifying and Studying Gifted Individuals

RETROSPECTIVE STUDIES   Using this approach, researchers locate eminent adults and, through biographical material, try to identify those factors that helped them become great.

Sir Francis Galton (1869)   Convinced of hereditary, race, and class bases for achievement, Galton identified eminent men in nine fields of endeavor (judges, statesmen, commanders, authors, scientists, poets, musicians, painters, and theologians) and then sought to show that achievement runs in families.

Galton classified his men of distinction as:

(a) Illustrious men among whom "many are as one in a million, and not a few as one of many millions. . . . They are men whom the whole intelligent part of the nation mourns when they die; who have, or deserve to have, a public funeral; and who rank in future ages as historical characters"; (b) eminent men—those who have "achieved a position that is attained by only 250 persons in each million of men, or by one person in each 4000"; (c) the third and lower grade is that of English judges—their average ability "cannot be rated as equal to that of the lower of the two grades" described above [Stein & Heinze, 1960, p. 20].

Galton estimated the chances for relatives of the most eminent men to achieve eminence themselves:

The chance of a father is 1 in 6; of a brother, 1 in 7; of each son, 1 in 4; of each grandfather, 1 in 25; of each uncle, 1 in 40; of each nephew, 1 in 40; and of each grandson, 1 in 29. For all more remote relatives, the chances are about 1 in 200, except first cousins whose chances are about 1 in 100 [Stein & Heinze, 1960, p. 23].

Women are conspicuously absent from Galton's study, except as relatives and breeders. Because of the smaller number of transmissions along the female line, Galton wondered about "an inherent incapacity in the female line for transmitting the peculiar forms of ability we are now discussing" or the possibility that the "aunts, sisters, and daughters of eminent men do not marry, on the average, so frequently as other women" (Stein & Heinze, 1960, p. 24).

Catharine Cox During the 1920s, psychologist Cox and two assistants at Stanford University selected 300 eminent individuals from biographical dictionaries. Through study of biographical material, they independently arrived at approximate minimum IQ scores that could account for a subject's known childhood performances. For example, Francis Galton learned to read at 2½, wrote a letter before he was 4, and had mastered almost the entire multiplication table by the age of 5. According to the weights given all these tasks in present-day intelligence tests, the child would have had to have had an IQ of 200, at the very least. The average minimum IQ score for the group as a whole was 155. Cox concluded that most eminent persons would have been identified as gifted children by standard intelligence tests, and that those gifted children who did go on to great achievement were characterized "by persistence of motive and effort, confidence in their abilities and great strength or force of character" (Cox, 1926, cited in Terman, 1947).

For more than half, later achievement was strongly foreshadowed by childhood interests—which were often disregarded by parents and teachers who tried to fit these youngsters into other molds. A problem of vocational guidance for gifted children arises from their versatility. Most of Cox's subjects were extraordinarily able in five to ten fields (White, 1931, cited in Terman, 1947).

Victor and Mildred Goertzel The Goertzels studied the childhoods of 400 eminent Americans and found a love for learning in almost all their childhood homes, as well as a high degree of opinionativeness among their parents. Most were middle class, were early readers, disliked school and teachers, and had trouble making friends. Many were faced with such major problems as poverty, broken homes, unhappy relationships with their parents, or physical handicaps, but practically none had nuclear family members who had to be hospitalized for mental illness.

Many of the children who were to become eminent possessed superior ability in reasoning and in recognizing relationships. They showed intellectual curiosity, had a wide range of interests, and did effective work independently [Goertzel & Goertzel, 1962].

A LONGITUDINAL STUDY

Lewis M. Terman   Many may have the potential for greatness, but very few achieve great success. What determines which ones will shine—and which will be overshadowed? Lewis M. Terman of Stanford University identified gifted children early in life and followed them to see which ones achieved success.

In 1922, Terman asked several teachers to give him the names of the three brightest children and that of the youngest child in the classroom, as well as that of the brightest child they had taught the year before.[1] Terman located more than 1300 children capable of earning an IQ of 140 or higher, a score reached by only 1 child in 200.

These children were tested for intelligence, school achievement, character, personality, and interests. They were examined medically, their physical measurements were taken, and their parents and teachers were interviewed for case-history material and ratings of the children's personalities. The data that emerged demolished the popular stereotype of the bright child as a puny, pasty-faced bookworm. On the contrary, Terman's gifted children were superior all-around. They tended to be taller, healthier, and better coordinated than the average child. They were also better adjusted and more popular with other children (Wallach & Kogan, 1965).

[1]Goertzel and Goertzel (1962) comment, "The teacher's ability to choose the child in her class who subsequently scored highest on the Stanford-Binet intelligence test was less than chance" (p. 279), but they also make the point that teachers are more likely to select children who score high on intelligence tests but relatively low in creativity (see the next section).

As adults, they still presented a picture of superiority, most notably in intellectual ability, scholastic accomplishment, and vocational achievements (Terman & Oden, 1959). They were healthy and numbered proportionately few alcoholics. They were just as likely as anyone else, though, to have problems in marriage, to suffer a mental breakdown, or to take their own lives.

How had these children's early promise been fulfilled? In middle age, most were still scoring close to the 99th percentile in mental ability. They were ten times more likely than an unselected group to have graduated from college, and three times more likely than other students to have been elected to the honorary societies Phi Beta Kappa or Sigma Xi. Because of different societal attitudes toward careers for men and women, the sexes were evaluated separately. Both sexes made a good showing: They were highly represented in listings such as *American Men of Science* (which also includes women), the *Directory of American Scholars*, and *Who's Who in America*. Both men and women had many publications to their credit, and 86 percent of the men were in the two highest occupational categories: the professions and the semiprofessions and higher echelons of business. By 1955, several dozen of the men had achieved national reputations, and eight or ten, international ones.

Terman's group was bright, but not notably creative. None became outstanding in the arts, music, or great literature. Terman himself said that he would be surprised to find more than sixty subjects achieving national reputations, more than twelve becoming really eminent, or even one of them considered among the thousand most eminent persons of history (1947). He compared the superiority of the children in his group, estimated at 1 in 200, to the 1 in 4000 ratio of Galton's eminent men, the 1 in about 2000 of listees in American *Who's Who*, and the 1 in 20,000 of scientists listed by Cattell.

Terman recognized the great difficulties in predicting greatness on the basis of childhood ability when he said that:

genius and eminence are far from perfectly correlated. Why they are so poorly correlated, what circumstances affect the fruition of human talent, are questions of such transcendent importance that they should be investigated by every method that promises the slightest reduction of our present ignorance. So little do we know about our available supply of potential genius; the environmental factors that favour or hinder its expression; the emotional compulsions that give it dynamic quality; or the personality distortions that make it dangerous! And viewing the present crisis in world affairs who can doubt that these things may decide the fate of a civilization! [1947, p. 42]

While most of these adults were more successful than the average person in our society, there was a range of achievement in the group itself. When the 150 most successful and the 150 least successful men were compared in relation to their life histories and personalities, a number of differences emerged. They differed most widely in "persistence in the accomplishment of ends," "integration toward goals," "self-confidence," and "freedom from inferiority feelings" (Terman & Oden, 1947). The two groups differed most in "all-round emotional and social adjustment, and in drive to achieve" (Terman & Oden, 1959, p. 149).

Creativity in Children

What is creativity? It is the ability to see things in a new and unusual light, to see problems that no one else may even realize exist, and then to come up with new, unusual, and effective solutions to these problems. Creativity involves *divergent*, rather than *convergent*, thinking, in Guilford's (1959) terms. Instead of trying to come up with one right answer, the creative person tries to pursue a problem along as many paths as possible, to find new alternatives.

Creative people often spend a great deal of time turning over problems in their minds, just letting their ideas bubble forth. While great discoveries almost always follow intensive work in a particular area, the new thought itself seems to spring full-blown from an observation of the moment. When Marie Curie realized that the radioactivity she was studying could not be accounted for by a description of any of the known elements, the daring thought that she might have discovered a new one popped into her head. Further research identified it as radium. Great creative discoveries rarely come about without years of arduous work. But they depend on their creators' willingness and ability to consider and see startling new possibilities.

MEASURING CREATIVITY   Recognizing the importance of creativity both for society and for individuals and aware that standard IQ tests don't measure it, researchers have put their own creative abilities to work to devise ways of assessing it. As of now, the special tests of creative aptitudes that have been developed are more important for research than for educational or vocational counseling. One problem with them is that they depend heavily on speed for their scoring—and creative people are not always lightninglike in their responses. Another problem is that while the tests are *reliable*—that is, consistent in their results even when administered by different testers—so far there is little or no evidence of their *validity*. That is, we don't know whether they really measure creativity in nontest situations (Anastasi, 1976).

Two major batteries of tests of creative aptitudes are the University of Southern Cali-

	Common answer	Creative answer
How many things could these drawings be?		
⬜ (with circles on top)	Table with things on top	Foot and toes
△ (triangle with circles)	Three people sitting around a table	Three mice eating a piece of cheese
(flower-like figure)	Flower	Lollipop bursting into pieces
⌒ ⌒ (two arches)	Two igloos	Two haystacks on a flying carpet
What do these things have in common?		
Milk and meat	Both come from animals.	Both are government-inspected.
How many ways could you use these objects?		
Newspaper	Make paper hats.	Rip it up if angry.

Fig. 8-1
Some Tests
of Creativity
(From Wallach
& Kogan, 1967)

fornia Tests from the Aptitude Research Project (ARP), developed by Guilford and his colleagues, and the Torrance Tests of Creative Thinking.

Guilford's ARP tests, which have been standardized for high school students and adults, measure divergent thinking. Some of the items ask test-takers to name things that belong in a given class ("things that will burn": gasoline, kerosene); to write four-word sentences, each word to begin with a given letter ("K—u—y—i—"; Kill useless yellow insects); to list as many uses as possible for a given object ("tin can": a vase, a cookie cutter); to write titles for short-story plots; and to make sketches of as many different recognizable objects as possible, based on a page full of identical figures, such as circles.

The Torrance tests, which were developed for use in schools and have been tested on schoolchildren, are grouped into three batteries. In *Thinking Creatively with Words*, test-takers name ways of improving a given toy to make it more fun to play with, list

unusual uses for common objects, and ask unusual questions about the same common objects. In *Thinking Creatively with Pictures*, test-takers draw pictures that take off from a colored curved shape, a few lines, or pairs of short parallel lines. *Thinking Creatively with Sounds and Words* uses long-playing records to give onomatopoeic words (like "crunch" or "pop," which imitate a natural sound associated with an object or action), to which test-takers respond by writing down what the sounds suggest.

FAMILY INFLUENCES ON CREATIVITY
Many researchers have studied the various ways in which the family influences children's levels of creativity. Miller and Gerard (1979) reviewed sixty-one reports on such studies and integrated the results into a set of conclusions that could be translated into the following guidelines for parents who want to have highly creative children.

• *Be of a high social class,* especially if you

want your children to be verbally creative. This may not always work for nonverbal creativity, but, in general, superiority in language skills will enhance creativity, especially for boys.

• *Have as many or as few children as you like.* Family size appears unrelated to creativity. So does birth order: Some studies show that the first-born is more creative, some less, and some show no difference. A few do find that the youngest sibling, after a big age gap, is relatively uncreative.

• *Have another child soon after the one whom you want to be the creative light of the family.* Highly creative children often have a younger sibling close in age.

• *Have a daughter if you want a child who is verbally creative, a son if you want one who's creative on figural tasks.* Gender differences don't show up at young ages, though, and are largest in cultural groups that stress differences between the sexes.

• *Don't worry about what other people think.* Highly creative children tend to have parents who feel secure and unconcerned about their social station, are uninhibited and unconventional, and are indifferent to social pressures.

• *Be capable yourself and develop your own interests.* For the mother, this may include going to work. For both parents, it may involve the pursuit of an intellectual or artistic hobby.

• *Treat your children with respect and confidence.* Expect them to do well, while granting them both freedom and responsibilities.

• *Don't strive for too much emotional closeness within the family.* Creative children often come from homes that are relatively cool, or in which the parents don't get along.

• *Don't be hostile, rejecting, or detached, either.* Creative children do not emerge from

home climates in which these qualities predominate, but rather from those that offer some emotional distance.

• Most important of all, *do not aim for rigid control of your children.* The most consistent and the best supported finding to emerge from this review of the literature is that parental vigilance, authoritarianism, dominance, and restrictiveness inhibit the development of creativity. Children who are constantly directed and molded apparently lose the confidence and the spontaneity essential for the creative spirit.

THE RELATIONSHIP BETWEEN INTELLIGENCE AND CREATIVITY

We all know bright people who do well in school or on the job but who exhibit "little evidence of the quality that advances rather than enhances the status quo" (Goertzel & Goertzel, 1962, p. 280). These people are high in intelligence but low in creativity. We also know people who test poorly and muddle their way through school but who constantly come up with original ideas. These people are high in creativity, low in intelligence. In an effort to measure creativity separately from intelligence, Wallach and Kogan (1967) studied 151 fifth-grade children, testing them in a relaxed, untestlike situation, since:

. . . creative awareness tends to occur when the individual—in a playful manner— entertains a range of possibilities without worry concerning his own personal success or failure and how his self-image will fare in the eyes of others [p. 88].

The children were also tested for intelligence, and the results of both tests were analyzed to produce four different groups:

1 *Intelligent and creative children* score high on both measures. They are friendly and popular, concentrate well on academic work, exude self-confidence, and are somewhat disruptive in the classroom, which may reflect the conventional conformity usually required

there. They see connections between events and show sensitivity to emotional clues in the environment. They report experiencing some anxiety—not so much as to cripple them, but enough to energize them.

2 *Intelligent children who score low in creativity* avoid risks, hesitate to express their opinions, are "model" students, and make conventional responses unless specifically asked to think of unusual answers, in which case they perform well. Other children want to be friendly with them, but they stay aloof. They are afraid of error and of criticism. Since they conform to expectations and do well in school, they exhibit little anxiety but show constricted behavior.

3 *Creative children who score low in intelligence* have the most trouble in school. They are least able to concentrate on their work and are disruptive and socially isolated. Other children keep away from them, and they keep to themselves. They are low in self-confidence and self-esteem. Yet they show creative thinking in unpressured testing situations. Their cognitive abilities may be stifled by the pressures of being evaluated in classroom testing situations.

4 *Children who score low in both creativity and intelligence* make up for their low status with social success. They are outgoing and relatively confident and self-assured.

The children in the two middle groups seem capable of better performance and better mental adjustment. Wallach and Kogan suggest that they are handicapped by personality problems caused by pressures. Intelligent but uncreative children—worried about what others think of them—try to avoid making mistakes. They are particularly at sea when there is no clear standard of evaluation for them to judge themselves by. Creative, unintelligent children are afraid of evaluation and perform best when they know they won't be judged. If both these types could learn to relax, they would perform better.

ACHIEVING CREATIVE SUCCESS At Harvard University's Project Zero (named a dozen years ago to reflect the considered state of knowledge on the topic of creativity), children are observed as they take part in a range of artistic activities. On the basis of his experience with the project and his examination of biographies of famous artists, Gardner (1979), codirector of the project, suggests three elements essential for artistic success:

1 *Inborn talent.* From a very early age some children show interest and ability in a certain field—music, drawing, facility with words or numbers, or a grasp of scientific principles.

2 *A favorable environment.* Even talented children need encouragement and instruction to become accomplished in their craft.

3 *Personality and character.* No matter how talented or proficient an artist is, if she or he does not possess the drive to excel, artistic greatness will not come.

[The creative person] must be willing to live with uncertainty, to return time and again to his project, until he satisfies his own exacting standards, while speaking with potency to others [Gardner, 1979, p. C17].

CHILDREN IN SCHOOL

School takes up so many hours and assumes such a central place in children's lives that it

Candi learns fast but works slowly.... I suspect her slowness is due in part to extra pains with the drawing and coloring, in part to her extreme fear of making a mistake.

Candi, age 6,
from *A Child Grows Up*, p. 222

In the long run, the structure of education is less important than the underlying attitudes and objectives. (Sam Falk/Monkmeyer)

affects and is affected by every aspect of their development.

The Ideal School
Nyquist and Hawes (1972) define the ideal classroom:

This is a classroom where freedom, responsibility, self-discipline, and consideration for others are learned by having to be practiced all the time. This is a classroom that accommodates the full range of individual differences, where individuality can be richly prized and given full expression—to such an extent that children of different ages often work together in it. This is a classroom where all children learn respect and trust by being treated with respect and trust. This is a classroom that provides abundant opportunities to develop intellectually in the way in which research has shown children naturally acquire powers of thought and logic—through their own action. This is a classroom where, with a skilled teacher, each child learns the meaning of good work, and in time becomes able to produce it in at least some things he or she attempts [p. 2].

Such classrooms herald the rise of a reform movement in American education. The most recent wave of reform washed over the schools in the 1970s, after many critical books indicted them for being inhumane and uncaring and particularly inept in education of disadvantaged children. American public schools were charged with being oppressive, grim, and joyless places where children's spirits were being mutilated every day (Silberman, 1970). Too often, the schools were using outdated, irrelevant curricula, avoiding meaningful social and personal issues, and ignoring the needs of individual children.

The Open Classroom
Many American schools have established "open," or "informal," classrooms, which originated in the "infant schools" of Great Britain. Since children learn best by doing, open education emphasizes their active involvement. In the open classroom, all the children are rarely doing the same thing at the same time. They do not sit at rows of desks, dutifully listening (or pretending to listen) as their teacher lectures. Instead, they scatter around the room working individually or in small

groups. Two youngsters might be stretched out on a rug, reading library books. The teacher is at the math table, showing four children how to use scales to learn about weights. Two children in the writing corner play a word game. Another takes notes about the nursing behavior of the class guinea pig. A sense of purpose pervades the room.

Open education is not a cure-all. Not all children can function in this relatively unstructured environment, and neither can all teachers. But many of the principles of open education can be incorporated into basically traditional classrooms, to the benefit of both teachers and pupils. In the long run, the structure of education is less important than the attitudes behind it. If children are to be respected as valuable human beings with their own individual needs instead of being considered receptacles for useless information; if the curriculum is designed according to what children want and need to know instead of what schools want to teach; if teachers offer helpful guidance instead of rigid command; if the emphasis is on successes instead of failures; and if warmth, understanding, and acceptance replace sarcasm and ridicule— then it matters little whether the children sit at desks, at tables, or on the floor. Their education will therefore be a happy, satisfying experience that advances development instead of stunting it.

The Teacher's Influence

A teacher's influence is especially powerful during the early years, when he or she becomes a parent substitute, an imparter of values, a contributer toward the child's self-concept.

When the superintendent of one suburban school district asked 2000 students from kindergarten through eighth grade "What makes a good school?" teachers headed the list (McPhee, 1966), "Understanding" emerged as the prime requisite of a good teacher. A kindergartner said, "Your teacher likes you even when you are bad"; a second-grader said, "Teachers shouldn't scream and yell

February 14, 1962. Today I rote a valentine for Miss _____. She said she liked it but she didn't take it home. it goes
Do you know how it works to be happy?
There is one way to do it and that is to give.
There are other ways too.
Another is love.
So here's some -- CATCH!

April 16. Today I rote a letter to Miss _____ (his teacher) It goes.
Dear Miss _____
Could I please have pameshen to speak to you privetly? It will only take a minit. It's very inportint becodes I have a probrom that MUST be solved imdyitly and I need your help. Otherwise I may end up with no glasses. So could I please speak today for just a minit.
From Howard.

Howard T. Bissell, age 7,
from *Small Voices*, pp. 98–99

over nothing"; and a sixth-grader felt that "a web of understanding should envelop teacher and pupils." Children also want teachers to teach. One first-grader said, "When you don't know something you ask the teachers and if you're wrong it's all right because that's why you're in school." And another first-grader said, "School is good when you have teachers that can get through to you, when they tell you something and you can understand them."

These children confirm Jersild's 1940 survey of 526 children who reported on the teachers they liked best. To them, the ideal teacher explains things in a way that the pupils learn; he or she is kind, sympathetic, considerate, interested in pupils as persons, fair, consistent in discipline, interested, enthusiastic, and attractive. Children like least teachers who ridicule, scold, assign too much homework, or show lack of sympathy, rigid or inconsistent discipline, and ill temper.

SELF-FULFILLING PROPHECY When the teachers feel that a certain child will do well in school, that child probably will do well. The *self-fulfilling prophecy*, by which people act as they are expected to, has been documented in different situations (Rosenthal & Jacobsen, 1968). In the "Oak School" experiment, some teachers in this California school were told at the beginning of the term that some of their pupils had shown unusual potential for intellectual growth. Actually, the children identified as potential "bloomers" had been chosen at random. Yet, several months later many of them—especially first- and second-graders—showed unusual gains in IQ. And the teachers seemed to like the "bloomers" better. Their teachers do not appear to have spent more time with them than with the other children, nor to have treated them differently in any obvious ways. Subtler influences may have been at work, possibly in the teachers' tone of voice, facial expression, touch, and posture:

It's amazing how much teachers gossip or talk about you. When you get there, the teachers already have a set opinion about you. They'll say, "Listen, I heard this or that about you." I haven't only had this just this year, it's been going on since I entered first grade .... They get this thing about you and it can really ruin you.

Robin, age 13,
from *Listen to Us!* p. 91

Regardless of where one stands concerning Rosenthal and Jacobson's original data, work by a large number of investigators using a variety of methods over the past several years has established unequivocally that teachers' expectations can and do function as self-fulfilling prophecies, although not always or automatically [Brophy & Good, 1974, p. 32].

This self-fulfilling principle has important implications for minority-group and poor children. Since many middle-class teachers are convinced (often subconsciously) that such pupils have intellectual limitations, they may somehow convey their limited expectations to the children, thus getting the little that they expect.

It is often difficult for teachers who either have been born into the middle class or have adopted its standards to understand or get through to children of lower socioeconomic status. Goals that the teacher takes for granted—neatness, punctuality, competitiveness—may not be held by the child's associates. When a child's family and friends hold values markedly different from the teacher's, the child will be loyal to familiar values and unimpressed with the teacher's. This may upset the teacher and cause problems in the teacher-pupil relationship. The closer students come to having their teachers' values systems, the higher their grades are likely to be (Battle, 1957). The advantage conferred on like-thinking students may be the result of more favorable interaction between teacher and student, which encourages the student to learn better, or it may be the product of bias in the grading process.

DO TEACHERS LIKE GIRLS BETTER? In the United States, elementary school is a girl's world, especially during the early grades. Girls read and write better than boys, are less likely to repeat grades or get into trouble, and are liked better by teachers (Brophy & Good, 1973; Baughman, 1971; Maccoby, 1966). In some other societies boys come out ahead (Brophy & Good, 1974). One explanation is that female teachers understand and like girls better and are less able to put up with the dirt and noise and aggression that swirl around little boys. But male teachers tend to show the same attitudes, generally scolding *and* praising boys more (Brophy & Good, 1973; Etaugh & Harlow, 1973). The result: Male-taught boys don't do any better (Brophy & Good, 1973).

The problem seems to lie in a conflict between the kind of behavior that our society says is appropriate for boys and the kind deemed appropriate for children in school. The ideal American boy is active, independent, and aggressive, while the ideal pupil is passive, docile, and quiet. (Girls have no such role conflict, since they are expected to act like "ideal pupils" all the time.) When these sets of expectations collide, it is usually the schoolboy model that falls by the wayside, since it is more important for most boys to show their friends and families that they are "real boys" than to show their teachers that they are good students. As education allows both sexes to be more active, assertive, and inquiring, all children should benefit.

Bilingual Education

In schools where many children come from families who speak a language other than English, bilingualism—the ability to understand and speak two languages—is often a major goal. Where this is so, the children learn both in English and in their native tongues. Bilingual education makes school a warmer, friendlier place for non-English-speaking youngsters; helps them learn basic skills like reading and arithmetic, which they would have great difficulty in mastering if they were taught in a language foreign to them; and helps enhance their self-image by encouraging them to identify with their cultural and linguistic heritage (Evans, 1975).

In the United States, bilingual education is most often geared to Spanish-speaking children—Mexican-Americans in the southwest and Puerto Ricans and Cubans in the east. It is, however, more of a goal than a reality: As recently as 1972, less than 3

percent of Mexican-American pupils in the southwest were in bilingual programs (Wright, 1973, in Evans, 1975). In those programs that do exist, over 80 percent are based on the *assimilation* model, which aims to shift the child's principal language to English by the end of the primary grades. Very few programs are built on the *pluralistic* model, which maintains the child's native language along with English.

Disadvantaged Children in School

Children from minority subcultures—black, Puerto Rican, American Indian, Mexican-American, Appalachian—have more difficulties in school. They tend to come from large, poor families and to speak little or no English (or an impoverished language that hinders communication). Instead of a close bond between school and home, there is often distance, suspicion, and lack of understanding. Parents may be too shy to come to school, and school personnel may have no empathy with parents and their way of life.

School systems across the country have tried a variety of approaches to help diminish the educational gap between middle-class and poor children. Disadvantaged children need compensatory education, beginning in early childhood and continuing throughout their school careers. They need small classes where they can receive individualized attention. They need special tutoring programs that emphasize the basic skills of reading, writing, and arithmetic. They need extra health services, psychological services, counseling, and social work. They need cultural enrichment, including pride in their own cultural heritage and their own identity. In teaching disadvantaged children—just as in teaching any children—teachers and administrators must understand all the nonacademic factors that facilitate learning: the image children

have of themselves, the motivation to succeed, the feeling of belonging, the awareness that other people care.

Other School-Related Problems

EDUCATING HANDICAPPED CHILDREN
Education for handicapped children has come a long way since the family of deaf-and-blind Helen Keller had to travel to distant cities and eventually hire a private tutor for their daughter. But many handicapped children still are not receiving the education that could help them to become fully functioning members of society. It has been estimated that about half of the nation's 7 million handicapped youngsters are not being educated adequately (Flaste, 1974). These children—about 10 percent of the school-aged population—are deaf, blind, mentally retarded, physically deformed, emotionally disturbed, speech-impaired, or afflicted with other problems. Some do not attend school at all because their local districts are unable or unwilling to meet their needs. Some are placed in regular classes where they cannot keep up or are channeled into the wrong kinds of special classes.

One of the controversies in special education today centers around *mainstreaming* versus segregated special classes. Under the principle of mainstreaming, handicapped children are in regular classes with nonhandicapped youngsters for all or part of the day. Proponents of this approach emphasize the need for handicapped people to learn to get along in a society where most people do not share their impediments and the need for normal people to get to know and understand handicapped individuals. Mainstreaming requires innovative teaching techniques that meet the needs of all students. Its critics maintain that handicapped children can be

taught better and more humanely in small classes by specially trained teachers. The best solution is probably a combination of the two approaches. A retarded child, for example, might be able to take physical education or shop in a regular class, while receiving academic instruction with slow learners. Or a child with cerebral palsy might be in regular academic classes but receive special physical training while classmates go to gym.

Deaf people can do anything that hearing people can do, and we look like everybody else. We graduate from school, and go to college, and get a job—it's just that we can't hear.

Diane, age 13,
from *Listen to Us!* p. 120

The goal of education for the handicapped is the same as the goal of education in general—to enable all children to fulfill their potential as much as possible, to lead rich lives in home and community, and to contribute to society to the best of their ability.

LEARNING DISABILITIES Many children of normal or above-normal intelligence have great difficulty learning how to read, write, or work with numbers. They see and hear perfectly well, but they have trouble processing what comes through the senses. As one child said, "I know it in my head, but I can't get it into my hand." Since school success is important for self-esteem, learning disabilities can have devastating effects on the psyche as well as on the report card.

There are a wide variety of specific disabilities, affecting one or more aspects of the learning process. Adam, for example, has problems with visual perception: He confuses up and down, and left and right, so that he has great difficulty learning how to read and do arithmetic. Barbara has problems with auditory perception: She cannot grasp what the teacher is saying when he stands up in front of the room. Charles has difficulties with small-motor coordination: He cannot color inside the lines, or draw and write clearly. Derek is clumsy in his large-motor movements, a deficit that is painfully apparent in the school yard when he tries to run, climb, or play ball. Ellen has speech problems: She began to speak quite late and still articulates so unclearly that she is embarrassed to speak out in class or to read aloud.

Since there is often a family history of reading disability, there is a possibility that the problems of some of these children are inherited. Other children are thought to have suffered brain injury before, during, or soon after birth. The injuries may not have been severe enough to show up in any obvious way, but they may have been severe enough to affect the learning process. The vague term *minimal brain dysfunction* has been coined to describe those children whose difficulties cannot be precisely pinpointed. For unknown reasons, many more boys than girls are affected.

If learning-disabled children are diagnosed early enough and are given special attention, they can very often overcome their difficulties well enough to lead satisfying, productive adult lives. Some go on to college and professional careers. Those whose problems are not recognized and dealt with often grow up feeling stupid and inadequate. Some observers have linked learning disabilities with juvenile delinquency (Brutten, Richardson, & Mangel, 1973).

Diagnosing specific learning disabilities often depends on a combination of different assessments—the observations of the classroom teacher; the results of tests that may be administered by a special teacher, a psychologist, or an educational specialist in learning disabilities; and possibly the results of neurological testing.

The child's IQ score is often sought, to establish the fact that he or she is not retarded. Because of the several subtests in the Wechsler intelligence tests, which yield separate scores, the WISC and the WPSSI give more clues than the Stanford-Binet IQ test about specific deficiencies, such as in the "perception and recall of visual patterns,

motor difficulties in the copying of forms, limitations of short-term memory, inability to handle abstract concepts, and many types of language disorders" (Anastasi, 1976, p. 480).

The Illinois Test of Psycholinguistic Abilities (ITPA), an individual test for children aged 2 to 10, measures three dimensions of the learning process: How children perceive through their eyes and ears; how they process information (their level of understanding, their association of past and present inputs, and their expression of ideas by words or gestures); and the levels on which they function in using what they have learned. In the ITPA manual expression test, the child uses his hands to "show what we do with" pictured objects like a pencil sharpener and a telephone. In the grammatical closure test, the child completes oral statements in response to pictures, such as "Here is a child. Here are three——." Since the items in the ITPA tend to be heavily loaded with cultural material, the test may be inappropriate for minority-group and disadvantaged children.

Another frequently administered test is the Frostig Developmental Test of Visual Perception, which has five subtests assessing visuomotor coordination, visual perception, and spatial relations. The emphasis in this is on movement skills.

A major element in determining the presence of specific learning disabilities involves *clinical* assessment—or a judgment arrived at after intensive individual case study. The clinician may be a psychologist, a counselor, or an educational specialist. The clinican gets information about the individual's life history; observes the child's behavior in testing, interview, or classroom situations; weighs the results of objective tests; and comes to a conclusion about the child's problems and what needs to be done about them. In those areas where suitable tests are not available, a clinician's judgment depends heavily on the ability, personality, training, and experience of the clinician.

After a child's difficulties have been diagnosed, a special educational program should be designed that builds on the child's strengths and overcomes his or her weaknesses. Barbara, for example, may receive special tutoring in which the teacher makes sure to write out what he says, so that she can see the words as well as hear them. On the other hand, Adam may learn better if he has access to a tape recorder so that he can talk his answers into it instead of always having to write them down. Charles and Derek will have special exercise regimes to help them develop the motor skills they need. Each child needs his or her own specially prescribed course of learning.

Sometimes children can get this special instruction by leaving their regular classrooms for two or three hours a day to be with a teacher who specializes in working with children with learning problems. Other times they may be placed in a small class made up of children with special needs. Or they may attend a public or private school especially geared for children with special educational requirements. In addition to the educational program, the parents can benefit from counseling to help them learn how to help their child at home.

SCHOOL PHOBIA Many people who have studied *school phobia* claim that it is misnamed—that *the unrealistic fear that keeps children from attending school* has less to do with a fear of school itself than it does with a fear of leaving their mothers. So many researchers are convinced of the basic "separation anxiety" underlying this problem that virtually no research has been done on the school situations of school-phobic young-

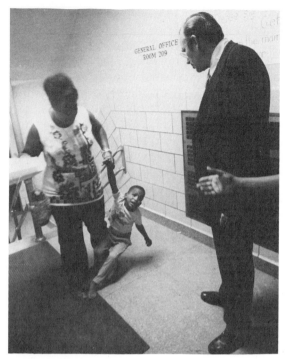

School phobia, the unrealistic fear that keeps children from attending school, often has less to do with a fear of school itself than it does with a fear of leaving the mother. (Leo De Wys, Inc.)

sters. We know very little about their perceptions of school, how they get along with their teachers and the other children, and whether there is a basic problem in the school itself, such as a sarcastic teacher, a bully in the schoolyard, or overly difficult work.

What, then, do we know about school-phobic children? In an extensive review of the literature, Gordon and Young (1976) have summarized findings about the children, their families, and the most favored means of treatment. First, these children are not truants. They are often good students whose parents know when they are absent. These absences extend for long stretches at a time. The children's ages are evenly distributed between 5 and 15, and they are as likely to be of either sex. They tend to be of average intelligence or higher and to perform at least at average levels in school. While they come from a variety of social class backgrounds, they seem to be overrepresented in the professional classes.

Typically, school-phobic children wake up on a school morning complaining of some physical ailment, such as nausea, stomachache, vomiting, or headache. Soon after they have received permission to stay at home, the complaint clears up. This may go on day after day, and the longer they are out of school, the harder it is to get them back. These children are often timid and inhibited away from home, but willful, stubborn, and demanding with their parents.

Not all school phobias are the same. In the "neurotic" type, which largely affects children from kindergarten through fourth grade, the avoidance of school comes on suddenly and the children continue to function well in other areas of their lives. In the "characterological" type, seen in early adolescence, the phobia has come on more gradually, the children are more deeply disturbed, and the outlook for the children's future is far less hopeful.

Not all family constellations are the same, either, although a few basic patterns predominate. The mother tends to be a perfectionist who can't live up to her own impossibly high standards, feels incompetent as a mother, is depressed, and has no interest in the world beyond her family. She is apt to have had an emotionally deprived childhood and has never resolved her dependence on her own mother. She is often ambivalent toward the phobic child. She encourages him to depend on her, tries to keep him immature, and shows her disappointment and resentment when he shows signs of independence. Then when he exploits his mother's overindulgence and makes demands that she resents, she feels trapped.

The father usually makes a good living and is conscientious and hard-working at his job. At home, though, he tends to be passive, dependent on his wife, and ineffectual as a parent. His relations with his own parents are often—like his wife's—still unresolved. He tends to hover at one of two poles of behavior:

Either he shows little interest in family matters or he becomes so controlling that he undermines his wife's already shaky self-confidence. While the marriage between these two is almost always enduring, it often suffers under the burden of poor communication and poor sexual relations. Husband and wife are often ambivalent toward each other, as well as toward their child, whom they treat inconsistently.

The most important element in the treatment of a school-phobic child is an early return to school. Most experts advise getting the child back to school first, then going on with whatever other steps may be called for, such as therapy for the child, for one or both parents, and possibly for the entire family. Getting the child back in school accomplishes a number of aims: It breaks up the extreme interdependence between mother and child, emphasizes the basic health of the child, keeps the child from falling behind in her work (which would aggravate her problems), restores her to a more normal environment, and removes the child from the phobic cycle.

The return to school is sometimes accomplished gradually, beginning with the parent's driving the child to school and just sitting in the car, then getting out and walking around the outside of the school together, next going with the child into the principal's office, and finally having the child go to school alone—first, possibly, for an hour a day, then several hours, and eventually for an entire day. An approach like this, of course, requires working closely with school officials.

Usually children can be returned to school without too much difficulty once treatment is begun. The few studies that have followed up these children in later years are unclear, though, in determining how well treatment helped their adjustment in general.

300

SUMMARY

1 Physical development is less rapid in middle childhood than in earlier years. Though boys are slightly taller and heavier than girls at the beginning of this period, girls attain the adolescent growth spurt at an earlier age and thus tend to be larger by the end of it. Wide individual and cross-cultural differences exist in height and weight. **2** In the middle years children's facial and bodily proportions change, and their vision becomes keener. Brain development is virtually complete. **3** It is possible to predict adult height from height at middle childhood. Of the techniques available, the most efficient is determination of *skeletal*, or *bone*, age. But all techniques are somewhat limited, and accuracy is greater the later the assessment is made. Hormone therapy can help the child who is not growing normally. **4** As a result of medical advances such as innoculations and antibiotics, many diseases that previously plagued schoolchildren have been controlled. Accidents still constitute a major problem in these years, and diseases such as tuberculosis, syphilis, gonorrhea, and hepatitis still affect too many children. **5** Because of improved motor development and coordination, boys and girls can now engage in a wider variety of physical activities than preschoolers. By adolescence, boys tend to outstrip girls in physical achievements. Social factors (it is "unfeminine" for girls to excell athletically) must be considered along with physical explanations. **6** The child from 6 to 11 is in the stage that Piaget refers to as *concrete operations*. The concrete operational child uses symbols (mental representations) to carry out operations. He or she is becoming increasingly more proficient at classifying, dealing with numbers, and conserving. Egocentrism is diminishing, as are certain primitive concepts of realism, animism, and artificialism. **7** Both Piaget and Kohlberg regard moral development as a process that coincides with cognitive development. Moral development is influenced by a child's maturational level, social role-taking skills, and interactions with adults and other children. **8** Piaget regards moral development as a two-stage process. The first stage, *morality of constraint* (heteronomous morality), is characterized by rigidity. The second stage, *morality of cooperation* (autonomous morality), is characterized by flexibility. Piaget formed these conclusions through study of children's understanding of rules, intentionality, and punishment. Kohlberg extended Piaget's view of morality to include six types of moral reasoning, organized on three levels: premoral; morality of conventional role conformity; and morality of self-accepted moral principles. **9** Learning-theory approaches to studying moral development claim that children learn their culture's moral values by identifying with or modeling themselves after parents, who reward or punish moral decisions. But research does not confirm generalizations or moral standards from the home to other institutions. *Values clarification* is a technique designed to help children learn to make moral judgments. **10** Psychoanalytic theory sees morality as the result of the Oedipus/Electra complex and the internalization of parents' moral standards through identification. **11** Most school-age children have not yet mastered exceptions to grammatical rules. Children's understanding of increasingly complex syntax develops up to and perhaps even after 9 years of age. A child's ability to communicate information to others improves with age and as egocentrism diminishes.   **12**   The intelligence of schoolchildren is assessed by individual tests (Stanford-Binet and Wechsler Intelligence Scale for Children) and by group tests (Otis-Lennon Mental Ability Test and Lorge-Throndike Multi-Level Battery).   **13**   A virtually impossible task confronting intelligence test constructors is to devise tests that measure innate intelligence without introducing cultural bias. But several *culture-fair* tests are purported to deal with experiences thought to be common in various cultures.   **14**   Cognitive functioning is correlated with individual temperment, cognitive style, sex differences, and parental child-rearing practices.   **15**   Studies of intellectually gifted children have been of two types: *retrospective* (analysis of biographical materials of individuals who have already achieved eminence) and *longitudinal* (long-term, follow-up studies of individuals identified as gifted during childhood). Gifted children tend to be superior in many respects—achievement, health, coordination, height, popularity—and as adults are superior in intellectual ability, scholastic accomplishment, and vocational achievement.   **16**   Creativity involves *divergent*, rather than convergent, thinking. The creative person sees things in new and unusual lights and devises novel solutions to novel problems. It is not always easy to measure creativity—"creative" tests are required. Many family factors—such as social class and parental attitudes—influence creativity in children. When children are assessed both by measures of creativity and by measures of intelligence, four performance patterns may result: Children may (a) score high on both; (b) score low on both; (c) score high on creativity and low on intelligence; or (d) score low on creativity and high on intelligence. Intellectual ability and creative ability are thus seen as separate constructs.   **17**   From 6 to 12, a child's development is influenced by school and the experiences that occur there. Academic and interpersonal successes (and failures) affect self-esteem, self-confidence, and basic outlooks on life. A child's school experience is influenced by various factors: type of classroom (open or traditional), teachers and attitudes, socioeconomic status, sex, and cultural membership. School-related issues include education of handicapped children, learning disabilities, and school phobia.

301

SUGGESTED READINGS

Baughman, E. E.   *Black Americans*. New York: Academic, 1971. A readable and fair-minded report about black people in society today. It presents and discusses research findings about intelligence, school achievement, family styles, self-esteem, and psychopathology.

Brutten, M., Richardson, S. O., & Mangel, C.   *Something's wrong with my child: A parents' book about children with learning disabilities*. New York: Harcourt Brace Jovanovich, 1973. A good overview of problems and their management.

Farnham-Diggory, S.   *Learning disabilities*. Cambridge: Harvard University Press, 1978. Presents current information on the diagnoses and treatments of learning disabilities such as dislexia, hyperactivity, and arithmetic disability.

Fincher, J. *Sinister people: The looking-glass world of the left-hander*. New York: Putnam, 1977. A comprehensive study of handedness that explores theories explaining left- or right-handedness, examines societal customs and the implications for left-handed people, delves into historical attitudes, and identifies a slew of famous "lefties."

Furth, H., & Wachs, H. *Thinking goes to school*. New York: Oxford University Press, 1975. Includes many "thinking games" based on Piaget's theory to be used with children.

Goertzel, V., & Goertzel, M. G. *Cradles of eminence*. Boston: Little, Brown, 1962. An absorbing study of the childhoods of some 400 prominent persons that seeks to relate early-life factors to eventual success in life. It brings together biography, autobiography, and professional literature about gifted children and adults.

Pomeranz, V. E., & Schultz, D. *The mothers' and fathers' medical encyclopedia*. Boston: Little, Brown, 1977. A source of up-to-date information about all aspects of children's health, including prevention and treatment of ills that affect young people from the cradle to college.

Simon, S. B., & Kirschenbaum, H. (Eds.) *Readings in values clarification*. Minneapolis: Winston, 1973. A collection of thirty-eight articles on the identification and development of values, goals, and ideals, by writers such as Carl Rogers, Lawrence Kohlberg, and Urie Bronfenbrenner.

Simon, S. B., & Olds, S. W. *Helping your child learn right from wrong*. New York: McGraw-Hill, 1977. A self-help manual for parents to aid in establishing moral values and emotional self-awareness in children. The authors explain why values themselves cannot be taught—but how parents *can* teach children a process for arriving at their own values.

MIDDLE
CHILDHOOD

9

PERSONALITY
AND
SOCIAL DEVELOPMENT

IN THIS CHAPTER
YOU WILL LEARN ABOUT

Freud's and Erikson's theories about human development during middle childhood

What life is like for schoolchildren—their games, humor, and peer-group influences

How children's self-concepts develop, and how prejudice and sex typing affect their views of themselves and others

The effects of family life on schoolchildren: What things matter

Some emotional disturbances in childhood, and how they are treated

CHAPTER OVERVIEW

THEORETICAL PERSPECTIVES ON PERSONALITY DEVELOPMENT

FREUD'S THEORY OF PSYCHOSEXUAL DEVELOPMENT: THE LATENCY PERIOD

Freud termed the elementary school years the *latency period*, considering it an island of relative sexual calmness between the turbulent preschool years (with their Oedipus and Electra complexes) and the storminess of adolescence. This concept of sexual latency does not, however, imply the absence of sexuality. During the years from 6 to 12, children are still sexual beings: They continue to masturbate, to be curious about sex, and to explore each other. In 1966, Broderick found that 90 percent of fifth-graders already had "steadies," 65 percent had been kissed, and 40 percent had gone on dates. By and large, though, by middle childhood youngsters have resolved their Oedipal conflicts, adopted their sex roles, and now turn their energies to acquiring facts, skills, and cultural attitudes.

Defense Mechanisms in Middle Childhood

The developing ego, or self-concept, of the school-aged child is threatened on all sides. To uphold its strength, children may develop defense mechanisms, many of which persist throughout adult life. These mechanisms include:

REGRESSION   During trying times, children often *regress*, showing behavior of an earlier age, to try to recapture remembered security. For example, a child who has just entered school or whose parents have separated may go back to sucking her thumb or wetting his bed. When the crisis is past, the babyish behavior usually disappears.

REPRESSION   In anxiety-producing situations, children may *repress*, or block, feelings that they formerly may have expressed freely. These emotions are now so raw and uncomfortable that they cannot let them rise to consciousness. They may repress their desires for forbidden candy by turning around so they cannot see it.

SUBLIMATION   Through *sublimation*, children channel their sexual energy, which now makes them uncomfortable and anxious, into such acceptable activities as schoolwork, sports, and hobbies.

PROJECTION   One way of dealing with unacceptable thoughts and motives is to attribute them to another; this is called *projection*. Thus, a child talks about how dishonest a brother is, or how mean a sister, or how jealous the new baby.

REACTION FORMATION   Children may say the opposite of what they really feel: Buddy says he doesn't want to play with Tony because he doesn't like him, when the truth is that Buddy likes Tony a lot but is afraid that Tony doesn't want to play with him. The tendency for school-aged children to play exclusively with others of the same sex may be considered a reaction formation.

ERIKSON'S THEORY OF PSYCHOSOCIAL DEVELOPMENT: INDUSTRY VERSUS INFERIORITY

During the school years, children learn the skills of their cultures in order to prepare for adult work. An Arapesh boy learns to make bows and arrows and to lay traps for rats, and an Arapesh girl learns to weed and plant and harvest. A young Eskimo learns to hunt and fish. An American child learns to count, read, and form letters.

This is the age when productivity becomes important. No longer are children content to play; they must become workers. Their beginning efforts to handle the tools of their society help them to grow and form a

February 5. I've been reading my first Shakespeare lately. I really like it, don't think it's hard to understand if you read carefully. The television is broken so I've accomplished something today. Cleaned room and downstairs, practiced music, read, helped Daddy on March of Dimes money.

Marilyn Bell, age 12
from *Small Voices*, p. 237

positive self-concept. These are crucial years for the development of self-esteem. Children who feel inadequate compared with their peers may go "back to the more isolated, less tool-conscious familial rivalry of the oedipal time" (Erikson, 1950, p. 260). Some children in this stage give work too important a place, so that they neglect their relationships with other people. The industrial tycoon who lives, breathes, and dreams business and rarely sees his family is, in Erikson's words, "the conformist and thoughtless slave of his technology" (1950, p. 261); such a person may have been pushed in this direction during the school years.

Erikson, too, sees middle childhood as a time of relative physical and sexual latency, and a time of rapid cognitive growth.

THE SOCIETY OF CHILDHOOD

Children today live, act, and think differently from those of years gone by. The great migration to the suburbs has drastically altered how children spend their time. Family mobility has forced children to keep making new friends and to grow up in communities where few adults know their names. Our relaxed views of morality have changed the flavor of children's talk (and taken away some of the great mysteries). More leisure has given parents more time with their children. Our expanding knowledge of psychology has increased our interest in how our minds work and has altered the ways parents deal with

their children, or, at least, how they think about the ways they deal with their children.

Technology has widened the boundaries of children's worlds. Travel, telephones, and television mean that children are not so sheltered from the adult world as they had been in recent years. Today's children are different in many ways from those of a generation or two ago. And yet there are still some eternal verities.

Children's continuing insistence on singing their own songs, telling their own jokes, playing their own games, and keeping among themselves what they don't want those alien intruders—adults—to know underscores the truth of Douglas Newton's observation that "the world-wide fraternity of children is the greatest of savage tribes, and the only one which shows no sign of dying out" (Opie & Opie, 1959, p. 285).

CHILDREN'S LORE, GAMES, AND HUMOR

After a ten-year study of some five thousand British children, Opie and Opie (1959) concluded that children have their own lore, which they hand down to one another. They rarely originate it. Rather, they imitate, they adapt, and they make creative mistakes. They pass along their pet superstitions—just ask Tom Sawyer how to get rid of warts. Consider what children were telling each other a few years back (R. P. Smith, 1959):

What we knew as kids, what we learned from other kids, was not tentatively true, or extremely probable, or proven by science or polls or surveys. It was so. . . . If you eat sugar lumps, you get worms. If you cut a worm in half, he don't feel a thing, and you get two worms. Grasshoppers spit tobacco. Step on a crack, break your mother's back. Walk past a house with a quarantine sign, and don't hold

your breath, and you get sick and die. Play with yourself too much, your brain gets soft. Cigarettes stunt your growth [pp. 18–20].

Children still parody the songs and poems of their elders; tell jokes that make fun of them; play time-honored tricks on teachers, parents, grouchy neighbors, and each other; and preserve a rich lode of traditional lore. Children are the great traditionalists. In line with Piaget's findings about the rigidity of children's conceptions of rules and morality, children pass on what they have heard as the Revealed Truth. They will not tolerate theories that contradict what they "know." Nor will they put up with alterations in familiar rhymes. While they eagerly seek out new jokes, stories, and rhymes, any slight variation in the old familiar ones is heresy.

Children's rhymes provide a safety valve for the release of anger, frustration, and aggression against parents and such other family members as pesky little brothers and sisters (Butler, 1973), as in the following jump-rope rhyme:

I had a little brother,
His name was Tiny Tim.
I put him in the bathtub
To teach him how to swim.
He swam down the river,
He swam down the lake,
He died last night
With an awful bellyache.

Jacks, marbles, ball games, wrestling matches, imaginative play that imitates the world of adults, making figures with string, rolling hoops, throwing dice, playing tag are all venerable pastimes of children, as popular today as they have been for thousands of years. In play, children discharge energy, prepare for life's duties, achieve difficult goals, and relieve frustrations. They get physical contact, discharge needs to compete, act aggressively in socially acceptable ways, and learn how to get along with others. They give their imaginations free rein, learn the trappings of their cultures, develop skills, and learn sex-appropriate behavior. In short, children's play is still children's work.

Children's Humor

Amid whispers and giggles, Dorie, 7, asks: "Do you want to hear a dirty joke?" To an eager nod, Dorie says, "A boy fell in the mud. Do you want to hear another one?" Again a nod. "A girl fell in the mud. Do you want to hear another? Yes? Okay, three came out." Raucous laughter follows snicker, and the joke is retold ad infinitum until every second-grader in the school knows it and repeats it to anyone who will listen.

Much children's humor derives from their abiding interest in excreta and sexuality. By telling jokes about these taboo and often mysterious subjects, children can deal with things they'd like to understand better but are embarrassed to talk about more matter-of-factly.

In the opinion of one psychoanalyst (Wolfenstein, 1954), play on the ambiguity of words, one of the earliest forms of humor, draws upon the basic ambiguities of sex and emotion.

At about 3, Vicky thinks it's the height of wit to say to a boy, "You're a girl." Behind this joke, says Wolfenstein, lie children's universal fears and wishes that their sex can be changed. As children become able to laugh at such comments directed toward themselves, they show their mastery of doubts about their own sex. At about 4, Vicky may expand upon this game by calling a boy by a girl's name and vice versa. Sometimes, just mixing the names of two children of the same sex is funny. Thus, children learn to overcome doubts about their individual identities.

Older children base entire jokes on made-up names that have a sexual significance. At 9, Vicky loves the "Heinie" jokes, which rely for their humor on the double meaning implicit in stories like the following:

A mother takes her little girl, named Heinie, out to buy her some underwear. She tells her child to wait in the alley while she goes into the store. When the salesman asks the mother what size underpants she needs, the mother answers, "Come out into the alley and I'll show you my Heinie."

Wolfenstein (1954) explains the humor in such jokes in this way:

By setting up a situation in which the mother calls the child "my Heinie," the loving union of child and mother is achieved in a mocking way: the child becomes again a part of the mother's body. . . . While the mocking love name accomplishes a symbolic fusion of mother and child, the action of the joke consists in the mother's unwitting self-exposure. Her concern for her child keeps impelling her to reveal an intimate part of her body. . . . The mother is exposed as both sexually accessible and foolish. . . . Her image is degraded; from having been ideally desirable she becomes ridiculous [pp. 83–84].

And thus, the child telling the joke retaliates to some degree against the powerful figure of the mother.

Not all children's humor takes place in bathroom and bedroom, though. Children minimize their anxiety about many different situations with the gift of laughter. Whatever children want to gain mastery over, they tell a joke about, as we can see in the following stories:

Hostility to siblings:
   "Boy, is my little sister spoiled!"
   "She is *not*."
   "Oh, no? You should see what the steamroller did to her!" (third grade)

Fears about death:
   "How do you make a dead baby float?"

"I don't know."
"Take a dead baby, some soda, and a couple of scoops of ice cream . . ." (sixth grade).

Many jokes are told for the sheer joy of showing mastery over language—using mispronunciations and wrong words, making puns, telling riddles, telling stories that depend for their humor on basic knowledge or on different meanings of a word, so that children can show off what they know. Goethe once said, "Men show their characters in nothing more clearly than in what they think laughable," and children show their rate of development the same way.

Prentice and Fathman (1972) confirmed the importance of children's cognitive development in their enjoyment and understanding of riddles, the favorite joke form for 6- to 11-year-olds. They posed thirty riddles from popular children's jokebooks to forty-eight children in the first, third, and fifth grades. The children were asked to rate them on a scale of enjoyment and to explain what was funny about each one. The children's *understanding* increased steadily from grade to grade, while their *enjoyment* increased from first to third grade but decreased in the fifth. These findings confirm Zigler's cognitive congruency principle (Zigler, Levine, & Gould, 1967) that jokes are funniest when they are moderately hard to understand. When we "get" a joke too easily, it's too obvious and not so funny.

Another factor that influences people's senses of humor is their cognitive style, as indicated by Brodzinsky's 1975 report. He determined whether a hundred thirty-five 6-, 8-, and 10-year-old boys were reflective or impulsive and then showed them over 250 cartoons of varying degrees of subtlety and emotional content. Again, the older the chil-

dren, the more likely they were to understand the cartoons. In addition, among the 6- to 8-year-olds, the reflective boys grasped the point of the cartoons faster than impulsive boys. By the age of 10, though, conceptual tempo no longer made any difference.

Brodzinsky suggests "that the specific skills needed to comprehend cartoon humor, particularly the more subtle, logically based humor, develop earlier in reflective than in impulsive . . . children" (p. 848).

The impulsive boys were more likely to laugh at *anything*, even pointless cartoons, indicating their greater emotional lability, or readiness to move quickly from one mood to another. This lability may tend to disrupt these children's ability to pay attention to what they are doing, and thus account for their lower comprehension scores.

LIFE IN THE PEER GROUP

Children influence each other from the cradle. Young infants begin to cry when they hear the wailing of other babies (Simner, 1971; Sage & Hoffman, 1976).

Toddlers imitate the way other children share and fight. Preschoolers' social behavior follows certain patterns that lead up to involvement with other children in the middle years. From age 2 to 5, children become more dependent on other children and somewhat less dependent on adults; they become more sympathetic and altruistic, as well as more competitive and aggressive (Hartup, 1970).

In middle childhood the peer group really comes into its own. During these years children spend more time away from their parents and more time with other children. Childhood subcultures exist in all societies, and they have always existed. Their strength and importance vary, however. At this time in the United States, the world of children may be more powerful than ever before. Our highly

mobile society has had to find substitutes for the bonds of kinship. Often the peer group fills this role, especially in heterogenous urban settings among working-class youth (Campbell, 1964).

Bronfenbrenner (1970) states that American children are no longer influenced by their parents as much as in the past, because they spend less time with them:

Urbanization, child labor laws, the abolishment of the apprentice system, commuting, centralized schools, zoning ordinances, the working mother, the experts' advice to be permissive, the seductive power of television for keeping children occupied, the delegation and professionalization of child care—all of these manifestations of progress have operated to decrease opportunity for contact between children and parents, or, for that matter, adults in general [p. 99].

Our society is now age-segregated to an unprecedented extent. Condry, Siman, and Bronfenbrenner (1968) heard from 766 sixth-graders that they spent an average of two or three hours a day over the weekend with their parents, while spending a little more time than this with groups of friends and an additional two or three hours a day with a single friend. They were spending twice as much time with children their own age as with their parents. How does this affect children?

Functions of the Peer Group

Peer groups serve many purposes in children's lives. They provide a realistic gauge for them to measure the development of their abilities. Only within a sizable group of people who are about the same age can people get a sense of how smart they are, how athletic, how skillful, how personable. Besides learning about themselves, children learn about the world from their peers: They learn what kinds of behavior are appropriate in various situations; they learn how to do a variety of things by seeing other children do them; and they learn how to get along with other people.

Peer groups help children form
attitudes and values. (Leo DeWys, Inc.)

January 5, 1952. Thinking it over it seems funny. First you go to a party and kiss a boy; and then you go to his house, and he acts like he never saw you before. I went to Rose's again and she said to me, "I was doing a nice slow burn when Michael kissed Janey." I'm beginning to think these kissing games are very silly. I have never kissed Johnny so far -- one of the reasons for our strong friendship.

Marian Cuca, age 11,
from *Small Voices*, p. 89

Peer groups help children form attitudes and values, by providing a forum for sifting through parent-derived values and deciding which to keep, which to discard. Siman (1977) looked at the behaviors and attitudes of 171 adolescents who were in established friendship cliques. Girls and boys in grades 6 to 12 were asked how often they engaged in thir-teen different behaviors such as doing volunteer or school work, taking part in sports, smoking, playing hooky, and so forth. They were then asked how they thought their parents and their friends felt about the various activities. The parents' standards for individual youngsters were compared with the average for the parents of all the members in each youngster's clique. The young people seemed to react not only to their individual parents' standards, but to the general group parental standards as they learned them from their friends. Thus the peer groups helped the individuals reinterpret parental values. Boys seemed more influenced by their peers than girls, and antisocial or negative behaviors reflected more peer influence. This may help to explain why boys get into more trouble than girls do.

Peers also offer emotional security: In some situations, another child can provide a kind of comfort that an adult cannot. Sometimes this comfort comes from learning that your friend has the same kind of "wicked" thoughts and behavior that would offend an adult. In fact, being able to work out forbidden fantasies in play with another child (like conspiring to poison a parent) can further emotional development (Asher, 1978).

Peer groups tend to be homogeneous with regard to age, race, sex, and socioeconomic status. In the elementary school years, groups are all-girl or all-boy, partly because of mutuality of interests, partly as an outgrowth of the group's function of teaching sex-appropriate behaviors, and partly because of the difference in maturity between girls and boys.

Influences of Peer Groups on Individuals

Peer groups often impose their own dominance on the emerging individual. It is usually mands of clearly defined situations seems a perfectly healthy response for a child (or for an adult, for that matter) [p. 312].

in the company of friends that children shop-lift, begin to smoke and drink, sneak into the movies, and do other antisocial acts. Sixth-graders who are rated more "peer-oriented" report engaging in more of this kind of behavior than do "parent-oriented" children (Condry, Siman, & Bronfenbrenner, 1968).

How does the group influence the individual? Berenda (1950) studied children's reactions to group pressures that contradicted what their own eyes told them. Ninety 7- to 13-year-olds were asked to compare lengths of lines on twelve pairs of cards in the company of the eight brightest children in their class, all of whom had been primed to give seven wrong answers out of the twelve. The group influence was powerful. Almost all the subjects had given correct answers to the seven critical questions in a previous test, while only 43 percent of the 7- to 10-year-olds and only 54 percent of the 10- to 13-year-olds answered them right in the group-pressure setting. Children become most susceptible to the influence of peers in middle childhood and are less conforming in adolescence (Costanzo & Shaw, 1966). The higher a child's status in the group, the less conforming he or she is likely to be. When material to be evaluated is ambiguous, children's judgments are influenced most strongly by the group. This carries grave implications for the individual trying to make sense out of a world with many ambiguous issues.

To some degree, conformity to group standards is a healthy, self-serving mechanism of adaptation, as Campbell (1964) comments:

The reasonable implication is that "conformity" is not solely the province of the anxious, the dependent, the maladjusted; unwitting conformity in the face of ambiguity may be so, but conformity to the socially accepted de-

Popularity

We all want people to like us. What our peers think of us matters terribly. Because acceptance by others has such a big effect on our self-esteem and often on our success in life, researchers have devised *sociometric techniques* to answer questions like the following: Why are some children more sought out than others? Why are some ignored or rebuffed? What characteristics do popular children have? What are unpopular children like?

One type of sociometric technique is a *sociogram*, a pictorial representation of group relationships. Researchers observe which children seek out others, which are chosen most and least often, and which are asked for help and advice. They ask children to name their three best friends or the three they like least. The questions can be more specific: Which three children do you like to sit near . . . walk home with after school . . . serve with on a committee . . . like to have on your gym team? The data then are plotted in pictorial form.

THE POPULAR CHILD By establishing which children are chosen most often and least often, researchers correlate acceptance with other factors. Popular children tend to be healthy and vigorous, well poised, and capable of initiative; but they are also adaptable and conforming. They are dependable, affectionate, considerate, and original thinkers (Bonney, 1947; cited in Grossman & Wrighter, 1948). They think moderately well of themselves, rather than showing extremely high or low levels of self-esteem (Reese, 1961). They radiate self-confidence without being overbearing or seeming conceited. Popular children show mature dependence on other children: They ask for help when they need it, and for approval when they think they deserve it, but they don't cling or make babyish plays for affection (Hartup, 1970). They are not

One of childhood's saddest figures is the one who hangs around the fringes of every group (Eva & Louis Millette)

goodie-goodies, but they make other people feel good to be with them (Feinberg, Smith, & Schmidt, 1958; Tuddenham, 1951). Popular children also tend to be more physically attractive than unpopular ones (Lerner & Lerner, 1977). This may reflect a desire by children to surround themselves with the "beautiful people." An alternative explanation is that the attractive child is used to favorable attention from parents and other adults, has developed more self-esteem as a result, and has turned into the kind of person who's enjoyable to be with.

THE UNPOPULAR CHILD One of childhood's saddest figures is the one who hangs around the fringes of every group, walks home alone after school, and sobs in despair, "Nobody wants to play with me." Children can be unpopular for many reasons, sometimes because they are withdrawn or rebellious (Y. H. Smith, 1950; Northway, 1944). They may walk around with a "chip on the shoulder," showing unprovoked aggression and hostility. Or they may act silly and babyish, showing off in immature ways. Or they may be anxious

and uncertain, exuding such a pathetic lack of confidence that they repel other children, who don't find them fun to be with. Very fat or unattractive children, children who act in any way that seems strange to others, and slow-learning youngsters are also outcasts.

How Adults Influence Children's Peer-Group Dynamics

Grownups cramp kids' style. Or they help to guide them through life. The personality, attitudes, and behavioral style of the adults who come into contact with groups of children exert a great influence on the individuals within those groups and on the group dynamics themselves. Would the boys in *Oliver Twist* or the girls in *The Prime of Miss Jean Brodie* have behaved differently under the tutelage of different adults? Undoubtedly.

Lewin, Lippitt, and White (1939) set up several clubs of 10-year-old boys, run in turn by authoritarian, democratic, and laissez faire leaders, so that each group experienced each type of leader. The children in the democratically led groups were more spontaneous, friendly, and fact-minded, while those in the other two groups showed more hostility toward each other. Under authoritarian leadership there was either a high level of aggression or a high level of apathy, which quickly gave way to aggression when the leader left the room or during periods of transition to a freer atmosphere. When the autocratic leaders left the room, work slowed down, sometimes to a halt, whereas the boys in the democratic groups continued to work whether the leader was present or not. Children do best under the leadership and guidance of a respected adult who respects them, and they do least well with repressive adult leadership or with no adult leadership at all.

Societal Recognition of Peer-Group Influences

Conscious, deliberate efforts are sometimes made to use peer-group influences to carry forward adult goals.

THE SOVIET UNION Russian adults foster a sense of the group to spur children on to socially approved behavior (Bronfenbrenner, 1970). Nursery school teachers emphasize sharing, cooperation, and joint activities. Grade school teachers emphasize mutual responsibility and encourage older children to help younger ones. Teachers encourage competition between groups rather than between individuals. Pupils sit up straight, stay neat and clean, do their homework, and observe classroom rules to make their row the best in the class. The children themselves exhort their row-mates to do better, for the good of the entire unit. Those groups that make the best showings win prizes, and youngsters who misbehave or fall behind in their schoolwork are often reduced to tears by "trials" by juries of their peers (Bronfenbrenner, 1970).

Russian children are less willing to engage in antisocial behavior than American, English, and West German children (Bronfenbrenner, 1967). Bronfenbrenner tested Russian and American 12-year-olds for their susceptibility to peer and adult influences. The children were confronted with thirty hypothetical situations involving their readiness to cheat, steal, play a practical joke on a teacher, neglect homework, and go against parental wishes. Some children were told that their classmates would see their answers; some were told that parents and teachers would see them; and some were told that only the researchers would see the answers. Both Russian and American children gave more socially approved responses when they thought adults would see their answers, with the Russians influenced more by this. Peer-group pressures took different directions for the two groups. They influenced the Russian children toward adult standards of behavior, while they influenced the American children away from adult-approved standards.

A study of Russian, American, English, and Swiss sixth-graders (Rodgers, Bronfenbrenner, & Devereux, 1968) found that Russian children were more likely to be clean, orderly, and polite but were less likely to tell the truth and seek intellectual understanding. In our efforts to encourage individualism and a constant search for one's own values, are we forced to accept a certain amount of rebelliousness against adults? If so, how much? How can we find the golden mean between unquestioning docility, on the one hand, and aggressive delinquency, on the other?

THE ISRAELI KIBBUTZ About 90,000 Israelis, some 2.8 percent of Israel's total population, live on the collective agricultural settlements known as kibbutzim (Government of Israel, 1973). The kibbutz way of life involves communal living, collective ownership of property, and communal rearing of children (Spiro, 1954).

A cornerstone of the kibbutz lifestyle is the individual's relationship to the group. In most kibbutzim, as soon as mother and baby leave the hospital, the mother returns to her apartment, and the baby goes to live in the infants' house to be cared for by a professional child-carer. Bettelheim (1969) says that babies often lose their appetites and become run down when a cribmate is taken out of the nursery. The babies move on together to the toddler house, to the kindergarten, and to the other houses they will progressively occupy. They are with each other constantly: They play together and go to school and on outings together. They become closer to each other than to their parents or siblings. Age-mates look out for each other, comfort each other, and exert group pressure on each other. The individual rarely goes against the group. At about the age of 12 or 14, children establish their own youth society, organizing along the same general lines as the kibbutz. They work, vote, and make policy. Their influence over each other becomes even stronger.

If the kibbutz children were not raised together, were not forced to depend upon each other for companionship and comfort, and did not have the power to resolve most problems of their age group, the peer group could not wield the power it does. Adult kibbutzniks want the peer group to have this power because it helps to reinforce adult standards and values.

THE UNITED STATES   A growing number of classroom teachers in this country enlist the help of their pupils to improve other children's behavior. The teacher of Diane, age 8, who regularly threw severe tantrums in class, began to give candy to all the children who didn't turn around to look at her while she was misbehaving. On each half-day when Diane threw no tantrums, the teacher would put a star on the board; after four stars, there would be a class party. Diane gradually threw fewer and milder tantrums. By the last month of school, she was throwing none; instead, she was making friends and reacting positively to school (Carlson, Arnold, Becker, & Madsden, 1968). By giving the other children a stake in Diane's good behavior, the teacher was able

to eliminate their reinforcement of her tantrums.

Bronfenbrenner (1970) urges adults to capitalize on peer-group influences. Teachers should set up teams to encourage mutual help and cooperative group competition. Schools should encourage older children to help younger ones. Family, neighborhood, and the larger community should all involve themselves more fully in the lives of children.

FRIENDSHIP IN MIDDLE CHILDHOOD

As children spend more time away from their parents and with their friends, the significance of their friendship patterns grows. Children's thinking about friendship, their reasons for choosing friends, and their ability to sustain a relationship undergo many changes during the six years or so of middle childhood.

According to Selman and Selman (1979), whose stage theory was introduced on page 248, children enter Stage 1, *One-Way Assistance*, at about age 4. This stage lasts until about age 9, overlapping with Stage 2. A child in Stage 1 considers someone as a friend only if the other person does what the first person wants him to. ("She's not my friend anymore, because she wouldn't go with me when I wanted her to.")

When Youniss and Volpe (1978) interviewed some hundred thirty 6- to 14-year-olds about friendship, they received answers that can be discussed in terms of Selman and Selman's stages. For example, the 6- and 7-year-olds thought of friendship in terms of playing together and sharing material goods. ("He lets me play soccer with him," or "They always say yes when I want to borrow their eraser.")

In Stage 2, *Two-Way Fair-Weather Cooperation*, which spans the years from 6 to 12, children acknowledge that friendship involves give-and-take. But they still see it as serving many separate self-interests, rather than the common, mutual interests of both parties to the friendship. ("We are friends. We do things for each other.")

The 9- and 10-year-olds who spoke to Youniss and Volpe saw sharing as a sign of friendship when one friend supplied something the other one didn't have. ("Somebody that plays with you when you don't have anybody else to play with.") At this age, children emphasized similarities between friends and pointed out states of equality and reciprocity. ("The group does things he likes to do," and "Shared everything they had. One wouldn't have more than the other. They'd have everything equal. If one was better than the other one, he wouldn't brag that he was.") Also, these children now recognized that a friendship is not between any two children who are thrown together, but between people whose personalities mesh: They share ideas, feelings, and interests.

By Stage 3 (ages 9 to 15), the stage of *Intimate, Mutually Shared Relationships*, children can view a friendship as having a life of its own. It is an ongoing, systematic, committed relationship that incorporates more than just doing things for each other. Friendship during Stage 3 tends to be treasured by the parties to it, who become possessive of the

intimate bond and who often demand exclusivity. ("It takes a long time to make a close friend, so you really feel bad if you find out that he is trying to make other close friends, too.")

Young adolescents interviewed by Youniss and Volpe described friendship in these terms: "When you need help, he helps you. . . . Never turns you down. If another person picks on you, he comes and helps you, if the other is bigger or smaller. Never runs away and leaves you." These 12- and 13-year-olds did not have substantially different concepts of friendship than did the 9- and 10-year olds. The older group simply carried further the same principles of equality and reciprocity that the younger ones had already grasped.

Not until Selman and Selman's Stage 4, the stage of *Autonomous Interdependent Friendships*, which begins at about age 12, do people respect their friends' needs for both dependency and autonomy. ("One thing about a good friendship is that it's a real commitment, a risk you have to take. You have to be able to support and trust and give, but you have to be able to let go, too.")

Selman and Selman have applied their stages in "friendship therapy" with children who have trouble making and keeping friends. By seeing how children deal with other young-

June 19. Today for the first time Gail Greenfield and I had a cut and we made blood sisters. This is how we did it. Paula Greenfield got some of my blood and put it on Gail's cut and got some of that blood and put it on my cut. And that's how we got to be blood sisters.

Susan Robben, age 8,
from *Small Voices*, p. 202

June 14. This year has been full of unforgettable experiences. Like Jenny's and my notes and giggles in science class, our first smoke (and last) on band trip, our split malts, troubles with teachers, skipping last hour, and oodles of other times. They were fun, but I do hope I mature next year! Most of this summer has been spent keeping up with the Giants and going to town with Nancy and planning trip to West Coast. Mother gave me a permanent yesterday and it was awful. So was the result, but I'm getting it all cut off so who cares?

Marilyn Bell, age 12,
from *Small Voices*, p. 239

Probably the most important key to success and happiness in life is a favorable self-image. (Charles Gatewood)

sters, a therapist can assess their levels of development and can sometimes help them to move on to the next stage. Helping children work out good relationships is important, since youngsters who have problems getting along with other children often have other problems later on: They are more likely to drop out of school, to have mental health problems, and to become delinquent (Lamb, 1978). There is, of course, a strong likelihood that both the difficulty in getting along with peers and later problems in adjustment stem from the same basic cause, but it is also clear that poor peer relationships in childhood will aggravate whatever other problems a person has.

THE SELF-CONCEPT OF SCHOOLCHILDREN

Probably the most important key to success and happiness in life is a favorable self-image. Lucky Patty, who likes herself! Confident in her own abilities, she approaches life with an open attitude that will unlock many doors for her. She can take criticism without going to pieces, and when she feels strongly about something she wants to say or do, she is willing to risk making other people angry. She often challenges parents, teachers, and other people in authority. She feels she can cope with obstacles; she is not overburdened by self-doubt. She solves problems in original, innovative ways. Because she believes she *can* succeed in the goals she sets for herself, she generally *does* succeed. Her success renews her self-respect and makes it easy for her to respect and love others. They, in turn, admire, respect, and enjoy her.

On the other hand, Peter, who does not feel good about himself, is hampered wherever he turns. Convinced he cannot succeed, he does not try very hard. His lack of effort almost always assures continued failure, resulting in a downward spiral of lack of confidence and lack of success. He worries a lot about whether he is doing the right thing, he is destructive both of material things and of people's feelings, and he is constantly plagued by one psychosomatic pain after another. He tries very hard to please others—often too hard, so that while he goes along

January 25. I'm not Eisenhower. I'm not MacArthur. I'm not Kefauver. I'm just Marian, a girl in 8-1, but I'm still running for president. I feel I'm qualified to run because I am interested in the activities of the students of our school. During my long years as a student I have held various jobs: In the first grade I was monitor of milk and crackers. In third grade I was paper monitor. In the fifth grade I was president of the photographic service in my public school. I was president of the first term of the 8th grade and I am now recording secretary of the civics club. Those are just thoughts, dear Diary, if I decide to make a speech and run for president of my class again.

Marian Cuca, age 11,
from *Small Voices*, p. 89

with what other people want, he often strikes them as "wishy-washy." Because of his self-doubts, he's not much fun to be with, and so he has trouble making and keeping friends—which, of course, drives his opinion of himself to even lower depths.

Coopersmith (1967) interviewed eighty-five 10- to 12-year-old boys and their mothers, tested their self-esteem, and concluded that people develop their self concepts according to four bases: *significance* (the way they feel they are loved and approved of by people important to them); *competence* (in performing tasks they consider important); *virtue* (attainment of moral and ethical standards); and *power* (the extent to which they influence their own and others' lives). While people may draw favorable pictures of themselves if they rate high on some of these measures and low on others, the higher they rate on all four, the higher they will rate themselves.

Parents of children with high-esteem love and accept their children, while making greater demands for academic performance and good behavior. Within clearly defined and firmly enforced limits, they show respect and latitude for individual expression and rely more on rewarding good behavior than punishing bad. The parents themselves have high levels of self-esteem and lead active, rewarding lives outside the family:

Rather than being a paradigm of tranquility, harmony and open-mindedness, we find that the high self-esteem family is notable for the high level of activity of its individual members, strong-minded parents dealing with independent, assertive children, stricter enforcement of more stringent demands, and greater possibilities for open dissent and disagreement. This picture brings to mind firm convictions, frequent and possibly strong exchanges, and people who are capable and ready to assume leadership and who will not be treated casually or disrespectfully [Coopersmith, 1967, pp. 252–253].

November 29.... I got angry and called Anna mean. Father told me to look up the word in the dictionary, and it meant "base," "contemptible." I was so ashamed to have called my sister that, and I cried.

Louisa May Alcott, age 10,
from *Small Voices*, p. 111

A variety of factors affect self-concept. Coopersmith found no relationship to height, physical attractiveness, or family size, and only a slim one to social status and academic performance. Sears (1970) contradicted some of these findings when he reported correlations between small family size and high self-concepts and such variables as high reading and arithmetic achievement. Both found that first-born and only children, children with warm parents, and boys with dominant mothers had higher self-esteem. Sears also found that higher sources of masculinity for both boys and girls correlated with higher self-esteem. Bledsoe (1964) found that fourth- and sixth-grade girls had higher self-concepts than boys, possibly because of the girls' earlier maturation or because of their more frequent contacts with adult women.

Age affects the way children see themselves. When ninety low-income black and white second-, fourth-, and sixth-graders were asked, "Who are you?" they described themselves differently at each consecutive age (Sheikh & Beglis, 1973). Second-graders thought in basic units of identification: "I am a boy"; "I live on Main Street"; "I am part of the Brown Family." Fourth-graders' responses reflected both their own individuality and their expanded worlds: "I get good marks in spelling"; "I have a lot of friends"; and "I like to play football." By sixth grade, students were referring more to their futures and were more aware of the opposite sex, and the girls were talking about physical appearance.

Black children described themselves more in terms of basic identification (sex, position in the family, year in school) and less often in terms of skills and accomplishments. Black sixth-grade girls showed racial identity and pride: "I am black and proud" or "I am black and beautiful."

The impact of school entrance raises children's self-concepts (Stendler & Young, 1951), perhaps because this is a well-recognized milestone of growing up. As children grow older, they become more accurate in evaluating themselves. McCallon (1967) asked fourth- and sixth-graders to compare their self-evaluations with the way they would like to be. The closer the two scores were, the higher the children's self-concept. Girls and older children felt closer to their ideal selves than did boys and younger children, indicating a relationship between self-esteem and maturity.

Curiosity level correlates highly with self-esteem in fifth-grade boys (Maw & Maw, 1970). Very curious children tend to be more self-reliant, less prejudiced, and more socially responsible, and they have a greater feeling of belonging. Children with poor self-esteem may not act very curious, because, expecting to fail, they don't stick their necks out. Or uncurious children may not explore their surroundings and fail to learn whatever might help them to gain a better opinion of themselves.

American Indian children often show lower self-esteem than Anglo children (Lefley, 1973), possibly because their cultures are in a state of transition, leaving them with neither the security of the old ways nor the strength of belonging to the dominant societal group. Younger children (7 to 10) have higher self-esteem than 11- to 14-year-olds, possibly because of the older children's greater awareness of the discrepancies between Indian and Anglo cultures (Lefley, 1974). In two tribes, both mothers and children of the less acculturated, more socially intact Miccosukee tribe had higher self-esteem than did those of the more highly assimilated Seminoles.

We might expect minority-group children from economically deprived homes to have lower self-concepts and sometimes they do. But two recent studies indicate that a child's intimate family situation probably exerts more influence than the broader social context on self-image. Soares and Soares (1969) looked at self-perceptions of 229 poor, mostly black and Puerto Rican children and those of 285 middle-class, mostly white children. The disadvantaged children had higher self-perceptions; poor boys had higher scores than poor girls; and middle-class girls thought more of themselves than middle-class boys did. Trowbridge and Trowbridge (1972) examined 1662 low-income and 2127 middle-class third- to eighth-graders and again found that the poor children had higher self-esteem. They were more likely to identify with statements like "I can usually take care of myself";

"I can make up my mind and stick to it"; "I'm pretty sure of myself"; "I can make up my mind without too much trouble"; and "If I have something to say, I usually say it." They see themselves as more popular and more likely to be leaders with other children.

Most surprising in view of the generally lower academic ratings of disadvantaged youngsters is the fact that those in this study saw themselves as more successful in school than did the middle-class children. They like to be called on in class, are proud of their school work, and don't have trouble talking in front of the class. Very few feel they are doing the best work they can. Children who think they are already doing their best consider their present status their upper limit, while those who feel they could try harder can save face and hold a loftier image of their abilities. When these poor children do poorly in school, they blame the school or the teacher. Middle-class children blame themselves. The challenge posed by these studies is how to motivate children to do their best while helping them to maintain good opinions of themselves.

HOW PREJUDICE AFFECTS CHILDREN

Children who speak a different language, who worship in other ways, or who look or act differently from the majority are often the butts of bigoted thinking, which may make them hate themselves and their backgrounds, with resultant emotional disturbance and antisocial behavior. The roots of prejudice run deep in our society. It is demonstrated by children as young as 2 years old, and it continues to flourish. Morland (1966) found that black and white preschoolers from both Virginia and Boston are already aware of racial differences

and imbued with the idea of white superiority. In studying racial attitudes of children in the first four grades, Williams, Boswell, and Best (1975a) found that both white and black children are biased in favor of whites. This bias is present among preschoolers and remains fairly constant for black children through the early school years, but for white children, it increases to second grade and then declines.

In nonracial situations, both black and white preschoolers tend to evaluate the color white more favorably than black. For example, they perceive a pictured white horse to be kinder than a black horse (Williams, Boswell, & Best, 1975b). Children who strongly prefer white over black carry this preference over to their attitudes toward people and demonstrate more of a prowhite, antiblack bias there, too (Boswell & Williams, 1975). The authors of these studies speculate that young children develop initial preferences for white over black as a result of their early personal experiences with light and darkness. This view is supported by findings that children who are afraid of the dark show more of this bias (Boswell & Williams, 1975).

Fortunately, there *are* ways to reduce racial prejudice. Katz and Zalk (1978) tested four different techniques to counter the racially biased attitudes of white second- and fifth-grade children who were found on tests of prejudice to have high levels. All four methods were effective on a short-term basis, and two held up for a longer time.

The four techniques were:

1 *Increased positive racial contact:* Children worked on interracial teams at an interesting puzzle and were all praised for their work.

2 *Vicarious interracial contact:* Children heard an interesting story about a sympathetic and resourceful black child.

3 *Reinforcement of the color black:* Children were given a marble (which could be traded in

for a prize) every time they chose a picture of a black animal instead of a white one.

4 *Perceptual differentiation:* Children were shown slides of a black woman whose appearance varied depending on whether or not she was wearing glasses, one of two different hairdos, and whether she was smiling or frowning. Each different-appearing face had a name, and the children were tested to see how well they remembered the names.

Two weeks after the experiment, the children's prejudice levels were measured again. All the groups who had been exposed to any of the four techniques showed less prejudice than did children in the control groups. Four to six months after the experiment, a second posttest showed that the children who had learned to tell the black faces apart and those who had heard the stories about black children had more positive attitudes than those in the other two groups. Younger children showed more gains, suggesting that prejudiced attitudes can be attacked more easily during the early grades. This study shows that young children's attitudes *can* be changed. As the authors point out, "Schools could probably be doing a good deal more to counteract racial prejudice in children than they are now" (p. 460).

"Children without Prejudice," the report of Forum 18 of the 1970 White House Conference on Children, offers some fifty recommendations to eliminate prejudice, including fostering open housing and education, greater emphasis on cultural contributions of minorities, more scholarships, recruiting and training minority-group teachers, allocating money for renewed or new housing, improving inner-city schools, developing drug education for elementary school children, and training police officers in human relations. The report concludes:

Children have a right to grow up in a society which stresses moral and ethical values, which

teaches the concepts of love of fellow man, which respects the right of individual religious beliefs, which develops the child's personality to include the virtues of honesty, integrity, good character, fairness, compassion, and understanding in all human relations [p.304].

SEX TYPING IN THE MIDDLE YEARS

In the 1950s a group of 8- to 11-year-old boys were asked to describe what men need to know and what they must be able to do:

They need to be strong; they have to be ready to make decisions; they must be able to protect women and children in emergencies; . . . they are the ones to do the hard labor, the rough work, the dirty work, and the unpleasant work; they must be able to fix things; they must get money to support their families; they need "a good business head." . . . They also need to know how to take good care of children, how to get along with their wives, and how to teach their children right from wrong [Hartley, 1959, p. 461].

And what do they think of women?

They are indecisive; they are afraid of many things; they make a fuss over things; they get tired a lot; they very often need someone to help them; they stay home most of the time; they are not as strong as men; they don't like adventure; they are squeamish about seeing blood; they don't know what to do in an emergency; they cannot do dangerous things; they are more easily damaged than men; and they die more easily than men. . . . They are not very intelligent; they can only scream in an emergency when a man would take charge.

. . . Women do things like cooking and washing and sewing because that's all they can do [Hartley, 1959, p. 462].

One boy epitomized rigid sex-role concepts:

If women were to try to do men's jobs the whole thing would fall apart with the women doing it. . . . Women haven't enough strength in the head or in the body to do most jobs. . . . If we had a woman in Congress and taking over everything, probably the Russians would attack tomorrow if they knew about it—if we had a war, they would tell everybody to put down their arms. They'd probably make it life imprisonment for any boy or man who strikes a girl. I wouldn't even trust a woman as a doctor. You never know what they are going to do next [Hartley, 1959, p. 463].

May. We selabrate Mother's Day because she does so many things for us and she loves us. She cooks and cleans for us, takes care of us, she teaches things to us, and she helps us with our problems. We love her.

June. We selabrate Father's Day because they work to get money to buy things for us, they read to us and teach us how to grow up. Fathers loves us and we love our fathers. Fathers take us places too.

Howard T. Bissell, age 7,
from Small Voices, p. 101

These attitudes now seem amusingly obsolete. In these days, children have very different ideas. Or do they? Some do, and some don't. A survey of 1600 fourth-, sixth-, eighth-, and tenth-grade suburban students from various social classes revealed some

Maggie is going to be a doctor when she is grone up and I am going to keep house and sew and cook but not wipe dishes.

We made bows and arrows and the first thing I did when I shot my arrows was to brake a window pane, because my arrow went the wrong way. Mama says its the safest to shoot right up in the air and thats just what I was doing when the window got smashed.

Mary Scarborough Paxson, age 9,
from Small Voices, p.15

decidedly stereotyped ways of thinking. But it also showed that many students, especially older girls, express a willingness to "grant women greater participation in the social, economic, and political spheres" (Greenberg, 1972, p. 9). While 70 percent of the boys thought a female doctor would be as good as a male, only 33 percent thought a trained female garage mechanic could fix a car as well. While 66 percent of the boys thought that "lady scientists" are as smart as males, only 35 percent thought we should have female astronauts. The students' social class did not affect their answers. Girls were consistently more egalitarian than boys, as were older students (after grade four for boys, six for girls), possibly because they understood and had thought more about the social issues involved.

Williams, Bennett, and Best (1975) told a series of stories to 284 children in kindergarten, second grade, and fourth grade. Twelve stories represented male stereotype adjectives as in this one, which represented the adjective grouping "*aggressive, assertive, forceful, tough*": "One of these people is a bully. They are always pushing people around and getting into fights. Which person gets into fights?" Twelve stories, like this one for the word grouping "*emotional, exciting, highstrung,*" represented female stereotype ad-

Sex typing becomes
more stable during the
school years, when
influences outside the
family are felt. (Erika
Stone/Peter Arnold, Inc.;
Everett C. Johnson/Leo
De Wys, Inc.)

jectives: "One of these people is emotional. They cry when something good happens as well as when everything goes wrong. Which is the emotional person?" The children were asked to answer by pointing to a picture of a male or a female.

The kindergartners were already thinking along stereotyped lines. Children's thinking became more stereotyped to the second grade but showed no increase over the next two years. The authors conclude:

The implication of these findings is that the child's earliest learnings regarding sex stereotypes occur during the preschool period, and that these are further reinforced by experiences occurring during the first year or two of school [p. 640].

Minuchin (1965) tried to relate children's sex-role concepts to the kinds of schools they attended and the kinds of families they came from. She found that both school and home orientations influenced children's attitudes. Children from traditional families and traditional schools (which stress facts, grades, competition, conformity, and adult authority) are more likely to play in sex-typed ways; boys are more aggressive, and girls are more oriented to family life. The more modern the background, the more open the children's attitudes. Children who veered most from conventional attitudes were girls who attended modern schools (which stressed individuality and flexibility), whose families were modern in outlook and of higher socioeconomic status.

THE CHILD IN THE FAMILY

Very often it is how children view their parents, as much as the parents' actual behavior and attitudes, that affects children most strongly.

HOW CHILDREN VIEW THEIR PARENTS

Young children tend to fear their fathers more than their mothers and to see them as more punitive, more dominating, and less nurturant (Kagan & Lemkin, 1960; Kagan, 1956), but children over age 10 usually consider their same-sex parent as the more punitive (Coopersmith, 1967). This may indicate a greater rivalry with that parent or may reflect more handling and disciplining by the same-sex parent.

Kagan, Hoskin, and Watson (1961) tested ninety-eight boys and girls 6 to 8 years old to assess their perceptions of their parents and themselves. Both boys and girls conceptualized themselves as closer to the same-sex parent and characterized their fathers as "stronger, larger, darker, more dirty, more angular, and more dangerous" (p. 635) than their mothers. Children generally see their fathers as the breadwinner and their mothers as homemaker and child-rearer (Lynn, 1974)—even in those families where both parents work and share child care. Since adults and children in other cultures also characterize men and women similarly, and since children develop these attitudes by the time they are 5 or 6, some factor outside the immediate family must be at work. After all, not all fathers are stronger, larger, dirtier, and more menacing than their wives. Why do most children see them so?

In Western culture the media help to confirm and communicate these views. Once a male child learns that his culture considers certain characteristics as masculine, he may perceive his own father in these terms, whether or not his father actually fits the description. Burger, Lamp, and Rogers (1975) found that middle-class second-graders feel that their mothers are more accepting than their fathers. As the children grow older, they report declining acceptance from both parents. First- to fourth-graders see their mothers as more controlling than their fathers, but as the children grow older, they report a gradual decrease of control. As psychological control diminishes, though, parental rule-making and limit-setting increase.

Some studies have shown that children from different social classes view their parents differently, reflecting differences in the ways their parents have treated them (Rosen, 1964). Middle-class parents have tended to be more tolerant of children's needs, more likely to consider motives and intentions, more accepting and egalitarian, and more likely to correct by reasoning or appealing to conscience rather than hitting. Lower-class parents—especially fathers—have tended to be more rigid and authoritarian and less accessible to their children. Traditionally, the lower-class father's only role in child rearing has often been as the agent of punishment, whereas the middle-class father has been more of a companion. Middle-class boys aged 9 to 11 have seen their parents as being more able and more ambitious, and they have seen their fathers as being more secure (Rosen, 1964). They have been much more likely to feel their fathers are interested in their school performance and are meeting their requests for attention. In recent years, however, the gap between lower-class and middle-class styles of parenting has been narrowing. People at all levels are becoming more aware of what children need, and fathers at all levels have been assuming larger roles within the family. It will be interesting to see whether these changes in parenting practices will be reflected in changing perceptions of parents by their children.

THE ONE-PARENT FAMILY

Two out of every ten children in the United States are growing up in a home with only one parent, usually because of desertion, separation, or divorce, and sometimes because their mothers never married. In some low-income black neighborhoods, the percentage jumps to 1 child in every 2 (Glick & Norton, 1977). In about 9 out of 10 cases the absent parent is the father. In 1975, while 13 percent of all families were headed by a woman without a husband, only 2 or 3 percent were headed by a man without a wife (Glick & Norton, 1977). About 10 million children are growing up in fatherless homes, and the proportion of children under 18 living in these homes doubled from 8 percent in 1960 to 16 percent in 1976 (U.S. Bureau of Census, 1978; Glick & Norton, 1977). School-age children are somewhat more likely to live with their fathers than are preschoolers, but despite the flurry of recent publicity given to fathers who care for their children, in 9 out of 10 divorce cases, the mother still gets custody (Espenshade, 1979).

How does growing up with only one parent affect children? It is hard to say. Practically no research has been done on the motherless family, and research on the fatherless family is often contradictory. The classic view (supported by some research but unsupported by other work) is that long-term absence of the father affects children's psychological functioning adversely, with especially devastating effects on their sexual identification and functioning. In an overview of the research on the effects of father absence on the personality of boys, Biller (1970) says that

Almost everybody I know has a father and mother. And I'm upset because sometimes kids will tease me because they've got a father and I don't. I don't have a father to stick up for me, or to help me fly airplanes, rockets, and so on. We need a man around the house sometimes to do certain things with me like going to the park, things like that. But sometime I think if he was around, he'd just get in the way.

Gene, age 11,
from *Listen to Us!* p. 81–82

father-absent boys have more trouble achieving a strong masculine identity, especially if their fathers have been away during the boys' preschool years, because the boys have not been able to identify with the fathers. It is harder for them to control impulses and accept delayed gratification because they have not learned to trust people, especially adult males. They're more likely to become delinquent. They score lower on tests of intelligence and academic achievement. They have more trouble making friends in childhood and developing long-term relationships with women later on. They are more anxious and more likely to suffer a variety of emotional problems. And they are not so highly motivated to achieve and, in fact, do not achieve as much career success as males whose fathers were present during childhood.

But Biller, and also Herzog and Sudia (1968), point out some problems in accepting these conclusions. Many studies on fatherlessness have severe deficiencies. Often they do not specify the age of the child during the father's absence, the length of absence, the child's sex, or the reasons for the absence. Often the numbers of children studied are too few. After reviewing some 400 studies, Herzog and Sudia concluded, "Existing data do not permit a decisive answer to questions about the effects on children of fatherlessness" (p. 181).

Children growing up in one-parent homes undoubtedly have more problems and more adjustments to make than children growing up in homes where there are two adults to share the responsibilities for child rearing, to provide a higher income, to more closely approximate cultural expectations of the "ideal family," and to offer a counterpoint of sex-role models and an interplay of personalities. But the two-parent home is not always ideal, and the one-parent home is not necessarily pathological:

It is obvious to any clinician that the two-parent system has its own pathology—the two parents may be in serious conflict as to how their parental roles should be performed; one parent may be competent but have his (or her) efforts undermined by the incompetent partner; the children may be caught in a "double bind" or crossfire between the two parents; both parents may be competent but simply unable to work together as an effective team in rearing their children; one parent may be more competent than the other but be inhibited in using this competence by the team pattern inherent in the two-parent system [LeMasters, 1970, p. 163].

Among a group of divorced women, one commonly cited advantage was the ability to raise one's children without having to cope with a spouse who disagrees with the day-to-day decisions about the children (LeMasters, 1970). Other research has concluded that the attitudes of a single parent are more important in determining the sexual attitudes of children than is the fact of single parenthood itself, that children of unwed mothers are no more likely to be emotionally disturbed than children with fathers (Klein, 1973), and that, in general, children grow up better adjusted when they have a good relationship with one parent than when they grow up in a two-parent home characterized by discord and discontent (Rutter, 1979).

To understand better how single-parent homes differ and how they affect children, it would be well to try to find answers to the following questions: How do tense, angry, unhappy intact homes compare with happy, well-ordered, one-parent homes? How do the parents in successful one-parent homes differ from those whose children have more problems? What are the strengths of one-parent homes? How are they similar to, as well as different from, two-parent homes? Who are the role models who substitute for absent parents and how effective are they? What are the differential effects of the timing and the reasons for parental absences? How do well-adjusted, one-parent children differ from poorly adjusted ones and what might account for these differences?

CHILDREN OF DIVORCE

Every year, more than 1 million American children experience the effects of their parents' divorce (*Monthly Vital Statistics Report*, 1978). Divorce is traumatic for everyone. The dissolution of a marriage stirs up powerful emotions of anger, hate, bitter disappointment, failure, and self-doubt in husband and wife. Children react to the breakup of their parents' marriage even more severely than they would react to the death of a parent, as seen in the fact that children from homes broken by discord are more likely to get into trouble than those from homes broken by death (Rutter, 1979). These children's antisocial behavior, however, appears to be due more to the discord in the home that caused the divorce rather than to the actual separation itself, since children from intact homes where there is a great deal of parental strife are also likely to get into trouble (Rutter, 1979).

No matter how unhappy the marriage has been, however, its breakup still often comes as a shock to the children, who need to adjust to an unfamiliar situation. During the process of adjustment, the children of divorcing parents often feel afraid of the future, guilty for their own (usually imaginary) role in causing the divorce, hurt at the rejection they feel from the parent who moves out, and angry at both parents. They may become depressed, hostile, disruptive, irritable, lonely, sad, accident-prone, or even suicidal; they may suffer from fatigue, insomnia, skin disorders, loss of appetite, or inability to concentrate; and they may lose interest in school work and in social life (McDermott, 1970; Sugar, 1970).

Hetherington, Cox, and Cox (1975) followed forty-eight divorced families for two years after the breakup and compared them with forty-eight intact families to assess the effects of divorce on children's development and family functioning. They found that after a divorce, family life is disrupted and disorganized on many levels. Both parents have a host of new stresses to deal with, including economic pressures (caused by the need to maintain two households), restrictions in social and recreational activities (usually felt more severely by the mother, especially an unemployed mother), and needs for intimate heterosexual relationships.

There are specific differences in parent-child interaction, too. Divorced parents communicate less well with their children, are less consistent, make fewer demands on them for mature behavior, and have less control over them. These differences are greatest during the first year. By the end of the second, a process of reequilibration seems to take place, especially between mothers and children. Over the course of the two years, the fathers become less and less available to their children. Since this study lasted only two years, it is impossible to say whether these divorced families would have continued to readjust until they more closely resembled intact families. All we can say with certainty is that the first two years after divorce are stressful for everyone in the family.

The way a child reacts to parental divorce is affected by his or her sex and age, the length of time the marriage has been in difficulty, and the duration between the first separation and the formal divorce (Sugar, 1970). Probably the most important factor in their lives is how well the parents deal with their children's sensitivities, fears, and anxieties. Things are made worse by a husband and wife who engage in drawn-out custody

A couple of times I thought I did it because of the times that day I was bad. I thought they must be fighting because of me.

Sally, age 8,
from *Listen to Us!* p. 75

fights, who communicate their bitterness toward each other through their children, who transfer their anger to the children, and who suddenly impose adult responsibilities on the children.

Egocentrism often makes children feel that they have caused the difficulties between their parents. One boy knew that his parents were arguing because of his father's infidelity; yet he could not help feeling that if he had not broken a dish that day, the argument might not have taken place (McDermott, 1970). One of the most important tasks of parents facing divorce is the need to reassure their children that they are not responsible for the break. Parents also can help their children by reestablishing regular routines, by finding adults who can help fill the gap left by the missing parent, and by not forcing the children to take sides. The emotional aspects of divorce, rather than the legal considerations, are hardest on children. Divisiveness and discord may go on for years in a legally intact marriage. While a divorce formalizes marital problems, it can eventually create a more harmonious home environment. The initial break is always painful, but many children thrive in an atmosphere that brings hope for a better life after the end of a troubled marriage.

WORKING MOTHERS

One of the most sweeping changes in our society over the past forty years has been the vast increase in women workers. Since the period immediately before World War II, the number of working mothers has increased

more than tenfold, and by 1978 more than half of all mothers with children under 18 were in the labor force (U.S. Department of Labor, 1979). The largest proportion of these women are mothers of school-age children.

Most women work for the same reasons men work: They need the money and they want to orient their lives around their work, as well as their families. Millions of women are the sole support of themselves and their children.

The fewer children a woman has, the older they are, the lower her husband's income, the higher her own education, and the higher the market value of her employment skills—the more likely she is to seek a job (Howell, 1973a). Because of more pressing financial needs and different vocational and sex-role expectations, black women are more likely to work. Many researchers have tried to find out how a mother's outside employment affects her children, but few answers have evolved. Says Howell (1973b):

Since parenting ability may be either enhanced or hindered by employment, it is not surprising that almost every childhood behavior characteristic, and its opposite, can be found among the children of employed mothers. Put another way, there are almost no constant differences found between the children of employed and nonemployed mothers; in general the more careful the methodology of a study, the smaller the differences found [p. 328].

In Hoffman's 1974 review of research on maternal employment, she found that a mother's working can have a variety of effects, depending on many individual factors. In general, she concluded that working mothers provide different role models than nonworking mothers, that employment "affects the mother's emotional state—sometimes providing satisfactions, sometimes role strain, and sometimes guilt—and this, in turn, influences the mother-child interaction," that different situational demands as well as the mother's emotional state affect child-rearing practices,

The children of working mothers do not differ with respect to peer relationships, school performance, IQ, emotional problems, or dependency or independence. (Michael Kagan/Monkmeyer)

If my mother was at home all day and not doing any work, she would do more cleaning and would always have everything ready for us. It's like babying you all your life, so I definitely think it's better that she works, because you become much more independent. You feel free that you make your own decisions, because you've proven that you can by doing it.

And my mother should definitely be able to work. Just because she's a woman, I don't think she should not have the opportunity to do something with her life rather than just sit home.

Melinda, age 13,
from *Listen to Us!* p. 47

and that working mothers provide less adequate supervision. Hoffman did not find that school-aged children suffer any deprivations from their mothers' working, but she could not carry the same conclusions to infants, since we do not have enough research data about very young children.

The timing of a mother's new job may affect children adversely. It is generally best if the parent who has been the baby's principal caretaker can avoid going to work for the first time during the third quarter of a baby's first year, when close attachments are being cemented; around the baby's second birthday, a crucial time for language development; and any time when a child faces other major adjustments such as the loss of a parent through death or divorce, the move to a new home, the birth of a sibling, or school entrance (Howell, 1973b).

Maternal employment can have salutary effects. Children of working mothers are more open in their sex-role views and have higher educational and career aspirations, and the daughters of employed mothers are more likely to select careers in traditionally male fields (Miller, 1974; Etaugh, 1973). Woods's 1972 study of 108 children of working mothers in an urban black ghetto found that mothers who worked full time were most consistent in disciplining their children, who in turn were better adjusted, had higher IQs, and did better in school than the children of mothers who worked occasionally or part time.

By most parameters, the families of women who earn a salary do not differ in any psychologically important way from those who engage in the work of homemaking. Their children do not differ with respect to peer relationships, school grades, IQ, emotional problems, or dependency or independence (Howell, 1973b). The healthy development of children rests on the quality of the care they receive, not on the quantity that is given by their own mothers. Whether the mother works outside the home or in it is less important than whether she enjoys what she is doing. Women who like their lives are more likely to communicate a sense of joy to their children, who, as a result, are likely to be better adjusted (Skard, 1965).

EMOTIONAL DISTURBANCES IN CHILDHOOD

Emotional disturbances in childhood are not uncommon, and they take a variety of forms. Sometimes they show up in uncharacteristic behavior. Sometimes they respond favorably to a relatively brief treatment of psychotherapy. At other times, psychological difficulties show up in other ways, call for other remedies, and are harder to resolve.

BEHAVIOR PROBLEMS

The most common way for children's emotional difficulties to surface is in their behavior. They show by what they do that they need help. They fight, they lie, they steal, they destroy property, and they break rules laid down by parents, school, and other authorities. Extreme forms of this behavior, which get youngsters in trouble with the law, will be discussed in the section about juvenile delinquency in Chapter 11.

Acting-out Behavior

Lying and stealing are among the most common forms of misbehavior in childhood. Almost all children make up fanciful stories as a form of make-believe, or lie occasionally to avoid punishment. But when children past the age of 6 or 7 continue to tell tall tales, they are often signaling a sense of insecurity. They need to make up glamorous stories about themselves to secure the attention and es-

teem of others. Or when lying becomes habitual or transparently obvious, children may be showing hostility toward their parents (Chapman, 1974).

Similarly, occasional minor stealing is common among children. While it needs to be dealt with, it is not a sign that anything is seriously wrong. But when children repeatedly steal from their parents, or steal so blatantly from others that they are easily caught, they are again often showing their hostility toward their parents and their parents' standards. In some cases, the stolen items appear to be "symbolic tokens of parental love, power or authority" (Chapman, 1974, p. 158). This seems to be the case, for example, with Ricky, a lonely boy who feels inadequate and seems to bolster himself by holding onto the money and objects he steals from his father. Any chronic type of antisocial behavior needs to be looked into and examined as a possible symptom of deep-seated emotional upset.

Hyperactivity

The story is an all too familiar one to many parents and teachers. Johnny can't sit still, can't finish a simple task, can't keep a friend, and is always in trouble. His teacher says, "I can't do a thing with him." The family doctor says, "Don't worry, he'll grow out of it." And the next-door neighbor says, "He's a spoiled brat." Finally Johnny's parents are told that he is a "hyperactive child."

What is *hyperactivity*, or *hyperkinesis*, as it is sometimes called? It often looks like the behavior of a seriously disturbed child. Sometimes it is, but often the emotional troubles come after the appearance of the hyperactive behavior, which is so trying to a child's parents, teachers, and friends. Basically, though, the syndrome is neither a disease nor an emotional disorder. It is a cluster of personality traits that appear normally in all children, but more intensely in about 4 percent of the school population (Stewart, Pitts, Craig, & Dieruf, 1966) and possibly 9 percent of boys (Werner, Bierman, French, Simonian, Connor, Smith, & Campbell, 1968).

Hyperactive children probably represent one end of a normal spectrum of personality types (Stewart & Olds, 1973). They are much more active than the average child, especially in situations—like the classroom—where a great deal of activity is considered inappropriate. They are also more impulsive, excitable, impatient, and distractible. All these characteristics create problems for them in their daily life, especially in school.

Hyperactive youngsters are likely to be of normal or above-average intelligence. Yet they have trouble with their schoolwork because they can't concentrate and can't show what they do know. It is difficult for them to sit in their seats long enough to hear a complete lesson or to complete a written assignment. When faced with an unfamiliar word or a perplexing arithmetic problem, they are more likely to blurt out the first thing that comes to mind instead of trying to work out the correct answer.

Parents and teachers can often help hyperactive children do better at home and school through a variety of special techniques. First, they have to understand and accept the child's basic temperament. Then they can teach the child how to break up his or her work into small, manageable segments; they can incorporate physical activity into the daily classroom schedule; and they can offer alternative ways of demonstrating what he or she has learned (such as individual conferences or tape-recorded reports, which take the place of written reports) (Stewart & Olds, 1973).

Sometimes one of a family of stimulant drugs is prescribed for a hyperactive child. These drugs apparently help the children to focus their attention on the tasks at hand and thus to concentrate better. The drugs do not help all hyperactive children do better in school, though. And even when they do appear to bring about an improvement in school performance, it is important to consider the long-range effects of giving drugs to solve a nonmedical problem. If, as many observers believe, these are basically normal children, what will be the ultimate effects of masking their true personalities? Because we don't yet know the answer to this and other equally important questions about the administration of stimulant drugs to children, it is best to consider these drugs only as a last resort, after more conservative ways of handling the problem have been tried.

In recent years, much attention has been given to the possibility of helping these children improve their behavior by putting them on a diet free of artificial food colorings and flavorings (Feingold, 1973). The original claims for improvement stemmed largely from parental comments about their children's improved behavior after having been put on the additive-free diets. Such testimonials, though, seem to represent a *placebo* effect. A placebo is a substance that contains no real medication; yet the patient, feeling that he or she is taking a potent medicine, is likely to report improvement. Wender (1977) observes:

Those researchers experienced in behavioral studies would expect a noticeable placebo effect when a treatment involves changing a family's pattern of eating plus increasing attention paid to the hyperkinetic child through the special shopping and cooking required to implement the diet [p. 4].

Apparently, this is what happened with the special diets, because in studies using a "double blind" technique, in which neither the child, the child's family, nor the researcher knew when the child was getting additives or not, behavioral differences were noticed either minimally or not at all (Harley, Matthews, & Eichman, 1978).

DEVELOPMENTAL DISORDERS

Some troubling behaviors appear to be caused by delays or abnormalities of development related to biological maturation. Children often outgrow these conditions but may suffer undesirable side effects in the meantime. For example, the child who wets his bed is handicapped in his social life because he can't sleep over at a friend's house or go away to summer camp. The child who develops a facial tic is humiliated when other children make fun of her. So the appearance of any of the following conditions calls for attention.

Bed-Wetting, or Enuresis

Most children stay dry, day and night, by the age of 3 to 5 years, but bed-wetting is the most common chronic condition seen by the typical pediatrician (Starfield, 1978). About 10 percent of children—twice as many boys as girls—continue to wet the bed regularly at the age of 5, about 5 percent at age 10, and 1 to 2 percent during the teen years. Most outgrow the habit without any special help (Barker, 1979). Less than 1 percent of bed wetters have any physical disorder, and researchers are still trying to find out why the other 99 percent can't stay dry at night. There are a wide range of theories, including emotional disturbance (children who wet the bed periodically often do so after some emotionally charged episode, although most enuretic children have no other symptoms of psychological disturbance); genetic factors (adults who wet the bed in childhood are more likely to have enuretic children, and identical twins are more likely than fraternals to be concordant for bed-wetting); physiological factors (enuretic children have functionally small bladders and some disturbance of sleep cycles); a lack of proper training; and delayed maturation of the nervous system (Chapman, 1974; Bakwin, 1971d; Starfield, 1978; Barker, 1979; Stewart & Olds, 1973). In most cases it is impossible to pinpoint the precise cause.

Part of the treatment includes reassuring children and parents that the problem is common, that in itself it is not serious, and that the child should not be blamed or punished. One guideline is for parents not to do anything unless the child himself sees his bed-wetting as a problem. Some of the most effective measures for treating enuresis include rewarding the child for staying dry; using electrical devices that ring bells or buzzers when the child begins to urinate; administering various drugs; and teaching the child to practice controlling the sphincter muscles that control bladder function (Chapman, 1974).

Soiling, or Encopresis

Soiling the underpants with fecal matter is a problem that sometimes begins simply because a child becomes so absorbed in play that he or she neglects going to the bathroom. It may also arise from constipation that makes defecation painful, from short-term emotional stress caused by such experiences as the birth of a sibling or the illness or death of a parent, or from more deeply entrenched emotional problems.

Encopresis, which is also more common among boys, usually disappears without treatment, although it may last two or three years. With treatment, it often improves in a few weeks or months. In any case, it is rarely seen after puberty. Yet it should be dealt with, since it can have severe emotional effects while it lasts, stemming from the fact that the encopretic child emits such a foul odor that he or she is subject to ostracism, ridicule, and scorn.

Treatments include structuring a definite time of day for defecating, with a reward for achievement; administering a laxative or bowel-softener; and counseling the parents to help them resolve situational stresses such as conflicts over toilet training, parental obsession with children's bowel functioning, or sibling rivalry (Chapman, 1974; Barker, 1979; Stewart & Olds, 1973).

Tics

Children often develop *tics*, or repetitive, involuntary muscular movements. They blink their eyes, hunch their shoulders, twist their necks, bob their heads, lick their lips, grimace, grunt, snort, and utter guttural or nasal sounds. More common among boys than girls, tics appear most often between the ages of 4 and 10, and usually go away before adolescence (Chapman, 1974).

Emotionally caused tics may arise from stresses in the child's past or current relationships. Some psychiatrists feel that children release emotional turmoil in this way. One 8-year-old boy, for example, exhibited several different tics. He was very passive and inhibited, substituting his tics for the aggressive things he wanted to say and do. After a year of weekly psychotherapy sessions, he became more assertive and gradually lost about 95 percent of his tics (Chapman, 1974).

Not all tics are emotionally caused, however. Some seem to have a neurological basis, as exhibited by those people who suffer from *Tourette's syndrome*, a disorder characterized by a variety of muscular and vocal tics (Shapiro, Shapiro, & Wayne, 1973). This malady appears to be physiological in origin, possibly the result of a chemical imbalance in the brain. The administration of a drug that is known to block the effects of one of the chemicals in the brain often provides dramatic relief. Tourette's sufferers often lose one tic, only to replace it with another, unlike youngsters who suffer from transient tics of childhood, which tend to disappear without being replaced.

Stuttering

At least four times as common in boys as in girls, this condition, also known as *stammering*, shows up in millions of young children in the form of halting speech with repetitive and inhibited sounds. It usually begins before the child begins school and is likely to disappear by early adolescence. Some 2 million American adults, however, continue to stutter (Pines, 1977).

The many theories about the cause of stuttering range over the physical, including faulty training in articulation and breathing,

mixed cerebral dominance (as in naturally left-handed children forced to use their right hands), and a defect in the system that provides feedback about one's own speech. Theories linking it to emotional causes point to parental pressures about proper speech or deep-seated emotional conflicts (Barker, 1979; Pines, 1977). Treatment is varied, also; it includes psychotherapy and counseling, speech therapy, the administration of certain drugs, and various other special techniques.

Most of the techniques concentrate on training stutterers to unlearn the patterns of learned motor responses that they have developed over the years. They are taught to speak slowly and deliberately; to breathe slowly and deeply, using abdominal muscles rather than those of the upper chest; and to start up their voices gently, as opposed to the abrupt and forceful way many stutterers use. Computers to monitor the voice, videotape machines, and metronomes worn like hearing aids are among the battery of technological developments that help stutterers. One program, which uses many of these aids and also has stutterers practice using the telephone, asking strangers for directions, and participating in other high-stress speaking situations, has found good success rates on follow-up but maintains that the ultimate success for any individual rests on how assiduously he or she continues to practice the skills learned in the course (Pines, 1977).

NEUROTIC DISORDERS

Everyone becomes anxious sometimes in dealing with stressful situations in life. What, then, constitutes a neurosis? Barker (1979) defines a neurotic disorder as a morbidly anxious reaction to stress, with the anxiety so severe and persistent that it interferes in some way with the individual's adjustment in society. People with neurotic disorders still have a fairly clear perception of the environment, as opposed to those suffering from psychoses. After conduct disorders, neuroses are the second most common group of psychiatric disturbances of childhood. In the conditions described below, the symptoms usually associated with one may alternate with or replace those of another.

Neurotic disorders include:

Anxiety neuroses, whereby the child expresses anxiety directly, through such symptoms as shyness, clinging, overdependence, social isolation, sleep problems, and psychosomatic ailments like nausea, abdominal pain, diarrhea, or headaches.

Phobias, in which the child shows irrational fear of particular objects or situations, such as snakes, dogs, buses, doctors, enclosed or open spaces, heights, or water. Phobias often respond well to behavior therapy. School phobia, discussed on pages 298–299, is the one most commonly brought to the attention of professionals.

Obsessive-compulsive neuroses, in which the child is consumed with *obsessions*, or thoughts and ideas he or she knows to be unreasonable but can't shake, and is driven to act out such thoughts in the form of *compulsions*. An example is the boy who is afraid something will happen to his parents if he does not carry out such rituals as getting his clothes out of the locker without touching the edges, bringing his books out of a box by taking them backward and forward four times across the side, and walking across the dining room only by one particular route (Barker, 1979).

Neurotic-depressive conditions, in which the child is sad and depressed, crying, showing little or no interest in people or activities, having eating and sleeping problems, and sometimes talking about wanting to be dead. These children are often dealing with real environmental stress, such as the loss or threatened loss of a parent through illness or separation, or the child's feeling that she or he cannot live up to parental expectations, say, in school or sports.

PSYCHOTIC ILLNESSES

Fortunately, *psychosis*, or a severe emotional disturbance that is characterized by a loss of contact with reality, is rare in childhood. When it does occur, it is often difficult to diagnose, but one fairly constant sign is the child's failure to make normal emotional contact with other people. Two of the most common childhood psychoses, which may even be variants of the same disorder, are autism and schizophrenia.

Early Infantile Autism

This disorder may begin as early as the fourth month of life, when the baby may lie in the crib, apathetic and oblivious to the people around him. In other cases, the baby may seem normal in infancy and then develop the symptoms at about 18 months of age (Bettelheim, 1967). Because of the nature of the symptoms, autistic children are sometimes misdiagnosed as mentally retarded, deaf-mute, or organically brain-damaged. They are twice as likely to be boys as girls.

These children seem to have erected a wall between them and all other people, even their parents. They do not make eye contact with others and don't even indicate that they've heard their parents speaking to them. They cannot empathize with others and have no ability to appreciate humor.

Autistic children usually have language disturbances. One out of three never develops speech at all, but only grunts and whines instead. Others repeat the same phrases over and over or parrot what other people have said to them. They are often devoid of inner language, as well, and cannot even play by themselves above a primitive, sensorimotor level (Barker, 1979).

Autistic children often fill the void left by the absence of interpersonal relationships in their lives with an overwhelming preoccupation with things. They become compulsive about the arrangements of objects and often engage in simple, repetitive physical activities with objects for long periods of time. If these activities are interrupted, they may react with fear or rage. One 4-year-old boy would play with crayons for several hours each day, over and over again letting them slide down a slanted surface and then moving the bottom crayon to the top. Others remain motionless for hours, like one 7-year-old girl who would look raptly at her clasped hands for hours every day (Chapman, 1974).

On intelligence tests, autistic children's scores range from severely abnormal to high average. Some show astonishing isolated skills: While functioning poorly in general, they may be able to recite long poems, sing unusually well, or perform difficult mathematical problems.

The cause of early infantile autism is unknown. Some psychiatrists speculate that these children did not develop normally because they did not receive enough parental warmth. Yet the disorder rarely occurs in more than one child in a family, and it is possible that parents often *become* cold and distant because they feel rejected by their autistic child. Other theories include metabolic or chromosomal defects as causes, but here, too, proof is lacking.

Knobloch and Pasamanick (1975) compared fifty autistic children with fifty who had organic brain injury, and followed the children for up to ten years. The authors found autistic children very similar to the others in their birth and medical histories and concluded that the autism was physically caused. They recommend the use of behavior modification techniques to manage the children's day-to-day behavior, but they discourage psycho-

therapy as being neither indicated nor effective.

The disease has a painfully discouraging prognosis. Only 5 percent of autistic children make good social adjustments in adulthood, while 20 percent make fair adjustments, and 75 percent are socially incapacitated and must be closely supervised (Chapman, 1974). Treatment may consist of outpatient psychotherapy, drugs, or long-term treatment in a residential center, but whether or not a child receives treatment—and the kind of treatment he or she gets—seems to make little difference in the long run.

Childhood Schizophrenia

The most common psychosis of childhood, schizophrenia is characterized by an escape from reality and a withdrawal from relationships with others. Again, the syndrome is much more common in boys. Most childhood schizophrenics have *some* contact with people: instead of a wall, there is a curtain between them and the rest of the world.

These children have facial expressions that are either habitually flat or habitually agitated. They are occasionally mute, but more often talk incessantly, using bizarre words in ways that make no sense to those around them. Their incoherent speech is often a frustrating attempt to express their deep fears and preoccupations. They often live in their own inner fantasy worlds, beset by hallucinations. One 8-year-old boy, for example, was making passing grades at school despite almost continual hallucinations. He had enough of a sense of reality to realize that people would think he was strange for having hallucinations, and so he told no one about them until he had had them for 18 months and finally told his mother (Chapman, 1974).

The disease is usually diagnosed when the child is in the first two or three grades of

In play therapy, the therapist gets clues about what is bothering the child from the way he or she plays with a doll family or other toys. (Sybil Shelton/ Monkmeyer)

school, but the child almost always has had problems before then in relationships with both children and adults.

Again, no one knows what causes schizophrenia. In our discussion of heredity on page 35, we pointed to a body of research that points to an organic basis for the disease, deriving from some dysfunction of the metabolic, hormonal, or central nervous systems. Some psychiatrists lean more toward explanations based on unhealthy personal relationships in the family.

Here, too, the prognosis is poor, with only about 5 percent of diagnosed schizophrenics making a complete recovery in adulthood and most continuing to have difficulties, often to the point of needing lengthy institutionalization (Chapman, 1974).

TREATMENT TECHNIQUES FOR EMOTIONAL PROBLEMS IN CHILDHOOD

The choice of a specific mode of treatment for any particular situation depends on many factors: the nature of the problem, the child's personality, the willingness of the family to participate, the availability of treatment in the community, the financial resources of the family, and, very often, the orientation of the professional first consulted.

Psychotherapy

Individual psychotherapy itself takes several forms. There is *preventive therapy*, which may be offered to a child at a time of great stress such as the death of a parent, even before the child exhibits any symptoms of disturbance. Then there is occasional *supportive therapy*, which offers the child the chance to talk about his or her worries with a friendly and sympathetic person, who can help the youngster cope more easily with the stresses in his or her life. In *play therapy*, the therapist gets clues about what is bothering the child from the way he or she plays with a doll family or other toys. In rare cases, the lengthy, intensive techniques of *child psychoanalysis*, which aim to restructure a child's personality, may be used. In most cases, however, children are not introspective enough to look that deeply into their personalities nor enough in control to make extensive changes.

Most psychotherapy tries to give the child insight into his or her personality traits, and into his or her relationships with others, both in the past and in the present (Barker, 1979). To accomplish these aims, the therapist accepts the child's feelings and helps the youngster to understand and cope with them. The therapist does this by interpreting what the child says and does, both in the therapy sessions and in everyday life, as reported in the sessions.

Child psychotherapy is usually much more effective when combined with some form of counseling for the parents. Often a different professional helps the parents to deal with their sense of inadequacy in having had to bring their child for treatment and with their guilt in feeling that they have caused the problem. They also focus on ways to cope most effectively with the present situation.

Family Therapy

In this approach the entire family is the patient. The therapist sees the whole family together, observes the way they act with one another, and points out to them their patterns in functioning—both the growth-producing patterns and the inhibiting or destructive ones.

Sometimes the child whose problem brings the family into therapy is, ironically, the healthiest member, responding in a relatively wholesome way to a sick situation. This was true in the case of 10-year-old Peggy, who had threatened her parents with a kitchen knife after they told her that her dog had died, when in fact they had taken him to the A.S.P.C.A. Therapy brought out an atmosphere of hostility and dishonesty permeating all the family relationships, an attempt by all members to avoid coming to grips with their problems, and, ultimately, a basic conflict between husband and wife that had set the stage for Peggy's problems and those of her 16-year-old brother, who was getting into trouble at school. Through therapy the parents were able to confront their own differences and begin to resolve them, thus taking the first step toward solving the children's problems as well.

Behavior Therapy

Also called behavior modification, this approach uses learning-theory principles to alter behavior—to eliminate undesirable behaviors like bed-wetting or temper tantrums, or to

January 22. Mama said if I want to be a lady when I grow up, I better start right now. We have a chart on the bathroom wall (to record washing, brushing teeth, cleaning nails, etc.) I get a blue star each day and a gold star for a perfect week. If I have twelve gold stars at the end, on Sunday I get a prize, which is 25 cents—that's the part I like. But the part I don't like is, if I miss I have to forfeit something.

Margaret O'Brien, age 10,
from *Small Voices*, p. 76

develop desirable ones like being on time or doing household chores. The therapist does not look for underlying reasons for the child's behavior and does not try to offer the child insight into his or her situation, but aims simply to change the behavior itself.

The approach is especially effective in dealing with specific isolated symptoms, such as phobic fears, which can be dealt with by systematic desensitization (see page 233), or bed-wetting, which responds well to the buzzer technique (see page 332). In operant conditioning, the child gets a reward like candy or praise or a token that can be exchanged for toys whenever she or he performs the behavior being encouraged (like putting one's dirty clothes in the hamper).

Parents and teachers who use this approach find it useful for dealing with many specific behaviors. When a child's problems are more deep-seated, though, behavior therapy needs to be supplemented by psychotherapy for the child and/or the parents.

Drug Therapy

Over the past three decades the number of available prescription drugs has mushroomed: Ninety percent of all the drugs available today were unknown thirty years ago (Stewart & Olds, 1973). With the proliferation of new drugs have come many that are used to treat emotional disorders in both adults and children. Today it is not uncommon to find tranquilizers prescribed for preschool insomniacs, antidepressants for bed wetters, stimulants for hyperactive children, and a range of other medications for children with a variety of behavioral, neurotic, or psychotic problems.

Giving pills to children in order to change their behavior is a radical step, especially since so many medicines have undesirable side effects, both known and unknown. Furthermore, the drugs themselves relieve only the symptoms of behavior and do not get at the underlying causes. At times the short-term prescription of a specific medicine may be indicated, but in most cases a psychotherapeutic or behavioral approach is likely to provide safer, longer-lasting effects in helping children resolve their problems.

SUMMARY

1 The middle child is in Freud's *latency period*, a time of relative sexual quiescence compared with the stormier preschool and adolescent periods. However, children maintain interest in sexual functioning and masturbate, engage in bodily explorations of each other, and talk about sexual matters. *Defense mechanisms* are used by the school-age child to combat anxiety; these include *regression, repression, sublimation, projection,* and *reaction formation.*   **2** *Industry versus inferiority* is the fourth of Erikson's eight developmental crises. Children learn those skills necessary for survival in their particular culture and face a sense of inferiority if they are much less successful in this pursuit than are their peers.   **3** *Childhood societies* exist in all cultures and throughout all recorded history. Older children pass down traditional lore, rhymes, humor, and games to younger children.   **4** The *peer group* assumes an important role during middle childhood, since a child spends more and more time away from the family and in the company of friends. The peer group is important in the development of identity, attitudes, and values, and as a socializing agent. The influence of the group is powerful, and a child's position in the group greatly influences self-concept. Adults also influence a child's standing in the group. In some cultures, such as Russia and Israel, the peer group has been used to carry out the goals of society. *Behavior modification* programs in American classrooms also might enlist the peer group to improve children's behaviors. Friendships are more significant now than in earlier years and children see friendship as involving give-and-take.   **5** *Self-concept* refers to one's self-image. Coopersmith isolated four factors that influence self-concept development: *significance, competence, virtue,* and *power.* The higher an individual rates on all four variables, the higher the self-regard. Self-concept is influenced by parental characteristics, early birth order, small family size, school success, and personality traits.   **6** Prejudice is shown in children as young as age 2. Recent research indicates that techniques such as telling positive stories about black children can reduce racial prejudice.   **7**   Sex typing becomes more stable during the school years. Extrafamily influences such as the school and textbooks are powerful in establishing sex typing.   **8**   Although a child spends a great deal of time with peers, the family still is an important influence. Children grow up in a variety of family situations—in homes with one or two parents, with mothers who work in or outside the home, in a nuclear family, in a kibbutz, or commune. In any of these home situations, an atmosphere of love, support, and respect for family members will provide an excellent prognosis for healthy development.   **9**   Emotional disturbances such as behavior problems, developmental disorders, and neuroses are not uncommon. A variety of treatment techniques—from psychotherapy to behavior therapy—are used.

SUGGESTED READINGS

Bettelheim, B.   *The children of the dream*. New York: Avon, 1969. A thorough study of communal child rearing in Israel. This book discusses both the strengths and weaknesses of this system and the possible future it has for ghetto children.

Bronfenbrenner, V.   *Two worlds of childhood: U.S. and U.S.S.R.* New York: Russell Sage, 1970. A comparative study of child-rearing methods of the United States and the Soviet Union.

Coopersmith, S.   *Antecedents of self-esteem*. San Francisco: Freeman, 1967. A thorough and thought-provoking report of an in-depth study of eighty-five boys, 10 to 12 years old, which correlated the boys' levels of self-esteem with parental attitudes and child-rearing practices, as well as with other aspects of the boys' functioning.

Gardner, R. A.   *The boys and girls book about divorce*. New York: Bantam, 1971. A sensitive guide for the children of divorced parents, written by a child psychiatrist, which presents in clear, straightforward terms many of the issues that trouble children, such as anger, blame, fear, and divided loyalties.

Gardner, R. A.   *The parents book about divorce*. Garden City, NY: Doubleday, 1977. A psychiatrist discusses the effect of divorce on children and deals with such thorny issues as how, when, and how much to tell the children; custody and visitation; and ways of helping children adjust to their new lives. He makes many controversial and thought-provoking suggestions.

Hoffman, L., & Nye, F.   *Working mothers*. San Francisco: Jossey-Bass, 1974. A collection of scholarly articles dealing with the mother who works outside the home and the consequences of her employment on self, husband, and child.

Hope, K., & Young, H. (Eds.)   *Momma: The sourcebook for single mothers*. New York: New American Library, 1976. A compilation of short articles by single parents giving a composite picture of what their lives are like and offering practical information about divorce, working, education, and helping children adjust to their parents' separation.

Lewis, M., & Rosenbaum, L. (Eds.)   *Friendship and peer relations*. New York: Wiley, 1975. A collection of articles focusing on the importance of peer relations in the child's development.

340

Liebert, R., Neale, J., & Davidson, E.   *The early window: Effects of television on children and youth*. New York: Pergamon, 1973. A report of the effects of television on aggression and social behavior. A discussion of television commercials and the question of government versus self-regulation of the television industry is included.

Olds, S. W.   *The mother who works outside the home*. New York: Child Study Press, 1975. A booklet that discusses the effects of a mother's working on her children and her marriage and offers practical suggestions.

Stewart, M. A., & Olds, S. W.   *Raising a hyperactive child*. New York: Harper & Row, 1973. A book for the lay reader that defines the characteristics of hyperactivity, explores possible causes, and offers practical suggestions to parents and teachers for the day-to-day management of hyperactive children.

Adolescence

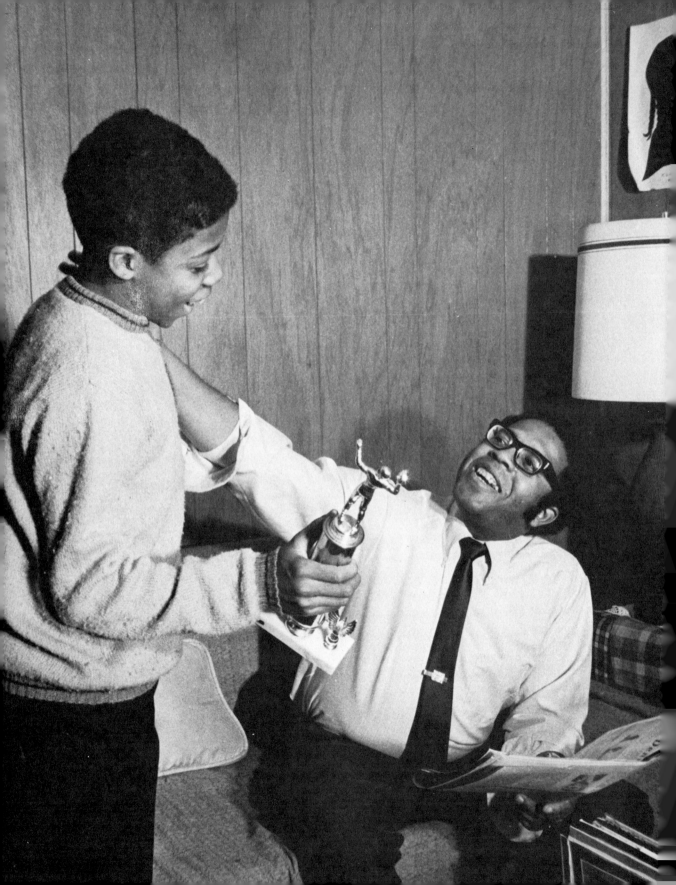

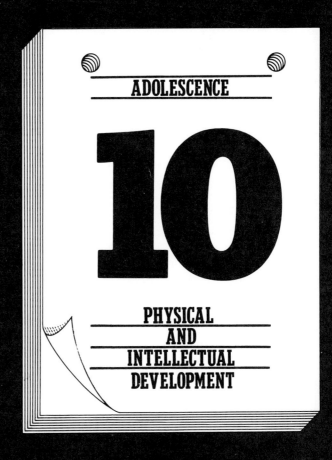

ADOLESCENCE

10

PHYSICAL
AND
INTELLECTUAL
DEVELOPMENT

IN THIS CHAPTER
YOU WILL LEARN ABOUT

Adolescence and youth as developmental stages

The physical changes adolescents go through during puberty, and how these changes affect personality development, especially self-concept

How adolescents' intellectual development enables them to consider *all* possibilities, and how this affects moral reasoning

The influence of status, sex, parents, school, and personality on vocational development

How going to college—or dropping out—influences development

CHAPTER OVERVIEW

ADOLESCENCE

Adolescence is the span of years between childhood and adulthood. In Western society it begins at about the age of 12 or 13 and ends at either the late teens or early twenties. Its beginning is heralded by the onset of *pubescence*, that stage of rapid physiological growth when reproductive functions and primary sex organs mature, and when secondary sex characteristics appear. Pubescence lasts about two years and ends in *puberty*, the point at which an individual is sexually mature and able to reproduce.

The end of adolescence is harder to mark. In some societies it ends at puberty. Intellectually, maturity is reached when the person is capable of abstract thought. Sociological adulthood is attained when an individual is self-supporting, has chosen a career, has married, or has founded a family. Legal adulthood comes when one can vote (at age 18), marry without parental permission (usually 18 for girls, 21 for boys), enlist in the army (17), or be responsible for legal contracts (21). Psychological adulthood is reached when one discovers one's identity, becomes independent from parents, develops a system of values, and is able to form mature relationships of friendship and love. Some people never leave adolescence, no matter what their chronological age.

ADOLESCENCE AS A DEVELOPMENTAL STAGE

Adolescence as we know it is a relatively recent phenomenon. Before the twentieth century it was not considered a developmental stage at all. Instead, children went through puberty and immediately entered some sort of apprenticeship in the adult world. Now, however, the period between puberty and adulthood is longer and has taken on a character of its own. It is longer for the physical reason that young people mature earlier today than they did a century ago, and for the sociological reason that our complex society requires a longer period of education and thus financial dependence.

In many contemporary primitive societies, children still move abruptly into adulthood at some preordained age, or at *menarche*, the first appearance of menstruation. Puberty rites take different forms, ranging from severe tests of strength and endurance that include mutilation such as circumcision (of both boys and girls), teeth filing, ear piercing, or elaborate tattooing or scarring. Or these rites can be relatively painless ceremonies that involve religious blessings, separation from the family, or acts of magic. The Bar Mitzvah for 13-year-old Jewish boys and the coming-out party for 18-year-old debutantes mark aspects of adult status, as do high school and college graduation, getting a driver's license, and giving up one's virginity. But in modern Western society, no *single* initiation rite signifies adulthood.

PHYSIOLOGICAL CHANGES OF ADOLESCENCE

THE TIMING OF MATURATION

Puberty is the time of life when the greatest sexual differentiation since the early prenatal stage takes place. At this point a person is sexually mature and able to reproduce.

Wednesday, 5 January 1944

I think what is happening to me is so wonderful and not only what can be seen on my body, but all that is taking place inside. I never discuss myself or any of these things with anybody; that is why I have to talk to myself about them.

Anne Frank, age 14,
from *The Diary of a Young Girl* in
Revelations: Diaries of Women, p. 37.

My voice was changing; and, curiously enough, I realize now why I began to be interested in singing. It was the pin-feather rooster starting to crow, though I did not know that my urge to sing, and that of other boys in school had its biological root....

So we young roosters used to roam about the town at night serenading chiefly our various "girls," though sometimes singing under windows of prominent citizens for the very joy of it.

William Allen White, age 14–15,
The Autobiography of William Allen White, p. 93.

Pubescence, the period during which an individual enters puberty, is characterized by the *adolescent growth spurt*, a sharp increase in height that occurs in girls between the ages of 8½ and 13 and in boys between 10 and 16. Soon after the growth spurt ends, the young person reaches sexual maturity. For girls, *menarche*, the beginning of menstruation, signals the onset of sexual maturation, although there is often a period of sterility after the first menstrual event. The presence of sperm in the male's urine may signal sexual maturation for boys. For both sexes, the appearance of pigmented pubic hair is a sign of sexual maturation.

During this time, changes in the primary and secondary sex characteristics occur, with individual variation in timing. The *primary sex characteristics* are those directly related to the sex organs, such as the gradual enlargement of the female's ovaries, uterus, and vagina, and of the male's testes, prostate gland, and seminal vesicles. The *secondary sex characteristics* include other physiological signs of maturity such as breast development in girls and broadening of the shoulders in boys. Other secondary sex characteristics that appear in both sexes are voice changes, skin changes, and the growth of pubic, facial, axillary (under the armpits), and body hair.

While the sequence of pubertal events also varies among adolescents, it is much more consistent than their timing. The first sign of pubescence for boys is generally the beginning enlargement of the testicles, accompanied by changes in the texture and color of the skin on the scrotum. Later, the penis enlarges and pubic hair appears. In girls the first sign of the approach of puberty is the development of breast buds some time between the ages of 9 and 13. This is followed by the growth of pubic hair (Tanner, 1978).

The Secular Trend in Growth and Maturation

People reach sexual maturity sooner, and grow faster and bigger than they used to, attaining adult height earlier. This trend toward larger size and earlier maturation is known as the *secular trend*.

In the United States the normal healthy son will be as much as 1 inch taller and 10 pounds heavier than his father. The normal healthy girl will be ½ to 1 inch taller, 2 pounds heavier, and will experience menarche about 10 months earlier than her mother [Muuss, 1970, p. 52].

Changes in size and age of maturity have occurred among children all over the world, including those from Poland, China, Japan, New Zealand, and Italy (Muuss, 1970). The most obvious explanation appears to be the influence of a higher standard of living. Children who are healthier, better nourished, and better cared for mature earlier and grow bigger. During famines and economic crises, the secular trend is often reversed (Tanner, 1968). It is also explained as a function of hybrid vigor, or the "bicycle effect": When improved methods of transportation brought together young men and women from different geographical areas, dominant genes—such as those for tallness—were able to reach more people.

The secular trend began about 100 years ago and now seems to have ended. A leveling off of growth showed up a few decades ago in the middle and upper classes. Boys entering Harvard University from *private* schools in 1958 and 1959 were not taller than boys from these same schools in the 1930s, but public school boys of the 1950s were taller than those of the 1930s, probably reflecting advances in living standards in less affluent families (Bakwin & McLaughlin, 1964). Now this leveling off is true of virtually the entire American population (Schmeck, 1976). This stability of stature for the population as a whole—except for those children who are the smallest for their age—probably reflects higher living standards in most, though still not all, sectors of the nation.

PHYSICAL MANIFESTATIONS OF ADOLESCENCE

Growth

One of the early signs of maturation is the *adolescent growth spurt*, a sharp increase in height that usually takes place in girls between the ages of 8½ and 13 and in boys between 10 and 16. Before the adolescent growth spurt, boys are only about 2 percent taller than girls; during the years from 11 to 13, the girls are taller, heavier, and stronger; after the male growth spurt, boys are again larger, now by about 8 percent. The male spurt seems more intense, and its later appearance allows an extra period for growth, since prepubertal growth is faster than postpubertal growth.

For both sexes, the adolescent growth spurt is comprehensive, affecting practically all skeletal and muscular dimensions. Even

the eye grows faster during this period, causing an upsurge of near-sightedness at about this age. The jaw usually becomes longer and thicker; both it and the nose project more; and the incisors of both jaws become more upright. These changes are greater in boys than in girls (Tanner, 1964), which helps to explain how it could have been acceptable to an Elizabethan audience to see a teenage male actor playing the part of Viola, the young woman in Shakespeare's *Twelfth Night*, who was passing as a young boy.

Before adolescence, boys are slightly stronger on the average than girls, but the difference is tiny. After the adolescent growth spurt, the male's larger muscles, larger heart and lungs, and greater capacity for carrying oxygen in the blood confer considerably greater strength and endurance (Tanner, 1964). Many adult women, however, are stronger than many men because of body build or a high rate of physical activity.

Boys and girls grow differently during adolescence, resulting in different body shapes. The male becomes larger overall, his shoulders wider, his legs longer relative to his trunk, and his forearm longer relative to both upper arm and height (Tanner, 1964). The female pelvis widens to make childbearing easier, and layers of fat are laid down just under the skin, giving the woman a more rounded appearance. Some boys continue to grow until about 25 years of age, and some girls till about 21; but most males reach adult height at 21 years, and most females at 17 (Roche & Davila, 1972).

Secondary Sex Characteristics

HAIR GROWTH Straight, fine hair, slightly darker than other body hair, begins to grow in the pubic area. After some months—or, sometimes years—this pubic hair becomes coarse and kinky. *Axillary hair* begins to grow under the armpits. And then, to the joy of adolescent boys, facial hair appears. The lesser amounts of facial hair that appear on some girls, often on the upper lip, are usually a cause of dismay

My hands and feet were....far from being feminine and dainty. For a sixteen-year-old my breasts were sadly undeveloped. They could only be called skin swellings, even by the kindest critic. The line from my rib-cage to my knees fell straight without a ridge to disturb its direction. Younger girls than I boasted of having to shave under their arms, but my armpits were as smooth as my face.

Maya Angelou,
I Know Why the Caged Bird Sings, p. 233.

and embarrassment, although it is perfectly normal, especially among dark-complexioned and dark-haired ethnic groups. Chest hair generally appears quite late in adolescence. Welcomed as a badge of manhood by many boys, girls who may perceive some wispy strands of hair that are growing between their breasts or around their nipples may be concerned, although such a phenomenon is also perfectly normal.

BREAST DEVELOPMENT   While a female's mammary glands begin to develop at about the sixth week of prenatal life and the principal milk ducts are already present at birth, outward manifestations do not appear before puberty. The nipples enlarge and protrude; the *areolas*, those pigmented areas surrounding the nipples, enlarge; and the breasts assume first a conical and then a rounded shape. They usually achieve their full growth before menarche. Sometimes one breast can grow more quickly than the other but, although one generally remains slightly larger, this difference is not noticeable upon maturity. (This left-right asymmetry also appears with regard to the size of feet, hands, testes, and virtually every other pair of body parts.)

Some adolescent boys experience temporary breast enlargement, which may last for some twelve to eighteen months before disappearing.

NOCTURNAL EMISSIONS   Very often the pubescent boy will awaken to find a wet spot or a hardened, dried spot in his bed. This will let him know that while he was asleep he had a *nocturnal emission*, or an ejaculation of semen. Often—but not always—such an emission occurs in connection with an erotic dream. Most youths who are not having sexual intercourse on a fairly regular basis experience these perfectly normal emissions.

SKIN CHANGES   The most obvious skin changes in adolescence are the outbreaks of pimples and blackheads that herald the appearance of *acne*. Caused by the increased activity of the sebaceous glands, which make the skin oilier, and by the enlargement of pores and coarsening of skin texture that occur at this time of life, acne is the bane of many a teenager's life. Most troublesome in boys, it is believed to be due to increased amounts of the male hormone *androgen*.

The activity of the sebaceous glands also makes the hair oilier during adolescence, and the sweat glands work overtime, causing the body odor to become stronger.

MENSTRUATION   She is dangerous because she can dry up the well and scare animals; she is good and can increase the food supply; she is especially susceptible to enemy magic; she is possessed of a powerful supernatural blessing. Who is she? The menstruating girl, as seen by several different cultures (Muuss, 1975). *Menstruation*, the monthly sloughing off of the lining of the unfertilized womb, first occurs when a girl's height spurt has slowed down, at an average age of 12.8 to 13.2 years. Usually, the early periods do not include ovulation, and most girls are not able to conceive for some twelve to eighteen months after their first menstrual period (Tanner, 1978).

Menarche has been occurring earlier over the past century. Like the secular trend in growth, this change also seems to have been caused by improved environmental conditions, and it, too, has apparently ended. The average age at which girls first menstruate has not changed over the last thirty years (Zacharias, Rand, & Wurtman, 1976). Climate has little or no effect—Nigerian and Eskimo girls have very similar menarchal ages—but other factors do. City girls mature earlier than country girls, as do girls from small families compared with girls from large families, and mildly obese girls compared with normal girls (but normal girls mature earlier than extremely obese girls); girls born early in the year menstruate sooner than those born at the end of the year; and girls from high altitudes menstruate later (Zacharias & Wurtman, 1969). All these relationships seem related to economic, especially nutritional, standards.

Genetics also appears to play a part in the timing of menarche. Identical twins differ by only 2.8 months, while fraternal twins differ by a year, sisters by 12.9 months, and unrelated women by 18.6 months (Hiernaux, 1968). Frisch (1972) hypothesizes that a critical weight triggers menarche, citing evidence that the mean weight at menarche of Caucasian girls has been about 106 pounds for more than a century. Other researchers, though, have failed to find support for this theory (Johnston, Roche, Schell, & Wettenhall, 1975).

Menstruation has different meanings in different societies, in different subcultures within a society, and in different families. In 1933, Conklin found that most American girls matter-of-factly accepted menarche; although some were ashamed and embarrassed, others were joyful and excited. Thirty years later, Shainess (1961) found that such differences appear to be related to how well prepared girls are for menarche, in terms of both information and attitudes. Of 103 upper-middle-class women surveyed, 21 percent had had no advance preparation, and several had been afraid that their bleeding was a result of injury. Among girls who had had some advance knowledge, 3 out of 4 still feared, worried about, or actually dreaded the onset of menstruation. Only 15 percent of all the mothers showed pleasure when their daughters had told them that their menses had come. Generally, girls have a more positive attitude when they know what to expect ahead of time, when they do not experience much monthly discomfort, and when their family and friends do not treat the menses as an illness or a cursed burden of womanhood.

In 1975, thirty-five white middle-class girls were found to experience menarche as a disturbing event; they showed fear, shame, and great concern with cleanliness, and they avoided their fathers. Whisnant and Zegans (1975) concluded that cleanliness and hygiene are overstressed for adolescent girls, at the expense of their psychological needs.

HOW PHYSICAL DEVELOPMENT AFFECTS PERSONALITY

Most young teenagers are more concerned about their physical appearance than about any other aspect of themselves (Jersild, 1952), and about one-third of all boys and one-half of all girls in one longitudinal study expressed worries about at least one aspect of their appearance (Stolz & Stolz, 1944).

What worries teenagers the most? Everything. But some things more than others. Boys want to be tall and broad-shouldered, while girls want to be slim though bosomy. Anything that makes a boy think he looks feminine (such as a slight physique or lack of a beard) or a girl think she looks masculine (a large-boned frame or facial hair) makes either one miserable. Both sexes want to look like everyone else and are uncomfortable when they mature much earlier or later than their peers.

Adolescent self-concepts depend largely

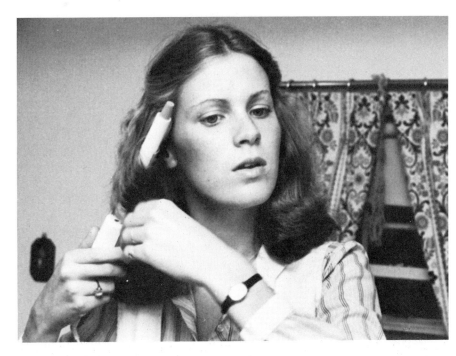

Most teenagers are more concerned about their physical appearance than about any other aspect of themselves. (Suzanne Szasz)

on how attractive young people consider themselves. Adults who considered themselves attractive during their teenage years have higher self-esteem and are happier than less comely people. Not until the mid-forties do the differences in happiness disappear for those who had been attractive or homely adolescents (Berscheid, Walster, & Bohrnstedt, 1973).

How is a teenager's weight level related to other aspects of his or her life? Hendry and Gillies (1978) categorized almost a thousand 15- and 16-year-olds as "overweight," "underweight," or "average," and then took a variety of other measures. They found surprisingly few differences, but those that did emerge differentiated more between overweight and other girls than among any of the other groups. This was especially true of ratings obtained from the students' physical education teachers.

What, then, were the findings? All the groups participated in sports to about the same extent, and no differences emerged in gym teachers' assessments of the students' friendliness, popularity, and reliability. There

were some differences, though: Fat teenagers were the least fit and disliked their bodies the most; fat girls were more likely to come from working-class homes, to have lower academic abilities than other girls, and to be seen by their teachers as less attractive, less enthusiastic, and less physically able than average girls; thin girls were more introverted and less competitive than other girls; underweight boys and girls struck their teachers as being more socially nervous; and both heavy and thin teens were less likely than average ones to have steady boyfriends or girlfriends.

According to classic studies performed in the 1950s, the timing of maturation also has psychological effects, usually more pronounced for boys. A high school boy whose growth has not yet spurted, whose voice is high, and whose cheeks are smooth looks like a little boy next to his earlier-maturing classmates. He can't compete with them either athletically or socially. An early maturer is generally considered and treated as more of a man, is more popular, and is more likely to be a school leader (Jones, 1957). Furthermore, he is likely to score, on the average, slightly higher than a later maturer of the same age in most tests of intellectual ability, an edge that he seems to retain in adulthood (Tanner, 1978). Mussen and Jones (1957) gave the Thematic Apperception Test (TAT) to thirty-three 17-year-old boys, sixteen early maturers and seventeen late maturers. The TAT is a projective test of personality that asks the testee to tell stoies about a series of pictures. Based on the boys' stories, the researchers concluded that late maturers are more likely to feel inadequate, to consider themselves rejected and dominated, to be dependent, to rebel more against their parents, and to think less of themselves. Early maturers showed self-confidence, independence, and the ability to play an adult role in interpersonal relationships. Mussen and Jones (1957) also found that late-maturing boys try harder to be accepted socially, but their attempts in this direction are often childish and affected. They exhibit more aggressive behavior, probably because of their basic insecurity.

Gross and Duke (1980) have reported on their analysis of data from the Cycle III on the National Examination Survey. Between 1966 and 1970, extensive health and behavioral data were collected on a probability sample of 3514 males and 3196 females aged 12 to 17 who were selected to mirror the adolescent population of the entire United States. Preliminary analysis indicated that late-maturing males were "educationally disadvantaged" compared to early and mid-maturers.

Among late maturing males 15% were characterized as above average in intellectual development compared with 27% of the mid-maturers and 52% of early maturers. This effect for late maturers was even more marked for the older boys who were obviously out of synchrony with their age mates [Gross & Duke, p. 75].

Another interesting finding in this study concerns body image: Early-maturing boys and girls report themselves as being thinner than the late maturers—but early-maturing boys are satisfied with their weight while early-maturing girls tend to express dissatisfaction.

Research findings about girls have been contradictory. When the TAT was administered to thirty-four early- and late-maturing 17-year-old girls, the early maturers seemed to be better adjusted; yet, ratings of these girls by both peers and adult observers over the previous six years had seemed to favor the late maturers (Jones & Mussen, 1958).

By adulthood, most differences between early- and late-maturing males have disappeared, but a few vestiges remain (Jones, 1957). Among twenty 33-year-old men, there were no differences between those who had matured early and those who had matured late in terms of size, physical attractiveness, educational attainment, marital status, or family size. While few personality differences showed up, the early maturers did seem to show earlier patterns of career success, and they were more concerned with "making a good impression." The late maturers were more flexible, assertive, insightful, self-indulgent, and touchy. Jones (1957) says:

We might speculate . . . that in the course of having to adapt to difficult status problems, the late-maturers have gained some insights and are indeed more flexible, while the early-maturing, capitalizing on their ability to make a good impression, may have clung to their earlier success pattern to the extent of becoming somewhat rigid or over-controlled [p. 120].

ANOREXIA NERVOSA

Stephanie, 15, weighed 67 pounds at the time of her death. She was a victim—not of poverty, parental neglect, or famine—but rather of a bizarre psychosomatic disorder that occurs almost entirely in adolescent girls. *Anorexia nervosa* is a prolonged and severe refusal to eat, which leads to death in 5 to 15 percent of anorexics in psychiatric treatment (Blum, 1974). Ten girls to every boy suffer from it (Forfar & Arneil, 1973).

The malady affects bright, friendly, well-behaved, appealing girls from apparently loving, stable, well-educated, well-off families. In these families there is often a great emphasis on food and eating. The girls themselves tend to be preoccupied with food—they like to cook, like to talk about food, and like to urge others to eat. They go on eating binges, but then follow these with extended fasting, self-induced vomiting, strenuous exercising, or excessive use of laxatives.

The condition often appears after someone has said something to the girl about getting fat, or else soon after menarche (Barker, 1976). Once the starvation begins, menstruation usually stops, along with such evidence of sexual development as the emergence of breasts and rounded hips. The girls have a distorted sense of body image and see themselves as beautiful when they are at their most pathetically and grotesquely skeletal.

Many psychiatrists see the disease as a fear of growing up, possibly because the girl sees growing up as a threat: It means having to become independent from her parents, and it means being put under heavy pressures to succeed in life. Some therapists also see the disease as an extreme symptom of family malfunctioning, theorizing that it may be a reaction to overprotective parents and to parents who have difficulty handling conflicts openly.

Treatment must be established as soon as the symptoms are recognized. The girl is likely to be put in the hospital, where she may be given a twenty-four-hour nurse, drugs to encourage eating and inhibit vomiting, and behavior therapy, which rewards her for eating by granting such privileges as getting out of bed and leaving the room. Such immediate measures need to be combined with psychotherapy, to change the basic attitudes that have brought her to this pass. Therapy, which almost always involves the family to some degree, is oriented toward getting the girl to

become more aware of her own feelings and needs and to become able to act in a self-directed, competent way (Bruch, 1977).

One hundred anorexics, all but twelve of whom had had refeeding and/or psychotherapy, were contacted four to eight years after they had first gone to the doctor (Hsu, Crisp, & Harding, 1979). Of these young women, forty-eight, or almost half, had a good outcome: Their weight was now about normal, they were menstruating regularly, and they appeared to be well adjusted, both socially and sexually. Of the others, the outcome was only fair for thirty, poor for twenty, and two had died. The patients who were doing poorly were likely to have had the illness longer and more severely; to have developed it at a later age; to have had such symptoms as vomiting, an insatiable appetite, or anxiety when eating with others; and to have had few or no friends in childhood and poor relationships with their parents.

INTELLECTUAL DEVELOPMENT IN ADOLESCENCE

Adolescents can now think in terms of what *might* be true, rather than just in terms of what they see in a concrete situation. Since they can imagine an infinite variety of possibilities, they are capable of hypothetical reasoning.

PIAGET'S STAGE OF FORMAL OPERATIONS

Adolescence ushers in a new level of intellectual development, demonstrated by differing reactions to this story told by Peel (1967):

Only brave pilots are allowed to fly over high mountains. A fighter pilot flying over the Alps collided with an aerial cable-way, and cut a main cable causing some cars to fall to the glacier below. Several peple were killed.

A child still at the Piagetian level of *concrete operations* said, "I think that the pilot was not very good at flying. He would have been better off if he went on fighting." This child assumes only one possible reason for an event. In this case of the crash, the likeliest explanation to him was that the pilot was inept. By contrast, a young person who had attained the level that Piaget calls *formal operations* said, "He was either not informed of the mountain railway on his route or he was flying too low also his flying compass may have been affected by something before or after take-off this setting him off course causing collision with the cable." This youngster was considering all kinds of possible explanations for the crash.

The development from stage to stage can be traced by following the progress of a typical child in dealing with a classical Piagetian problem in formal reasoning, the *pendulum problem*. This child is shown the pendulum, which consists of an object hanging from a string, and is then shown how he can change the length of the string, the weight of the object, the height from which the object is released, and the amount of force he can use to push it. He is then asked to determine which of these factors, either alone or combined with others, determines how fast the object swings.

When Jason first saw the pendulum, he was not yet 7 years old. At that time he was unable to formulate a plan for attacking the problem, but instead tried one thing after another in a hit-or-miss manner. First he pushed a long pendulum with a light weight, then he swang a short pendulum with a heavy weight, and then he removed the weight entirely. Not only was his method completely slapdash, but he couldn't even understand or report what had actually happened. He was convinced that his pushes made the pendu-

lum go faster, and even though this was not so, he reported it as observed fact.

The next time Jason was faced with the pendulum, he was 11. His more advanced age showed in the way he tackled the problem this time. He did look at some possible solutions, and he even hit upon a partially correct answer. But he failed to try out every possible solution in a systematic way. He varied the length of the string, and he varied the weight of the object, and he thought that both length and weight affected the speed of the swing. He was still failing to keep one dimension constant while he varied the other.

Not until Jason and the pendulum met again in adolescence did he go at his old friend in a thorough, well-organized manner. He now realized that any one of the four factors, or some combination of them, might affect the speed of the swing. So he carefully designed an experiment to test all the possible hypotheses, holding constant one factor while he varied another. By carefully doing this, he was able to determine that one factor—the length of the string—is the only one that determines how fast the pendulum swings. (This description of age-related differences in the approach to the pendulum problem is adapted from Ginsburg & Opper, 1979.)

By solving the pendulum problem the way he did, Jason illustrated his arrival in the stage of *formal operations*, a cognitive level, which, according to Piaget's theory, begins at about the age of 12. Jason can now think in terms of what might be true and not just what he sees in a concrete situation. Since he can imagine an infinite variety of possibilities, he is, for the first time, capable of hypothetical reasoning. Once he develops a hypothesis, he can then construct a scientific experiment to test that hypothesis and to deduce whether it is true. He is now capable of *hypothetico-deductive* reasoning. He considers all the possible relationships that might exist and goes through them one by one, to eliminate the false and arrive at the true. This systematic process of reasoning operates for all sorts of

In the process of living and learning, individuals integrate what they have learned to plan their future careers and lifestyles. (Charles Gatewood)

problems. People can now integrate what they have learned in the past with their problems of the present and their planning for the future. They apply these thought processes to the mechanics of day-to-day living, and also to the construction of elaborate political and philosophical theories.

As adolescents' neurological structures develop, their social environment widens, and opportunities for experimentation arise. The interaction of these factors brings about the maturation of the cognitive structures. According to Piaget, by about the age of 16, a person's way of thinking is almost fully formed. After this time, the cognitive structures do not undergo further modification. There are no more qualitative leaps. The mental structures—well enough developed now to enable

adolescents to handle a wide variety of intellectual problems—are said by Piaget to be in an advanced state of equilibrium. But if teenagers' culture and education have not encouraged them to engage in hypothetico-deductive reasoning, they may never attain this stage, even though they have the necessary neurological development.

In fact, Kohlberg and Gilligan (1971) report that almost half of American adults never reach this stage at all. Their conclusions are based on several studies of the degree of success attained by people of various ages on different formal operations tasks. In one experiment, for example, among 265 persons given the pendulum task, the percentages of those passing it at different ages are as follows:

ages 10 to 15:   45 percent

ages 16 to 20:   53 percent

ages 21 to 30:   65 percent

ages 45 to 50:   57 percent

Going by this criterion and the figures from this cross-sectional study, we see that it is not until after the age of 21 that a strong majority of people reach the level of formal operations. A large proportion of Americans may never develop the capacity for abstract thought.

Ginsburg and Opper (1979) summarize some thoughts about adolescent intellectual activity:

The effect of the adolescent's intellectual achievements is not necessarily limited to the area of scientific problem-solving. Piaget finds repercussions of formal thought on several areas of adolescent life, although his remarks probably hold more particularly for certain subgroups within European cultures than for American culture. In the intellectual sphere,

...information was exciting for itself alone. I burrowed myself into caves of facts, and found delight in the logical resolutions of mathematics.

Maya Angelou,
I Know Why the Caged Bird Sings, p. 243.

the adolescent has a tendency to become involved in abstract and theoretical matters, constructing elaborate political theories or inventing complex philosophical doctrines. The adolescent may develop plans for the complete reorganization of society or indulge in metaphysical speculation. After discovering capabilities for abstract thought, he then proceeds to exercise them without restraint. Indeed, in the process of exploring these new abilities the adolescent sometimes loses touch with reality, and feels that he can accomplish everything by thought alone. In the emotional sphere the adolescent now becomes capable of directing emotions at abstract ideals and not just toward people. Whereas earlier the adolescent could love his mother or hate a peer, now he can love freedom or hate exploitation. The adolescent has developed a new mode of life: the possible and the ideal captivate both mind and feeling [p. 201].

THE EGOCENTRISM OF ADOLESCENCE

Despite adolescents' abilities to conceptualize ideas and to take a scientific approach in looking at phenomena, their thought is not yet completely adult in nature because of their lingering egocentrism. No longer children, they now recognize that other people have their own thoughts too. However, since they are preoccupied with themselves, they believe that these thoughts of others invariably focus on them. "It is this belief that others are preoccupied with his appearance and behav-

ior that constitutes the egocentrism of the adolescent" (Elkind, 1967, p. 1030). This egocentrism does, therefore, interfere with their ability to think abstractly and hypothetically.

Two illustrations of adolescent egocentrism are the *imaginary audience* and the *personal fable*.

When Josh hears his parents whispering, he "knows" they are talking about him. When Amanda passes a couple of boys laughing raucously, she "knows" they are ridiculing her. Many adolescents feel under constant scrutiny from everyone and think that others are as admiring or as critical of them as they are of themselves. This belief "that others in our immediate vicinity are as concerned with our thoughts and behavior as we ourselves are" (Elkind & Bowen, 1979, p. 38) is known as the *imaginary audience*.

To confirm this concept. Elkind and Bowen (1979) administered to almost 700 students in the fourth, sixth, eighth, and twelfth grades a scale of questions designed to test the young people's levels of self-consciousness and their willingness to reveal themselves to an audience. Situations covered included finding a grease spot on their dress or pants at the beginning of the most exciting dress-up party of the year and being asked to get up in front of their class to talk about a hobby or read a story they had written. The eighth-graders—especially the girls—turned out to be more self-conscious and less willing than older or younger students to reveal themselves to an audience, thus validating the concept of the imaginary audience in early adolescence.

A counterpart to the imaginary audience, the *personal fable* is the adolescent's belief that he or she is special because so many people are interested in him or her. Wendy *knows* that no one ever before in the history of the world has felt the way she does. No one ever loved so much; no one was ever so misunderstood; no one was ever so sensitive to injustice. Her belief in her uniqueness leads to a belief that she is not subject to the rules

Sometimes I reflect with horror
that when I am grown up I
shall be just an ordinary young
girl, with a simple, grey little
life, so that in the end there
won't be any difference between
me and other people: that all
my dreams and feelings are
only the ferment of youth. Deep
pain comes over me and something tightens in my heart. "Am
I really but one of the crowd?" I
ask myself despairingly. "Just
that" is the sad answer.

Nelly Ptaschkina, age 15,
The Diary of Nelly Ptaschkina, pp. 148–149.

at a mature level of thinking (Looft, 1971). As the thought process of adolescents mature, they are better able to think about their own identities, to form adult relationships with other people, and to determine how and where they fit into their society.

ADOLESCENT MORAL DEVELOPMENT

Not until adolescents have attained the Piagetian stage of abstract formal operations can they reach the most highly advanced stages of moral development, according to Kohlberg. People have to be capable of abstract reasoning to understand universal moral principles. Advanced cognitive development does not *guarantee* advanced moral development, but it *must exist* for the moral development to take place. Kohlberg and Gilligan (1971) state that people cannot shift from conventional to postconventional stages of moral thinking until they have a grasp of the relative nature of moral standards. They need to understand that every society comes up with its own definition of right and wrong, and that what is totally acceptable in one culture may be considered a grave sin in another. Many young people discover this concept of relativism in college, which probably explains why college students often score at the postconventional level. (This emphasis on the influence of college learning is one basis for charges that Kohlberg's theories are elitist.)

Kohlberg's first two stages of moral reasoning (see Table 8-4) generally characterize childhood thought, although some delinquents—as well as other adolescents and adults—still think in terms of stage-2 precepts of self-interest. In general, though, adolescents range through conventional stages 3 and 4, and postconventional stages 5 and 6. Most adolescents—like most adults—are at Kohlberg's conventional stage of moral devel-

that govern the rest of the world. She is magically protected from the things that can happen to other people. The personal fable makes a girl think that *she* can't get pregnant or a boy think that *he* can't get killed on the highway. "These things only happen to other people, not to me" is the unconscious assumption that helps to explain much adolescent risk-taking.

Overcoming Adolescent Egocentrism

Elkind (1967) feels that egocentrism diminishes at about age 15 or 16, when the young person "gradually comes to recognize the difference between his own preoccupations and the interests and concerns of others" (p. 46). At this time the imaginary audience becomes the real audience, and the personal fable gives way to the understanding that one is like other people.

Eventually, adolescents realize that others are not preoccupied with them, but that they have their own concerns about themselves. With this realization, they overcome egocentric thinking. The more they talk about their own personal theories and listen to those of other young people, the sooner they arrive opment (level II). They conform to social conventions, are motivated to support the status quo, and think in terms of doing the right thing to please others or to obey the law.

College-educated middle-class youth are those most likely to think at stages 5 and 6. Only 1 out of 10 adults reaches stage 6. As we listen to "law and order" political campaign speeches, we realize how many adults are functioning at stage 4.

The different ways adolescents react to the moral dilemmas posed by Kohlberg illustrate the differences in their reasoning. Let's look at the sequence of moral development in respect to the value of human life (Kohlberg, 1968):

Stage 1: When Tommy, 10, is asked, "Is it better to save the life of one important person or a lot of unimportant people?", he says, "all the people that aren't important because one man just has one house, maybe a lot of furniture, but a whole bunch of people have an awful lot of furniture. . . ."

He is confusing the value of people with the value of their property.

Stage 2: Tommy, 13, is asked whether a doctor should "mercy kill" a fatally ill woman requesting death because of pain. He answers, "Maybe it would be good to put her out of her pain, she'd be better off that way. But the husband wouldn't want it, it's not like an animal. If a pet dies you can get along without it—it isn't something you really need. Well, you can get a new wife, but it's not really the same."

He is thinking of the woman's value in terms of what she can do for her husband.

Stage 3: At 16, Tommy answers the same question by saying, "It might be best for her, but her husband—it's a human life—not like an

animal; it just doesn't have the same relationship that a human being does to a family. . . ."

He identifies with the husband's distinctively human empathy and love, but he still doesn't realize that the woman's life would have value even if her husband didn't love her or even if she had no husband.

Stage 4: At 16, another boy, Richard, answers by saying, "I don't know. In one way, it's murder, it's not a right or privilege of man to decide who shall live and who should die. God put life into everybody on earth and you're taking away something from that person that came directly from God, and you're destroying something that is very sacred, it's in a way part of God and it's almost destroying a part of God when you kill a person."

He sees life as sacred because it was created by God, an authority.

Stage 5: At 20, Richard says: "There are more and more people in the medical profession who think it is a hardship on everyone, the person, the family, when you know they are going to die. When a person is kept alive by an artificial lung or kidney it's more like being a vegetable than being a human. If it's her own choice, I think there are certain rights and privileges that go along with being a human being."

He now defines the value of life in terms of equal and universal human rights in a context of relativity, in a concern for the quality of that life, and out of concern for the practical consequences.

Stage 6: At 24, Richard answers, "A human life takes precedence over any other moral or legal value, whoever it is. A human life has inherent value whether or not it is valued by a particular individual."

Richard now sees the value of human life as absolute and not because it is derived from or dependent on social or divine authority. There is a universality to his thinking, which transcends cultural boundaries.

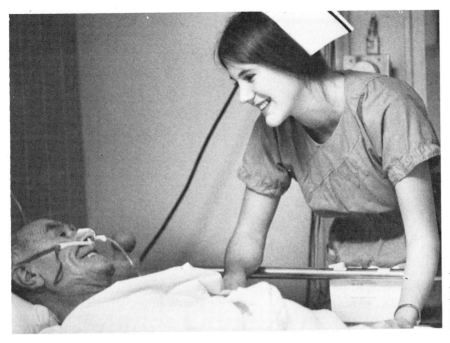

The adolescent search for identity is closely tied to vocational aspirations. (Sherry Suris/Photo Researchers, Inc.)

Kohlberg is committed to the belief that people can be taught to elevate their moral thinking—not by moralizing or preaching, or by rewarding or punishing, but by confronting people with difficult moral dilemmas and helping them to develop their thinking in regard to them. Such help can be given by exposing them to people whose thinking is one stage advanced or by offering them opportunities to take the roles of persons with different moral orientations. Social interaction with peers is essential for reorganizing and restructuring earlier ways of thinking. Adolescents who rate high in social participation and social interaction advance more rapidly through the moral stages than those who are socially inactive, either through lack of opportunity or psychological reluctance (Keasey, 1971). Arbuthnot (1975) found that role-taking among 17- to 21-year-old college students can either advance or retard their moral judgment. Those students who assume the role of a person at a higher level of moral reasoning will enhance their thinking. The thinking of those who role-play a person at a lower level will regress. So teachers and parents who want to advance young persons' moral reasoning should pro-

vide them with opportunities for discussing, interpreting, and role-playing moral dilemmas.

VOCATIONAL DEVELOPMENT

The adolescent search for identity, discussed in Chapter 11, is closely tied to vocational aspirations. The question "Who shall I be?" is very close to "What shall I do?" and it is a major preoccupation of this age. Many factors affect a person's search for meaningful work. Socioeconomic status, parental ambitions and encouragement, schooling, individual ability and personality, sex, race, societal values, and the accident of particular life experiences all play their parts.

Monday, August 12

Oh dear! How am I going to be an author and thumb the dictionary all the while looking up the right spelling? We girls have an elegant plot. We just got that worked out yesterday. Oh its scrumptious!

Kathie Gray, age 13,
Kathie's Diary: Leaves from an Old, Old Diary, pp. 54–55.

Socioeconomic Status

Most of us are greatly influenced in our vocational goals by the kinds of homes we grow up in. Generally, the lower the social class, the lower the goal. Most people are more comfortable in familiar situations, and most people are more familiar with people of similar social class. Children who grow up in working-class neighborhoods are more likely to know adults who work as plumbers, postal workers, and hairdressers rather than doctors, lawyers, and professors. They become more familiar with both the jobholders and the jobs, which then appear more attainable. While young people often aim to reach higher socioeconomic levels than those of their parents, generally they aspire only to the next higher rung.

Hollingshead (1949) asked high school students what kinds of jobs they aspired to. Only 7 percent from the lowest social class in the study aimed for business and professional careers, while 77 percent from the two highest classes had such goals. At that time upper- and middle-class high school students had more of an idea of what they wanted to do than did teenagers from working-class homes. Today the proportions might well be reversed. Many first-year college students have only the haziest notion of the type of work they want to do, and some are still at sea after they receive their diplomas. Some volunteer for service projects like the Peace Corps until they come to grips with what they want to do. Others take low-level jobs while clarifying their ultimate occupational goals.

Parents

If parents do not encourage children to pursue higher education and are not willing to help them through college, it is that much harder for the students. Some do work their way through school, or take out loans, or win

At the age of sixteen when I let everyone know that I was going to be a great writer, my friends and family took the news quite calmly, my mother included. She did not become angry. She quite simply assumed that I had gone off my nut. She was illiterate and her peasant life in Italy made her believe that only a son of the nobility could possibly be a writer.

from Mario Puzo, "Choosing a Dream: Italians in Hell's Kitchen," quoted in *Generations: Your Family in Modern American History*, eds. Jim Watts and Allen F. Davis (New York: Alfred A. Knopf, 1978), p. 42.

scholarships. But, by and large, parental encouragement and financial support influence aspiration as well as achievement. When parents are ambitious for their children and reward them for good school work, the children aspire to occupations higher than their parents' (Bell, 1963). Parental encouragement is a better predictor of high ambition than is social class.

School

The particular school students attend can affect their choice of occupation. Studies of high school students have shown that the sons of manual workers have higher educational and career aspirations when they attend largely middle-class schools than when they go to school mostly with other children of the working class. Similarly, sons of professionals have higher goals when they go to school with other upper- and middle-class youths than when they attend schools that have a high proportion of students from lower-class families (Boyle, 1966; Wilson, 1959). This effect is more pronounced in large, heterogeneous communities.

Personality

Huey Long, the controversial politician, was brash and egotistical all his life. He would go to almost any length to get attention, he manipulated people for his own ends, and he made up his own rules for behavior. Commented Williams (1969, p. 37), "These are qualities that make an ordinary person the opposite of endearing—but in a politician they are called genius."

The typical successful politician has a very different personality from the typical successful nuclear physicist. A restless, energetic, outgoing person is more likely to succeed in politics, sales, or military life than in accounting or scientific research. A shy, thoughtful person would be happier as a librarian than as a trial lawyer.

Most jobs require certain personality traits as well as particular talents. People who know themselves well enough to pick work that suits them temperamentally are more likely to be successful. A study of 638 bright, college-bound high school seniors found that the students had formed definite ideas of personality types common to various occupations, and they saw their own personalities in terms of vocational stereotypes (Holland, 1963 I, 1963 II). These students saw engineers as practical and useful builders, physicists as dedicated intellectuals, teachers as patient and helpful, accountants as precise but dull, artists as creative and temperamental, and business executives as smart, busy, and ambitious (Holland, 1963 I). Girls who expressed interest in scientific vocations saw themselves as analytical, curious, precise, and thorough, while girls interested in social work thought of themselves as easygoing, accepting of others, friendly and understanding. Boys who looked to business careers considered themselves aggressive, dominant, energetic, and *not* artistic, idealistic, quiet, or scientific; while boys with artistic leanings saw themselves as dreamy, idealistic, impractical, and sensitive (Holland, 1963 II).

People also tend to enter occupations in which job duties match what they are good at. Boys who expressed interest in skilled trades said they most enjoyed working with their hands, tools, equipment, or apparatus; girls attracted to accounting jobs said they were most competent in solving numerical problems (Holland, 1963 III).

People also go into particular careers to fill basic personality needs. A woman may become a psychiatrist to clear up questions about herself, or a man may become a business executive because he wants to wield power. High school seniors who were asked to rate jobs according to the personality needs they fulfill showed that they viewed the jobs and the jobholders quite differently. They considered scientists and engineers to be motivated by needs for achievement, but not by needs for affection. Physicians and nurses emerged as being much warmer, with needs for close human relationships (Dipboye & Anderson, 1961).

THE COLLEGE EXPERIENCE

Those high school seniors who go on to college go for many reasons: to earn a degree that they need to pursue a profession they have already decided upon (such as accounting, medicine, law, psychology); to explore different fields of study in an effort to find out what they do want to do with their lives; to earn more money later in life; to expand their intellectual horizons; to establish social contacts; to find someone to marry; to gain some time to continue to grow up; to mark time till they know what to do; or because they can't think of any reason *not* to go to college. Bird (1975) says, "The main thing college does for students is to get them away from home without having to break with their parents or earn their own living" (p. 17).

Not all students benefit from college, and a number of influential observers now recommend that fewer of them go directly from high school to college. Bird (1975) recommends a number of alternatives to college that fulfill many of the above objectives, including vocational training, travel, apprenticeships and learning jobs, working in the arts, mastering a craft or skill, owning a business, joining the armed forces, doing independent study, volunteering full time at a public service task, and working out of doors or at a temporary low-level job. In view of the large numbers of students who do go to college—some 9 million in 1975 (Bird)—there is surprisingly little research on the intellectual and personality development that takes place during these years.

Perry (1970) studied intellectual development in the college years by interviewing sixty-seven Harvard and Radcliffe students over their four undergraduate years. In the ways these students responded to academic and social challenges, they demonstrated a progression in their thought, from extreme rigidity to flexibility and an ultimate commitment. First, students see the world in polar terms, in which every question has a right answer known to an Authority, who must teach it. Then as they encounter a wide variety of ideas, both within the academic curriculum and from other students, they move through positions in which they accept pluralism and uncertainty as legitimate—but still temporary. (Eventually, they still expect to learn the one right answer.) Next they see the relativism of all knowledge and values, recognizing that different societies, different cultures, and different individuals have to work out their own value systems. Finally they realize what this relativism means in terms of their own life choices, and they affirm their identity through the values and commitments they choose for themselves.

One study that sought to find out how success in college relates to success in later life came up with some important findings. Heath (1978) followed up sixty-eight graduates of Haverford College, a small and highly selective men's liberal arts college. Ten to fifteen years after graduation, these men's

> I remember little about that first year in Emporia College, except that it was fun to get the best of old Dr. Cruickshank, the Greek professor... and I stumbled through the year of Greek as a thick-headed blunderer as ever thumbed a pony. But my Latin was good.
>
> William Allen White, age 17,
> *The Autobiography of William Allen White*, p. 103.

> My happiest memories of those college days involve sports. In freshman year I played on the Poet lings (Whittier College) basketball team, and we had a perfect season for the year: we lost every game. In fact, the only trophy I have to show for having played basketball is a porcelain dental bridge. In one game, jumping for a rebound, a forward from La Verne College hit me in the mouth with his elbow and broke my top front teeth in half.
>
> Richard M. Nixon,
> *Memoirs of Richard Nixon* (New York: Grosset & Dunlop, 1978), p. 19.

maturity and competence as professional and family men had virtually no relation to their college academic records. In fact, the honor students—those who had earned the highest grades and won the most awards—tended, in their thirties, to be more depressed, less involved with their children, less close with their wives, and more tense and distant with their colleagues than men who had achieved more modestly in school. These men were now, on the average, more mature and competent in their thirties. Since they had also been more mature and competent as students, Heath concludes that colleges should orient both their admissions and educational policies toward character development, emphasizing an awareness of self and a respect and sensitivity toward others, instead of concentrating so much on academic superiority.

Kurfiss (1977) found that college students are most likely to advance first in those areas in which they are most closely engaged such as those relating to their education, after which they apply this concept to other areas. She suggests that both educational planning and career counseling can be more effective if they take into account students' positions in this progression from rigidity to flexibility, and thus, to self-determination.

Madison (1969) bases his theories of personality development in college on biographical data gathered from a number of students. After analyzing these, he concludes that the college student is more a mixture of child and adult than most people have recognized, and that a major impact of college lies in the student's questioning many of the incorrect assumptions held over from childhood, replacing them with more adult concepts, and in the process advancing the establishment of adult identity.

Individuals change in response to the diversity of the student body, which poses challenges to one's long-held views and values; to the student culture itself, which is structured differently from society at large; to the curriculum, which may offer new insights and new ways of thinking; and, occasionally, to members of the faculty, who take a personal interest in a student and provide a new set of role models.

The form that changes may take can be seen in the process of choosing a major and career. Trixie, one of the students studied by Madison, first made a tentative choice of a career in astronomy, based upon what astronomy represented to her before she got to college ["adventure, being a pioneer, being superior, being like a man, being different from Lucy, being strong like Father, being the opposite of weak Mother" (p. 52)]. At college she discovered psychology, which was better suited to her interests in herself and in other people, as well as her scientific leanings. So she reorganized her life more realistically as a result of her discoveries about herself and about the specific academic disciplines.

Sex Differences in Development in College

Male and female students have tended to develop differently, both intellectually and with regard to personality, and in recent years the disparities have been increasingly questioned.

One problem is that women students have lower self-esteem and lower aspirations than men. When 3347 undergraduates at six prestigious colleges were questioned, 61 percent of the men said they felt confident that they were well prepared for graduate school, compared to only 49 percent of the women. More men than women expected to earn a doctorate, go on to medical or law school or into business management, while more women than men prepared assignments before each class, took careful class notes, and panicked over exams or assignments (Leland et al., 1979). Says one of this study's coordinators, "Women underestimate their academic ability by overpreparing for exams and so on and they underestimate their career goals. If these women, who are the cream of the college crop, don't have high aspirations, it's very likely that others feel the same way" (New York Times, 1978, p. 85).

Sternglanz and Lyberger-Ficek (1975) were puzzled at the shift between girls' superiority in school during the early years and through high school, which then changes to inferior performance at the higher levels. They studied students and lecturers of sixty college classes to determine patterns of differences by sex. They found that there were more male students in all classes, except those taught by women; in these, the sexes were divided equally. They also found that men raised their hands more and were more likely to respond to the instructor in most classes—again, except for classes taught by women, where both sexes behaved similarly. Both male and female professors treated male and female students equally, and so the differences in student behaviors were apparently not direct responses to teacher cues.

The authors suggest that women may be less inhibited in female-taught classes because of the effect of having a female model in front of them—which makes a good case for colleges' hiring more women on their faculties. The differences in interaction in the male-taught classes, despite the professors' apparently equal treatment of both sexes, may be a result of students' having been treated differently earlier in life and, as a result, not recognizing the equal treatment they are now receiving.

These findings may have implications for graduate study. Since most professors are male and since women students respond better in female-taught classes, women may not receive as much encouragement to pursue graduate training. If colleges hire more women and make special efforts to train female students to be more assertive in male-taught classes, more women may elect to go on to graduate school.

Madison (1969) attributes the differences in the development of college women to their preoccupation with boyfriends and thoughts of marriage, maintaining that this preoccupation retards the intellectual development even of many women who enter college planning to pursue a definite career. These women often experience a confusion about identity, because they need to establish themselves in terms of their present abilities and future roles in society—and at the same time have a much more readily accepted identity as a dating partner and future wife. While college men also have an identity as a dating partner and future husband, their major preoccupation at this time of life is with developing their career potential. The young man's identity problems

are just as pressing, says Madison, but are "more straightforward" than the young woman's. He concludes (1969):

Exposing bright and ambitious girls to a fine college is not enough. Powerful forces are at work in society that shape a different course for the girl. By the time she arrives as a freshman, these shaping influences have already become so much a part of the girl's personality structure that she offers only weak resistance to the forces that push her in traditional directions . . . Something different is called for in the college girl's life, some different kind of college and some teaching procedures that would allow [a bright woman] to develop her potential [p. 150].

One thing that colleges can focus on is getting across the message that a successful woman can still be womanly, that she need not be, in Mead's (1939) words, "unsexed by sucess." Many women, though, do fear success for just this reason. Horner (1970) asked female students to write a story based on this situation: "After first-term finals, Anne finds herself at the top of the medical school class." Male students were given the same sentence, about "John." Of ninety women, fifty wrote stories representing fear of success; they expressed their fears of rejection, concern about their femininity, or denial of the success itself. Of eighty-eight men, only eight wrote such stories.

Leaving College

The college "dropout" is variously defined as a student who leaves a college and takes some time off before resuming studies at the same school ("stopping out"), or transfers to another school, or ends college studies altogether. Cope and Hannah (1975) report that only 40 to 50 percent of entering B.A. and B.S. students earn their degrees in four years; 20 to 30 percent graduate later; and 30 to 40 percent never earn degrees. Students are most likely to leave during their first two years, and the dropout rate varies enormously from

The college experience can be an opportunity to explore and expand intellectual interests and abilities. (Susanne Anderson/Photo Researchers, Inc.)

10 percent at some prestigious highly selective small private colleges up to 80 percent at less selective state and community colleges.

There is no one "dropout personality." Students leave college for all sorts of reasons. While leavers usually have lower average aptitude scores, most of those who leave are doing satisfactory academic work (at least a C average). Students leave school because they change their occupational plans, or they don't like various aspects of the college

I quit because I was tired of being broke too. I had worked my way, in my brief time that I was [in college]. In high school, I worked in a library, and a 7-11 store during summers so I could save up. And it was really hard to find jobs, so I did baby-sitting and stuff like that. Then once I was at school, I just wasn't able to get a job at all.

Cathy Tuley , born 1950, a secretary in Nancy Seifer, *Nobody Speaks For Me!, Self-Portraits of American Working Class Women* (New York: Simon and Schuster, 1976), p. 224.

they're enrolled in, or they want to move to be close to a loved one, or they get married. Leaving school before graduation seems to be a matter of a particular student's interacting with a particular campus environment at a particular point in time.

Timmons (1978) took a random sample of 432 first-year students at a large university and looked at the answers they had given early in the year to an orientation questionnaire. He then compared the profiles of those who had withdrawn with those who had stayed on at the college. The withdrawers had been more dissatisfied with their lives at the time of admission. The men seemed to be following their parents' goals rather than their own and were less interested in their courses than the continuers were. The women did not get along with their parents as well as the continuers did, and were also more likely to feel lost, lonely, and socially isolated. For some of these students, withdrawal was an active step toward separating from their parents and forming their own identities.

The decision to leave college is often a positive step. Many students gain more by working for a while, enrolling at a more compatible institution, or just allowing themselves time to mature than they would have gained by remaining at the original school. Colleges need to make dropping out more acceptable by making it easier for students to take leaves of absence, to study part-time, and to earn more credit for independent study, life experiences, and work done at other institutions. Cope and Hannah (1975) urge the college door to

be one that revolves freely to allow an entrance and an exit for students at appropriate times—to reassess, to lower tension, to get married, to relax, to play on the one hand; and to return, to think, to study, to learn on the other [p. 110].

Formal education need not—and usually does not—end in one's early twenties. It can and should continue throughout adulthood. An indication of the trend toward life-long learning can be seen in the fact that adult part-time students in two-year colleges or technical-vocational schools are almost equal in number to those in four-year colleges or universities (U.S.D.H.E.W., 1979). We will discuss the place of educational programs in the lives of older adults in later chapters.

YOUTH

In recent years a new stage of development has been conceptualized, that of *youth*, a stage which bridges the transition between adolescence and adulthood. According to Keniston (1970), this stage is not unique to the United States, but it is assuming new importance to our society.

Many people reach an age and stage of psychological development when they are no longer adolescents. They have made the psychological commitment to their own sense of self. Yet they have not made the social commitments ordinarily thought of as going along with adulthood—settling upon a career, choosing a marriage partner, deciding to raise children. They have not rejected these actions (which would signify a commitment not to do them), but they are still in the process of deciding about these activities. To characterize the growing number of people, usually in their twenties, who seem to fit this pattern, Keniston (in Erikson, 1965) has defined the concept of youth as a new stage of life:

The youth culture is . . . not so obviously transitional, but more like a waiting period, in which the youth is ostensibly preparing himself for adult responsibilities, but in which to adults he often seems to be armoring himself against them . . . The youth culture has roles, values, and ways of behaving all its own; it emphasizes disengagement from adult values, sexual attractiveness, daring, immediate pleasure, and comradeship in a way that is true neither of childhood nor of adulthood. The youth culture is not always or explicitly anti-adult, but it is belligerently *non*-adult [p. 210].

The youth culture involves young people from all sectors of society, including affluent, blue-collar, and ghetto backgrounds.

The emergence of this stage of life may spring from a fear of growing up and assuming adult responsibilities. It can be of real positive value to society by providing a breathing space during which young people can work through their reservations about attaining adult status. During youth they can resolve the tension between the self they are becoming and the society they live in. They can integrate their sense of who they are and can decide how they want to relate to society.

This life stage has several themes (Keniston, in Silverstein, 1973):

An emphasis on the present rather than on the future

A continued search for identity in careers and values

A redefinition of the relationship to one's parents, to childhood, and to the childhood self, often through new relationships the youth forms with a sweetheart, a counselor, or a group of peers

The search for commitments of ultimate worth and value, which may include an idealistic pursuit such as the Peace Corps, a philosophic or religious inquiry, an artistic in-

volvement, or individual private experience (leisure, sports, or personal relationships)

Thus, the youth culture offers time for the psychological work that prepares one for adulthood.

SUMMARY

1 *Adolescence* is a period of transition from childhood to adulthood. It begins with *pubescence*, a period of rapid physical growth and maturation of reproductive functioning and primary and secondary sexual characteristics. Pubescence lasts about two years, ending with *puberty*, when sexual maturity and reproductive capacity are complete. The end of adolescence is not clear-cut; in Western societies, no single sign indicates that adulthood has been attained. In some societies, adolescence ends at puberty and is signified by *puberty rites*, which take a variety of forms.   **2** Dramatic physiological changes mark adolescence. Most notable and obvious is the appearance of *menarche* in females. Males experience *nocturnal emissions*. Both sexes undergo sharp growth in height, weight, and muscular and skeletal development—the *adolescent growth spurt*. A *secular* trend in growth and maturation occurs so that the children reach sexual maturation and adult height earlier than before, a trend—influenced by today's higher standard of living (improved nutrition and health care)—that seems to be leveling off.   **3** An adolescent's rapid body changes affect self-concept and personality. Particularly important is the effect of *early* or *late maturing*, which is pronounced during adolescence but seems to disappear by adulthood.   **4** The adolescent years correspond to Piaget's stage of *formal operations*, during which an adolescent develops the ability to think abstractly. This enables young people to deal flexibly with problems to test hypotheses, and to engage in hypothetical, deductive reasoning. Environment plays a more important role in the attainment of this stage than in earlier stages of cognitive development.   **5** Although an adolescent is not egocentric in the sense that a child is, this concept does apply. *Adolescent egocentrism* is seen in the adolescents' notion that other people's thoughts are focused on them, just as they are preoccupied with themselves. Manifestations of adolescent egocentrism include the *imaginary audience* and *personal fable*. Adolescent egocentrism is gradually overcome as an adolescent realizes that other people have their *own* concerns. Selection of an occupation enables the individual to become less self-involved and thus contributes to the demise of adolescent egocentrism.   **6** Most adolescents are in the conventional stages of moral development (Kohlberg's stages 3 and 4).   **7** The search for identity is closely linked to vocational choice, which is related to and influenced by socioeconomic status, sex, parental attitudes, schooling, and personality.   **8**   The college experience affects personality and intellect as college students question many childhood assumptions. Some 30 to 40 percent of college students drop or stop out for reasons including marriage and changes in vocational plans.   **9**   In recent years a new stage of development—*youth*—has been conceptualized as a transitional stage between adolescence and adulthood.

SUGGESTED READINGS

Bird, C.   *The case against college*. New York: McKay, 1975. Presents the view that college, although good for some, may be inappropriate for the majority of high school graduates. Discusses alternatives such as vocational training, travel, and the armed services.

Bruch, H.   *The golden cage: The enigma of anorexia nervosa*. Cambridge, MA: Harvard, 1978. A clearly written, informative book about this puzzling illness, written by a psychiatrist who has done extensive research on eating disorders.

Cottle, T. J.   *Time's children: Impressions of youth*. Boston: Little, Brown, 1971. A well-written collection of essays about children's experiences, feelings, fears, and wants. It is an interesting observation on how children grow up and how the world around them affects their development.

Inhelder, B., & Piaget, J.   *The growth of logical thinking from childhood to adolescence*. New York: Basic Books, 1958. An account of the research of Piaget on the development of intelligence through the various levels of human growth. Piaget and Inhelder show how a child's mind develops characteristics of adult thinking.

Minton, L.   *Growing into adolescence: A sensible guide for parents of children 11 to 14*. New York: Parents' Magazine Press, 1972. A very readable book that uses many examples to explain the dynamics of early adolescence, as they revolve around such issues as burgeoning sexuality, need for independence, developing values, and the many day-to-day problems common in these years.

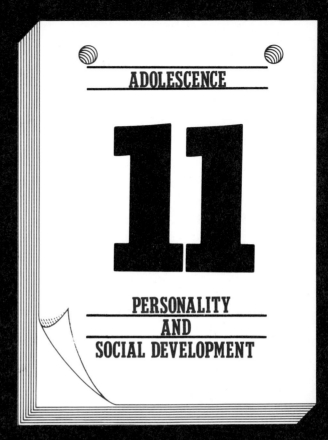

ADOLESCENCE

11

PERSONALITY
AND
SOCIAL DEVELOPMENT

I remember a very definite change when I reached what in modern child psychology is called the "latency period." At this stage, I began to enjoy using slang pretending to have no feelings, and being generally "manly".

The Autobiography of Bertrand Russell,
Bertrand Russell (1872-1914), p. 43.

Probably the most important task of adolescence is the search for identity. Teenagers need to develop their own values, and to be sure they are not just parroting their parents' ideas. They have to find out what they can do and be proud of their own accomplishments. They want to develop close relationships with boys and girls their own age, and to be liked and loved and respected for who they are and what they stand for. Says Jones (1969):

The adolescent enters the threshold of personhood seeking an image he does not know in a world he rarely understands, with a body that he is just discovering. He has a mixed desire to be an individual who wants to assert himself while at the same time fearing to lose the little security and reassurance that only family can offer [p. 332].

Many different theories offer explanations of the significance of adolescence and its effects on the individual.

THEORETICAL PERSPECTIVES ON ADOLESCENCE

G. Stanley Hall (1916) contended that genetically determined physiological factors cause psychological reactions. Hall saw adolescence as a period of *Sturm und Drang*, or "storm and stress": a period of vacillating, contradictory emotions. Margaret Mead (1961) studied adolescence in other cultures and found that Western adolescence is not a universal phenomenon. When a culture decrees a serene and gradual transition from childhood to adulthood, as does Samoa, there is an easy acceptance of adulthood. Societies that permit young children to see adult sexual activity, watch babies being born, become close to death, do necessary work, exercise assertive and even dominant behavior, engage in sex play, and know precisely what their adult roles will involve have fairly stress-free adolescences.

Even in our society adolescence is often calm. In his studies of Midwestern adolescent boys, Offer (1969) found little "turmoil" or "chaos." He did find a high level of "bickering" over relatively unimportant issues between 12- and 14-year-olds and their parents. In a recent follow-up study of these same boys eight years later, Offer and Offer (1974) were able to divide most of them in three groups. Almost 1 in 4 fell into the "continuous growth" group; these teens were happy, had a realistic self-image, and showed little sign of crisis or turmoil. More than one-third fit into the "surgent growth" group of reasonably well-adjusted youths who had somewhat more difficulty dealing with unexpected trauma and often regressed to more immature behavior or became angry at difficult times. Less than 1 adolescent in 5, however, fit the "classical" picture of "tumultuous growth."

Adelson (1979) claims that the picture so many people have of the "typical" turbulent teenager has been painted by the tendency of researchers to pay attention to a small proportion of the adolescent population. As a result, we know a disproportionate amount about the upper-middle and lower classes, but very little about youths from the lower-middle class. Researchers have also dwelled on the problems of the emotionally disturbed, the irreligious or "eccentrically" religious, the politically alienated. Among college students, we know more about those who study the humanities and the social sciences, but very little about those in science, technology, and business. Our knowledge of adolescent development is largely a knowledge of the development of adolescent males, with virtually no sense of the way girls turn into women. As a result of all these gaps, we know surprisingly little about normal teenagers. Yet from what we do know, from those studies that *have* concentrated on "ordinary" young peple, Adelson (1979) concludes:

Taken as a whole, adolescents are *not* in turmoil, *not* deeply disturbed, *not* at the mercy of their impulses, *not* resistant to parental values, *not* politically active, *not* rebellious [p. 37].

Bandura (1964), who also found a preponderance of good feeling between teenagers and their parents, feels that a stormy adolescence is often a self-fulfilling prophecy:

If a society labels its adolescents as "teenagers," and expects them to be rebellious, unpredictable, sloppy, and wild in their behavior, and if this picture is repeatedly reinforced by the mass media, such cultural expectations may very well force adolescents into the role of rebel. In this way, a false expectation may serve to instigate and maintain certain role behaviors, in turn, then reinforce the originally false belief [p. 230].

Sigmund Freud (1953) considered the *genital stage* of mature sexuality the keynote of adolescence. This is a reawakening of the sexual urges of the phallic stage, which now are directed into socially approved channels—heterosexual relations with people outside the family. Because of the physiological changes of sexual maturation, adolescents no longer repress sexuality as they did during the latency stage of middle childhood. Their biological needs make this impossible. They typically go through a homosexual stage, which may manifest itself in hero worship of an adult or in a close chum relationship, which is the forerunner of mature relationships with persons of the opposite sex. Before these can be achieved, young people have to free themselves from dependency upon their parents.

Anna Freud (1946) considered the adolescent years more important for the formation of character than her father had. The glandular changes that produce physiological changes also affect psychological functioning. The *libido*, the basic energy that fuels the sex drive, is reawakened and threatens the id-ego balance maintained during the latency years. The resultant conflicts cause anxiety and possibly fears and neurotic symptoms, which call forth defenses of repression, denial, and displacement. To avoid being overwhelmed by instinctual urges, adolescents employ ego defense mechanisms, such as *intellectualization* (translation of their perceptions into abstract thought) and *asceticism* (self-denial).

Erik Erikson (1950, 1965, 1968) identified adolescence as a crisis of *identity versus role confusion*. Rapid body growth and new genital maturity emphasize to young people their impending adulthood, and they begin to question their roles in adult society. The most important task of adolescence is to discover "Who I Am." A significant aspect of this search for identity is the young person's decision about a career.

Erikson sees the prime danger of this stage as identity confusion. He says this can express itself in a young person's taking an excessively long time to reach adulthood, and he offers Hamlet as an "exalted example." Adolescents may also express their confusion by acting impulsively to commit themselves to poorly thought out courses of action, or by regressing into childishness to avoid resolving conflicts. He sees the cliquishness of adolescence and its intolerance of differences as defenses against identity confusion. He also sees falling in love as an attempt to define identity. By becoming intimate with another person and sharing thoughts and feelings, the adolescent offers up his or her own identity, sees it reflected in the loved one, and is better able to clarify the self.

During the "psychosocial moratorium" (Erikson, 1950, p. 262) that adolescence and youth provide, many young people's efforts are focused toward a search for commitments to which they can be faithful. These commitments are both ideological and personal, and the extent to which young people can be true to them determines their ability to resolve the crisis of this stage.

THE SEARCH FOR IDENTITY

Implicit in the adolescent voyage of self-discovery is the young person's seesawing between childhood and maturity. At one moment Vicky climbs onto her father's lap, puts her arms around him, and talks baby talk. At the next she argues for the right to stay alone over a weekend and bitterly berates him for treating her like a child. Most teenagers object when older people think of them as children, or even use the term "adolescents," even though they themselves are likely to concede, "In some ways, I still think and act somewhat like a child" (Sorensen, 1973, p. 38).

Erikson (1960) emphasizes that the adolescent effort to make sense of the self and the world is not "a kind of maturational malaise," but is instead a healthy, vital process that contributes to the ego-strength of the mature adult (1960). The search for identity is, of course, a life-long enterprise. It does not end in adolescence. The importance of this time of life is as a launching point for the quest.

RESEARCH ON IDENTITY
Marcia has based several studies on Eriksonian theories, trying to determine the ways by which young people's commitments—one to an occupation and one to a set of beliefs—help them to form their identity. He developed a thirty-minute semistructured interview (see page 373) to evaluate an individual's identity status as being in one of these four categories (Marcia, 1966):

1 *Identity achievement:* After a crisis in which the person has spent a great deal of effort actively searching for choices, he or she now expresses strong commitment.

2 *Foreclosure:* This person has made commitments, but instead of undergoing an identity crisis, she or he has accepted other people's plans. She becomes a devoutly religious housewife because her mother was, or he becomes a Republican farmer because his father was.

3 *Identity diffusion:* Uncommitted, this person may be a playboy type who actively avoids commitment or may be an aimless drifter, without goals.

Friday, October 5, 1877

In the studio all distinctions disappear. One has neither name nor family; one is no longer the daughter of one's mother, one is one's-self,--an individual,--and one has before one art, and nothing else. One feels so happy, so free, so proud!

Marie Bashkirtseff, age 17, artist, *Marie Bashkirtseff: The Journal of a Young Artist,* p. 135.

4 *Moratorium:* Still in crisis, this person is heading for commitment and will probably achieve identity.

In 1967, Marcia evaluated seventy-two male college students on ego-identity status according to the four categories above. He then administered measures of self-esteem and tested the stability of their levels of self-esteem by arbitrarily giving them positive or negative information about their competence on another test that they took. The students in the first and last categories—identity achievement and moratorium—had the strongest sense of self. Their levels of self-esteem varied less in response to attempted manipulation than did those of the students in the foreclosure and identity diffusion groups. This study seems to show that the harder that young people work toward resolving their identity crises, the stronger will be their sense of themselves.

Orlofsky, Marcia, and Lesser (1973) looked at the relationship between ego-identity status and Erikson's sixth crisis, that between intimacy and isolation, which typical-

ly occurs during young adulthood. For the thirty-three college juniors and seniors in this study, the findings support the Eriksonian idea that people need to resolve their identity crises before they can achieve true intimacy with another person.

This study found that "foreclosure" and "identity-diffusion" students had superficial and stereotyped relationships with other people, that "moratorium" subjects were most variable, and that those individuals who seemed to have the greatest capacity for intimate relationships were in the "identity-

---

**IDENTITY-STATUS
INTERVIEW**

SAMPLE QUESTION ABOUT OCCUPATIONAL COMMITMENT:
"How willing do you think you'd be to give up going into————if something better came along?"

TYPICAL ANSWERS FOR THE FOUR STATUSES:

Identity achievement: "Well, I might, but I doubt it. I can't see what "something better" would be for me.
Foreclosure: "Not very willing. It's what I've always wanted to do. The folks are happy with it and so am I."
Identity diffusion: "Oh sure. If something better came along, I'd change just like that."
Moratorium: "I guess if I knew for sure I could answer that better. It would have to be something in the general area—something related . . ."

SAMPLE QUESTION ABOUT IDEOLOGICAL COMMITMENT:
"Have you ever had any doubts about your religious beliefs?"

TYPICAL ANSWERS:

Identity achievement: "Yeah, I even started wondering whether or not there was a god [sic]. I've pretty much resolved that now, though. The way it seems to me is . . ."
Foreclosure: "No, not really, our family is pretty much in agreement on these things."
Identity diffusion: "Oh, I don't know. I guess so. Everyone goes through some sort of stage like that. But it really doesn't bother me much. I figure one's about as good as the other!"
Moratorium: "Yes, I guess I'm going through that now. I just don't see how there can be a god [sic] and yet so much evil in the world or . . ."

Source: Marcia, 1966.

achievement" status, or in a new category defined as "alienated achievement." Students in this last status refused to commit themselves occupationally, apparently after much thought. They had reached ideological positions from which they defied convention and society, and they seemed to base their identity strength more on their relationships with other people than on their occupational and ideological choices.

Teenagers from cultural or racial minority groups are thrust into a particularly intense identity crisis. They have to deal not only with the same life changes as other teens but also with a host of other problems caused by their minority status. Raised by adults who generally do not share the value system of the dominant culture and who rarely achieve positions of importance within it, minority-group adolescents often have trouble finding role models to identify with.

The teacher thought I was stupid. Couldn't spell, couldn't read, couldn't do arithmetic. Just stupid. Teachers were never interested in finding out that you couldn't concentrate because you were so hungry, because you hadn't had any breakfast.

Dick Gregory, from *Nigger*
in *Childhood Revisited*, p. 115

For many adolescents, the teenage years are a time of great idealism, when they become convinced of the need for social change, become outraged at the hypocrisy and the complacency of society, and try to change the world. Their efforts are genuine, and when society can channel their energies constructively, their contributions can be meaningful.

RELATIONSHIPS WITH PARENTS

Strife between parents and teenagers is common, but it need not be a constant fact of life. Bandura and Walters (1959) showed a comfortable acceptance of each other by parents and teenage sons. Another recent study found that parents are troubled by many facets of teenage life, but they are generally positive about the young people themselves. Parents say: "We love their fresh insights, surprising evidences of maturity, their idealism and eagerness to learn"; "It's great becoming friends as well as parents"; and "They make me feel alive and involved. I was 'old' when they were young, but now I'm younger than my years" (*McCall's*, 1973, p. 34).

Sorensen (1973) found that most teenagers say they really know, like, and respect their parents. Among teenagers, 3 out of 4 feel that they really know their mothers, and 3 out of 5 feel that they really know their fathers. About 78 percent feel strong affection for their parents, 88 percent have a lot of respect for them as people, and almost all feel that their parents, in turn, care for them. Still, there is a substantial minority of teenagers who feel that they have never really gotten to know their parents, and 1 teen out of 4 can't stand to be around them. Usually these youths blame their parents for having failed in some specific way, for showing a lack of understanding or an unwillingness to help with a problem in the youngsters' lives.

AMBIVALENCE: INDEPENDENCE OR DEPENDENCE

Young people feel constant conflict between wanting to be independent of their parents and realizing how dependent they actually are. Boys see their fathers as being the more powerful parent, while girls consider their mothers more powerful (Grinder & Spector, 1965). In the pursuit of independence, adolescents often repulse their parents' attempts to guide them, dismiss their opinions as hopelessly out of date and irrelevant, and deliber-

In the search for identity and independence, the young engage on many levels for proof of individuality. (Sybil Shackman/Monkmeyer)

ately say and do things to shock them. As Erikson (1950) says:

In their search for a new sense of continuity and sameness, adolescents have to refight many of the battles of earlier years, even though to do so they must artifically appoint perfectly well-meaning people to play their roles of adversaries [p. 261].

This attitude continues through the college years for many young people. Allport (1964) feels that not until about the age of 23 are most people able to deal with their parents in a mature way. We remember Mark Twain's words: "When I was 14 my father knew nothing, but when I was 21 I was amazed at how much the old man had learned in those seven years."

Young people trying to find their own values in a confusing society are concerned with the genuineness of the people they look to as models. They are quick to accuse parents and teachers of hypocrisy whenever they detect any deviation between professed ideals and actual behavior. Former images

Fall 1536
Cousin John, yesterday I was asking you if principles didn't make one too dogmatic. You answered, "The lack of principles leads to superficially and indecision." I accepted this response with great respect. I wonder, however, if one's principles cannot change over time. Can't I embrace today what I rejected yesterday, without being accused of indecision? I will discuss my doubts with Father, who will surely clear them up.

Mathilde von Buddenbroch, age 16,
Le Journal de Marguerite, p. 161.

of their parents as perfect, all-knowing models come tumbling down, never again to be reassembled. From this time on, parents are only people like anyone else. But because they once were invested with much more power than anyone could possibly have, this toppling of ideal models comes as a grievous blow. If only our parents had been perfect, if only they had raised us perfectly, how perfect we could be! As Oscar Wilde once put it: "Children begin by loving their parents. After a time they judge them. Rarely, if ever, do they forgive them."

Adolescents need the freedom to make up their own minds. They want to know where their parents stand on issues, but they also want to come to their own conclusions. While they are searching for answers, they want to be listened to, respected, and—above all—taken seriously.

FORMING THEIR OWN VALUES

Teenagers tend to hold the same political and religious attitudes as their parents (Bealer, Willits, & Maida, 1964). The campus protesters of the 1960s tended to come from liberal, activist families. While their parents were often dismayed by the radicalism and illegality of their children's activities, the students themselves tended to feel they were just carrying their parents' ideas one step further (Keniston, 1967).

Conflicts between the generations occur less often over broad values than over timing. Adolescents want to do things that their parents think they're not ready for. Once the parents and the child achieve some sort of balance between what is permitted and what isn't, the temporary nature of this type of conflict is over.

RELATIONSHIPS WITH PEERS

Parents often express the fear that teenagers will get into trouble just to go along with the crowd. The herd instinct *is* strong during adolescence, as is the desire to be accepted by the crowd. Indeed, a major governmental study involving over 3000 teenagers concluded that an adolescent's friends have more influence than his or her parents in determin-

ing whether he or she will become involved in serious juvenile delinquency (*The New York Times*, 1977). But the influence of the peer group is not all-powerful. The same government study indicated that the parents are more influential in relation to less serious troubles such as truancy and running away from home.

Brittain (1963) posed a variety of hypothetical dilemmas to 280 ninth- to eleventh-grade girls from urban and rural high schools in Alabama and Georgia. For each instance, one solution was favored by a hypothetical teenager's parents, a different one by her friends. The girls showed that they valued the opinions of both their parents and their peers; whichever one carried more weight depended on the particular situation. When deciding how to dress or how to resolve school-centered situations and other problems with immediate consequences, the peers' opinions were more influential. But when deciding about which job to take, or how to resolve deeper moral conflicts, or other long-range issues, the girls leaned more toward parental opinions.

There appear to be differences in the ways boys and girls respond to peers and parents. Emmerick (1978) followed up Brittain's study, with forty-nine boys and forty-nine girls from two ninth-grade and two twelfth-grade classes. The students were asked to provide solutions for ten conflict situations and were asked to choose between alternates suggested by peers or by parents. In two different forms of the tests, which were divided among the students, alternate courses of action favored by parents on Form I were shown as favored by peers on Form II, and vice versa.

The ninth-grade boys chose parent-approved alternatives more often than either the girls or the older boys. While the girls' responses tended to remain stable between the ninth and the twelfth grades, the boys' responses tended to change. However, in line with Brittain's findings, the particular situation a student was considering influenced his or her leaning toward the opinion of parent or peer.

There is no one peer group for all teens. The subgroup that they are drawn to depends partly on socioeconomic status (since most adolescent cliques are class-bound), partly on the values picked up from home, and partly on their own personalities. Once they become members of a particular set, adolescents influence each other in their dress, their social activities, their sexual behavior, their use or nonuse of drugs, their pursuit or nonpursuit of academic work, their vocational aspirations—the basic patterns of their lives. But not all adolescents run with the herd. Some are independent and individualistic even now; some are already pursuing life goals that keep them too busy; some prefer fewer but more intimate friendships; and some are excluded by every crowd in town.

No matter which crowd a teenager is part of—or even if he or she is a loner—a young person is still more likely to identify with other adolescents, no matter what their background or interests, than with older or younger people. American teenagers are caught up in "generational chauvinism" (Sorensen, 1973). They see themselves as part of a group, they think this group is better than any other, and they define the group strictly by age, taking seriously the phrase, "Don't trust anyone over 30."

Adolescents identify with other teenagers rather than with other people of their own race, religion, community, or sex (Sorensen, 1973), maybe because they feel that most other teens share their personal values, but that most older people do not. Comparing themselves with people in their forties and fifties, adolescents consider themselves more idealistic, less materialistic, healthier sexually, and better able to understand friendship and the important things in life (Sorensen, 1973). Perhaps young people have always felt this way, but in other countries or other times, when society venerated the wisdom of old age, young people tacitly went along with the opinion that not until one reaches adult status

does one have a true understanding of life. These days, when *youth* is venerated, many young people feel they have nothing to learn from their elders. What their peers can teach them seems much more valuable, and so they spend a great proportion of their time with people their own age.

FRIENDSHIP IN ADOLESCENCE

During the teen years, friends become vitally important, as young people pursue the task of separating from their families, seeking their own identities, and, in the process, looking for kindred spirits with whom they can make the journey. Friends give each other the emotional support that adolescents need, but often no longer can accept from their parents. According to one sociological point of view, the friendships of adolescence "are formed when the lack of a strong sense of boundaries to the self permits one to become deeply emotional and to express one's deepest sense of self to others who, having similar vulnerabilities, cannot be considered agents of a hostile world" (Bensman & Lilienfeld, 1979, p. 60).

In many cases these friendships forged out of mutual need endure throughout life. The qualities that teenagers look for in a friend are very similar to those sought out at later stages in life. Adolescent friendships can be considered, then, the cornerstones of adult friendship patterns.

Sunday, August 11 (1877)

Journal Jessie and I are going to be Authers! We are going to "colaberate" and write our first books together. Isn't that a glorious union for us two most special friends?

Kathie Gray, age 13,
Kathie's Diary: Leaves from an Old, Old Diary, p. 54.

Adolescents search out
kindred spirits with
whom they can make
the journey to adulthood.
(Dorri Olds)

In one study of friendship, people at four stages of life—high school seniors, newlyweds, parents whose youngest child was about to leave home, and people getting ready to retire—described their friendship networks: the number of friends they had, their age and sex, how long they had been friends, and how often they saw each other (Weiss & Lowenthal, 1976).

While the adolescents reported having the fewest number of friends (a mean of 4.7, compared to the 4.8 reported by the middle-aged, 6 by the preretirement group, and 7.6 by newlyweds), they saw them more often than did people in any of the other groups. Three-quarters of the high school students saw their friends every day. Not surprisingly, the younger the person, the shorter the duration of the friendship, with high school students reporting that about three-quarters of their friends had been important for five years or less.

People in all four life stages held very similar views of the meaning of friendship and of the qualities they looked for in a friend. The five specific dimensions of friendship that showed up in the subjects' detailed discussions of three friends each, were *similarity* (in personality, values, or attitudes, with an emphasis on shared activities or experiences); *reciprocity* (helping, understanding, and accepting each other, with an emphasis on mutual trust and ability to share confidences); *compatibility* (enjoyment in being together); *structure* (geographic closeness, convenience, or long duration of acquaintance); and *role-modeling* (admiration and respect for the friends' good qualities).

Some variations through the life cycle showed up. Similarity, which was very important to the adolescents, became less important as people grew older. Explain Weiss and Lowenthal, "These late adolescents are in the process of attempting to establish a separate, unique identity, but they also still have dependent family relationships; their self-concept may well be strengthened by a recognition of similarities with their peers" (p. 58).

In another study, adolescents and adults were asked to compare their present life with what it had been ten years earlier and the way they expected it to be ten years in the future

September 14, 1940

All the same, I don't care for the physical aspects of love. A kiss is too wet, and I cease to love when I have given it. What is so nice about him, this friend of my heart, is that he understands and accepts it. He told me he loved me above and beyond kisses. Here's a man worthy of my love at last.

Flora Groult, age 16,
Diary in Duo, p. 183.

(Gamer, Thomas, & Kendall, 1975). The teenagers mentioned friends most often, feeling that it was important to have many friends, as well as "good" friends. In view of the finding cited above that adolescents have fewer friends than older people, teenagers may have unrealistic expectations of the number of friends they "should" have at their age and may, therefore, often set themselves up for disappointment.

There seems to be a tie between the emerging sexuality of adolescents and their friendship patterns. Weiss and Lowenthal, for example, in their 1976 study of friendship across the life span, found that while most people have friends of the same sex, adolescents and newlyweds are more likely than older people to name a friend of the other sex. While this may indicate a growing societal acceptance for opposite-sex friends, it probably also reflects the intermingling among adolescents of courting behavior and friendships. Bensman and Lilienfeld (1979) feel that sexuality influences friendship in another way, as young adolescents try to find meaning and expression for their sexuality:

Combating the fear of failure in sexual relations, celebrating success, and exchanging information, accurate or not, are all means for providing social support for universal biological drives that are either not deeply supported or denied at family and public levels [p. 60].

SEXUALITY

Sexuality comes to the fore during adolescence, but one study recently concluded that it is generally not the predominant focus of interest even in these years. Kermis, Monge, and Dusek (1975) asked 430 boys and girls from grades five through eleven, along with 102 college students, to list and rank topics according to their interest in receiving more information about them. Arts, crafts, sports, future work, and understanding other people were some of the topics that generally ranked higher than sexuality-related topics such as birth control information, sexual relations and reproduction, and dating and going steady. While these researchers concluded that adolescents are not "bedeviled by emerging sexuality," they did see sexuality as a topic of definite interest to teenagers.

Young people's images of themselves

Sexuality comes to the fore during adolescence, although it is generally not the predominant focus of interest. (Charles Gatewood)

and their relationships with peers and parents are all bound up with their sexuality. At this age sexual activity—from casual kissing, to necking and petting, to intercourse—fulfills a number of important needs, probably the least of which is physical pleasure. More important is the ability of sexual interaction to enhance communication, to exemplify a search for new experience, to prove one's maturity, to be in tune with the peer group, to find surcease from pressures, and to investigate the mysteries of love.

Many adults believe that today's teenage sex scene is one huge orgy, with most girls on The Pill and ready to jump into bed with a boy as easily as their mothers used to bestow a good-night kiss. This is most certainly an exaggeration even though, as we shall see, many changes in young people's attitudes and behavior have taken place over the last generation.

COMMUNICATING WITH PARENTS

Attitudes toward sexuality and sexual behavior have changed among both young people and their parents. Many parents are now in a transitional stage: They recognize their children's premarital sexual activity, but they cannot fully accept it. Parental values are more liberal today, especially concerning girls. Today's parents are less likely to punish or cast out a pregnant daughter than they are to help her. Today's parents may worry about where to put their daughter's boyfriend when she brings him home for a weekend; twenty years ago they would not have admitted that they knew she was sexually involved with him (and she would not have told them).

Yet communication about sex still remains a problem for most parents and teenagers. Young people generally want to be able to talk freely with their parents about sexual behavior and problems, but don't, for many reasons.

They feel they cannot be open with their parents because their parents are not open with them; because their parents' views are so different that they would not understand them; because they are afraid of their parents' disapproval, lectures, or punishment; because they feel their parents will be hurt, disappointed, or shocked to discover their children's "loss of innocence"; because they are embarrassed; or, occasionally, because of their own desire for privacy (Hass, 1979).

Teenagers are more likely to feel comfortable talking about sex with their parents if both generations have similar sexual values, either liberal or conservative, and mothers and daughters are more successful in communicating about sexual matters than any other parent-child combination (Hass, 1979).

When parents and children do discuss sex, conversations are usually abstract rather than particular. When 625 fifteen- to eighteen-year-olds were asked, "What kinds of things about your own sex life do you tell your parents?", the most common response by far (45 percent for boys and 51 percent for girls) was, "I only talk in a general way about sex, not specifically about me" (Hass, 1979, p. 175). College students report that their childhood questions about sex were more likely to have been answered satisfactorily than were their inquiries during puberty and adolescence when sexual curiosity and anxiety are at their peak (Shipman, 1968). Occasionally young people resist sexual information, denying even to themselves that they have heard such things from their parents' lips. This may be caused by a universal taboo against incest. In some nonliterate societies, the taboo is expressed by avoiding the children at certain times or by evicting them from the parental hut; in our society it surfaces in the lack of communication about sex, especially between a child and the parent of opposite gender (Shipman, 1968).

The ever-present adolescent ambivalence can be seen in young people's feelings about talking about sex with their parents. While they say they would like to be open and frank with their parents about their sexual behavior, they don't like to be questioned and they tend to consider their sexual activities nobody else's business. But when parents are obviously aware of their children's sexual activities and ignore them, the children often become puzzled and angry. Said one 16-year-old girl:

I'm not going to pretend that I don't know what's happening. If my daughter comes in at five in the morning, her shirt backwards and wearing some guy's sweater, I'm not going to ask her, "Did you have a nice time at the movies?" . . . I don't plan to fail! [Sorensen, 1973, p. 61]

Teenagers who are able to talk freely to their parents about sexual matters often express their gratitude for their parents' non-judgmental understanding and reassurance. These young people generally rate their parents as being willing to share their own sexual values and to acknowledge that they are sexual beings themselves. Says Hass (1979):

Communication between parent and child should not await adolescence. It must start early. A feeling of trust and openness about sexuality will generalize from a relationship which has been that way in other areas throughout life [pp. 178–79].

CURRENT SEXUAL PRACTICES

Teenage virgins are not extinct, although they are becoming rarer all the time. Hunt (1974) reported information about sexual behavior collected in 1972 from more than 2000 adults in twenty-four cities around the country. Half of the men in the study who had gone to college reported having had premarital sexual intercourse by the age of 17, and 3 out of 4 noncollege men had had their first coital experience by this age. For women, educational levels were less important than marital status at the time of the survey. Among married women, nearly 1 in 5 reported having had sexual intercourse by the age of 17; 1 in 3

single women were no longer virgins by 17. (These figures are for white women only. They are given in this way to make it possible to compare them with Kinsey's figures, which had been based on a white population. See Tables 11-1 and 11-2).

How do these figures compare with those of the past? They show a dramatic increase in premarital intercourse for both sexes. For males, the biggest change has occurred among those who go on to college. The rates of premarital sexual activity for these young men have doubled since Kinsey (1953).

The most striking changes overall have been among girls and women of all educational levels. Across the board, the percentage of women in their late teens and their mid-twenties who have had sexual intercourse before marriage has also doubled since Kinsey's figures (Hunt, 1974). In 1953, when Kinsey reported on his interviews with more than 5000 white women, only 3 percent had parted with their virginity by age 15, and only 23 percent had done so by age 21. A generation later, Zelnik and Kantner (1972) found that 11 percent of white females were no longer virgins at age 15, while 40 percent were nonvirgins by age 19. When the figures include both white and black girls, the nonvirgin rates go up to 14 percent at age 15 and 46 percent at age 19.

By 1977, Zelnik and Kantner found that the rate of adolescent sexual activity had continued to escalate. Between 1971 and 1976, sexual experience among never-married 15- to 19-year old girls increased by 30 percent. Girls were beginning intercourse at earlier ages, with the median age of first intercourse down to 16.2 years in 1976. They were having intercourse with more partners: Five out of ten now reported sex with more than one partner, compared to less than four in ten back in 1971, with 48 percent of the sexually active girls saying they had not had sex at all in the four weeks before the interview, compared with 40 percent previously.

In recent years, the differences in sexual experience patterns between black and white girls have narrowed. Black girls are still twice as likely as whites to be sexually experienced, with 63 percent of unmarried black teenagers reporting that they had had sexual intercourse in 1976, compared to 31 percent of the white girls. The rate of increase in sexual activity among whites, however, was more than double the black increase from 1971 to 1976.

Sorensen (1973) found that 56 percent of all nonvirgin girls (or 30 percent of *all* the girls surveyed) and 71 percent of the nonvirgin boys (or about 44 percent of *all* the boys) had had their first sexual intercourse by the age of 15; some had had intercourse even before they were 12.

Many young people today are having sexual intercourse at quite early ages. Adolescents who might in earlier days have been content with necking and petting are now culminating their relationships with intercourse. This relative precocity may be an attempt to form significant relationships. These teenagers are acting in intimate ways, although they have not yet determined enough of the sense of self that Erikson (1950) postulates as a prerequisite for a genuinely intimate relationship.

Many youths now feel pressured *into* sexual relationships. College students sometimes worry about their normality if they are still virgins at age 19 or 20; they may engage in intercourse just to get rid of a burdensome virginity, and they may feel that the pressures from family, friends, and society at large are forcing them into sexual activity before they are ready for it. A Yale University physician (Lee, 1973) comments:

Adolescents are as ambivalent and anxious about sex as their elders ever were. Yes, there has been a youth rebellion against Victorian morality, but rather than liberating, it has transformed sex into an ideology. The new ideology is that sex is good and good sex means orgasm and anybody can. The result has been to turn the pleasures of sex into a duty. Along with all this goes the "knowledge" that if you don't have intercourse, you'll go crazy—and that virginity is a hang-up [p. 92].

Sorensen's (1973) finding that very few nonvirgins had waited until age 18 or 19 to have intercourse contrasts with a 1969 study by Luckey and Nass, which found that of the 58 percent of college men and 43 percent of college women who were no longer virgins, the average age of first intercourse was 17.9 for the men and 18.7 for the women. These disparities in age may reflect different practices among college-bound and non-college-bound youth: The Luckey and Nass study surveyed only college students, while the Sorensen study surveyed people from a range of socioeconomic levels. Those from lower socioeconomic groups tend to become more sexually active at a younger age (Zelnik & Kantner, 1972). This accounts for at least part of the difference between white and black teenagers, since more blacks have been trapped in the lower classes. Zelnik and Kantner (1972) found that 32 percent of all 15-year-old black girls are no longer virgins, and by age 19, 81 percent have had intercourse. The black girls were less promiscuous than the whites, with 11 percent of the black nonvirgins reporting intercourse with four or more partners, compared to 16 percent of the whites.

In general, teenagers are not promiscuous. They tend to enter into sexual relationships that have meaning for them, and they plan to honor their relationships with fidelity. Of the girls interviewed by Zelnik and Kantner (1977), 40 to 48 percent had not had intercourse at all during the past month, and 70

	1938-1949 (KINSEY, 1953)	1971 (ZELNIC & KANTNER, 1972)	TABLE 11-1
By age 15	3%	11%	Premarital Intercourse among Single White Females, 1938-1971
By age 19	18-19%*	40%	

*Data incomplete.

	KINSEY, 1953		HUNT, 1974		TABLE 11-2
	BORN BEFORE 1900	BORN 1910-1919	BORN 1838-1947	BORN 1948-1955	Partners of Premarital Intercourse for Married White Females
Fiancé only	40%	42%	49%	53%	
Other males only	20%	12%	8%	3%	
Fiancé and other males	40%	46%	43%	43%	

percent had engaged in it only once or twice. Of the nonvirgins, 60 percent had had only one sexual partner, and half of these expected to marry him. In sum, teenagers seem to be more sexually active than they used to be, especially younger teens and girls, but anyone looking for directions to the orgy will be hard put to find them.

CURRENT SEXUAL ATTITUDES

Change is even more evident in attitudes toward sexuality than in behavior. Says Hunt (1974):

The young have indeed increasingly come to view premarital intercourse as right, if the people involved have a deep emotional commitment to each other, or even if they merely feel strong affection that might someday become something deeper [p. 151].

Almost three-fourths of the teenage boys questioned by Sorensen (1973) say they do not lose respect for a girl who goes to bed with a boy before marriage. And 65 percent of the boys do not believe that girls should stay virgins until they find the boys they want to marry; these boys do not insist on virginity for their future wives. Some of the pressures against premarital sexual activity for girls have

disappeared. When nonvirgins feel guilty, it is usually because they are uncomfortable about deceiving their family or friends, not because of the behavior itself. As late as 1969, Mussen, Conger, and Kagan stated:

In no study available to us did a majority of students approve of premarital sexual relations for couples who are not in love or engaged, and in most studies, less than 50 percent approved even when there was a formal engagement [p. 640].

In the Sorensen study (1973), 76 percent of the boys and 66 percent of the girls approve of living together without marriage.

Young people have strong ideas of right and wrong about sex. More than 8 out of 10 have strong feelings about what is right and wrong for them, but they are tolerant and reluctant to condemn others. The prevailing ethic is that "anything two people want to do sexually is moral, as long as they both want to do it and it does not hurt either one of them" (Sorensen, 1973, p. 106). Only 1 out of 4 believes it's immoral for unmarried persons to have sex; almost half believe that sex without love is still moral; but almost 9 out of 10 think it's immoral for a boy to force a girl into sex. Modern teenagers express strong opinions against exploitation, such as a boy's telling a girl he loves her just so that she'll have intercourse with him.

SEX DIFFERENCES AND THE DOUBLE STANDARD

Boys and girls differ in the nature of their sex drives and in their sexual behavior. Boys are aroused much more easily. They are likely to have an erection when they inadvertently touch a girl or see one, when they read or hear about sexual activities, when they look at erotic pictures, when they think about sex, and when they neck or pet. They are often embarrassed by these erections but are rarely able to control them. Once aroused, they feel an intense urgency toward sexual release, an urgency concentrated in the genital area. By the age of 15, most boys are having orgasms two or three times a week—mostly from masturbation, sexual dreams, and petting (Pomeroy, 1969). They reach their sexual peak during their late teens, and while they may remain sexually active well into old age, the rate of activity gradually decreases. Boys are more sexually active than girls: They start earlier, have more partners, are less likely to be constrained by social standards, and are less likely to insist on love as a prerequisite for sex.

For most adolescent girls, sex is not so much a part of daily life. Far fewer of them

There was a housemaid whom I used to induce to accompany me to this underground [hideaway], where I kissed and hugged her. Once I asked her whether she would like to spend the night with me, and she said she would die rather, which I believed.

Bertrand Russell,
The Autobiography of Bertrand Russell (1872-1914), p. 45.

Edward rushed in at tea time with the smell of horses on him. Me heart lept. He gave a kiss. Twas the first time a boy kissed me and if that's all there's to it, a great todo is made about nothing. Edward says he can marry me in six years.... Tis a happy woman I am. I think tis betrothed I am.

Maggie Owen Wadelton, age 11 (1908),
The Book of Maggie Owen, p. 32.

experience orgasm, for one thing. When 15- to 18-year-old girls were asked whether they had ever had an orgasm, 42 percent said "yes," 25 percent said "no," and 33 percent said, "I am not sure" (Hass, 1979). By and large, females don't reach their sexual peak until their thirties or forties, although this may well be due more to psychological than physiological reasons.

In any case, teenage girls are more likely to want romance and affection in a relationship rather than sexual satisfaction. Their sexual feelings tend to revolve more around the person they are with and less on specific physical pressures. Some girls, though, become aroused as easily as most boys. These girls are stimulated by seeing, reading, and thinking of sexual things. They have orgasms frequently, quickly, and easily, and they often undergo a real struggle to keep out of trouble in a society that does not approve of such behavior. They may also have difficulty in their own teenage society, when most of the other girls are not so free sexually (Pomeroy, 1969, p. 31).

It is hard to say whether the difference in sexual response between the sexes is based on biology or culture. Mead (1949) hypothesizes differences based on structural anatomical differences: Males masturbate earlier and more frequently, and are more responsive to sexual stimulation, because their sexual organs are more accessible. Other writers suggest that the greater intensity of the adolescent boy's sex drive is strictly hormonal: Sexuality is different for boys and girls because biology is different. This would explain why the more urgent sexual needs of boys require physical release, and why the more diffused sexual yearning of girls find fulfillment in emotional relationships. On the other hand, because of the woman's more vulnerable position and the man's need for reassurance that he is the father of his wife's children, girls are sex-socialized quite differently from boys all over the world.

The recent sexual revolution has affected girls and women much more than boys and men. It will be interesting to see whether, in this freer climate, female sexuality will become identical to male sexuality, or whether there always will be a difference between the sexes in sexual attitudes, expression, and needs.

HOMOSEXUALITY

Homosexuality is coming out of the closet in American society. While the rate of homosexual activity may not be on the rise, it is becoming a more visible phenomenon. More people are openly asserting their sexual preference for others of their own sex and demanding that they not be penalized for this preference. "Gay liberation" protests and marches demand an end to discrimination against homosexuals. The American Psychiatric Association finally voted to remove homosexuality from its official list of mental disorders. No longer classifying it as an illness, the APA now designates it a "Sexual orientation disturbance"—and Gould (1974) considers that definition relevant only for homosexuals who "are either disturbed by, in conflict with, or wish to change, their sexual orientation." "Homosexual behavior on a continuous basis and self-acknowledgement of one's own homosexuality are generally an adult rather than an adolescent phenomenon in contemporary American society" (Sorensen, 1973, p. 285). Only 9 percent of all adolescents (11 percent of the boys and 6 percent of the girls) report having had any homosexual experiences, and only 2 percent of the boys and almost no girls

report having had any homosexual experiences during the preceding month (Sorensen, 1973).

After interviewing sixty young men aged 16 to 22 who had had at least one homosexual experience to orgasm, Roesler and Deisher (1972) found that before a youth considers himself a homosexual, certain significant events have usually taken place over a period of time, including early homosexual sex play, seeking out homosexual partners in adolescence, and "coming out," or participating in the gay world.

They found that, on the average, it takes four years for a youth to go from his first homosexual orgasm to the point of considering himself a homosexual. These four years are often a time of extreme emotional turmoil. Almost half the young men in this study (48 percent) had visited a psychiatrist during this time of transition, and almost one-third (31 percent) had made what they considered a significant suicide attempt. Their unhappiness shows their difficulties in accepting themselves as homosexuals.

Comment Roesler and Deisher:

The depth of revulsion toward homosexual activity in our society is such that there are very few places a young person can turn to discuss his problems without being condemned. The institutions from which young people usually derive security—church, school and family—are often nonsupportive when a youth reveals homosexual feelings and experiences. It is usually after such institutions have failed that a physician is called to answer the cry for help [p. 1023].

Some youths apparently find it easier to accept their homosexual identities. More than half of this group, for example, did not seek psychiatric help, and more than two-thirds did not attempt suicide, not even as a cry for help.

Most boys and girls feel that homosexuality is abnormal, and few say they would participate in it themselves. More than half support laws against homosexuality, and only about 40 percent feel that "if two boys/girls want to have sex together, it's all right so long as they both want to do it" (Sorensen, 1973, p. 289).

Theories abound about the nature and the causes of homosexuality, with very little concrete knowledge about it. Male homosexuality is more common in our society than female homosexuality, but no one knows why. Either kind is thought to be a pathological dysfunction by some, or merely a variant of normal sexuality by others; at least one psychiatrist feels that "if there were no social restrictions on sexual object choice, most humans would be functioning bisexuals" (Gould, 1974).

PROBLEMS OF ADOLESCENCE

As we have said, most people weather the adolescent years quite well. And yet many serious problems do make their first appearance during these years. Some of the signals that can portend serious trouble for the individual are dropping out of school, running away from home, abusing alcohol and other drugs, and getting into trouble with the law. The inability to handle the responsibility of sexual behavior often results in an unplanned pregnancy or in the contraction of a venereal disease. Serious emotional illness, such as depression or schizophrenia, often comes to the surface in adolescence. It is important to remember that these problems are not "normal," not "typical," but that they are, instead, signals that a young person is in trouble and needs help. The danger in assuming that

turmoil is a normal, necessary part of adolescence is that we will fail to recognize a teenager in trouble and will fail to get that young person the help that she or he needs.

Let us look at some of the most common problems of adolescents.

VENEREAL DISEASE

The rates for diseases that are spread through sexual contact have soared for all ages over the past twenty years. The increase in the eight major venereal diseases, of which the best known are syphilis and gonorrhea, has had a particularly severe effect on adolescents. During 1972 more than half a million victims of syphilis and gonorrhea were under 21, and a substantial number were under 15 (Gordon, 1973). About 11 percent of nonvirgin boys and 10 percent of nonvirgin girls have had VD themselves, and almost all adolescents over 15 know at least one friend who has had it (Sorensen, 1973).

The reasons for this rise of venereal disease among young people are manifold: increased sexual activity among all age groups; the oral contraceptive, which does *not* protect against VD, replacing the condom, which does; the complacent attitude that VD can be cured easily; the *personal fable* viewpoint, which makes youths think they and their lovers are immune; and the willingness to take risks because people want sexual intercourse more than they don't want VD.

Most teenagers know the basic health facts—that VD is transmitted through sexual contact, that anyone can get it, and that it is serious (Sorensen, 1973). But they are often reluctant to seek help because they are afraid their parents will find out, and they are ashamed and embarrassed to alert their sexual partners. Most of the educational campaigns aimed at eradicating venereal disease focus on catching and treating it early. Not until at least equal prominence is given to preventing it and to the moral obligation to avoid passing it on will headway be made in stopping this epidemic.

With increasing sexual activity among teenage girls, the rate of teenage pregnancy has increased proportionately. (Mary Ellen Mark/Magnum)

ADOLESCENT PREGNANCY

At a time when the birthrate among American women, in general, is on the decline, there is one group for whom it is rising—unmarried teenagers. Over the last decade, out-of-wedlock births have increased by 75 percent among younger adolescents and 33 percent among 18- to 19-year-olds (McKenry, Walters, & Johnson, 1979). One in ten American girls gets pregnant by the age of 17; 1 in 4 does so by the age of 19; and 8 in 10 are not married when they conceive (Zelnik, Kim, & Kantner, 1979). The proportion of white girls who conceive has increased in recent years as a direct result of their increasing sexual activity. About 1 in 4 sexually active girls has been pregnant at least once by the age of 17, and 1 in 3 by the age of 19. While 1 out of 3 girls do terminate their pregnancies by abortion (American Academy of Pediatrics, 1979), this still leaves a staggeringly high number of babies born to unmarried young girls. In 1977, for example, there were some 600,000 babies born to mothers under the age of 20 (Conger, 1978).

Although one-third of the abortions in this country are performed on teenage girls, more than half of all pregnant adolescents see their pregnancies through to delivery of the child (*The New York Times*, 1977). Teenage mothers bear one-fifth of our nation's children and are responsible for half of all illegitimate births (Mothner, 1977).

The Consequences of Teenage Parenthood

Nine out of ten pregnant girls from lower socioeconomic levels keep their babies (Gordon, 1973). Sometimes they raise the children themselves, whether or not they marry the father, or they turn them over to their own mothers. Middle- or upper-class girls usually have an abortion, put the baby up for adoption, or get married. From one-half to three-quarters of all teenage marriages are "shotgun weddings," and about half of all teen marriages end in divorce (Gordon, 1973; Wagner, 1970). Teenage marriages are two to four times as likely to split up as those of older people (Gordon, 1973).

The consequences of this increase in teenage parenthood are great for the young mothers, their babies, and society at large. The girls themselves are more prone to a number of complications of pregnancy, including anemia, prolonged labor, and toxemia (McKenry et al., 1979). Young mothers are twice as likely to bear low-birthweight and premature babies, two to three times more likely to have babies who die in the first year, and 2.4 times more likely to bear children with neurological defects (McKenry et al., 1979). Recent research seems to indicate that a major reason for the health problems of teenage mothers and their children is social, not medical. In two large-scale university hospital studies, one American and one Danish, the teenage pregnancies turned out better than those of any other age group, leading the authors to conclude that "if early, regular, and high quality medical care is made available to pregnant teenagers, the likelihood is that pregnancies and deliveries in this age group will not entail any higher medical risk than those of women in their twenties" (Mednick, Baker, & Sutton-Smith, 1979, p. 17).

Even with the best of care, however, and the best of physical outcomes, the lot of teenage parents and their children is often not a happy one. The Danish study cited above found that the teenage mothers in the group had more trouble rearing their children, and that by 1 year of age, their infants were showing a deterioration, while the babies of older mothers were improving (Rebenkoff, 1979).

In another study, Furstenberg (1976) compared the life experiences of 400 girls who became mothers by the time they were 17 with the lives of classmates who did not become pregnant in early adolescence. Almost all the young mothers said they wanted to finish high school, but half did not, showing a dropout rate five times greater than that of their classmates. Two-thirds of the young mothers married within five years after their babies were born, and 3 out of 5 of these marriages broke up within six years. Their marriages were twice as likely to break up as those of their classmates. After five years, only 48 percent of the young mothers were holding jobs, compared with 63 percent of their classmates. They were three times more likely to be entirely dependent on welfare. Obviously, teenage motherhood can have disastrous effects on a girl's life, so much so that unmarried pregnant girls attempt suicide more often than other girls their age (McKenry et al., 1979).

Why Teenagers Get Pregnant

Why, in an age of improved contraception, do so many girls get pregnant? Few sexually active girls openly express a desire to have a baby outside of marriage, but some theorists believe that many a teenager gets pregnant to satisfy underlying psychological needs. She is thought to be acting out Oedipal fantasies in which she substitutes her boyfriend for her father, is trying to prove her maturity to her parents, tries to place herself on an equal footing with her mother, sees the baby as the person who can give her the unconditional love missing from her life, has the baby to overcome penis envy, or has any number of other personality problems. Many other observers feel that pregnant teenagers are no different psychologically from nonpregnant sexually active girls.

Furstenberg (1976) found that the young mothers in this study did not differ much from their classmates in their sexual practices, suggesting that they had not engaged in sex because they wanted to have a baby at this time in their lives, but had instead become pregnant by accident.

Recent findings show that girls are particularly at risk for pregnancy in the first few months after they begin having intercourse, with half of first premarital pregnancies to teenagers occurring in the first six months and

*Just as gratefulness was con-
fused in my mind with love,
so possession became mixed up
with motherhood. I had a baby.
He was beautiful and totally
mine. No one had bought him
for me.*

Maya Angelou,
I Know Why the Caged Bird Sings, p. 245.

1 out of 5 in the first month after beginning intercourse (Zabin, Kantner, & Zelnik, 1979). While sexual activity is beginning at younger and younger ages, teenagers seldom seek contraceptive help until they have been sexually active for a year or more. The younger the girl is when she begins to have sex, the longer she delays in seeking contraception.

Pregnancy among teenagers is usually the result of using no contraception at all. Shah, Zelnik, and Kantner (1975) asked almost 1000 sexually active teenagers about their contraceptive practices, and 4 out of 5 indicated that they had engaged in intercourse without using any means of birth control. Of these, 7 out of 10 said that they did not use contraception because they thought they could not become pregnant. Some were ignorant of the facts of reproduction, thinking they could not conceive because they were too young, because they had sex infrequently, or because it was the wrong time of the month.

Then the *personal fable* plays its part. About 1 girl out of 3 believes that a girl who does not want a baby will not have one (Sorensen, 1973). Said one 18-year-old:

Like when I'm having sex, I don't really connect it with getting pregnant, cause I've never been pregnant, you know, and a lot of my friends have but I just can't picture it happening to me. And like you really don't connect it, you know, until once you've been pregnant. Because when it's never happened you say, "Why should it happen?" or, "It's never happened yet," you know. You always look at the other person and say, "It happened to them, but it'll never happen to me" [p. 324].

The second most important reason for not using birth control, according to Shah, Zelnik, and Kantner's study (1975), is the nonavailability of contraceptives to teenage girls. About 3 out of 10 girls said they did not know where to get contraceptives, thought they were too expensive, did not have anything at the time of intercourse, or did not know about them.

Some girls are ignorant of the most effective methods, especially the diaphragm or the intrauterine device; some are afraid their parents will find their contraceptives. Some are reluctant to disturb the spontaneity of the sex act by appearing too well prepared ahead of time. Some feel that contraception is too much trouble, or they forget to take adequate measures. Some feel it is their boyfriends' responsibility. As abortions are legalized and easier to get, some feel they can turn to this afterward.

The phrase "I'm not that kind of girl" sums up a major reason why many girls do not use birth control (Wagner, 1970). These girls feel that sexual intercourse is wrong and that they should not be engaging in it. They either deny to themselves that they are sexually active or keep making resolutions that this night is going to be different. They avoid the appearance, even to themselves, of planning to "go all the way." They save their self-respect by considering themselves as having been so swept away by love that they could not help themselves. Unpremeditated sex is acceptable, while carefully planned sex is something only "bad" girls engage in.

This attitude is borne out dramatically by Furstenberg's (1976) finding that nearly half the pregnant teenagers in his study said that it was very important for a woman to wait until marriage to have sex. Explaining the discrepancy between words and deeds, he says:

Many of the youths were paying allegiance to a

sexual code to which they were unable to adhere. This ambivalence made it especially difficult for these women to deal with the consequences of their sexual behavior [p. 150].

There has been a dramatic increase in the quality and consistency of teenage contraception in recent years. Zelnik and Kantner (1977) found that the percentage of sexually active adolescents using the most effective birth control methods—The Pill and the IUD—virtually doubled from 1971 to 1976, possibly because teenagers have been availing themselves of the services of family planning clinics. Despite this increase, though, teens' knowledge of the risk of pregnancy remains poor, they rarely use birth control methods when they first begin to have sexual intercourse, and many wait until after the first unplanned pregnancy.

Since the most common method of teenage birth control today is The Pill, many boys automatically assume that their girlfriends have taken precautions. More than 60 percent of boys who had had intercourse during the preceding month never used a condom (Sorensen, 1973), once the most common contraceptive for young people. Some boys are afraid that if they bring up the possibility of pregnancy, their partners will change their mind about wanting sexual intercourse (Scales, 1977).

Unmarried fathers do not seem to have deep psychological motivations for siring children. Compared with other boys, teenage fathers are quite similar in personality and intellectual functioning (Pauker, 1971). Scales (1977) urges counselors to

Increase males' concern with the possibility of pregnancy and to encourage their willingness to share responsibility for preventing pregnancy as a necessary part of nonexploitative relationships [p. 220].

Needs of Unmarried Teenage Parents

Pregnant girls have special needs. Any pregnant woman needs reassurance of her ability to bear and care for a child and of her continued attractiveness. She needs to communicate her anxieties and to receive sympathy and reassurance. The unmarried teenager is especially vulnerable. She realizes that emotionally and intellectually she is far less mature than she had thought. Whatever she decides to do about the baby, she has conflicting feelings. At the time a pregnant girl needs the most emotional support, she often gets the least. Her boyfriend may be frightened by the responsibility and turn away from her. Her family may be angry with her. She may be isolated from her friends by not being able to attend school with them. This emotional isolation in a time of great tension can disrupt the adolescent search for identity. To alleviate these pressures, the pregnant teenager should be able to discuss her problems with an interested, sympathetic, and knowledgeable counselor.

While the major impact of an illegitimate pregnancy is felt by the mother, the teenage father's life is often affected as well. A boy who feels emotionally committed to the girl he has impregnated also has decisions to make. He may pay for her abortion, at some financial sacrifice. Or he may take the more long-lasting step of marrying his girlfriend, a move that will affect his educational and career plans. The adolescent father also needs someone to talk to, to help him sort out his own feelings and make the best decision for himself, his sweetheart, and the new life they have conceived.

DROPPING OUT OF SCHOOL

Students who leave school before earning their diplomas are likely to have serious vocational and social problems. In our highly technological society, the number of jobs for unskilled workers is shrinking, day by day. Many employers will not hire anyone who is not a high school graduate for any job. Fewer adolescents drop out these days. Between 1970 and 1977, high school dropouts across the country had declined from 17 percent of the population aged 14 to 34 to 13.6 percent. The total for blacks, though, remained at 20.4 percent (Hechinger, 1979).

The need to stay in school is high for several reasons, which have to do with the increasing technology of our society and the current state of the economy. When technology is important, even entry-level jobs require a higher basic level of education. When unemployment is high, youths are urged to remain in school so that they will remain out of the labor market a little while longer. The combination of these pressures serves to keep more young people in school for a longer period of time. In 1960 there were a million school dropouts, compared with only 800,000 in 1971. But 800,000 minimally educated, minimally trained, and minimally employable youths are too many.

Who Are the Dropouts?

Poor black students are most likely to drop out, although 4 out of 5 dropouts are white, and financial need is very rarely the primary reason for leaving school (Cervantes, 1965a). Girls drop out as often as boys; dropouts are likely to have been left back, to score lower on intelligence tests, and to have reading problems (Combs & Cooley, 1968). But most dropouts are of at least normal intelligence, and some have IQs of 110 or more (Combs & Cooley, 1968; Cervantes, 1965a). At least half and maybe three-fourths of these students have the ability to graduate from high school. Why don't they?

Why They Drop Out

Reasons for leaving school are many. Voss, Wendling, and Elliott (1966) set up three categories: the *involuntary dropout*, who must leave school because of physical disability or family emergency; the *retarded dropout*, who

is incapable of doing high school work; and the *capable dropout*, who has the ability to graduate. Those in the first category are relatively rare, and those in the second case can be explained easily. Retarded dropouts usually leave school early. In one study, three-fourths of those who dropped out in seventh grade had IQ scores below 85, compared to only one-third of those who left between seventh and twelfth grades (Voss et al., 1966). Capable dropouts present the greatest challenge.

Combs and Cooley (1968) tested a large and diverse number of ninth-graders in 1960, and four years later they compared those who had dropped out with those who graduated but had not gone on to college. As ninth-graders, the dropouts generally scored lower in general academic ability, but some scored in the highest quarter. The dropouts showed more interest in labor and skilled trades—boys in music, and girls in mechanical and technical fields. Some may have felt that further academic schooling would be neither relevant nor helpful.

Differences in personality and school activity showed up. Both male and female graduates saw themselves as tidier, calmer, more vigorous, more cultured, more mature, more sociable, and more self-confident than did the dropouts. The dropout boys considered themselves leaders more often, but they also saw themselves as more impulsive. They had a lower sense of self-esteem. Dropout boys dated more and had more trouble studying. Girls who dropped out were more likely to come from poorer families than graduates, but there was no such difference for the boys. Financial need was not, then, what caused the boys to leave school. It may not have been the determining factor for girls, either, since most got married and moved away from home instead of contributing to family income.

It is almost impossible to pin down the precise reasons for dropping out. Three-fourths of the girls said they left to get married. But did they want to marry because they weren't doing well in school, because they became pregnant, or because they wanted to get away from home? The boys gave a variety of reasons for leaving—they were needed at home, didn't like school, were failing, got married, or felt too old to be in school—but these explanations tell very little about underlying reasons. Whatever their reasons, more than half regretted having left school (Combs & Cooley, 1968).

Cervantes (1965b) compared 150 white lower-class high school seniors with 150 dropouts and concluded that a major difference lay in family relationships. Among the dropouts, 4 out of 5 did not feel understood or accepted by their families, while 4 out of 5 seniors felt mutual understanding and acceptance. The seniors' families communicated with each other better than the dropouts' families did, and they enjoyed each other's company more. These differences may not apply to minority-group members, whose reasons for dropping out may have more to do with alienation from the educational structure and society at large than from their immediate families.

DRUG ABUSE

From the beginnings of history, humankind has sought to relieve the ills that flesh and spirit are heir to by developing a medicinal arsenal. People have always relied on drugs to alleviate unhappiness and ill health, and to give a lift to their lives. The ancient Greeks got drunk on alcohol; marijuana was used in China and India well before the birth of Christ; and cocaine was a staple among sixteenth-century Incas. If drugs are such a constant, why are we so concerned about contempo-

rary drug use? For one reason, because so many people today are using drugs at a very young age. And while certain drugs may not be harmful in moderation, adolescents are not known for being moderate. In these years of identity crisis, they often turn to drugs as shortcut answers to their problems, and they endanger their physical and psychological health while failing to resolve the problems. Youthful drug use seems to be on the downswing since its peak during the 1960s, but many young people are still ingesting legal drugs like alcohol and nicotine, and illegal ones like marijuana, LSD, cocaine, amphetamines, barbiturates, and heroin.

Of 7414 high school students surveyed by Yancy, Nader, and Burnham (1972), 85 percent had used alcohol, and 27 percent had used marijuana. Only 8.6 percent had tried LSD, and less than 3 percent had used heroin. Curiosity led most of them to try drugs, and many experimented once and stopped. The authors concluded: "Drug use, in itself, may not be evidence of psychopathology, but a result of the normal adolescent curiosity and desire to experiment" (p. 744). This, of course, would not apply to those teenagers who continue to use drugs regularly and heavily. In Milman and Su's 1973 survey of 551 middle-class, white, private high school students, they found that an illicit drug user was more likely to be an older boy who also smoked and drank, who got poor grades and was not interested in going on to college, who had drug-using friends, was sexually active, had a history of difficulty with the police, and was generally unhappy.

Youthful drug-taking patterns generally follow those of the adult society (Lennard, 1971). Just as adults take barbiturates and stimulants to alleviate unhappiness, depression, and day-to-day pressures, so do youths. Pharmaceutical companies and drug-oriented adolescents alike extol the use of drugs in virtually every human situation. The danger in this attitude is that opting for a chemical solution obscures the nature of the real problems facing young people and can impede

Most teenagers drink moderately and have no problems, but some, like some adults, cannot handle alcohol. (Paul Conklin/Monkmeyer)

recognition that social systems need to be altered or new social arrangements need to be created (Lennard, 1971).

Alcohol

Many of the same people who are deeply worried about illegal marijuana use are brought up short when reminded that alcohol is also illegal for most high school and many college students—and it is a much more serious problem. Alcohol is the most heavily abused drug in the United States today. It is certainly the most frequently used, with some 80 million drinkers in this country, many of whom are young people.

More than 1 million teenagers drink daily or on weekends. A nationwide survey done for the National Institute on Alcohol Abuse and Alcoholism of 13,122 seventh- to twelfth-graders found that most American adolescents drink (Rachal, Williams, Brehm,

Cavanaugh, Moore, & Eckerman, 1975). More than half drink at least once a month, and only about 1 in 4 of these 13- to 18-year-olds don't drink at all or drink less than once a year. About 1 in 4 who are 13 years old or younger drink often enough and in large enough quantities to be classed as at least moderate drinkers, and more than half of those 17 or over are in this category. Boys drink more often and more heavily than girls; beer is the favorite teenage drink, followed by wine and then hard liquor; and children tend to follow the drinking patterns of their parents:

The abstainer is most likely to come from an abstaining home; the moderate drinker from a home in which the parents drink moderately; and the heavy drinker from homes in which heavy drinking has been the pattern [Akers, 1970, p. 277].

Most teenagers drink moderately and infrequently and have no problems with alcohol; but some youths, like some adults, cannot handle this potent psychoactive drug. The most troubling finding of this NIAAA survey was its high proportion of young problem drinkers, defined as those who had been drunk at least four times in the past year or who had gotten in trouble with friends, school authorities, or the police at least twice in the past year because of drinking. More than 1 out of 4 could thus be classified as problem drinkers.

The typical teenage problem drinker is a boy, 15 or older, who rarely goes to church, does poorly in school, and comes from a family with drinking parents. Interestingly, he is likely to have first tried alcohol at about the age of 12, later than the youngster who drinks more moderately (Rachal et al, 1975).

Most teenagers start to drink because it seems a grown-up thing to do, and they continue to do so for the same reasons adults do—to put a pleasant glow on social situations, to reduce anxiety, and to escape from problems. Teenage drinking is closely linked with delinquent behavior (Akers, 1970), but it appears that many young people drink for the same reasons they engage in antisocial behavior. The problem drinking does not cause the delinquent behavior, but both grow out of the same needs.

Marijuana
While many teens use marijuana the same way their parents used alcohol, the fact that they are using a drug outside the ken of their parents' generation enhances the appeal for youth and the anxiety for adults. Marijuana has been known all over the world for centuries, but its use among Western middle-class youth is a recent phenomenon.

In 1976, the National Institute of Drug Abuse surveyed 17,000 high school seniors from 130 schools and found that 53 percent had tried marijuana, 5 percent more than had reported using it the previous year. Thirty-two percent of these students considered themselves current marijuana users, while 70 percent voiced disapproval of regular marijuana smoking. In another study reported by the institute, 53 percent of 18- to 25-year-olds and 22 percent of 12- to 17-year-olds reported that they had tried marijuana, with 25 percent of the older group and 15 percent of the younger students indicating that they used it currently on an occasional or regular basis. The young adults used cigarettes and alcohol more frequently than marijuana, but the high school seniors were likely to consider tobacco a more serious health risk than marijuana (*Pediatric News*, 1977; *Capital Times*, 1976).

Students and nonstudents the same age are just as likely to smoke (Brecher, 1972), and even those who don't use it themselves

generally accept its use by others (Tec, 1972). The use of marijuana has risen steadily in recent years. In 1967 a Gallup poll of college students found that 5 percent had smoked marijuana; in 1974, a similar study found that 55 percent had smoked it; and a 1979 inquiry found that 66 percent of college students had tried it (*The New York Times*, 1979).

Marijuana smokers are more likely to drink, and heavy users tend to be heavy drinkers (Rachal et al., 1975). One probably does not cause the other, but the correlation reflects the fact that certain personalities turn toward drugs to solve problems.

Marijuana is not physically addicting, but some people apparently become psychologically dependent on it. Furthermore, it may cause some physical problems. Recent research on healthy young adults indicates that chronic marijuana smoking may impair the large airways to an extent not observed in habitual tobaccco smokers, and marijuana smoke is said to contain 50 percent more cancer-causing materials than does tobacco smoke (Doyle, 1979). More definitive research is necessary to determine the effects of marijuana on the body.

Tobacco
Sneaking a cigarette behind the barn has become a humorous staple of adolescent lore. But the amused, indulgent smiles accepting youthful forays into regular use of tobacco have turned to concern, with new awareness of health hazards. The publication in 1964 of the U.S. Surgeon General's report clearly brought out relationships between smoking and lung cancer, heart attack, emphysema, and other diseases.

Adolescents got the message. Most 13- to 18-year-olds feel that smoking causes cancer and increases the chance of heart attack (Lieberman, 1970). Yet 1 out of every 4 teenagers smokes, and many who hold these opinions are regular smokers. Most young smokers feel that they will stop smoking in five years or less, apparently unaware of the tremendous difficulty many people experience in giving up this habit. In fact, many scientists feel that smoking is not just a habit but an actual physiological addiction (Brecher, 1972).

While fewer adults are smoking these days, more teenagers—most especially girls—are taking it up. The proportion of adolescent girls who smoke almost doubled between 1968 to 1974, so that now teenage girls smoke as much as teenage boys (Howard, 1978). If this trend continues, one type of equality women will achieve will be the equal chance of contracting such smoking-related diseases as lung cancer and heart attack, as preliminary reports are already indicating (Brody, 1973). Each year, about 1½ million adolescents begin to smoke, and this age group now accounts for some 6 million regular smokers (National Institute of Child Health and Human Development, 1978). In 1977, 1 in 5 high school seniors were smoking ten or more cigarettes daily (McAlister, Perry, & Maccoby, 1979).

Why do teens start to smoke? Most drift into it. Children often smoke their first cigarette sometime between the ages of 10 and 12, and rarely enjoy it. Yet many force themselves to have another, those who will become smokers usually do so at 12 or 13 years of age, and smokers become physically dependent on nicotine at about 15 (NICHHD, 1978; McAlister et al., 1979).

Young people are most likely to smoke when their friends and families do. If one parent smokes, a child is twice as likely to do so than if neither parent did. If both parents, or one parent and an older brother or sister, smoke, the chances are 4 to 1 that a youngster will follow suit. And if a child's best friend smokes, chances soar to 9 out of 10 that the child will also (NICHHD, 1978).

Smoking is somewhat of a class phenomenon: Young people who do not plan to go on to college are more than twice as likely to smoke as are those who do (McAlister et al., 1979). It is also related to personality. Teen smokers are likely to be more rebellious, better able to tolerate ambiguity, want to be older, achieve less well in school, and go out less for sports (McAlister et al., 1979).

Many efforts have been made to discourage young people from smoking, but the only kind that seems to show any promise at all is one that relies heavily on peer leadership. Since peer pressures seems so effective in inducing people to smoke, its influence in the other direction may be the best preventive mechanism (McAlister et al., 1979).

JUVENILE DELINQUENCY

There are two kinds of juvenile delinquency. One type of delinquent is the *status offender*. This is the young person who has been truant, run away from home, been sexually active, not abided by parental rules, or done something else that is ordinarily not considered criminal—except when committed by a minor.

Then there is the person who has done something that is considered a crime no matter who commits it—like robbery, rape, or murder. If the person is under 16 or 18 (depending on the state), she or he is usually treated differently from an adult criminal. The court proceedings are likely to be secret, the offender is more likely to be seen and sentenced by a judge rather than a jury, and the punishment is usually more lenient.

Children between the ages of 10 and 17, who make up only 16 percent of the population, accounted for almost half of all arrests in 1974 for violent crimes and theft (Chambers, 1975). Many people feel that the large amount of juvenile crime is caused by the law's treating juvenile offenders differently from adults. The controversy in dealing with young delinquents, then, is between two forces. There are those who feel that sentences should be meted out depending on the youth's own needs, with emphasis on social solutions such as probation and therapeutic guidance. The other camp would base sentences on the seriousness of the crime rather than the age and special needs of the young person who committed it. The latter point of view seems to be gaining ground and probably will lead to many changes in dealing with young offenders (Chambers, 1975).

Studies of adults have shown that many young people commit offenses which are officially classifiable as delinquent but that few receive any kind of handling by the police which would label them as young criminals (Perlman, 1964). Youths from socially and economically deprived backgrounds probably commit more crime than middle-class youth—and are *much* more likely to get police records for minor offenses. Since much delinquent behavior among middle- and upper-class adolescents never comes to the attention of authoities, it is impossible to estimate its real prevalence.

According to statistics drawn by the Federal Bureau of Investigation from reports received from police departments around the country, 23 percent of the arrests in 1978 were for people under the age of 18 and 7 percent for those under 15 (FBI, 1979). Even though crimes went up 11.7 percent between 1969 and 1978, the arrests of juveniles decreased by 10 percent from 1974 to 1978. Many more boys and men still get arrested compared to girls and women. However, as in so many other aspects of life these days, the women are catching up. For all ages in the population, the male crime rate rose by 5.5 percent between 1969 and 1978, while the female crime rate rose by considerably more—39.1 percent. The males accounted for 90 percent of violent crimes, while larceny was the prime crime of females.

The major increases in crime by girls under 18 were in these categories: robbery; forgery; counterfeiting; fraud; buying, receiving, and possessing stolen property; embez-

zlement; prostitution and commercialized vice; offenses against family and children; and driving under the influence of alcohol. For boys under 18, the major increases were for embezzlement; prostitution and commercial vice; drug abuse; offenses against family and children; and driving under the influence of alcohol.

Girls are now becoming more like boys in their delinquency. Proportionately more of them are engaging in the same kinds of aggressive crimes that characterize male delinquency, as opposed to the misbehavior (like running away, sex offenses, and ungovernable behavior) that had previously characterized most female delinquency.

Who Is the Delinquent Youth?

The typical delinquent is a boy of 15 who lives with one parent and several brothers and sisters. The family lives in an overcrowded apartment in a deteriorating neighborhood in a big city. The boy has done poorly in school for years; he's gotten low grades, was left back, and is now about to drop out (President's Commission, 1967). The neighborhood plays a large part in delinquency, since a child from a poor family who lives in an upper-class area is less likely to become delinquent than one surrounded by other deprived families (President's Commission, 1967). Studies of many ethnic groups—Germans, Irish, Poles, Italians, and blacks—show that crime is heaviest in the inner city and lowest as families are able to move out (President's Commission, 1967). The persistently high crime statistics for black youths reflect in part their families' greater difficulty in getting away from the high-crime urban core.

The Delinquent's Family

The picture of the family of delinquent youths that emerges from many different studies, as reviewed by Cavan and Ferdinand (1975), is one of parents who are harsh, rejecting, or indifferent, but rarely affectionate; who neglect or beat their children, are erratic in their discipline, and rarely exercise consistent, firm guidance; and who are themselves unhappy, insecure, inadequate at coping with life, and unable to offer their children qualities to admire and copy. They tend to be separated or unhappily married and are often so burdened with their own emotional and social problems that they have little time, energy, or sensitivity for their children's. Most research has been done on the families of lower-class boys, and relatively little is known about middle-class and female delinquents.

The Delinquent's Personality

Not all children from deprived neighborhoods and unhappy families are destined for a life of crime, of course. What makes one child get into trouble, while another from the same street, or even the same family, stays law-abiding? Recent research has focused more on the psychological profiles of delinquents, rather than on their sociological backgrounds.

After studying fifty-five delinquents who had been patients at the Illinois State Psychiatric Institute, Offer, Ostrov, and Marohn (1973) concluded that delinquency is not a class phenomenon, but a result of emotional turmoil that affects young people from all levels of society. The affluent delinquents get taken to psychiatrists, while the ones from poor families get booked by police.

These psychiatrists identified four different kinds of delinquent youths: the *impulsive* delinquent, who acts without thinking and has no controls; the *narcissistic* delinquent, who focuses only on himself, feels he has been hurt, and sees his only way of maintaining self-esteem as getting back at the people who have hurt him; the *emotionally empty* delinquent, who is passive, unfeeling, and a loner; and the *depressed* delinquent, who acts out to relieve the pain of his internal conflict.

Other recent research has related physical causes to delinquency. Lewis, Balla, Pincus, and Shanok (1979) divided ninety-seven boys at a correctional school into two groups: violent offenders, who had committed assaults, rape, and murder; and less violent or nonviolent offenders, who had set fires, been

in fistfights, or threatened people. The violent youths had more serious and more extensive medical histories, had suffered more head injuries early in life, had been the victims of more physical abuse, and had shown more neurological symptoms, like blackout spells and falling (often symptoms of epilepsy). Furthermore, they had more psychiatric symptoms, like paranoia (an obsessive conviction that other people want to hurt you), delusions, and hallucinations. Identifying medical causes as contributing factors to delinquency may make it possible to treat some youthful offenders with medications such as anticonvulsants and antidepressants.

EGO STRENGTHS OF ADOLESCENTS

There are many positive aspects to adolescent life. Normal adolescence is exciting: All things appear possible; one is on the threshold of love and life's work and participation in the broader society; one is getting to know the most interesting person in the whole world, oneself. Yet few adolescents recognize and value their positive attributes.

Researchers who gave blank sheets of paper to 100 high school students and asked them to list their strengths found that out of a total of nineteen categories (see Table 11-3), the average student listed only seven strengths. Say Otto and Healy (1966):

This indicates a limited self-perception of personality strengths not too markedly different from that of adults. In similar studies which have been conducted, adults have listed an average of six strengths but at the same time were able to fill one or more pages with listings of their "problems" or "weaknesses" [p. 293].

Most of the young people listed relation-

TABLE 11-3
Adolescent Strength
Categories

1 *Health*—this includes being in general good health, promoting and maintaining health, and having energy and vitality.

2 *Aesthetic strengths*—included here are the ability to enjoy and recognize beauty in nature, objects, or people.

3 *Special aptitudes or resources*—this includes special abilities or capacities such as having special skills to repair things, ability to make things grow, or "green thumb," having ability in mathematics or music, etc.

4 *Employment satisfaction*—enjoyment of work or duties, ability to get along with co-workers, pride in work, superior satisfaction with work.

5 *Social strengths*—having sufficient friends of both sexes, use of humor in social relations, and the ability to entertain others were included here.

6 *Spectator sports*—attendance or interest in football, baseball games, the reading of books, fiction, plays, etc., were listed under this category.

7 *Strengths through family and others*—included here were getting along with brothers and sisters and parents, ability to talk over problems with father or mother, feelings of closeness or loyalty to family, etc.

8 *Imaginative and creative strengths*—use of creativity and imagination in relation to school, home, or family, expression of creative capacity through writing, etc.

9 *Dependability and responsibility strengths*—listed here were ability to keep appointments, trust placed in respondent by other people, keeping promises, and perseverance in bringing a task to conclusion.

10 *Spiritual strengths*—attendance at church activities and meetings, church membership, reliance on religious beliefs, feeling close to God, using prayer, meditation, etc.

11 *Organizational strengths*—ability to lead clubs, teams, or organizations, capacity to give or carry our orders, having long- or short-range plans, etc.

12 *Intellectual strengths*—included here were an interest in new ideas from people, books, or other sources, enjoyment of learning, interest in the continuing development of the mind, etc.

13 *Other strengths*—listed here were such items as ability to risk oneself, liking to adventure or pioneer, the ability to grow through defeat or crisis, etc.

14 *Emotional strengths*—ability to give and receive warmth, affection, or love, capacity to take anger from others, being aware of the feelings of others, etc., capacity for empathy, etc.

15 *Expressive arts*—included here were participation in dramatic plays, ballroom and other types of dancing, sculpting, playing a musical instrument, etc.

16 *Relationship strengths*—this category includes such items as getting along well with most of the teachers, being patient and understanding with people, helping others, accepting people as individuals regardless of sex, beliefs, or race; other people confiding in respondent, etc.

17 *Education, training, and related areas*—this included good grades received, the acquisition of special skills, such as typing, selling, or mechanical drawing, etc.

18 *Hobbies, crafts, etc.*—listing of any hobbies or interests such as stamp or coin collecting, sewing or knitting, hairstyling, etc.

19 *Sports and activities*—participation in swimming, football, tennis, basketball, etc., and enjoyment or skill in the foregoing activities or outdoor activities such as camping, hiking, etc., were listed here.

SOURCE: From Otto & Healy, 1966.

Normal adolescence is exciting: All things appear possible. (Bonnie Freer/Photo Researchers, Inc.)

ship, intellectual, or emotional strengths; more girls listed social and dependability strengths, while more boys listed sports and activities. While the listings of boys and girls differed somewhat, they were more alike than dissimilar.

These authors gave adolescents more credit for personality strengths than the young people did themselves, listing the following as "personality resources or strengths" of adolescents, which differ qualitatively from those of adults and appear in unique and distinctive patterns:

1   Considerable energy or drive and vitality

2   Idealistic, and have a real concern for the future of this country and the world

3   More often exercise their ability to question contemporary values, philosophies, theologies, and institutions

4   Have heightened sensory awareness and perceptivity

5   Courageous, able to risk themselves or stick their necks out

6   Have a feeling of independence

7 Possess a strong sense of fairness and dislike intolerance

8 Are responsible and can be relied on more often than not

9 Flexible and adapt to change more readily

10 Usually open, frank, and honest

11 An above average sense of loyalty to organizations, causes, etc.

12 Have a sense of humor which (more) often finds expression

13 Have an optimistic and positive outlook on life more often than not

14 Often think seriously and deeply

15 Greater sensitivity and awareness of other persons' feelings

16 They are engaged in a sincere and on-going research for identity [p. 296]

If we can help more young people to recognize and build upon their strengths as they are about to enter adult life, the adolescent search for identity can bear richer fruit.

SUMMARY

1 Various theoretical intepretations of adolescence exist. G. Stanley Hall views adolescence as a time of *storm and stress*, marked by vacillating, contradictory emotions. Margaret Mead is concerned with the way cultural factors influence adolescence; she claims that adolescence may be stressful or smooth, depending upon how a particular society responds. Albert Bandura says adolescence, even in America, is not as stressful as Hall implies. Sigmund Freud places adolescents in the *genital stage*, the stage of mature adult sexuality. This stage is biologically determined and occurs when reawakened sexual urges no longer are repressed as during latency. Now sexual gratification is aimed at developing satisfying heterosexual relationships with people outside the family and in finding a suitable reproductive partner. Anna Freud expanded Sigmund Freud's work on defense mechanisms. These include *intellectualization* and *asceticism*. Erik Erikson's fifth crisis involves the adolescent's search for *identity*, or role *confusion*. Career choice is viewed as an important step in identity formation.   **2** Probably the most important task for the adolescent is the search for identity, which can occur in many ways: by developing one's values, by developing pride in one's achievements, and by developing close relationships with peers.   **3** The relationship between teenagers and parents is not always smooth. Adolescents often feel conflict between wanting independence from parents and realizing how dependent they are. Many adolescents have trouble talking freely with parents—especially about sexual matters.   **4** Teenagers are highly influenced by their peer group. They strongly identify with others in this group and tend to do what their crowd does. Teenagers identify with other teenagers rather than with other people of their own race, religion, community, or sex. And they consider themselves more idealistic, less materialistic, healthier in their sexuality, and better able to understand friendship and the important things in life than are members of the older generation. **5** Adolescent sexual experiences have repercussions on budding identity. Many conflicts between parents and adolescent children focus on sexuality. **6** About half of all 19-year-old girls and almost half of 19-year-old boys are virgins. It is difficult to compare these data with information from past generations. Teenagers tend to enter into meaningful, monogamous sexual relationships, rather than promiscuous ones. **7** Current sexual attitudes are more liberal than in the past. Most males do not lose respect for females who have intercourse before marriage, and most members of both sexes approve of living together before marriage. Still, males tend to be more active sexually. **8** Poor black students are most likely to drop out of school, although 4 out of 5 dropouts are white, and financial need is rarely the cause for dropping out. Females leave school as often as males. **9** Adolescent problems include drug abuse, dropping out of school, juvenile delinquency, and sexual problems such as venereal disease and unwanted pregnancy. **10** Even with all the difficulties of establishing a personal, sexual, social, and vocational identity, adolescence is typically an interesting, exciting, and positive threshold to adulthood.

SUGGESTED READINGS

Berry, J. R. *Kids on the run*. New York: Four Winds Press, 1978. The stories of seven teenage runaways told in their own words, with comments from social workers and others who work with adolescents.

Erikson, E. *Identity: Youth and crisis*. New York: Norton, 1968. Erikson's classic discussion of the development of identity during the adolescent years.

Freud, A. *The writings of Anna Freud, Volume VII (1966–1970): Problems of psychoanalytic training, diagnosis and the technique of therapy*. New York: International Universities Press, 1971. A beautifully illustrated collection of Anna Freud's writings. The clear and lucid text deals with present psychoanalytic training issues and child analysis.

Gordon, S. *The sexual adolescent: Communicating with teenagers about sex*. North Scituate, MA: Duxbury Press, 1973. Everything a teenager wants to know about sex. Information on adolescent pregnancy, abortion, contraception, VD, sex education. Written by a nationally recognized authority on adolescence.

Hunt, M. *Sexual behavior in the 1970's*. New York: Dell, 1974. A survey of premarital, marital, and extramarital sex in the United States during the 1970s.

Hyde, J. *Understanding human sexuality*. New York: McGraw-Hill, 1979. A textbook covering a wide range of topics in the area of sexuality: physical and hormonal factors, contraception, sex research, variations in sexual behavior, sexual dysfunction, and sex and religion, the law, and education.

Konopka, G. *Young girls: A portrait of adolescence*. Englewood Cliffs, NJ: Prentice-Hall, 1976. An intensive study of the lives of almost 1000 adolescent girls in the United States today. Includes discussion of adults, friends, sexuality, drugs, and political concerns.

Maynard, J. *Looking back: A chronicle of growing up old in the sixties.* New York: Doubleday, 1974. The fascinating personal remembrances of a 19-year-old woman who grew up in the 1960s.

Mead, M. *Culture and commitment: A study of the generation gap.* Garden City, NY: Natural History Press/Doubleday, 1970. Mead examines our present knowledge of culture, with its basis in the model she derives from primitive society. She explores living cultures of different degrees of complexity, all existing at the same time, and emphasizes the differences between primitive, historic, and contemporary post–World War II cultures.

Muuss, E. *Theories of adolescence* (3d ed.). New York: Random House, 1975. A systematic and comprehensive picture of different theoretical positions on adolescent development that shows the relationships among them.

Sorensen, R. C. *Adolescent sexuality in contemporary America.* New York: World, 1973. A major report on adolescents' attitudes and behaviors, primarily in the area of sexuality.

Young Adulthood

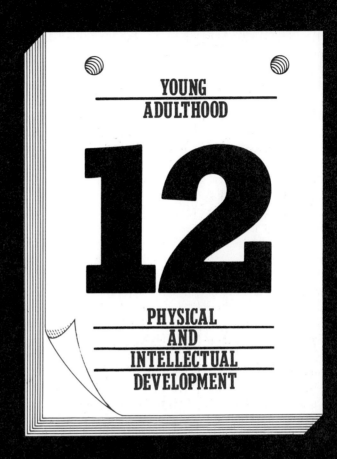

YOUNG
ADULTHOOD

12

PHYSICAL
AND
INTELLECTUAL
DEVELOPMENT

IN THIS CHAPTER
YOU WILL LEARN ABOUT

The general physical health of young
adults (it's good), and how factors such as
education, sex, and marital status affect it

The intellectual functioning of young
adults, including moral development and
creativity

Career choice and job satisfaction, and
how sex affects vocational development

Special situations of those couples in
which both spouses pursue careers
outside the home

CHAPTER OVERVIEW

Physical Development of Young Adults
*Health Status | Women and Hormonal
Fluctuations*

Intellectual Functioning of Young Adults
*Moral Development | Moral Development:
The Woman's Perspective | Creativity*

Career Development
*Career Choices | Job Satisfaction | Sex
and Vocational Development |
Dual-Career Families*

The twenty-year span between the time people emerge from adolescence, at about 20, till they enter midlife, at about 40, is a busy time. If, as many believe, childhood and adolescence are periods of preparation for adulthood, then young adulthood is the time people have been preparing for.

This is the time when people choose their life paths and begin to walk independently along them. People choose their careers. They decide on their family lifestyles—marriage or the single life, parenthood or childlessness, monogamy or extramarital sexual activity—the very structure of life itself. They establish networks of friends, engage in leisure activities, and begin to invest time in civic and community involvement.

Young adults are moving away from their parents' homes to establish their own independent residences and become financially, psychologically, and socially self-supporting. They now sense their chance to live according to their own independent values, unhampered by parental demands; they still, however, are influenced by parental attitudes. They take their first steps in a vocation, even though their first jobs may bear little relationship to their long-range careers. An important part of most young adults' lives are the intimate sexual and emotional relationships they form, which often lead to marriage. Most married people have children during these years and devote much of their time and their emotional and physical energy to raising them. A small but growing segment of the population opts for the single life or for the child-free married one. Most young adults are at their peak physically and intellectually and are rarely held back by dysfunction in either area. During the young adult years people become more secure in their own identity, but they are still constantly growing, developing, expanding, pursuing, and changing their goals.

When does young adulthood begin? As indicated in Chapter 10, the transition from adolescence to adulthood varies widely. No single societal event marks the transition for most people, although in our materialistic society the usual criterion for considering someone an adult is his or her ability to be self-supporting. Children from middle-class families tend to remain financially dependent on their parents until they finish college in their early twenties. Those who pursue graduate education may well be supported by their parents into their thirties. Even if they marry during this time, their financial dependence keeps them from fully assuming an adult role. Working-class young people tend to complete their educations earlier, to marry earlier, and to consider themselves independent adults at an earlier age.

Financial independence is not the only transitional point, of course. Some people who support themselves economically are still their parents' babies emotionally, and some people whose parents still give them money are independent in every other respect. As with the other stages of life, adulthood varies with each individual, according to many different indices.

PHYSICAL DEVELOPMENT OF YOUNG ADULTS

The typical young adult is the ideal physical specimen. Strength, energy, and endurance characterize this time of life. From the middle twenties, when most body functions are fully developed, until about the age of 50, declines from this peak are so gradual they are hardly noticed.

Most men reach their full adult stature at 21.2 years, although 1 out of 10 continues to grow until 23.5 years; most women reach full growth at 17.3 years, although 1 in 10 continues to grow until 21.1 years (Roche & Davila, 1972). Today's 20-year-olds tend to be taller than their parents because of the secular trend in growth, discussed in Chapter 10. Between the ages of 30 and 45, height remains the same; at that point it begins to decline (Tanner, 1978).

The peak of muscular strength occurs sometime around 25 to 30 years of age (Bromley, 1974), followed by a gradual 10 percent loss of strength between 30 and 60 years. Most of the weakening occurs in the back and leg muscles, with a little bit less in the arm muscles. Manual dexterity is most efficient in young adulthood; agility of finger and hand movements begins to lessen after the mid-thirties (Troll, 1975).

The senses are also at their sharpest during young adulthood. Visual acuity is keenest at about age 20 and doesn't begin to decline until about 40, when a tendency toward farsightedness begins to make people resort to reading glasses. Hearing is best at about 20; from this time there is a gradual loss, especially for higher tones. Taste, smell, and sensitivity to touch, temperature, and pain remain stable, with no diminution until about 45 to 50 years.

HEALTH STATUS

Young adults are the healthiest people in the population. More than 9 out of 10 people aged 17 to 44 view their health as good or excellent (U.S. Department of Health, Education, and Welfare, 1976). People in this age group get far fewer colds and respiratory infections than they did as children; and when they do get them, they shake them off easily. Generally, they have outgrown their childhood allergies, and they have fewer accidents. Many young adults are never seriously sick or incapacitated. Very few have chronic conditions. Fewer than 1 percent are limited in their ability to get around and do things because of chronic conditions or impairment.

Women see doctors more frequently than men do, partly because of routine visits that focus on the reproductive system (during pregnancy, during efforts to become pregnant, at the time of abortion, and for such routine tests as the Pap smear, which detects cervical cancer). Another reason for women's more frequent doctors' visits came out in an analysis of the 1975 statistics of the National Ambulatory Medical Care Survey, which collected information on 50,000 visits to doctors around the country (Duffy, 1979). Women seem to be more sensitive to their bodies: They perceive symptoms sooner than men do, act upon them sooner, and have a more elaborate vocabulary for describing them.

About half of all acute conditions experienced in young adulthood are respiratory, and another 20 percent are injuries. The most frequent chronic conditions, which are more common in low-income families, are back or spine problems, hearing impairments, arthritis, and hypertension. The most frequent reasons for hospitalization in these years are childbirth, accidents, and digestive and genitourinary system diseases (U.S. Department of Health, Education, and Welfare, 1976).

Despite the general state of good health in this time of life, frequency of death from all causes increases sharply after age 30. At all ages, the death rate for males is higher than that for females, and between the ages of 15 to 24, the male death rate is almost triple the female, largely because of the high rate of violent deaths among males (Fuchs, 1974). Out of every 4 deaths among men in this age range, 3 are caused by accidents, suicide, or homicide. If violent deaths are excluded, the differential between male and female deaths is only 40 percent—about the same range as for infants and children. The differential begins to fall during the late twenties and continues to do so until about the age of 40, when the male death rate is about 75 percent above the female (Fuchs, 1974). The differential then rises again.

In our society, the biggest killer of young men is accidents, mostly auto accidents. Of every 1000 men under 25, 11 will lose their lives accidentally. The biggest threat to black men is homicide: 30 out of 1000 will lose their lives this way before the age of 55. Very few young men die of disease. Twenty years ago the overall death rate among this age group was 15 percent lower, and the rate for violent deaths was 40 percent lower, despite steady advances in medical care since then. Why, then, are we losing so many of our young? Says Fuchs (1974):

Numerous theories have been advanced to explain the increase in violent deaths among the young—affluence, the Vietnam war, the decline in religious belief, overly permissive parents, and so on—but the only thing we can be certain of is the increase itself. The suspicion also exists that the self-destructiveness of the young is a symptom of more widespread problems in society at large [p. 42].

As people reach the age of 35, they are less likely to die violently; but for men 35 to 44, 3 out of 10 deaths are still violent ones. Cardiovascular problems increase throughout life: Blood pressure has been rising slowly and gradually from early childhood, and cholesterol levels increase steadily between the ages of 21 and 35, when heart attack becomes the leading killer in the United States. It maintains this position throughout life, with men having more heart attacks than women, and those in sedentary occupations having more than more active people (Troll, 1975). Cancer is the second most frequent cause of death for people over 35—breast and uterine cancer for women, and lung cancer for men (American Cancer Society, 1975).

The Effects of Lifestyle on Health

Good health is not just a matter of luck; it often reflects the way we live. A study of 7000 people, aged 20 to 70, found that their observance of seven common health habits (see Table 12-1) was directly related to their health

(Belloc & Breslow, 1972). Those people who followed all seven habits were the healthiest of all, followed by those who followed six, then those who followed five, and so on.

The effects of certain activities can often be seen directly in the incidence of certain health conditions. Smokers, for example, are more likely to contract lung cancer and to suffer from heart ailments (Kakvan & Greenberg, 1977; Walker, 1977); drinkers, to get cirrhosis of the liver (Lieber, 1976); and women who begin sexual intercourse early and engage in it frequently with many different partners, to develop cancer of the cervix (Meisels, Bégin, & Schneider, 1977).

The more education people have, the healthier they tend to be (Fuchs, 1974). Why should this be? First, people with more education tend to come from families with more money, who can afford better medical care. Second, good education may lead to more sensible work and living habits. Formal schooling may increase self-confidence and decrease stress, often a factor in causing or aggravating such diseases as hypertension, heart attacks, stroke, and ulcers. Finally, it is possible that people who are sophisticated enough to see the benefits of a good education are also aware of the importance of a healthy way of life.

Sex differences in mortality may result partly from the beneficial effects of the female hormones. Equally, if not more important, though, are the different lifestyles of most men and women. As female lifestyles become more like those of men, their vulnerability increases, too. Today, for example, more women are dying from lung cancer and heart

TABLE 12-1
Seven Health Habits

1 Eating breakfast
2 Eating regular meals and not snacking
3 Eating moderately to maintain normal weight
4 Not smoking
5 Drinking alcohol moderately or not at all
6 Exercising moderately
7 Sleeping regularly 7–8 hours a night

Married people are healthier than the separated or the widowed. They have lower rates of chronic illness and disability. (© Joel Gordon 1979)

attacks, probably because they are smoking more, drinking more, and assuming more stressful positions in the working world.

Marriage is healthy. Analysis of 1960 and 1970 census data, as well as other governmental health surveys, shows that married people are healthier than the separated or the widowed (Verbrugge, 1979). Married people have low rates of chronic limitation and disability; when they do need to go to the hospital, their stays are generally short. Single people, who have never been married, rank next to the married, followed by the widowed. The least healthy group consists of those who are divorced or separated. These people show high rates of acute conditions, of chronic conditions that limit social activity, and of disability because of health problems.

A number of explanations are possible for the relationship between marital status and health—that people with health problems are less likely to marry in the first place, or to stay married; that married people lead a healthier and safer lifestyle; that the ability of spouses to take care of each other means that hospitalization or institutionalization is needed

less often; that married people merely *seem* healthier, since their family responsibilities keep them from taking time off from work; and that being married is less stressful than the other states. This last explanation finds confirmation in studies on the relationship between stress and illness, which indicate that the life event that causes the most stress is the death of a spouse, closely followed by divorce, and then separation (Holmes & Rahe, 1976).

After asking more than 5000 people to talk about the life events that had taken place in the year before their illnesses, Holmes and his colleagues found strong evidence that the more stress a person was under, the more likely it was that the person would become ill (Holmes & Rahe, 1976; Holmes & Masuda, 1972). Surprisingly, many of these stressful events seemed very positive in nature—such as marriage, a new baby, a new home, or an outstanding personal achievement. Even happy events, though, require some adjustment to change in one's life; this change induces stress, and stress seems to make people more likely to fall sick.

Based on people's assessments of the

TABLE 12-2
Life Events
and Weighted
Values

LIFE EVENT	VALUE	LIFE EVENT	VALUE
Death of spouse	100	Son or daughter leaving home	29
Divorce	73	Trouble with in-laws	29
Marital separation	65	Outstanding personal	
Jail term	63	achievement	28
Death of close family member	63	Wife beginning or stopping	
Personal injury or illness	53	work	26
Marriage	50	Beginning or ending school	26
Fired at work	47	Revision of habits	24
Marital reconciliation	45	Trouble with boss	23
Retirement	45	Change in work hours	20
Change in health of family	44	Change in residence	20
Pregnancy	40	Change in schools	20
Sex difficulties	39	Change in recreation	19
Gain of new family member	39	Change in social activity	18
Change in financial state	38	Change in sleeping habits	16
Death of close friend	37	Change in number of family	
Change of work	36	get-togethers	15
Change in number of		Change in eating habits	15
arguments with spouse	35	Vacation	13
Foreclosure of mortgage	30	Minor violations of law	11
Change of responsibility			
at work	29		

SOURCE: Adapted from T. H. Holmes and R. H. Rahe, "The Social Readjustment Rating Scale," *Journal of Psychosomatic Research,* 11 (August 1976), 213. Reprinted with permission from the authors and Pergamon Press Ltd.

amount of adjustment various life events required, these researchers assigned numerical values to the events (see Table 12-2). Research indicates that people who have experienced 200 or more life change units in a single year are likely to be under intolerable stress. Such people should try to avoid making further changes in their lives or should seek counseling for help in adjusting to the changes they are facing.

WOMEN AND HORMONAL FLUCTUATIONS

For some forty years of a woman's life—from about 12 until about 50—her body undergoes marked fluctuations of hormonal levels in connection with the menstrual cycle. An increasing amount of research has been conducted in recent years to determine the effects of these hormones on a woman's physiological, intellectual, and emotional state.

Various studies have reported that anywhere from 15 to 95 percent of women experience depression, irritability, anxiety, and low self-esteem during the days immediately preceding menstruation (Bardwick, 1970). Dalton (1964) found that many women who commit suicide or acts of criminal violence do so during the premenstrual and menstrual phases of their cycles. She also found that women were more likely to report sick, seek admission to the hospital, or need psychiatric help at these times. (But women still have lower crime, suicide, and accident rates than men do.)

Other writers have also correlated women's well-being with hormonal levels.

Ivey and Bardwick (1968) studied a group of twenty-six college women over two menstrual cycles, asking them twice at ovulation and twice at premenstruation to speak for five minutes about some experience. When their stories were analyzed for themes, it was found that hostility, depression, and inability to cope dominated the stories told during the premstrual phase, while self-satisfaction over success or the ability to handle things characterized the stories told at ovulation. One young woman said premenstrually:

They had to teach me how to water-ski. I was so clumsy it was really embarrassing, 'cause it was kind of like saying to yourself you can't do it and the people were about to lose patience with me [p. 341].

At ovulation, this same young woman said:

So I was elected chairman. I had to establish with them the fact that I knew what I was doing. I remember one particular problematic meeting, and afterward, L. came up to me and said, "You really handled the meeting well." In the end it came out the sort of thing that really bolstered my confidence in myself [p. 341].

Golub (1975) measured fifty women, ages 30 to 45, during the premenstrual phase and again, two weeks later, on tests of depression, anxiety, and cognitive functioning. While she did find significant premenstrual increases in anxiety and depression, she found no statistically significant differences in performance on eleven of the thirteen cognitive tests that measured such factors as perception, memory, problem solving, inductive reasoning, concept formation, and creativity.

It appears, then, that levels of anxiety and depression may be higher premenstrually, but they are not high enough to affect cognitive function. The amount of premenstrual anxiety in these women was less, in fact, than that seen among students taking exams. In general, women are no more adversely affected in the performance of their duties by cyclic hormonal fluctuations than men are by their greater susceptibility to ulcers, heart attacks, and strokes.

Paige (1973) offers a cultural explanation for women's mood and action changes during their menstrual cycles.

In studying Catholic, Jewish, and Protes-

tant women—all of whom presumably have the same cyclic fluctuations of hormones—she found that Catholics showed an extreme jump in premenstrual anxiety, Protestants showed little change, and Jewish women were anxious throughout the entire cycle. These differences, then, seem related to varying cultural attitudes toward menstruation and toward women in general, which are most constraining among Jews and Catholics. Those Jewish women who follow orthodox social and hygienic menstrual rituals and abstain from sexual relations during their periods are most likely to have menstrual problems, and so are Catholic women who regard menstrual distress as an integral part of the traditional female role. In all three groups, those women who hewed most closely to the traditional female sex role were more likely to suffer menstrually related cramps and depression than were ambitious career women.

One recent study (Englander-Golden, Willis, & Dienstbier, 1977) set up two control groups to compare to menstruating women: one of men, and one of women taking oral contraceptives which keep hormone levels fairly constant throughout the monthly cycle. The researchers did not tell the subjects that they were focusing on premenstrual tension. Participants looked at videotapes showing various kinds of interaction among people, and then gave their opinions on the amount of pressure on various characters in the stories. The menstruating non-Pill women showed the most variation in their responses across a two-week interval, sometimes perceiving a great deal of pressure, sometimes far less. The women taking Pills were more consistent, and the men were the most consistent of all. These researchers concluded that mood swings during the menstrual cycle have a physiological, rather than a psychological, basis, but add that they feel further research is needed.

So is there a premenstrual syndrome or not? There does seem to be evidence that women's moods change cyclically, but recent research is also beginning to find cyclical changes in men's functioning, and the full significance of mood variability in either sex has yet to be understood.

INTELLECTUAL FUNCTIONING OF YOUNG ADULTS

Intellectual functioning is at a high level in young adults, who show a new flexibility of thought and, in many ways, a steady increase in performance. For many years it was believed that general intellectual activity peaked at about the age of 20 and then declined. This theory was based on the results of cross-sectional studies, which gave intelligence tests to different groups of people in varying age groups and found that young adults did best (Doppelt & Wallace, 1955; Jones & Conrad, 1933; Miles & Miles, 1932).

In any cross-sectional study, though, such differences may result from cohort differences. That is, people born more recently may have a larger store of information because of more extensive schooling, and they may have developed their intellectual abilities more than they would have if they had been born twenty or thirty years earlier. The superior intellectual performance of young people may not reflect diminishing intelligence with age but a different outlook, depending on when one grows up and is educated. Longitudinal studies, which test the same people periodically over the years, seem to bear out this latter view, since they usually show that general intelligence appears to increase until at least the fifties (Owens, 1966; Bayley & Oden, 1955).

While intellectual functioning is at a high level in young adults, moral development and creativity often peak later. (© Ray Ellis/Photo Researchers, Inc.)

The picture is complicated further by the existence of different kinds of intellectual abilities. Cattell (1965) and Horn (1967, 1968, 1970) have proposed a distinction between "fluid" and "crystallized" intelligence. *Fluid intelligence* involves the processes of perceiving relations, forming concepts, reasoning, and abstracting. It is tested by tasks in which the problem posed is novel for everyone or else is an extremely common cultural element. People are asked to group letters and numbers, to pair related words, or to remember a series of digits. This type of intelligence is considered dependent on neurological development and relatively free from the influences of education and culture. Measured by such tests as the Raven Progressive Matrices test, it reaches full development in the late teens and begins to decline in the twenties.

Crystallized intelligence, on the other hand, involves tasks that have to have been specially learned and are therefore more

Intellectually, the month of September 1900 was the highest point of my life. I went about saying to myself that now at last I had done something worth doing, and I had the feeling that I must be careful not to be run over in the street before I had written it down .... With the beginning of October I sat down to write The Principles of Mathematics, at which I had already made a number of unsuccessful attempts,

Bertrand Russell, age 28,
The Autobiography of Bertrand Russell, 1872–1914,
p. 218–219.

dependent on education and cultural background. It is measured by tests of vocabulary, general information, and social dilemmas. People continue to do better on tests of crystallized intelligence until near the end of life. So far, though, much of the basic research on fluid and crystallized intelligence is cross-sectional, and so the reservations regarding this testing method need to be borne in mind.

In tests regarding Piagetian concepts of conservation, formal operations, animism, and egocentrism, young adults do quite well. In general, they do better than either children or middle-aged adults. Conservation performance is high except for volume, in which middle-aged people do better than college students (Papalia, 1972). Elkind (1962) found that 92 percent of college students conserve mass and weight, but only 58 percent do volume. Tomlinson-Keasey (1972) found that college women surpassed elementary school girls and middle-aged women on formal tasks. Clayton and Overton (1973) found that college women surpassed elderly women on the pendulum task, a measure of formal operations that asks the subject to analyze what determines the speed of a swinging pendulum. Both groups, however, performed well on tests of transitivity, concrete tasks that state the relationship between two items and ask

the subject to infer a relationship to a third.

Piaget (1972) says that while all normal subjects attain the stage of formal operations sometime between 11 and 20 years of age, they reach this stage at different times and in different areas of thought, depending on their particular aptitudes and areas of specialization: "The period from 15 to 20 years marks the beginning of professional specialization and consequently also the construction of a life program corresponding to the aptitudes of the individual," he writes (p. 209). For example, people studying law will use superior logic while discussing legal concepts, while carpenters' apprentices will be able to reason hypothetically to solve problems involving construction. Yet the research cited above suggests that some normal subjects *never* attain formal operations.

Piaget calls for further research to find out whether it is possible to demonstrate cognitive structures at this level of development that are common to all indivuals but will be used differently by each one according to his or her particular abilities.

Young adults show a great deal of apparent animistic response by attributing life to biologically nonliving stimuli such as the moon or the sun in violation of Piagetian theory, which would not predict animistic reasoning past the age of 12 (Papalia-Finlay, 1978; Sheehan & Papalia, 1974).

It is possible that college students may be exhibiting a broader concept of life and reflecting characteristics of thought that enable them to deal with concepts flexibly rather than in a rigid, restricted manner.

When compared with old people, young adults are clearly less egocentric and better able to put themselves in the place of another, at least on a specific task of spatial perception (Looft & Charles, 1971). College students aged about 19 were better able than septua-

genarians to select a spatial pattern that represented what another person saw from another side of the table.

We would expect older people to be *less* egocentric, since they have had more experiences, more opportunities to observe how other people react to situations, and therefore more chances to study others' points of view. The increased egocentrism noted in this particular study may be a manifestation of the decreased social interactions experienced by these elderly persons or of some loss of neurological functioning caused by aging. Or it may simply be an artifact of the cross-sectional study method; that is, these older subjects may *never* have had the ability in question.

In a review of research, Looft (1972) says there is very little on egocentrism relating to adults. What there is indicates that adults are *not* egocentric, at least in communicating. Most adults have learned that they need to be sensitive to their listeners' needs, and when they get a signal that they are not being understood—such as a blank stare or a questioning look—they modify the messages. Werner and Kaplan (1963) asked adults to write two descriptions of a drawing: One was for the subject's own reference at a later date; the other was designed to describe the drawing to someone who had not seen it. The descriptions the subjects wrote for themselves were only about half as long as those designed for someone else. Obviously, these people realized that someone who had not seen the drawing would need more details. Adds Looft (1972):

This factor is revealed also in the frequent occasion of an undergraduate student asking to borrow the lecture notes of another. The often-heard reply of the lender in this situation is something like, "You can borrow my notes, but I don't think you'll be able to get much out of them" [p. 81].

Piaget (1962) cited an example of adult development to less egocentric communication:

Every beginning instructor discovers sooner or later that his first lectures were incomprehensible because he was talking to himself, so to say, mindful of only his own point of view. He realizes only gradually and with difficulty that it is not easy to place oneself in the shoes of students who do not yet know what he knows about the subject matter of the course [p. 5].

MORAL DEVELOPMENT

Of six stages of moral reasoning postulated by Kohlberg (see Chapter 8), fully principled thinking (stages 5 and 6) is an adult development, typically not reached until the late twenties or later—if ever. Development at the upper levels requires personal social and moral experiences to a much greater extent than does moral development in childhood and adolescence, which is largely a function of cognitive growth.

In the development of moral reasoning, "live and learn" is the byword. In order for people to develop to the highest stages of ethical reasoning, they need to undergo experiences that lead them to transform their ways of judging what is right and fair. Usually the experiences that promote such change have a fairly strong emotional component, which triggers rethinking in a way that hypothetical, impersonal discussions can never do. As people undergo such experiences, they are called upon more and more to take the perspectives of others with regard to social and moral conflicts.

Bielby and Papalia (1975), for example, noted that some adults spontaneously offer personal experiences as reasons for answering the Kohlbergian moral dilemmas (Chapter 8) in a certain way. Someone who had had actual experience with cancer was more apt to condone a man's stealing a precious drug to save his dying wife, and to give his or her own illness or that of a loved one as an explanation for that answer.

Two signal experiences that Kohlberg maintains advance moral development are "the experience of leaving home and entering a college community with conflicting values" and "the experience of sustained responsibility for the welfare of others." Moral change, according to Kohlberg (1973), is clearly a focal point for adult life in a way cognitive change is not, since the crises and turning points of adult identity are often moral. In sum, he feels that while the cognitive awareness of principles develops in adolescence, commitment to their ethical use develops only in adulthood.

The cognitive stage, then, seems to set the upper limit for moral growth potential. Someone whose thinking is still at the level of concrete operations would be unlikely to advance to the moral stage of postconventional morality. This requires a more sophisticated cognitive level.

The Watergate affair—the political scandal of the 1970s that involved breaking into the Democratic party headquarters, stealing documents, taping conversations without the participants' knowledge, and then trying to hide these and other events from public knowledge—involved adults of varying ages and varying moral stages. Candee (1975) feels that at least one young adult experienced growth in moral reasoning as a result of this experience. Egil Krogh, who authorized the break-in at a psychiatrist's office for the purpose of obtaining a patient's file, originally reasoned from a stage-4 perspective, in which his "primary duty was to fulfill the requirements of his role, not to insure human rights" (Candee, 1975, p. 11), Said Krogh,

I see now that the key is the effect that the term "national security" had on my judgment. The very words served to block my critical analysis . . . to suggest that national security was being improperly invoked was to invite a confrontation with patriotism and loyalty and

so appeared to be beyond the scope and in contravention of the faithful performance of the duties of my office . . . the very definition of national security was for the President to pursue his planned course [*The New York Times*, 1974, p. 16].

Krogh, however, went on to question the moral validity of the social system in which he was operating and thus to achieve a stage-5 level of moral reasoning:

But however national security is defined, I now see that none of the potential uses of the sought information could justify the invasion of the rights of the individuals that the break-in necessitated. The understanding I have come to is that *these rights are the definition of our nation* [italics added by Candee]. . . .

I hope they [young men and women who are fortunate enough to have an opportunity to serve in government] will recognize that the banner of national security can turn perceived patriotism into actual disservice. When contemplating a course of action, I hope they will never fail to ask, "Is this right?" [*The New York Times*, 1974, p. 16].

MORAL DEVELOPMENT: THE WOMAN'S PERSPECTIVE

Kohlberg's initial research was done only with male subjects. As a result, the male way of thinking became his norm, and women have not come out too well when measured on the traditional Kohlberg tasks. Women generally come out at stage 3, with a strong orientation toward an interpersonal definition of morality. They "have trouble making the transition" to stage 4, which requires recognition of a societal definition of morality, or an orientation toward law and order. Critics claim that this poorer showing of women demonstrates sex bias in Kohlberg's scheme and a failure to

consider the different quality and developmental sequence of women's moral thinking.

According to Gilligan (1977), women have unique concerns and perspectives. While our society equates manhood with independent assertion and judgment, it defines womanhood in terms of concern for the well-being of others, and of self-sacrifice to ensure that well-being. So woman's central moral dilemma is the conflict between herself and others.

To determine the way women develop morally, Gilligan decided to look at their reasoning in an area of their lives in which they have choices. Focusing on the control of fertility, she interviewed and gave Kohlberg dilemmas to twenty-nine women referred by abortion and pregnancy counseling services, who talked about their pregnancies and the ways they were arriving at their decisions about them.

These women spoke in "a distinct moral language whose evolution informs the sequence of women's development" (Gilligan, 1977, p. 63). They see morality in terms of selfishness and responsibility, as an obligation to exercise care and avoid hurt. People who care for each other are the most responsible, whereas those who hurt someone else are selfish and immoral. While men think more in terms of justice and fairness, women think more about specific people.

Gilligan identified a sequence of moral development for women:

LEVEL 1: ORIENTATION OF INDIVIDUAL SURVIVAL

The woman concentrates on herself—on what is practical and what is best for her.

Transition 1: From Selfishness to Responsibility

The woman realizes her connection to others, and thinks about what would be the responsible choice in terms of other people (such as the unborn baby), as well as herself.

LEVEL 2: GOODNESS AS SELF-SACRIFICE

This conventional feminine wisdom dictates sacrificing the woman's own wishes to what other people want—and will think of her. She considers herself responsible for the actions of others, while holding others responsible for her own choices. She is in a dependent position, one in which her indirect efforts to exert control often turn into manipulation, sometimes through the use of guilt.

Transition 2: From Goodness to Truth

She assesses her decisions not on the basis of how others will react to them, but on her intentions and the consequences of her actions. She develops a new judgment that takes into account her own needs, along with those of others. She wants to be "good" by being responsible to others, but also wants to be "honest" by being responsible to herself. Survival returns as a major concern.

LEVEL 3: THE MORALITY OF NONVIOLENCE

By elevating the injunction against hurting anyone (including herself) to a principle that governs all moral judgment and action, the woman establishes a "moral equality" between herself and others, and is then able to assume the responsibility for choice in moral dilemmas.

Gilligan provides a dramatic illustration of the two contrasting concepts of morality: Kohlberg's morality of rights and her own morality of responsibility. The abstract morality exemplified by Kohlberg's stage 6 led the biblical Abraham to be ready to sacrifice the life of his son when God demanded it as a proof of faith; Gilligan's person-centered morality can also be seen in the Bible, in the story of the woman who proved to King Solomon that she was a baby's mother when she agreed to give up the infant to another woman rather than see it harmed.

Acknowledging the female perspective on moral development enables us to appreciate the importance for both sexes of our connections with other people and of the universal need for compassion and care.

CREATIVITY

If intellect and energy are both at their zenith during young adulthood, we might reasonably expect this to be the wellspring period for great works. And yet this is not the case. Dennis (1966) studied 738 eminent scholars, scientists, and artists—all of whom lived till the age of 79 or later. In every group, productive output in the decade of the twenties was less than in the thirties, usually only half or less than half as great. In some groups output in the twenties was only 2 percent of their total lifelong work, and in no group did it represent more than 15 percent of the total.

Among scholars and scientists, the twenties represented their *least* productive decade. Only in some of the arts were the twenties more productive than the seventies. Leonardo da Vinci's first signed work appeared when he was 21, Mozart wrote his first mass at 26, and Beethoven composed his first symphony at 29. Chamber musicians and poets are particularly productive during the years from 20 to 29. The thirties are generally much more productive than the twenties, but less productive than the forties—except for chamber musicians, who achieve more in their thirties than their forties. Of the scientists, those who are most productive in their early years are the mathematicians and chemists.

There are lights. The excitement. The audience. The tension. The part that was to live its own life. Weep with a role. Laughter and fury borrowed from an imaginary person. Emotions I had scarcely known. The eyes and expressions of my colleagues. Sometimes we were so close it seemed unreal there existed other relationships outside the theatre.

Liv Ullmann,
in *Changing*, p. 100.

The reasons for these differences in different fields of endeavor probably have a lot to do with the nature of the output in different professions. Says Dennis (1966): "The musician and the poet, by intense effort, may sometimes complete a contribution within a very short period of time, but a history of Rome or a record of the voyage of the Beagle cannot be dashed off in a week" (p. 110). Scholars and scientists often need long periods of study and data collection before they can produce important work.

CAREER DEVELOPMENT

When people embark upon their first full-time jobs, they are carving out an important aspect of their identity, achieving independence, and demonstrating their ability to assume adult responsibilities.

CAREER CHOICES

Some factors that influence an individual's choice of careers come to the fore during adolescence—socioeconomic status, parental encouragement, school, and individual abilities and personality (see Chapter 9). But the final choice of career usually does not take place until young adulthood or later. Among people questioned at the age of 45, the average age at which they chose their final occupations was 28 (Flaste, 1976).

A major element that affects people's first jobs—and sometimes their lifetime occupations—is what Stockmal (1976) calls a "critical event": a chance meeting, a major illness or tragedy, or a stroke of luck. Some of these jobs work out well. (Just as spouses in the old arranged marriages learned to love each other, workers often come to love their jobs.) When they do not, jobholders often change jobs. The pattern of change can vary widely: One person may try a succession of different jobs before landing one that she or he really likes and will stick with thoughout life; another may stay with one occupation for twenty years before making a major career shift.

The editor offered me a job which he said, with more truth than he realized, would not bring me much money, but would give me a chance to learn a trade that was profitable, and that I could use when I went back to school. As I took that letter out of Box 10 at the Emporia post office, I did not realize that I had received my life's calling; that I had channeled my entire life without deviation or break from the letter that I held in my hand.

William Allen White,
The Autobiography of William Allen White, p. 109.

JOB SATISFACTION

A 1974 survey of workers of different ages found that 75 percent of people under 21 were satisfied with their jobs, as were 84 percent of those in their twenties, and over 90 percent of people over 30; this percentage continued to increase with age (Quinn, Staines, & McCullough, 1974). People rated their jobs in terms of interest level and challenge, pay, and working conditions. Younger people may be more dissatisfied with their jobs because they are still in the process of finding work that will be personally fulfilling, while older people are more likely to have settled upon their niche in life. Or this may be another instance in which we are dealing with cohort differences— younger people may be less likely to be satisfied with work in general.

A 1975 study of 400,000 workers who had been out of high school for eleven years found that 80 percent called their jobs rewarding, and only 8 percent said they wished they were

in different types of work (Wilson & Wise, 1975). These 30-year-olds were more concerned with emotional fulfillment than with pay. The greatest regrets came from those who married early and did not seek as much training after high school as they thought they should have.

In 1977, a national survey of 1515 workers representing all occupations, all industries, and 74 different geographic areas in the United States found that workers were less satisfied with their jobs than they had been in 1969 or in 1973 (Quinn & Staines, 1978). Workers today feel more pressured by conflicting demands from other people; are less happy with pay, promotions, and fringe benefits; and are less likely to feel they can use and develop their own special abilities on the job. One out of three respondents feels that work and leisure activities interfere with each other, and 1 out of 3 married workers feels that jobs interfere with family life. Men show more of a decline in job satisfaction than women; blue-collar workers more than those in professional, technical, and managerial occupations; and wage and salaried workers more than the self-employed.

The 1977 survey was the first in this series of three conducted for the United States Department of Labor to include questions about the relationship between work and life away from the job, and here may rest one clue for the drop in job satisfaction. Apparently, more workers are expressing their feelings that job satisfaction depends not on the job alone, but on how it fits into their lives in general.

A 1978 survey of 23,008 readers of the magazine *Psychology Today*, a highly professional (43.4 percent) and young (43.5 percent from 25 to 34 years) group, found that workers want more psychological satisfaction from their jobs. They want more chances to learn, to grow, to exercise their talents, to achieve something worthwhile (Renwick, Lawler, & *Psychology Today* staff).

Most of the readers who returned the 77-point questionnaire were fairly positive

Women now make up more than 40
percent of the civilian labor force
(A.T. & T. Photo Center)

toward their jobs: Twenty-one percent were
very satisfied and 20 percent had some
dissatisfaction. Those in higher-status occupations were most satisfied, and the most
dissatisfied were black workers under the age
of 24 who were earning between $5000 and
$10,000 a year. Least likely to plan to change
their jobs in the next five years were professionals; most likely were semiskilled and cleri-
cal workers.

SEX AND VOCATIONAL DEVELOPMENT

The sex of an individual often has more to do
with that person's eventual career than with the
person's abilities, interests, or personality.
Many women have devoted a major portion of
their working lives to homemaking, the care of
children and of the home, which is rarely even

recognized as a vocational choice but is just
something women "are supposed" to do, no
matter what their individual interests or talents. Current efforts to achieve societal recognition of the value of homemaking (including
Social Security benefits) may even result in an
increase among men opting to spend part of
their lives staying at home with the children.

Yet many woman have always worked
outside the home. At some time in their lives, 9
out of 10 hold jobs; and women now make up
more than 40 percent of the civilian labor force
(U.S. Department of Labor, 1979). Like men,
women work to earn money, to achieve recognition, and to fulfill personal needs.

Laws providing for equal opportunity in
employment underline the rights of both sexes
to be considered equally for jobs, to be paid
equally, and to be promoted equally. At the
present time, however, reality falls far short of
the goal. Working women average only 59
cents for every dollar earned by men, and
women have to work nearly nine days to gross
the same earnings that men gross in five (U.S.
Department of Labor, 1979). The earnings
differential has remained at about the same
level since 1961, in contrast to the gains
women have been making in employment
over the past few years. This is so for two
reasons: Even though more women are getting better jobs these days, most are still in
low-paid jobs that have been traditionally held
by women. Then, as more women have entered the labor force, many have come in at
entry-level jobs.

Many careers have disproportionate
numbers of one sex or the other. U.S. Department of Labor (1979) statistics show that
women were in the following occupations in
the following ratios:

Registered nurses	97%
Dietitians	93%

Elementary school teachers	84%
Health technicians	70%
Physicians	11%
Attorneys	13%
Engineers	3%

In recent years, the career picture for women has changed dramatically. During the 1970s, the percentage of female lawyers and judges doubled and that of bank officials and financial managers almost doubled. In 1970, women accounted for less than 9 percent of all physicians in the country; by 1978 they had inched up to more than 11 percent. Over the decade the proportion of women accountants rose about 5 percent to 30.2 percent, and many more achieved a foothold in the upper ranks of business. Among sales managers and department heads in retail trade, the female percentage went from 24 to 37 percent.

Some of the disparities in occupational status and in income result from discrimination in the marketplace. Some result from societal expectations that affect women's ambitions for themselves. A major roadblock to female accomplishment is what Horner (1970) has called "fear of success." Many capable students feel, either consciously or subconsciously, that vocational success is not compatible with femininity. While ostensibly striving for career success, these women are afraid of achieving it. As students they may refuse to divulge their good marks, preferring to talk about their failures. They often change their career plans toward goals that they consider to be more traditional, more feminine, and less ambitious. Middle- and upper-class white women whose fathers are successful professionals or businessmen are more likely to fear success than are black women or women from lower- or lower-middle-class homes whose fathers have not been successful.

Some of the traditional barriers to women's fulfillment of their potential seem to be crumbling, as evidenced by the greater numbers of first-year college women who plan to pursue traditionally male careers: law, medicine, engineering, and—most popular—business. Over the last nine years the number of female students in these fields has almost tripled, although it is still less than half the male figure (up from 5.9 to 16.9 percent for women, and down from 48.9 to 39.4 percent for men).

What makes a woman break from the traditional mold? If her own mother works, she is likely to have higher career aspirations and to be more likely to choose a career in a male-dominated field (Etaugh, 1973). Personality is also significant. Bachtold and Werner (1971) found that female psychologists were significantly more confident, inner-directed, aloof, intelligent, dominant, flexible, adventuresome, radical, and self-sufficient than women in general. And O'Leary and Braun (1974) summarized the literature on professional women and found them to be nonconforming, self-reliant, independent, flexible, autonomous, self-directed, and high in ego strength.

Women also may be influenced by their love relationships. Married women are more likely to choose traditionally female careers

I was not aware that there was anything unusual about my continued dedication to becoming an artist. When male students started making comments about my sex, I took them to task and assured them that neither ideas nor art had sex, feeling very confident about myself and my rights.

Judy Chicago,
Through the Flower, p. 20.

than are single women and to be less committed to their careers. Those married women who do show career commitment in an untraditional job usually have their husbands' support and encouragement (Bielby, 1975). The question still stands, though, whether it is the man's encouragement that gives a woman the freedom to pursue her interests—or whether professionally committed women marry only those men who support their aspirations?

DUAL-CAREER FAMILIES

In recent years there has been an increase not only in the number of women who work but in the number whose careers are as important to the wives as the men's careers are to the husbands. These marriages, in which husband and wife both pursue careers outside the home and share the duties within it, represent a considerable change from traditional family patterns in American society and offer both advantages and disadvantages.

The benefits of a dual-career marriage include increased family income, a more egalitarian relationship between husband and wife, a closer relationship between father and children, a sense of integrity for the woman who is developing her personal potential and for the man who is not holding her back, and an enhanced capacity for each partner to function and develop in both work and family roles. Some of the stresses for these couples include the energy taxation caused by the need to fulfill both roles, possible restriction of both careers caused by family responsibilities, competitive rivalry between husband and wife, anxiety and guilt over whether the children's needs are being met, and resentment expressed by relatives, friends, neighbors, or the children's schoolteachers.

The husband and wife in a dual-career family are part of three role systems: the work system of the wife, the work system of the husband, and the joint family system. Each role makes demands on the individuals at different times, for example, in the family when there are young children and at work when one is trying to reach a senior position.

Couples have to decide which roles should peak first—the family, the husband's career, or the wife's career. The difficulty of setting priorities among these roles causes many stresses for career couples (Rapoport & Rapoport; cited in Skolnick & Skolnick, 1974).

In many cases, of course, the reason for a married woman's going to work is financial. With the inflationary prices of recent years and people's desire for a higher standard of living, two paychecks are often necessary. Sometimes, however, there is a choice around whether a woman goes to work. Are there advantages to her staying at home that will compensate for the family's living at a somewhat lower economic level? In families that are financially comfortable, what makes one woman decide to pursue her own career outside the home while another works in the home as a homemaker?

The reasons behind people's decisions in this area, as in so many other life choices, are complex, growing as they do out of many sociological and psychological factors. One explanation lies in the personalities of both men and women. Burke and Weir (1976) compared 189 Canadian couples: husbands and wives in both two-job marriages and those in which only the man brought in an income. The men were all engineers or accountants; the women, some of whom worked full-time and some part-time, held a wide range of jobs. The members of two-career families were younger, had been married a shorter period of time, and the husbands earned less money. They differed in other ways, too. In their answers to a personality test, the members of the two-career families showed themselves to be more self-reliant and self-sufficient, and less interested in seeking gratification through relationships with other people.

The homemakers were more willing than

the working wives to let other people take charge, make decisions, and assume power and authority over their lives. They also had the strongest needs for affectionate, intimate relationships. Their husbands were more competitive and power-seeking than the husbands of working wives, less concerned with developing close relationships, but more likely to prefer to initiate any expressions of affection themselves.

By contrast, working wives were more self-assertive and more interested in being in control of their own lives. Their husbands were less assertive and less concerned with power and authority than the other men.

Personality needs undoubtedly play a large role in people's decisions to be in a single- or a dual-career marriage. The question remains, though: Are these differences that people have had since childhood, or are they the result of an adaptation to social norms, and will they then change along with social customs, as the two-job marriage becomes the norm? Longitudinal studies may yield some findings on the origin of such personality differences.

As more couples adopt this lifestyle, society will no doubt make institutional changes to alleviate the strains for them and their families. Living and working environments could be redesigned, for example, so that people could more easily pool domestic services and thus split their time more easily between home and workplace. More jobs could be structured on a part-time basis; more employers could automatically provide child-care services; and other changes could be made to fill the needs of parents, children, and society at large.

SUMMARY

1 The period of young adulthood, from about 20 to 40 years of age, is characterized by making decisions about careers, family lifestyles, and commitment to friends and community. **2** The physical and sensory status of young adults is typically excellent. Accidents account for most deaths among young adults, and the death rate is three times higher for males than for females. **3** Hormonal fluctuations have been noted in connection with the menstrual cycle. These fluctuations appear to influence mood but not intellectual functioning. Cultural factors such as religious membership must be considered in explaining these findings. **4** Intellectual functioning (both standardized intelligence tests and Piagetian cognitive tasks) is generally at a high level during young adulthood. Compared with older adults, young adults show less egocentrism on spatial and communication tasks, and higher levels of moral reasoning. However, not all young adults reach the Piagetian stage of formal thought. **5** Musicians and poets are particularly creative during their twenties and thirties, while members of other professions, especially scientists and scholars, are more productive during later developmental periods. **6** During young adulthood most people make long-range career choices. Job satisfaction increases with age and is tied to the type of work one does. **7** Although 90 percent of women hold jobs at some time in their lives, discrepancies in occupational status and income still exist between men and women. Horner has proposed the idea of "fear of success" to explain why bright women—afraid of social rejection and loss of femininity—reject traditionally male careers. Even so, today more women are pursuing careers in business, law, medicine, and engineering.   **8** Dual-career families, in which both wife and husband pursue careers outside the home, are becoming more prevalent. As more couples adopt this lifestyle, society will no doubt make institutional changes to alleviate the strains of setting priorities among the competing roles of spouse, parent, and worker.

SUGGESTED READINGS

Bernard, J. *The future of marriage*. New York: World, 1972. Examines the impact of marriage on men and women, and concludes that marriage is more beneficial for men than for women.

Bird, Caroline. *The two-paycheck marriage*. New York: Rawson, Wade, 1979. A fascinating report on working couples and what the massive influx of women into the labor force means for marriage, child rearing, employment, and society in general.

Bolles, R. N., *What color is your parachute? A practical manual for job-hunters and career changers*. Berkeley, Ca: Ten Speed Press, 1980. A practical and entertaining step-by-step guide to deciding on life goals and finding the work that will help to implement them.

Bolles, R. N., *The three boxes of life. . . and how to get out of them*. Berkeley, CA: Ten Speed Press, 1978, A lively introduction to life/work planning that emphasizes integration throughout life of the three elements of education, work, and leisure.

The health consequences of smoking for women, a report of the Surgeon General. Washington, DC: U.S. Dept. of Health, Education, and Welfare, 1980. A comprehensive 400-page report to Congress that brings together in one volume all the scientific documents pertaining to women and smoking. It includes information on the effects of smoking on problems before, in, and after childbirth; on women's increased lung cancer rates; and on other effects.

Kundsin, R. (Ed.) *Women and success: The anatomy of achievement*. New York: Morrow, 1974. A collection of papers on aspects of women and careers. Includes articles on the influence of family attitudes, education, and economics on career choice.

Sheehy, G. *Passages: Predictable crises of adult life*. New York: Dutton, 1976. An absorbing account of the personality changes adults go through, from 18 through middle age, with comparison between men's and women's developmental rhythms.

Terkel, S. *Working*. New York: Random House, 1974. The subtitle of this powerful book tells its story: "People Talk about What They Do All Day and How They Feel about What They Do." The book is made up of transscripts of tape-recorded interviews with workers in a wide range of occupations.

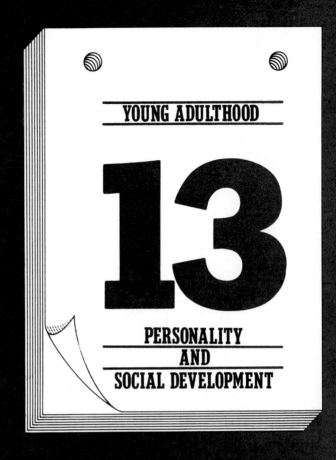

YOUNG ADULTHOOD

13

**PERSONALITY
AND
SOCIAL DEVELOPMENT**

IN THIS CHAPTER
YOU WILL LEARN ABOUT

Recent research which indicates that
human personality continues to evolve
during adulthood

Two theories that describe the continuing
development of personality

How the choice of lifestyle affects
personality and social development during
young adulthood: the issues and effects of
romantic love, marriage, single life,
parenthood, stepparenting,
nonparenthood, and divorce

The impact of friends on the young adult

CHAPTER OVERVIEW

Theoretical Perspectives on Adult
Development
*Bühler's Theory | Erikson's Crisis VI:
Intimacy versus Isolation*

Research Studies of Adult Development
*The Grant Study of Adult
Development | Levinson's Studies of
Men | Gould's Studies of Men and
Women*

Choosing a Personal Lifestyle
*Romantic Love | Marriage | Single
Life | Cohabitation | Parenthood |
Stepparenting | Nonparenthood | Divorce*

Friendship in Young Adulthood

THEORETICAL
PERSPECTIVES ON
ADULT DEVELOPMENT

Hindu texts written in the second century described life as "a series of passages, in which former pleasures are outgrown and replaced by higher and more appropriate purposes" (Sheehy, 1976, p. 355). From that point until the twentieth century, the concept of development throughout adult life was ignored by scientists and recognized only by artists such as Shakespeare, who in *As You Like It* immortalized the "seven ages of man."

The dissemination of Freud's ideas at the beginning of the twentieth century and the birth of the new study of child development led to the acceptance of the concept of development throughout childhood. Then, early in the century, Charlotte Bühler, a clinical psychologist in Vienna, undertook an ambitious project to look at development throughout the life span. Her work and the five-stage theory she first published in 1933 inspired studies by Else Frenkel-Brunswik (in Neugarten, 1968), who outlined five stages in personality development throughout adulthood. These stages in turn foreshadowed Erikson's eight crises of development, which served as the underpinning for the research cited later in this chapter.

BÜHLER'S THEORY

Bühler (1933) emphasized goal-setting in her five-phase theory of human development, which concentrates largely on development in adulthood (see pp. 480–481).

Phase two: adolescence and young adulthood (about ages 15 to 25)

During these years people first grasp the idea that their lives are their own. They are interested in analyzing the life experiences that have shaped them so far, and they may write their first autobiographies. They are idealistic in their search for cosmic goals: They want a partner to love, a God to believe in, answers to the meaning of life, and a chance to realize their dreams. People resolve this phase adequately by being mature enough to analyze and consider their own potentials as well as their needs, to clarify the values they believe in and want to live for, to handle normal problems and conflicts, and to be adaptable to changing attitudes and circumstances.

Bühler (1968) points to David, age 22, as a person who handles this phase well. A science student, his plans for the immediate future include studying for his college degree and earning enough money to support himself. Then he plans to become a college teacher and marry his fiancée, and eventually to become a professor.

Phase three: young and middle adulthood (about ages 23 to 45 or 50)

People now go from tentative to more specific, definite goals. Ideally, individuals become clearer about their values and goals, and they have a better grasp of their potential for development. This is the time of a rich personal life—usually including marriage and children, when one is at the peak of one's sexual capacity, at a stable point in one's career, and amidst a circle of friends. Yet, while this is the ideal, few people are able to overcome the many hindrances they encounter in their efforts to settle down. Sometimes they are disappointed because they feel they chose the wrong career or marriage partner. Sometimes they are too immature to integrate their lives into any stable pattern. And sometimes they have to use up so much psychic energy in emotional conflicts that they don't have enough to make their adjustments to life. Experiences of success help a person to achieve the goals of this phase, while experiences of failure can be disabling.

Phase four (mature adulthood) and phase five (old age) will be discussed in detail in Chapters 15 and 17.

ERIKSON'S CRISIS VI:
INTIMACY VERSUS ISOLATION

The young adult, having developed a sense of identity during adolescence is now ready to fuse this identity with that of others. He or she is now ready to make a commitment to a close, intimate relationship with another person. At this point, healthy people are willing to risk temporary ego loss in such emotionally demanding situations as coitus and orgasm, in the kinds of very close friendships that call for personal sacrifices and compromises, and in other situations requiring self-abandon. Those people who are afraid to give themselves over to such situations may end up feeling isolated and self-absorbed. As young adults resolve the often-conflicting demands of intimacy, competitiveness, and distance, they develop an ethical sense that Erikson considers the mark of the adult.

It is not until this stage that "true genitality" can occur, because up until now people's sex lives are dominated either by the search for their own identity or by "phallic or vaginal strivings which make of sex-life a kind of genital combat" (1950, p. 264). Now, though, the young adult can aspire to Erikson's "utopia of genitality," which should include mutual orgasm in a loving heterosexual relationship, in which trust is shared and the cycles of work, procreation, and recreation are regulated, with the ultimate aim of securing to the children of the union all the stages of their own satisfactory development. Erikson sees this not as a purely sexual utopia but rather as a more all-encompassing accomplishment. This position is restricted in several respects—in its advocacy only of *heterosexual* sex that culminates in *mutual* (or simultaneous) *orgasm*, and ultimately leads to *procreation*.

While the research on adult development cited in the next section underscores the search for intimacy in young adulthood, confirming this Eriksonian stage, it does not bolster his contention that the typical young adult has found his or her identity in adolescence. On the contrary, most of young adulthood seems to be a continuation of the search for identity. Another omission in the Eriksonian concept is the great emphasis on career development during young adulthood, which he places largely in middle childhood and adolescence. The case histories of the subjects in the research on adult development demonstrate that vocational development is at least on a par with interpersonal development at this time of life, and that it evokes just as much emotion and is a major part of the search for identity.

RESEARCH STUDIES OF ADULT DEVELOPMENT

Just as in every other phase of life, everyone functions in a unique way during young adulthood. People enter it with different abilities, different strengths and weaknesses, and different traits of personality and temperament. Everyone's life circumstances are unique. And yet studies of adult development can throw some light on the general developmental course that runs like a common thread through the lives of so many people. In discussing these findings, as in discussing developmental findings throughout this book, we have to remember the diversity in common experiences. And we have to remember that all ages are approximate: Ages for passing through developmental stages vary from one person to another, and the stages themselves often overlap in the same person.

THE GRANT STUDY OF ADULT DEVELOPMENT

This study of normal adult development began in 1938 with a group of 268 eighteen-year-old Harvard students who were considered healthy both emotionally and physically. By following up the average subject into his fifties, the researchers, have drawn a number of conclusions about adults in generally favorable circumstances (Vaillant & McArthur, 1972). The self-summary of one subject shows the typical pattern for these bright and achieving men:

At 20 to 30 I think I learned how to get along with my wife. From 30 to 40 I learned how to be a success at my job. And at 40 to 50 I worried less about myself and more about the children [unpaged].

At age 20 many of the men were still their mothers' sons, very much under parental dominance. The decade of the twenties—and sometimes the thirties—was spent winning autonomy from their parents, finding women they wanted to marry and marrying them, having and raising children, and deepening friendships that had begun during adolescence. Of those men who at age 47 were considered most well adjusted, 93 percent had achieved a stable marriage before 30 and were still married at 50:

From age 25–35, the men worked hard at their careers and devoted themselves to the nuclear family. . . . Poor at self-reflection, they were not unlike latency children—good at tasks, careful to follow the rules, anxious for promotion, and accepting many aspects of the "system." They tended to sacrifice playing and instead worked hard to become specialists. Rather than question whether they had married the right woman, rather than dream of other careers, they changed their babys' diapers and looked over their shoulders at the competition. Self-deception about the adequacy of both marital and career choice was common [Vaillant & McArthur, unpaged].

During the decade of their thirties, the men's careers were the focal points of their lives. Many of them seemed to the anthropolo-gists studying them to be no more than "hard working, bland young men in grey flannel suits." Before age 30, it was impossible to determine any individual's eventual career or his success in it, but by 40 the men's occupational futures seemed clear. There was only one valid predictor of success: Those men judged to have stable personalities at age 27 turned out to be more successful in their careers.

The men who were best adjusted at age 47 viewed the years from 21 to 35 as the unhappiest in their lives, and the period from 35 to 49 as the happiest. The least well adapted 47-year-olds looked back nostalgically at their young adult years.

LEVINSON'S STUDIES OF MEN

In another study of adult development, Levinson, Darrow, Klein, Levinson, and McKee (1974) interviewed in depth forty men aged 35 to 45—ten in each of four occupations: hourly workers in industry, business executives, academic biologists, and novelists. The interviews focused on all aspects of their lives—education, work, religion, politics, leisure, and their relationships with parents, siblings, wives, children, and peers. The interviewers put special emphasis on the men's late adolescent and adult years, with a view to grasping the connections among the various segments of life and their patterns and evolution over the years. The men also took personality tests.

From this multidisciplinary study, conducted by researchers with backgrounds in psychology, psychiatry, and sociology, Levinson (1977) constructed his theory that the goal of adult development is the building of a *life structure*. This structure has its external aspects—participation in the sociocultural world that includes a person's religion, race, ethnic heritage, family, and occupation, as well as such major societal events and conditions as wars and economic depressions. It also has an internal side made up of the person's values, dreams, and emotional life. As people shape their life structures, they go through *stable* periods that generally last some six to eight years, when they make choices and build their lives around them. Overlapping these are *transitional* periods lasting four to five years, when people reappraise their lives and explore new possibilities for the next stage. The following four of Levinson's stages occur during young adulthood.

LEAVING THE FAMILY (AGES 17 TO 24[1])

During this period, which for any given individual may take three to five years, a man[2] needs to move out of preadulthood and into adulthood. This happens as he moves out of his parents' home and becomes more independent both financially and emotionally. The youth who goes to college or into the army enters an institutional situation midway between being a child in the family and reaching full adult status.

GETTING INTO THE ADULT WORLD (AGES 22 TO 28)

Sometime during his early twenties, the balance shifts so that the young man is now a "novice adult," more in the adult world than in the family. During his twenties, he needs to perform two major and contradic-

---

[1] All ages are approximate.
[2] While women *may* follow parallel patterns of development, these researchers focused only on men and drew conclusions only for men.

My real feelings at this time were simple. I wanted to make my life a thing of great importance. That is to say, I wanted to live everyday, every hour, every moment with the greatest possible intensity, with the most complete awareness of being alive. But how could I do that unless I escaped from the middle-class environment that I lived in and which I saw stretching forward inexorably and with stifling dullness into the future?

Gerard Brenan
A Life of One's Own, p. 119

tory tasks—to explore his life possibilities by avoiding strong commitments and keeping his options open to all opportunities, and at the same time to become responsible and form a stable life structure. Some men are tentative during these years as they create a loose structure without investing much of themselves; some commit themselves strongly to marriage, occupation, and other goals, showing continuity from the previous stage and toward the next one; and others combine stability and change, sometimes making a strong commitment in one sector (like work or marriage) and not in others.

Many people enter adulthood with a dream of their future, often couched in an occupational setting. Their vision of becoming a world-renowned novelist or a Nobel Prize winner spurs them on and vitalizes them throughout much of their adult development. Many adult crises are precipitated by the realization that such cherished dreams will not be fulfilled. The way people deal with reorienting their goals, which may include substituting a more attainable ambition, determines how they will be able to cope with life.

THE AGE-30 TRANSITION (AGES 28 TO 33)

A couple of years one side or the other of age 30, people take another look at their lives. They wonder whether the commitments they made over the past decade were premature—or they make strong commitments for the first time.

Some people slide through this transition of growth and change fairly easily, even as they modify their lives, whereas others experience a developmental crisis, in which they find their present life structure intolerable yet seem unable to form a better one. Problems with marriage are high now, and the divorce rate peaks. The role of work shifts as a man changes jobs, gets promoted, or settles down

At about age 30, people take another look at their lives. They wonder whether the commitments they made over the past were premature—or they make strong commitments for the first time. (© Joel Gordon 1976)

after a period of uncertainty. Some men enter psychotherapy to help them clarify their goals.

Levinson (1977) considers this move from the end of the age-30 transition crucial. If the choices made now are sound, they will provide a strong foundation for the life structure. If they are poor, they may dangerously weaken the next period. No matter how good the structure, however, it will continue to change.

In her interviews with both men and women, Sheehy (1976) found that many women also experience an age-30 transition, often leading to a radical change in their direction in life. This is the time, for example, when a career woman may shift to a life revolving around home and children—or when a homemaker decides to go back to school and prepare for a profession.

In 1898 I attained the age of thirty.
My name now appeared on the
Gazette's masthead as W. A. White.
I felt that there was something
irrevocably sad about being thirty-
middle aged. I felt impatient at
the futility of my life, that I had
done so little and now it was about over.

The Autobiography of William Allen White, William Allen White
p. 311.

SETTLING DOWN (AGES 32 TO 40) The
early thirties usher in this period, when people
make deeper commitments to work, family,
and other important aspects of their lives.
They set specific goals for themselves (a
professorship, a certain level of income, a
one-person show) with a set timetable, often
the milestone age of 40. As they work at
establishing their niche in society and "making it," they work out a life plan.

BECOMING ONE'S OWN MAN (BOOM) In
the middle to late thirties, generally at age 36
or 37, comes a period when a man feels
constrained and oppressed by people who
have power and influence over him. He wants
to be more independent and to speak more
with his own voice, but he also wants affirma-
tion and respect, which he may jeopardize by
breaking away from the authorities in his life.
During Boom a man is often at odds with his
wife, children, lover, boss, friends, and co-
workers. At this time a person discards the
mentor, a slightly older person who has shown
interest in him and has helped to advance his
career development. Levinson identified three
different patterns within this period:

**Sequence A: Advancement within a stable life
structure** This is usually marked by a key
event like a job promotion or some other
achievement that gives a person outside
recognition and enhanced self-esteem.

**Sequence B: Failure-decline within a stable
life structure** This failure may be obvious, or

it may come in a person's own eyes, even
though he seems successful to the rest of the
world.

**Sequence C: Changing structure, or breaking
out** The man who finds his life so intolerable
that he considers a radical change like quit-
ting his job, leaving his wife, or moving across
the country experiences a major emotional
crisis whether he actually does change his
direction in life and invests energy and time in
creating a new life structure, or whether he
eventually decides to stay where he is and
come to terms with his present life.

**This crisis involves a terrible dilemma. The
man fears that if he stays put, he faces a living
death, a future without promise, a self-
betrayal. Yet to make a major change at this
point may be hurtful to his loved ones as well
as himself; his hopes for a better life may be
only a pipe dream that will soon end in failure,
disappointment, and remorse [Levinson, 1977,
p. 106].**

GOULD'S STUDIES
OF MEN AND WOMEN
The only major study of adult development to
include women is that done by Gould (1972;
1978), who examined attitudes and life histories of psychiatric outpatients in seven age
groups ranging from 16 to over 60, and of 524
nonpatients of comparable ages. The responses of these men and women echo many
of the findings in each of the other two studies.

In the 18-to-22 age group, people feel
halfway out of the family and sense a great
need to get all the way out. They have a
tenuous sense of their own autonomy and feel
that the real adult life is just around the corner.

Between 22 and 28, people feel like
adults. They are established in a chosen

lifestyle, independent of their parents, and they pursue immediate goals without wasting time in introspective questioning about whether they are following the right course.

Between 29 and 34, people begin to ask themselves, "What is this life all about now that I am doing what I am supposed to?" and "Is what I am the only way for me to be?" They are committed to marriage and career and raising children, but they strive to account for some inner aspect of themselves. They feel resentful against their spouses, who see them as they were and not as they could be.

This study sees a transitional period between ages 35 to 43, when people continue to question their lives and their values with an increasing awareness that their time is limited. They look back and wonder whether they've done the right thing; they look around them and wonder how best to deal with their adolescent children in the limited time the children will be home with them; and they look ahead and wonder what the future holds for them.

The samples these studies have drawn on are limited by being mostly white, mostly middle-class, and almost all male. Research is needed to determine whether the approximate sequence, if not the ages, of the developmental stages are appropriate for people of other socioeconomic levels and other races, and for women. But even the limited findings they have produced confirm the premise that personality continues to evolve throughout life, that the end of adolescence does not mean the end of growth, and that each age period is significant.

CHOOSING A PERSONAL LIFESTYLE

It is during the young adult years that most people decide whether they will marry or stay single and whether or not they will have children.

These are also the years when they act upon these decisions. For most young adults, an intimate relationship with a person of the opposite sex—a love relationship—is a pivotal factor in their lives, whether or not this relationship leads to marriage and parenthood.

ROMANTIC LOVE

Love—why we fall in love, whom we fall in love with, and what love is, anyway—has long been a favorite topic for poets, novelists, and songwriters. Over the past ten years or so, it has become increasingly popular with social scientists, as well, who have been coming up with some well-researched and illuminating findings about "this thing called love."

What makes two people choose each other to fall in love with? People often *do* marry the boy or girl next door or down the block, but this may have less to do with a preference for the familiar than with the fact that, as Barry (1970) says, "one must meet one's future spouse in order to select him or her" (p. 43). Some element of self-love must be involved in the selection of a loved one, since lovers tend to resemble each other on many traits: physical appearance and attractiveness, mental and physical health, intelligence, popularity, warmth, their own parents' marital and individual happiness, and such other family factors as socioeconomic status, race, religion, education, and income (Burgess & Wallin, 1953; Walster & Walster, 1978).

The more well balanced a couple are in the attributes each brings to the relationship, the happier they tend to be (Walster & Walster, 1978). This balance need not, however, stem from being alike in every aspect. The beautiful young woman who marries a rich and powerful older man is a familiar stereotype of the way two people sometimes balance out their contributions. Equality in the relationship can be achieved in other ways, too: A very intelligent woman who has difficulty getting along with people may value the warmth and friendliness exhibited by a man who is less intellectual than she is. When a man and woman discover that their relationship seems to favor one or the other, they usually react in one of three ways: They try to make it fairer (either the partner who feels cheated demands more, or the one who feels guilty gives more), they talk themselves into believing that things are fairer than they seem, or they end the relationship (Walster & Walster, 1978).

One value of research on such an elusive quality as love is that it helps to dispel many of the myths that have grown around this major element in the lives of most people. For example, when Neiswender, Birren, and Schaie (1975) looked at the quality of love in adulthood, they found:

Men and women do *not* experience love differently. Women, for example, are not more emotional, nor are men more physical.

Married love is not qualitatively different from unmarried love. It is neither more realistic and mature nor less idealistic.

Love is not only for the young. While people of different ages do experience love somewhat differently, older people love just as much as younger ones do.

These researchers divided twenty-four couples, all of whom had been nominated by people who described them as being "very much in love," into four age groups: adolescents (average age 19), young adults (average age 28), middle aged (average age 50), and elderly (average age 73). They identified six types of love, each of which was characterized by statements like the following:

Affective: "I feel complete because of him."

Cognitive: "I think she makes good decisions."

Physical: "Our sexual relationship is both physically powerful and tender."

Verbal: "He finds it easy to confide in me."

Behavioral: "Doing unpleasant tasks is more fun if we do them together."

Fantasy: "I constantly dream and imagine what the future holds for us."

The first four of these components—involving the heart, the mind, the body, and the spoken word—turned out to be of equal importance in the experience of love, while the last two are relatively unimportant. These investigators found that the dimensions of love vary in importance across the life cycle, thus providing a basis for a developmental study of love. In young adulthood, for example, physical intimacy is an important element; this dimension increases steadily from adolescence to middle age. Young adults, like people in midlife, are the most realistic about the strengths and weaknesses of those they love, as compared to adolescents and old people, who tend to idealize their loved ones more.

Walster and Walster (1978) describe two very different forms of love, *passionate* and *companionate*. Passionate love, the kind celebrated in popular songs and romantic stereotypes, is, they say, "a wildly emotional state, a confusion of feelings: tenderness and sexuality, elation and pain, anxiety and relief, altruism and jealousy" (p. 2). Companionate love, on the other hand, just as deep—often more so—but less intense, is marked by "friendly affection and deep attachment" (p. 2). After interviewing and/or testing more than 100,000 people over the past fifteen years, Walster and Walster found that passionate love is quite short-lived, for most couples lasting from 6 months to about 2½ years. As the intensity, the insecurity, and the newness of passionate love fade away, the love—if it lasts—turns into companionate love. In this kind of loving friendship, people enjoy being together, share a commitment to a joint future, and show trust and loyalty to each other.

MARRIAGE
Of all the states in the United States, the

Of all the states in the United States, the married one is the most popular. (© Joel Gordon 1976)

married one is the most popular. Some 95 to 98 percent of our population gets married (Carter & Glick, 1970), and most of these people wed for the first time during their young adult years. After a drop in the marriage rate that began about 1973 and reached a low of 10 marriages per 1000 people in the population in 1976, it began to creep up again until in 1978 it reached 10.3 marriages per 1000 population (National Center for Health Statistics, 1979). People have been tending to marry later, and now the typical first-time bridegroom is 22.9 years old, and the typical bride 20.4 years (Glick & Norton, 1977).

Predicting Success in Marriage

What is success in marriage? Different researchers have relied on people's ratings of their own marriages, on the absence of marital counseling, or on the number of years a couple stay together. But all these criteria are flawed. People are sometimes less than honest with themselves; some people find it easier to acknowledge problems and seek help; some people will put up with more unhappiness than others; and a couple may

stay together for sixty years, even though each makes the other miserable. Even so, these three criteria are still the best ones we have in rating marriages.

Age at marriage is an important predictor of a marriage's success. Teenagers have high divorce rates for many reasons. Early marriage may affect career or educational aspirations, restrict both partners' potential for growth, and lock a couple into a relationship neither one is mature enough to handle. People who wait until their late twenties or later to marry have the highest chances for success (Kieren et al., 1975; Troll, 1975).

A marriage has the highest chance for success if both partners are of the same religion and practice that religion; if they come from the same social class and if that class is in the upper echelon; if the bride is not pregnant; and if the couple has known each other for a long time (Stephens, 1968; cited in Kieren et al., 1975).

Personality factors are an important element of marital success. Happily married persons have been characterized, on the basis of personality tests, as "emotionally stable, considerate of others, yielding, companionable, self-confident, and emotionally dependent'' (Burgess & Wallin, 1953; cited in Barry, 1970).

According to research performed over the years, factors relating to the husband have exerted more influence on the success of a marriage than those pertaining to the wife (Barry, 1970). It has generally been more important for the future of the marriage if the husband had a close relationship to his father; if his parents had been happily married; if his educational and socioeconomic levels were high; if he is well adjusted emotionally; and if he is rated highly by his wife on emotional maturity and on filling his role as a husband. This may have been because women were willing to work harder at marriage—any marriage—than men were, because it meant more to them in their personal visions of success in life. Now that more women are seeking to achieve identity through career goals and more women are choosing to remain single, they may have a more independent attitude toward marriage, and this disparity may cease to exist.

Emotional Development in Marriage

People develop emotionally through an intimate reciprocal adult relationship. Their former relationships with their parents may have been and continue to be intimate—but parent-child relationships cannot be reciprocal in the same way as a relationship between contemporaries. They may have had close relationships with siblings, same-sex friends, or sweethearts—but marriage introduces a new commitment. The effort to fulfill this commitment often helps each partner to develop more fully.

People grow, for example, in a relationship in which they can share their innermost thoughts. By talking through their ideas, feelings, and plans for the future, they become clearer in their own minds, and often change and grow in response to each other. They also grow through the constant adjustments that marriage requires. Husband and wife have to

work out systems for making decisions about issues that affect them both. They have to work through important life decisions— whether both will pursue careers and how their working lives will mesh with their home lives; whether they will have children, and if so, when and how many, and how they will structure their family life; how they will handle money; how they will spend leisure time; and what their relationships will be with both sets of families and with their friends.

Problems in these areas can erupt into crises that may serve as catalysts for future growth, or they may cause nothing but discord, from which neither partner learns. People who can resolve these crises, either by themselves or with the aid or professional counseling, often learn about themselves and come through the experience as more mature individuals. In the process, the couple often forges a stronger bond.

Benefits of Marriage

The ubiquity of one form of marriage or another throughout history in every society around the world attests to it as a human need. The marriage bond is usually considered the best way to ensure an orderly raising of children and thus a continuation of the species. In most societies marriage also provides economic benefits, providing for an orderly division of labor and a manageable consuming and working unit. It provides an available and regulated outlet for sexual activity. And in a highly mobile, fragmented society like ours, marriage *ideally* provides a safe place where each partner can bask secure in the knowledge that his or her partner will be an almost-constant source of friendship, affection, and companionship. (Our high divorce rate attests to the difficulty of attaining this ideal, but the high remarriage rate among divorcees shows that people keep trying.)

Marriage does seem to make people happy—or else happy people tend to be married. Campbell, Converse, and Rodgers (1975) asked more than 2000 adults around the country about the quality of their lives. Married men and women of all ages reported higher feelings of satisfaction and general good feelings about their lives than the single, the divorced, or the widowed. The happiest of all groups were married people in their twenties with no children, and heading these were young married women. After marriage, women report feeling much less stress; but young husbands, although happy, report feeling more stress. Apparently marriage is still seen as an accomplishment and a source of security for a woman, but as a responsibility for a man.

Yet Bernard (1973) concluded that, while popular opinion holds that women gain more from marriage, it is actually men who are the big winners. Married women say they are happier, but they are less well adjusted than single women and suffer more from depression, nervous breakdowns, anxiety, and alcoholism. They also exhibit poorer mental health than their husbands.

In general, though, marriage is healthy. In all developed countries married people live longer, and this difference is particularly notable for men. Divorced and widowed men have higher death rates than single men, who are closest to the rate of married men. Fuchs (1974) suggests that divorced and widowed men may have such high rates because they have less desire to live after they lose their wives. This theory is bolstered by a breakdown of death statistics: Widowers die more from presumably self-destructive causes such as lung cancer, cirrhosis of the liver, motor accidents, homicide, and suicide—but there is far less difference between widowed and single men in rates for diseases in which individual behavior has less effect, such as vascular lesions, diabetes, and leukemia.

Types of Marriage

In a classic study of marriages, Cuber and Harroff (1965) interviewed more than 200 people who had been married ten years or more and had never seriously considered separation. They identified five types of marriages, described below.

The *conflict-habituated marriage* is lived out to the rhythms of constant quarreling and nagging. Such a couple's apparently mutual needs for conflict and tension keeps the marriage together, often for a lifetime of battling. (When asked whether she had ever considered divorce, one wife said, "Divorce? Never! Murder? Every day.")

In the *devitalized marriage*, husband and wife look back to their early wedded days and remember their love, their exciting sexual relationship, and their close identification with one another. Now, though, they are in a boring rut. They go through the motions of togetherness—they raise the children and keep up with household and social obligations. But while there is little conflict in such a marriage, there is also little intimacy and little passion.

The *passive-congenial marriage* is like the devitalized one, except that the passivity has been there all along. Husband and wife

So far we have never had any words between us nor any disagreement; and I have ceased to feel bashful when we go out visiting or sight-seeing. Now each of us seemed to think only of how to please each other; and I felt sure that nothing would ever separate us. May our relation always be thus happy!

from *A Woman's Diary*
(Diary of an unknown Japanese woman), 1895
in *Revelations: Diaries of Women*, p. 168.

seem to have drifted together because each wanted to get married, but neither one ever seemed to have wished for an intense emotional involvement with the other. Many people in such marriages devote their real life force to careers or children and find the marriage itself a convenient backdrop to their major life interests.

Couples in a *vital marriage* find their prime joy in life in each other, but they still maintain their separate identities. They enjoy doing things together and sharing their feelings, and they consider their relationship the most important thing in their lives. When conflict does occur, it generally revolves around important rather than trivial matters, and it tends to be resolved quickly.

The *total marriage* is like the vital marriage, only more so. The couple's togetherness dominates their entire lives, and their very existences seem to become intertwined. Husband and wife share all aspects of their existence, and they experience few areas of tension.

These five types of marriage revolve around relationships and what people think marriage should be, rather than around personalities. Occasionally a marriage changes from one type to another, but generally it remains within its type. These classifications help us to understand the many different long-term relationships people are capable of and the many forms marriage can take.

Marital Sex

"Sexual liberation," writes Hunt (1974), "has had its greatest effect . . . within the safe confines of the ancient and established institution of monogamous marriage" (p. 194). The most extensive survey of sexual activity in the United States since Kinsey's has found that sex within marriage has become much more vital. It's more of an equal-opportunity activity these days, with husbands being more concerned about their wives' enjoyment of sex and wives being more willing to initiate and take responsibility for it. Husbands and wives are having more frequent sexual intercourse

than their counterparts in the same age brackets did in the past several decades. They are also engaging in more varied sexual activities. Most important, though, is the fact that married people now seem to be deriving more pleasure from the sexual side of their marriage than has been the case in this country for many years.

We can attribute this change to many factors in society. Since the beginning of the twentieth century, a generally more liberated attitude has emerged on the part of marriage counselors, the clergy, and the medical profession, veering away from the older beliefs about the wickedness of sex. Increasingly, sexual activity—especially in marriage—has been held to be normal, healthy, and pleasurable. More information about sex has been available in the public press, in professional journals, and from practitioners of the new profession of sex therapy pioneered by Masters and Johnson (1966).

The greater reliability of contraceptive methods and the availability of legal and safe abortion also contributed to this change, as husbands and wives are freed from fears of unwanted pregnancy. And the women's liberation movement has helped many women to acknowledge their sexuality.

SEXUAL DEVELOPMENT IN MARRIAGE

One of the most important areas of mutual development revolves around the sexual relationship. Sexual adjustment often requires a complete reversal of previous attitudes and behavior. From having held back physical desires and perhaps even feeling guilty about having them or acting upon them, the now-married couple suddenly seeks to adopt a philosophy of complete sexual freedom. Some couples have difficulty making this adjustment and carry their former sexual inhibitions to the marriage bed.

TABLE 13-1

Summary of Contraceptive Methods

METHOD	USER	EFFEC-TIVENESS RATING	ADVANTAGES	DISADVANTAGES
Birth control pills	Female	Excellent	Easy and aesthetic to use	Continual cost; side effects; requires daily attention
IUD (IUCD)	Female	Excellent	Requires little attention; no expense after initial insertion	Side effects, particularly increased bleeding; possible expulsion
Diaphragm with cream or jelly	Female	Very good	No side effects; minor continual cost of jelly and small initial cost of diaphragm	Repeated insertion and removal; possible aesthetic objections
Cervical cap	Female	Very good	Can be worn 2-3 weeks without removal; no cost except for initial fitting and purchase	Does not fit all women; potential difficulties with insertion
Condom	Male	Very good	Easy to use; helps to prevent venereal disease	Continual expense; interruption of sexual activity and possible impairment of gratification
Vaginal foam	Female	Good	Easy to use; no prescription required	Continual expense
Vaginal creams, jellies, tablets, and suppositories	Female	Fair to good	Easy to use; no prescription required	Continual expense; unattractive or irritating for some people
Withdrawal	Male	Fair	No cost or preparation	Frustration
Rhythm	Male and female	Poor to fair	No cost; acceptable to Roman Catholic Church	Requires significant motivation, cooperation, and intelligence; useless with irregular cycles and during postpartum period
Douche	Female	Poor	Inexpensive	Inconvenient; possibly irritating
Abortion	Female	Excellent	Avoids unwanted pregnancies if other methods fail	Expensive; possible medical complications; psychologically or morally unacceptable to some
Sterilization	Male or female	Excellent	Permanent relief from contraceptive concerns	Possible surgical/medical/psychological complications

SOURCE: From Katchadourian & Lunde, 1975, p. 167.

Husband and wife have to develop skills to communicate their sexual needs. Instead of expecting the other person to guess what will be sexually fulfilling, each partner has to become more attuned to his or her own body rhythms and sensitivities, and then to let the partner know what is most satisfying. People who have had previous sexual experiences need to consider the quite-different feelings, attitudes, and physical needs of the present partner. As Kieren, Henton, and Marotz (1975) emphasize, mates must, if necessary, "change some of [their] values and ways of thinking about sex to bring them closer to those of the partner" (p. 198). They need to make decisions about birth control; and if they plan to space the births of their children or not to have any at all, they must decide upon the method that is most satisfactory to both husband and wife (see Table 13-1). Finally, the physical act of sex may require adjustments in both partners' daily routines. Instead of fitting it in whenever there is time left from other activities, couples can strengthen their sexual relationship by setting time aside just for each other.

The time required to make a good sexual adjustment varies from couple to couple and is often contingent on other aspects of the marriage. Problems in the sexual relationship may be a symptom of other marital difficulties, or they may simply result from the couple's sexual naivete. In either case, professional marriage counseling can sometimes help a couple to develop a more satisfying sexual relationship.

Extramarital Sex

Infidelity means different things in different cultures, and to different people within the same culture. Cuber and Harroff (1965) found that infidelity occurs in 4 out of their 5 types of marriage—in all except the total marriage—but in entirely different contexts. In the conflict-habituated marriage, a partner may engage in casual sex out of anger toward the mate; a member of a devitalized marriage may stray to recapture a remembered joy or to seek a more vital relationship; a person in a passive-congenial marriage may be drawn into adultery out of boredom; and a person in a vital marriage may be showing an excess of vitality in a spirit of bohemian emancipation that may or may not be shared openly with the partner.

Over the past generation, there has been no measurable increase in the number of American husbands who have had extramarital sexual experience, and only a limited increase among wives (Hunt, 1974). What changes there are, are greatest for men and women under 25. Just under half of all married and divorced white men have at some time had extramarital sexual intercourse.[1] Women

are less likely to have had such experiences: In Hunt's study, 52 percent of the divorced white women had had extramarital intercourse, but only 17 percent of those presently married. The greatest increase in extramarital sexual activity has been among white women aged 18 to 24, who are three times as likely today to have an affair as women in this age group were a generation ago. This probably signals a change from a double to a single standard, rather than any sweeping values revolution.

Hunt (1974) comments:

The majority of people have always experienced extramarital desires, at least from time to time, and kept them hidden; in today's climate of open discussion, those desires are being manifested in the form of discussion and of an unconcealed appetite for vicarious experience. At the same time, most people continue to disapprove of such behavior because they believe that when it becomes a reality rather than a fantasy, it undermines and endangers the most important human relationship in their life. [p. 256].

In one survey of 800 married persons, Athanasiou and Sarkin (1974) found that people who had had extensive premarital sexual experience were most likely to have extramarital affairs, especially if their marriages were at all unhappy.

It seems, then, that despite the moral, religious, and legal sanctions against adultery—and despite the dangers most people feel it carries for their marriages—it fulfills the need of many married persons.

Violence between Spouses

In our increasingly violent society, wife-beating is one form of aggression that is often accepted as an integral part of many "happy"

---

[1]Hunt broke his figures down by race so that he could make more accurate comparisons with Kinsey's statistics, which were based on a largely white population.

marriages. Straus (1975) cites a recent experiment in which a series of violent scenes were staged in the street. Male passersby intervened in fights between two men or two women, but not when a man was hitting a woman; they apparently assumed the man was her husband and, as such, had the right to hit her.

There are few data about the incidence of husband-wife fights, but in one study of 600 applicants for divorce, Levinger (1966) found that more than 1 out of 3 wives listed "physical abuse" as one of their complaints. Women of lower socioeconomic status were much more likely than middle-class wives to complain of this.

Violence between spouses is more common in families where there is unemployment, poverty, and membership in a subculture that accepts violence as an acceptable way to discharge aggression (Lystad, 1975). Very often an abused wife will feel that she deserves the brutal beatings she receives from her husband; at other times the wife knows how pathological her situation is, but she is afraid to leave for fear she will be beaten more, or even killed.

In recent years, more attention has been paid to the plight of these women and to their need for protection. Even today in many states a wife cannot sue her husband for assault and battery, and police officers called to break up a fight between husband and wife will rarely arrest the husband. Some of these attitudes *are* beginning to change: Shelters exist in many communities where battered wives can go with their children, and the legal system is becoming more responsive to these families' needs.

SINGLE LIFE

Not everyone wants to be married. The U.S. Census Bureau reports that from 1970 to 1975 the number of adults aged 25 to 34 who have never married increased by 50 percent; and the number of unmarried women aged 20 to 24 increased from 28 percent in 1970 to 40 percent in 1975 (*The New York Times*, 1976). Among 20- to 35-year-olds, 1 in 4 is single. The number of adults under the age of 35 who live alone more than doubled between 1970 and 1977 (Reinhold, 1977).

People who once might have felt pressure to marry now seem to feel more freedom to stay single for a longer period of time. Some want the freedom to try new experiences and do not want to hedge this freedom by assuming the emotional and financial obligations of marriage. Since single persons do not need to consider how their actions will affect spouse and children, they are freer to take social, economic, and physical risks. They can decide more easily to move across the country or across the world, to take chances on new kinds of work, and to devote more time to the pursuit of individual interests such as furthering their education or engaging in creative activities. Some people stay single because they like being alone and prefer not to have to be with others much of the time.

Given the poor prognosis for teenage marriages, the decision of many young adults to postpone marriage may end up lowering the divorce statistics, which are now running at 4.8 per 1000 population, the highest in history (U.S. Department of Health, Education, and Welfare, 1976).

The 30-year mark signals a turning point for the single woman. Most under-30 singles want to get married some day, and most eventually do. After the age of 30, though, it is less likely. Says Adams (1971):

By 30 most women who are still unmarried are beginning to build up economic independence, an investment in work, and a viable value system that allows them to identify and exploit major sources of personal and social satisfaction in other areas than marriage and family. Even those whose first preference is marriage are compelled to readjust their social sights

People who once might have felt pressure to marry now seem to feel more freedom to stay single for a longer period of time (Ginger Chih/Peter Arnold, Inc.)

and relationships because the number of eligible men will have thinned out and their married peers will be caught up in a web of social and domestic activities with which they cannot identify and that do not meet their needs. At this juncture the unmarried woman, if she is not to be plagued by a constant sense of dissatisfaction, must take stock of her situation and carefully evaluate both its negative features and its assets [p. 491].

In interviewing more than sixty single men and women, aged 22 to 62, Stein (1976) found a number of "pulls" (positive advantages in being single) and "pushes" (negative aspects of being married) that made many people opt for the single life. Among the "pulls," singles cited career opportunities, self-sufficiency, sexual availability, an exciting lifestyle, mobility, the freedom to change, and opportunities—to have sustaining friendships, a variety of experiences, a plurality of roles, and psychological and social autonomy. Among the "pushes" were restrictions within a monogamous relationship (feeling trapped, obstacles to self-development, boredom, un-

happiness, anger, and role playing and conformity to expectations), poor communication, sexual frustration, lack of friends, and limited mobility and availability of new experiences.

From an in-depth study of seventy-three college-educated, never-married men and women over the age of 30, Schwartz (1976) found them a highly diverse group of people. She identified six patterns of lifestyles, based on individual behavior, attitudes, and values.

The most common pattern in this group was the *professional*, which consisted of twenty-eight people who organized their lives around their work. These individuals identify strongly with their occupational role and invest most of their energy in their careers. The next common category, with eighteen people, was the *social*, made up of individuals whose lives revolve around their personal relationships. While these people often enjoy their work, they do not give it priority in their lives: They put more time and energy into joining organizations, pursuing hobbies that put them in close contact with other people, and visiting with family and friends. The sixteen people in the *individualistic* category focused on their search for self-identity and self-growth. Individualists appreciate the independence, freedom, and privacy being single gives them, they like to spend time alone, and they use their free time for learning or for self-expression. They have the most hobbies of any of the categories.

Of the other singles interviewed, five were *activists*, who centered their lives around involvements in politics or the community; four were *passive*, spending most of their free time alone, showing the least initiative in shaping their lives, and having the most negative outlooks on life; and two women—one a teacher and the other a nurse—fell into the *supportive* pattern, in which they saw the purpose of their lives as being of help to others.

Most of the people interviewed reported being moderately or highly satisfied with their lives, with women showing considerably more satisfaction than men (perhaps because they report having more sources of support from family and friends when problems arise). The most satisfied men were those in the professional and individualistic categories; the most satisfied women, in the supportive and activist groups. Well over half the women in this sample were professionally oriented.

Despite their diversity in personality and lifestyle, these singles have one thing in common: All must learn how to get along in a society that is predominantly oriented toward marriage. Concludes Schwartz (1976):

Singles have to learn how to be single and how to adjust to the advantages and disadvantages of this state just as married people learn to adjust to the demands and satisfactions of that state. The difference, however, is that early socialization is tailored to prepare people for marriage. Guidance and counseling for alternative life careers, including that of being permanently single, is almost nonexistent [p. 13].

The problems of single people range from practical ones like finding a job, getting a place to live, and being totally responsible for themselves to the intangibles of wondering where they fit into the social world, how well they are accepted by friends and family, and how their single status affects their self-esteem. Single people may be stereotyped as being single because they are sexually unattractive, or have unresolved early psychosexual conflicts, or cannot make an emotional commitment, or are homosexual, although these views seem to be diminishing.

Single people who want to enjoy some of the benefits of family life without being married are meeting their needs in a number of ingenious ways. Some are developing informal "communes of unattached individuals who are not close and intimate friends but operate among each other on the basis of shared needs and reciprocal services" (Adams, 1971, p. 496). One social structure that helps to meet their needs is the deliberately created "extended family" formed by some church and community groups. These "families" consist of persons of various ages and family structures (married, single, divorced, widowed) who get together regularly and offer their members the same kind of practical and psychological support that biological families provide (Olds, 1975).

Unmarried Sexual Activity

Being single does not mean being celibate. More and more young people are having sexual experiences before marriage; and the later people marry, the less likely they are to be virgins on their wedding day. Yet most people engage in premarital sex for a very brief part of their adult lives—over a period of five to six years for most men and one to two years for most women (Hunt, 1974).

By the age of 25 nearly half of the married white women in Hunt's survey and nearly 75 percent of the single ones had had premarital sexual intercourse, about twice the proportion that Kinsey had found twenty and thirty years earlier. Among younger people, sexual activity is generally bound up with an affectionate relationship, and there is little promiscuity. There is more casual sex among older single people and separated and divorced persons. Those young adults who do *not* engage in premarital sex hold back for a number of reasons: moral or religious scruples, fear of pregnancy, fear of public opinion, or fear of how it would affect their future marriages. Women express these fears more than men do, indicating that the double standard still lives.

COHABITATION

A relatively new social development is *cohabitation*, or the open living together of an unmarried couple. This type of living arrangement doubled from the years 1970 to 1978 to reach a total of 1.1 million households (Reinhold, 1979). The cohabiting woman is twice as likely to move in with the man as he is to move into her residence, and 8 out of 10 of these unmarried couples share their living quarters with only one other person, while the rest have one or more children living with them (Glick & Norton, 1977).

Among people under 25 years old, the number of unmarried couples living together increased eightfold since 1970, with 1 out of 4 of these couples including at least one college student (Reinhold, 1979; Glick & Norton, 1977). Most such couples live together for a relatively short time—63 percent for less than two years—before they either marry or separate (Glick & Norton, 1977).

Comparing 138 student cohabitators with 153 college students who were not living with someone of the other sex, Henze and Hudson (1974) found the cohabitators less conventional in several aspects of their lives. They were less likely to go to church, more likely to consider themselves liberals, and more apt to use drugs. One way in which cohabitators perpetuate traditional attitudes, however, is in the double standard: Males are more likely to be the breadwinners, and are more apt to

have cohabited one or more times in the past. No differences showed up in the family backgrounds of the two groups, such as parental education, parents' marital happiness, or disciplinary practices.

In a more extensive study of a nationwide random sample of 2510 twenty- to thirty-year-old men, Clayton and Voss (1977) found that while only 5 percent were living with a woman at the time of the interview, 18 percent had done so in the past for six months or longer. Of these, 65 percent had lived with only one woman. Cohabitators were more likely than noncohabitators to be black, residents of large cities, nonstudents or high school dropouts, from the Western or Northeastern sections of the country, early initiates into sexual intercourse, illicit drug users, and participants in unconventional activities such as studying an Eastern religion. For some of these young men cohabitation seemed to have served as a prelude to marriage. For others, especially those who had been married and divorced, it offered a temporary or permanent alternative to marriage.

The impact of cohabitation on society is not clear. Its growing popularity indicates that we can think of it as an increasingly accepted courtship pattern. For many young people it is the modern equivalent of dating and going steady. It is not a "trial marriage," nor does it seem to serve as practice for marriage. In fact, it does not seem to have any effect one way or the other on eventual marital adjustment. Jacques and Chason (1979) studied eighty-four married college students, 65 percent of whom had had at least one cohabitation experience before marrying. After questioning the students about many different aspects of their marital relationships, the researchers found no significant difference between those who had lived with someone premaritally and those who had not.

Why do so many couples decide to live together? With the longer length of time between physiological and social maturity (because of the secular trend toward earlier sexual maturation and the societal trend toward more extended education), many young people want close sexual relationships and yet are not ready for marriage. Living with someone helps many young adults to know themselves better, to understand what is involved in an intimate relationship, and to clarify what they want in marriage and in a mate. For many, the experience is a maturing one.

Yet these relationships are not without problems. Some are similar to those encountered by newlyweds—the overinvolvement in the other person, the working out of a sexual relationship, the felt loss of personal identity, an overdependency on the other, and a growing distance from other friends. Other problems are specific to the nature of cohabitation: discomfort about the ambiguity of the situation, jealousy, or the desire for a commitment that is not there. More than two-thirds of cohabiting women who took part in a study at Cornell University had tried to conceal the relationship from their parents, and almost half succeeded. Those who felt guilty did so mostly about being dishonest with their parents, not about the relationship itself. The couples had practically no problems with others in the outside world—friends, school authorities, or landlords. The benefits still outweighed the problems: More than half rated the relationships as very successful, and more than 80 percent felt they were both maturing and pleasant (Macklin, 1972).

Among 18- to 34-year-old adults in the New York area who responded to a newspaper survey, some 60 percent approved of such relationships (New York *Daily News*, 1975). The reason for young people's problems with their parents can be seen in the disparity between the age groups that answered the survey: Among people over 50, only 17 percent approved of such relationships. Macklin (1972) emphasizes society's need for help in adjusting to this new phenomenon. Parents need help in understanding the reasons behind the pattern and in learning not to view it as necessarily unhealthy or immoral. Students need counseling at earlier ages to help them consider the complexities of intimate relationships and to decide their own lifestyles.

PARENTHOOD

The birth of a first baby marks a major transition point in its parents' lives. Moving from an intimate relationship involving two people to one involving a third—a helpless being totally dependent on these two people—changes people and changes marriages. The research in this area has been inconsistent: Some studies show the birth of a child as a troublesome crisis that creates a major upheaval for both parents and for their marital relationship (LeMasters, 1957; Dyer, 1963); other studies see this event more as a time of transition that involves some difficulty than as a major crisis (Hobbs & Cole, 1976; Hobbs & Wimbish, 1977); and still other studies find both kinds of reactions and attempt to look for factors that differentiate couples whose lives are enhanced by having a baby and couples who experience problems around new parenthood (Feldman, 1971; Rollins & Galligan, 1978).

What seem to be the major effects of becoming a parent? The baby's birth brings

I realized how much we have changed in the past three months; how much I have learned about loving. I had expected that like a little girl, mocking love to her doll, my love would at once envelop my baby; instead I had to learn it, grow into it.

Frances Karlen Santamaria,
in *Revelations: Diaries of Women*, p. 114.

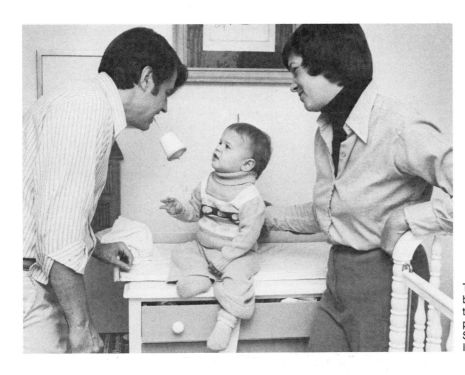

The birth of a first baby marks a major transition point in its parents' lives. (Erika Stone/Peter Arnold, Inc.)

home to a couple more dramatically than any other event in their lives the recognition that they are no longer children, but adults. But along with the joy and excitement that parents may feel upon holding their new baby and the feelings of achievement that they may experience upon reaching this new status come a host of conflicts and anxieties. The addition of a totally dependent third person who demands a great deal of time and attention often creates strains and tensions in a marriage.

The mother—especially the highly educated, career-oriented mother—often resents the new demands made on her time and energy, as well as the interruption of her professional life. For even in these "liberated" times, when the roles of men and women are undergoing great changes, in most homes most of the responsibility for raising the children still falls to the mother. It is not surprising, then, that both black and white women have more difficulty than their husbands in adjusting to their new roles as parents (Hobbs & Cole, 1976; Hobbs & Wimbish, 1977).

In a study of 271 middle- and working-class couples whose first babies were between 6 and 56 weeks old, Russell (1974) found that women are bothered most by fatigue, interrupted sleep and rest, feeling "edgy" or emotionally upset, worry about their personal appearance, and worry about their loss of figure. Those women whose health was excellent, who had had easy pregnancies and deliveries, and had been married a longer time had the most positive reactions to their babies' birth. The more highly educated a woman was, the more trouble she had adjusting to parenthood.

Russell found that different issues came up for men. While, like their wives, the new fathers in her study were most bothered by interrupted sleep and rest, their other concerns were different. They were bothered by the necessity of changing plans because of the baby, the additional work and money problems the baby brought, and interference in child rearing from their in-laws. Those men who had prepared for parenthood by attending classes, reading books, or taking care of other people's children were most likely to

enjoy being fathers, as were those who saw their role of "father" as one of the most important of all their life roles and wanted more children.

Those couples who were happily married at the time of the study (when the babies were from 6 to 56 weeks of age) and who had planned for the birth of this first baby had the most positive adjustments to parenthood.

In their study of sixty-five white couples with a first child of about 6 months of age, Hobbs and Cole (1976) found that more than 3 out of 4 couples were having either no difficulty in adjusting to the new baby or only slight difficulty, leading the investigators to conclude, "It is more accurate to think of beginning parenthood as a transition, accompanied by some difficulty, than a crisis of severe proportions" (p. 730). In Hobbs and Wimbish's 1977 study of thirty-eight black parents, they found that black parents had slightly more trouble adjusting to their first child, but that their difficulties were not of crisis proportions, either. Both black and white parents indicated that the single most bothersome aspect of becoming a parent was the interruption of their lifestyles.

Why People Have Children

Throughout the years and around the world, having children has traditionally been regarded as "the fulfillment of a marriage, if not the primary reason for marriage. It was taken for granted that a couple married, produced children, and later enjoyed their grandchildren" (McCary, 1975, p. 289). In preindustrial societies families needed to be large. The children were needed to help with the family's work and someday to care for their aging parents. Because the economic and social reasons for having children were so powerful, parenthood—and especially motherhood— was invested with a unique emotional aura.

Only the woman who became a mother was truly fulfilled; only the woman who viewed sex as primarily procreative was given permission to enjoy it; and only the woman who wanted children was considered normal.

Today, though, economic and cultural reasons demanding universal parenthood are diminishing. Overpopulation is one of the world's major problems. Technological progress requires fewer workers. Improved medical care ensures the survival of most children. Social Security and other government programs ensure the care of the aged. Furthermore, it has become clear that children can have negative, as well as positive, effects on a marriage.

As a result of all these influences, people are taking advantage of the extremely effective birth control devices available today and are having fewer children. In 1967, 26 percent of 18- to 24-year-old wives wanted four or more children, while only 8 percent wanted this large a family in 1974 (*U.S. News & World Report*, 1975).

An interesting counterpoint, though, to this trend toward smaller families in a time of improved contraception is an increase in the number of premarital births, which went from 5 percent in 1960 to 14 percent in 1975 (Glick & Norton, 1977). This may be explained in part by the increased acceptance of premarital sex, which makes conception out of wedlock less of a disgrace and by the resulting decision among some young women to bear and keep their illegitimate children rather than have abortions or give the babies up for adoption.

People are having smaller families these days, but they are still bearing and rearing children. There are many interpretations for people's procreative urges (Skolnick, 1973). Psychoanalytic theorists maintain that women have a deep instinctual wish to bear and nurture infants; that they thus replace their own mothers; and that their babies are substitutes for the penises they will never have. Ego-psychologists such as Erikson define parenthood in terms of the growth of skills and personality resources, seeing *generativity*, or a concern in establishing and guiding the next generation, as a basic developmental need. Functional sociologists attribute reproduction to people's needs for immortality, which they achieve by replacing themselves with their own children. Still another interpretation sees parenthood as a part of nature common throughout the animal world. Then there are cultural pressures that make many people feel impelled to have children as a response to assumptions—on the part of media, schools, employers, family, churches, etc.—that all normal people want to have children.

An international study undertaken in Korea, Indonesia, the Philippines, Taiwan, Thailand, Turkey, West Germany, Singapore, and the United States sought to find out what parents see as the psychological satisfactions of having children, and how these satisfactions affect the number of children they choose to have (Hoffman & Manis, 1979). Among the answers given by the American subjects—1569 married women under age 40 and 456 of their husbands—love, fun, and stimulation headed the list. Other satisfactions often reported were those relating to expansion of the self—giving a purpose to life, providing a learning experience, self-fulfillment, carrying on the family name, and immortality. Children are also seen as conferring adult status on their parents and as giving their parents something useful to do. (These responses were given most often by women with more traditional views of sex roles and by those who did not work outside the home.)

Nonparents were more likely than parents to cite the sense of achievement, competence, and creativity one gets from producing, rearing, and watching a child develop. The authors comment, "Possibly creativity and a sense of achievement through parenthood exists more in anticipation than in the actual day-to-day experience of parenting and, for parents, the relationship between the effort and the effect may seem less clear" (p. 589). The economic value of children seemed more important to rural and to black parents.

While few parents directly cited the moral worth of being a parent—putting the needs of others first and becoming less selfish—as a reason for having children, 13 percent of the mothers and 11 percent of the fathers indicated that they felt they had become a better or less selfish person as a result of parenthood.

In some of the countries with higher birthrates, values associated with having several children, such as economic worth, offering adult status and social identity, and moral worth, ranked higher than in the United States where the most common responses indicated satisfaction with just one or two children.

PARENTAL SEX PREFERENCES Parents' desires for a child of one sex or the other are linked to their reasons for having children in the first place. Parents who prefer a son usually want a child to carry on the family name and bring honor to the family, while those who want a daughter want a child who is lovable, easier to raise, able to help with housework, and is fun to dress (Williamson, 1978). Around the world, boys are generally preferred to girls. In the United States, couples who want only one child usually hope for a boy, those who want two want one of each, and those who want three prefer two sons and one daughter. Husbands are especially likely to express a strong preference for a boy.

In developing countries and in societies in which the status of women is low, boys are highly preferred. In these societies, a woman's marital security and status may depend on her producing sons (even though we have seen, in Chapter 2, that it is the male who determines the sex of his offspring!). In some of these countries, boys are given better medical care, are fed better, and are given more schooling. Female infanticide is rarely practiced today, but the mortality of females is sometimes higher because baby girls are

often neglected in those countries that under-value them.

Adoptive parents, on the other hand, both in Europe and in the United States, tend to prefer girls. This may reflect the greater yearning for children of women—who are more likely than their husbands to want daughters. Couples may also feel it will be easier to take in a girl, believing she will be less aggressive, more obedient, neater, more adaptable, and less disruptive than a boy.

The Effects of Children on Their Parents' Marriage

From his studies of lower-class, working-class, middle-class, and upper-middle-class parents, Feldman (1971) concluded that "parenthood has a pervasive influence on the marriage" (p. 24). One of the major sources of dissension that he found among married couples was a difference in their beliefs about the ways children should be raised. As he points out, "Conflicts about child rearing cannot usually be resolved by compromise, i.e., when he cries the baby cannot be picked up one time and left to cry it out the next" (p. 9). Our attitudes about the right way to bring up children are often deep-seated, stemming from our own childhoods, our cultural and economic backgrounds, and a host of varied experiences over the years. Yet this is a topic which most engaged and newly married couples spend very little time discussing.

Couples most likely to report an increase in marital satisfaction with the birth of their first child were those who had known each other a long time before they had married and who had pursued their individual interests during the marriage rather than being unduly dependent on each other. Furthermore, women who were not very happy while pregnant but exhibited such maternalistic attitudes as a desire to breast-feed, a concern about the

baby's crying, and a child-centered approach to feeding, and who expected their husbands to assume a large role in taking care of the baby were likely to see the birth of the first baby more positively.

Several studies have shown "a decrease in marital happiness with the coming of the first child and an apparent increase of marital happiness at the later stages in life when the children were all gone" (Feldman & Feldman, 1977, p. 1). Yet this does not, of course, hold true for all marriages. In Hobbs's 1974 study, for example, most couples reported that their marriages had either improved (42 percent) or stayed the same (43.5 percent) since the birth of their first child. (Those parents who did not return Hobbs's questionnaire may, of course, have experienced more crises, and, thus, affected her results.)

What are the differences between couples whose marriages improve as they become parents and those whose marriages get worse?

Rollins and Galligan (1978) feel that children are least likely to lower their parents' marital satisfaction in families where the couple wanted the children very much, when the parents can draw on outside resources to help care for the children, and where they have a greater ability to manage time, energy, and money. They have found that a decline in marital satisfaction during the child-rearing years is more common among working-class than middle-class families, possibly because of the working-class families' diminished resources.

It is interesting to note that even when parenting has a negative effect on the marriage, it may have a positive effect on the parents' self-concepts and on their work roles (Feldman & Feldman, 1977). This seems to indicate that becoming a parent can indeed contribute to the development of an individual.

Parenthood as a Developmental Stage

Those people who do choose to become parents develop through this experience as they do through other life experiences. We often forget that children affect their parents and that the experience of being a parent spurs development in certain ways, as, for example, when parents relive their own childhood experiences as their children grow up. The Group for the Advancement of Psychiatry (1973) puts it this way:

Parents are not just "vehicles" for the care of children. They are people, and parenthood is one phase in their total development as human beings, a development that never stops but continues from birth to death [p. 18].

Parenthood should be—and can be—a creative self-growth experience when parents remember their own needs for continuing development. Adds GAP: "It would be much better for everyone—especially for the child—if parental needs were understood and met in a healthy way" (p. 20).

The Group for the Advancement of Psychiatry (1973) specifies four phases of parenthood:

1 *Anticipation:* thinking about parenthood. During pregnancy, people think about the meaning of parenthood and how they will raise their children. They are often ambivalent about wanting to assume this responsibility and need to change their self-image from their parents' children to their children's parents.

2 *Honeymoon:* a time of adjustment and learning. During the first months after the birth of a baby, attachments are formed between parents and child, and family members learn new roles in relation to one another.

3 *Plateau:* the middle period of parental life, from infancy through the teenage years. In each stage, parents have to adapt their behavior to the level of the child.

4 *Disengagement:* the period leading to the end of an *active* parental role, generally upon the child's marriage. Some parents cannot disengage because a child's mental or physical handicap continues to require active par-

enting; others have difficulty disengaging because of their own needs to be needed by their children.

As these phases point out, the parenting role changes as the child grows. And the parent grows also in the experience of parenting. When children fulfill their parents' expectations (which are sometimes extremely unrealistic), the parents are deeply gratified and satisfied with the job they have done. Self-esteem is closely tied in with the ways in which children turn out—especially for the mother, who is usually given more responsibility in child rearing. But parents need to remember that no matter how good they are at parenting, "the final product is not entirely within their control" (GAP, 1973, p. 43). Children have their own abilities and temperaments; they are subject to many influences outside the home; and they often develop values that their parents cannot agree with but that are valid for the children.

Adoptive parents develop basically the same way as biological parents, even though they face experiences and encounter attitudes special to their own situation. In addition, they have to deal with special challenges—the acceptance of their own infertility (if this is the reason they have chosen to adopt), the awareness that they are not duplicating the experience of their own parents, the need to handle the issue of adoption with their children, and the jealousy they may feel when their children express an interest in learning about their biological parents.

The Father's Role

In some primitive societies, biological paternity is not even recognized. The inhabitants of the Trobriand Islands in the South Pacific and the Aranda think that intercourse is for fun, not for babies (Mead & Newton, 1967). But most societies do recognize the father's role in procreation, and all prescribe their own mores for social fatherhood. Usually the man provides materially for his sexual partner and their children; only rarely does he take an active role in the care of the children.

In the United States the traditional role of the prospective father has been one of supporting and protecting his wife, but one in which he was relatively uninvolved with the pregnancy. Today, however, the rapid proliferation of classes for expectant parents has involved many more prospective fathers with the physiological and psychological aspects of pregnancy. With the growing popularity of prepared childbirth (during which the woman is active and participating) and of prenatal classes that include fathers, more and more men find that they do indeed have a valuable role at delivery. A supportive husband can coach his wife in her breathing, can massage her back during contractions, can provide emotional encouragement, and can enjoy the feeling that he is participating actively in his child's birth, as he did in its conception.

Paternal patterns of child care are changing. Billions of words have been written about mother-child relationships, but child-care professionals have virtually ignored the father's relationship to his child, especially in infancy. But this is changing, now that we are seeing more examples of what one psychologist has called "the new father" (*Life*, 1972). This man "no longer considers child care to be strictly woman's work. He is much more aware of his child's emotional needs and he actively, intimately nurtures them."

In a review of new books for and about fathers, Levine (1979) notes "signs of a new sensibility toward fathering, no doubt occasioned in large measure by the women's movement and the reassessment of parental roles it has stimulated" (pp. 158–159).

An important corollary of men's attitudes and behaviors toward their children came out in a study of divorced and separated fathers (Keshet & Rosenthal, 1977). A group of 127 predominantly white, professional men fell into four categories: fathers who saw their children at least two days a month, those who saw them weekly or about two days a week, those with joint custody who cared for their children half-time, and men who had full custody. As these men assumed varying degrees of responsibility for the care of their children, they grew to like themselves better, express emotion more easily, better understand women, and view their careers as less important. The greater their involvement in child care, the more involvement they desired. Many tried to get greater flexibility at work so they could spend more time with their children.

Confirming the role that parenthood plays as an agent in parents' own development, Keshet and Rosenthal conclude that "men who, following separation, take on some major responsibility for the care of their children, find that the demands of that responsibility can become an important focus for their own growth" (p. 18).

In a survey of 160 black and white men who were living with their wives, working full-time, and parents of at least two children between the ages of 3 and 16, Price-Bonham and Skeen (1979) found that fathers from these two racial backgrounds are more similar than dissimilar.

Both black and white men rate the *best* things about being a father as having someone to love and love them, someone to take care of them in their old age, and feeling that their children make them feel respectable. Both rate highly the *worst* things about being a father as having problems of discipline and increased responsibilities. Both hold similar goals for their children: that they live a religious life, be good athletes, be happy, obey laws, respect society, and do their best. Three out of four said they would give financial support, guidance, teaching, and praise to help their children reach these goals. Both

When surveyed, both black and white
men agreed that one of the best things
about being a father is having someone
to love and being loved in return. (Bob
Adelman/Magnum)

*In 1952, I had me a son, Robert
Le Roy. He's built just like
me. I don't know for sure if he
will be a pitcher. A daddy likes
to think his boy is going to be
what he is, but he never knows.*

LeRoy (Satchel) Paige
Maybe I'll Pitch Forever, p. 184.

Bonham and Skeen recommend extensive education for fatherhood, beginning early in the school curriculum. They suggest emphasis on the value of time spent with children as compared to the value of time at work, on different methods of discipline (to break intergenerational patterns of spanking, beating, and failing to explain reasons for discipline), and on planning programs to encourage father participation.

STEPPARENTING

The word "stepparent" conjures up vivid images from the tales of our childhood—of the wicked stepmother who orders a woodsman to cut out the heart of an innocent young girl or the cruel stepfather who treats his wife's son worse than he does his pet dog. Unfortunately, these images often sabotage the efforts of the kindest of today's stepparents to forge close, warm relationships with the children of their spouses. Yet more are making the effort, and many do succeed.

With today's high rates of divorce and remarriage, families made up of "yours, mine, and ours" are becoming more common. Some 25 million adults are now stepparents to more than 6 million children, some 1 in every 8 (U.S. Bureau of Census, 1975).

The stepfamily—also called the "blended," or "reconstituted," family—is different from the "natural" family. For one thing, it has a larger supporting cast, including ex–spouses, ex–in-laws, and absent parents, as

groups of men felt that fatherhood was a bigger job than they had thought it would be, and many decided that, if they could do it over, they would not have children. Many felt their children had made life financially harder, and had interfered with what they had wanted to do in their lives.

Black and white men did differ in some respects. Black fathers felt it was more important to give their children spending money, to help them develop athletically, and to have their children be like themselves, whereas white fathers felt it was more important to help their children with their homework, and considered themselves stricter and talked with their children more often.

On the basis of their findings, Price-

With today's high rates of divorce and remarriage, families made up of "yours, mine, and ours" are becoming more common. Mr. and Mrs. Wade Whitney, Jr., just married, are seen here with fourteen of their sixteen children, seven his and nine hers, from previous marriages. (United Press International)

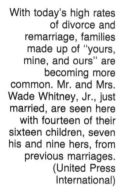

well as assorted aunts, uncles, and cousins on both sides. Furthermore, as Einstein (1979) points out, it is "contaminated with anger, guilt, jealousy, value conflicts, misperceptions, and fear" (p. 64). It is, in short, burdened by much baggage not carried by an "original" family. Obviously, it cannot expect to function in the same way. Yet this unrealistic expectation and a lack of preparation for handling some of the special situations and problems that arise lead to divorce in 4 out of 10 of these families within the first five years of marriage (Einstein, 1979).

The area of greatest stress for stepparents is, not surprisingly, that of child rearing. When the stepparent and the biological parent have very different notions about how to raise children, they clash, the children become confused and often manipulative, and an atmosphere of anger and distrust pervades the home. On the other hand, those parents who agree about child-rearing poli-

cies and present a united front to all their children have the greatest chance of creating a harmonious family. Other problems for stepparents include adjusting to the habits and personalities of their stepchildren and gaining their acceptance (Kompara, 1980).

"Stepping" is generally regarded as more difficult for the mother than for the father. Aside from the more familiar "wicked stepmother" of the fairy tales, she also has a harder act to follow in real life. In our society children are usually closer to their mothers and spend more time with them than with their fathers, making it that much harder for anyone else to step into the role of the biological mother (Kompara, 1980).

Some stepparents have an easier time of it than others for several reasons. Young women, for example, are more likely to have excellent relationships with their stepchildren compared to mothers over 40. Young children and adult children accept stepparents more easily than do adolescents. And women whose natural children live in the same home as the stepchildren generally have more positive stepparenting experiences (Kompara, 1980).

Kompara (1980) cautions stepparents not to try to rush the relationship. Rather, a gradual moving together of adult and child will be more likely to result in mutual affection and trust.

NONPARENTHOOD

An increasing number of people are choosing not to have children at all—some 5 percent of American married women, according to the 1973 report of the U.S. Bureau of the Census.

After interviewing fifty-two voluntarily childless wives, Veevers (1973) identified two characteristic paths: that in which a couple decides before marriage never to have children, and that in which the couple keeps postponing conception until they finally reach a point when they decide that they do not ever want children. The latter path was taken by two-thirds of these wives. Often, childless women began to have doubts about ever having children while still in their own adolescence.

What makes people come to this decision? Some couples decide at an early age that they don't have what it takes to make good parents and that they'd rather have contact with other people's children than full responsibility for their own. In some cases people have such heavy commitments to their careers that they do not want to take time away from them to raise a family. Some couples feel that having children might be an intrusion in their relationship. And others enjoy the freedom to be able to travel or to make spur-of-the-moment decisions, and they do not want the financial burdens children entail.

In a comparison of twenty-seven voluntarily childless couples and fifty-four voluntary sets of parents, Ory (1978) found that both groups had wanted children when they themselves were children, adolescents, and engaged young adults, but that from the begin-

ning those people who later became parents always wanted more children than those who never had any children. The difference was greater between the two groups of women than between the men, and this difference widened as people grew older and married. Both sets of parents recognized prevailing American values that consider two or three children an ideal family size, and one or none to be undesirable.

Houseknecht (1977), who interviewed fifty-four unmarried college women in depth, found that those who desire children appear more concerned with society's negative attitudes toward childlessness than those who do not want children. These seem less concerned with the attitudes of other people—even close friends and relatives—but they do manage to find some sources of support for their own positions. They are not total nonconformists.

Nonparents tend to find support for their own inclinations by minimizing contact with parents and friends who pressure them to have children and by joining an organization like NON (National Organization for Nonparents) or seeking new childfree friends (Ory, 1978).

Judging from the results of a 1977 survey of voting-age adults, Blake (1979) concludes that a large increase in voluntary childlessness is not likely. Most people feel that having children brings certain advantages to their parents, that they are a hedge against loneliness in old age, give life meaning, provide fulfillment for women, and strengthen marriages. Belief in the last three advantages are more likely to be held by people without a college education. Since men are more likely than women to see the "plusses" in having children, Blake concludes that men:

. . . **may be willing to help women lower the opportunity costs of childbearing and rearing** in order to have a family—a small family, perhaps, but a family nonetheless. Equal sharing of household and childbearing responsibilities between mates could have the effect of mitigating many opportunity costs for women and allowing couples to experience parenthood if they wish to do so [p. 256].

A number of studies have indicated that marriages without children are happier (Rollin, 1970; in Skolnick & Skolnick, 1971) and that marriages are happiest before children are born and after they leave home (Campbell, 1975). Children do place added demands on a marriage, and many people either do not want to or are not able to meet these demands.

Yet when Houseknecht (1979) compared fifty mothers with fifty voluntarily childless wives between 25 and 40 years of age, she found a very small difference in overall marital adjustment. The differences she did find favored childless women: They were more likely to engage in outside interests, and to work on projects with their husbands, to have frequent exchanges of stimulating ideas, and to discuss things calmly with their husbands. The childless wives also expressed a stronger desire and determination to continue the marriage, and they agreed more with their husbands on division of household tasks, leisure time activities, and career decisions. Overall, however, the women in both groups reported similar levels of agreement and expression of affection.

Most studies show that childfree wives are better educated, more likely to be employed, and less religious than mothers. Since this study matched both groups of women for these three variables, perhaps the smaller difference in marital adjustment between the two groups indicates that these aspects of women's lives are as important to their marital

happiness as the decision whether or not to have children.

In any case, since unwanted children suffer a variety of handicaps, including more frequent illness, poorer school grades, and more behavior problems than children whose births had been desired (Dytrych, Matejcek, Schuller, David, & Friedman, 1975), the decision of some people not to have children is undoubtedly the wisest one they could make for themselves and for society.

DIVORCE

The United States has one of the highest divorce rates in the world. The rate has risen steadily over the past half-century, until by September 1976 divorces over the previous year exceeded 1 million for the first time in our nation's history (*Newsday*, 1976). From 1965 to 1976, the divorce rate doubled, from 2.5 to 5.0 per 1000 population, and it continued to rise in 1977 and 1978 (Glick & Norton, 1977; Wegman, 1979).

Divorce is primarily a phenomenon of young adulthood, with people divorcing sooner than they used to, even though there has also been a rise in midlife and late-life divorce. In 1971, the median age of first divorce was 31.6 (Kimmel, 1974), while by 1975, it had dropped to 27 for women and 29.1 for men (Glick & Norton, 1977).

The "seven-year itch" is more than folklore, since this is a peak time for divorce. Divorce rates are highest in times of national prosperity and, for various reasons, are highest for marriages between teenagers, between people whose own parents had been unhappy or divorced, between childless couples, among black people, and for marriages with pregnant brides (Kimmel, 1974).

Some reasons for the current high divorce rate in this country are the difficult readjustment to a postwar economy after Vietnam, a more liberal attitude toward personal behavior which makes divorce more acceptable than it used to be, and a lower birthrate which makes it easier for nonparents to return to singlehood (Glick & Norton, 1977).

The rising divorce rate is a circular phenomenon. It is spurred by changes in societal attitudes, and these changes come about because more and more people get divorced. The rise in the divorce rate appears to result largely from people's increasing expectations for marriage. As the economic and social bases have become less important, emotional reasons have become more so. As more people live farther away from their extended families, they turn to spouses for the functions that parents, other relatives, and old friends used to fill. People today expect a marriage partner to make their lives richer, to help them develop their potential, and to be a loving companion and best friend. These increased demands can't always be met—but people keep trying.

When a marriage falls short of the partners' expectations, few people consider it shameful or immoral for them to seek a divorce. Divorce does not carry the social stigma it once did. Yet separation is still not taken casually. The breakup of any intimate relationship is painful, especially a marriage for which both partners once held such high hopes, and especially when children are involved. Individuals in an unhappy marriage are concerned with failure, ranging from their inability to select the right mate to their inability to make the marriage work. The difference now is that people in an unhappy marriage are less likely to accept the situation than they might have done years ago. They are more likely to recognize that the marriage will not get better by itself and that the present situation is likely to damage the personalities of both spouses and their children. And they are more likely to do something. Some couples try professional marriage counseling. This may help them work out their difficulties and save the marriage, or it may help both individuals to decide that separation is best for everyone and to handle it in the best way possible.

Bohannon (1971) has described six aspects of every divorce: the emotional (the deterioration of the marital relationship); the legal; the economic; the coparental (revolving around the children's needs); the community (changes in relationships with people and institutions outside the family); and the psychic (the individual's need to regain personal autonomy). In any marriage, some of these aspects are more intense than others, but all cause stress. Says Bohannon (1971): "They are the more painful and puzzling as personal experiences because society is not equipped to handle any of them well, and some of them not at all" (p. 34).

According to Bohannon, "A 'successful' divorce begins with the realization by two people that they do not have any constructive future together" (p. 62). The decision to separate may be a positive one that represents growth and maturity, a new understanding of oneself and one's needs, and a new appreciation of what one must do to make a marriage work. A person's adjustment afterward depends largely on feelings toward the self, toward the partner, and toward the way the divorce was handled.

No matter how "successful" the divorce, there is always a painful period of adjustment. The divorcee is somewhat estranged from previous friends, especially those who had been friendly with both spouses, and from in-laws with whom one may have been close. She or he faces a certain degree of ambiguity and isolation in the community, as well as a host of practical problems revolving around caring for the children, meeting financial obligations, making new friends, developing new relationships with members of the opposite sex, and coming to terms with the personal psychological significance of the divorce.

Relatively few divorced people stay single. Four out of five remarry, usually within two to three years. From 1967 to 1975, people have tended to marry later and divorce sooner, and to shorten the interval between remarriage and redivorce (Glick & Norton, 1977). At every age, divorced people are more likely to marry than those who have never been married at all. While the divorce rate for remarriages is higher than that for first marriages, 60 percent of second marriages last until death. The higher divorce rate may be a reflection of the remarried person's awareness that he or she managed one divorce and could handle another in search of an ideal mate, or simply a happier life alone.

The present increase in divorce is not a sign that people don't want to be married. It represents their desires to be happily married and their conviction that the pain and trauma of divorce may be necessary for a better life.

FRIENDSHIP IN YOUNG ADULTHOOD

Friends continue to be important in these years. Adult friendships, in fact, may recapitulate the developmental stages in making friends as described by Selman and Selman (1979). Two adults, for example, meeting for the first time, may first look at each other's physical appearance or consider the benefits to themselves of becoming friendly with the other person, as in the child's stage 0. They might explore each other's superficial likes and dislikes and enjoy each other's company on a surface level, as in stages 1 and 2. Then they may develop a deeper friendship, as in stages 3 and 4.

Many adults, however, still have trouble holding onto the intimacy and mutuality of stage 3 while rising to the autonomy and interdependence of stage 4. They cannot be intimate with another person and at the same time allow that person independence. According to Selman and Selman, those who combine these two levels of friendship in one relationship attain the most meaningful bond.

Young couples often meet the people who will become their close friends at college, on the job, through their children, or in community activities. Athanasiou and Yoshioka (1973) looked at friendships among 275 young women from a large housing complex. These women (average age 29) tended to be white, married, and mothers of small children. The women were most likely to be close friends with their next-door neighbors, and the friendships of their children under 3 years old influenced the friendships of the mothers. Women tended to be friendly with other women who had the same marital status, were close in age, had about the same number of children, and were at about the same level of household income. Friendship between next-door neighbors was not affected by the women's education or race, or by their husbands' occupation and education. However, when women lived farther away from each other, occupation and education played a larger role in determining who would be friends.

In Weiss and Lowenthal's 1973 study of friendships across the life span, they found that newlyweds have more friends than any of the other three age groups they studied— adolescents, middle-aged people, and the elderly. Different friends are likely to serve different functions. A man may ride to work with one friend, bowl with another, and talk about family problems with a third. In another study of friendship through the life cycle reported by Gamer, Thomas, and Kendall (1975), people in their twenties and thirties talked about being selective in their choice of friends, as they commented on the great variability among people. As reported in Chapter 11, the same basic determinants of friendship apply to all age levels—similarity, reciprocity, compatibility, convenience, and respect.

During the young adult years, people make friends along a new dimension—as couples, an element that makes forming friendships more complex. Newly married people often find that they do not care for each other's friends from single days, and then have to decide whether they will see their friends separately, whether they will put up with each others' friends, or whether they can work out some sort of compromise. Another difficulty for many couples is the difficulty of four people becoming friends, as opposed to two. Very often people will enjoy the friendship of one member of a marriage, but not the other. Yet in a couple-oriented society like ours, it is difficult to see one without the other. Leefeldt and Callenbach (1979) point out one way by which many couples manage to stay friends as a foursome. They allow a kind of "discount" for couple friendships; that is, they

do not expect the same level of intimacy they would look for in a single friendship. The friendship meets their needs for involvement with other people besides themselves and their families, allows them to avoid isolation and to see each other in outside situations, and offers an extra source of stimulation for each couple.

SUMMARY

1 Clinical psychologist Bühler proposed a five-phase theory of human development that emphasizes goal-setting from childhood to old age. *Self-fulfillment* is the key to healthy development. During childhood (to age 15), people have not yet determined their life goals. In adolescence and young adulthood (15 to 25 years), they set tentative, idealistic goals. In young and middle adulthood (about 23 to 45 or 50 years), people set more specific, realistic goals.   **2** Erikson's sixth psychosocial crisis is intimacy versus isolation. According to Erikson, to develop successfully, young adults must fuse their identity with another person in a close, intimate, heterosexual relationship that leads to procreation. The negative outcomes of this period may include isolation and self-absorption.   **3** Studies of adults indicate that development continues throughout adult life as people confront the "crisis" of leaving home, deciding on a career, establishing a family, and setting lifetime goals.   **4** During young adulthood most people decide whether to marry or stay single, with 95 percent marrying. Marriage partners tend to come from similar backgrounds. Successful marriages are most likely to occur between couples in their late twenties or older; between people of the same social class, especially the upper levels; between partners who have known each other for a long time; and when the bride is not pregnant at the time of marriage. People develop as emotional and social beings during marriage, with married men and women generally reporting higher feelings of satisfaction about their lives than single, divorced, or widowed people.   **5** Today, greater numbers of people feel free to remain single until a late age or to never marry. The advantages of being single include opportunities for career exploration, travel, and self-sufficiency. Possible negative aspects include difficulties in finding a job and place to live and in being accepted by friends and family.   **6** Having a child marks a major transition in couples' lives, from sharing reciprocal responsibilities to having total responsibility for a new life. Parenthood has a mixed impact, with couples today opting for fewer children than in past decades as the economic and cultural forces demanding universal parenthood are diminishing. An increasing number of people are choosing not to have children at all. **7** The United States has one of the highest divorce rates in the world. Highest divorce rates occur between people who were married as teenagers; between people whose parents were unhappily married or divorced; between childless couples; among black people; and in marriages in which the bride was pregnant. However, 4 out of 5 divorced people eventually remarry. **8** Individual friendships are very important during young adulthood. Now, people make friends as couples, as well as individuals. Although complex, couple friendships allow the partners to be involved with others, avoid isolation, and have an extra source of stimulation.

SUGGESTED READINGS

Boston Women's Health Book Collective. *Ourselves and our children.* New York: Random House, 1978. Looks at the experience and demands of parenthood at various times in the life span. Has information on how parents can help each other and find professional help.

Fabe, M., & Wikler, N. *Up against the clock.* New York: Random House, 1979. Examines the issues involved in deciding for or against having a child, including combining children and a career, the decision to be a single mother, and choosing to be childfree.

Glickman, B. M., & Springer, N. B. *Who cares for the baby? Choices in child care.* New York: Schocken Books, 1978. An analysis of various child-care issues, with suggestions for choosing a particular type of care.

Hope, K., & Young, H. (Eds.) *Momma: The sourcebook for single mothers.* New York: New American Library, 1976. Personal statements by single mothers discussing their feelings and problems; offers practical, legal, financial, and social advice.

Group for the Advancement of Psychiatry (GAP). *The joys and sorrows of parenthood.* New York: Scribners, 1973. A perceptive book that analyzes parenting from the parent's point of view, raising questions about the expectations people have of parenting, and about the learning and growth that take place through the experience.

Klein, C. *The single parent experience.* New York: Avon Books, 1973. A practical guide for the single parent, male or female. Chapters dealing with adoption, homosexual parents, and child care.

Lerner, R., & Spanier, G. *Child influences on marital and family interaction: A life-span perspective.* New York: Academic, 1978. An outstanding collection of articles by leading researchers that examine the child's development and its effects upon parent-child interaction across the life span. Includes chapters on the impact of children with developmental dysfunctions and physical handicaps on marital quality and family interaction.

McBride, A. B. *The growth and development of mothers.* New York: Harper & Row, 1973. A sensitive blend of personal anecdotes and theoretical analyses of motherhood as a developmental experience.

midlife

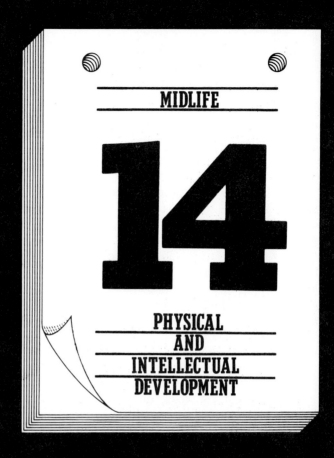

MIDLIFE

14

PHYSICAL
AND
INTELLECTUAL
DEVELOPMENT

**IN THIS CHAPTER
YOU WILL LEARN ABOUT**

The physical changes that men and
women confront during the middle years,
and how they cope with them

Middle-aged adults' intelligence, moral
development, and creativity, and the
incentives to continue an education or
adjust a career

CHAPTER OVERVIEW

Physical Functioning in Middle Age
*Health | Menopause | Male
Cycles | Sensory
Functioning | Psychomotor
Functioning | Coping with Physical
Change*
Intellectual Functioning in Middle Age

The Adult Learner | Career Adjustment

Salud, amor y pesetas—y el tiempo para gustarlo

The Spanish toast quoted above ("Health, love and money—and time to enjoy them") inspired the authors of a book about middle age (Hunt & Hunt, 1974) to use it as a chapter title, finding it the "ideal summary of what middle age can offer" (p. 23). Does this sound as though they are looking at middle age through rose-colored glasses? Are they putting the best face on the years that to many of us stand for stodginess, wrinkles, paunches, aches and pains, and the just as painful knowledge that we are no longer young? Not to the many people in their middle years who consider this time the best in their lives.

People in middle age are usually in fairly good health both physically and psychologically, and they are in the most secure financial position of their entire life. The fact that they have lived long enough to accumulate valuable social, professional, and personal experience which they can apply to all sorts of situations is one of the greatest strengths of middle age. Says Bromley (1974, p. 243):

The physical vigor of youth may have passed or the supposed tranquility of old age not yet arrived, but overall "middle" age compares favorably with other ages, and is indeed sometimes referred to as the "prime" of life.

This "prime" time still has its own crises. The middle-aged adult realizes that his or her body is not what it once was. Wrinkles crease the once-smooth skin; the waist is thicker; minor (and sometimes major) ailments cause a variety of twinges; and muscles can't always do what they used to do. Men generally become more distressed at the changes in what their bodies can do, particularly regarding sexual vigor, while women are more upset at changes in appearance—the wrinkles, the less firm flesh, the gray hairs.

Middle-aged people are coming to terms with their ultimate career potential, as tney reevaluate their earlier aspirations and either resign themselves to achieving a less lofty goal than they had originally aspired to—or change goals completely as they embark upon a new career or lifestyle.

Within the family, middle-agers often feel caught between generations. They are still often responsible for dependent children and have also assumed a new and often more psychologically burdensome responsibility—that for aging parents. Under pressure from both ends of the age spectrum, they may feel crushed by the responsibilities. Marriage undergoes reevaluation, especially as the children leave home. Once in the "empty nest," husband and wife may find that they have nothing to hold them together any more. Or, more happily, they may recapture the early honeymoon quality of their marriage.

Sometime during the middle years most people undergo a switch in time orientation. From thinking in terms of the years they've already lived, suddenly they begin to think in terms of the time they have left to live (Neugarten, 1967). With this switch they realize that they can't possibly live to do everything, and they are eager—sometimes desperately so—to make the most of their remaining years. They may decide to switch careers, to get out of a marriage, or to retire early.

Middle-aged people reflect on and evaluate their lives. They check over the high and the low points, the decisions they're happy about and the ones they regret, their accomplishments and their mistakes; and they often indulge in "if only . . ." fantasies of what might have been.

Reevaluation of oneself and one's life is, of course, a continuous process. It is somewhat special in middle age, though, since people in these years recognize that the decisions and events of the past have shaped their lives up to the present and have more or less turned them in a certain direction. At this juncture they have to decide whether to continue in the same direction or whether to make a massive upheaval in their lives and change direction while there is still time. They look in the mirror and ask, "What do I want to do with the rest of my life?" "Where am I going?" "What is the meaning of life?" "What is the meaning of *my* life?" Questions like these give rise to the "midlife crisis," discussed later in this chapter.

This kind of reevaluation at midlife is essential, since as Jung (1933) has written:

We cannot live in the afternoon of life according to the programme of life's morning. . . . The afternoon of human life must also have a significance of its own and cannot be merely a pitiful appendage to life's morning. Whoever carries over into the afternoon the law of the morning (money-making, social existence, etc.) must pay for so doing with damage to his soul. [pp. 108–109].

When does "the afternoon of life" begin? It is even harder to establish this turning point than to set adulthood itself, since there are no biological markers for middle age.

The age of 35 is the midpoint of the Biblical life span of threescore years plus ten, but with today's improved health and medical standards, most 35-year-olds still retain much of the glow and vigor of youth. Bromley's (1974) midpoints for the adult portion of life, after which each sex can expect to live another twenty-five years, are 45 to 50 years for men and 50 to 55 years for women. These figures, though, are mere statistics without any biological or psychological significance. Another opinion is that people are not middle-aged until they feel middle-aged, and this can be as late as 60 for some.

For the purposes of this discussion, we'll say that middle life begins at age 40 and continues for another twenty-five years. As people enter middle age, then, they have well over half their adult lives before them. As Hunt and Hunt (1974) say, "Middle age isn't the leftover tag end of life; it's a very major part of it" (p. 24). In this time of life, as in every other, there are wide individual differences among people. While one 40-year-old may fit the stereotype of a settled, established, experienced, and mature solid citizen, another may still undergo an identity crisis and strive energetically to establish a new life.

PHYSICAL FUNCTIONING IN MIDDLE AGE

From young adulthood through the middle years, biological changes do take place but are so gradual that they are hardly noticed—until one day a 50-year-old woman realizes that she gets winded after running a short distance that used to be easy, or a 55-year-old man recognizes that he cannot play as many sets of tennis as he once could. People look back on what they used to be able to do, notice the differences, and feel their aging.

I finished up the season with eleven wins and only four losses and an earned-run average of 1.86. I was the top pitcher in the league. That ain't bad when a man's past fifty.

LeRoy (Satchel) Paige,
Maybe I'll Pitch Forever, pp. 244–245.

HEALTH

While there are some indisputable bodily changes and while certain chronic conditions are more common during middle age, most of the changes from young adulthood are minor ones. Only a small minority of middle-aged adults are affected by ailments that are so disabling that they need to bring about a

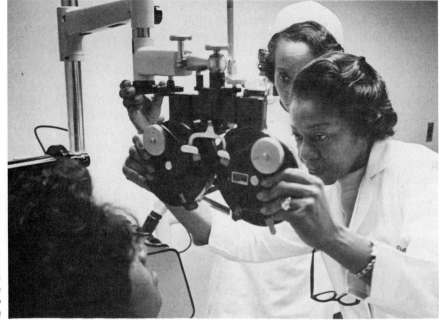

During middle age there is typically a slight loss in sensory abilities and in maximum physical strength and coordination; but these rarely affect an individual's life in an appreciable way. (Bruce Roberts/Photo Researchers, Inc.)

change in lifestyle or have a real fear for the future (Hunt & Hunt, 1974).

A major change is the loss of reserve capacity, which provides a backup in times of stress, or dysfunction of one of the body's systems. The common physical changes as summarized by Schanche (1973) are:

The heart of a 40-year-old can pump only 23 liters of blood per minute under stress, compared to the 40 liters per minute that could be pumped at age 20.

The kidneys lose their reserve capacity to concentrate waste.

The gastrointestinal tract secretes fewer enzymes, which sometimes leads to indigestion and constipation.

The diaphragm weakens, and the chest increases in size in response.

The male's prostate gland, the organ surrounding the neck of the urinary bladder, enlarges, often leading to bladder and sexual problems.

Male sexual capacity declines.

While in Dallas, rehearsing, I got a call from my brother the gynecologist. Come back to New York right away, he ordered; those routine physical tests turned up a cancerous growth in the pelvic region that has to be removed. So I missed *Lucrezia*. But a fast healer, I was back on stage in three weeks, doing *The Daughter of the Regiment* in San Francisco and *I Puritani* in Los Angeles. I didn't want people to think I was dead!

Beverly Sills
Bubbles: A Self Portrait of Beverly Sills, p. 217.

The most common chronic ailments of the middle aged are asthma, bronchitis, diabetes, nervous and mental disorders, arthritis and rheumatism, impairments of sight and hearing; and malfunctions or diseases of the circulatory, respiratory, digestive, and genitourinary systems. But these ailments do not necessarily come on in middle age:

According to figures published by the Metropolitan Life Insurance Company, two fifths of all people between the ages of 15 and 44 already have one or more of these chronic conditions, and . . . between the ages of 45 and 64 the figure reaches only three fifths [Hunt & Hunt, 1974, p. 25].

High blood pressure affects many middle-aged people, especially among blacks, more than half of whom over 45 have high blood pressure, compared to only one-third of the white population (U.S. Department of Health, Education, & Welfare, 1976). Some chronic conditions—asthma, bronchitis, and other respiratory infections, peptic ulcer, and nearsightedness—level off or even decline in middle age.

General health during middle age is better than most people expect it to be, but the trend in these years *is* downward. Middle-aged people do suffer more from a variety of ailments, mostly minor. They don't sleep as well as they used to; they can't eat as many rich and spicy foods without suffering indigestion; they throw their backs out unexpectedly. They see their doctors more often—up to six times a year on the average, and from the age of 45 they are more likely to miss work because of illness (Bromley, 1974).

Lifestyle Differences

This is the time of life when habits carried over from earlier years show striking effects on health. Belloc and Breslow's 1972 study shows that 55-year-old men who observe seven health practices (see Table 12-1) function as well or are as healthy as 35-year-old men who observe none of them. And a comparison of death rates between Utah and Nevada residents in their forties seems to underscore this point (Fuchs, 1974). While the two states are similar in climate, income, schooling, hospitalization, and medical care, the death rate for 40- to 49-year-old Nevadans is more than half again the rate for Utah residents. Says Haggerty (1977): "The difference is very likely to be due to the Mormon-

oriented abstemious lifestyle in Utah and a more hard-living style in Nevada" (p. 277).

These, then, are the years when such smoking-related illnesses as cancer of the mouth, throat, and lungs, and emphysema are likely to appear. So are such other lifestyle-related ailments as heart disease (linked to inactivity, high cholesterol levels, smoking, drinking, and overweight), anemia (iron-deficient diet), cirrhosis of the liver (overuse of alcohol), cancer of the cervix (early multiple sexual contacts), and obesity (too much food, too little exercise) (Turner & Helms, 1979; Haggerty, 1977).

Obesity is a critical health problem. For people who are 30 percent or more overweight, the probability of dying in middle age increases by 40 percent. Some of the disorders that can be attributed in part or in whole to obesity are hypertension, digestive disorders, and complications of diabetes (Turner & Helms, 1979).

The main causes of death during the middle years are heart disease, cancer, strokes, and respiratory disease.

Sex Differences

Men and women show different patterns of health, with a number of ailments likely to affect one sex more than the other. Men have more heart disease, more digestive disease (such as ulcers and hernias), more emphysema, more injuries, and poorer vision and hearing (Neugarten, 1967; Lewis & Lewis, 1977). Women are more likely to suffer from varicose veins, gallbladder disease, colitis, anemia, and diabetes (Lewis & Lewis, 1977). Men have higher death rates at this time of life, as at every other stage in the life cycle. Women, however, go to see the doctor 1½ times more than men do, are hospitalized more often, and have more operations (Lewis & Lewis, 1977). Their superior longevity may be linked to their willingness to seek health care and to assume the role of the patient more frequently than men.

Some middle-aged men become quite anxious about their health, turning to exercises, diets, medicines, and other protective strategies to maintain their bodies at desirable levels of performance and appearance. Often, however, men tend to ignore symptoms of illness, partially out of the societally induced attitude that to admit to being sick is weak and unmanly. By and large, women are more health conscious for their families as well as for themselves. As mothers, wives, and as daughters of aging parents, women tend to arrange for health services for the entire family. In fact, Lewis and Lewis (1977) say, "Females, more so than physicians, might be viewed as the principal determiners of the health status of all members of society" (p. 867). These authors then pose an important question: "If females become more equal (i.e., like males), who will look after them?"

As the roles of men and women have changed in recent years, we have so far seen only negative effects on health—more stress experienced by women, compounded by more smoking and more drinking, resulting in more of the ills formerly in the male province. But equality does not have to mean women's taking on of men's bad habits. It can mean men's taking on more of the so-called "feminine" habits, which include a heightened consciousness of health and an awareness of what it takes to preserve and restore it.

MENOPAUSE

This biological event in every woman's life when she stops menstruating and can no longer bear children, comes at different times for different women, although the median age is 49.2 (Olds, 1970). The time span of some two to five years during which a woman's body undergoes the various physiological changes that bring on the menopause is known technically as the *climacteric*.

Menopause is caused by a decrease in the production of estrogen, which brings about the end of ovulation. Its onset may be sudden or gradual, with the woman noticing nothing more than the cessation of the menses or experiencing any of some fifty different symptoms that she may associate with the menopause.

The only symptoms that seem directly related to the reduction of estrogen production are "hot flashes" (sudden sensations of heat that flash through the body, often followed by chills); thinning of the vaginal linings (which can make sexual intercourse very painful); and urinary dysfunction (caused by tissue shrinkage).

The administration of artificial estrogen often dramatically resolves these problems. Recent studies, however, have shown that women who have received estrogen replacement therapy have a higher risk of cancer of the endometrium, the lining of the uterus (Hoover, Gray, & Fraumeni, 1977; Finkel, 1975; Smith, 1975). While middle-aged women who take estrogen are twenty times more likely to get cancer, their risk can decline to almost the same level as that of nonusers once they stop taking the hormone (Jick et al, 1979). Since some physicians feel that short-term use of estrogen, over a period of a few months, is relatively safe, the benefits of this treatment must be weighed against its risks.

Many other symptoms commonly associated with menopause—insomnia, fatigue, anxiety, palpitations, and so forth—do not seem to have a hormonal basis. Others may be keyed to the psychological aspects of menopause, which dramatically signal to a woman that she has passed a milestone in her life.

Menopause does not seem to have the serious consequences for women that the old wives' tales would have us believe. Neugarten, Wood, Kraines, and Loomis (1963) surveyed several hundred women from 21 to 65 years of age on their attitudes toward menopause and found that women who had been through it had a much more positive view than women who had not. A typical comment was, "I've been healthier and in much better spirits since the change of life. I've been relieved of a lot of aches and pains" (cited in Neugarten, 1968, p. 200).

MALE CYCLES

In recent years there has been much talk of a "male menopause" (a contradiction in terms, since "menopause" means the cessation of the menses). This time of a man's life is more correctly referred to as the *male climacteric*. Despite the fact that men retain the ability to father children until quite late in life—into the seventies or eighties—there *are* some biological changes in middle-aged men. These include a decreased rate of testosterone production, decreased fertility and frequency of orgasm, and an increase in impotency (Beard, 1975). Furthermore, men appear to have cyclic fluctuations in the production of hormones (Kimmel, 1974).

When Doering, Kraemer, Brodie, and Hamburg (1975) examined the plasma testosterone levels in twenty men over a period of sixty days, they identified cycles for twelve of the men that ranged in length from three to thirty days. These researchers, however, found no relationships between hormone levels and mood changes.

Then Parlee (1978) observed fifteen men over a ninety-day period and did find cyclical patterns in mood states. She found predominant cycles of from six to ninety days, with one cluster between seven and twenty-three days and others at thirty and forty-five days. By analyzing variations in a total of 200 different mood states (including elation, vigor, anger, and depression), she found repeating patterns of fluctuation in 120 of these states. Parlee concluded:

Both men and women experience biological and psychological cycles, with periods of 24 hours and longer. If we can acknowledge that

"men have them too"—and if we can get away from the preoccupation with negative aspects of menstruation—we can begin a serious exploration of rhythmic phenomena in human experience [p. 91].

SENSORY FUNCTIONING

Sight

It is during middle age that many people become so farsighted that for the first time in their lives they need reading glasses. There is a small loss during the forties—about 10 percent or a little more—in visual acuity, convergence, and accommodation. Middle-aged people need about one-third more brightness to compensate for the loss of light reaching the retina (Belbin, 1967). Nearsightedness, though, levels off.

IT GOT SO I COULDN'T READ THE NEWS-PAPER WITHOUT FALLING ASLEEP. THE LETTERS JUMPED ROUND ON THE PAGE. MY WIFE TOLD ME, "WHY DON'T YOU GET YOUR EYES CHECKED? MAYBE YOU NEED GLASSES."

quoted in *Making it from 40 to 50*
by Joel Davitz and Lois Davitz,
p.26

Hearing

There is also a gradual loss of hearing ability during middle age. Hearing losses for speech begin to decline in the twenties, and the ability to hear sounds at the upper frequencies drops off by about 10 percent between ages 20 and 40. Most hearing loss during these years is not even noticed, since it occurs to levels of sound that are unimportant to behavior. Auditory aging occurs at much later ages among some African tribespeople than it does among white populations in Europe and the United States, possibly because people in the

Western countries are suffering the effects of living in a high-noise environment (Timiras, 1972).

Taste and Smell

There is a decrease in the number of taste-buds after childbirth, and the sensitivity of taste decreases starting from the middle years (Soddy & Kidson, 1967). There also seems to be a steady loss in the sense of smell, rising to a plateau between ages 37 and 51, and decreasing later (Smith, 1942).

Most of the losses in sensory abilities during middle age can be compensated for quite easily. They are rarely so great as to change an individual's life in any appreciable way.

PSYCHOMOTOR FUNCTIONING

Although there is a gradual decline of about 10 percent in maximum physical strength from its peak in the twenties to lower levels in the middle years, this is often not noticed, since few of us really need maximum strength and coordination in our daily lives. The only people seriously affected by this drop are manual laborers and competitive athletes. In the 1976 Olympics, a television commentator referred to one graceful and highly skilled ice skater as approaching the end of her career. "After all," he said, "she's 26 now." In such highly demanding physical endeavors, one enters middle age early. For most of the rest of us, the gradual declines in strength and coordination may lead us to play doubles tennis more often than singles or to get help lifting extremely heavy loads, but our lives go on basically as before. Simple reaction time is at its speediest at age 25 and is maintained until about 60, when the reflexes slow down (Woodworth & Schlosberg, 1954).

When we talk about complex rather than simple motor skills, the picture becomes more complicated. Complex motor skills increase during childhood and youth and gradually decline after people have achieved their full growth. One example is driving, which requires several skills, including coordination, quick reaction time, and sensitivity to glare. After the age of about 30 to 35, each of these individual abilities declines (DeSilva, 1938; cited in Soddy & Kidson, 1967). And yet, driving ability is better at this age than before (McFarland et al., 1964). The improvement that comes from experience more than makes up for the decrements that come from getting older.

The same is true elsewhere. Skilled industrial workers do not lose their abilities in their forties and fifties. In fact, they are usually more productive than ever, partly because they are generally more conscientious and careful (Belbin, 1967). Persons aged 45 to 54, for example, have been found to sort mail more consistently than 35- to 44-year-olds. Furthermore, middle-aged workers are less likely to have disabling injuries on the job—a function, no doubt, of experience and good judgment, which more than compensates for any diminution of coordination and motor skills (Hunt & Hunt, 1974).

COPING WITH PHYSICAL CHANGE

People deal with the physical changes of middle age in many different ways. One may turn into a hypochondriac, calling the doctor upon feeling the slightest twinge, or reading and talking obsessively about health and worrying constantly about the possibility of death. Another may ignore obvious danger signals and avoid doing anything about them until becoming extremely ill. Another may become obsessed with physical appearance, going on one crash diet after another, buying large quantities of cosmetics, and dying the hair to cover the gray. And still another may initiate a succession of extramarital affairs to prove his or her continuing vitality, attractiveness, and appeal to the opposite sex.

A "double standard" of aging in our society allows men to age without penalty in several ways that women may not, most notably in physical appearance. Facial lines, wrinkles, and gray hair may indicate strength and maturity in a man, while they only serve to make a woman sexually ineligible and unattractive. On the other hand, middle-aged women do not feel anxious if they haven't succeeded at anything, while men who have not achieved career or financial success feel old before their time:

In effect, people take character in men to be different from what constitutes character in women—women's character is thought to be innate, static—not the product of her experience, her years, her actions [Sontag, 1975, p. 38].

I look at my daughter, and I am envious. She has the figure I had at her age. There isn't much I can do. The pounds slip on. It's a daily fight in a losing battle.

quoted in *Making It from 40 to Fifty* by Joel Davitz and Lois Davitz, p. 135.

Men, then, are expected to *do*, while women are expected only to *be*. The attempts to conform to these expectations put different strains on the sexes.

INTELLECTUAL FUNCTIONING IN MIDDLE AGE

It may be true that "you can't teach an old dog new tricks," but this adage cannot be applied to human beings. Middle-aged and even old people *can* continue to learn new tricks, new facts, and new skills, and they can remember those they already know well. Longitudinal studies of intelligence indicate that IQ performance increases at least until the mid-fifties. There is no evidence of decline in many types of intellectual functioning before age 60,

and there are even increases in some areas, such as concept mastery. Middle-aged people can learn new skills and abilities with a great deal of ease—unless they think they can't.

Intelligence testing of adults is different from that of children. Serious questions need to be posed. For example, since the major purpose of IQ tests is to predict school achievement, what is the purpose of testing adults? How can adult intelligence tests be validated? Is it appropriate to use standardized IQ tests with adults? What do their results tell us?

The results of intelligence tests taken by adults are not always easy to interpret. Since many of these tests were originally designed for use with children, the questions and tasks seem childish and silly to some adults. Then there is the question of motivation. Children and adolescents are often highly motivated to do their best on such tests, largely because some payoff such as college admission may be based, in part, on test performance, and also because of a youthful need to prove their ability in this way. Adults, however, and especially those of advanced age, do not seem to have a similar payoff to spur them on to their best efforts. Finally, these tests may not be tapping the abilities that are most central to what intelligence means in adulthood, such as wisdom, or the ability to function well in various situations of daily life.

Yet plotting the course of intellectual development in the adult years is of more than theoretical interest. It has practical implications in determining retirement policies, in evaluating an individual's competence to live alone, and in making community plans that take into account the needs and interests of the aging population.

Performance on many aspects of intelligence tests seems to increase during adulthood, with different abilities peaking at different times. Certainly, verbal abilities rise, especially among people who use their intellectual powers regularly, either on the job or through reading or other mental stimulation. Although people in middle age may take a little longer to complete certain tasks and may not be as adept at tests of short-term memory, they often compensate for this kind of change by the wisdom garnered from a range of experience that is necessarily wider than that of younger people. Adults who achieve higher IQ scores are, not surprisingly, healthier, better educated, and in the higher social classes. Furthermore, they generally had high IQ scores as children (Turner & Helms, 1979).

Kangas and Bradway (1971) did a thirty-eight-year follow-up study of forty-eight people, first tested for intelligence as preschoolers, then as junior high school students, young adults, and in early middle age. They found an increase in IQ across the four testing periods, indicating continued mental growth during middle age and possibly even beyond.

Interesting sex differences emerged from these findings. Women whose IQs had been high as children gained less than those with medium or low preadult IQs, and less than males with any level of preadult IQ. On the other hand, the higher the level of a male's preadult IQ, the greater his adult gain. These findings have interesting implications in light of Horner's (1970) theory of bright women's fear of success. Are these women who tested so high as girls inhibiting their intellectual potential?

In tests of Piagetian cognitive functioning, middle-aged adults show considerable variability on some tasks and little on others (Papalia & Bielby, 1974). In most studies that have assessed these abilities across the life span, results are similar for young and middle-aged adults, and few changes are

noted until old age. Papalia (1972) found high levels of conservation ability in adults aged 30 to 64, with the highest overall performance being among those aged 55 to 64. The tasks measured were number, substance, weight, and volume conservation. Tests of classification found that adult subjects above and below 40 years of age classified differently, with the middle-aged subjects seeming to prefer conplementary-based categorizations rather than categorization according to similarity (Annett, 1959).

Formal reasoning ability, the ability to deal with abstract concepts, is especially interesting to study in middle-aged subjects, because while Piaget (1972) claims that formal thought should develop during adolescence, the research shows that not all middle-aged people can solve formal operations problems. Tomlinson-Keasey (1972) looked at formal operations in sixth-grade girls, in college women, and in middle-aged women; they found that formal operational ability was considerably less than 100 percent in each age group. The college students, whose average age was 19.7 years, did the best, with 67 percent passing the test. The middle-aged subjects, at an average age of 54, did next best, with 54 percent passing. Formal operations ability seems to depend largely on an individual's past experiences, education, and perhaps even personality.

The same reservation about cross-sectional studies applies here as elsewhere. We can never say conclusively that a particular Piagetian ability has deteriorated unless we have data indicating it was there in the first place, which we can know only through longitudinal studies.

Further moral development in adulthood has been acknowledged by Kohlberg (1973), who attributes adult changes to increased role-taking opportunities. Bielby and Papalia (1975) substantiated some of his theory by measuring moral judgment and perceptual role-taking egocentrism in subjects aged from 10 to over 65. Those in early middle age—ages 35 to 49—scored highest of all. Further

Lifelong education has proven a boon for colleges, which are eager to expand their departments of continuing education to absorb a new group of students who can fill the seats left empty by declining undergraduate enrollments. (© 1977 Laimute E. Druskis)

research should try to determine which experiences in people's lives influence their moral thinking.

Creative productivity is at a high point during middle age. At the age of 40, Frank Lloyd Wright designed Roble House in Chicago; at 44, Aaron Coplan composed *Appalachian Spring*; at about 52, Leonardo da Vinci painted the *Mona Lisa*; at 56, Picasso painted *Guernica*; and at 57, Handel composed the *Messiah*. In studying scholars, scientists, and artists, Dennis (1966) found that the highest rate of output is generally in the forties or soon afterward, and that productivity remains relatively high for many people in their sixties and seventies. Lehman (1953) found that different types of creative production peak at different times. As Troll (1975) reports:

In general, the more unique, original and inventive the production, the more likely it is to have been created in the 20s and 30s rather than later in life. The more a creative act depends on accumulated development, however, the more likely it is to occur in the later years of life [p. 39].

THE ADULT LEARNER

A 41-year-old homemaker enrolls in law school to fulfill a lifelong dream. A 56-year-old automotive mechanic takes a not-for-credit night course in philosophy. A 49-year-old physician signs up for a seminar in recent advances in endocrinology. These three students exemplify the boom across the country in continuing education, today's fastest-growing arm of education.

Who is the adult learner? According to the profile that has emerged from a number of different studies summarized by Arbeiter (1976–1977), she or he is likely to be relatively well educated. Thirty-two percent of college graduates participate in adult education, compared to 20 percent of those with some college, 12 percent of high school graduates, and 4 percent of those who did not finish high school. Adult learners tend to have higher incomes: Seventeen percent of adults from families with incomes of $15,000 or more take courses, double the rate for those with incomes under $10,000. Almost half of adult education participants are over 34, and 15 percent are over 44. Adults between 55 and

65 years of age are least likely to attend classes and lectures and most likely to study with an individual instructor or at a local social organization.

Why do middle-aged adults go to school? For many reasons. Some seek training that will help them do their present jobs better, and some study to move up the career ladder. People who are changing career directions become part- or full-time students to prepare themselves for new professions. Persons who see retirement looming ahead expand their minds and their repertoires of skills to make more productive and interesting use of their retirement years. Professionals in rapidly expanding fields like law, medicine, teaching, the sciences, and engineering need to keep up with new developments.

Lifelong education has proved a boon for colleges, which are eager to expand their departments of continuing education to absorb a new group of students who can fill the seats left empty by declining undergraduate enrollments. In their eagerness to meet adult students part way, an increasing number of colleges are granting credits for practical life experience. They are also becoming more flexible in scheduling, providing more opportunities for students to matriculate part-time and to do much of their work independently. At Empire State College, part of the State University of New York, students may follow custom-designed academic syllabi, working at home and checking in from time to time with supervising tutors at centers throughout the state.

Colleges are not the only places, of course, that offer adult education courses. They are also provided by local public school districts, community organizations, businesses, labor unions, professional societies, and government agencies. In addition, Stubblefield (1977) urges the encouragement of "self-directed learning projects," particularly for those people who are more interested in acquiring knowledge than credentials. Such students might, with guidance, design their own programs, which could include going directly to resource persons and to libraries, and working as a volunteer in a relevant field.

As Stubblefield points out, "In our modern complex society, no one ever completes his or her education. Learning throughout the life-span is a requirement, not an option" (p. 351).

CAREER ADJUSTMENT

Typical career adjustment during the middle years is likely to have one of two faces: Either a worker is at the peak of the career she or he chose during young adulthood, earning more money, exerting more influence, and commanding more respect than at any other period in life; or a person is on the threshold of a new vocation, exemplifying the not uncommon trend toward a multicareer lifetime, possibly spurred by the reevaluation of self that takes place during the midlife crisis (discussed in the next chapter).

People who follow the first pattern are reaping personal benefits and also letting society benefit from their years of experience in a chosen field. Most officeholders, business leaders, academic giants, and other prominent persons in our society tend to be in their middle years. Outstanding accomplishments of people much younger than 40 or much older than 65 usually rate special notice. As Hunt and Hunt (1974) point out, "in 'traditional' societies it was the elders who held the power, but in most modern societies, power, wealth, and prestige tend to be concentrated among the middle-aged" (p. 102).

Generally, people attain positions of power during their middle years as a result of having accumulated wisdom and experience in their chosen fields. Most of them continue to enjoy the work area they have settled into. More than 90 percent of workers older than 30 report that they are satisfied with their jobs, and this percentage increases with age (Quinn, Staines, & McCullough, 1974).

Continued job satisfaction during middle age may reflect the stability of vocational interests throughout adulthood. A group of people tested when they were about 40 years old showed the same general areas of vocational interests that they had shown eighteen years earlier in college (Strong, 1959).

Changing Careers in Midlife

At age 40 the president of a multimillion-dollar corporation left his prestigious position to go back to school to study architecture; eventually he opened his own architectural firm. At age 50 a homemaker who had held a variety of part-time jobs while her children were growing up enrolled in a school of social work; with her master's degree, she found a good job as a community organizer, which enabled her to draw on many of her past experiences. A 45-year-old engineer, laid off because of cutbacks in the aerospace industry, went back to his first love and became a full-time portrait artist and art teacher; his wife, who had earned a law degree but had postponed practicing while she raised four children, now became a member of a corporate legal staff.

Stories of such midlife career changes abound these days as people seek new careers for a variety of reasons. With today's longer life expectancies, many middle-aged people realize that they don't want to keep doing the same thing for the next twenty years, and strike out in a totally new direction. Others are forced by technological or economic unemployment to seek a second career.

Thomas (1977) looked at the relationship between change in career and change in what Levinson (1974) has called "life structure." *Life structure* consists of an individual's goals; of participation in society; of various roles, such as family member, churchgoer, worker, and so forth; and of more personal elements, such as values, dreams, and emotional life. A career is part of a person's life structure, but only a part. In his analysis of this relationship, Thomas divided people into four categories:

Changers are those individuals who experience both a major change in life structure *and* a change in career. The two are often related, as people move from the success goals they have absorbed from their culture (i.e., "making a lot of money") to more personal views of success ("work that makes a difference to the world"). This kind of change is seen in the case of a successful interior designer who left her high-paying career to get a degree in psychology so that she could work with retarded children.

Pseudo-changers make a switch in career but retain the same life structure. An example is the engineer who left a corporate job to start his own company. He continued to pursue the same success goals and the same lifestyle as he and his family continued to live in the same neighborhood, visit the same families, and carry out the same activities.

Crypto-changers experience a change in life structure but remain in the same career. A university professor continues to hold the same tenured post, but her changed values are apparent in her refusal to conduct conventional research, in her new communal living arrangements, and in her "hippie" dress and appearance.

Persisters move through their middle years, adhering to the same goals, values, and lifestyle they have pursued since early adulthood, and continuing to do the same work. Sometimes this stability reflects a conscious sense that they are already living the best of all possible lives and, therefore, see no need to change. At other times, it reflects a failure to examine their lives closely, sometimes because of a fear of moving into unfamiliar territory. Like some unhappily married couples who stay together until one partner dies, some unhappy workers stay "married" to a job they don't like until they retire. And just as we can't judge a marriage by the number of years it lasts, neither can we judge career satisfaction by time alone.

As we see the different patterns people's lives assume, we see that "career change by itself is only a rough indicator of what is going on in an individual's life during the mid-life period" (Thomas, 1977, p. 326).

What are some of the common events in middle age that affect life structure in general and careers in particular? In a summary of influences on careers, Heald (1977) names the "emptying of the nest" as one of the most important. In most cases, as we shall see in our discussion of this event in the next chapter, marriages improve when the youngest child leaves home and a couple are once more alone. In other marriages, couples who have found the children their primary shared interest now find that they have little to keep them together any more, and they separate. In any case, this time of transition often leads to a reorientation from family concerns to an evaluation of career directions.

Financial concerns also influence career changes. A pair who have finally paid off their mortgage or sent their last child through college are now less pressured by economic needs. Thus, they are free to change careers to those that may bring in fewer dollars but more personal satisfaction. Other couples suddenly realize that they are ill-prepared for retirement and focus renewed energies on accumulating a nest egg while they are still capable of substantial earnings.

Other events arouse anxiety. The husband of the woman who goes to work for the first time may have difficulty accepting her as an equal partner in the marriage and as a worker with an outside life that does not include him. Her excitement about her new career may make him restless enough with his job so that he looks for a new line of work as well. A middle-aged worker may feel pres-sured by younger workers moving up the career ladder and may prefer to change jobs entirely rather than deal with the competition. Or, in lofty positions, guilt sometimes sets in as workers achieve high ranks and become anxious about accepting the fact that they are now earning more money with less effort. Their guilt may make them fail in their jobs, be fired, and be forced to seek a lower-paying position.

In any case, no matter what propels a person to change careers in midlife, the fact is that more and more people are doing this. As a result, a special need in society is in the area of counseling to help middle-aged adults recognize the possibilities that are open to them and understand how they can make the most of these possibilities. Sometimes the workers themselves resist change most strongly. Belbin and Belbin (1966) found that "it is a formidable problem to steer older workers into training," and that many workers who lost their jobs were more inclined to seek downgrading instead of retraining for other skilled jobs.

In a study of thirty-seven "career dropouts"—people aged 30 to 55 who had chosen voluntarily to leave successful white-collar or professional careers—Roberts (in Entine, 1974) found that most of these people "were alienated from the concept of work in an established career system as the means to personal satisfaction" (p. 36). They experi-ence value conflicts with their employers, were bored, chafed at a lack of meaning in their jobs, and felt exploited. All in this group were happy with their new jobs and lifestyles, most of which involved less income and hard work at odd jobs and rural households. Dimin-ished income was more than compensated for by what they saw as a better quality to their lives.

This is what vocational counselors and adult educators need to concentrate on—helping people find jobs that will give them fulfillment, satisfaction, and an improved qual-ity of life.

SUMMARY

1 The main focus of the middle years is on reevaluating oneself and one's life. Although there is no biological marker or universally accepted behavioral sign marking middle age, we consider it to include the years between ages 40 and 65.   **2** Most middle-aged people are in good health, and most physical changes between young adulthood and middle age are relatively minor. There is typically a slight loss in sensory abilities and in maximum physical strength and coordination; but these rarely affect an individual's life in an appreciable way.   **3** Major causes of death during the middle years are heart disease, cancer, stroke, and respiratory diseases, and death rates are twice as high for men as for women. In addition, men have more heart and digestive diseases, more emphysema, and poorer vision and hearing. While men may become quite preoccupied about their own health, middle-aged women often become more concerned about their husbands' health and arrange for the family's health services."   **4** Menopause, the cessation of menstruation and reproductive ability, occurs at the median age of 49.2. Menopause is caused by a decrease in the production of estrogen, which brings about the end of ovulation. Estrogen replacement therapy, though highly successful in resolving menopausal symptoms, has recently been linked to cancer of the endometrium, and it thus should be used with extreme caution. Women who have been through menopause typically have more positive views about it than do premenopausal women. Decreased hormone production (for example, of testosterone) has also been noted in males.   **5** Longitudinal studies of performance on standardized IQ tests indicate performance increments at least until the mid-forties. High levels of performance on Piagetian tasks such as conservation have been noted, though not all adults have attained formal thought or principled (postconventional) morality.   **6** Creative productivity is at a high point for scholars, scientists, and artists during the mature years.   **7** Continuing education and career adjustment are becoming more commonplace during the middle years. Participation in adult education programs in order to prepare for career changes may be triggered by the self-evaluation process that occurs during midlife.

SUGGESTED READINGS

Hunt, B., & Hunt, J.   *Prime time*. New York: Stein & Day, 1974. A good, clear, easy-to-read book addressed to middle-aged readers, giving practical suggestions to make the most of the middle years in terms of health, marriage, sexuality, work, and leisure time.

LeShan, E.   *The wonderful crisis of middle age*. New York: Warner, 1973. A personal account of what it's like to be middle-aged, bolstered by many anecdotes. Presents basically traditional viewpoints of women's roles, offers interesting analysis of middle-aged extramarital affairs, and gives good discussions of relationships between the middle-aged, their grown children, and their aging parents.

Peterson, R., and Associates.   *Lifelong learning in America*. San Francisco: Jossey-Bass, 1979. Contains information on federal, state, and local policies and practices of lifelong learning in the United States. Extensive information on resources available.

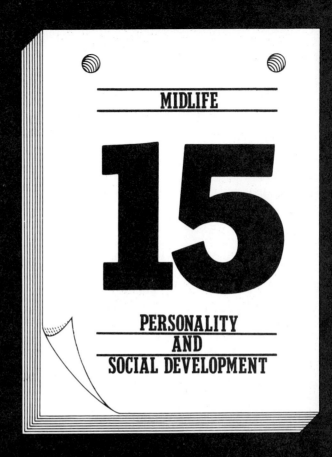

MIDLIFE

15

PERSONALITY
AND
SOCIAL DEVELOPMENT

"I'm a completely different person now from the one I was twenty years ago," said the 47-year-old architect, as the six other people in the room, all in their forties and fifties, nodded in agreement. The notion that personality is unalterably fixed in childhood, never to change, has few adherents. Observers of middle age, as well as middle-agers themselves, recognize that personality continues to change throughout adulthood, as a result of the experiences, relationships, and self-evaluation that occur during these years.

In 1968, Neugarten identified some changes characteristic of each decade, which, of course, do not apply to everyone. At that time, she found that 40-year-olds see boldness and risk-taking as rewarding and see themselves as energetic and ready to seek the world's rewards. During the fifties, people are at a turning point in their lives as they become more introspective, reflective, and self-evaluative. By the sixties, people tend to see the world as a complex and dangerous place, one whose demands the individual must try to conform to, rather than try to change.

In more recent years, Neugarten (1980), along with other observers, has been taking a less age-oriented view of people, feeling that chronological age of itself is a poorer predictor of the way people think and live than are the experiences those people have had. Still, of course, many experiences do tend to come at predictable points in the life cycle, resulting in certain similarities among people in the same age bracket. Let us look, then, at what many people are like in their middle years.

SELF-CONCEPT DURING MIDDLE AGE

How do middle-aged people view themselves? On the whole, quite positively, espe-

> *I have learned more about who I am and what I want to be in life since the age of 40, than in all the years before.*
>
> Eda LeShan
> quoted in "Middle Age Needn't Be Like Dark Ages,"
> *The New York Times*, March 29, 1973.

> *A milestone in my life had been that bright, crisp day in February, 1918, when I celebrated my fiftieth birthday.... Sallie had arranged a dinner for a dozen of our old friends.... Coming down before the guests were assembled, I amazed the family by sitting down midway on the stairway landing and bursting into tears. To be fifty was definitely to leave youth and young manhood, and to begin to be an old man.*
>
> *The Autobiography of William Allen White,*
> William Allen White, p. 626.

cially as judged by a survey of 100 well-educated, successful men and women aged 40 to 60 (Neugarten, 1967). They are more sensitive to their position in society and become wrapped up in assessing themselves and evaluating their lives. They see middle age as a unique time of life, qualitatively different from other ages. People look at different aspects of themselves in their self-assessments—how they are in their families, in their careers, and in their bodies. They see themselves as neither young nor old, but rather a "bridge between the generations." Middle-aged people feel a responsibility to the younger generation and feel closer to the older one. As friends and relatives die, and as they see more obituaries for people of their own age, they get a new sense of the finiteness of time and the reality that someday they too will die.

Middle-aged people rarely dwell on this, however. They are too busy running their lives with a new sense of power and competence.

They are enjoying the fruits of their years of experience and are making them work for them. As one news magazine called them, they are—and feel themselves to be—"the command generation."

[They] recognize that they constitute the powerful age-group vis-a-vis other age groups; that they are the norm-bearers and the decision-makers; and they live in a society which, while it may be oriented towards youth, is controlled by the middle-aged [Neugarten, 1967, p. 93].

These conclusions were based on the responses of a rather privileged group; such a favorable self-concept in the middle years may not be true of people in the lower socioeconomic strata. But, with optimal education and work opportunities, such a middle age is what society can strive to obtain for all individuals. Hunt and Hunt (1974) attribute much of this positive attitude to the experience that middle-aged people have gained in their social situations, as well as in other areas. They write:

The middle-aged . . . have a general awareness of most of the problems in human relationships, a capacity to perceive and interpret meanings in words and behavior, an ability to make essential discriminations among those meanings and to be appropriately compassionate—or appropriately critical; above all, they have the self-assurance that they can cope easily and effectively with almost any situation they encounter.

These are general terms; let's be specific. Can you remember how, as a young person, you suffered when you had to walk alone into a roomful of people, particularly if most of them were strangers to you? Or when you couldn't think of anything interesting to say to someone attractive you had just met, or someone you were dating for the first time? Can you recall how hideously embarrassing it was when you had to walk into a store and ask the manager for a summer job? Or tell a professor that you

thought he had made an error in grading your exam? Or ask your boss for a raise? Or ask a friend if it was true that he'd made some derogatory remarks about you to someone else? Or tell someone you'd been seeing regularly that it wasn't working out and that you wanted to be free to see others?

What made these and innumerable other situations so agonizing when you were young was that you simply lacked experience: you did not know exactly how to speak or act in the situation, you did not know how to predict the other person's responses, you could not anticipate how you would react to those unpredictable responses, you did not know whether you would be unnerved, inept, speechless, helpless, or whether you would manage to deal with the situation effectively [p. 112].

THEORETICAL PERSPECTIVES ON PERSONALITY DEVELOPMENT AT MIDLIFE

Let us look at the applications to middle age of some of the major theories that offer explanations for the way personality develops throughout the life span.

THEORIES FOUNDED ON PSYCHOANALYSIS AND EGO PSYCHOLOGY

Erikson's Crisis VII: Generativity versus Stagnation

Individuals deal with this crisis of development at about age 40. Erikson (1950) defines *generativity* as "concern in establishing and guiding the next generation," and identifies this basic impulse to teach and guide and foster the development of the young as an element of virtually all institutions in society, such as churches, schools, and even one's place of work.

People need not have children themselves in order for the generative impulse to flourish. Generativity can emerge from productivity and creativity in various areas. Also, having children does not necessarily guarantee generativity. Erikson feels that some young parents are retarded in their generative abilities, either because they never developed a sense of trust themselves or because they had to work too hard at building their own personalities.

Generative adults expand their ego-interests and grow in a psychosexual as well as a psychosocial sense. Those who do not develop this aspect of themselves stagnate: They indulge themselves (becoming generative toward themselves, as if they were their own children) and may even lapse, from self-concern, into early physical or psychological invalidism.

Robert Peck

Expanding on Erikson's concepts, Peck (1955) specifies four psychological developments as critical to successful adjustment in middle age:

1 VALUING WISDOM VERSUS VALUING PHYSICAL POWERS "Wisdom," defined as the ability to make the best choices in life, appears to depend largely on sheer life experience and the opportunities of encountering a wide range of relationships and situations. Sometime between the late thirties and the late forties most successfully adjusted people appreciate that the wisdom they now have more than makes up for their diminished physical strength, stamina, and youthful attractiveness.

2 SOCIALIZING VERSUS SEXUALIZING IN HUMAN RELATIONSHIPS People redefine the men and women in their lives, valuing them as individuals, as friends, and as companions rather than primarily as sex objects.

3 CATHECTIC FLEXIBILITY VERSUS CATHECTIC IMPOVERISHMENT The ability to shift emotional investments from one person to another and from one activity to another becomes especially crucial during middle age. This is the time when people are likely to experience breaks in their relationships because of the deaths of parents and friends, and because of the maturing and independence of children. They may also have to change their activities because of physical limitations.

4 MENTAL FLEXIBILITY VERSUS MENTAL RIGIDITY By middle age, many people have worked out a set of answers to life. But when they let these answers control them rather than continuing to seek out new ones, they become set in their ways and closed to new ideas. Those people who remain flexible use their experiences and the answers they've already found as provisional guides to the solution of new issues.

None of these adjustments need arise for the first time during middle age; some may be functions of the mature personality from early adulthood. If they don't take place by the middle years, however, it is doubtful that the individual will be able to make a successful emotional adjustment.

Charlotte Bühler

The fourth phase in Bühler's (1968) concept of personality development takes place in the years from about 45 to about 65. Healthy people take stock of their past and revise their planning for the future in the light of their present physical condition, job status, and personal relationships. Immature people avoid assessing themselves and fail to make effective decisions. They don't recognize those traits in their personalities that cause problems in their relationships with other people or in their professional lives, and thus they cannot do anything to change unsatisfactory patterns. As people assess themselves and their lives, they either feel fulfilled by the effective decisions they have made or feel unfulfilled because of disappointments and failures, many of which they recognize as attributable to their own personality problems.

Abraham Maslow
Maslow's (1954) theory of self-actualization, briefly described in Chapter 1 (page 18), offers still another explanation of the functioning of the mature personality.

SOCIAL-PSYCHOLOGICAL THEORY
Social psychologists (who study the ways people get along with each other and in society) and some other theorists define personality as a product of a person's experience in life and the various social roles that individual plays, rather than as a single construct that holds across a variety of situations. In other words, the commonly observed fact that when some aspect of a person's situation changes, that person's behavior is likely to change, too, leads these theorists to conclude that personality is fluid and adaptable to social requirements.

Change in adulthood often centers around changing social situations: We go away to school, take a job, change jobs, meet someone we like, leave that relationship and enter a new one, get married, become parents, move to a new community, suffer losses through death, and so forth. According to the social-psychological perspective, these environmental factors affect adults more than biological markers of development like growth and maturation, which accompanied so many changes in childhood. (Adult change may come as a direct response to such biological factors as losses of physical faculties, especially in cases of marked disability.) Since everyone's social environment—the way in which we interact with other people—is constantly changing, adult development cannot be stable, but is instead "part of a dramatically changing organism" (Ahammer, 1973, p. 284).

Neugarten (1977) points out that the social learning framework underlying this point of view does not deal with the individual's sense of consistency and continuity over the years, even though these issues are important as a person sets goals and works to meet them. We also need to remember that while many studies have shown short-term changes in people's behavior in response to social situations, they offer little help in understanding the long-term picture of personality development through the life span.

Much recent research, such as that of Levinson, Vaillant, and Gould, has sought to explain adult development by observing what people do and how they think at various stages in their lives, how much their chronological place seems to influence their actions and attitudes, and how they respond to the modifications in their environment. In other words, some of the theories that have evolved from this newer research seem to blend the psychodynamic and situational explanations for understanding human beings.

RESEARCH IN PERSONALITY DEVELOPMENT AT MIDLIFE

Are there, in Neugarten's (1977) words, "orderly and sequential changes related to age"? If so, are they "significant in accounting for differences in behavior" (p. 632)? According to the work of Levinson, Gould, and Vaillant, whose findings on personality in middle age will be discussed below, the answer to both these questions is a resounding yes. These three recent studies stand apart from most of the research on middle age, both in their efforts to include other periods of adulthood, and most of all in their emphasis on actually describing what people do and how they feel. These studies are not, of course, the only ones that have looked at personality development

at this time of life. What has some of the other research found?

Single Dimensions of Personality

Are middle-aged people more cautious than younger ones? More likely to conform than older people? How egocentric are they? How creative? A great deal of research has focused on single dimensions of personality such as these to see whether differences exist across age levels. In almost all areas, the findings are contradictory. The one clear exception is introversion, which shows up in most studies as a personality trait that, for adults, increases with age (Neugarten, 1977). For all the other characteristics, the studies vary so much from each other on defining concepts, choosing measures, deciding on samples, and all the other factors that go into setting up a research project that it is almost impossible to compare them.

Furthermore, the great reliance these studies place on cross-sectional samples means that *cohort* differences may be confused with *age* differences. So if middle-aged people turn out to be less likely to take risks than younger people, we don't know whether people do, in fact, become more careful with age, or whether these middle-aged adults were reared in an age when prudence was valued over "foolhardiness."

Multiple Dimensions of Personality

Studies such as those done by Neugarten and her colleagues (1964) have the advantage of large, representative samplings of 40- to 80-year-old people and longitudinal study over a ten-year period, but many questions remain unanswered. One is the problem of deciding which personality traits are independent of each other. Says Neugarten (1977):

While we deal with "separate" traits for purposes of analysis, a personality is essentially a

whole, or a set of systems within systems, and our analytic units are usually not separable in the real world of behavior [p. 637].

These researchers found no differences between middle-aged and old people in coping styles, or satisfaction with life, or the processes that people could consciously control, like behavior that was being performed to meet some goal. Age differences did show up, though, in "intrapsychic" dimensions: With advancing age into late adulthood, people become more passive and more wrapped up in their own inner worlds.

Adaptation, or Coping Styles

The way people respond to various events in their lives depends strongly on two factors—their stage of life and their personality.

The life stage is important because people's preoccupations vary, depending upon where they are in the life cycle. Even though we are becoming what Neugarten (1980) has called an "age-irrelevant society," in which people are ruled less rigidly by an internal time clock that guides people into "age-appropriate" behaviors, certain tasks are more common at specific times of life. The concern with forming intimate relationships, traditionally thought of as a young adult's task, becomes important for the growing numbers of people whose initial relationships have been severed by divorce and who are now dealing with this task all over again. Middle-aged people may be just entering this stage, or they may be becoming parents for the first time, or they may be with a new spouse for the first time.

Yet even though society has become much more accepting of variations in the courses of individual lives, people often have certain expectations of the way their lives will proceed. When their lives turn out differently, they have to adjust their thinking. This adjustment may be liberating in the way it frees them to lead adventurous, fulfilling lives. Or it may be traumatic. In either case, it seems to be a significant factor in the way people handle various issues and events.

The woman who adjusted well to work, marriage, and parenthood will probably take in her stride such transitional events as menopause, the empty nest, and retirement. (Sybil Shelton/Monkmeyer)

Noberini and Neugarten (1975) feel that the time a life event occurs affects the degree of trouble a person has in adapting to it. So the man who is widowed in early adulthood or the mother whose grown child lingers in the home are both apt to experience these events as crises, whereas widowhood forty years later and an empty nest four years earlier would have constituted a more easily accepted transition. Aside from the emotional loss of his wife, the young widower has not had the opportunity to "rehearse" for his new status. Her death is a totally unexpected blow. On the other hand, the mother of the 25-year-old who still lives at home has rehearsed her role of the emancipated parent so well that she is eager to play the part. Her expectations, too, have been violated. "Off-time" events probably have more crisis-causing potential than do those that come in predictable places in an individual's expected life script.

The impact of personality on adaptation to life can be seen in the consistency over time of different people's coping patterns (Noberini & Neugarten, 1975). Thus, the woman who adjusted well to work, marriage, and parenthood will probably take in her stride such transitional events as menopause, the empty nest, and retirement.

SEX DIFFERENCES IN PERSONALITY DEVELOPMENT

Men and women usually respond to different events in middle age. Women—even those with careers—tend to define their age status in terms of events in the family cycle, especially the time when the children leave home; and single women discuss the children they might have had. Men place themselves in the age cycle in terms of their work setting. They take stock of themselves professionally and compare what they have achieved with what they had expected or hoped to achieve. And they become keenly aware of the state of their health.

At this time in their lives, some couples experience a disharmony of moods that could be described by Sheehy's (1976) term, "the sexual diamond." She coined it to describe the variations in the male and female sexual life cycles, in which the two sexes are most alike before birth, at age 18, and over 60.

From the age of 18, they start to move apart. In relation to sexual activity, they are farthest from each other, or at opposite ends of the diamond, at about age 40, after which point they begin to come closer to each other until they reach what Brim (1974) has called the "normal unisex of later life."

In middle age a man and a woman are often at opposite poles in their perspectives on life, too. This is especially true for those couples who have followed a traditional life-style in which the wife stayed home to rear the children while the husband devoted most of his energy to his career. By now he is apt to be feeling bored or pressured on the job and wondering whether this is his destiny for the rest of his life. Meanwhile, now that the children are older and more on their own, the wife is likely to feel an exhilarating sense of freedom and excitement as she sets about exploring the interests and developing the abilities that she subordinated for the past fifteen years or so.

Both men and women become freer during these years to shake off many of the stereotyped attitudes they have held. Men often become more open with their feelings, more interested in developing intimate relationships, and more nurturing. Meanwhile, women tend to become more assertive in speaking up for and going after what they want (Neugarten, 1968). Yet Neugarten (1968) still found that some of the older, more traditional patterns persist: Men continue to cope with the environment in increasingly abstract and cognitive terms, while women are increasingly affective and expressive. Both men and women become more attuned to their own personal needs and concentrate on satisfying them.

Livson (1975) interviewed forty-five psychologically healthy men and women aged 50. Those whose emotional health had re-mained high and stable from ages 40 to 50 tended to fit the traditional sex-typed roles in our society: The men were intellectual and overcontrolled, while the women were gregarious, nurturant, and domestic. Those whose mental health was poor at age 40 but improved significantly by 50 tended to be more unconventional: The men were emotionally expressive, sensuous, talkative, and outgoing; the women were skeptical, insightful, unconventional, and oriented toward intellectual mastery.

Apparently the poor mental health of the nontraditional men and women at age 40 was the price they paid as they suppressed their natural tendencies to function successfully in conventional adult sex roles. By age 50, though, people were able to relax more and let their true personalities emerge. This may be because this is a time of life when women can disengage from motherhood and men come to terms with their achievements, or it may simply be a function of age. In either case, the fit between personality and societal sex roles seems to have a great effect on personality. Livson finds that "middle age can open fresh options to diversify sex roles—and expand the boundaries of the self" (p. 5).

THE MIDLIFE CRISIS: FACT OR FICTION?

"How *am* I?" responded the attractive speech therapist. "I'm going to have my fortieth birthday in two weeks, and I can't talk to anyone for ten minutes without mentioning it. So I guess I'm having my midlife crisis. Isn't everybody?"

I spent a large portion of my 44 years living to take care of and please others. I feel that I am not promised a tomorrow and that I probably won't pass through this way again.

Toni Martinazzi, who quit her job to take a one-year long hike across country. *New York Times*, April 14, 1980, page A16.

What *is* the *midlife crisis*? The term has become a trendy catchphrase, quick to pop up as an explanation for a depression, an extramarital affair, a career change, or almost any other event that occurs in the life of someone between the ages of 35 and 55. First enunciated by such writers as Jung (1968) and Jacques (1967), the midlife crisis is generally understood to be a period of emotional, and sometimes behavioral, turmoil that heralds the onset of middle age. It may last for several years, with the exact time and duration varying from person to person. In men, this crisis has sometimes been called the male climacteric and has been associated with reduced intensity of sexual behavior. In women, it has often been linked to the menopause. The crisis is an often-unsettling time of questioning former goals, losing one's mooring for a time, and bridging the transition to the second half of life. The crisis is closely keyed to people's awareness that they have begun to grow old. The first part of adult life is over: You have formed your family, established your occupation, achieved independence from your parents, and are tasting freedom from the daily responsibilities of child care. You are in the "prime of life" when fulfillment seems possible, but suddenly you realize that time is limited. You have only a measured number of years in which to achieve that fulfillment, and it is clear that you will not do all you had once hoped to.

But does this realization necessarily signal a time of trauma? Or can it mark a relatively smooth transition to the next stage of life? Is crisis too strong a word for a time that can be very positive indeed, as Jacques (1967) points out:

The gain is in the deepening of awareness, understanding, and self-realization. Genuine values can be cultivated—of wisdom, fortitude, and courage, deeper capacity for love and affection and human insight, and hopefulness and enjoyment [p. 35].

Let us see what recent research findings tell us about the existence of the midlife crisis—whether it is inevitable, when it is likely to occur, what form it takes, and whether it can be avoided.

Levinson's Studies

Levinson and his associates (1974)[1] identified a midlife transition lasting from about 40 to 45 and providing a bridge from early to middle adulthood. Most of the forty men they interviewed were found to question virtually every aspect of their lives at this time, asking such questions as:

What have I done with my life? What do I really get from and give to my wife, children, friends, work, community—and self? What is it I truly want for myself and others? What are my real values and how are they reflected in my life? What are my greatest talents and how am I using—or wasting—them? What have I done with my early dreams and what do I want with them now? Can I live in a way that best combines my current desires, values, talents, and aspirations [Levinson, 1977, p. 107]?

Eighty percent of the men in this small sample found this a time of moderate or severe crisis, during which they often feel and act irrational. While more research is needed in this area, many researchers and theorists do consider confronting the basic structure of one's life to be a normal and vital task of middle age. Says Levinson (1977):

The desire to question and enrich one's life stems from the most healthy part of the self. . . . A profound reappraisal of this kind cannot be a cool, intellectual process. It must also involve emotional turmoil, despair, the sense of not knowing where to turn or of being

[1]See Chapter 13 for a discussion of the Levinson, Grant, and Gould studies.

stagnant and unable to move at all. . . . Every genuine reappraisal must be agonizing, because it challenges the assumptions, illusions, and vested interests on which the existing structure is based [pp. 107–108].

Why is such a painful reevaluation necessary for so many people? Levinson answers this question: "We need developmental transitions in adulthood partly because no life structure can permit the living out of all aspects of the self" (1977), p. 108). At midlife, people look back over the choices they have made and the priorities they have set and wonder whether they now need to encourage some aspects of themselves that have been neglected. They also come to terms with many of the illusions they have held, including the dreams of their youth, and thus can now get a more realistic view of themselves. Those who do not work on the tasks of the midlife transition may emerge from it into a rather constricted middle age, or may keep busy, well organized, involved—and unexcited. The most successful individuals of all find middle age fulfilling and creative, an opportunity to allow new facets of their personalities to flower and flourish.

At midlife, people look back over the choices they have made and the priorities they have set and wonder whether they now need to encourage some aspects of themselves that have been neglected. (© 1979 Marjorie Pickens)

The Grant Study

In their longitudinal study of Harvard men, Vaillant and McArthur (1972) also identified a midlife crisis at about age 40. Around this time many of the men abandoned the "compulsive calm of their occupational apprenticeship" to "experience once more the *sturm und drang* of adolescence." For most of the men, in fact, this period of the forties was stormier than their teenage years had been. During this "second adolescence," they reassessed their past, came to terms with long-suppressed feelings about their parents, and reordered their attitudes toward sexuality. These turbulent years were marked by difficulties in getting along with teenage children, and often by overt depression. And yet, as troubling as these years were, the best-adjusted men in the group saw the years from 35 to 49 as the happiest in their lives. The best-adjusted were also much more likely to have achieved generativity than the poorly adjusted, as measured by having responsibility for other people on the job, by giving money to charity, and by raising children whose academic achievements equaled their fathers'. Vaillant and McArthur (1972) state:

Perhaps the most important conclusion of the

Grant Study has been that the agonizing self-reappraisal and instinctual reawakening at age 40—the so-called mid-life crisis—does not appear to portend decay. However marred by depression and turmoil middle life may be, it often heralds a new stage of man [unpaged].

Gould's Studies

Gould (1972) saw a transitional period corresponding to the midlife crisis in both men and women between the ages of 35 and 43. During the next seven years, to age 50, people are living with the issues that they questioned earlier. The early forties mark a period of personal discomfort, a feeling that one's personality is pretty well set, and that life does not change much from year to year. During the decade, marital happiness and interest in friends and social activities all increase. People in the later forties tend to feel that the "die is cast," and they become resigned to their past experiences and present personalities, although with some bitterness toward their parents, dependency on their spouses, anxiety over their children, and negative feelings toward life in general.

In the fifties this negative cast diminishes. The awareness that time is running out may help to mellow people so that they can accept their parents, see their spouses as companions, and want their children's happiness more than they want them to achieve. People seek approval from their spouses, their children, and themselves. The perceived finiteness of life makes people think about how meaningful their lives have been and what contributions they have made to the world.

Other Research and Thinking

In her summary of four different research papers, which used both longitudinal and cross-sectional data, Nydegger (1976) found little evidence for a midlife crisis. The women and men in these studies—almost all white, middle-class, relatively successful in socioeconomic terms, and currently in middle age—show up as being quite satisfied in their forties with their jobs, their marriages, and their lives in general. They are quite stable emotionally. Instead of worrying about the "empty nest" and a decline in job involvement, most of the people surveyed are relieved by them, seeing such changes as very liberating.

While there *are* stresses at this time of life (as at any other), they do not produce disorganization in people's lives. Quite the contrary: "One's overwhelming impression of middle age is certainly not that of anxiety or despair, but rather of satisfaction and anticipation of even better times ahead" (Nydegger, 1976, p. 138). Nydegger concludes that while some people undeniably undergo crisis at this time, "there is no support in these studies for a crisis interpretation of midlife as *typical*" (p. 138).

Layton and Siegler (1978) also believe that even though important changes do take place at midlife, "crisis is no more inevitable at this time than at any other. The processes underlying the so-called crisis at mid-life are the same processes at work elsewhere in the life span" (p. 1). How can we understand these processes and how can we predict whether a given individual is likely to go through crisis? First, say Layton and Siegler, we need to understand three elements: identity, efficacy, and evaluation.

Identity is the way people think of themselves in a variety of contexts—how they look and feel, how they achieve on the job, how they relate to members of their family and to other people, and what values and beliefs they hold and act by.

Efficacy is the desire to be effective—to do things competently and to feel good about one's mastery.

And *self-evaluation* is triggered by such everyday events as looking in the mirror or having a birthday or by "marker" events like being promoted or having the children leave home. At such times, people evaluate themselves in relation to the self they have been in previous years, and also in comparison to others.

When people feel they are doing better than they could have expected, efficacy is intact. But when someone else gets the promotion, beats you in tennis, or looks ten years younger, efficacy is threatened. To maintain a favorable identity, people try to restore efficacy. The woman who has been passed over for promotion looks for another job or proves her competency as a weekend gourmet cook; the man who came in last in the 5-mile race joins a health club or takes up another sport.

Crisis is most likely to occur, say Layton and Siegler, when a person cannot overcome the loss of efficacy—when she cannot find another job *and* her soufflés keep collapsing, or when he cannot build up his energy level and continues to give a poor athletic performance. Crisis could be predicted, they suggest, by knowing when the likelihood of restoring a person's efficacy is minimal. This theory has not yet been put to the test of research, but it seems to hold a promise of being able to predict which people will experience turmoil in middle age.

Attention has recently been paid to a sizable group of women—an estimated 2 to 3 million—whose situation in middle age seems to fit these criteria for crisis (Targ, 1979). Known as *displaced homemakers*, these are women who were homemakers all their adult lives, were then widowed or divorced in middle age, and suddenly find that they have lost their (unpaid) jobs. They are now faced with multiple problems: supporting themselves, dealing with being alone, and restoring their self-esteem. Societal help has appeared for these women in the form of laws

providing counseling, job training, and other supports (Olds, 1976).

In discussing the male midlife crisis, Brim (1977) points out that most people undergo marked personality change through the adult years. They change their appearance, their social lives, their interests, and also their ways of feeling and showing their emotions. The recent attention paid in the United States to personality change at midlife may reflect the fact that we live in a highly mobile, constantly changing society, compared to the more stable environment of the past. People in our society may actually undergo more personality change than people in more tranquil cultures.

If personality change is spurred by life events, then middle age offers an especially fertile soil for change. Some of the life events that Brim (1977) points out as important possible triggers for midlife crisis in men are the gradual decline in the secretion of male hormones, beginning in the thirties; the gap between a man's early aspirations and what he has actually achieved; the need to confront the certainty of his own death; and the changes in his relationships with his growing children and his changing wife. Some changes may stretch out over ten or twenty years, and so may a person's adjustments to them.

Brim suggests that a man is most likely to experience crisis when he has to deal with several stressful events occurring at about the same time—such as the death of his parents, the awareness that his children are not turning out according to his hopes for them, and the realization that he will never achieve the professional success he had dreamed of. Yet he, like a number of other observers, concludes that:

The "growing pains" of mid-life, like those of youth and old age, are transitions from one comparatively steady state to another, and these changes, even when they occur in crisis dimensions, bring for many men more happiness than they had found in younger days [1977, p. 16].

HAPPINESS IN EARLY AND MIDDLE ADULTHOOD

Our nation's Declaration of Independence did not guarantee happiness to its citizens—only "the *pursuit* of happiness." Happiness is a difficult state to define, since everyone means something different by the term: What one person might find utter bliss another would consider total boredom. So each of us is free to pursue happiness in our own way.

I guess what I most enjoy in my life is my children. I enjoy being with them, doing things with them, and I like being at home. And I like my church work, community work, things like that. There's nothing about my life I really don't like. I mean you get discouraged and downhearted, but everybody has those periods. As a whole, I enjoy my life.

Anita Cupps, born 1948, a mine worker's wife
Nancy Seifer, *Nobody Speaks for Me! Self-Portraits of American Working-Class Women*, p. 372.

What makes people happy? What do people mean by happiness? In recent years, more researchers have been trying to find out the ingredients of this elusive, much sought after condition. It is somewhat difficult to interpret their findings, however, since those studying happiness or life satisfaction often do not define these terms and sometimes use them interchangeably. In addition, the people taking part in the surveys often impose their own definitions and answer accordingly. This, of course, is consistent with the idea that happiness is a very personal construct: "I don't have to judge my happiness by what I think would make someone else happy. And if I say I am happy, I can be presumed to be happy." With these reservations in mind, let us look at some of the data.

Clemente and Sauer (1976) asked 1347 Americans over the age of 18 to rate their satisfaction with their family life, friendships, activities, and the place where they lived. When they analyzed the answers in terms of the people's age, race, socioeconomic status, marital status, how healthy they consider themselves to be, and their degree of religious and political participation, two factors stand out from the rest. The most important? Race and health. Not surprisingly in our society, whites are more satisfied with their lives than blacks are. And, not surprisingly in any society, healthy people are happier than those who suffer from illness and disability. Married people and people who are active in religion and politics are slightly happier than the unmarried and the uninvolved, but the difference is not great. People at higher socioeconomic levels are happier than those at lower, but neither education nor income makes the difference by itself, indicating that there are other factors involved that are hard to isolate. While a number of other studies have found younger people happier than older ones, this survey found just the opposite.

When fifty-four middle- and lower-middle-class men and women at midlife were asked to evaluate their happiness at various times in their lives, they reported more high than low points throughout their lives (Lowenthal & Chiriboga, 1972). The ratio of high-to-low points was higher for men than for women, which may mean that men are happier—or simply that they are more prone to repress any expression of unhappiness.

The women's lowest point of life happiness was early middle age, while the men's unhappiest time was young adulthood. Two transitions often thought of as crisis—the empty nest and retirement—were "up" periods for both sexes. When the men spoke of current frustrations, they were most likely to bring up money or job, whereas the women's frustrations centered more around problems with their husbands or their children. When focusing on things they were proud of, however, both sexes referred to their marriages and their children.

How happy as adults are people who have been identified as gifted children? To answer this question, Sears (1977) followed up 430 women and 486 men, aged 48 to 70, who had been among the original group of bright children chosen by Terman in the 1920s. These people grew up during World War I, lived through the Depression, and raised their children during World War II. While, overall, the men rated their occupational satisfaction higher than the women did, the *employed* women rated this measure as highly as the men. Women were happier with friends and cultural life than men were, but both the women and the men gave their highest satisfaction scores for family life.

Sears focused chiefly on the women and found that most of them—69 percent—said they would choose their work lifestyle again. Those who had never had children were happier with their lifestyle, but the mothers drew more satisfaction from family life. Those women who were happiest with their lifestyle had been working outside the home for some years, had been single for a considerable length of time (sometimes after an earlier marriage), and had no children. Family income—which covered a wide range—did not seem to affect a woman's satisfaction with her work pattern.

In many ways these women were ahead of their times and in tune with contemporary thinking and mores. They were better educated than the average woman of their day, more likely to have a better job, better satisfied with work outside the home than within it, apt to have fewer children, and more prone to divorce and remarry. When asked how they would live their lives if they could do it all over again, most said they would prepare themselves for and pursue a career except for the years when they were raising their children. As they looked back over their lives from the vantage point of 1972, this seemed like a more fruitful choice than either remaining a homemaker or working at whatever income-producing job came along.

What about people who are young and middle-aged today? Some answers about their happiness showed up in two surveys—one of 52,000 women who read *Redbook Magazine* and one of 2000 male readers of *Esquire*. Both groups are very select: overwhelmingly white, young, well-educated, and in the $10,000 to $40,000 income brackets. Two-thirds of the women are married, and a little over a third have no children. The average age of the women is 31, the men two years older (Sheehy, 1979).

What goals do these people hold? The women place the top value on family security (which includes taking care of loved ones), on mature love, and on inner harmony, while the men value a sense of accomplishment equally with a comfortable life and mature love. The only women who put accomplishment among their three top goals are middle-aged—between 46 and 55 years old. In general, women want to be at peace with themselves, while men tend to take more risks in trying to outwit the culture.

On the graph of happiness through life (see Figure 15-1), women are seen to be quite happy at age 21, least happy in their late forties, and then happier as the years go on. In fact, women in their mid-fifties show up as even happier than 21-year-olds, and their satisfaction with life continues to increase during the sixties. The men's happiness curve is much more volatile. It rises and falls markedly every five years or so, with their peaks showing up first in late adolescence, then again in the late thirties and in the late forties. It dips sharply in the mid-fifties, to increase gradually through the sixties. (We need to remember, of course, that both these surveys

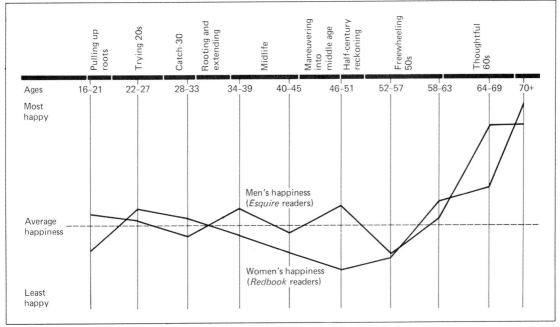

Fig. 15-1

are cross-sectional, and so we don't know whether individuals' happiness levels change over the years, or whether some cohorts are happier than others.)

Many young people dread middle age. They are sure they will no longer be feeling young by the time they celebrate their thirty-sixth birthday and will be feeling and acting positively old by their fifty-fifth (Sheehy, 1979). Yet the responses from people actually in these age brackets indicate that the younger adults' prophecies are ten years premature and paint a far grimmer picture of middle age than that actually experienced by people already there.

The happiest middle-aged women are better-educated, better-paid, and more likely to be professionals than the other women who answered the happiness questionnaire. While still in their twenties, the happiest women made their commitments to both marriage and career, but married later and had fewer children (one, on the average). Their lives were rarely calm and untroubled. On the contrary, almost all had known extremely unhappy times, from childhood to the present. They describe just as many painful situations as the most unhappy women: handicapped children, alcoholic husbands, miserable childhoods, trouble with money, marriages, jobs—the gamut.

The critical difference is that the happiest women have usually faced the difficulty, picked themselves up and taken the painful steps necessary to extricate themselves from a trap or to surmount a tragedy. Indeed, an important ingredient in their sense of well-being is the exhilaration of having freed themselves and the self-validation they find possible once they stop trying too hard to please everyone else [Sheehy, 1979, p. 59].

This conflict between pleasing others and pleasing oneself is one that recurs throughout life for many women, as Gilligan (1977) points out in her analysis of women's moral development. Most of the women who answered the *Redbook* survey did not overcome their need for other people's approval until they reached their mid-forties and, for the first time, developed a clear sense of their own identity.

FAMILY RELATIONSHIPS

MARRIAGE

Marriage at midlife is very different from what it used to be, historically. When life expectancies were shorter, with women often dying in childbirth, it was the rare couple indeed who lived with each other for twenty-five or thirty or forty years. The most common pattern was for marriages to be broken by death and for the survivors to remarry, often remarrying others who had been widowed. In these marriages or in those in which both partners did grow old together, households were usually alive with children. People had children early and late, had more of them, and expected them to live at home until they married. As a result, it was relatively rare for a middle-aged man and woman to be alone in their marriage.

Today this is far more common. Even though more marriages are sundered by divorce', the couple who have managed to stay together can often look forward to twenty or more years together after the last child has left the home. What is this postparental stage of marriage like for most people? Research has produced contradictory results, indicating that there is a diversity of marital styles in later life (Troll, Miller, & Atchley, 1979).

Pineo (1961) studied adults married up to twenty years and found a general drop in marital satisfaction and a loss of intimacy that he characterized as "disenchantment." He explains this disenchantment on the premise that at the time of marriage a couple are as happy as they can be. Since they wouldn't be marrying each other unless they felt extremely positive toward each other, it would be hard for the relationship to get better; perforce, it must get worse. This theory does not take into account the many relationships that seem to deepen over the years as husband and wife share both joys and sorrows, deal with the complexities of each other's personality, and forge a greater intimacy.

Burr (1970) feels that the notion of gradual decline in marital satisfaction is inaccurate. Instead, satisfaction with such different aspects of the marriage as sex, children, and money rises and falls at different times. In general, after the stage in which the children are of school age, the marriage seems to get better in regard to companionship, money, sex, task performance, and relations with the children.

Couples in the "launching stage," when one or more children are still at home, say they are quite satisfied with their marriages—more so than any age group except honeymooners and old people (Feldman, 1964). They still focus on their children—being involved with their lives, talking about them, and fighting about them. While Feldman found that couples in which the wife is under 65 and all the children have left home are less happy in their marriages, other researchers have found that the years after the children are gone rival the honeymoon for happiness levels (Feldman & Feldman, 1977; Campbell, 1975; Brim, 1968; Deutscher, 1964).

These postparental years give both husband and wife a chance to breathe a sigh of relief, now that they have done their duty by their children. In this "second honeymoon" stage, they have the privacy they haven't had for years, the freedom to be spontaneous, fewer money worries, and a new opportunity to get to know each other as individuals.

Troll and Smith (1976) differentiate between attraction and attachment in a marriage and find an inverse relationship between the two. *Attraction*, which could be equated with Walster and Walster's (1978) definition of passionate love (see page 432), is high for newlyweds, while *attachment* (or *companionate love*) is low. As the mystery between two people is dispelled by the intimacy of their day-to-day life together, attraction decreases but attachment deepens. A marriage that has been basically good over the years is apt to be better than ever now.

Sex during middle age—far from being only a memory or an occasional foray into pleasures of the past—can be a vital part of life. (© Joel Gordon 1978)

When a marriage has long been shaky, however, midlife may present a crisis. The children have been launched, and you feel your parental duties are over; you look at each other and realize that one or both of you have changed and you have little in common; you look ahead to the twenty-five or so years looming before you and ask yourself whether you want to continue to spend it with this person. When the answer is no, you head for the divorce court. In 1965, 51,700 couples who had been married for twenty or more years were divorced, and a decade later, in 1975, that number soared to 72,920 (Johnson, 1977). These couples are separating for many of the same reasons younger couples do— their greater expectations from marriage and their growing willingness to end an unsatisfactory relationship; the growing acceptance of divorce, even for older couples; and the less stringent divorce laws across the country.

SEXUALITY

The various myths about middle-aged sexuality, many of which are believed by the middle aged themselves, have served in the past to diminish this time of life for many people. And yet, recent advances in health and medical care, more liberal attitudes toward sex throughout all strata of society, and new studies of sexual activity have reinforced the awareness that sex during middle age—far from being only a memory or an occasional foray into pleasures of the past—can be a vital part of life. The most recent extensive national survey of sexual activity in the United States (Hunt, 1974) found that middle-aged people are engaging in sexual activity more often and in more varied ways than ever before.

Sexual activity *is* different during the middle years, partly because of physiological changes in males. They usually do not experience sexual tension as often as in younger

From thirty-five to forty-five women are old; but at forty-five the devil takes over and they become beautiful, splendid, maternal, proud. The acidities are gone and in their place reigns calm. These women are worth going out to find and because of them some men never grow old.

Jean-Baptiste Troisgros in Garson Kanin, *It Takes a Long Time to Become Young*, p. 37.

days: Men who eagerly sought sexual activity every other day may now be content to go three to five days between orgasms. Their erections arrive less often on their own accord, now needing direct stimulation. Their orgasms come more slowly and sometimes not at all. And they require a longer recovery time after one orgasm before they can ejaculate again.

However, men who have been sexually active during their younger years and throughout the thirties are likely to continue to be sexually active during their middle and even older years (Masters & Johnson, 1966). Very often a decrease in sexual activity can be attributed to one of six nonphysiologic reasons: monotony in a sexual relationship, preoccupation with business or money worries, mental or physical fatigue, overindulgence in food or drink, physical and mental infirmities of either partner, and fear of performance failure associated with or resulting from any of these causes (Masters & Johnson, 1966).

The couple who are aware of these potential blocks to sexual fulfillment and who recognize the normal changes of middle age and can design their sex life around them can still find great satisfaction together. Hunt and Hunt (1974) make several recommendations that can enhance the sex life of middle-aged couples: the use of a lubricating substance in those instances when a woman's natural lubrication is inadequate; longer and more inventive foreplay to arouse both partners; close attention to overall physical condition; capitalizing on the longer sexual act made possible by the male's slower orgasm; and the continuation of regular and frequent sexual activity.

PARENTHOOD

It is ironic that the two times of life most frequently linked with emotional crisis—middle age and adolescence—often live in the same house. It is, after all, middle-aged adults who are the parents of adolescent children. While dealing with their own special concerns at midlife, they have to deal daily with young people who are undergoing their own great physical, emotional, and social changes. In fact, sometimes parents' own long-buried adolescent fantasies resurface as they see their children turning into independent, sexual beings. Furthermore, seeing their children at the brink of adulthood makes some parents realize even more sharply how much of their adulthood is behind them. The contrast between the years ahead of their children and the years behind the parents sometimes creates resentment and jealousy on the part of the parent—and sometimes an over-identification with the child's fantasies (Vahanian, 1980).

Another parenting issue that middle-aged people need to face is an acceptance of their children as they are—not as the people the parents had hoped and dreamed they would turn out to be. Levinson (1977) emphasizes the "de-illusionment" that occurs at midlife. This coming to terms with reality is a major issue in parenting, as in other quarters of a person's life. People now realize that they do not have total control over their children, that they cannot mold them into carbon copies of themselves or even somewhat improved versions. For better or for worse, their children's characters are fairly well set now, and their

I WAS NEARLY FIRED A FEW YEARS AGO. I WENT BEFORE TOWN COMMITTEES FIGHTING FOR MY POSITION BECAUSE MY SON WASN'T LIKE HIS FATHER. HE WAS A DRAFT RESISTER.... IT DIDN'T MATTER THAT I HAD A PURPLE HEART, BELIEVED IN THE SYSTEM, HAD FOUGHT FOR THE SYSTEM. IT WAS MY SON OR MY JOB. BUT MORE THAN THAT, MY SIN KEPT TALKING TO ME. I STOOD BEHIND HIM.

quoted in *Making It from 40 to 50*
by Joel Davitz and Lois Davitz, p. 95.

directions in life may be very different from the one their parents had wanted them to follow.

This acceptance is so difficult for many parents, and the need to break away so strong for many youths, that the years of adolescence are sometimes hard on everyone in the family. The most frequent area of disagreement among the middle-aged couples interviewed by Lowenthal and Chiriboga (1972) was that of child rearing. As one father of three said, just after his youngest child had gone off to college, "They make the last couple of years at home so miserable that their going doesn't come as a trauma—it's a relief!" Perhaps this is nature's way of preparing parents for the empty nest.

For years people have talked about the "empty nest crisis" that afflicts women who have invested much of themselves into mothering. Recent research has shown, however, that while some women do experience such a crisis, they are far outnumbered by those who find it liberating not having children in the home any more. Little study has been done on the effect of the empty nest on fathers, although there is some evidence that some fathers react to their children's leaving the home with regrets that they had not spent more time with them when they were younger (Rubin, 1979).

Among fifty-four middle- and lower-middle-class men and women whose youngest child was about to leave the home, this transition stage represented the lowest point in the life satisfaction stage for only three women and two men (Lowenthal & Chiriboga, 1972). And even among these five, none explained their low levels of happiness by referring to their children's imminent departures. On the other hand, thirteen of these parents found the period of their children's adolescence their most trying period, when they had problems with their children and, sometimes, conflicts with their spouses over the children. Their attitude toward the empty nest could be summarized by the words of one mother, who said:

I feel my job with them is done. I don't have to discipline them anymore, it's their problem. . . . I hope I can always be a mother, but we'll treat each other as adults. I have a much more relaxed feeling now [pp. 9–10].

Harkins (1978) compared "empty nest" women whose youngest child had graduated from high school within the past eighteen months with "post-empty nest" mothers who had experienced this event more than 2½ years previously and "pre-empty nest" mothers whose children were juniors or seniors in high school at the time of the study. She found that most women do not believe the empty nest to be a particularly stressful transition, and, in fact, that those in the transitional period are often in an especially good frame of mind. The most distressed women are those whose children do *not* become successfully independent when their parents had expected them to.

Among 160 women who had asssumed the traditional role of homemaker and mother for at least ten years after the birth of their first child and who tended to see mothering as their career, only one failed to respond to the departure of her children with a decided sigh of relief (Rubin, 1979). Most of the women found jobs and reorganized their day-to-day lives to better fit their new situation. Apparently, the only women who do experience this time as a crisis are those who have not looked ahead to it and have not thought about what they would do with their lives after their children were no longer at home (Targ, 1979).

THE MIDDLE-AGED CHILD OF AGING PARENTS

Young, newly married adults are closely tied to their middle-aged parents, who often help them financially or with various services, like babysitting or helping them get their first homes in order. They often visit back and forth, and the young couples spend a great deal of time talking about their parents (Troll, Miller, & Atchley, 1979). In general, the parents continue to give more than they get.

While relationships toward parents evolve constantly through the years, they seem to change most abruptly sometime during the children's middle age. It is at this time that many people, for the first time, are able to look at their parents objectively, neither idealizing them and being unable to acknowledge their shortcomings nor being bitter toward them for their mistakes and inadequacies. The coming of maturity helps people to see their parents more as individuals in their own right, with both strengths and weaknesses.

I'm feeling low at the moment mostly because of my parents. They've both getting older. I don't want to face it. They've always been very full of life, and I can't see them slowing down, and I'm bothered when they bring up the subject.

quoted in *Making It from 40 to 50* by Joel Davitz and Lois Davitz, p. 194.

Something else happens at about this time, too. The children suddenly look at their parents and see how old they have become. No longer pillars of strength to lean on, parents are starting to lean themselves. They begin to seek their children's help in making decisions. With the loss of physical faculties and earning powers, they may become dependent for the performance of daily tasks and for financial support. And as they become ill, infirm, or senile, their children are called upon to assume total responsibility for managing their lives. Middle-aged children often have to make decisions about their parents' living arrangements, and it may be painful to weigh one's responsibilities toward parents as against those toward one's spouse and children.

Adults and their elderly parents generally prefer to live near each other, but not in the same home. Since both generations want their independence, they generally live together only when such a living arrangement seems absolutely necessary. Most often, this need arises from the ill health or poverty of an aging, single parent who can neither live alone nor afford an attractive alternative for care. When two generations do live together, the most common pattern is that of mother and daughter in the same home, reflecting the tendency of mothers and daughters to maintain closer family ties throughout adulthood than any other combinations of family members (Troll et al., 1979).

Support is still not all one-way, though. Upper- and middle-class parents often continue to help their middle-aged children financially, while among working-class families aid flows the other way (Troll et al., 1979).

While much current myth portrays the abandonment of old parents by their middle-aged children who simply turn them over to the Social Security system for aid, we have not become so heartless a society. Recent research turns up no evidence that children neglect their aging parents. The best relationships seem to exist when both parent and child are functioning well and neither *needs*

Many of the friends of midlife are old friends, and by the mid-forties, the circle is well established. (© 1976 Chester Higgins, Jr./Photo Researchers, Inc.)

help from the other (Clark & Anderson, 1967), but when the elderly cannot take care of their own needs, they expect—and they get—help from their children (Bleckner, 1965).

FRIENDSHIP

Middle-aged people sometimes seem to have less time and energy available to invest in friendships than do people in other stages of the life cycle. They are often heavily involved with family, between spouses, children, and aging parents, and there is sometimes an "almost obsessive concern" with building up security for impending retirement (Weiss & Lowenthal, 1976). As a result, people at midlife tend to have fewer friends than either newlyweds or people about to retire, and their friendships are less complex than those in the age groups before and after. That is, they use fewer adjectives to describe the dimensions of their friendships. It is possible that people are just too busy at this time of life to devote as much time to their friends as they have before and will again.

Yet friendships do persist throughout middle age. Many of the friends of midlife are old friends, and by the mid-forties, most people have a circle of friends as large as they want (Hurlock, 1968). People still make some new friends. Middle-aged men and women tend to be fairly heavily involved in formal organizations (Troll, 1975), and they often meet and become friendly with people through these activities. Friendships also evolve from similarities in life stage, such as age of children, duration of marriage, or occupational status, rather than chronological age (Troll, 1975).

While people often make new friends on the basis of closeness and convenience, by the time they reach middle age, these factors are less important. Among 150 middle-aged, middle-class couples who had moved within the past five years, most named as a "best friend" someone from the community where they had lived before (Hess, 1971). Their second-best friends, though, were likely to be new neighbors.

So we see that with friendships, as with so many of the other concerns in midlife, there is some consolidation of the past, some reaching out toward the future, and always growth and development.

SUMMARY

1 Middle-aged people tend to have strong self-concepts, especially when they have had the advantage of optimum educational and occupational opportunities. **2** Erikson's seventh psychosocial crisis, occurring during middle age, is generativity versus stagnation. The generative individual has concern for establishing and guiding the next generation. One who fails to develop a sense of generativity suffers from stagnation, self-indulgence, and, perhaps, early physical and psychological invalidism. **3** Expanding on Erikson's concepts, Robert Peck specified four psychological developments critical to successful adjustment during middle age: valuing wisdom versus valuing physical prowess; socializing versus sexualizing in human relationships; cathectic flexibility versus cathectic impoverishment; and mental flexibility versus mental rigidity. **4** According to Charlotte Bühler, people between ages 45 and 65 must evaluate their past and revise their future plans in light of present physical conditions, job status, and personal relationships. **5** Social-psychological theorists see change in adulthood as primarily a function of environmental factors rather than biological ones. **6** Research indicates that the early forties is the time of midlife transition, a period which may involve considerable personal turmoil. Several factors precipitate this event, including awareness of one's own mortality and the need for new goals and challenges, personality, coping style, and sex differences; and the occurrence of several stressful events simultaneously influence how the midlife transition is handled. **7** The period of the fifties is often characterized by a period of stabilization and mellowing. **8** Surveys of middle-aged people indicate that they are quite happy, especially if they are healthy, wealthy, and white. **9** Research on the quality of marriages during midlife is contradictory. Marriages are seen as relatively more or less happy during midlife than during early adulthood depending upon the dimensions assessed. Middle-aged people today are engaging in sexual activity more often and in more varied ways than in the past. **10** Much research indicates that the postparental years—when children have left the nest—are among the happiest. During the middle years, people often change their relationships with their parents, who are viewed more objectively. Middle-aged children may begin to act as parents to their own parents. **11** Middle-aged people tend to invest less time in developing friendships, especially new ones, since their energies are devoted to family, work, and building up security for retirement.

SUGGESTED READINGS

Arnstein, H. *Getting along with your grown-up children*. Philadelphia: Evans (Lippincott), 1970. This book, written for middle-aged parents, is interesting reading for young adults, too, as it spells out the many ways in which the parental relationship changes over the years and gives insights into parenthood during middle age.

Gould, R. *Transformations*. New York: Simon and Schuster, 1978. A practical book which explains growth and change in adulthood and how people can cope with crises and changes.

Levinson, D.   *The seasons of a man's life*. New York: Knopf, 1978. Describes the developmental course of adulthood based on Levinson's interviews with forty male executives, biologists, factory workers, and novelists. Includes analyses of the nature and timing of emotional crises, marriage, and career problems, and the importance of "mentors."

Lowenthal, M., Thurnher, M., and Chiriboga, D.   *Four stages of life*. San Francisco: Jossey-Bass, 1975. A study of men and women facing the "incremental" transitions of leaving home and starting a family and the "decremental" transitions of "empty nest" and retirement.

Rubin, L.   *Women of a certain age: The midlife search for self*. New York: Harper & Row, 1979. A report of in-depth interviews with 160 women aged 35 to 54 covering topics such as the "empty nest syndrome," depression, and sexuality.

Troll, L. E.   *Early and middle adulthood: The best is yet to be—maybe*. Monterey, CA: Brooks/Cole, 1975. A survey of research findings on physical status, personality, and intellectual functioning in early and middle adulthood by a leading developmental researcher.

Troll, L. E., Israel, J., and Israel, K.   *Looking ahead: A woman's guide to the problems and joys of growing older*. Englewood Cliffs, NJ: Prentice-Hall, 1977. A series of practical articles written by authorities on midlife.

Vaillant, G.   *Adaptation to life*. Boston: Little, Brown, 1977. A report of the Grant study of adult development which focuses on styles of adaptation and mental health in men.

Late Adulthood

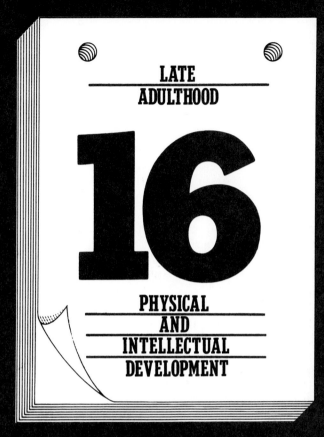

LATE
ADULTHOOD

16

PHYSICAL
AND
INTELLECTUAL
DEVELOPMENT

IN THIS CHAPTER YOU WILL LEARN ABOUT

The onset of late adulthood: what it means in terms of physical and mental health, life expectancy, and physical changes

Some theories about biological aging and the factors influencing this

Intellectual functioning in late adulthood: intelligence, cognition, learning and memory ability, and how we may improve performance

What changes are needed if the elderly are to participate actively in our society

CHAPTER OVERVIEW

Physical Functioning
When Late Adulthood Begins | Health Status Life Expectance and Causes of Death Sensory Abilities in Late Life | Anatomical and Physical Changes | Psychomotor Skills | The Nature of the Aging Process

Mental Health
Mental Illnesses Common in Late Adulthood

Intellectual Functioning in Late Adulthood
Intelligence Testing throughout the Life Span | Piagetian Abilities | Influences on Test Performance in Later Life | Can the Intellectual Performance of the Elderly Be Improved through Training? | Learning and Memory in Late Adulthood | Implications of Research

Work and Retirement
Women and Retirement | Making Retirement a Positive Experience

Old age. The very term sounds so bad to so many people that those advanced in years are hardly ever referred to simply as old people. Instead, they are called "senior citizens," "golden agers," "elderly persons," persons in the "harvest years" or the "twilight years," or, most recently, "older Americans."

What is so bad about late adulthood that people can't talk about it without covering it in a cloak of euphemisms? Is it really so bad? How much of what we believe about it is true? What can people reasonably expect of their later years?

The stereotypes of the old are many. There is the positive one, that with old age comes tranquility, a "golden age" of peace and relaxation when people can harvest the fruits of their lifelong labors.

Most of the stereotypes, though, are negative: Old people are poorly coordinated, feel tired most of the time, and easily fall prey to infections. They have many accidents in the home and spend most of their time in bed. They tend to live in hospitals, nursing homes, or other institutions suitable for people whose health and abilities are steadily declining. They are not so smart any more, unable to remember the simplest things or to learn new facts and skills. They have no interest or desire in sexual relationships. Isolated from family and friends, they sit around watching television or listening to the radio. They don't spend their time productively. Their personalities are very different from what they used to be, and they're now grouchy, self-pitying, touchy, and cranky (Butler, 1975; Saul, 1974).

"Baloney!" shouts more than one observer of late adulthood.

While the lives of millions of vigorous, productive, and cheerful old people belie these stereotypes, society's widespread acceptance of these viewpoints helps to perpetuate them. *Ageism*, or prejudice against the elderly, runs rampant. How does it hurt old people? A physician who assumes that a 75-year-old heart patient is no longer interested in sex and who does not bring up the subject is denying the patient a fulfilling aspect of life. An adult child who becomes patronizing and overprotective forces an aging parent to become infantile. A social worker who accepts depression as an expected part of old age in effect abandons an elderly client. Attitudes like these affect the way old people live. Furthermore, such viewpoints are reflected in old people's feelings about themselves. Many old people are among the most ardent believers of the myths of aging.

What, then, is the truth about old age? In recent years the science of *gerontology*, or the study of the elderly and of the process of aging, has expanded. *Geriatrics*, the branch of medicine concerned with the aged, attracts more practitioners. More and more people are now studying the biological, psychological, and sociological aspects of aging.

This recent interest in aging and the aged stems largely from the fact that the proportion of old people in our society is much larger now than it used to be. As medical science has advanced, more people are living to and past the biblical life span of threescore years and ten. Elderly citizens are more of a presence in our culture, and it is important from a societal point of view as well as from a personal one to help them make the most of their lives.

In 1900 there were only 3 million Americans over age 65. By 1976 there were 22.9 million (almost 2 million of whom were over 85); and by the year 2000 there are expected to be about 32 million, including 13 million people over 75 (U.S. Department of Health, Education, and Welfare, 1978). In 1975, while 1.2 million people over 65 died, 1.8 million celebrated their sixty-fifth birthday. This gave the United States a net increase of 555,000 older citizens, or 1510 per day (USDHEW, 1978).

A disproportionate number of elderly

people live in seven states. In 1976, 46 percent of them lived in California, Florida, Pennsylvania, Texas, New York, Ohio, and Illinois, with the first four showing the greatest increase since 1970 of their elderly populations (NCOA, 1978). They are slightly more likely than other age groups to live outside the country's metropolitan areas (31 percent, compared to 26 percent for younger people) (USDHEW, 1978).

In 1977, 8 percent of the nation's black population, 11 percent of the white, and 4 percent of the Hispanics were 65 and older (USDHEW, 1978). Why these racial differences? Largely because of the higher birthrates for nonwhite groups, which increase their proportion of younger people, and also because white people in our society have longer life expectancies.

Between 1900 and 1960 the elderly population increased twice as quickly as the nation's population as a whole, by 5 times as compared with 2½ times (Blau, 1973). By the year 2020, 1 out of every 5 Americans will be over 65 (Henig, 1979).

This "graying" of our population has many causes. The high birthrates in this country in the late-nineteenth and early- to mid-twentieth centuries, combined with high immigration rates early in this century, swelled our population with people now in the over-65 brackets. Medical advances have lengthened our average life expectancy—largely because fewer people now die in childhood and early adulthood.

In view of the increasing numbers of old people, it is important to help younger people understand and get along with the elderly in the family, on the job, and in the community. You who are reading this book have even greater expectations of reaching old age yourselves. The more you know about what to expect during your latter years, the better prepared you can be to make the most of them.

From a theoretical point of view, developmentalists who study the life cycle from conception through death recognize that old age

is a normal period of the life span, with its own special characteristics and its own developmental tasks.

What, then, do we know about old age?

PHYSICAL FUNCTIONING

As in every other stage of the life cycle, there is no arbitrary dividing line when middle age ends and old age begins. One person says at 50, "I hope I never get as old as I feel"; another, at 84, talks about putting aside money for the "twilight years."

WHEN LATE ADULTHOOD BEGINS

Neugarten (1975) sets up a category of people from ages 55 to 75 whom she calls the "young-old," people distinguished from the middle aged because they have already retired from full-time work and distinguished from the "old-old" because of their "continued vigor and active social involvement." Butler (1975) refers to early old age (ages 65 to 74) and advanced old age (75, the point at which physiologic changes occur to a marked degree, and above).

The trouble with any classification is that the diversity which we have noted throughout life is still present and, in fact, appears to be even more pronounced in old age than in the earlier years. Senescence, the period of the life span during which one grows old, begins at different ages for different people. Declines in bodily functioning begin early for some people, but late for others, and this physical aging is an important marker for the beginning of late adulthood. Chronological years are a less satisfactory index of aging than the way a person feels or acts.

For the purposes of this discussion we have somewhat arbitrarily chosen the age of 65 to mark the beginning of late adulthood. This is the age when people become eligible for full Social Security benefits, when many organizations and businesses expect employees to retire, and when people are often eligible for "golden age" bus and movie passes.

HEALTH STATUS

When Charlotte M., aged 77, woke up on a typical morning, she was tired because she hadn't slept well. She had been kept awake by a headache and a stuffed nose, apparently caused by deterioration of the cartilage in the back of her neck. Her lower back and knee were stiff from a recent fall, and she was somewhat uncomfortable because of indigestion. And yet she did not consider herself a sickly old woman. She recognized that her symptoms were not serious, shrugged at their annoyance, and refused to let them interfere with the busy life she led as a salesperson. None of Charlotte's discomforts are unique to people of her age:

The special problem in the elderly is the fact that a given illness is usually superimposed on an assortment of preexisting chronic illnesses and on organ systems which have lost their wide margin of reserve capacity. The elderly patient thus represents a delicately balanced mechanism in which even a "minor" illness can lead to major consequences [Estes, 1969, p. 124].

The majority of elderly persons are reasonably healthy, although the rate of illness in the elderly is higher than that for younger age groups. Only about 25 percent of men over 65 and 10 percent of women cannot do paid work or housework because of chronic health problems. While an additional 21 percent of the men and 30 percent of the women have some limitations, these are not major. Only 2 percent are bedfast; 6 percent are house-

bound; and 6 percent are ambulatory with difficulty. Nonwhites are more likely to be handicapped than whites, probably as a reflection of different socioeconomic circumstances for the two groups and poorer medical care for nonwhite people.

Chronic conditions (those of long duration) do increase with age and do cause disability. The most common conditions that limit the activities of older persons are heart conditions, high blood pressure, arthritis, rheumatism, orthopedic impairments, and mental and nervous conditions (U.S. Department of Health, Education, and Welfare, 1971; Estes, 1969). It's interesting to note, though, that some of these so-called "diseases of old age," like heart attack and arthritis, begin to appear among people in their thirties (Ledger, 1978). Other chronic conditions common among the elderly include obesity, abdominal-cavity hernias, cataracts, varicose veins, hemorrhoids, and prostate disorders. Many people have a combination of chronic ailments, but most are only mildly limited (Estes, 1969). Chronic conditions that show no consistent increase past middle age are asthma, hay fever, diabetes, peptic ulcers, and chronic bronchitis (Riley, Foner, & Associates, 1968).

In 1975, about 1 person in every 10 *under* the age of 65 was hospitalized, compared to 1 in 6 of those 65 and over (U.S. Department of Health, Education, and Welfare, 1978). Older persons are hospitalized a few days longer, on the average, as are nonwhites.

Persons over 65 seem to have one health advantage over younger people—they have fewer colds, flu infections, and acute digestive problems. They may be more immune to common germs, may go out less and thus be exposed to fewer, may be less aware of symptoms, or may pay less attention to them. When acute illness does strike an old person, though, it generally leads to more days of restricted activity than it would for a younger person. Even so, this still amounts to an average of less than ten sick days a year for people over 65 (Estes, 1969).

Probably at least 1 out of 5 older persons spends some time in a long-term care facility—a mental hospital, convalescent or nursing home, or other institution (Kastenbaum & Candy, 1973). Women and whites are much more likely to be institutionalized than men and nonwhites. Since women live longer than men and usually outlive their husbands, they are more likely to be alone and to need outside help when they get sick. The fact that old black people are institutionalized at less than one-third the rate that their population would indicate may result from overt racial discrimination as well as from financial problems. Or it may point to cultural differences: There may be more of a commitment for the children of aging black parents to take their parents into their own homes than there is among white families.

With the establishment of the Social Security system, and then the additions of Medicare, which pays for much of the health care of persons over 65, and of Medicaid, which pays for much care for low-income people, being sick is no longer the crushing financial burden it once was to the elderly and their families; however, families still bear the costs of private institutionalization.

Old people do, of course, need more health care. In 1975, the average cost of health care for someone over 65 came to $1360, nearly three times as much as the $472 required for the average younger adult. Of the $103 billion spent for health care in that year, some 30 percent went to pay for care for the 10 percent of our population who are 65 or older. Fortunately for individual pocketbooks, however, two-thirds of the health-care expenditures for older persons came from national public funds (NCOA, 1978).

We really don't have any evidence to show whether elderly people of any given age are in better or in worse health than in earlier decades. We do know that as medical progress has stemmed the scourges that took many people earlier in life, more people are now living to ages characterized by long-term illness. But such illness is not inevitable. Poor

health is not a necessary, inescapable result of aging. Says Levin (1971):

Aging itself is not a disease and most older people are not in poor health. However, aging is accompanied by physical changes and *increases the possibility of the development of chronic illness* [p. 19; emphasis added].

Busse (1969) distinguishes between primary aging and secondary aging. *Primary aging* results from inborn and inevitable biological changes that are independent of stress, trauma, or disease and that do not effect all people the same way. *Secondary aging* comes about as a result of trauma and chronic disease. Primary aging results in decreased efficiency of various functions, but often what is considered to be a part of aging is really a characteristic of secondary aging or of disease. If the changes usually attributed to old age are in reality the results of disease, then we can develop a far more optimistic attitude toward the health of the old. Says Bromley (1974):

The pattern of physical and mental disease in old age could be altered by changes in medical and psychiatric care, and by social and economic changes in, for example, social attitudes and living standards . . . Old age is not entirely a consequence of biological degeneration; it is partly the product of political, economic, and historical conditions [p. 118].

LIFE EXPECTANCY AND CAUSES OF DEATH

In ancient Rome and during the Middle Ages, the average life expectancy was between 20 and 30 years. By the middle of the nineteenth century, Americans could expect to live to an average age of 40 years. By the turn of the twentieth century, it was 49 years. Children who were born in 1975 can expect to live for 77.2 years if they are white females, 69.4 years if they are white males, 72.3 years if they are nonwhite females, and 63.6 years if they are nonwhite males (Population Reference Bureau, 1979). A man who has already reached the age of 65 can expect to live another fourteen years, while a 65-year-old woman has eighteen years ahead of her (U.S. Department of Health, Education, and Welfare, 1978). Many people do, of course, live longer. In 1971, the Social Security Administration paid benefits to 5000 centenarians (Saul, 1974), and the 1970 census counted up more than 106,000 people over the age of 100 (Butler, 1975).

The gains in life expectancy result primarily from declines in infant and child mortality rates, which dropped dramatically during the first half of the twentieth century. It's improbable that people can expect to live to much later ages than they now do, "short of a further biological and medical revolution" (Bromley, 1974, p. 112). Bromley maintains that 110 years of age is about the upper limit of human longevity, and that the average 80-year-old of today can expect to live only a little longer than 80-year-olds of previous centuries.

Since the beginning of this century, the United States death rate has declined sharply, and with this decline we have seen changes in the leading causes of death. For the population as a whole, for example, there have been fewer deaths from infectious diseases and from childbirth, and more deaths from heart disease, cancer, and stroke (Riley et al., 1968). These last three diseases account for 3 out of 4 elderly deaths, with heart disease accounting for 44 percent of elderly deaths, cancer for 18 percent, and strokes for 13 percent (U.S. Department of Health, Education, and Welfare, 1978). Other leading causes of death in old age are influenza,

pneumonia, arteriosclerosis (hardening of the arteries), accidents, and diabetes.

Shifts in the causes of death result from societal factors such as improvements in sanitation, immunization against many diseases that used to kill (like diphtheria and whooping cough), and the widespread use of antibiotics, which have taken some of the scare away from bronchitis, influenza, and pneumonia. The population as a whole has risen to a higher standard of living, is eating better, and is more knowledgeable about health. Along with these positive changes have come some negative ones—the increase in smoking and in carcinogenic agents in foods, in the workplace, and in the air we breathe, which lead to more deaths from cancer; the faster pace of life, which contributes to hypertension and heart disease. The very fact that more people are now living to advanced ages means that they are more likely to contract conditions and diseases that are characteristic of old age.

Sex Differences in Mortality

The same tendency observed during the fetal period holds true in old age, too: Males are more vulnerable than females. For every 100 white women 65 and over, there are only 69 white men. When we look at people past the age of 75, there are only 58 men to every 100 women. For some reason, sex differences in life expectancy—while still present—are less pronounced among blacks and Hispanics (NCOA, 1978).

In later life there appear to be both biological and environmental reasons for the lower mortality rates among women. Environmental factors can be seen in the fact that men are more likely than women to die from accidents, suicide, and homicide (Bogue, 1959; cited in Riley et al., 1968). They are also more likely to die from heart disease, lung cancer, emphysema, and asthma—all have been linked with environmental causes. According to the U.S. Department of Health, Education, and Welfare (1972), the only disease that claims more women is diabetes, possibly a reflection of different eating habits.

Yet different lifestyles for men and women cannot be the only factor accounting for different mortality rates. For one thing, the sex difference in the fetal stage and in infancy supports the notion of an inborn difference in resistance. Second, when men and women in similar Roman Catholic teaching orders were subject to similar kinds of lifestyles free from the sex roles of ordinary life, the nuns still had a longer life expectancy than the brothers (Madigan & Vana, 1957; cited in Riley et al., 1968).

SENSORY ABILITIES IN LATE LIFE

With age the sensory and perceptual functions decline, with great variation among individuals in the maintenance of these abilities.

Vision

Middle age brings farsightedness, but this tendency stabilizes at about age 60. People over 65 have other visual problems. They are likely to have 20/70 vision or less, are not as able to perceive depth or color, and cannot see as well in the dark, a handicap that keeps many older persons from driving at night (Bell, Wolf, & Bernholz, 1972; Corso, 1971; Riley et

At ninety-one her carriage was as erect as ever. The hip fracture did not make her lame, but it had left her a bit timid, and she had come to use a cane, emphasizing to her friends that it was needed not for support but merely to give her confidence on unfamiliar terrain, for she did not like to admit that her eyes were not so sharp as they had been

from Hannah Josephson,
Jeannette Rankin: First Lady of Congress
(Indianapolis: Bobbs-Merrill Co., 1974), p. 201.

al., 1968). Half of the legally blind persons in the United States—more than half a million— are over 65 (White House Conference on Aging, 1971). Extensive losses in visual acuity are higher for nonwhites (U.S. Department of Health, Education, and Welfare, 1966). Fortunately, with the development of improved corrective lenses and of new surgical techniques for the removal of cataracts, many vision losses are at least partially correctible. Some 92 percent of the elderly wear glasses or contact lenses (U.S. Department of Health, Education, and Welfare, 1978).

Hearing

Older people suffer marked hearing losses, especially at high frequencies. The ability to hear speech also drops off with age (Riley et al., 1968). It is especially hard for many older people to follow a conversation when there is competing noise—from radio or television, outside noises, or the buzz of many people talking at once (Kalish, 1975).

Older people are more likely to suffer hearing impairment than visual impairment. Of those between ages 65 and 74, 13 percent suffer impairment of hearing, as do 26 percent of those 75 and over. Of an estimated 4½ million persons with a serious hearing loss, some 55 percent are over 65 (Kalish, 1975). Only 5 percent of older people use hearing aids, however (NCOA, 1978), probably largely due to the difficulty many people have in adjusting to their use. Hearing loss is more common among elderly men than women (NCOA, 1978).

Other Senses

Testing results for taste and smell are contradictory, but there does seem to be some diminution in perception. When older people complain that their food doesn't taste as good any more, this may be because they have

Older people often suffer marked hearing losses, with a diminishing ability to follow conversation. (Hella Hammid/Photo Researchers, Inc.)

fewer tastebuds in the tongue and because they have experienced atrophy of the olfactory bulb, the organ at the base of the brain that is responsible for the perception of smell (Bromley, 1974).

The vestibular senses, which help to maintain posture and balance, seem to lose efficiency. This may be one reason why old people fall frequently. Dizziness is a common cause of falls in this age group, and deaths from falls are more common among the elderly than are deaths from traffic accidents (Rodstein, 1964).

Touch and movement perception also seem to decline with age, but there is little evidence to show that the perception of pain, heat, and cold weakens.

ANATOMICAL AND PHYSICAL CHANGES

Many of the changes of old age are readily apparent to even the most casual observer. The skin becomes paler and more splotchy, taking on a parchmentlike texture and losing some elasticity. Since some subcutaneous fat and muscle disappear, the inelastic skin

tends to hang in folds and wrinkles. Varicose veins are more common. The hair becomes thinner in both men and women, and what is left turns white.

Old people shrink in size because the discs between their spinal vertebrae atrophy, and the slight loss of stature that ensues is exaggerated by the tendency to stoop. Osteoporosis, a thinning of the bone that affects some women after menopause, may cause a "widow's hump" at the back of the neck. Chemical composition of the bones changes, causing an increased chance of bone fractures.

The bodies of old people adjust less quickly to cold and become chilled more easily. Exposure to cold and poor living conditions may cause an abnormally low body temperature, a serious risk for the aged. Old people cannot cope as well with heat, either, and they cannot work as effectively in moderately high temperatures. The reflexes respond more slowly, and incontinence—loss of bladder or bowel control—sometimes occurs, much to the distress of the individual.

All the body systems and organs are

more susceptible to disease, but the most serious change affects the functioning of the heart. After age 55, the rhythm of the heart becomes slower and more irregular; deposits of fat accumulate around it and interfere with its functioning; and the blood pressure rises. On the whole, the digestive system remains relatively efficient. The smooth muscles of the internal organs continue to operate well, and the liver and gall bladder hold up well. When obesity is present, it affects the circulatory system, the kidneys, and sugar metabolism; it contributes to degenerative disorders and tends to shorten life.

Dental Health

Tooth and gum problems become common in old age, with the loss of teeth the most common dental problem. More than half of all people over 65 have lost all their teeth, with the problem being especially bad among people from low income levels. In all age groups, men have more dental problems than women. Some people—albeit a very small proportion—retain all their teeth until very late in life. Dental health is related to a combination of innate tooth structure and lifelong eating and dental health habits. The relationship between poor dental health and poor dental care may be seen in the fact that in 1975, 47 percent of people 65 and older had not seen a dentist for five or more years (U.S. Department of Health, Education, and Welfare, 1978; NCOA, 1978; Bromley, 1974).

PSYCHOMOTOR SKILLS

Old people can do most of the same things that younger people can do, but they do them more slowly. They do not have the strength they once had, and they are severely limited in activities requiring endurance or the ability to carry heavy loads. Their general slowing down affects the quality of their responses as well as the time taken for them. Different physical activities slow down at different rates, with activities requiring the most stamina or the most muscular involvement showing the greatest decline (Salthouse, 1976).

Birren (1974) maintains that a big factor in the high accident rates of the aged is the slowdown that comes in the processing of information by the central nervous system. It takes longer for old people to assess their environment, take in all the appropriate factors, and make a decision fast enough to take the right action. This slowness in processing information shows up in all aspects of old people's lives. It makes them do more poorly on intelligence tests, especially those of the timed variety. It interferes with their ability to learn new information and to retrieve from memory information that they already have.

Combined with their decreased efficiency in sensorimotor coordination, old people's slower reaction times have practical implications in terms of driving. People over 65 have a disproportionate share of accidents compared with middle-aged drivers—usually because of improper turning, starting, and stopping, rather than speeding (California Department of Highway Patrol, 1958; cited in Riley et al., 1968). In fact, drivers over 70 have been termed "very similar to teenagers" in their high accident rates (Zylman, 1972). And yet the ability to drive can make the difference between an old person's active participation in society or enforced isolation. Instead of discouraging them from driving, we need to institute measures that will protect them and others and yet enable those who can continue to drive to do so. This would include regular retesting of older drivers' vision, coordination, and reaction time. It might also include staggering the work times of older workers so that they would not have to battle rush-hour traffic. And it might include a shorter work day, in recognition of the fact that many older drivers cannot see well enough in the dark to drive at night.

Society needs to recognize the slowdown and the sensory changes that come with age and to redesign environments that are more supportive of older adults in helping them to manage their lives safely and comfortably.

Physical exercise throughout adulthood appears to diminish losses in speed, stamina, and strength, and in various underlying functions such as circulation and breathing (Bromley, 1974). The substantial improvements that follow physical training probably mean that many of the effects we associate with aging result more from lack of use of our bodies and their adaptation to nondemanding physical circumstances than from our chronological age. Physical training does not extend the normal life span. It does seem to extend the energetic part of life and help people be more resistant to physical ailments that might otherwise be fatal, such as heart attacks (Bromley, 1974).

THE NATURE OF THE AGING PROCESS

Eos, a mythological goddess, asked Zeus to allow Tithonus, the mortal she loved, to live forever. Zeus granted Tithonus immortality, and the lovers lived happily—but not forever. Tithonus began to grow old until he became so infirm that he could not move. Yet he was denied the gift of death, and to this day he lives on, where Eos finally put him away, "a helpless, driveling vegetable." Eos had made a grievous error—she had forgotten to ask Zeus to grant eternal youth along with eternal life.

In recognition of the tragedy of life too long extended, the Gerontological Society has as its motto: "To Add Life to Years Not Just Years to Life." The goal of research in aging is, says Hayflick (1974), to understand the aging process not for the sake of "extension of longevity per se, but the extension of our most vigorous and productive years" (p. 40).

There are many different theories of aging, but none of them has been universally accepted as the definitive answer. We still do not know exactly why advancing age makes our bodies lose their abilities to function. We do know that aging is a complex process influenced by many different factors, including heredity, nutrition, disease, and various environmental influences. Heredity provides us with a good example of one of these influences. A good piece of advice we can give to someone who wants to live for a long time is "Choose your parents wisely." Children of long-lived parents are more likely to live long themselves, and identical twins have more similar life spans than do fraternal twins (Kallman, 1957, cited in Moore, 1968; Jarvik et al., 1960; Kallman et al., 1956). The mother's longevity seems more influential than the father's, although his bears a close relationship, too, especially for sons (Bromley, 1974). Some of this familial influence is also environmental—related to a family's diet, health, and exercise habits and other aspects of its lifestyle.

But knowing that the way we age is affected by the families we are born into does not explain how the process takes place. We do know that the cells in the body that make up our various organs lose their capacity to increase in number as we get older (except for cancer cells, which increase uncontrollably). The big questions, then, are "What happens to these cells? How do old cells differ from young cells? What happens to make them different?" Various researchers have provided different answers to these questions.

Most of the theories on biological aging fit into two basic approaches. The first is that aging is a programmed process, one that is pre-set for every species and is subject to only minor modifications. The other line of thought is that aging is the result of accumulated "insults" to the body. These two approaches have very different implications: If we are programmed to age in a certain way, there is nothing much we can do to retard the process, but if we age only because of the stresses our bodies are subject to, we may be able to extend our lives by eliminating some of those stresses. The truth very likely lies in a combination of these two different approaches. Let us look at some of the most prominent theories along both these lines:[1]

The Programmed Theory

Since each species has its own pattern of aging and its own life expectancy, aging must be built into the organism in some way. By programming the future lifescript so that an individual reproduces, then ages, and finally dies, the forces of nature help the new generation to survive and play out its own part in the program (Wilson, 1974). While this theory provides an intriguing explanation for *why* we age, it gives us no clues as to *how* the process takes place.

The Gene Theory

This theory has three variations:

1   Each individual is born with one or more harmful genes that become active later in life, causing aging and eventual death.

2   People have two different kinds of genes, one that provides well-being in youth and one that causes decline later in life. Early in life the "good" genes predominate, and in middle age the "bad" genes take over.

3   Only one set of genes is involved, but they change their character in middle age from helpful to hurtful.

An example of this theory is the age-related scripting of *estrogen* in the human female. In a woman's youth, this hormone enables her to reproduce and also seems to protect her against hardening of the arteries and subsequent heart disease. Then after menopause, estrogen production slows to a near halt, the woman can no longer conceive, and she is much more susceptible to heart attack.

[1]We are indebted here to Rockstein and Sussman's (1979) excellent overview of the most commonly talked about and most plausible current theories of aging.

The Running-Out-of-Program Theory

According to this theory, there is a set amount of basic genetic material (DNA) in each cell. As the cells age, the DNA is used up, and the cells die. This theory is supported by research reports that certain enzymes decrease with age, and also by Hayflick's (1974) findings that cells will divide only a limited number of times (about fifty for human cells). He concludes that about 110 years is the maximum expectancy for human life and that reports of longevity much beyond this are scientifically inaccurate.

The Somatic Mutation Theory

On the basis of research that found more chromosomal abnormalities in older mice than younger ones, more in short-lived mice than in those from a long-lived strain, and more in mice and guinea pigs exposed to x-rays and chemicals than in unexposed animals, Curtis (1971) concluded that over the years *mutations*, or changes, occur from various causes in the chromosomes, and that these changes cause aging.

The Cross-Linkage Theory

After Bjorksten (1974) noted that the protein gelatin used in an early copying machine was irreversibly changed by certain chemicals, he suggested that the proteins in the human body can be similarly altered by various compounds. Such alteration interferes with the normal function of these proteins and causes the tissues and organs in the body to age.

The Free Radical Theory

This special application of the cross-linkage theory proposes that *free radicals*, chemical components of cells that exist for only a second or less before they react with other substances such as fats, can damage the cells as they react with these other substances and can cause chromosomal mutations. As they react, free radicals continue to produce new free radicals, which in turn cause more damage. Since certain compounds like vitamins C and E can lessen the production of free radicals, some people argue that taking these vitamins will extend the human life span, but so far we have no firm evidence that this is so.

The Clinker Theory

In the belief that "bad" drives out "good," adherents of this theory maintain that aging is a result of the accumulation over time of harmful substances in various parts of the body. These substances include chemical byproducts of metabolism, which interfere with the normal functioning of organ tissues because they displace the good, functioning substances.

The Error Theory

This is a popular theory, one that is talked about a great deal, but one whose thesis is relatively unsubstantiated, according to Rockstein and Sussman (1979). What is its thesis? That alterations occur in the DNA and that these errors are transmitted to RNA and eventually to newly synthesized enzymes. When the number of defective enzymes reaches a high enough level, cells die; and when enough cells die, so does the individual itself (Busse, 1969). Recent research, however, has shown enzymes to be less active with age, but has not shown any *qualitative* changes in them to indicate that they are defective.

The Wear and Tear Theory

Comparing our bodies to machines whose parts eventually wear out through continual usage, this theory also proposes that internal and external stresses (which include the accumulation of harmful byproducts) aggravate the wear-and-tear process. Then as the cells grow older, they are less able to repair or replace damaged components, and so they die. What we know about the way aging takes place in the heart and skeletal muscles, and in all the nerve cells, including those of the brain, seems to support this theory. The cells involved in these organs do not divide and cannot, therefore, replace themselves after they have been injured or destroyed.

The Autoimmune Theory

Our bodies' immune systems were designed to repel such harmful substances as viruses, bacteria, and foreign proteins. With age, this system may become "confused," so that it cannot distinguish elements of its own host body, such as its own proteins, and it attacks itself. This explanation is another one that explains *what* happens, but not *how*.

As we said in our introduction to this awesome list of theories, the truth about how people age probably lies in some combination of these explanations. Rockstein and Sussman (1979) suggest, for example, that genetic programming may determine an outside limit for the length of human life. Within this genetic program, wear and tear takes place; mutations occur in some cells; other cells are damaged by cross linkage or free radicals, or both; and a self-attacking autoimmune system develops. All these factors play their separate though interconnected roles in the aging process.

MENTAL HEALTH

Most old people, like most people of any age, are emotionally healthy. As such, they generally want to participate actively in life, to be as self-sufficient as their health and circumstances permit, and to maintain satisfying relationships with other people. Old age can be a time of consummation, of enjoyable productivity, and of consolidation of the abilities and knowledge built up over a lifetime. But the emotional resources of the elderly are often strained by the many crises they must face—loss of health, loss of job, loss of loved ones, and loss of income. Old people expend a great deal of psychic energy in mourning these losses, in adjusting to such changes, and in reorganizing their lives.

Even though most old people are emotionally sound, there is a relatively high incidence of mental illness among the aged, partly because of an increase in depression as a response to multiple life stresses, and partly because of an increase in organic brain disorders.

Despite the need, however, many elderly people do not receive treatment for their emotional problems. Only about 2 percent of persons seen in psychiatric clinics are over 60, and only 4 to 5 percent of those seen in community health centers are over 65 (Butler & Lewis, 1977). There are several reasons for this. Old people who could benefit from some type of psychotherapy may not be aware that the symptoms making them unhappy—such as depression, for example—represent a form of illness that can be treated. They may be proud about solving their own problems and reluctant to admit that they need help. They may be frightened of being mentally ill and feel that seeking help means they are "crazy." They may have mistaken ideas about psychotherapy: One elderly woman, for example, thought that going to a psychiatrist meant going into analysis, a lengthy and costly process, whereas help is often offered on a short-term, limited basis. Many old persons feel that going for help is a waste of time at their age, that they're "too old to change."

Since these attitudes are often shared by other family members, they don't seek help for the old person, either.

Even when people are receptive to—or eager for—help, they don't always receive it. Private treatment is expensive, and low-cost mental health services do not exist in every community. Furthermore, practitioners who do see the elderly are not always sensitive to their problems. Some clinicians dismiss treatable disorders as irreversible senility. Others feel that it is a waste of their time to treat people who are going to die soon, anyway. And others have so much difficulty facing up to their own inevitable aging and death that they cannot deal with elderly clients.

Yet therapy can benefit the elderly. One type is offered at the University of Pennsylvania's Center for Cognitive Therapy. *Cognitive therapy* aims to relieve the depression of elderly people by improving such functions as concentration, attention, and memory; by helping them to see themselves in realistic terms; and by involving them in interesting activities (Ledger, 1978).

Group therapy can be especially helpful to old people, as it offers the chance to share common worries and helps to overcome loneliness (Butler, 1975). As many as 75 percent of patients over age 65 who receive treatment in private mental hospitals improve and return to their own homes within two months (Gibson, 1970; cited in Butler, 1975, p. 479).

MENTAL ILLNESSES COMMON IN LATE ADULTHOOD

Senility

Senility is defined as an irreversible mental and physical deterioration associated with old age. But, as Butler (1975) points out:

[The term] is not a medical diagnosis, but a

I always regret my age because there were so many things I could do and I can't do now. But if there's not much physical satisfaction, there's still a great mental satisfaction.

Frederick the Francophile, 81,
In *The View in Winter*, by Ronald Blythe, p. 147.

wastebasket term for a range of symptoms that, minimally, includes some memory impairment or forgetfulness, difficulty in attention and concentration, decline in general intellectual grasp and ability, and reduction in emotional responsiveness to others [Butler, 1975, p. 232].

This condition is not a necessary result of aging but a reflection of any of a variety of different problems, some based in organic illnesses and others in functional ones.

Senility is far from inevitable. The great majority of old people show no signs at all of mental deterioration for as long as they live (Henig, 1978). Those who do are often suffering from one or more of some 100 physical ailments whose symptoms can mimic senility (Henig, 1978). For example, a person who has just undergone surgery may be disoriented as to time or place, as can someone suffering from poor nutrition or poor health. Infections within the body, undiagnosed diabetes, or other physical problems sometimes cause senilelike symptoms.

Chronic brain syndromes are usually behind what is generally called senility. One common type is Alzheimer's disease, a disorder that causes intellectual impairment in some ½ to 1½ million American adults (U.S. Department of Health, Education, and Welfare, 1979). Characterized by a number of changes in the brain, primarily the degeneration of brain cells, the disease is diagnosed through a variety of physical, neurological, and psychiatric evaluations. Blood tests, brain scans, electroencephalograms (EEGs), and special studies of spinal fluid are sometimes required for diagnosis, along with an assessment of the patient's medical history, mental status, and symptoms.

What are its symptoms? There are a number, which range in severity, including forgetfulness, confusion, irritability, restlessness, agitation, and impairments of judgment, concentration, orientation, and speech. As the disease progresses, the symptoms become more pronounced and disabling.

At present, there is no known way either to prevent or to cure Alzheimer's disease. Drugs can sometimes relieve agitation, lighten depression, or help the sufferer sleep. Proper nourishment and fluid intake are important, and a planned exercise regimen and physical therapy may be beneficial. During the early phases of the disease, the patient can usually be cared for at home, but as it progresses, a nursing home may be indicated.

About 1 out of 2 old people with severe intellectual impairment suffers from this disease. About 1 out of 4 suffers from vascular disorders—either multiple strokes or *cerebral arteriosclerosis*, a hardening of the blood vessels in the brain. Both these conditions cause injury by blocking the flow of oxygen and nutrients to the brain. The other quarter suffer from a variety of other conditions, such as abnormal thyroid function, anemia, brain tumors, and abnormalities in the spinal fluid system (U.S. Department of Health, Education, and Welfare, 1979).Careful diagnosis is important, since some of these other conditions can be treated much more easily than Alzheimer's.

A major problem with elderly people is drug intoxication. With today's expanding arsenal of pharmacological solutions to life's problems and an increasing tendency for people to see a variety of medical specialists, it is not uncommon for an old person to be taking up to a dozen different medications prescribed by several different doctors. Because physicians do not always ask what other medicines a patient is taking, they sometimes prescribe drugs that interact in a harmful way. In addition, because of age-related changes in the metabolism of the body and because an older person may be small and thin, a dosage that would be appropriate

General intellectual decline in old age may be largely a myth. One who disproves the myth is Millicent Fenwick. After a distinguished career in publishing and public service, she entered politics at the age of 59 and was elected to the New Jersey State Assembly. At the age of 64 she was elected to the U.S. Congress, where she has served since 1974. (United Press International)

for a 40-year-old constitutes an overdose for an 80-year-old (Henig, 1979). The side effects sometimes look like senility.

Another major problem in old age is depression. People who are suffering from a variety of more or less disabling aches and pains; who have lost spouses, siblings, friends, and sometimes children; and who feel they have practically no control over their lives are bound to be depressed. And depression can make people disorganized, absentminded, careless, apathetic, unable to concentrate, uninterested in the world around them. Beck (quoted in Ledger, 1978) speaks of a "vicious cycle":

A person slows down a bit because he is depressed; this is "considered a sign of some kind of cerebral impairment. Since he's already depressed, he begins to think his brain is deteriorating. As he believes that, he begins behaving that way even more, and it sends him into a deeper depression." Consequently, the depression becomes masked—"the person more and more is treated as if his brain is deteriorating, and he becomes unhappy and may even commit suicide" [p. 21].

INTELLECTUAL FUNCTIONING IN LATE ADULTHOOD

Leah W., aged 75, was recently taken aback when one of her daughter's friends told her how "alert" she seemed. The elderly woman considered the comment patronizing and gratuitous—as well she might. When we consider that Golda Meir was Premier of Israel in her mid-seventies and William O. Douglas was a Supreme Court Justice in his, and that many other old people lead richly stimulating intellectual lives, often into their nineties, the notion that elderly people who have their wits about them are rare exceptions is outlandish. And yet, this belief—that to be old is to be addled—is pervasive. Recent research supports the contention that "general intellectual decline in old age is largely a myth" (Baltes & Schaie, 1974, p. 35). Many intellectual abilities hold up quite well with age.

INTELLIGENCE TESTING THROUGHOUT THE LIFE SPAN

One element that fuels the argument that intelligence does decline with age is the fact that old people *do* tend to exhibit lower levels of performance on various IQ and Piagetian measures. However, in recognizing this fact, we have to make the distinction between *performance* and *competence*. While the term *competence* refers to a person's underlying ability, this ability may not be reflected in that individual's *performance*, or test score. Given optimal conditions, performance should give us a measure of competence. But conditions are not always optimal, especially in old age, when many factors may operate to depress performance and lead us to underestimate competence. We will discuss some of the individual factors, such as test anxiety, boredom, cautiousness, and self-defeating attitudes, in a following section. We also have to take into account the method of data collection—cross-sectional, longitudinal, or sequential—and the particular test used. These factors, too, influence the measurement of performance and the resulting conclusions about competence.

Cross-Sectional Testing

Early studies on intellectual functioning in the elderly pointed to mental deterioration with age. These surveys were cross-sectional: They looked at age differences in IQ test performances among groups of subjects of different ages. Researchers concluded that intelligence increased through childhood, peaked in adolescence or very early adulthood, and then declined (Doppelt & Wallace, 1955; Jones & Conrad, 1933; Miles & Miles, 1932; Willoughby, 1927). But as we have pointed out in our discussion of cross-sectional and longitudinal studies, cross-sectional studies which involve one-shot testing of different age groups often confound age and cohort effect. Societal influences such as war, economic depression, and trends in education may influence performance. People born more recently may have received a better education and may perform better on tests for this reason, not because of their age.

Another problem with the early tests is that they contained many different types of questions, combining both verbal and performance items, which show differential trends across the life span. Only by isolating the different types of abilities and by repeatedly testing one or more people can we get information about their development throughout the life cycle. For example, the different abilities comprised by fluid and crystallized intelligence peak at different ages, as indicated earlier.

Longitudinal Testing

Longitudinal studies do not reveal a marked decline in intelligence after early adulthood, as the cross-sectional studies did. Owens (1966) tested people at an average age of 50 and again at 61 on the army Alpha test, which the subjects had first taken as college freshmen in 1919. Scores did *not* decline. They *increased* substantially over the years between 1919 and 1950. From 1950 to 1961, the scores remained quite stable, showing no decrease from the ages of 50 to 61. Most of the earlier increase had been in age-related learning abilities:

A large part of the increase seen in most of the longitudinal studies was traced directly to age-correlated increases in vocabulary, verbal ability, and general information. These factors, which operate to the advantage of the same individual as he grows older, actually operate to the disadvantage of older age groups in the cross-section studies [Riley et al., 1968, p. 257].

Of course, longitudinal testing also has its methodological problems. People may be-

If you are smart and manage to stay healthy, you'll also stay smart, although it may take you longer to demonstrate that fact at sixty-five than it did at twenty-five, and the print in which the questions are written may need to be larger.

Ward Edwards
quoted in *A Good Age*, by Alex Comfort, p. 183.

come sophisticated in taking the tests and may do better on successive tests, masking any downward changes that might be a result of age. The people who are lost to the experiment through death, disappearance, or some other reason may constitute a special segment of the population, making the final sample skewed in favor of people at upper levels of intelligence. (There may, for example, be a correlation between intelligence and physical health.)

Cross-Sequential Testing
Schaie and Strother (1968) tried to overcome the drawbacks of both cross-sectional and longitudinal intelligence testing by combining the two methods in what they call the *cross-sequential method*. They repeatedly tested individuals in a cross-sectional sample. Then they analyzed the test scores for different abilities: verbal meaning (understanding ideas expressed in words); space (thinking about objects in two or three dimensions); reasoning (solving logical problems); number (working with figures and solving simple quantitative problems); and word fluency (writing down previously learned verbal material). They found significant cross-sectional age changes for all variables, but longitudinal age changes only for those where the speed of response was important. Age changes over time within a given individual seem much smaller than the differences between cohorts, and these differences may result from changes in environmental opportunities and/or from

genetic changes in the species. More recent studies (Schaie & Labouvie-Vief, 1974) show similar results.

PIAGETIAN ABILITIES
According to research on various Piagetian measures of cognitive functioning (virtually all of which is cross-sectional in design), elderly people do not perform as well as younger adults. This is an important finding in terms of Piaget's theories, since he has implied that the formal operations stage is the apex of thought, is attained at adolescence, and will be maintained throughout life (Piaget & Inhelder, 1969). If elderly people do less well than adolescents and young adults, this theory would be refuted, or at least modified.

Papalia (1972) studied cognitive functioning in adulthood and old age. She tested subjects, from the age of 6 to over 65, on four types of conservation ability—number, substance, weight, and volume. As a group, the over-65 subjects performed less well than the younger adults did on substance, weight, and volume. *All* subjects aged 11 and over conserved number. A structural similarity in thought processes between children and old people seems to be given some support by the responses of the nonconserving elderly in this experiment, who often said, as children do, "It's more now because it's larger."

Other studies have also found lower levels of conservation performance in old people, as compared with young and middle-aged adults (Rubin, Attewell, Tierney, & Tumolo, 1973; Sanders, Laurendeau, & Bergeron, 1966). And institutionalized old people have been found to do significantly less well than noninstitutionalized persons on conservation tasks (Rubin, 1973). This may result from restricted social interactions among the institutionalized persons, as compared with those who live in the community; or it may be related to the reasons for the institutionalization in the first place. (Perhaps people who do not reason as cogently are more likely to be placed in institutions.)

Elderly people appear to be more egocentric than younger adults (Bielby & Papalia, 1975; Rubin et al., 1973; Looft & Charles, 1971) and to have lower average Kohlbergian moral-stage designations (Bielby & Papalia, 1975). Old people have also been found to approach classification problems differently from middle-aged adults and similarly to children (Denney & Lennon, 1972).

Adults of all ages often respond animistically; that is, they attribute life to inanimate objects. We do not know why this is so. Elderly people who respond this way may *never* have had a "mature," or biological, life concept. Only longitudinal studies can determine this. They may be choosing to use nonbiological criteria in attributing life, based on whimsy or the feeling that all in nature is alive. Some have suggested that they may be returning to immature levels of response, but this explanation does not take into account the high levels of animism throughout the adult years (Sheehan & Papalia, 1974).

These studies raise a number of questions. We don't know why, for example, children and old people tend to group objects in a complementary way (according to a relation between them, such as sand and pail) rather than according to similarity (pail and glass, both of which are containers). Is it because they are not able to see similarities? Or is it because, at their ages and in their lifestyles, a complementary relationship seems to make more sense?

Because all the Piagetian studies so far have been cross-sectional, we do not know whether people who are old today ever possessed the abilities in question. We need longitudinal and sequential analyses to deter-

mine that old people did have these abilities when they were young before we can say that they have lost them because of age. If it turns out that these cognitive abilities are indeed lost with age, then we have to look for reasons. So far, attempts to explain why certain subjects do poorly on the Piagetian tasks have yielded inconsistent results. For example, there is a positive correlation in some studies between ability and educational level, but not in others. There is a great need for more and different kinds of research before any conclusions can be drawn about how age affects the Piagetian abilities.

INFLUENCES ON TEST PERFORMANCE IN LATER LIFE

If the findings of those studies that show some decline with age in intellectual competence (most of which are cross-sectional in design) are valid, there are a number of possible reasons that could explain the poorer showings of older people. We set forth these reasons below, but note that the phenomenon they seek to explain may be nothing more than an artifact of testing methods.

Neurological Deterioration

Hooper, Fitzgerald, and Papalia (1971) suggest that the brain, along with the rest of the body, exhibits a slowdown with aging. Old people's poorer showings on tests of fluid intelligence are pointed out to bolster this theory.

Physical Limitations

Because of old people's diminished capacities to see and hear, they often have difficulty perceiving instructions or executing a task. Execution is also affected by their poorer powers of coordination and agility.

Physiological Factors

People with relatively low blood pressure, with a lesser incidence of systemic disease, and with fewer negative neurophysiological indicators all do better on intelligence tests. So do adults who engage in physical fitness exercises (Schaie & Gribbin, 1975). The performances of old people who do not fit these categories are poorer. Furthermore, pretest fatigue significantly suppresses the intellectual performance of old people and makes their performances differ most markedly from those of younger persons (Furry & Baltes, 1973).

Speed
Elderly subjects perform least well on tests with a speed requirement. When tested under "power" conditions—in which they are allowed as much time as they need—they do better than when they are timed (Bromley, 1974; Horn & Cattell, 1966). Some abilities seem to be more affected than others by the emphasis on speed. If all the physical and psychological processes of the body slow down with age, as Birren (1974) maintains, this would explain old people's poor showings on timed tests. We then need to ask whether speed is a required characteristic of what we call intelligence, or whether our culture arbitrarily places too much emphasis on its importance.

Test Anxiety
Fear and lack of familiarity in the testing situation may influence performance (Schaie & Gribbin, 1975). For example, old people who have never seen a machine-scored answer sheet often become confused as they try to follow the instructions, focus their eyes on innumerable rows of identical parallel lines, and then struggle to find the right pair of lines to mark and actually make their marks in the correct place.

Says Krauss (1976), who has devised new tests using several styles of playing cards and requiring practically no writing:

To assume that test performance of any individual who is trying to cope with the mechanics of test taking although not familiar with the routine testing of the academic world can be compared to that of a college-age or young adult individual is simply not reasonable [p. 5].

When old people know they are being timed, their anxiety heightens, since they are usually well aware that it takes them longer to do things now than it used to. Furthermore, as elderly persons grapple with the mechanics of taking the test and finishing within the time limit, they often become nervous at the thought that everyone else in the room knows how much trouble they are having. Their self-consciousness makes them even more anxious.

Inappropriateness of Tasks
Intelligence tests were originally developed to predict how well children would do in school. They do predict academic performance quite well, from elementary school through college. Yet, as Krauss (1976) very sensibly points out, elderly people do not usually aspire to become full-time college students. So what are we measuring when we give old people tests that were "developed for use with a young population, standardized on a young population, and validated for a young population" (p. 1)?

While intellectual development during childhood and adolescence usually involves acquiring new skills and abilities, intellectual functioning in adulthood demands applying these abilities to life situations that have social consequences (Schaie, 1976). Adults, says Schaie, demonstrate their intelligence by the degree of competence they show in coping with the problems of everyday life. First, they assess a situation by getting the right information, next they take some kind of action to achieve their goals, and then they evaluate the degree to which their action has been successful, so that they can apply what they have learned to the future.

To measure intellectual functioning in adulthood, therefore, we should devise tests that measure people's abilities to deal with the kinds of situations they are likely to encounter. How, for example, could we predict an elderly person's ability to balance a checkbook, read a railroad timetable, or make informed decisions about one's own medical problems? Schaie (1976) emphasizes the need to develop meaningful test tasks to predict competence in these and other real-life situations.

Cautiousness

Old people are consistently more cautious than the young. They avoid taking any course of action if this is a permissible alternative; but when risk-taking is required, they plunge ahead (Botwinick, 1966). They may take fewer risks because they are afraid of being embarrassed. Perhaps instructions need to be worded differently for older test-takers, so that they are forced to take risks.

Self-Defeating Attitudes

Carey (1958) found that old people, especially women, have deprecatory attitudes about their own abilities to solve problems. They do not expect to do well and thus may enact their own self-fulfilling prophecies. While these negative attitudes have nothing to do with the task at hand, they inhibit people from doing as well as they could.

Lack of Continued Intellectual Activity

Blum and Jarvik (1974) tested a group of people in their eighties who had been tested twenty years earlier. They were divided by educational level ("higher" were those who had entered high school, and "lower" were those who had not gone beyond elementary school) and by ability levels, based on vocabulary test scores. Both higher initial ability and higher levels of education were related to intellectual performance late in life, perhaps because the people at the higher levels

remained more intellectually active. Social isolation mitigates against intellectual ability and is considered by Denney and Lennon (1972) to hold people back by not granting them the opportunity to interact as much with others or to extend themselves intellectually.

Terminal Drop

Death seems to send its harbinger in the form of lessened intellectual ability. By testing people, retesting after a period of time, and comparing the initial scores of those who were retested with those of people who had died in the meantime or refused to be retested, researchers have learned of the phenomenon known as *terminal drop*, a sudden drop in intellectual performance shortly before death (Riegel & Riegel, 1972; Reimanis & Green, 1971; Jarvik, 1962).

Terminal drop is not necessarily a function of age, since it is also seen in younger subjects. The poor showings of old people in cross-sectional studies may reflect actuarial reality: More old people than young are likely to die in the near future, and more old people are, therefore, exhibiting terminal drop.

The concept of terminal drop has a very practical use. If it is possible to predict a person's nearness to death through a battery of simple tests, it may also be possible to institute measures that could change that prediction. As Botwinick, West, and Storandt (1978) point out, "Such a battery might one day be useful as part of routine biomedical assessments of the elderly patient. Just as a measurement of high blood pressure, for example, puts the physician on the alert, so might a behavioral indicator" (p. 759). After noting low scores on such a battery, a doctor might recommend preventive or remedial medical care, or an individual might decide to make changes in his or her lifestyle.

There are several simple tests—short, easy to give, and easy to take—that have recently been found to predict closeness to death. Botwinick and his associates (1978) administered a battery of such tests to 380 healthy men and women, aged 60 to 89, who were all living on their own at the time of testing. Within five years after taking the tests, eighty-three of these people died. By comparing their test scores with those of the survivors, the researchers identified several tests that, in combination with each other, offered clues to imminent death.

Among the most accurate predictors were two tests of verbal skills (vocabulary, and the identification of similarities between words) and one psychomotor test, the Digit Symbol task, which times people on their ability to decode numbers that are associated with geometric figures. (For example, the digit "3" might be coded by the symbol "E." The subject has to hold one element in short-term memory while hunting for the other. This test is responsive to the general slowing down with advancing age and also to the decline in short-term memory.) There were also two effective personality tests. One, which identified depression, confirmed earlier findings that depressed people are closer to death. Another, which assessed the degree of control people feel they have over their lives, found that those who felt they had less control were more likely to die. One surprisingly simple test asked people to rate themselves on health, on a scale of 1 to 10. This self-rating differentiated the two groups better than did the detailed physicians' reports. Perhaps each of us has a finer tuned sense of our own state of health than we realize.

CAN THE INTELLECTUAL PERFORMANCE OF THE ELDERLY BE IMPROVED THROUGH TRAINING?

In keeping with the distinction we pointed out between performance and competence, several researchers have looked into the possibility of raising old people's performance levels on intelligence tests. These investigators have tried a number of different techniques, which include trying to decrease anxiety over taking tests, teaching people how to solve problems more effectively, and encouraging them to analyze their own actions.

Crovitz (1966), for example, found that the elderly were less likely to put into words the correct basis for sorting cards in a test of visual discrimination. When elderly subjects were trained to ask themselves during the test, "How did I sort these cards?" they did much better than untrained subjects. Meichenbaum (1974) suggests that the elderly can be trained to break down the processes involved in problem solving into separate components. Poor problem solvers can be taught to talk to themselves, either silently or out loud, and can thus improve their abilities to organize information, generate alternative solutions, and distinguish relevant and irrelevant information.

Training studies have focused on a variety of tasks, including Piagetian conservation tasks (Hornblum & Overton, 1976) and figural relations, considered an aspect of fluid intelligence (Plemons, Willis, & Baltes, 1977). In tests of figural relations, the testee is asked to identify relationships between figures in a pattern and to produce a missing element.

Plemons and her colleagues (1977) trained fifteen people between the ages of 59 and 85 in this ability and then compared them with an untrained control group. Six months after the initial test, a posttest revealed that the trained group had improved their performance on tasks that were similar to the one they had been trained on, but not on tasks that were considerably different. The fact that significant improvement did take place led these researchers to conclude that it is easier to improve intellectual performance in old age than people had previously thought. This study is particularly interesting when we look at intelligence from a theoretical point of view. Since fluid intelligence is not supposed to be related to environmental factors (see page 412), it shouldn't be "trainable." And yet these results indicate that it is.

LEARNING AND MEMORY
IN LATE ADULTHOOD

"I can't remember whether or not I already put the sugar in that cake," says Pauline B., at age 73 a professional caterer. "I guess I really am getting old if I'm this forgetful." Yet Pauline remembers the telephone numbers of a wide circle of friends, relatives, and customers; she never forgets an appointment and keeps most of her recipes in her head. Is her memory really failing—or is she having trouble concentrating because she is distracted by worries about her health? Failing memory is a traditional sign of aging. Yet, in the maintenance of memory as in other capabilities, old people vary enormously.

Memory is usually studied and discussed in conjunction with learning, since it is hard to separate the two. One must first learn something in order to remember it. Welford (1958; cited in Inglis et al., 1968) has described a sequence of phases in the learning-memory continuum: perception, short-term storage, evolution of a durable trace, endurance of such a trace, recognition, recall or retrieval, and the use of recalled material. Changes with age seem to affect several of these phases.

Perception is vital. If poor sight or hearing prevents someone from perceiving information correctly, she or he will not be able to store it in the mind. *Short-term storage*, or *short-term memory*, deals with the initial reception of material and is thought to be temporary, lasting anywhere from thirty seconds to fifteen minutes. If information is fed in too rapidly, some will fail to register or will be wiped out by subsequent information. Most recent memory research has been on short-term memory and seems to show it to be more efficient in young people than in older ones. Most of this research, though, is cross-sectional. Welford's "evolution of a durable trace" and "endurance of such a trace" both

refer to *long-term memory*. When information passes from short-term into long-term storage, it is thought to alter the operation or structure of the brain permanently.

Older people are able to learn new skills and information, but they need more time for the learning than do younger people. They learn best when material is presented slowly, at length, and over a longer period of time with intervals in between, rather than in concentrated form (Chown, 1972). Their ability to learn depends largely on the nature of the task, on how it relates to previous experiences, and on the method of training. Older people cannot acquire as much speed in complex rhythmical tasks or in those that require sensorimotor coordination. It is particularly hard for them to learn new skills that involve unlearning deeply ingrained habits. For example, people who already know how to touch-type on a regular typewriter have more difficulty learning how to type on a braille typewriter than do those who never learned to type at all (Chown, 1972). Old people may find it hard to learn from lectures in which material is presented quickly; they do much better when they have some control over the pace of their learning.

Inglis, Ankus, and Sykes (1968) suggest that there may be a loss of efficiency in short-term memory storage that accounts for the slower learning of older people. They studied learning and short-term memory in 240 subjects between the ages of 5 and 70. In one learning task they found an increase in accuracy between the ages of 5 and 10, which they considered a function of maturation, and then they found that there was no change between the ages of 11 and 70. In another task, which involved material that had presumably been in short-term storage, they found an increase in accuracy from 5 to 10 years, a plateau or slight increase between 11 and 30, and then a decrease from 30 to 70.

An important aspect of memory is the way items are organized in the mind when they are first learned. Hultsch (1971) feels that older people experience some deficit in organizing information. He found that the more amenable material is to being organized, the more trouble older people, as compared with younger ones, have in recalling it. He also found that old people who had scored low in verbal facility showed decrements with age when asked to recall a group of words; but when they were instructed to recall them alphabetically, they did just as well as younger subjects. Apparently they had problems organizing the material for themselves, but they could respond when presented with an organizational scheme—in this case, alphabetizing.

Another reason for memory loss with age may be a decrease in the ability to retrieve information from storage, rather than any problem in the storage system itself. In one experiment, old people had some trouble *recalling* items they had learned, but they did just as well as younger people in *recognizing* the items (Hultsch, 1971). In other words, if asked a question, they might have difficulty in coming up with the right answer themselves; but if presented with a multiple-choice problem, they could recognize the correct answer.

The general slowness of the elderly person's responses is a critical factor in learning and memory. Anders, Fozard, and Lillyquist (1972) asked people in three different age groups (19 to 21, 33 to 43, and 58 to 85) to memorize from one to seven items. The subjects were then asked whether a certain item had been in the list. All the groups made very few mistakes, indicating that they were equally successful at registering and storing the information. But while the old people were able to retrieve the information as *accurately* as the young and middle aged, they could not do so as *quickly*. It took them longer to respond, for any of a number of possible reasons: It seems to have taken them longer to search their memory, to make a decision, and then to express that decision. The youngest group performed twice as fast as either the middle-aged or old group, and the oldest performed slowest of all. Since it takes old people longer to retrieve information from

memory, they are at a disadvantage: They have more time in which forgetting can occur. This can happen when the amount of information taken in exceeds the span of immediate memory.

Older people often become very distressed by their inability to remember a variety of everyday things, feeling that they have begun a downward slide into mental deterioration. Yet they can compensate for some of their memory problems by resorting to a number of different memory-nudging techniques. The man who always kept his schedules in his head may now turn to writing them down in an engagement calendar; the woman who takes several different medicines may take out each day's quota and put them in a place where she is sure to see them throughout the day; a daily "to do" list may come in handy. Busy executives often resort to such devices; there is no reason why they cannot be just as helpful to the elderly.

IMPLICATIONS OF RESEARCH

It is impossible to draw any definitive conclusions about intellectual functioning in old age—whether the apparent deficit in functioning is only an artifact of measurement or environment; or, if it is actual, what causes it. We do know that old people are no more homogeneous than young ones and that in fact they may be more heterogeneous. On many studies, the elderly show more variability than do younger people. We also know that many people continue to function well, far into old age. For those who don't, we have some clues about why their performance may not be a true measure of their competence.

If, as current thought is leaning more and more, intellectual decline in old age is largely a myth, then we as a society are wasting a precious resource—the potential contributions of a growing portion of our population.

Many of our elderly are ignoring their years of learning and experience and fading into the background, even though they are able to participate actively in society. To enable this participation, we need to make significant changes in the areas of adult education, variable retirement ages, and segregation by age (Schaie, 1974)

Adult Education

We need an expansion of adult education programs. While the average person over 65 now has nine completed school years behind him or her, 37 percent of older Americans have been graduated from high school, and 8 percent have finished four or more years of college (U.S. Department of Health, Education, and Welfare, 1978). Education rates have been rising steadily since the present older generation was in school, however, and as those who came after them reach old age, we will see an elderly population that is more inclined toward continuing their education. Adult education programs will, therefore, be even more relevant and necessary in the years to come.

Some adult education programs should be in the nature of job-training sessions to upgrade skills so that unemployed, underemployed, or just plain bored middle-aged and old people can find employment in new occupations. Special attention needs to be paid to the problems of older women who have never worked for pay and now need to, for either financial or emotional reasons. We need to determine which sociocultural skills today's old people have missed and to make provisions to offer these skills.

These programs should be especially designed for older learners. While they may cost more to administer, the eventual results should prove their worth. For example, an employer that funds programs for older trainees can realize a savings, since the increased cost of the special training will be more than offset by the lower job turnover among older workers.

Courses need to be offered in a way that takes into account the physiological changes occurring among old people. Reading matter should be in fairly large print. Audiovisual materials should be clear and easily understandable by students whose physical faculties are not as keen as they once were. Programmed teaching aids should embody repetition and adequate time for responses.

Courses for older learners also have to take into account the psychological needs of this age group. To counter older persons' cautiousness and avoidance of risk situations, rewards could be offered for participation; special discounts could be granted; and pressures could be eliminated by minimizing competition and grades. Trainers can give suggestions for organizing material in the mind, so that it will be remembered better. Some mechanism should be built into courses to allow students to exert some control over the pace of their instruction. It may sometimes be best to hold separate classes for older students.

Older people often become discouraged in training programs because they do not learn as quickly as their younger classmates or as quickly as they learned in their own younger years. Instructors need to be sensitive to these feelings and need to encourage older students to complete their training by assuring them that it may take them a little longer but that when they finish they will be just as capable as their younger colleagues.

One innovative low-cost, on-campus summer program is Elderhostel, which offers college courses specially geared to people over 65. Students sign up for several one- or two-week sessions to study Shakespeare, geography, weaving, early American music, and a variety of other topics. The program, which began at the University of New Hampshire, is being expanded nationwide (*The New York Times*, 1976).

Other exciting new educational efforts include provisions at the City Colleges of Chicago that allow older adults to attend college without having to pay enrollment fees; a comprehensive project in postretirement education offered by four community colleges in cooperation with the University of Michigan–Wayne State University Institute of Gerontology; and Program 65 at Ohio State University, which lets students over age 65 audit courses free of charge. One 93-year-old in this last program is studying the American presidency; his life has spanned seventeen administrations (News-CASE, 1976).

WORK AND RETIREMENT

A 72-year-old furniture salesman loses his job because of the death of his employer, and he gets three offers of employment, one of which he takes. A 65-year-old woman works day and night as a practical nurse helping new parents take care of their infants. An 81-year-old physician is the only one in his community to continue to make house calls.

In 1975, the most recent year for which we have statistics, more than 3 million older people, or some 21.7 percent of men over 65 and 8.3 percent of women, were in the labor force or actively seeking work (NCOA, 1978). This represents a great decrease from 1900, when two-thirds of all men over 65 were in the work force (U.S. Department of Health, Education, and Welfare, 1978). By 1960, only about 1 out of 3 men and 1 out of 10 women over 65 were working, and by 1990, only 17 percent of older men and 7.5 percent of women are expected to be working (*Changing Times*, 1978). During World War II, the percentage of older workers rose, indicating that people this age can work when they are needed and wanted. Well-educated men in professional or managerial positions stay on the job longer. In 1960, more than half of college graduates over age 65 were working,

compared to less than 1 in 4 of those with a fourth-grade education or less (Back, 1969). However, people generally *want* to retire. Most retirements are voluntary.

Since women are more likely to be working outside the home now than they were earlier in the century, their increased entry into the labor force balances the present tendency toward earlier retirement.

Retirement is a major transition point. In Holmes and Rahe's Social Readjustment Rating Scale (1967) (see page 410), retirement comes tenth in a list of forty-three life crises, after such events as the death of a close family member, divorce, going to jail, and one's own illness.

Often, however, retirement is less stressful than a person's worries about it ahead of time. Haynes, McMichael, and Kupper (1974) looked at mortality patterns among men working in the rubber industry and found higher mortality rates among 60-year-olds and 64-year-olds. The researchers cannot explain the high death rates of 60-year-old men, but they attribute the high rate among 64-year-olds to stress connected with the fact that they are only one year away from retirement. Retirement *per se* does not lead to a higher probability of death.

Some people, of course, eagerly await retirement while others dread it. The way workers react to giving up their jobs depends on how much they like their work, how much they need the money, whether they themselves made the decision to stop work or were forced to retire, whether they had planned ahead for this change in their work lives, what other interests they have, and a host of other factors. Generally, the higher the level of education and the higher the job status, the less eager a worker is to retire. People who work at tedious, low-level jobs which require hard physical labor are often eager to stop working; and when they do stop, their health is apt to improve (Butler & Lewis, 1977; Shanas et al., 1968).

In a recent national survey (Sandoz, 1976) a majority (59 percent) of 1500 physicians, who specialize in treating older patients, stated that emotional factors—such as feelings of inadequacy and uselessness—are the most important cause of declining health among retired people. Only 13 percent named the aging process itself, while 32 percent cited such changes in lifestyle as inactivity or irregular habits. These doctors found that the greatest complaint of retirees is depression, which 6 out of 10 physicians attribute to idleness and the inability to use free time, 2 out of 10 lay at the door of financial difficulties, and almost 2 out of 10 attribute to domestic problems.

Retirement can put a strain on a marriage as husband and wife find themselves together twenty-four hours a day. The wife may find it difficult to adjust to having her husband "under foot" all day, interfering with the schedule she has worked out for herself. The husband is likely to be restless and irritable until he finds some outlet for his energies. Says a psychiatric social worker who presents a workshop for retired couples:

It's ironic. We pay attention to retirement in financial terms, making ourselves as economically secure as possible, but we rarely pay attention to how we are going to survive as people. We don't get ready for the emotional backlash [Delatiner, 1980, p. 8 L.I.].

WOMEN AND RETIREMENT

Up to now, retirement has generally had a more significant impact on a man's life than on a woman's, since men have taken much more of their self-concept from their work roles than women have. In the 1976 Sandoz survey, this group of geriatric physicians noted that career-oriented men suffer rapid decline after retirement four times more often than career-oriented women. However, 53 percent of these doctors found that retired working women have a wider variety of problems than homemakers of the same age (Sandoz, 1976).

There has been surprisingly little research on the effects of retirement on women. Now, however, as more human-relations professionals recognize the central force that work represents in the lives of many women, it is likely that a closer look will be taken at women's reactions to this major transition in their lives.

In one study of 2398 women aged 65 and over, Jaslow (1976) compared retired women (54.1 percent), working women (6.3 percent), and women who had never worked (39.6 percent). Working women had the highest morale, the most positive feelings about their health, were in the best financial position, and were considerably younger than the women in the other groups. The relationship between work and morale was affected by the women's ages, health, and income. Among women whose income was above $5000 per year, those who had retired had higher morale than those who continued to work. Women who had never worked outside the home had the lowest morale of the three groups.

In another study, twenty-five women who had recently retired from jobs at a university were interviewed, along with their husbands (Szinovacz, 1978). Most of the women had held service, secretarial, or maintenance jobs; only 8 percent had been in professional or semiprofessional positions. For these women, retirement tended to be an important life transition, but not a critical one. Less than 1 in 3 used their time to do more household chores, and, in fact, several expressed feelings that they were having trouble "settling down" to them. They found that work in the house was not a satisfactory replacement for the gratifications of work outside the home and the social contacts that went along with it.

In the postretirement years, many people relish the first long stretches of leisure time they've had since childhood and enjoy exploring new interests they never had time for before. (Alon Reininger/Leo De Wys, Inc.)

Most of these couples did not experience serious marital problems upon the wives' retirement, and most enjoyed their increased leisure time together.

MAKING RETIREMENT A POSITIVE EXPERIENCE

The years after retirement are often happy ones. In a newspaper survey of 444 Long Islanders, 30 percent of the respondents who were over the age of 65 said that the years after retirement were the best ones of their lives (*Newsday*, 1977). People in this age group mentioned this period more often than any other time of life.

There is no feeling in life thus far quite like those first days and weeks when we wakened to realize that Bob didn't have to be anywhere at nine o'clock. It was October, and we revelled especially in things that happened on weekday mornings. Walking on the beach and around the marshes at low tide, contemplating snowy egrets and eider ducks, gathering armfuls of the last goldenrod, watching gulls soar over the white-caps and blue, blue water offshore. Undeniably all of this could have been equally fine on any Saturday or Sunday, but it has a very particular charm when it occurs on Monday morning at ten and when you are just retired.

Jean and Robert Hersey, *These Rich Years—A Journal of Retirement* (New York: Charles Scribner's Sons, 1969), p. 8.

In the postretirement years, many people relish the first long stretches of leisure time they've had since childhood, enjoy exploring new interests they never had time for before, and like spending time with family and friends. What can individuals and society do to allow more people to enjoy this time of life? Let us look at some of the steps we can take.

Planning for Retirement

Those people who can anticipate what their lives will be like after they stop working and who actively plan ahead tend to have the richest postretirement lives. To encourage more people to do this, many community organizations have begun offering workshops for people in their middle years, new books on this topic are appearing regularly, and a growing number of companies are instituting programs for employees. Ossofsky (1979) cites research that confirms that:

Pre-retirement programs can improve produc-tivity and morale by enabling employees to make fact-based decisions about when to retire, rather than staying on out of fear of retirement and the unknown [p. 63].

An effective planning program, says Os-sofsky, will help workers to recognize their own responsibilities in providing for their retirement, to realize how much control they have over their future and what they can do now (such as buying a house or choosing the best insurance policy), to know what they have to do to provide financial security (in addition to any contributions to be made from government or their employers), and to be emotionally and physically prepared.

One program, developed by the National Council on the Aging (1979) in cooperation with a number of corporations and unions, helps workers plan for their retirement by raising issues around the topics of lifestyle and financial planning, health, interpersonal relations, living arrangements, new careers, and community services.

Some of the developmental crises throughout life, including retirement, could be

alleviated if we planned our entire adult lives differently. Right now, young adults plunge themselves into pursuing an education and then into building a career. Middle-aged adults expend most of their energies earning money. Old people are hard put to fill their time with leisure activities. If we wove work, leisure, and study into our lives in a more balanced way at all ages, young adults would feel less pressure to establish themselves early, middle-aged people would feel fewer burdens of supporting both younger and older generations, and old people would be more stimulated and more useful.

Using Leisure Time Well

Some people enjoy being able to sleep late, being free to go out fishing, take in an afternoon movie, or visit with family and friends. Others, however, find more gratifica-tion from using the fruits of their professional and personal experiences in a more struc-tured way. For people in this second category and for those who can benefit from their acquired wisdom, a number of programs have sprung up to tap this valuable resource. The Retired Volunteer Service Corps at the Univer-sity of Maryland has enlisted forty-seven retired men and women to tutor, counsel, and offer career advice to undergraduates (*The New York Times*, 1979). Project ASSERT (Ac-tivity to Support the Strengthening of Educa-tion through Retired Technicians) at Ohio State University has enlisted retired blue-col-lar workers in the technical fields of drafting, automotive repair, electronics, and computer technology. In New York City and elsewhere retired business people share their experi-ence with budding entrepreneurs.

Doing Away with Compulsory Retirement

In view of a body of research that shows employees from 65 to 70 years of age, and sometimes older, performing as well as younger workers in jobs that don't demand heavy physical labor, a growing chorus is calling for an end to arbitrary retirement ages

(Shapiro, 1977). The American Medical Association, for example, long opposed mandatory retirement at 65 on the grounds that people's work opportunities affect their health.

People age differently and have different spans of productivity. Employers should devise new ways to appraise the best ages for people to retire, perhaps by examination, as is already done for pilots and certain other professions. When people do retire, they should receive some preparation for this new phase of their lives and should, of course, have financial security.

In April 1978, the United States Congress outlawed some mandatory retirement policies and severely limited others in an amendment to the Age Discrimination in Employment Act of 1967. Most nonmilitary federal workers cannot now be forced to retire at any age, and most other public and private workers cannot be made to retire before they turn 70. There are a few exceptions: air-traffic controllers, fire fighters, some law-enforcement workers, executives entitled to certain high pensions, and people who work for companies that have fewer than twenty employees.

Most people will probably continue to retire at or before age 65 if they can afford it, but those who wish to keep working will be helped by this amendment, and also by recent changes in the Social Security laws. These changes will reward those older workers who postpone retirement: For every year workers stay on the job past the age of 65,

they will receive a 1 percent increase in benefits when they do retire. In 1982, this yearly increase will go to 3 percent.

Another change in the Social Security regulations partly redresses another inadequacy in the law. Until now, these laws had been contributing to the idleness of many able-bodied people by their requirement that persons aged 65 to 72 who earn money by working have to pay the government back one dollar for every two they earn, over a certain amount. As a result, many older workers have stopped working, cut back their hours more than they would have liked to, or worked far below their potential level. Such regulations have penalized older people holding paid employment, while not affecting retired millionaires. (Once a person becomes eligible for Social Security payments, she or he does not have to forfeit a penny of it even if the individual is enormously wealthy.)

A modest reform has been effected in this provision, which in 1982 will lower from age 72 to 70 the point at which a worker is allowed to earn any amount of money and still collect full Social Security benefits. We need to continue to make reforms in laws which will permit people to extend their working lives to the limits they are capable of and interested in.

SUMMARY

1 Most stereotypes of the elderly are negative, as are the attitudes of other age groups to them. Ageism refers to prejudice against the elderly.   **2** Senescence, the period of the life span when one grows old, begins at different ages for different people; the designation of age 65 as the beginning of old age is arbitrary. The number and proportion of old people in our society today is greater than ever before.   **3** Most elderly persons are reasonably healthy, but the rate of illness and days hospitalized is higher for the elderly than for other age groups. Although many elderly have one or more chronic conditions, most are not severely hampered by them.   **4** Life expectancy has increased markedly from the turn of this century. Children born in 1975 can expect to live for 77.2

years if they are white females, 69.4 years if they are white males, 72.3 years if they are nonwhite females, and 63.6 years if they are nonwhite males. The major causes of death are heart disease, cancer, and stroke.   **5**   Sensory and perceptual abilities decline during old age, with vast individual difference in the timing and extent of decline. Anatomical and physical decline are common, and there is a general slowing down with advancing age.   **6**   Aging is a complex process influenced by heredity, nutrition, disease, and other factors related to socioeconomic status. No theory of aging is universally accepted; possible causes of aging include alterations in the structure of DNA, errors in cell division, and defects in the immunological system with age. Most of the theories of aging fall into one of two categories: aging as a programmed process and aging as the result of accumulated "insults" to the body.   **7**   Even though most elderly are emotionally healthy, there is a relatively high rate of mental illness among them. Problems include depression, "senility," and drug intoxication. Many elderly do not receive adequate care for these problems since they are often (wrongly) assumed to be an inevitable part of aging.   **8**   Cross-sectional studies of intellectual functioning in the elderly indicate mental deterioration with age, as well as lower levels of functioning on Piagetian tasks; longitudinal studies do not show the same marked decline. New data collection techniques (such as the cross-sequential method) have been designed to overcome the shortcomings of cross-sectional and longitudinal techniques.   **9**   Besides mental deterioration and methodological shortcomings, other factors may influence intelligence test results. Such factors include neurological deterioration, physical limitations, physiological factors, speed requirements of tests, test anxiety, boredom and lack of motivation, cautiousness, self-defeating attitudes, inefficient problem-solving techniques, lack of continued intellectual activity, and terminal drop.   **10**   Learning and memory are interrelated, since one must learn something in order to remember it. Studies indicate that old people *can* learn new skills and information, provided it is presented slowly, at length, and over a longer period of time with intervals between exposures. A distinction is made between short- and long-term memory. *Short-term memory* refers to the initial reception of material, a process that seems to be more efficient in young age groups. *Long-term memory* refers to the storage of material, a process that appears to hold up well with age. Memory loss with age may result from an old person's difficulty with organizing material or from a decrease in the ability to retrieve information from memory.   **11**   The notion of intellectual decline in old age may be largely a myth. We need to restructure society to allow the elderly to participate actively. To enable this participation, we must make changes in adult education, retirement policies, and practices of age segregation.

SUGGESTED READINGS

Butler, R. N. *Why survive?* New York: Harper & Row, 1975. An angry book by a noted gerontologist who details the problems of being old in America today. This Pulitzer Prize–winning book offers suggestions on both personal and social levels, gives case histories, and provokes thoughts on major social issues.

Institute of Gerontology. *No longer young: The older woman in America*. Ann Arbor, Michigan: University of Michigan, Wayne State, 1975. A collection of papers on the plight of older women today.

Jones, R. *The other generation: The new power of older people*. New Jersey: Prentice-Hall, 1977. A fascinating account about the impact of the growing number of people over 65 on our society. Jones includes discussions of ageism, the growing militancy of the elderly, and the impact of the changing ratio of workers to nonworkers.

Puner, M. *To the good long life: What we know about aging*. New York: Universe Books, 1974. Popular presentation about recent findings from the fields of psychology, biology, and sociology.

Saul, S. *Aging: An album of people growing old*. New York: Wiley, 1974. An anecdotal series of vignettes by or about older people compiled by a social worker who has done much work in institutions.

Weinstein, G. W. *Life plans: Looking forward to retirement*. New York: Holt, Rinehart and Winston, 1979. A guide for the individual who is thinking about retirement, which raises many of the issues involved, such as deciding whether to move, how to plan one's time, how to manage money matters, and so forth. Offers exercises to help readers clarify their thinking, as well as facts about retirement and suggestions for making the most of these years.

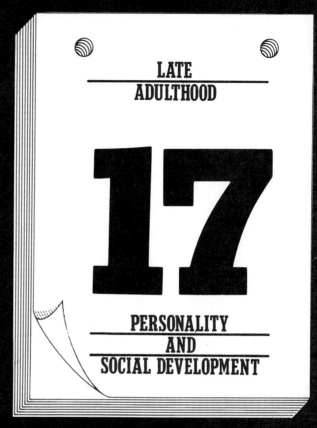

LATE
ADULTHOOD

17

PERSONALITY
AND
SOCIAL DEVELOPMENT

IN THIS CHAPTER
YOU WILL LEARN ABOUT

Prejudices and stereotypes against the
elderly

Factors which contribute to successful
aging and happiness

How physical, social, and emotional
changes come to bear on the daily life of
old people

The importance of family and friends

Patterns of aging among members of
minority groups and other cultures

CHAPTER OVERVIEW

Successful Aging
Theories of Successful Aging

Personality Change in Late Adulthood

Happiness in Late Adulthood
Self-Esteem | Life Satisfaction

Theoretical Perspectives on Aging
*Erikson's Last Stage: Ego Integrity versus
Despair | Peck's Theory of Psychological
Development in Late Adulthood | Bühler's
Theory of Intentionality*

Aging and the Family
*Marriage in Late
Adulthood | Sexuality | Widowhood | Being
Single in Late Adulthood | Family
Relationships | Parenthood | Grandparenthood*

Some Social Issues Related to Aging
*Friendship in Late
Adulthood | Income | Housing | Crime
and the Elderly*

Cross-Cultural Patterns of Aging
*Minority Groups in the United
States | Aging in Other Cultures*

The years beyond age 65 constitute a normal stage of development, during which people can experience growth as well as crisis. But the position of old people in our society brings cries of outrage from people who share this view. Many students of aging in America agree with Estes (1979) when she says that the biggest problems faced by the elderly are the ones we create for them, and that politics and economics affect the status of the aged more than the aging process does.

One problem with the role of the elderly in the United States is that our society is in a transitional stage. A young country, we were founded by people who were young and vigorous themselves, who had left elderly parents and grandparents behind on foreign soil. Life was hard here, and life expectancy was short. We had few elderly to integrate into the life of the nation, and so we built no traditions for doing so. Now the picture is very different. With improvements in sanitation, epidemic control, and medical care, we suddenly have large numbers of old people among us. We are not prepared for them.

Our society does not allow many of our elderly to experience their last years positively. We don't respect old people for their wisdom and experience, but instead dismiss their ideas as outdated and irrelevant. We don't allow them to use their abilities productively, but force them into retirement when they are still eager and able to work. We don't sustain them financially, but allow them to waste away in a state of poverty that crushes the spirit. We accept illness as an inevitable part of old age and consider many pathological conditions irreversible.

Yet old age does not have to be the "low-water mark" of the life cycle. If we as a society resolve to do something about it, we can create an atmosphere that will enable people to live out their final years in dignity,

comfort, and continuing development. As Roscow (1962; cited in McTavish, 1971) has said:

It should be clear that the crucial people in the aging problem are not the old, but the younger age groups, for it is the rest of us who determine the status and position of the older person in the social order [p. 90].

The young and the middle-aged among us determine not only the fate of people who are now old but also our own futures. We perpetuate our youthful stereotypes of the face of old age; we believe them ourselves as we grow older; and we govern our attitudes toward our elders (and eventually toward ourselves) by them.

These attitudes develop very early in childhood and persist throughout the life span. Third-graders already perceive old people in unrealistic extremes—as being either very kind or very mean and as being very lonely, bored, and inactive, and with time hanging heavily on their hands (Hickey, Hickey, & Kalish, 1968). One source for children's views of old people is in the books they read, which tend to carry stereotyped portrayals of the elderly. In one study of nearly 700 books available to children through a local library system, Ansello (cited in Flaste, 1977) found that only 16 percent had any older characters at all and that those which did usually showed them unfavorably. More than 75 percent of the elderly characters had no real function nor position and were most frequently described as "sad" and "poor."

Adolescents and young adults tend to consider old age risky, unpleasant, and without significant positive values (Kastenbaum & Durkee, 1964), thus setting up barriers toward their own positive aging:

Many attitude studies about old people have been conducted in the last 15 years or so. Generally speaking, one could say that the over-all results have shown that the college and adult population (including the elderly themselves) see old people as living in a social climate which is not conducive to feelings of usefulness, adequacy, and security [Hickey, Hickey, & Kalish, 1968, p. 218].

Successful aging *is* possible. Many people do experience the last stage of life positively. Our job as a society is to discover the ingredients of successful aging—and then to reorganize our thinking and our societal structures so that we can foster successful aging for more of us.

SUCCESSFUL AGING

Too many discussions of the elderly focus only on the problems associated with this time of life. These problems are important. It is also important, though, to realize some of the positive developmental characteristics "connected with the unique sense of having lived a long time and having accepted the concept of life as a cycle from birth through death" (Butler & Lewis, 1977, p. 28). Butler and Lewis emphasize the important place aging has in the human life span when they say:

·Old age does have unique developmental work to do. Childhood might be defined as a period of gathering and enlarging strength and experience, whereas a major developmental task in old age is to clarify, deepen, and find use for what one has already attained in a lifetime of learning and adapting. The elderly must teach themselves to conserve their strength and resources when necessary and to adjust in the best sense to those changes and losses that occur as part of the aging experience. The ability of the elderly person to adapt and thrive is contingent on his physical health, his personality, his earlier life experiences, and on the societal supports he receives: adequate finances, shelter, medical care, social roles, recreation, and the like. An important point to emphasize is that, as true for children, adolescents, and the middle-aged, it is imperative that older people continue to develop and change in a flexible manner

I have seen much of the world now, but there is much more, and I want to keep refreshing my mind for as long as I live with new places and new experiences.

I feel much the same way about people. There are those I love dearly and whose welcome could never wear out. There are friends whom I cherish and want to see often; and, of course, friends whom I don't see often — because of distance or other complications— but still cherish.

Rose Fitzgerald Kennedy,
Times to Remember (Garden City, NY: Doubleday & Company, 1974), p. 497.

if health is to be promoted and maintained. Failure of adaptation at any age or under any circumstance can result in physical or emotional illness. Optimal growth and adaptation can occur all along the life cycle when the individual's strengths and potentials are recognized, reinforced, and encouraged by the environment in which he lives [pp. 19–20].

THEORIES OF SUCCESSFUL AGING

There is more than one way to age successfully. Research indicates that people make a variety of healthy adjustments as they grow old, depending on their individual personalities and unique life circumstances. There are two major theories proposed to explain successful aging: the *activity theory* and the *disengagement theory*. Both are insufficient explanations, because each one is dogmatic in trying to characterize successful aging as being of one type only. A relatively new theoretical attempt to explain aging is the theory of *social reconstruction/social break-down*.

Activity Theory

According to the activity theory, the more active old people remain, the more successfully they will age. Ideally, the old person remains as much as possible like a middle-aged person in keeping up as many activities as possible and finding substitutes for those that have been lost through retirement or the deaths of spouse or friends. A person's roles (as worker, spouse, parent, and so on) are the major sources of satisfaction in life, and the greater the role loss (through retirement, widowhood, distance from children, infirmity, etc.), the lower the life satisfaction.

One study that tried to test the assumptions of this theory failed to support the thesis that high activity levels are necessary for successful aging. Lemon, Bengston, and Peterson (1972) categorized three separate types of activity: *informal*, including social interaction with relatives, friends, and neighbors; *formal*, including participation in voluntary organizations; and *solitary*, including reading, watching television, and pursuing some hobbies. They interviewed 411 people, aged 52 to over 75, assessing their degrees of activity and their degree of life satisfaction; they found that activity in and of itself had little relationship to whether people were satisfied with life.

Disengagement Theory

This theory, proposed by Cumming and Henry (1961), was for some time considered the only "right" way to age. It says that aging is characterized by a mutual withdrawl by the old person, who voluntarily cuts down activities and commitments, and by society, which forces retirement and encourages segregation by age. Disengagement is normal, as is the old person's increased preoccupation with the self and decreased emotional investment in others. The decline in social interaction helps old people to maintain their equilibrium and is beneficial both to the individual and to society. Since the old person welcomes this withdrawal and voluntarily contributes to it, morale is high.

The theory of disengagement has generated considerable research over the years, much of which has failed to support its prediction that low morale would accompany high activity and its contention that disengagement is inevitable, universal, and sought by the elderly themselves (Maddox, 1968; Havighurst & Tobin, 1965; Reichard, Livson, & Peterson, 1962).

Critics point to this theory's failure to recognize the fact that disengagement seems to be related less to old age itself and more to the factors associated with aging, such as poor health, widowhood, retirement, and impoverishment. Instead of being an inevitable result of aging, it is influenced by the social environment. For example, when people work (and are, thus, economically engaged), they continue their work-related associations— trade union activities, professional friendships, reading in the field. When they lose or give up their jobs, however, they tend to give up these activities.

One important influence on disengagement seems to be an individual's awareness of his or her closeness to death. Lieberman and Coplan (1970) measured degrees of engagement among eighty old people, and then went back more than two years later to compare the levels of those people who had died in the meantime with those who were still alive. They found that the people who had died had shown signs of disengagement two years before their death, while the survivors had not. These researchers concluded that disengagement is probably a short-lived process, taking about two years rather than the twenty-five or thirty originally proposed.

Those who feel that the facts about old people don't support the disengagement theory contend that it is a rationalization on the part of a society that wants to "shelve" old people and that justifies a lack of attention to their needs by stating that they themselves want to disengage (Hochschild, 1975).

Social Reconstruction Syndrome

Neither the activity nor the disengagement theories of aging fully explain the relationships among social activity, personality, and psychological well-being in old age. Bengston (1973) proposes a new model based on the *social breakdown syndrome* originally proposed by Zusman (1966), in which a person's social environment interacts negatively with his or her self-concept. The individual has a problem with identity, possibly because he, along with others around him, holds unrealistic standards; other people label him as incompetent, or wanting in some way; he accepts the label and learns behavior appropriate to it, in the process forgetting his previous skills; he has now become more dependent and incompetent and feels inadequate.

Kuypers and Bengston (1973) feel that the negative interaction between a person's self-concept and the environment explains many of the problems of aging in our society. To break its vicious cycle, they propose the *social reconstruction syndrome*. How would this work? In three major ways. First, we need to liberate old people from an age-appropriate view of status. The belief that self-worth depends on a person's productivity immediately negates the value of the retired or unemployed person. So education for society at large and counseling for older people are needed to help them adopt more humanitarian values in judging themselves. As Fischer (1977) has said:

The values of our society rest upon a work ethic—an ethic of doing—that gives highest value to people in the prime of their productive years. We should encourage a plurality of ethics in its place—not merely an ethic of doing, but also an ethic of feeling, an ethic of

sharing, an ethic of knowing, an ethic of enduring, and even an ethic of surviving [p. 33].

Second, we have to provide old people with the social services they need to help them cope with life—including housing, transportation, medical care, help with housekeeping. And third, old people need to have more control over their own lives. Bengston (1973) suggests, for example:

. . . an old age home whose personal and decision-making bodies are exclusively comprised of the elderly themselves. While the nursing and social service staff, for example, might be younger people, they are servants of the elderly board of directors, the elderly committee structure, and the elderly administrators [p. 49].

Actual Patterns of Aging

Empirical research, along with everyday observation, shows that there are different styles of both successful and unsuccessful adjustment to old age. Two major studies indicate that the ways in which people adapt to old age seem to depend less on their degree of activity and involvement in life around them than on the personality traits and habits of response that have characterized them throughout their lives.

Reichard, Livson, and Peterson (1962) studied eighty-seven men, aged 55 to 84, half of whom were still working and half of whom had retired. Just over half the subjects—forty-seven—fit rather neatly into one of five patterns of aging, while the others could not be categorized. Three of these patterns were considered successful, in that the individuals who followed them were rated "well-adjusted." These people were effective in overcoming frustrations, resolving conflicts, and achieving socially acceptable satisfactions and achievements. They tended to be happy, sociable, confident, productive, and high in self-esteem.

Of the successful patterns, the largest group comprised those who were judged best-adjusted of all, the "mature." These men enjoyed life, accepted themselves realistically, were basically self-sufficient, and found genuine satisfaction in personal relationships and in activities that reflected well-developed interests. They took old age for granted and made the best of it, without regrets for what had happened in the past and with optimism for the future.

The second successful group was made up of "rocking-chair men," whose generally satisfied state rested on a more passive base. These men welcomed the opportunity to retire, to be free of responsibility, and to indulge their needs for dependency. They were content to rely on others to provide for their material well-being and emotional support.

The third successful group, the "armored," stayed happy by keeping busy. Anxious and fearful about growing old and infirm, they defended themselves against the specter of aging by compulsive activity, clinging to old habits, and tight control over their emotions.

The two unsuccessful patterns of aging in this group characterized people who demonstrated a great deal of hostility. The "angry" men blamed others for keeping them from achieving their life goals, could not reconcile themselves to growing old, were afraid of death, and were especially resentful toward the young. The "self-haters" turned their hostility toward themselves. As they became depressed, pessimistic, and regretful about their past lives, they looked toward death as a release from their present unhappiness.

The Kansas City Study of Adult Life analyzed styles of aging by looking at personality, activity level, and life satisfaction. From intensive interviews with 159 men and women aged 50 to 90, Neugarten, Havighurst, and Tobin (1965) identified four major personality types, which they correlated with varying levels of activity in eleven different social roles (parent, spouse, grandparent, kin-group member, worker, homemaker, citizen, friend, neighbor, club-and-association member, and church member); they then rated people according to their levels of life satisfaction. After analyzing the data for the fifty-nine 70- to 79-year-olds in the study, the researchers came up with eight patterns of aging that fit fifty out of the fifty-nine in this age group.

There were three kinds of people considered to have *integrated personalities*—well-functioning, with complex inner lives, competent egos, intact cognitive abilities, and high levels of life satisfaction. The *reorganizers* were highly active; they had reorganized their lives, substituting new activities for old, and were currently engaged in a wide variety. *Focused* people showed medium levels of activity; they had become selective, currently devoting energy to and gaining satisfaction from one or two roles (like the retired man now preoccupied with his roles of homemaker, parent, and husband). The *disengaged* showed low levels of activity; by personal preference they had withdrawn into a self-contained, contented life.

The *armored-defended personalities* (striving, achievement-oriented, and tightly controlled) fell into two groups. Those in the *holding-on* pattern held on as long as possible to the patterns of middle age; with high or medium activity, they were high in life satisfaction. *Constricted* individuals tried hard to defend themselves against aging by limiting their energies, their social interactions, and their experiences. They were able to achieve high or medium life satisfaction while exhibiting either low or medium activity.

Passive-dependent personalities were of two kinds. The *succorance-seeking* have strong dependency needs; as long as they can lean on one or two other persons, they can maintain high or medium life satisfaction with high or medium activity. *Apathetic* people seemed to have been passive all their lives; doing little, they achieve medium or low life satisfaction.

Finally, the *unintegrated personalities* showed a disorganized pattern of aging. They had gross defects in psychological functioning, loss of control over their emotions, and deterioration in thought processes. They managed to stay in the community, but with low activity and low life satisfaction.

This study shows that activity level is a less important measure of life satisfaction than the impetus behind that activity level, or the personality structure of the individual. People who are very satisfied with life may be very active or quite inactive. The authors conclude:

In normal men and women, there is no sharp discontinuity with age, but instead an increased consistency. Those characteristics that have been central to the personality seem to become even more clearly delineated, and those values the individual has been cherishing become even more salient [Neugarten, Havighurst, & Tobin, 1965; cited in Neugarten, 1968, p. 177].

Maddox's findings (1966) also support this point of view. In longitudinal analyses of people reevaluated at two-year intervals, he found a persistence in lifestyle, rather than a change. This contradicts disengagement theory, which would predict decreased amounts of social involvement over time. In sum, the underlying personality structures and patterns of living that people have developed in their earlier years are still dominant features of their old age.

PERSONALITY CHANGE IN LATE ADULTHOOD

Cross-sectional personality testing has identified a number of personality traits commonly

associated with old age, such as rigidity, restraint, cautiousness, passivity, and concern with self (Riley et al., 1968).

It is possible that some personality characteristics may have survivorship value in old age. Lieberman (1975), for example, talks about the "adaptive paranoia" of old age, and Gutmann (1971) found a pattern of combativeness among very old men in various primitive cultures. A different kind of personality "fit" in old age was described by Albert Einstein (1950) in his autobiographical writing, in which he expressed his feeling that old age was the most becoming time for his particular personality, which tended to be solitary and reflective.

Other personality characteristics that may not show up in a testing situation but that are commonly observed in old people include the desire to leave a legacy, the wish to pass on the fruits of one's experience, an attachment to familiar objects, a new awareness of time and of the life cycle, continued creativity and productivity, and a sense of fulfillment in a life well spent (Butler & Lewis, 1977).

HAPPINESS IN LATE ADULTHOOD

SELF-ESTEEM

The way people regard themselves is the basic factor in their overall happiness and adjustment to life. Self-esteem is developed by a continuous interaction between the individual and the environment, which includes the other people in one's life. As people act in a competent way, they receive feedback from their environment that allows them to define their social roles, personal traits, and work and leisure activities in a meaningful and positive way (Schwartz, 1975).

A major flaw in the quality of life for people in their seventies and older is occa-

Like people in every other age group, old people thrive by demonstrating their competence. (© Joel Gordon 1979)

They don't come to see me just because I take the trouble to look as good as I can. They come because I represent something—courage, stamina, faith, motherhood, who knows? Sometimes they just sit there in stunned silence, amazed that I'm still alive and moving.

Marlene Dietrich, in her seventies quoted in *It Takes a Long Time to Become Young* by Garson Kanin, p. 47.

sioned by the losses that tend to accompany these years, which erode their sense of effective control over their lives—the deaths of loved ones, the loss of work roles, and sensory deprivation caused by losses in physical faculties.

Like people in every other age group, old people thrive by demonstrating their competence. This competence may take many forms. People feel competent when they exert control over their own lives. The more options they have, the more in control they are, and the healthier they will be. In an institution, for example, privacy is important in achieving competence, because people whose privacy is assured have more options (Schwartz, 1975). They can decide when they want to be alone and when they want to be with other people, and they can avoid stressful situations. They have one more way to control their environment. Those who live with and work with old people need to understand how important it is for them to have alternatives that permit as much mastery over the environment as possible.

LIFE SATISFACTION

Toward the end of his life, Samuel G., a civil engineer who worked full-time at his profession until he was 81 when his health began to fail, turned to philosophizing. As he saw his savings dwindle, one of his favorite aphorisms became, "It's better to be healthy and rich

In old age, one becomes more aware of what has, and what has not, been achieved. What one can further do becomes a smaller proportion of what has already been done, and this makes personal life less feverish.

Bertrand Russell
from "Pros and Cons of Reaching Ninety," *The Observer*,
May 13, 1962; reprinted in *The Autobiography of
Bertrand Russell, 1944–1969*, p. 185.

instead of sick and poor." Recent research indicates that many elderly people—not surprisingly—share this view of life.

An increasing amount of research has been devoted to finding relationships between various aspects of the life of an elderly person and the degree of satisfaction that person expresses. In one recent study of 141 working- and lower-class women and men over the age of 60, Markides and Martin (1979) found that health and income are the factors most closely related to life satisfaction.

These influences are critical, say these researchers, because when people feel good and have enough money, they can be more active. And their research also shows that people who are active—who go to church or to the movies, to meetings or museums, on sightseeing excursions or picnics—are happier with their lives than those who tend to stay at home.

Men's satisfaction is more likely to be influenced by their levels of education and income, reflecting cultural differences between the sexes. Income may be more important for men because they may prefer activities that cost more money than those that women enjoy—and also because the double standard requires many men to treat their female companions. Education may be more important to men because of its effect on their past careers, since satisfaction with one's accomplishments in the past often affects one's present feelings about life. As today's more highly educated, more highly placed working women become older, this factor may turn out to be more important for women, too.

THEORETICAL PERSPECTIVES ON AGING

ERIKSON'S LAST STAGE: EGO INTEGRITY VERSUS DESPAIR

Ego integrity is the culmination of the successful resolution of the seven previous crises in development throughout life. It implies, according to Erikson (1963), "a post-narcissistic love of the human ego—not of the self—as an experience which conveys some world order and spiritual sense, no matter how dearly paid for" (p. 268). This love of the ego implies an acceptance of the life one has lived, with no regrets for what could have been or for what one should have done differently. It implies acceptance of one's parents as people who did the best they could and thus are worthy of one's love, even though they were not perfect. It implies an acceptance of one's approaching death as the inevitable end to a life lived as well as the individual knew how.

The person who has failed to meet this crisis is desperately afraid of death. "Despair expresses the feeling that the time is now short, too short for the attempt to start another life and to try out alternate roads to integrity" (1963, p. 269).

PECK'S THEORIES OF PSYCHOLOGICAL DEVELOPMENT IN LATE ADULTHOOD

Peck (1955) expanded Erikson's discussion of psychological development in late adulthood, emphasizing three major crises that old people must resolve for healthy psychological functioning.

1 Ego-Differentiation versus Work-Role Preoccupation

Peck sums up the chief issue in this crisis with the question each person must ask: "Am I a worthwhile person only insofar as I can do a full time job; or can I be worthwhile in other, different ways—as a performer of several other roles, and also because of the kind of person I am?" (1955; in Neugarten, 1968, p. 90).

This is a crucial question to ask in old age. Especially upon retirement, people need to redefine their worth as human beings beyond their work role. The more successful they are in finding attributes about themselves that they can point to with pride, the more successful they are likely to be in maintaining their vitality and sense of self. The woman whose major work has constituted serving as a wife and parent faces this kind of crisis when her children leave home or her husband dies. Whether a career was centered on the market-place or the home, those adjusting to its loss need to explore themselves and find other interests to take the place of those that formerly gave direction and structure to life. They need to recognize that their egos are richer and more diverse than the sum of their tasks at work.

2 Body Transcendence versus Body Preoccupation

The physical decline that generally accompanies old age signals a second crisis. People who have emphasized physical well-being as the axis of a happy life may be plunged into despair by any diminution of their faculties or any appearance of bodily aches and pains. Those who can instead focus on satisfaction from relationships with people and from ab-sorbing activities that do not depend on a peak state of health are able to overcome physical discomfort. An orientation away from preoccupation with the body needs to be developed by early adulthood, but it is critical-ly tested in old age. One of the goals of life may well be the cultivation of mental and social powers that can increase with age, along with attributes such as strength, beauty, muscular coordination, and other hallmarks of physical well-being that are likely to diminish over the years.

3 Ego-Transcendence versus Ego-Preoccupation

Old people need to deal with the reality that they are going to die. Successful adaptation to the prospect of death "may well be the most crucial achievement of the elder years" (Peck, 1955; in Neugarten, 1968, p. 91). How can people transcend their ego of the here and now to gain a positive viewpoint toward the certainty of their coming death? By recog-nizing that the way they have led their lives will allow them to achieve enduring sig-nificance—through the children they have raised, the contributions they have made to the culture, the personal relationships they have forged. Essentially, they transcend the ego by contributing to the happiness or well-being of others, which, says Peck, "more than anything else, differentiates human living from animal living" (p. 91).

BÜHLER'S THEORY OF INTENTIONALITY

In Bühler's (1968) theory, which is built around the goals people strive toward, the fifth phase of life is marked by old age, beginning at about 65 to 70 years. At this time most people can finally rest from concentrating on achiev-ing their goals. As they cast off the strictures that have kept them focused toward the aims they defined in earlier years, they may regress to the pleasure-seeking patterns they followed in childhood before they built their lives around goals. If they are healthy, they may enjoy leisure activities such as travel or hob-bies, which they never took the time for before. Or they may do volunteer work for a cause they believe in. Or they may continue to work, but with a more relaxed and less striving attitude. If they are ill, they may have no choice but to become inactive.

The most important aspect of the fifth

phase is a gradually evolving sense of the totality of one's life. Looking at one's life as a whole brings to some people a feeling of fulfillment, of a life well lived, of goals met. Others look back with despair and depression because they feel they have wasted their lives and failed to achieve the goals they set. Bühler found that most of the old people whose lives she studied showed neither of these extremes; instead, they exhibited a combination of partial fulfillment, tempered by many disappointments and culminating in a state of resignation.

AGING AND THE FAMILY

MARRIAGE IN LATE ADULTHOOD

With the lengthening of life expectancies, we are also lengthening marital expectancies. Years ago it was not uncommon for a man to lose one or more wives in childbirth, or for either partner to lose one or more mates to flu or pneumonia. The surviving spouse would remarry, and the pressures to work at a marriage over the span of a long lifetime were eased by death. Today, fiftieth-anniversary parties are more common, but so are divorces. The strain of keeping both partners interested in each other as intimate companions and friends over a very long period of time is simply too much for some marriages.

Those couples who are still together in their late years are less likely than younger ones to say that their marriages are full of problems. This may sometimes be a denial of reality, but in other cases represents the simple truth. For one thing, now that divorce is readily attainable, those marriages that have lasted over the years are apt to be self-selected: They are the happier ones. Furthermore, many couples who were in marriages that were difficult in earlier years have been able to work out their differences and arrive at mutually satisfying relationships. While Yarrow, Blank, Quinn, Youmans, and Stein (1971) found some deterioration in up to one-third of elderly marriages, they also found that older marriages are less likely to end in divorce than

death. The decision to divorce usually comes within the early years of a marriage. This may be a cohort difference reflecting the fact that people who are old today are less likely to turn to divorce, while younger people, facing a lifetime together with a partner who isn't living up to the other's expectations, decide to end the marriage. Or the difference may be a result of development: As people mature, they may be able to be more flexible and make a relationship work; they may reach a point where they either resolve their problems or decide that they can live with them.

How happy are the marriages of older people? Often they are at a level that many younger couples might well aspire to. Stinnett, Carter, and Montgomery (1972), for example, contacted 408 men and women, aged 60 to 89 (mostly between 65 and 69) and queried them about their marriages. The greatest proportion rated their marriages as very happy (45.4 percent) or happy (49.5 percent). More than half reported that their marriages had become better over the years and that the happiest time of married life was the present.

What makes a marriage happy? For these people, the most rewarding aspects were companionship and being able to express their true feelings to each other. They were still romantics, stating that being in love was the most important factor in achieving a successful marriage. The two most important characteristics of such a marriage, they said, were respect and the sharing of common interests. The largest proportion of these older married people reported a trouble-free marriage, but of those who did have problems, the most common were differences in values, in philosophies of life, and in interests. While most of these people named this period of their lives as their happiest, the three major problems of their old age were housing, poor health, and money.

The marital happiness of older couples is often at a level that many younger couples might well aspire to. (Rollie McKenna/Photo Researchers, Inc.)

How important is marriage on the morale of an older person? Very, according to a body of research which shows that married elderly people are happier than the unmarried, and especially happier than the divorced and widowed (Lee, 1978). Does marriage itself make the difference, or is it the quality of the relationship that's important? To find out, Lee gave a 28-page questionnaire to 439 married men and women, aged 60 and over, in which he scattered six questions relating to morale and five designed to measure marital satisfaction (see Table 17-1).

The returns showed that the degree to which people are satisfied with their marriages influences their general sense of well-being, especially for women. For both sexes, the other two factors that correlate highly with morale are health and satisfaction with standard of living.

Ill health often has a major effect on the morale of both partners, even when only one of them is sick. It may separate the couple, reduce sexual interest, affect the ability to engage in enjoyable activities, and drain a couple's financial resources. Furthermore, the healthy partner must take on the responsibility of taking care of the ill one and of assuming the major responsibilities of keeping the household together. The stresses sometimes seem too much for the healthy partner to bear, and the result may be depression, anger, or illness on the caretaker's part. Says Medley (1977): "Health is an integral factor in marital adjustment" (p. 7).

Lee (1978) found that a man's morale does not seem to be related to whether or not he is employed; he did not examine the effect of employment on a woman's morale, possibly because few of the elderly women in his sample were working at the time. Education has a small effect on morale. Age and length of marriage bear a small relation, too, but in an unexpected way: Older people and those married for a shorter time have higher morale scores.

The findings from this study offer an indication that marriage seems to mean something different to men and to women. Men value marriage, but they usually value occupational success to the same degree, and their morale is apt to hinge just as much on

TABLE 17-1 Morale Scale and Marital Satisfaction Scale

MORALE SCALE*
1 On the whole, life gives me a lot of pleasure.
2 On the whole, I am very satisfied with my way of life today.
3 Things just keeping getting worse and worse for me as I get older.
4 All in all, I find a great deal of happiness in life today.
5 I have a lot to be sad about.
6 Nothing ever turns out for me the way I want it to.
MARITAL SATISFACTION SCALE
1 If you had it to do over again, would you marry the same person?
2 How satisfied are you with the love and affection you receive from your spouse?
3 How satisfied are you with the amount of understanding of your problems and feelings that you get from your spouse?
4 How satisfied are you with the amount of companionship you have—doing things with your spouse?
5 All things considered, how satisfied are you with your marriage overall?

*Each item was followed by four response categories, ranging from strongly agree to strongly disagree.
SOURCE: Lee, 1978.

how well they have done in their work lives as on their family lives. For many of the women in this cohort, however, their marriages have been their work lives. They are, therefore, doubly dependent on it as a source of gratification. As more women seek fulfillment through careers, it is probable that their profiles may resemble men's more closely. Satisfying primary relationships will continue to be important to both sexes, even though this difference between them is likely to become smaller.

Even though people who are old today grew up at a time when roles were more clearly delineated for each sex, it is interesting to note that happy elderly couples live less by rigidly defined sex roles than is the case among unhappily married couples (Clark & Anderson, 1967). Apparently, many couples, in the interests of working out their relationships, ignore sex-role structures and are more flexible about who does what in the marriage.

Remarriage in Late Adulthood

After Mrs. N.'s good friend died, her widowed husband moved out of town. Some years later, back in town on a visit to his son, he called on Mrs. N., now widowed herself, and took her to lunch. She recalls:

We began to write, and he called me up. Before I knew it, we decided to get married. I guess I didn't think I ever would [get married]. I didn't think I wanted to. [But] as he came, I kind of missed him when he didn't come, see? The more we saw of each other, the better we liked each other. It just worked into something [Vinick, 1978, p. 361].

This story is part of a growing phenomenon: In the space of only thirteen years, from 1960 to 1973, the number of brides 65 and older more than doubled to over 16,000, and the number of grooms almost doubled to over 33,000 (U.S. Department of Health, Education, and Welfare, 1964; U.S. Bureau of Census, 1975). Every year, more than 35,000 couples in which at least one member is over 65 say their marriage vows.

In an effort to find out more about these relationships, Vinick (1978) interviewed twenty-four elderly couples who had remarried when both partners were over 60 years of age. In many ways, the courtship and remarriage of Mrs. N. are typical. Most of the remarried couples in this study had been widowed rather than divorced; most had known each other during their previous marriages or been introduced by a friend or a relative; in most, the man took the initiative in beginning the relationship. While most couples did not fall in love at first sight, more than half married less than a year after they began seeing each other as single people.

One can still be in love at any age without being ridiculous. It's not the same sort of love that young people go in for, but must one resign oneself to living alone just because one's old? It's dreadful going back to lonely lodgings. It's at my age that one most needs one's heart warmed up again.... It's not right to laugh at old people who get married again; you need the company of someone you love.

Henri Rousseau, age 65,
quoted in *It Takes a Long Time to Become Young,* by
Garson Kanin, p. 53.

Why had these elderly people decided to marry again? Most sought companionship and relief from loneliness. Men were most likely to cite these reasons, while women were somewhat more likely to mention their feelings toward or the personal qualities of the man they married. Most received the backing of their adult children, although some got negative feedback from their friends, sometimes because the friends felt abandoned or envious.

Almost all of these people—who had been married from two to six years—were very happy in their marriages. Of the few who were not, most felt they had been forced into these marriages by circumstances beyond their control. These were, however, in a tiny minority. The typical response was like this one:

We're like a couple of kids. We fool around—have fun. We go to dances and socialize a lot with our families. We enjoy life together. When you're with someone, you're happy. [Vinick, 1978, p. 362].

The women's happiness tended to be tied to external factors—their friends' approval, enough money, and satisfactory housing. The men's was related more to internal states—how they had felt about remarriage beforehand, how they had gotten along with their children, and their present state of mental and physical health. These marriages tended to be calmer than marriages earlier in life, with a "live and let live" attitude toward each other. Much of this serenity seemed to stem from the absence of some of the strains on an early marriage, such as raising children, striving for career success, and getting along with in-laws.

Not only does remarriage in old age enhance life for the pair themselves—it also takes a burden off society. Single old people, for example, are more likely to need help from the community or to have to go to an institution than are married ones. For both humanitarian and pragmatic reasons, then, it behooves society to encourage remarriage among the elderly. Some of the measures suggested by Vinick are increased accessibility of men and women to each other in housing and senior citizen groups; more public programs that bring men and women together, such as shared meals; and provisions for retaining widows' pensions and Social Security benefits, even after their remarriage.

SEXUALITY

Occasionally we open up a newspaper to see a story reporting a marriage between two very old persons. Generally the tone of the reporting is somewhat of the "aren't they cute" variety, falling into one of our most prevalent stereotypes: that old people *are* sexless and *should* be sexless, and that those who are *not* are perverted. Only recently have researchers begun to gather information on sexual behavior of the elderly. They have found that sexuality can be a vital force throughout life.

Sex serves many purposes besides the purely physical. An active sexual relationship assures both partners of the other's love and affection and of their own continuing vitality.

People who have had an active sexual life during their younger years are likely to continue to be sexually active in old age. (Bruce Davidson/ Magnum)

Furthermore, the physical aspects of sex in old age represent a normal, healthy aspect of human functioning.

While Kinsey's studies of male and female sexuality (1948, 1953) gave some attention to the elderly, most of their conclusions were based on data from younger people. In-depth scientific facts about sexuality in old age did not appear until Masters and Johnson's work and the findings of the Duke Longitudinal Study.

After interviewing men and women over age 60, Masters and Johnson (1966) concluded that people who have had an active sexual life during their younger years are likely to continue to be sexually active in old age. The most important factor in the maintenance of effective sexuality is consistent sexual activity over the years. A healthy man who has been sexually active can usually continue some form of active sexual expression into his seventies or eighties. Women are physiologically able to be sexually active as long as they live. A major bar to a fulfilling sexual life for

older women is the unavailability of interested partners.

While sex is present in old age, it is different. Older people do not feel as much sexual tension, are likely to have less frequent sexual relations, and experience some diminution in the intensity of the experience. A man over 60 takes longer to become aroused, longer to develop an erection, and longer to achieve ejaculation. Some of the accompanying physiological signs of arousal, such as sexual flush and increased muscle tone, are present but less intense. Sexual responses of older women are similarly affected. Breast engorgement, nipple erection, increased muscle tone, clitoral and labial engorgement, and other signs of sexual arousal are not as intense. However, older women are still able to reach orgasm, especially if they have been sexually active over the years. With these changes, though, both men and women are still able to enjoy a fulfilling and satisfying sexuality in late life.

At the Duke University Center for the

Study of Aging and Human Development, a longitudinal study of sexual interest and activity has confirmed Masters and Johnson's findings that many people over 60 are sexually interested and active (Pfeiffer, 1969).

At the start of the study, 254 men and women, aged 60 to 94, were asked about their sexual interest and activity. The findings were quite different for men and women, possibly because of biological differences between the sexes, but also undoubtedly because of the cultural double standard that expects men to be more sexually interested than women. About 80 percent of the healthy, well-functioning men were interested in sex, and about 70 percent were regularly sexually active. Ten years later, about the same proportion expressed interest, but only 25 percent were still sexually active. Among the women, only about one-third of those who were healthy and functioning well socially and intellectually reported continuing sexual interest at the start of the study, and only about one-fifth were having sexual intercourse regularly. Both these proportions remained stable over the next ten years. Most of the women said that it was their husbands who had stopped intercourse, and the men tended to agree that this was so. The women stopped having sexual intercourse at a median age of 60, compared to the male median of 68, which probably reflects the reality of women's tending to marry men a few years older than themselves.

Another difference between the sexes seems a clear reflection of a cultural double standard. In old age as in earlier life, married men are not very different from unmarried men in terms of their sexual interest and activity, while married and unmarried women differ greatly. Only one-fifth of the unmarried women reported any sexual interest, and very few of these reported any activity. Some 20 to 25 percent of the men and a smaller percentage of the women became more interested in sex and more active as they grew older, possibly—especially in the case of unmarried men—because they had found new partners.

While much more research is needed to assess sexual attitudes and capabilities in old age, it is clear that sexual expression is a normal and enjoyable part of life for many old people. It could be an even more significant part of people's lives if young and old alike appreciated this fact. Old people need to accept their own sexuality without shame or embarrassment. Younger people need to avoid ridiculing or patronizing old persons who show evidence of healthy sexuality. Medical and social workers need to take people's sexual activity into account when prescribing therapies (avoiding when possible those drugs that interfere with sexual functioning) and need to be matter-of-fact about discussing sexual activity (by, for example, raising the issue with a heart patient who may be embarrassed to bring up the subject). Persons planning housing arrangements for old people need to provide opportunities for men and women to socialize, with enough privacy so that those who are interested in sexual relationships can pursue them.

WIDOWHOOD

"As long as you have your husband, you're not old," said one recently widowed 75-year-old woman. "But once you lose him, old age sets in fast." Any discussion of marriage in late life has to be linked with a discussion of widowhood, one of the hardest burdens of old age, especially for women. While 8 out of 10 elderly men are married, less than half of all women over 65 have husbands (NCOA, 1978). This is largely because women live longer than men and usually marry older men. Even when men have been widowed, their chances for remarriage are twice as good as women's, because there are more possible mates for them to choose from. Women over

65 outnumber men by 3 million; in addition, men tend to marry younger women. The reverse of this situation—the older woman who marries a younger man—is not acceptable to most people in our society. Elderly black people are less likely to live with their spouses than are elderly whites, partly because of the shorter life expectancy of black men (which creates a greater proportion of widowed black women—60 percent compared to 53 percent among white women (U.S. Department of Health, Education, and Welfare, 1978)—and partly because of economic pressures in the black community that cause dissolution of marriage earlier in life.

While we will discuss the specific issues in mourning the loss of a loved one in Chapter 18, we will look here at some of the ramifications that losing a spouse has for the day-to-day life of the survivor.

Adjusting to the Death of a Spouse

When one partner in a marriage that has been of long duration dies, the surviving spouse faces a host of emotional and practical problems. The survivor of a happy marriage has lost a lover, a confidant, a good friend, and a steady companion. There is a great emotional void in the survivor's life. Even in a bad marriage, the survivor feels the loss. For one thing, the role of spouse has been lost. The woman who has structured her days according to the meals she'll cook, the shirts she'll wash, and the apartment she'll clean suddenly feels that she has nothing to do, no one to do things for, and no reason to live.

One's social life changes, too. While friends and family usually rally to the mourner's side immediately after the death of a spouse, eventually they all return home and go about their own lives, leaving the widow or widower alone to carve out an entirely new life structure. Friends sometimes become upset when bereaved people talk about their grief, a disturbing reminder that it can happen to anyone. As a result, they may avoid the

widowed when they are most sorely needed. Although no one can substitute for the lost partner, people do need relationships with others and seek to fill the void in their lives as much as possible. The social problems are different for men and women, although both often feel like a "fifth wheel" among couples they have been friendly with for years. Men are more likely to form relationships with other women and to remarry. Women are more likely to find companionship with other widows, but they have a hard time forming heterosexual relationships.

Living as a Widow

Lopata (1973) surveyed the attitudes, experiences, and lifestyles of 301 widows aged 50 and over. Since the experiences of a woman widowed at age 50 are likely to be quite different from one who lost her husband at age 75, we need to be careful about applying generalizations from such a broad range to elderly women.

Over half of these women felt that they had changed in at least one—and often more—specific ways as a result of widowhood, and most felt that the change was beneficial. Even many women who had been very happily married came to consider themselves more independent or competent after they were widowed. These same women often considered loneliness the worst problem of widowhood, and they missed their husbands' love and companionship.

Women who reported no change after widowhood tended to be the least educated and to be more socially isolated than women who reported changes. These women seemed to have been more isolated from other people even while they were married. While they considered "being shunned by other people" the major problem of widowhood, they may not have realized how much they contributed to their own isolation.

Like any other life crisis, widowhood affects people in different ways. Much has to do with what the married relationship was like. Ironically, many women who could not get along with their husbands when they were alive have more trouble adjusting to their deaths, possibly because of the guilt they now feel. A woman's personality and lifestyle also affect how she will react to her husband's death. The more a woman has been dependent on her husband for her own identity, the more keenly she will feel his absence.

It would seem that the most important thing that a woman can do to prepare herself for the probability of eventual widowhood is to gain a strong sense of her own identity. She is less likely to be devastated by her husband's loss if, while he is still alive, she has pursued her own interests and her own social activities and assumed a large role in every aspect of family planning and management, including the financial.

BEING SINGLE IN LATE ADULTHOOD

People who have never married may constitute a "distinct type of social personality" (Gubrium, 1975). When twenty-two 60- to 94-year-old never-married people were interviewed about their feelings regarding old age, they expressed fewer feelings of loneliness than the typical person in the same age bracket. This may indicate that loneliness is more a result of having loved and lost than never having loved at all. It may also indicate that some people choose not to marry because they don't feel the need that most people do to have such an intimate relationship. These single old people seemed to be less affected by old age than most elderly persons; they were more independent, had

fewer social relationships, and were generally satisfied with their lives.

FAMILY RELATIONSHIPS

What is the quality of family life for the elderly? How do they feel about it themselves? When Seelbach and Hansen (1980) asked 367 old people how satisfied they were with various aspects of family relations, they received a heartening response. Eight out of 10 indicated that they were quite happy with the way their families treated them.

There were a number of differences among the people in the sample, however. For example, while 88 percent overall said they were perfectly satisfied with the treatment they received from their families, the "old-old" (over 80) were more satisfied than the "young-old" (65 to 80). While 87 percent said their families were the finest in the world, the marrieds and the old-old were more likely to agree with this statement than the single (81 percent of whom were widowed) and the young-old. Even though institutionalized people (about 40 percent of the total group) were slightly less likely to agree than were those who lived in the community, they still produced an 81 percent agreement rate. More than 81 percent of the total sample reported that they were now receiving as much love and affection from their families as they ever had, and again, the old-old and the noninstitutionalized were more likely to agree.

Institutionalized persons may feel more estranged from their families because they don't see them as often, or because they feel that a family who places an elderly member in a nursing home doesn't love that person as much. On the other hand, some people may go into nursing homes precisely because their family relationships are not as strong to begin with.

Few of these old people expressed negative feelings about their families. Fewer than 1 in 3 wished that their families would pay more attention to them, and less than 16 percent felt their families either didn't care about them or tried to boss them. It is possible, of course, that some of these people may have exaggerated the positive aspects of their family relationships to save face in front of the interviewers. Even allowing for some puffery, however, it seems that, by and large, old people have better relationships with their families than popular mythology would have us believe.

PARENTHOOD

In our society, the relationship between old people and their children is complex. We do not have the easy flow of a cycle of care, common in some more primitive societies, where old people expect to be personally cared for in their children's homes. Parent-child relations simmer in a complex mixture of love and resentment, of conflicting pulls between duty toward parents and obligations toward spouse and children, between wanting to do the right thing and not wanting one's present style of life to change.

Most adult children do help their parents in many ways. Hill (1965) analyzed the patterns of help given by one generation to another among more than 100 three-generation families. The grandparent generation received a great deal of help from both their children and their adult grandchildren. This help took the form of emotional gratification, household management, and aid given during illness. The grandparents were much more likely to receive help than to give it.

Of course, help goes in the other direction, too. Parents of handicapped persons may maintain their protective roles as long as they live. Older people may help their children by looking after grandchildren while the parents go to work or school. They may open their homes to a separated or divorced child while she or he reorganizes and starts a new life. In such cases parents and grown children may both benefit from sharing the same household. (Circumstances like the latter two, though, are more likely to occur in the lives of middle-aged, rather than elderly, grandparents.)

In most instances, adult children and

elderly parents do not live together. Most old people do not want to live with their children. Of those who do, women are more likely to do so than men, and the widowed of both sexes are more likely than the married (Shanas, 1969). Lopata's (1973) survey of widows found that most women felt it would be difficult to live with their married children's families. They knew they would have trouble keeping quiet about mistakes they felt their children were making—in bringing up their own children, getting along in their marriages, handling their finances, and other aspects of daily life. They knew that the advice they felt compelled to give would rarely be welcomed.

Unfortunately, both for the old (who have reserves of experiences and wisdom to draw on) and for the young (who have much to learn), people in our society rarely look to their elders for advice, especially when those elders are their own parents. A spirit of independence, of the felt need to learn from one's own mistakes, and of the supposed obsolescence of older people's experiences has interfered with the age-old cycle in which the old taught and counseled the young.

Other factors also operate against parents' and children's living together. People today tend to live in smaller quarters than in former days, often making it inconvenient to absorb an extra person into the household. The older people themselves may be hampered by moving in with a child. They have little privacy, which limits their social life; they may resent having to account to their children for the ways they spend their time; and they may become so afraid of being a burden or an intruder that their own spontaneity suffers.

Even though elderly parents and their children rarely share the same household, they do see each other often. Most older persons live quite close to at least one of their children. While fewer than 3 old persons in 10 live with a child, an additional 5 to 10 live within half an hour's distance; and only about 1 in 20 are more than a day's journey away from the nearest child (Shanas, 1969). A 1974 study found that 8 out of 10 old persons had seen at least one of their children within the past week (Rabushka & Jacobs, 1980).

In sombre contrast to these cheerful findings of close ties between aging parents and their grown children are the disturbing reports that have begun to appear of abuse toward old people who are dependent on their children and too frail to defend themselves (Wallace, 1980). According to a number of reports by those studying domestic violence, the most common type of abuse is neglect, as in those cases when adult children withhold food, shelter, clothing, medical care, money, or other assets from the parent. Then there is the psychological aspect—tongue-lashings or threats of violence or abandonment.

More and more cases of actual violence, however, are coming to light: of beating, punching, or burning elderly parents. In Connecticut, one year after passage of a law requiring the reporting of suspected abuse against people over 65, some 400 cases of physical abuse came to the attention of authorities (Wallace, 1980).

What makes children turn so fiercely on their parents? Sometimes they themselves had been beaten as children and are now following their parents' aggressive example. Sometimes the adult children are responding to the strains on their time, energy, and finances of long-term care of an old person, and to the major changes in their lives as a result. Sometimes they react angrily and violently to the elderly parent's personality, manifestations of emotional disturbance, alcoholism, or total dependency. In any case, when matters reach such a sorry state, separation of the old person from the family is best for all concerned, even if institutionalization is the only answer.

GRANDPARENTHOOD

The role of grandparent varies in different societies. Indulgent, warm relationships are the rule in those cultures in which grandparents do not exert their authority, and formal, authoritarian stances are more common in societies in which the old have economic power and prestige. In our diversified society, Neugarten and Weinstein (1964) found five major styles of grandparenting: the *formal*, in which grandparents leave all child rearing to the parents and confine their interest in the children to occasional babysitting and the offering of special treats; the *fun seeker*, who becomes a playmate to the grandchildren in a mutual relationship that both enjoy; the *surrogate parent*, who assumes actual caretaking responsibility, usually because the children's parents are both working and have left the children in the grandparent's care; the *reservoir of family wisdom*, an authoritarian role in which the grandparent dispenses special skills or resources; and the *distant figure*, who has occasional contact with the grandchildren on holidays and birthdays but is essentially remote from their lives.

Half of the seventy sets of grandparents interviewed in this study were either fun seekers or distant figures, both styles in which neither authority nor nurturance is a major component. Grandparents over age 65 are more likely to adopt the formal style. This may reflect cohort differences, by which people of different eras see their roles differently; or it may reflect the fact that the older the grandparents get, the less interested they are in spending days at the zoo or in playing with little children.

It is also interesting to look at the viewpoints of children toward their grandparents and the qualities that they value. Kahana and Kahana (1970) asked children of different ages—4 to 5, 8 to 9, and 11 to 12—a variety of questions about their grandparents and about old people in general. The closest relation-

When people can talk with friends about their worries and pain, they can deal better with such crises of old age as widowhood, retirement, and general decrease in social interaction. (© 1977 Warren D. Jorgensen/Photo Researchers, Inc.)

ships for children in all age groups were with the maternal grandparents, and the favorite grandparent was most often the mother's mother.

The youngest children preferred those grandparents who gave them love, food, and presents (the formal grandparents of Neugarten and Weinstein's study). The 8- and 9-year-olds focused on mutuality in the relationship and emphasized shared activities, thus preferring the fun seekers. And the oldest children again preferred the indulgent style of grandparenting, showing less interest in a mutual relationship. Other studies (Kahana & Coe, 1969) have shown that grandparents feel increasingly distant from their grandchildren as the children grow older. Kahana and Kahana (1970) suggest:

It is possible that different styles of grandparenthood fit in best with the child's needs at different stages in his development [p. 99].

Importance of Close Personal Relationships

Our relationships with others are important throughout life. Not only is old age no exception, but it seems that relationships become even more essential to the happiness of the elderly. Lemon, Bengston, and Peterson (1972) found that people who had an active friendship circle were more satisfied with life.

Even more important than having friends at all is the nature of the friendship. People who have a close, intimate, stable relationship with a person in whom they can confide their deepest feelings and thoughts are more likely to weather well the vicissitudes of aging (Lowenthal & Haven, 1968). A confidant is more important for good mental health and high morale than is high social interaction or role status. When people can talk about their worries and pain, they can deal better with such crises of old age as widowhood, retirement, and general decrease in social interaction. The only circumstance that a sympathetic listener does not seem able to improve is poor physical health.

In a survey of 280 people aged 60 and older (Lowenthal & Haven, 1968), a profile emerged of people most likely to have confidants. The married are more likely to have someone they can confide in than are the widowed, who in turn are more likely to have a confidant than singles. Very often, the spouse is the confidant, especially for a man. The very fact that someone has chosen to get married may indicate that that person is able to enjoy the intimacy of a close relationship.

Confidants are not likely to be brothers or sisters. Aside from spouses and children, they are likely to be of the same sex. In their study of 234 people aged 70 or older, Powers and Bultena (1976) found that only 1 out of 10 women's friendships crossed sex lines, and only 1 out of 3 of the men's. Women and men whose intimate friends were of the other sex were more likely to be single or widowed.

Age differences are more readily overcome, with 2 out of 5 of the men's intimate friends and 1 out of 4 of the women's being at least sixteen years younger.

Lowenthal and Haven (1968) found that people between ages 65 and 74 are more likely to have confidants than are those under 65 and over 75. Education does not matter, but occupational status does, at least for men: White-collar workers are more likely than blue-collar workers to have confidants. People who like to be with other people and people who live through their roles are more likely to have confidants than people rated low on these variables.

SOME SOCIAL ISSUES RELATED TO AGING

FRIENDSHIP IN LATE ADULTHOOD

How do old people choose their friends? Largely on the same bases that younger ones do. For example, old people tend to be friendly with those who live nearby. In addition, as in younger years, similarity strongly characterizes friendships in old age. Friends are likely to be of the same sex, same marital status, same race, same socioeconomic status, and about the same age (Rosow, 1970).

A change in status often brings about a change in friendships. Blau (1961) found that people who are widowed at an earlier age than most of their friends and those who retire before most of their friends do find their social lives restricted. They don't fit in as well anymore. The widow or widower tends to feel out of place among couples; and the early retiree finds not only that most of his friends are working during the day and are thus unavailable to him but also that by not being in the working world any longer, he feels "out of it" when the conversation revolves around his friends' working lives. As their friends' statuses change, both widows and retired persons come back into the social swim.

Social class has an effect on friendship patterns, too. Middle-class old people have more friends than those from the working class, and they are more likely to distinguish between friends and neighbors. Working-class people, on the other hand, tend to make friends with people who live in their neighborhoods and to make little or no distinction between friends and neighbors (Rosow, 1970).

Sex Differences in Friendship Patterns

In old age, as in earlier periods of the life span, men and women differ on the place of friendship in their lives. In Lowenthal and Haven's 1968 study of intimate friendship in old age, they found that women are more likely to have someone they can confide in than men are. When a man does have someone he can open up to, that person is likely to be his wife. A married woman, though, is more likely to confide in a child, a relative, or a friend instead of her husband.

Vinick's 1978 report on elderly remarried couples confirms this tendency of women to have closer relationships than men do with children and other relatives, and to be more likely to have friends. While eight of the twenty-four men in this sample said they had no friends, none of the women made this statement. Even those men who did have friends saw them less after their wives' deaths and after their retirement, while women found sustenance in the companionship of other women in what Blau (1971) has called the "society of widows." The men reported being lonely after being widowed more often than did the women. Undoubtedly, the women's friendships helped to ease their loneliness.

Powers and Bultena's 1976 report seems to contradict this picture of women being more friend-oriented—until one looks at the quality of the friendships held by both sexes. These researchers found that men see more people than women do on a regular basis, including friends and children. The men in this study had half again as much contact with their children and families as the women did, and they were twice as likely to see friends. However, they were less likely to number *intimate* friends among these contacts. Close friends were important for elderly women, though, who tended to see their good friends almost as much as they did their husbands.

Furthermore, this difference was not attributable to the fact that women live longer than men and thus are less likely to have lost close friends due to death. More men than women had *never* had an intimate friend. While only 3 out of 10 women said that they did not have a close friend at the time and had never lost one, more than 4 out of 10 of the men gave this response. Furthermore, when the women's dear friends died or moved away, they were much more likely to make a new close friend than the men were.

Women value their friendships consistently in good times and bad, while men reach out for friends more often in times of need. Men who are recently widowed, who are retired, who are in poor health, and who have little money are more likely to have an intimate friend than men who do not suffer from these troubles. While close friendships may not be essential to enjoying old age—and there are those people who seem to be relatively content in the absence of intimacy—many people

find that having someone who can sympathize with their problems and listen to their stories about their grandchildren and consider them to be important in his or her own life is a special blessing in these later years.

Family, Friends, and Neighbors

Relationships with people in these three categories mean different things to different people. For financial help, for example, old people virtually never go to friends or neighbors. They go first to their grown children, then to other close relatives. For care when they are ill, however, people look first to their children, but neighbors play a close second. Relatives and friends who do not live in the immediate neighborhood play a minor role in helping them when they are not well.

Among those old people who have the heaviest burdens—those who live alone, are widowed, retired, or sick, and have no adult children living nearby—there is an inverse relationship between contact with their children and with their neighbors and friends. The less they see of their children, the more they see of friends and neighbors. For these people, friends and neighbors become substitutes for their children. Interestingly, this is most common among elderly parents whose children live in the same town but are not as available to them as the parents would like them to be, rather than among parents whose children live at a distance. So it seems that these old people turn to their neighbors out of a sense of emotional deprivation. Those parents, for example, who are the *most* emotionally dependent on their children and who have no other emotionally meaningful relationships are most likely to transfer this dependence to their neighbors. According to Rosow (1970), this kind of compensatory socializing with neighbors represents an effort to keep busy rather than a social interest in its own right.

These parents still feel deprived, since seeing neighbors "is not an effective emotional substitute for constant contact with their children" (p. 62).

INCOME

The biggest problem affecting old Americans is poverty. One-fifth of our total population is poor, and one-fifth of the poor are over 65 years of age (Butler, 1975). Over half the elderly are so deprived that they do not get enough to eat, cannot buy the medicines they need, and cannot keep a phone to link them with the outside world. In 1975, 65 percent of families headed by persons over 65 had an annual income of under $11,000. The median income of elderly families was $8057, compared to $14,698 for younger families (NCOA, 1978). While 1 out of every 3 elderly couples had an income of $10,000 or more, 1 out of every 7 had an income less than $4000 (U.S. Department of Health, Education, and Welfare, 1978).

Many people, after a lifetime of hard work, become poor for the first time in old age. They outlive their savings. Social Security payments and pensions—for those lucky enough to receive them—rarely allow for more than a subsistence existence.

As a result, the elderly spend relatively larger amounts on basic necessities such as housing, food, and medical care than do younger people (U.S. Department of Health, Education, and Welfare, 1978). Widows, single women, and minority-group men and women are among the most desperately poor old people.

More than half the income of elderly persons comes from some kind of retirement or welfare program; a little over one-fourth comes from continuing employment; and 19 percent comes from investments and contributions. Among the elderly poor, 92 percent

of their income comes from public sources, compared to one-third of the income of the nonpoor (U.S. Department of Health, Education, and Welfare, 1978).

In view of the large proportion of their income that comes from fixed sources, inflation hits especially hard at the aged. Says Peterson (undated):

Although social security benefits were raised several times in the last ten years, the increases have only kept income close to poverty with rising prices. No increases have been given to allow older people to share in the rising standard of living of the working population. Private pensions have been less flexible since most have not been adjusted at all to meet price increases [p. 2].

While our society has made enough medical progress to enable people to live for many more years, it needs to make economic progress to allow more of these old people to live decently. Butler (1975) recommends a universal pension system that would "incorporate under one umbrella all private and public pension plans, including Social Security." It would allow for rises in the cost of living; two-thirds would be financed from general federal tax revenues, and one-third from trust funds. Such a plan would ensure that old people would not have to add poverty to the other problems of aging. As Peterson puts it:

When a nation as affluent as America discovers widespread poverty afflicting so large a group of its citizens, it is imperative that corrective action be taken. At a time when social consciousness has revitalized the American ideal of social justice, failure to mobilize our resources to meet the needs of our older population is not only incomprehensible but inhuman [p. 45].

HOUSING

Contrary to another stereotype, which visualizes the typical old person in some kind of institution, almost all old people live in the community. Most elderly persons—more than 8 out of 10 men and almost 6 out of 10 women—live in families. About 1 in 3 live alone or with nonrelatives, with the proportions in this kind of setting about 2½ times higher for women than for men, reflecting women's greater longevity and more common widowhood (U.S. Department of Health, Education, and Welfare, 1978).

As people grow older, they are less and less likely to live in a family setting, but still only 5 percent of old people live in nursing homes, hospitals for the mentally or physically ill, or other institutions (U.S. Department of Health, Education, and Welfare, 1978).

Old people who live in the community are most likely to live in older houses in the older sections of central cities and in older suburbs (Shanas, 1969). The federal government's annual housing survey showed that the elderly's homes are in no worse shape than those owned by younger people and that only 3 percent of elderly homeowners said their houses had a serious problem they would or could not fix because of lack of money (Rabushka & Jacobs, 1980).

Living arrangements often become a major problem as people age. When they have companionship—a spouse, a sibling, or a friend—and are reasonably healthy, they can make their own arrangements. Pride of ownership, a feeling of independence, and a preference for the familiar make it generally desirable for people to remain where they are, when possible. But it is not always possible. One partner may become too infirm to manage three flights of rickety steps. A neighborhood may deteriorate, with frail-looking old people becoming prey to young thugs. Either mental or physical disability may keep a person living alone from being able to manage.

Keeping Old People in the Community

Creative social planning can enable old people to remain in the community, out of an institution. For example, the staff of one geriat-

ric hospital recognized that there were many people in the community who did not need to live at the hospital but could benefit from many of its services, and that these services could be especially helpful to families who wanted to keep aging parents with them but could not maintain full-time supervision. The hospital established a day-care program that picked up people in the morning and brought them to the center, where they were served their meals, bathed, given medication and treatment, offered recreational activities, and then taken back home in the early evening (Kostick, 1972).

Another type of service involves going directly to old people in their homes, providing help with marketing and food preparation, house cleaning, dressing and personal care, transportation, and other nonmedical services (Kistin & Morris, 1972; Evans, 1979). Meals on Wheels programs deliver one hot meal a day at a nominal fee to housebound elderly people.

Still other innovative efforts concentrate on changing the housing situation itself. In New York State, "Enriched Housing" units feature apartments that have been especially designed for elderly people who can live independently if they have a little help (Evans, 1979). In these units, tenants eat their midday meal together in a common dining room. Building staff prepare these meals, clean the apartments, and stop in every day to see each tenant.

In a suburb of Denver, Colorado, six old people share a split-level house owned by a local nonprofit organization (Pascoe, 1976). The tenants get their own breakfasts, eat a hot lunch at a nearby church, and have their evening meal at home, where it has been prepared by a hired cook. They share the chores, but lead separate social lives with their own friends and families.

In Seattle, Washington, an agency called Home Sharing for Seniors matches elderly homeowners with tenants of varying ages who offer such services as cooking, gardening, or light housework, as well as companionship, for free room, and sometimes free room and board (Rogers, 1980). Another program, Project Share, in Hempstead, New York, makes similar matches between people 60 years or older (Shaman, 1979).

We need more programs like these to meet the needs of the elderly, whose problems are made worse by a society that is not structured for their comfort. There is little housing at rents low enough for most old people to afford. What exists is often located in communities where transportation, shopping, and recreational and medical facilities are poor.

Close to three-quarters of a million older people live in housing built especially for them—low-rent public housing, lower-middle-income assisted housing, or open-market retirement centers (Lawton, 1975). Many older people prefer such housing, as indicated by the fact that waiting lists for high-cost housing are just as long as those for low-cost. This alternative is not for everyone, of course: Some 2 out of 3 old people prefer to live among people of various ages (Lawton, 1975a), but other studies (Rosow, 1967) have found that older people tend to be better integrated socially when they live in apartment buildings with numbers of other old people. There is obviously a great need for more special housing, especially designed to meet the needs of the elderly.

Living in Institutions

Most old people don't want to live in institutions, and most families don't want to place their parents there. The old person often feels that placement is outright rejection by his or her children, and the children tend to place their parents reluctantly, apologetically, and with great guilt feelings. Sometimes, though, because of the old person's needs, or the family's circumstances, such a placement seems to be the only solution.

About 1 out of every 5 Americans will spend some time during old age in an institution offering long-term care—a hospital for the mentally or physically ill, a convalescent home for the aging sponsored by a nonprofit organization or government agency, or a commercial nursing home operated privately for profit (Kastenbaum & Candy, 1973). About 80 percent of institutionalized older persons—almost a million men and women—are in commercial nursing homes (Butler, 1975).

Who are America's 1 million nursing home residents? They are old: Seventy percent are over 70 years of age, and their average age is 82. Most are women, who outnumber men by 3 to 1. Most are widowed, and only 1 in 10 has a living spouse. More than half have no living relatives or only very distant ones, and more than 6 out of 10 have no visitors at all. Almost all are white. Most have more than one physical ailment and are disabled: Less than half can get around by themselves, more than half are mentally impaired, and one-third are incontinent. They stay an average of 2.4 years, and only 1 in 5 returns home. The vast majority die in the nursing home, 1 out of 3 in the first year of admission (Moss & Halamandaris, 1977; Butler, 1975).

The decision to place a relative in a nursing home is often made with a heavy heart. Some of the homes are beautifully run, but these are often beyond the financial reach of most families or have long lists of people waiting for admission. At least half the country's 23,000 nursing homes are inadequate, according to the Senate Special Committee on Aging (Hess, 1975).

According to a U.S. Census Bureau report (1978), however, the overwhelming majority—about 90 percent—of nursing home residents and their families are satisfied with

Sometimes, because of the old person's needs or the family's circumstances, the placement of an old person into an institution seems to be the only solution. (© 1975 Michael Philip Manheim/Photo Researchers, Inc.)

their care. The residents' biggest complaint is about their meals, but even here only 14 percent say they don't like the food service.

Despite this indication of approval, society cannot afford to be complacent about conditions in nursing homes. Because of the helplessness of their residents and the insufficiency of alternatives, it is far too easy for abuses to creep into the system. A few years back, governmental investigations did uncover many such abuses. They found many instances in which proprietors economized at the expense of the old people within their care. In such homes, there were too few staff workers to give adequate care, meals were not nourishing enough, and patients were overdrugged to make them easier to handle (Mendelson, 1974).

The Ideal Nursing Home

Ideally, such an institution should be a homelike, lively place with a trained administrator, a caring and capable medical director, and a full range of social, therapeutic, and rehabilitative services. It should be safe, hygienic, and attractive. It should provide stimulating

activities and opportunities to socialize with other people—of both sexes, all ages (Butler, 1975).

The model nursing home should also provide its residents with the right to make many of the decisions about their care and their day-to-day lives. A dramatic demonstration of the importance that decision making and control over their own lives hold for nursing home residents can be seen in the results of an experiment by Langer and Rodin (1976).

Two groups of residents in a highly rated nursing home took part in this experiment. The forty-seven people in the first group were told that they were responsible for seeing that they got good care, for making decisions about how they spent their time, and for changing things they did not like. They were also asked to choose and care for a plant. The forty-four people in the second group were told that the staff was responsible for caring for them and for making them happy. They were handed a plant and told that the nurses would water and care for it.

Before the experiment began, all these

residents answered questionnaires indicating how happy and active they felt and how much in control of their own lives they considered themselves to be. They were also rated on various measures by nurses who knew nothing of the experiment. Both groups were about the same. Three weeks after the experiment began, however, a posttest showed two very different profiles. Among those encouraged to take more responsibility, 93 percent became more active, more alert, and happier, and they became involved in many different kinds of activities. In the other group, however, 71 percent became weaker and more disabled.

These findings confirm Seligman's (1974) premise that the loss of control over one's life can lead to depression and even death. Says Seligman:

We kill many of our senior citizens by denying them choices, purpose in life, control over their lives. Many of these deaths are premature and unnecessary [p. 84].

CRIME AND THE ELDERLY

"Oh, I never go out after dark any more. I'm too afraid I'll get knocked down like my neighbor across the hall," says Rose T., aged 72. Mrs. T. is not alone in her fear of being the victim of violent crime. This fear is a serious obstacle against mobility and freedom of lifestyle for the elderly. Even though the elderly are more often victims of crimes against property than against the person (NCOA, 1978), their frailty makes them vulnerable to the purse-snatchers and muggers who prey upon victims who can offer little or no resistance.

At least 700,000 older men and women were victimized in 1975 (NCOA, 1978). Many of these people were taken in by "con" artists who defrauded them of their savings, sometimes leaving them virtually penniless. Most

likely to be victimized are poor women who live alone. Older black people are about twice as likely as older white people to consider the fear of crime a "very serious" problem personally, probably because they are more likely to live in neighborhoods with higher crime rates in general.

CROSS-CULTURAL PATTERNS OF AGING

MINORITY GROUPS IN THE UNITED STATES

In 1964 the National Urban League described the plight of the black aged as a state of "double jeopardy," in which they suffer from discrimination based on both age *and* race. This could be expanded to "multiple jeopardy" for a variety of subgroups in our population, such as Mexican-Americans, American Indians, and Puerto Ricans. All the problems of old age that face the aging population in general are even more troublesome for old people in these subgroups. They tend to be poorer; to be more affected by illness and less likely to have it treated; to be less well educated; to have a history of unemployment and underemployment; to live in poorer housing; and to have shorter life expectancies. Furthermore, while their needs for social and medical services are greater, they live in areas where services are least available.

A particularly poignant irony exists in the inability of so many minority-group workers to benefit from Social Security and Medicare, which they need the most. Even if they contributed during their working years, they die too soon to collect any benefits. The life expectancy for black men, for example, is only 63.6 years, compared to the 69.4 years a white man can expect to live (Population Reference Bureau, 1979). And only 4 percent of the Spanish-surname population in the Southwest is over 65, compared to 9 percent of the white population (Moore, 1971). Furthermore, since many of the jobs held by minority-group members during their working years were not covered by Social Security, the minority elderly are more likely to be on Old Age Assistance.

Family and cultural patterns vary from group to group. Popular mythology states that there is more cohesiveness and mutual concern in black families, and that as a result old black people are more likely than their white counterparts to live in extended families. But in 1960, half of all black people aged 60 and over lived alone or with only one other person, and 16 percent lived entirely alone. Elderly blacks are more likely than whites to have people other than their spouses living with them (20 percent compared to 12.5 percent) and to have relatives under 18 in the home (14 percent versus 3 percent; Butler & Lewis, 1973; Hill, 1971). These differences are probably based more on economics than on family solidarity. It is more common in the black community for grandparents to care for their grandchildren so that the mothers can go out to work. There is an even greater disparity among family living arrangements of elderly black men and women than between white men and women: Half of all black elderly men live with their spouses, while only 1 in 5 women do (Hill, 1971).

Among Asian-Americans, it is more common to see old men living alone. Because of immigration patterns earlier in this century, many old men have no family in this country. Among this group, too, the myth of reverence for the elderly ignores the needs of many old people (Kalish & Yuen, 1971).

The very concept of old age varies from group to group. Mexican-Americans consider themselves old at much younger ages than do most other people. This is reflected in the fact that senior citizens' clubs in the Chicano area of East Los Angeles begin taking members at the age of 50 (*Human Behavior*, 1976).

AGING IN OTHER CULTURES

Every day an ancient Russian farmer climbs up and down steep hills to reach the fields where he does half a day's hard work. A wizened old Ecuadorian woman is kept busy gathering strands of sheep wool and spinning

it into cloth. A Kashmiri, gray with advanced age, dances vigorously at a wedding. These three old people are typical of the aged population in three scattered locations around the world: Abkhazia, in the southern Soviet Union; Vilcabamba, an Andean village in Ecuador; and the principality of Hunza in Pakistani-controlled Kashmir (Leaf, 1973). Patterns of aging vary widely from culture to culture. It would be impossible for us to describe all such patterns, and so we will mention only a few examples of old people in these three socities, where people seem to live much longer and remain vigorous much longer than in most other places around the world.

Leaf (1973) tried to confirm the ages of certain members of these societies. Since birth records were rarely present, he turned to baptismal records, passports and other documents, dates carved in doors, the ages of children and grandchildren, and memories of outstanding events such as war service or natural diasters. While original reports stated that people well over 100 were very common, further investigation showed many of them to be "youngsters" of 70 or 80 or thereabouts. Leaf satisifed himself that even if the people exaggerated their ages somewhat, there was no doubt that they were very old. Most significantly, despite their great age, they were vigorous, healthy, and respected. Surely we in America can learn much from them about successful aging.

What is it about life in these three communities that produces so many healthy old people? Several aspects of their lives—both physical and psychological—are very different from that of people in our society. For one thing, the social status of the elderly is high. Old people live with members of their family, who respect and admire them and appreciate the useful contributions they make to the family and to the community. Second, there is no forced retirement. People work as long as they are able to.

On a regular, daily basis very old people pick tea, feed poultry, weed, do laundry, clean house, tend animals, and care for small children. In Hunza a council of elders made up of twenty wise old men meets every day to resolve disputes among citizens. Then, people have a different outlook toward life. They expect to live a long time and consider the normal life span to be about 100 rather than our "threescore and ten." They consider themselves young for a much longer time. Many, in fact, feel that youth extends to about 80 years of age.

The major physical differences between them and us involve diet and exercise. In all three of these long-lived communities, people eat less than we do. In 1968 the U.S. National Academy of Sciences recommended that men over age 55 consume 2400 calories daily, women 1700. Instead, the average American takes in some 3300 calories a day. In these three socities, people consume a low-calorie diet throughout life, a pattern of eating that undoubtedly influences health in middle and old age. The old people consume less than 2000 calories a day, with a low of 1200 among the people of Vilcabamba. There and in Hunza people eat very few fats of animal origin—very little meat and few dairy products. Such dietary habits seem to delay development of *atherosclerosis*, fatty deterioration of the heart arteries, a prominent ailment among elderly Americans. The Abkhas-

ians eat somewhat more from the meat and dairy group, but they still keep to a relatively low-fat diet. The old people drink homemade wine regularly, sometimes consuming two or three glasses a day with meals. They drink a little vodka, too. Obesity is nonexistent among the first two groups and only occasional among the Abkhasians.

Another factor contributing to the populace's health is the high level of physical activity common to all three cultures. The normal activities of everyday life—the walking and climbing over mountainous terrain, the work involved in farming, sheep herding, hunting, and other daily pursuits—maintain good muscle tone and cardiovascular fitness.

It is also probable that some genetic factors are involved. Very old people in our country, as well as in these three, often have parents who lived to advanced ages, possibly because long-lived individuals have been blessed genetically. They may not have genes that carry predispositions to fatal or disabling diseases. Heredity becomes particularly important in small isolated communities like Vilcabamba and Hunza, where there is a great deal of intermarriage.

An active interest in the opposite sex is associated with longevity. One study of 15,000 people older than 80 found that, with rare exceptions, only married people attain extreme age (Leaf, 1973).

The most important lesson such long-lived communities can teach us is not how to reach a very old age—but how to make old age a good age. At a time when more and more old people are adding pages to their books of life, we need to think about and look for ways to make their final chapters rewarding, fulfilling endings to their lives.

SUMMARY

1 In our society, the prevailing attitude among all age groups toward the elderly is a negative one, which affects old people's feelings toward themselves as well as society's manner of dealing with the aged. **2** Three theories of aging are the activity theory, the disengagement theory, and the social reconstruction/breakdown theory. Activity theory holds that the more active elderly people remain, the more successfully they will age. Disengagement theory postulates that normal, successful aging is characterized by mutual withdrawal between society and the elderly. Social reconstruction/breakdown theory holds that an elderly person's social environment interacts negatively with the elderly person's self-concept. **3** The eighth and last stage of Erikson's theory of psychosocial development is ego integrity versus despair. Aged individuals either develop an acceptance of their lives and impending death, or they become desperately afraid of death. **4** Peck specified three psychological developments critical to successful aging: ego-differentiation versus work-role preoccupation; body transcendence versus body preoccupation; and ego-transcendence versus ego-preoccupation. **5** Bühler regards the fifth phase of life, old age, as a time when one develops a sense of the totality of one's life. Most of the elderly look upon their lives with a sense of partial fulfillment. **6** As life expectancy increases, so do the lengths of marriages. Divorce is relatively uncommon in elderly couples, many of whom are quite happy in marriage. Major problems for the elderly include caring for an ill spouse and widowhood. **7** Elderly persons who have never married express fewer feelings of loneliness and are more independent than typical elderly people. **8** Although elderly parents usually do not live with their adult children, they frequently see each other and offer mutual assistance. The role of grandparent varies in different societies, and there are several styles of grandparenting in our society. **9** Although the popular stereotype is that the elderly years are sexless, they need not be. Many people over 60 are sexually interested and active. **10** Some problems associated with aging include: lowered income, substandard housing, institutionalization, crime, and coping with retirement. **11** Elderly members of ethnic minority groups face all these problems, but to a greater degree. **12** Aging in other cultures may be a very different experience from aging in America today. Cultures where the elderly are respected and active and are permitted to perform useful work produce many happy, healthy old people.

SUGGESTED READINGS

Brown, R. N. *The rights of older persons: The basic ACLU guide to an older person's rights*. New York: Avon Books, 1979. A comprehensive guide that focuses on the rights of elderly persons with regard to Social Security benefits, pension, mandatory retirement, employment, and other issues, with suggestions for combating age-based discrimination.

Burnside, I. (ed.) *Sexuality and aging*. Los Angeles: University of Southern California, 1975. A collection of articles about various aspects of aging and sexuality. Includes implications for nurses, physicians, counselors, and teachers.

Butler, R. N., and Lewis, M. I. *Sex after sixty*. New York: Harper & Row, 1976. An easy-to-read guide to sex in the later years, which covers normal physical changes, common medical and emotional problems, the situations of people without partners, and other aspects of a topic about which there is much embarrassment and ignorance.

Jones, R.   *The other generation: The new power of older people*. New Jersey: Prentice-Hall, 1977. An interesting book about the impact of increasing numbers of people over 65 on our society. Discusses many practical issues related to aging today: retirement, ageism, and political groups developed to further the causes of the elderly.

Pfeiffer, E.   *Successful aging: A conference report*. Durham, NC: Duke, 1974. A collection of papers by leading researchers on adulthood and aging organized around the theme of "successful aging."

Seligman, M.   *Helplessness*. San Francisco: Freeman, 1975. A fascinating account of Seligman's theory that anxiety and depression arise from a feeling of learned helplessness, that is, loss of control, a situation which characterizes many elderly in our society. He demonstrates how allowing an individual a measure of control over the environment guards against helplessness.

Endings

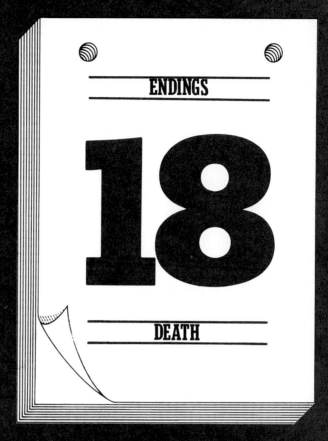

ENDINGS

18

DEATH

IN THIS CHAPTER YOU WILL LEARN ABOUT

Attitudes people of different ages have about death and dying

The content and purpose of death-education programs

The stages people go through in facing their own deaths, and the psychological changes that accompany the final period of life

Some ethical issues—such as euthanasia—surrounding death, and some new ways—such as the hospice movement—to help dying people

Normal and morbid grief and ways to deal with this

CHAPTER OVERVIEW

Death: the inspiration for some of the greatest music, painting, poetry, drama, and fiction the world has ever known. Death: the mystery upon which philosophers have pondered and devolved entire systems of approaching life. Death: the impetus for the values frameworks in the world's many religions. Death: the challenge to scientists in a wide range of disciplines.

Once, death was very much a part of most people's daily lives. They expected some of their children to die in infancy or childhood. They saw family and friends succumb to a frightening array of fatal illnesses. People feared death, and yet they accepted its presence, hovering in the corners of their lives.

Since about the turn of the twentieth century, however, death has been receding farther and farther into the background of the life of the ordinary person in our society. Because of advances in medicine, children are more likely to reach adulthood, adults are more likely to reach old age, and old people are able to overcome illnesses that were once fatal. Furthermore, the twentieth century has seen no war fought on American soil.

As death has become less of a threat, most people have been able to push it to the periphery of their consciousness. We meet it face to face far less often. Care of the dying and the dead, for example, is no longer an aspect of family life. Instead, these functions have become the province of professionals. People go to hospitals to die, and morticians prepare their bodies for burial. We rarely even speak directly of death; instead, people have turned to euphemisms like "passing away," "passing on," and "going to meet one's Maker."

Yet the more of a taboo death has become, the more attention it has demanded. "We do not escape death, but it returns as a preoccupation of our culture, which both denies death and is obsessed by its observation," says Pattison (1977, p. 8), who refers to the "pornographic" treatment of death in popular culture, such as that seen in horror movies and violent TV shows. These, says Feifel (1977), "bring to our awareness disaster and battlefield deaths, but they are usually removed from the realm of feeling to that of impersonal statistics, black comedy, and fictive experience" (p. 5).

Recently, we have seen the birth of a healthier attitude toward death—an attitude that seeks to understand it, to explore the emotional, the moral, and the practical issues surrounding it, and to try to make this inevitable outcome of every person's life as positive as possible. *Thanatology*, the study of death and dying, is arousing a great deal of interest as people recognize the importance of integrating death into life.

Bromley (1974) sums up the need to make the terminal stage of life a significant and valuable portion of the life cycle:

To be educated for dying as well as for living does not mean that we need become morbidly preoccupied with death. The realization that each of us will die gives us a common interest; it helps to focus our attention and energies on the present and the near future, and on the absurdities of some of our present values and social practices [p. 287].

Bromley emphasizes the need to "familiarize ourselves with the psychological and behavioral aspects of dying while we are still alive and well" through firsthand observation of the dying, through literature and the arts, and through open discussion and scientific inquiry. By preparing ourselves for the last stage of our lives, we can make it a positive interval—a last chance for us to exhibit our best qualities—rather than the negative one it now is for most people.

There are at least three facets of dying: the biological, the social, and the psychological (Bromley, 1974). Current medical debate focuses on when biological death occurs: when the heart stops beating, when breathing stops, or when electrical activity in the brain ceases. The criteria for death have assumed a new importance with the development of medical apparatus that can prolong the basic signs of life indefinitely. People in deep comas can be kept alive for years, even though they may have suffered irreversible brain damage and may never regain consciousness.

The social aspects of death revolve around its legal significance, such as the redistribution of power and wealth and around funeral and mourning rituals. A major problem in our society is that we have few conventions for how people should act when they know they are dying, how those around them should act, and how survivors should behave after the death of a loved one. One convention we do have that is rarely helpful for either dying people or those close to them is to isolate the dying in a hospital or nursing home, to refuse to discuss their condition with them, to separate from them before death by visiting less often, and thus to leave them alone to cope with their imminent death.

The psychological aspects of death involve the way we feel both about our own impending death and about the deaths of those close to us. With the general erosion of a strong religious climate that carries firm belief in an afterlife, most people today have a great deal of trouble coming to terms with the meaning of death. We need a more positive approach that accepts the reality of death as a natural and expected phase of the life cycle.

ATTITUDES TOWARD DEATH ACROSS THE LIFE SPAN

One topic of interest to thanatologists and developmentalists alike is the way people of different ages think and feel about death, and how they are influenced by their cognitive, emotional, and experiential development.

CHILDHOOD

Children 2 or 3 years old rarely get upset by the sight of a dead animal or the news of a dead person, because they usually have no idea what death means. Children vary considerably in the age at which they begin to understand death, and in their reactions to it. The pioneer in exploring children's understanding of death was Maria Nagy (1948), who observed children in Hungary right after World War II. She found an evolution of their ideas about death between the ages of 3 and 10, a concept that has since been supported by some researchers and refuted by others.

According to Nagy, children's understanding of death goes through three age-related stages. In the first stage, when children are less than 5 years old, they consider death a continuation of life and think it is temporary and reversible. So a child sees death as a separation, but thinks that the dead person might return again. Children of this age also think that dead people eat, hear, see, and think, even though they don't do these things as well as living people do. In the second stage, between the approximate ages of 5 to 9, children recognize that death is final and permanent, but they still don't see it as inevitable and don't relate it to themselves. They often personify death, seeing it in the form of a skeleton, a circus clown, an angel, or a spirit. By the third stage, which they reach at about 9 or 10, children realize that death comes to everyone, and, therefore, that they too will die.

A number of observers have found that these stages do not apply neatly to all children. Kastenbaum (1972), for example, cites the case of a 6-year-old boy who realized his own inevitable mortality, and, shocked, said, "But I had been planning to live forever, you know" (p. 281). And Anthony (1965) tells of the 4-year-old who said, "Every day I'm afraid of dying. . . . I wish I might never grow old, for then I'd never die, would I?" (p. 324). Koocher

(1973) found that American children rarely personify death in the way that Nagy's Hungarian children did. (On the other hand, Kastenbaum and Aisenberg (1972) found that adults often do, seeing death as a gentle comforter, the grim reaper, or a wrinkled old woman.) A number of researchers have found that children's social, economic, and cultural backgrounds influence their concepts of death. Bluebond-Langner (1977) reports findings that show children from poor families are more likely to associate death with violence, while middle-class children refer to disease and old age.

Koocher (1975) confirms Nagy's general progression, which he relates to cognitive development. Under the age of 6 or 7, children think in magical, egocentric terms about the causes of death. They may say it is caused by "eating a dirty bug" or "going swimming alone when your mother says no." They cannot understand the concept, because death is outside their own experience—that is, even if someone close to them has died, they have not died themselves.

The idea of reincarnation is common among children. Anthony (1965) tells of two 5-year-olds who believed that dead people are reborn as babies: One, whose father had died two years before, asked, "Mama, is papa borned yet?" Children often believe that dead things can be brought back to life if you "take them to the emergency room" or "keep them warm and give them hot food." This belief in rebirth and the impermanence of death is fed by fairy tales like "Little Red Riding Hood," in which the dead grandmother comes back to life by emerging from the wolf's body, and by animated cartoons, which regularly show characters falling from airplanes and cliffs, being blown up in explosions, being mashed flat by steamrollers—and always coming back to life in the next frame.

Between 7 and 11 years of age, children cite more concrete causes of death such as "cancer," "guns," "dope," and "poison." They can now incorporate the experiences of others into their thinking, and they now realize that death is irreversible. At about the age of 7, 8, or 9, when they are starting to understand the concept, many children become consumed with questions about death.

By early adolescence, at about age 12, virtually all children realize that death comes to everyone and that its coming need not be seen as punishment or an act of violence, but as part of the normal life cycle. By this time young people turn to more abstract, general explanations for death such as "illness," "old age," and "accidents."

From her studies of children who had a terminal illness, Bluebond-Langner (1977) concluded that all the views of death in Nagy's stages—separation, personification, and a biological universal—are present at all stages in development. The way children view death at any particular time reflects their own individual lives and their own social, psychological, and intellectual experiences and concerns. Experience, rather than age, determines their understanding of death and explains why chronically ill children often learn of their own imminent death at a very early age.

How Dying Children Learn about Death

Bluebond-Langner (1975) focused on forty children, aged 3 to 9, all of whom had leukemia and were patients in a hospital where they were cared for in the same facilities as children who were not mortally ill. She found that dying children go through five stages in which they learn their real condition, whether or not anyone ever tells them. As the children learn more about their disease, they also pass through different definitions of themselves. (See Table 18-1.)

First, these children learn that "it" is a serious illness, and they have a radical change in self-concept: From having thought

TABLE 18-1
Stages in Dying
Children's Think-
ing about Death

STAGES	UNDERSTANDING OF DISEASE	SELF-CONCEPT
Before diagnosis of leukemia	———	I am healthy and normal.
STAGE 1 (After diagnosis)	"It" is a serious illness.	I am seriously ill.
STAGE 2 (After beginning of treatment)	These are the drugs used to treat this illness, and this is the side effect of this treatment.	I am seriously ill, I am getting treatment, and I will get better.
STAGE 3	This is the purpose of these treatments. Certain symptoms mean that certain procedures will be followed. Some of treatments are performed to treat the side effects of the other treatments.	I am always ill, but I am going to get better.
STAGE 4	This disease is a cycle of remissions and relapses. People can get sick over and over again in the same way, and the medicines don't always last as long as they are supposed to.	I feel better for awhile, and then I get sick again, and this is how it is going to be. I am always ill, and I will not get better.
STAGE 5 (Often after learning of the death of another leukemic child)	This cycle does not go on forever. It has an end, and that end is death.	I am going to die.

SOURCE: From Bluebond-Langner, 1977.

of themselves as normal, healthy children like other children, they now think of themselves as people who are seriously ill. Second, they learn the names of the drugs they are being treated with and the side effects of the chemotherapy, and they think of themselves as people who are seriously ill but who will get better. Third, they learn the purposes of the procedures used to treat them, and they think of themselves as *always* ill, but still going to get better. In the fourth stage, they see their disease as a cycle of remissions, in which they feel better, and of relapses, in which they feel sick. While they do not yet think of death, they say, "I am always ill and will not get better." Finally, they realize that for them leukemia will be a fatal illness and that they themselves are going to die. They often enter this fifth stage after hearing of the death of another child who also had leukemia.

These children's passage from one stage to another depended on the specifics of their own experience—the number of times they had been to the clinic, the extent of their conversations with other leukemic children, the number of their relapses and remissions, and the knowledge of another child's death. Age and intellectual ability had little to do with the speed or completeness with which the children passed through these stages, and Bluebond-Langner points out that some 3- and 4-year-olds of average intelligence know more about their status than some very intelligent 9-year-olds.

What have these dying children taught us about helping other children deal with death?

Since personal experience plays such a major part in helping children understand death, Bluebond-Langner emphasizes the importance of introducing the concept into their lives at a very early age and giving them the experience of talking about death and the issues surrounding it. The death of a pet—even the death of flowers—may provide a natural framework for raising these questions. Two of the most important concerns for children are their fear of being deserted and left alone if someone close to them dies and their sense of guilt for having in some way caused the death.

Children, especially adolescents, often become depressed upon the death of a parent, but generally young children have less severe and less prolonged grief reactions than adults do. There is no particular link between the death of a parent and the conduct disorders or delinquency of a child. Children often react more to the many family difficulties caused by a parent's death rather than to the death itself (Rutter, 1979). These

Children suffering from leukemia and other fatal diseases undergo a radical change in self-concept: From thinking of themselves as normal, healthy children, they begin to think of themselves as seriously ill. Pictured is Chad Green with his mother shortly before his death in 1979. (Daniel Bernstein)

> *May 12. I can't believe Mother is dead and that we will never see her again. Mother was killed when the hospital was bombed. I cried almost all night and I am ashamed of what I did in front of everybody.... I tried to get out into the street to fight the Germans.... I was all right until the bombs started to fall around midnight and then I couldn't stand it. I know I yelled and bit Uncle Pieter in the hand, but I don't know why. I think I was crazy.*
>
> Dirk Van Der Heide, age 12, from *Small Voices*, p. 20.

difficulties may include financial uncertainty, unstable care arrangements, moving around to a succession of new homes in strange neighborhoods or even different cities, and the inability of a bereaved and depressed widow or widower to focus closely enough on the needs of the child.

ADOLESCENCE

The death rate is very low in adolescence, and teenagers have generally had very little experience with death. Between the ages of 15 and 24, mortality rates are only about 1 in 1000, with the leading causes for both sexes being accidents, homicide, cancer, and suicide. As Shneidman (1977) points out:

The school years are obviously a time of life when the threats to life itself are not so much from internal disorders of the [body], but rather from threats by others in the environment and from imprudencies from within the self [p. 68].

Most young people have not been in the kind of setting that would help them develop mature attitudes toward death. That lies ahead. In these years, they rarely think about death, or about how long they will live. Instead, they think more about *how* they will live. "Adolescents make brave soldiers," says Pattison (1977, p. 23), "because they do not fear annihilation so much as whether they are brave and glorious." Because of their drive to live out their newly discovered identities, adolescents often have highly romantic ideas about death.

Furthermore, many are still thinking in egocentric ways and are in the grip of the personal fable (described on page 354). They feel they can take virtually any kind of risk without danger. In fact, in a spirit of rebellious perversity, some teens go out of their way to do just what their parents and other adults have warned them against. They hitchhike, they drive recklessly, and they experiment with potent drugs—often with tragic results.

When adolescents are terminally ill, they face death, says Feifel (1977), "in the contradictory and perplexing ways adolescents seem to face life" (p. 177). The mysticism and intense interest in religion that is ordinarily common in adolescence often becomes heightened. At the same time, mortally ill youths often tend to deny their real conditions and to talk as if they are going to recover when, in fact, they know they are not. This denial, and the accompanying repression of their emotions, is a useful device that helps many sick young people deal with this crushing blow to their expectations for life. Ill teenagers are far more likely to be angry than depressed. They think about suicide much less than adults in similar circumstances do and are much more likely to cast about

looking for someone to blame. Their anger at the unfairness of their fate often erupts toward their parents, doctors, friends, or the world in general. A saving grace for many of these young people is the "black humor" they often turn to in order to defuse the tension they are under. In one group of adolescent cardiac patients, for example, a number who had recently had pacemakers implanted referred to themselves as "Ever-Ready," "Dry Cell," and "Hot Shot" (Galdston, 1977).

There is, of course, no "one way" in which adolescents act. The way they respond to the imminence of their own deaths often reflects the basic kinds of personalities they had before they fell ill. As Schowalter (1977) says:

Some patients are placid, others rage; some question, others do not; some become more mature, others regress. One must not rely on formulae but expect just as wide a range of behavior in dying adolescents as one expects in the living [p. 202].

In his report on the attitudes about death of ninety college students, as revealed in their answers to a questionnaire that appeared in the magazine *Psychology Today*, Shneidman (1977) sees many changes over the last few generations in people's views of death. Contemporary college students, he says, "have made themselves the center of their own universe, and have put themselves back into their own deaths" (p. 71). They recognize death and dying as aspects of living and see themselves as able to affect their own destinies. Ninety-six percent believe that psychological factors can influence or even cause death, and half believe that most people participate in their own deaths, either consciously or unconsciously.

From late adolescence on, the most common view of death in the opinion of people responding to this questionnaire (which was answered by people of all ages) is simply as "the final process of life." Only 30 percent of college students believe in an afterlife, and they feel that the most upsetting single thing about death is the inability to have any experiences. One student wrote:

Death means the end of consciousness. Like dreamless sleep, like before birth—no memories. Nothing. The body decays, its elements become part of the earth so when one dies he gives back to the earth [p. 73].

And another:

Death signifies the termination of all meaning your life has begun to assume through careful working through of your ideas. It comes, and it drops one into a void from which he can never return [p. 73].

YOUNG ADULTHOOD

Young adults are not so very different from adolescents in their attitudes toward death. They, too, have very low death rates. They, too, are relatively unlikely to have their lives disrupted by the death of someone close to them or by the foreboding of their own deaths. They tend to have finished their preparations for life—education, training, courtship—and are now living life as grown-ups. Recently embarked on a career, in a marriage, or in parenthood, they are eager to live the life they have been preparing for all these years.

As a result, when young adults are suddenly taken ill or badly injured, they feel more intensely emotional about their imminent deaths than do people at any other stage of the life cycle (Pattison, 1977). They feel extremely frustrated at the inability to fulfill their dreams. To have worked so hard—for nothing! This frustration turns into rage, and this anger

often makes young adults difficult hospital patients.

They are troublesome patients for another reason as well—the fact that the hospital staff responsible for their care are also usually young adults themselves, who find it difficult dealing with the thought of death for a person around their own age. As Kastenbaum (1977) points out, much adult thought about death is evasive. People don't like to think about the possibility of their own deaths.

MIDLIFE

When the Chicago community organizer Saul Alinsky was once asked what had made him decide to devote his life to organizing working-class people, he recalled a time when he had been gravely ill:

I realized then that I was going to die. I had always known that in some abstract sense, of course, but for the first time I really *knew* it deep inside me. And I made up my mind that before I died I would do something that really made a difference in the world.

For most people it is in middle age that they really *know* deep inside themselves that they are indeed going to die. With the deaths of their parents, they are now the oldest generation. As they read the obituary pages—which they do more regularly these days than they used to—they find more and more familiar names. Their bodies send them signals that they are not so young, agile, and hearty as they once were.

With this inner knowledge of their own deaths, the way middle-aged people perceive time undergoes a change. Previously, they have thought of their lives in terms of the number of years they have lived since birth, but now they think of the number of years left to them until their deaths (Neugarten, 1967).

The realization of death's certainty is often an impetus for making a major life change. Faced with the awareness that their time on this earth is finite, people reassess and take stock of their careers, their marriages, their relationships with their children, their friendships, their values, the way they spend their time. Feeling that life is short and that they owe it to themselves to make the most of the years they have left, people may make major changes in any of these areas. Or they may just look at them in different ways—and concentrate more on the positive aspects.

Appreciations of some of the elemental things that people tend to value more highly as they age—human love and affection, insight, pleasures of the senses, nature, children—are probably a result of the restructuring and reformulation of concepts of time, self, and death [Butler & Lewis, 1977, p. 312].

LATE ADULTHOOD

The 79-year-old woman looked very small and frail in the middle of the hospital bed. "Don't feel sorry for me when I'm gone," she told her daughter. "I'm not afraid of death—I'm only afraid of living like this."

This woman was speaking for many old people when she expressed her feelings. Lonely since the death of her husband and her closest friends, sick and unable to pursue the activities she had engaged in over the years, and concerned about becoming a burden on those who were left, she was ready to embrace death. In general, elderly people are less anxious about death than are the middle-aged (Bengston, Cuellar, & Ragan,

I think more about death than I did years ago. I think about how little time I have left - ten years, five years .... Looking forward to even ten years is only looking forward to tomorrow. .... I accept death as a natural thing, even a rather nice and beautiful thing! I think of death and zoology.

Father Edmund, 75, in *The View in Winter,* by Ronald Blythe, p. 250.

1975). Through the years, as people have lost friends and relatives, they have gradually reorganized their thoughts and feelings in acceptance of their own mortality. Old people often feel like outsiders in a world running by values they do not share. Their physical problems and some of the other troubles of old age diminish their pleasure in living. Thus, both positive and negative factors combine to prepare old people for their deaths. Those who feel that their lives have been meaningful are usually more able to accept the prospect of their own death than are those who are still wondering about the point of having lived at all.

FINDING PURPOSE IN LIFE

The hero of Tolstoy's short story, "The Death of Ivan Ilych" (1946) is wracked by an illness that he knows will be fatal. In despair, he asks himself over and over again:

Then what does it mean? Why? It can't be that life is so senseless and horrible. But if it really has been so horrible and senseless, why must I die and die in agony? There is something wrong! . . . .

Turning his face to the wall he continued to ponder on the same question: Why, and for what purpose, is there all this horror? [p. 462].

Even greater than his physical suffering is Ivan Ilych's mental torture as he lies dying and becomes more and more convinced that he has wasted his life, that his life has been without purpose, and therefore that his death is equally pointless.

What Tolstoy brought to us in a literary way, contemporary social scientists are investigating in the laboratory. Their findings bear out the great writer's thesis. Frankl (1965) proposed that people need to find meaning in their own deaths if they are to feel that their

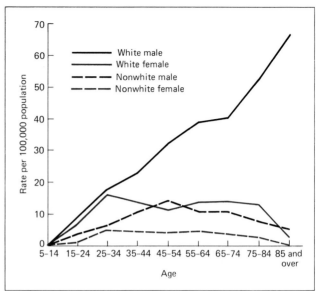

Fig. 18-1
Suicide Rates by Age
and Color. Source: *Vital
and Health Statistics*,
Series 20, 1967, p. 5.
National Center for
Health Statistics

lives are meaningful. Conversely, the greater purpose one's life has, the less one fears death.

To test this theory, Durlak (1973) administered scales designed to measure people's feelings about "purpose in life" and "fear of death" to thirty-nine women whose average age was 76. He found a significant negative correlation between "fear of death" and "purpose in life," thus supporting Frankl's theory. A National Institute of Mental Health study (reported in Butler & Lewis, 1973) found that more than half the healthy old people seem to have resolved the problem of their death; about 1 in 3 showed denial; and 15 percent openly expressed fear.

SUICIDE

A handbook complete with instructions for committing suicide as painlessly as possible, with an appendix listing the lethal doses of various medicines: a macabre section of a science-fiction novel? No, a thoughtful— though controversial—effort of a British organization dedicated to its aim of "the right to die with dignity" (Borders, 1980). While the book

is oriented toward terminally ill patients, some of its critics fear that it might seem to offer too easy a solution for people whose problem is depression rather than physical disease. This is a very real concern, because in recent years the suicide rate has been alarmingly high, especially for young people.

SUICIDE AMONG YOUNG PEOPLE

During the eight years between 1968 and 1976, the suicide rate for 15- to 24-year-olds more than doubled; presently, some 5000 people in this age group are killing themselves each year (Graham, 1978). Suicide is the second highest cause of death for this age group, topped only by accidents. Even children aged 10 to 14 are more suicide-prone now, with 158 suicides in 1976, compared to 116 in 1968. Young male suicides outnumber female by more than a 4:1 ratio, but young women are twice as likely to attempt it.

Why do young people try and sometimes succeed in killing themselves? What makes life so intolerable to them? Suicide attempters feel lonely, isolated, and alienated, and they consider themselves unloved by parents and peers. Some constitute a new, more aggressive group of delinquent youths who abuse drugs and alcohol and are sometimes under the influence of these substances when they make their attempts. Ironically and tragically, many of these young people—even those whose attempts end in death—do not want to die. They only want to change their lives, and their suicide attempts are desperate pleas for attention and help.

What are young suicide attempters like? After the first two years of a suicide prevention program for teenagers, which operated from a hospital serving an inner-city, low socioeconomic black population, Rohn, Sarles, Kenny, Reynolds, and Heald (1977) issued a report on a group of sixty-five adolescents who had tried to kill themselves. Ranging in age from 7 to 19 years, they had a median age of 16, and 75 percent were girls.

These young people tended to be social isolates, with half described as "loners." Seventy-five percent were doing very poorly in school: Nineteen percent had failed one or more grades and thirty-five percent were dropouts or chronic truants. Another 35 percent had behavior or discipline problems. In a subgroup of twenty-five who received psychological testing, 60 percent were judged to suffer from minimal brain dysfunction, with attendant learning difficulties and the poor self-image and feelings of hopelessness that often accompany academic failure. Their families were troubled, with a high proportion of separated and divorced parents (59 percent were in single-parent homes), a number of alcoholic parents (31 percent had at least one), and a large number of youths living away from their parents (25 percent). This study adds a new element—that of minimal brain dysfunction—and confirms other studies that have found that adolescents who try to kill themselves have experienced very different patterns of life from other young people.

In their study of fifty 14- to 18-year-old suicide attempters, Jacobs and Teicher (1967) had found that these youths had had problems in childhood, an escalation of these

problems during adolescence, and a final phase in the weeks and days just before the suicide attempt, when they suffered the loss of meaningful social relationships.

The suicide attempters were more alienated from their parents and more likely to have been depressed during the five years before they tried to take their lives. Seeking to establish an alternative intimate relationship, they often became involved in intense romances. Involved with their loves, they ignored or broke off ties with other friends; and if the romance failed, they were left alone with no one to turn to. Of those teens involved with sweethearts, 58 percent of the suicide attempters' romances were breaking up at the time of the attempt, compared with none of the control adolescents' affairs.

About 3 out of 4 suicide attempters were girls, and of these, five were either pregnant or worried that they might be pregnant, compared with none of the controls. When they told their boyfriends or their parents about their pregnancies, they often were rebuffed by both. Jacobs and Teicher (1967) conclude:

The state of depression characteristic of adolescents who attempt suicide stems from a series of real life experiences. Although most people accept as a truism that "we all have our ups and downs," the perspective of the suicide attempter at the time of his interview was that his life was not characterized by ups and downs, but only "downs." We feel it is unwarranted to attribute this belief to a restricted view of reality stemming from a "state of depression." By comparing the life histories of the experimental and control adolescents, there is good evidence to show that this *Weltanschauung* is justified by the suicide attempters' real life experiences [pp. 147–148].

Among older adolescents, college students are more likely to commit suicide than nonstudents. Yet academic pressures do not seem to be responsible, since suicidal students were found to have higher grade point averages and to have won more scholastic awards than their peers (Seiden, 1966). Cantor (1977) offers one explanation:

We might hypothesize that these students needed to achieve in order to feel worthwhile and when they actually did achieve they found that the victory was hollow, that self-worth did not necessarily evolve from good grades [p. 435].

Seiden (1966) found that students are likely to commit suicide not toward the end of the semester or during final exams, but in October or February, at the beginning of the term. Precipitating crises are often concern over studies, physical complaints such as an inability to eat or sleep, and difficulties with relationships, sometimes because of stormy love affairs and at other times because of social isolation. A particularly tragic case of the latter was the student who had been dead for eighteen days, unmissed and unnoticed before he was found in his room.

In her studies of young women who have attempted suicide, Cantor (1977) found them to be impulsive and to have a low tolerance for frustration and stress. Suicidal young women are often in conflict with their parents, are unable to call upon them for support, and often cannot communicate with or count on their fathers. Many are first-borns, and many have experienced father absence, especially during adolescence.

Potential suicides can often be helped by friends who offer the kind of involved attention the depressed person needs, who make themselves available when needed, and who can openly discuss their friends' suicidal thoughts (Cantor, 1977):

Most young people who attempt suicide are profoundly unhappy and want to change their lives. But they do not want to die. They want to change their lives enough to make it possible to continue to live [p. 442].

SUICIDE AMONG THE ELDERLY

People over 65 account for at least 1 out of 4 suicides, even though they make up only one-tenth of the population. They may even be ending their lives at higher rates, since many deaths may not be recognized as self-inflicted. Some suicides among old people may look like the consequences of accidental overdoses of drugs or the forgetful failure to take life-preserving medicine. However, old people who take their own lives seem to plan carefully and to know just what they are doing, judging from the fact that 1 in every 2 attempts in this age group ends in loss of life, compared to only 1 in every 7 among adolescents. Those most likely to end their lives are white men in their eighties (National Council on Aging, 1978). Elderly white men kill themselves at a rate nearly three times as high as that of nonwhite men and nearly five times as high as that of all women of the same age (Flaste, 1979).

What makes the elderly so suicidal? One explanation is their "irreversible progression of losses":

One's work is gone, and so are friends. A spouse has died. The children have moved away. Even the past is lost as memory fails. Painful illness has replaced physical well being. Self disdain has replaced self esteem. Hope has disappeared. There is a sense of passivity and helplessness [Flaste, 1979, p. C2].

Some explain the high rates among elderly white men by referring to the disparity between the heights achieved by younger members of this group, which makes it more difficult for them to face the deprivations of old age. Another contributing factor may well be their overidentification with their work roles, which leaves them without an identity after they have stopped working.

Often the depression of old age can be lifted to some degree by supportive psychotherapy, by practical measures that reduce a person's feeling of isolation, or by medication, so that the person will regain an interest in life. At other times—especially when an old person has a disabling or painful illness—all efforts fail. There is a growing level of support around the nation for "right to die" legislation, which removes the criminal connotations from suicide and gives mature people the right to end their lives when they see fit.

DEATH EDUCATION

"Why did my guinea pig die? When will it be alive again?"

"What can I say to my friend when she says she's going to kill herself?"

"How much should I tell a terminally ill patient about his disease and his limited life expectancy?"

These are just a few of the questions that are dealt with in courses about death, which are now being aimed at various age levels and groups within the community. Educators have realized that it is important to understand our attitudes toward death, to be familiar with various cultural ways of handling it, and to be sensitive to its emotional ramifications, both for the person who dies and the one who survives. Courses about death are being offered to high school and college students; to social workers, doctors, nurses, and other professionals who work with dying people and their survivors; and to interested members of the community. Even early childhood teachers are introducing discussions about death at appropriate times, when they fit into the curriculum or into the children's experience. Learning about death helps people of all ages to deal with it in their personal and professional lives.

What, specifically, can we expect death education to accomplish? The goals are different, depending on the ages and needs of the students, but some are important for everyone. Here are some of the most important aims, which draw on a list suggested by Leviton (1977):

• To help children grow up with as few death-related anxieties as possible

• To help individuals to develop their own personal belief systems about life and death

• To help people see death as a natural end to life

• To help people prepare for their own deaths and the deaths of those close to them

• To help people be comfortable around the dying and to treat them humanely and intelligently for as long as they live

• To help both laypeople and health-care professionals, such as doctors and nurses, get a realistic view of the professional and his or her obligation to the dying and their families

• To understand the dynamics of grief and the way different age groups react to loss

• To understand and be able to help a suicidal person

• To help consumers decide what kind of funeral services they want for themselves and their families, and how to purchase them most wisely

• To make dying as positive an experience as possible, by emphasizing the importance of minimizing pain, offering warm, personal care, involving family and close friends in the care of the dying person, and being sensitive to that person's wishes and needs

As part of an elementary school class on life and death, these children have made a field trip to the cemetery. (Robert E. Egington/*Time Magazine*)

FACING DEATH

How do people face the approach of their own deaths? What are the processes by which they accept the fact that their life will soon end? In recent years, a number of professionals who have closely observed dying persons have evolved theories to explain the dying person's thought processes. Let us look at the most important ones.

THE STAGE THEORY OF ELISABETH KÜBLER-ROSS

A physician who worked with dying patients and who encouraged them to talk about themselves, Kübler-Ross (1969) is widely credited with having revitalized the current interest in death and dying. She found that most of the patients she had contact with welcomed the opportunity to speak openly about their conditions. And she found that most of them had a very accurate picture of their closeness to death—even when they had not been told. After speaking with some 500 terminally ill patients, Kübler-Ross proposed

that there were five stages in coming to terms with death: denial, anger, bargaining, depression, and ultimate acceptance.

1 Denial Most people respond with shock to the knowledge that they are about to die. Their first thought is, "Oh, no, this can't happen to me." When people around the patient also deny reality, he or she has no one to talk to and, as a result, feels deserted and isolated. When allowed some hope along with the first announcement and given the assurance that they will not be deserted no matter what happens, people can drop the initial shock and denial rather quickly.

2 Anger After realizing that this is happening to them, people become angry as they ask, "Why me?" They become envious of those around them who are young and healthy. They are really angry not at the people themselves, but at the youth and the health that they themselves don't have. They need to express their rage to get rid of it.

3 Bargaining The next thought may be, "Yes, it's happening to me—*but*." The *but* is an attempt to bargain for time. People pray to God, "If you just let me live to see my daughter graduated . . . *or* my son married . . . *or* my grandchild born . . . I'll be a better person . . . *or* I won't ask for anything more . . . *or* I'll accept my lot in life." These bargains represent the acknowledgment that time is limited and life is finite. When people drop the *but*, they are able to say, "Yes, me."

4 Depression In this stage people need to cry, to grieve for the loss of their own life. By expressing the depths of their anguish, they can overcome depression much more quickly than if they feel pressured to hide their sorrow.

February 2, 1892

This long slow dying is no doubt instructive, but it is disappointingly free from excitements: "naturalness" being carried to its supreme expression. One sloughs off the activities one by one, and never knows they're gone, until one suddenly finds that the months have slipped away and the sofa will never more be laid upon, the morning paper read, or the loss of the new book regretted; one revolves with equal content within the narrowing circle until the vanishing point is reached, I suppose.

Alice James (dying of cancer), age 44, in *Revelations: Diaries of Women*, p. 204.

5 Acceptance Finally, people can acknowledge, "My time is very close now, and it's all right." This is not necessarily a happy time, but people who have worked through their anxieties and anger about death and have resolved their unfinished business end up with a feeling of peace with themselves and the world. Says Kübler-Ross (1972):

People who have been able to sit through this stage with patients and who have experienced the beautiful feeling of inner and outer peace that they show will soon appreciate that working with terminally ill patients is not a morbid, depressing job but can be an inspiring experience [p. 259].

Kübler-Ross's five stages are not invariant for all people, however, and should not be held up as the criterion for the "good death." Butler and Lewis (1977) noted that in their experience, people generally don't go through the stages as neatly and orderly as in the theoretical model. They caution that while the stages offer useful guidelines for understanding death, they should not be regarded too rigidly.

And Leviton (1977) emphasizes the individualistic style of dying unique to each person, in which it may be just as normal and healthy for a person to die in a state of denial or anger as in that of acceptance. He goes on to say:

Elisabeth Kübler-Ross has probably done more to make the public aware of the needs of the dying than any person working in the field today. She hypothesized that the dying person goes through five psychological stages prior to death. Further, she explicitly stated that the stages should be tested under more rigorous conditions. What has happened? We find not only novices but experienced death educators and thanatologists accepting the five stages as invariant, as gospel. Health-care givers find themselves being forced to think in terms of whether they were "unsuccessful" in meeting the ultimate goal, the big number 5— "acceptance" of death [p. 259].

THE "DYING TRAJECTORIES" OF E. MANSELL PATTISON

The dictionary defines a trajectory as "the path of a moving particle or body, especially such a path in three dimensions" (*American Heritage Dictionary*, 1971, p. 1362). Pattison (1977) defines his *trajectory of life* as our own anticipated life span and the plans we make for the way we will live out our life. When illness or injury forces us to face the fact that we will die much sooner than expected, the trajectory we hold has to change. We have to change our thinking and our plans to deal with the present and with our shortened future. Between the time we first learn of our impending death—what Pattison calls "the crisis of knowledge of death"—and the actual point of death, we are in what he calls the *living-dying interval*. In this interval, we shape our *dying trajectory*.

The Living-Dying Interval

This interval is composed of three stages: the acute crisis phase, the chronic living-dying phase, and the terminal phase. The goal of those caring for the patient is to help him or her cope with the shock of the acute phase, live as effectively as possible through the chronic phase, and, finally, move into the terminal phase.

THE ACUTE PHASE   During this time, people face what is probably the most severe crisis of their lives—the pronouncement of doom, the awareness that their lives will soon be over, the need to face the fact that they will never get the chance to do all that they had hoped. To cope with the enormously high state of anxiety such a crisis provokes, indi-

viduals turn to whatever defense mechanisms help them cope best. In the first part of this phase, people are often immobilized and have the sense that "This is not happening to me; I'm just watching." Next may come overwhelming feelings of inadequacy, bewilderment, and confusion. Denial, anger, and bargaining, the first three of Kübler-Ross's stages, often appear in this acute phase. During this time, dying persons need emotional support and help in focusing on the reality of their condition and whatever future they have left to them.

THE CHRONIC LIVING-DYING PHASE
During this period, the dying person has to confront a number of fears. Professionals and caring family and friends can help the patient to separate each issue and deal with them, one at a time. The major concerns are fear of the unknown, fear of loneliness, fear of sorrow, fear of loss of family and friends, fear of loss of body, fear of loss of self-control, fear of suffering and pain, fear of loss of identity, and fear of regression (withdrawal from life). Dying people can overcome these fears by mourning their losses, exerting as much control as possible over their lives, and placing their lives in perspective within their own personal histories, families, and human traditions.

THE TERMINAL PHASE   This stage begins when dying people begin to withdraw into themselves. This withdrawal seems to be set off by internal body signals that tell people they need to conserve their energy. During this phase, patients' hopes of getting better change from expecting their hopes to be realized to recognizing that their hopes represent what they would *like* to happen but that they don't *expect* to happen. It is at this point that people accept the reality of their imminent death.

Different Kinds of Dying Trajectories

No one trajectory is the "ideal" for every individual. Each person's dying trajectory is different, depending on the individual's own personality and life circumstances. Furthermore, there are various possible trajectories that depend on the nature of the life-threatening condition:

Certain death at a known time. In acute leukemia or a massive accident, for example, the dying process is so quick that it remains within the acute phase of the living-dying interval.

Certain death at an unknown time. This typical trajectory of chronic fatal illness poses the challenge of living effectively in a time of uncertainty.

Uncertain death but a known time when the question will be resolved. In radical surgery the outcome is often clear immediately after the operation: Either the surgery is unsuccessful and the patient has died or will die soon, or it is successful and the patient has a good chance of living for a long time.

Uncertain death and an unknown time when the question will be resolved. Victims of diseases like multiple sclerosis go on for years not knowing what course their disease will take, how severe it will become, and when it may prove fatal.

Different Kinds of Death

Four different kinds of death occur, often "out of phase" with each other (Pattison, 1977). The interplay among them can lead to emotional and ethical confusion on the part of the dying person, the survivors, and society at large. (See page 586 for a discussion of ethical issues surrounding death.) What are these different kinds of death?

Sociological death: the withdrawal and separation from the patient by others

Psychic death: the acceptance of death by the individual

Biological death: "brain death," or the point at which the organism no longer exists as a human being with a functioning mind and body, even though "life-support" machines may keep the heart and lungs going

Physiological death: the point at which all vital organs have stopped functioning.

PSYCHOLOGICAL CHANGES BEFORE DEATH

Even before physiological signs indicate that a person is dying, psychological changes often begin to take place. In Chapter 16 we noted a "terminal drop" in intellectual functioning, experienced by people shortly before death (Riegel & Riegel, 1972; Riemanis & Green, 1971). Personality changes also show up during the terminal period.

Lieberman and Coplan (1970) suggest that there may be a "total system decline" in individuals near death. They tested eighty people aged 65 to 91, studied them over a three-year period, and administered a battery of psychological tests. Afterward, the researchers compared the scores of those subjects who had died within a year after the last testing session with the scores of those who lived an average of three years beyond the last session.

The subjects who were going to die within the year had lower scores on cognitive tests. They were also different in terms of personality—less introspective, less aggressive, more docile in their self-image. Those who were dealing with some sort of crisis in their lives and were close to death were more afraid of and more preoccupied with death than people who were beset by similar crises but not close to death. Persons who were close to death but whose lives were relatively stable at the time showed no special fear of or preoccupation with death. These changes suggest a psychosomatic relationship, in which physiological changes in the body trigger psychological changes. The changes are not, though, simple elements of disease. People who recovered from acute illnesses did not show the same pattern of personality decline as those who later died from the same kinds of illness.

The old people in this study talked quite freely about death. Many of them had worked out its meaning for themselves and had integrated it into their philosophies of life. Death is not, though, the focal point toward which the last decade of life is oriented. It becomes most meaningful and most important a year or two before it actually happens.

THE LIFE REVIEW

They live by memory rather than by hope, for what is left to them of life is but little compared to the long past. This, again, is the cause of their loquacity. They are continually talking of the past, because they enjoy remembering [Aristotle, *Rhetoric*, 367–347 B.C.].

Old people's tendencies to talk about the people, events, and feelings of previous years used to be tolerated as a result of aging and an indication that their memory for recent events was fading. Butler (1961) postulates that such reminiscence is part of a normal life review process, which helps people to deal with unresolved conflicts, and gives new significance and meaning to their lives and thus prepares them for death:

Some of the positive results of reviewing one's life can be a righting of old wrongs, making up with enemies, coming to acceptance of mortal life, a sense of serenity, pride in accomplishment, and a feeling of having done one's best. It gives people an opportunity to decide what to do with the time left to them and work out emotional and material legacies [Butler & Lewis, 1973, p. 44].

The Swedish film *Wild Strawberries* is an evocative portrayal of the value of the life review. As an elderly physician dreams and thinks about his past and his coming death, he realizes how cold and unaffectionate he has been for much of his life and becomes warmer and more open in his last days. This film underscores the fact noted in real life that personality can indeed change at any time in the life span, including old age.

In real life, too, many old people experience a creative ordering of their lives as a result of the life review. In other instances, the review can bear tragic witness that a person has wasted his or her life, has done irreparable injury to others, and has no chance to live life over again:

In the course of the life review the older person may reveal to his wife, children, and other intimates, unknown qualities of his character and unstated actions of his past; in return, they may reveal heretofore undisclosed or unknown truths. Hidden themes of great vintage may emerge, changing the quality of a lifelong relationship. Revelations of the past may forge a new intimacy, render a deceit honest; they may sever peculiar bonds and free tongues; or they may sculpture terrifying hatreds out of fluid, fitful antagonisms [Butler, 1961; cited in Neugarten, 1968, p. 496].

ETHICAL ISSUES AROUND DEATH

Immediately after birth an infant is found to have several disabilities. One is Down's syndrome, which will prevent him from ever functioning at a normal intellectual level. Another is an obstruction that makes it impossible for him to swallow, and, thus, to eat. The physician asks the infant's parents whether they want an operation to remove the obstruction. If not, the baby will die.

A child has been so badly beaten by her stepfather that, according to a team of neurosurgeons, her brain has died. There is no chance, they say, that she could ever walk, speak, or even think. The stepfather's attorney is attempting to prevent the hospital from disconnecting the respirator as the mother has requested, so that his client cannot be tried for murder. If hospital personnel do turn off the machines that are maintaining the child's breathing and heart action, who is responsible for her death—the stepfather or the hospital employee?

A 55-year-old woman is suffering from terminal cancer. With medical care she may live another couple of years, but the likelihood is that she will become so weak that she will be confined to her bed most of the time. She is apt to be in a great deal of pain. She asks her physician to give her a potent drug. He knows that an overdose of this medicine will bring death, and he strongly suspects that the woman plans to end her life at a time of her own choosing.

These are only a sampling of the many ethical issues that hover around the presence of death. Dying people themselves, their families, and those who treat them are often faced with hard choices. Many revolve around the importance of the quality of life, as opposed to its length. Many are new to our generation, spurred by technological advances that create situations that never existed before.

For example, before the discovery of antibiotics, elderly people often succumbed fairly quickly and easily to pneumonia, sometimes dubbed "the old person's friend." Now pneumonia can be treated, and the elderly survive this illness, often to fall prey to a long, debilitating, and uncomfortable parade of other ailments. Before the invention of respirators, biological death was synonymous with physiological death. Now the decision about keeping someone alive with artificial support systems has many ramifications. Decisions about organ transplants are, of course, another virtually uncharted sea. As life becomes more complex, death becomes more complicated.

The questions that arise are endless.

When a doctor knows she can prescribe a medicine that can relieve a patient's pain but that may also shorten his life, does she give the drug? When a doctor can save only one life, as in the case of a traumatic childbirth, whom does he save—the mother or the baby? Is abortion murder, or is there a point that distinguishes between a medical procedure on the mother's body and the killing of a new life?

Do people have the right to take their own lives? If so, under what circumstances? What is the legal liability of anyone else who might help them? Can assistants to a suicide be charged with murder?

When a doctor has diagnosed a terminal illness, how shall she tell her patients? Should they be given an approximate time frame for their lives so they can put their affairs in order and better prepare for their deaths? Or will knowing the prognosis hasten their deaths, becoming a self-fulfilling prophecy?

Who makes the decision that a life is not worth prolonging? Who decides when to stop treatment? The patient? The family? The physician? A hospital committee? What abuses are possible? How can they be prevented?

None of these questions has simple answers. Each requires soul searching by everyone involved. Each situation is unique and, therefore, each solution must be unique.

EUTHANASIA

On June 20, 1973, Lester Zygmaniak walked into a quiet hospital, aimed his sawed-off shotgun at a bedridden patient, and with one blast killed him. The dead man was the killer's 26-year-old brother, George. Victim of a motorcycle accident that had left him paralyzed from the neck down, George had begged Lester to kill him. When Lester complied, he was practicing what is known as *euthanasia*, or mercy killing, a prime example of the kind of dilemma we have been discussing.

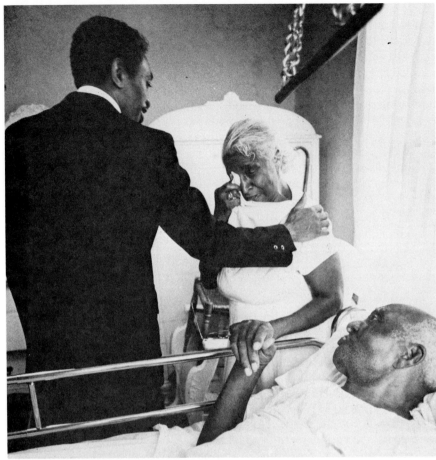

New institutions, called hospices, have recently been set up to help ease the pain and treat the symptoms of the terminally ill, make them comfortable, and help their families deal with the patients' illness and subsequent death. (Linda Bartlett/Woodfin Camp and Assoc.)

Lester's act, described in a book titled *Act of Love* (Mitchell, 1976), was *active* euthanasia, in which some action is deliberately taken with the purpose of shortening a life. *Passive* euthanasia describes those situations in which a person is allowed to die by withholding treatment that might extend life.

Euthanasia has been gaining wider acceptance in recent years. In a 1973 Gallup poll, 53 percent of those questioned agreed with active euthanasia, compared with 36 percent in 1950. In 1969, 87 percent of American physicians approved of passive euthanasia, and 80 percent admitted sometimes practicing it (Schulz, 1978). In 1973, doctors attending the convention of the American Medical Association supported the use of *living wills*, which let individuals make crucial decisions about their own deaths (see box on facing page).

NEW WAYS TO HELP TERMINAL PATIENTS

THE HOSPICE MOVEMENT

"I had a fast-growing conviction," writes Norman Cousins in his book *Anatomy of an Illness* (1979), "that a hospital is no place for a person who is seriously ill" (p. 29). Many who are concerned with the terminally ill are convinced that hospitals are even worse places for these patients. The typical hospital is set up to treat acute illness, with the goal of curing people and sending them home well. This goal is doomed to be thwarted for the terminal patient. As a result, dying patients are often

This directive is written while I am of sound mind and fully competent.

I insist that I have the complete right to refuse any medical and surgical treatment unless a court order affirms that my decision would bring undue or unexpected hardship on my family or on society.

Therefore:

If I become incompetent, in consideration of my legal rights to refuse medical or surgical treatment regardless of the consequences to my health and life, I hereby direct and order my physician or any physician in charge of my care to cease and refrain from any medical or surgical treatment that would prolong my life if I am in a condition of:

1 Unconsciousness from which I cannot recover
2 Unconsciousness over a period of 6 months
3 Irreversible mental incompetency

However, although mentally incompetent, if conscious, I must be informed of the situation, and if I wish to be treated I am to be treated in spite of my original request made while competent.*

If there is any reasonable doubt of the diagnosis of my illness and the prognosis, then consultation with available specialists should be obtained.

This directive to my physician also applies to any hospital or sanitarium at which I may be at the time of my illness, and relieves them of any and all responsibility in the action or lack of action of any physician acting according to my demands.

If any action is taken contrary to these express demands I hereby request my next of kin or my legal representatives to consider—and if necessary, to take—legal action against those involved.

I hereby absolve my physician or any physician taking care of me from any legal liability pertaining to the fulfillment of any of my demands.

Signed_____

*This paradox must be understood. It is the only time a request or demand made while incompetent can override one made while competent. It is conceivable, although rare, that next of kin may attempt to take advantage of such a state of incompetency and to too readily take advantage of a prior directive ordering cessation of therapy.
SOURCE: From Garfield, 1978.

subjected to needless tests and useless treatments, are given less attention than patients whose chance of recovery is better, and are subject to hospital rules that have no relevance for them.

In response to a felt need for special facilities for these patients, a number of special institutions called *hospices* have sprung up. The one on which most of the American ones have been modeled, St. Christopher's Hospice in a suburb of London, was founded in 1948 by Cicely Saunders, a medical social worker, who aimed to make it "something between a hospital and the patient's own home; combining the skills of the one with the warmth and welcome, the time available, and the beds without invisible parking meters beside them of the other" (Saunders, 1977, p. 160).

Since that time, many other hospices have been established, so that now there may be as many as 130 operating in the United States (Porter, 1979). The first hospice expressly for terminally ill children has just been set up by St. Mary's Hospital in New York City (Teltsch, 1980). In these facilities, warm, personal care is the key. Staff, personnel, and volunteers help to ease the pain and treat the symptoms of patients, keep them as comfortable and as alert as possible, show interest and kindness to them and their families, and help the families deal with the patients' illness and subsequent death. A team of doctors, nurses, social workers, psychologists, clergy, family, friends, and volunteers all work together to alleviate the different kinds of pain that trouble the dying patient (see Figure 18-2).

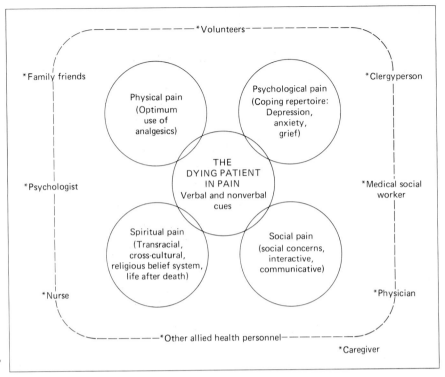

Fig. 18-2
The Hospice Pain
Model. Source: Garfield,
1978, p. 366

MAKE TODAY COUNT

The death rate for any generation is 100 percent. We *all* die. However, I know what will probably kill me, while most people do not. We have no guarantee of how long we will live. But I believe it is truly the quality of life, not the quantity, that is most important [Kelly, 1978, p. 63].

So wrote Orville Kelly, a man who had been diagnosed as suffering from terminal cancer. Spurred by his own difficulty in dealing with his diagnosis and his changed life before he arrived at this point of view, Kelly founded Make Today Count as an organization where seriously ill patients and their families can get together to talk about their feelings and the problems of living with life-threatening conditions. It now has more than eighty chapters in thirty states.

THE SHANTI PROJECT

The Shanti hot-line number, 415-524-4370, is likely to ring at any hour of the day or night, with requests from all over the country. One caller may ask for a volunteer to break the news of the imminent death of an elderly woman to her and to her family; another for someone to counsel a patient about to undergo chemotherapy to let him know what to expect and to support him through the ordeal; a third to help the wife of a dying man cope with her own feelings and be of as much help as possible to her husband. The project, named for the Sanskrit word for "inner peace," was founded in the San Francisco Bay area by Charles Garfield, a psychologist deeply concerned with offering compassionate care for the dying and their families.

Shanti volunteers range in age from 22 to 73 years and come from all sorts of personal and religious backgrounds. The major requisite is that they have "the willingness, emotional strength, training, and sensitivity to confront humanely the realities of death and dying without resorting to evasion and denial" (Garfield & Clark, 1978, p. 364). A newsletter is available from the Shanti Project, 1137 Colusa Ave., Berkeley, CA 94707.

BEREAVEMENT, MOURNING, AND GRIEF

A major problem for bereaved people in America is our lack of universal mourning rites that help them express their grief and that provide some structure for "filling up the emptiness caused by the loss," as Butler and Lewis (1977, p. 41) express the task ahead of them. Mourners are expected to be brave, to suppress their tears, and to get on with the business of living. Yet feelings of loss run deep. They need to be expressed and dealt with before people can reorganize their lives. Without such expression survivors often have trouble accepting the reality of what has happened and are, therefore, unable to heal the wound in their lives.

What do we actually mean when we use these words of survivorship that head this section? Let us define them:

Bereavement   This is the objective fact, the change in status of the survivor. When someone close to us dies, we change from being a wife to being a widow, from a child to an orphan, a mother to a childless woman, a brother to an only child. Even when the status does not change—when, for example, one sibling of several dies, the survivors are still bereft of that person's presence in their lives.

Mourning   The term refers to the behavior followed by a bereaved person or community after a death. It is the Irish wake, to which friends and family come to view and keep vigil over the body of the dead person and to toast his memory with food and drink. It is the Jewish *shiva*, the week following a death when

After I saw him in his coffin and said goodbye, Janice and I went to the beach. We stood on the sand and I felt the wind on my cheeks. I could hear the waves, and I suddenly knew that I was alone forever, that I could lose the people I loved anytime, any moment, and the only thing I had in this life was myself.

Judy Chicago,
in *Through The Flower*, p. 25.

the family covers all the mirrors in the house, renounces the wearing of shoes, and remains at home to visitors, who often bring gifts of food. It is the flying of a flag at half-mast to observe the death of a public person. As many of these customs fall into disuse in modern society, bereaved people lose some of their most valuable supports for coping with their grief.

Grief   This is the emotional response of the bereaved person, which can be expressed in many different ways, ranging from a feeling of emptiness to a feeling of rage. Let us look at some of the forms that grief can take:

Anticipatory Grief
The family and friends of a person who has been ill for a long time often prepare themselves for the loss to come by experiencing many of the classic symptoms of grief while the person is still alive. This often helps the survivors, enabling them to handle the actual death more easily when it does come. If such anticipatory grief, however, makes the survi-

vors disengage themself from the dying person while she or he is still alive, it can create a devastating sense of isolation for the terminally ill patient.

Normal Grief

This often follows a fairly predictable pattern, in which the bereaved person is likely to experience waves of strong emotions in a sequence that may parallel the responses to one's own oncoming death. Schulz (1978) identified three phases in the expression of normal grief:

1   The *initial phase* lasts for a few weeks after the death. During this period survivors tend to react with shock and disbelief. They are often dazed and confused. As their awareness of loss sinks in, the initial numbness gives way to overwhelming feelings of sadness, often expressed by almost constant crying. Toward the end of this period grievers sometimes become afraid that they cannot handle their sorrow and that they are heading for an emotional breakdown. Some deal with this anxiety by using alcohol or tranquilizers. Such physical symptoms as shortness of breath, an emptiness in the abdomen, loss of appetite, and insomnia are common.

August 22, 1916

.... made a drawing: the mother letting her dead son slide into her arms. I might make a hundred such drawings and yet I do not get any closer to him. I am seeking him. As if I had to find him in the work.

Käthe Kollwitz, age 53
in *Revelations: Diaries of Women*, p. 245.

2   The *intermediate phase* begins about three weeks after the death. At about this time the people who have rallied around the widow or other principal mourner have gone back to their own lives, leaving her to cope with the resumption of day-to-day life without the dead person. This phase lasts for about a year. The widow will relive her husband's death, going over all the details in her mind and in her conversation, in an obsessive search for the meaning of his death. From time to time she is seized by a feeling that her dead husband is present: She will hear his voice, sense his presence in the room, even see his face before her. With time, all these sensations diminish.

3   The *recovery phase* begins at the start of the second year after the death. While the widower still misses his dead wife, he knows that life must go on, and he becomes more active socially, getting out more, seeing people, resuming old interests, perhaps discovering new ones. Many survivors feel stronger and proud of themselves once they have reached this point and they realize that they have survived an event they had always dreaded.

Morbid Grief

Reactions similar in nature to those of normal grief but much more intense and long lasting are considered pathological. At other times morbid grief reactions take on a different complexion. The bereaved person may at first react with a sense of well-being inappropriate to the loss. By forcing the grief inward, he or she may develop physical problems like asthma or colitis. After the initial period of apparent calm, bereaved people often show changes in personality, becoming hostile, irritable, and so immobilized that they have to be pushed to initiate any activities. They may become depressed, unduly worried about their own health, phobic, or panicky. Some are overcome by guilt, blaming themselves for the death.

GRIEF THERAPY

With the help of family and friends, most bereaved people are able to work through their losses and come through the crisis to resume a normal life. They do not forget the dead person, of course, and they may have recurrent bouts of sadness, particularly around special times like birthdays and holidays, but somehow they are able to pick up the pieces and go on with their lives. For about 1 out of 4 bereaved people, however, some kind of further help seems indicated (Schulz, 1978).

Such lay organizations as Widow to Widow, Catholic Widow and Widowers Club, and Compassionate Friends (for parents whose children have died) emphasize the help that one person who has lost someone close can give to another. This help takes many forms, from showing empathy for the feelings of the newly bereft, to demonstrating the possibility of going on without the dead person, to offering such practical help as arranging transportation and helping to find new housing arrangements.

Professional therapists focus on helping bereaved people express their sorrow and their feelings of loss and guilt, of hostility and anger. They encourage their clients to review their relationships with the deceased and to integrate the fact of the person's death into their lives so that they can be freed to develop new relationships and new ways of acting with surviving friends and relatives. Schulz (1978) maintains that this work can generally be concluded in eight to ten visits.

We need to be able to accept the eventual coming of death of those whom we love, just as we need to realize that our own time on this earth is limited. With death comes the final rounding of the circle, the close to whatever we have made of life, to the changes we have undergone, the growth and development we have experienced from that initial moment of conception.

SUMMARY

1 Recently, there has been an upsurge in interest in our society about the topic of death and dying. *Thanatology* refers to the study of death and dying. **2** People of different ages have different attitudes toward death and dying. **3** The suicide rate has increased in recent years. White men in their eighties are most likely to commit suicide. **4** The function of death-education programs which are aimed at different age levels and groups within the community is to help people understand their attitudes toward death, to be familiar with how various cultures deal with death, and to be aware of the needs of the dying person and his or her survivors. **5** Elisabeth Kübler-Ross, a pioneer in the study of death and dying, says that there are five stages in coming to terms with death: denial, anger, bargaining, depression, and acceptance. These stages are, however, not invariant for all people nor do all people reach the stage of acceptance. **6** E. Mansell Pattison has described the stages of dying in terms of dying trajectories. **7** Psychological changes preceding death include intellectual and personality change as well as the "life review" during which a person reminisces about the past. **8** Euthanasia is gaining wider acceptance today. **9** Programs and movements such as the hospice movement,

Make Today Count, and the Shanti Project are designed to help seriously ill and dying patients and their families. **10** Normal grief, the emotional response of the bereaved person, may be described in three stages: During the initial phase, which lasts a few weeks, the survivor feels shock and disbelief. In the intermediate phase, which lasts about a year, the survivor must cope with daily life. The recovery phase generally begins at the start of the second year after the death when the survivor becomes more active and shows renewed interest in life. For about 1 out of 4 survivors help through such organizations as Widow to Widow or through professional therapy is needed for dealing with bereavement.

SUGGESTED READINGS

Cousins, N. *Anatomy of an illness as perceived by the patient*. New York: Norton, 1979. The story of a remarkable recovery from a supposedly irreversible crippling disease, explained by the author in terms of his having assumed the responsibility for his own health.

Feifel, H. (Ed.) *New meanings of death*. New York: McGraw-Hill, 1977. A collection of readings by a distinguished group of scientists, clinicians, and educators covering topics such as death education, effective treatment for the dying person and his or her family, and the function of grief for mental health.

Kübler-Ross, E. *Death: The final stage of growth*. Englewood Cliffs, NJ: Prentice-Hall, 1975. A collection of essays by different writers, including doctors, nurses, sociologists, clergy, people facing death themselves, and bereaved persons, showing how coming to terms with death is an essential step in human development.

Kübler-Ross, E. *On death and dying*. New York: Macmillan, 1979. A moving book that started the recent birth of a new interest in death; E. Kübler-Ross draws upon case studies and actual dialogues with dying patients to back up her pioneering concept that there are five stages in the outlook of the dying person.

Lerner, G., *A death of one's own*. New York: Simon & Schuster, 1978. The story of the death of the author's husband from a brain tumor, the shared decision of husband and wife to face the death together, at home, and the meaning of this experience for the woman who survived.

Mitchell, P. *Act of love: The killing of George Zygmaniak*. New York: Knopf, 1976. A powerful tale of a real-life "mercy killing," which describes the events leading up to the shotgun killing of one brother by another, recreates the trial, and in the process raises legal and moral questions.

West, J. *The woman said yes*. New York: Harcourt Brace Jovanovich, 1976. A moving account of two sisters—one, who was terminally ill, asked the other to help end her life in the way she chose.

accommodation Change in existing schemata to include new experiences.

acting out behavior Situation where a child's emotional difficulties surface in his or her behavior (e.g., lying, stealing).

activity theory Theory of aging which holds that in order to age successfully an individual must remain as active as possible.

adaptation Term given to complementary processes of assimilation and accommodation.

adolescent egocentrism Belief, held by an adolescent, that other people are preoccupied with his or her appearance and behavior.

adolescent growth spurt Sharp increase in height that typically occurs in girls from 8½ to 13 years and in boys from 10 to 16 years.

ageism Prejudice against the elderly.

allele Pair of genes affecting a trait. When alleles are identical, an individual is *homozygous* for a trait; when alleles are dissimilar, the individual is *heterozygous*.

amniocentesis Prenatal medical procedure by which a sample of the amniotic fluid is withdrawn and analyzed to determine the presence of certain birth defects.

amniotic fluid Liquid in which embryo is suspended within the uterus.

amniotic sac Fluid-filled membrane encasing the conceptus.

anal stage According to Freud, the psychosexual stage of toddlerhood (12 to 18 months) in which children receive pleasure through anal stimulation; toilet training is the critical situation.

androsperm Y-carrying sperm.

animism Piagetian term for the attribution of life to inanimate objects.

anorexia nervosa Prolonged, severe refusal to eat.

anoxia Lack of oxygen to fetus, which may lead to brain damage at birth.

anxiety neurosis Situation in which the child expresses anxiety directly.

Apgar Scale Medical technique to measure adjustment of neonate at birth; measures appearance, pulse, grimace, activity, and respiration.

artificialism Piagetian term for the belief that the universe is man-made.

asceticism Adolescent defense mechanism, described by Anna Freud, which is characterized by self-denial.

assimilation Incorporation of new object, experience, or concept into existing schemata.

attachment An active, affectionate, reciprocal relationship specifically between two individuals; their interaction reinforces and strengthens the bond.

autonomy versus shame and doubt According to Eriksonian theory, the second critical alternative of personality development. Between 18 months and 3 years, the child develops a sense of autonomy (independence, self-assertion) or the feeling of doubt and shame.

autosomal dominant inheritance Pattern of inheritance in which a specific gene is dominant; that is, if it is inherited, it manifests itself in the individual.

autosomal recessive inheritance Pattern of inheritance in which a trait appears only if an individual has inherited two genes for it, one from each parent. If the individual inherits only one gene for the trait, it will not appear in the individual but may be passed on to children.

autosomes Nonsex chromosomes (twenty-two pairs).

babbling Stage of prelinguistic speech that begins at around 3 to 4 months; characterized by repetition of simple consonant and vowel sounds.

baby biography Journal of development of a child. Source of some of our earliest knowledge of child development.

basic trust versus basic mistrust According to Eriksonian theory, the first critical alternative of personality development. From birth to 12–18 months, an infant develops a sense of whether or not the world can be trusted; feeding situation is an important determinant of the outcome of this stage.

behavior modification Use of operant conditioning procedures to shape behavior.

behavior therapy A therapeutic approach using learning theory principles to alter behavior. Also called behavior modification.

birth without violence Technique of childbirth advocated by LeBoyer in which the trauma during birth is minimized by bringing the baby into a darkened, quiet delivery room.

blastocyst Fluid-filled sphere resulting from cell division of zygote.

centration Tendency to focus on one aspect of a situation and to neglect the importance of other aspects; characteristic of preoperational thought.

cephalocaudal principle Principle that development proceeds in a head-to-toe direction; upper parts of the body develop before lower parts do.

cervix Opening of the uterus.

cesarean delivery Delivery of baby through abdominal surgery. About 5 percent of all births are cesarean.

childhood schizophrenia The most common psychosis of childhood, characterized by an escape from reality and a withdrawal from relationships with others.

chromosomes Tiny rod-shaped particles that carry genes, the transmitters of inheritance.

classical conditioning Learning in which a previously neutral stimulus (conditioned stimulus) acquires the power to elicit a response (conditioned response) by association with an unconditioned stimulus that ordinarily elicits a particular response (unconditioned response).

classification Ability to sort stimuli into categories according to characteristics (for example, color or shape).

climacteric Medical term for menopause and the changes that occur then.

clinical study (clinical method) Study that combines observation with careful, individualized questioning.

cognitive development Development of the ability to think logically. According to Piaget, cognitive development occurs in four stages: *sensorimotor*, *preoperational*, *concrete operational*, *formal operational*. In each stage, intellectual abilities are qualitatively different.

cohabitation Living together and maintaining a sexual relationship without being legally married.

conceptus Product of fertilization of egg by sperm; depending on stage of development, may be *zygote*, *embryo*, or *fetus*.

concrete operational stage Third stage of Piagetian cognitive development (from 7 to 11 years), during which children develop logical, but not abstract, thinking.

conservation Piagetian term for the awareness that two stimuli which *were* equal (in length, weight, amount, etc.) remain equal in the face of perceptual alteration, so long as nothing has been added to or taken away from either stimulus.

constructive play Goal-directed play.

conventional stage of moral development According to Kohlberg, the second level of moral development; characterized by observation of standards of others because child wants to please other people.

cooing Stage of prelinguistic speech that occurs at around 6 weeks; characterized by squeals, gurgles, and bleats.

coordination of secondary schemata Fourth substage of sensorimotor stage described by Piaget; characterized by simple problem solving that makes use of responses mastered previously.

correlation Statistical relationship of the direction and magnitude of the relationship between/among variables. Range from -1.0 to $+1.0$.

critical period Specific time during development when an event will have its greatest impact.

cross-sectional study Study in which more than one group of subjects (of different ages, sexes, etc.) are measured on one occasion.

cross-sequential design A technique of data collection combining longitudinal and cross-sectional strategies.

crystallized intelligence A type of intelligence proposed by Cattell and Horn involving the ability to remember stored information. Influenced by education and cultural factors.

decentering Piagetian term for considering all aspects of a situation in making conclusions.

deferred imitation Piagetian concept involving internal imitation; child sees something, stores its mental symbol, and, later, imitates the stored behavior.

developmental disorder Emotional disturbance caused by delays or abnormalities of development related to biological maturation.

disengagement theory Theory of aging which holds that successful aging is characterized by withdrawal of society and of the elderly.

dizygotic twins (*fraternal twins*) Twins conceived by the union of two different eggs and two different sperms.

DNA (deoxyribonucleic acid) Molecules possessing hereditary information that determines makeup of cells.

drug therapy A therapeutic technique which includes administration of drugs.

early infantile autism A childhood psychosis characterized by impoverishment of interpersonal relations, language disturbances, and a preoccupation with things.

echolalia Stage of prelinguistic speech that occurs at around 9 to 10 months; characterized by imitation of sounds of others.

ego According to Freudian theory, the aspect of personality generally known as common sense; operates on reality principle to mediate between *id* and *superego*.

(ego) integrity versus despair According to Eriksonian theory, the eighth and last critical alternative of personality development, characterizing old age. A sense of acceptance of one's own life allowing one to accept death; the developmental alternative is despair, characterized by failure to accept one's life and, thus, one's ultimate end.

egocentric speech Speech that fails to take into consideration the needs of the listener and thus is not appropriate for communication.

egocentrism Inability to consider another's point of view; characteristic of preoperational thought.

elaborated code Type of speech pattern identified by Bernstein (1964) that is characterized by complex, detailed messages; used by middle class. (See also *restricted code*.)

Electra complex The female counterpart of the *Oedipus complex*.

electronic fetal monitoring Monitoring of fetal heartbeat by machine during labor and delivery.

embryo Conceptus between 2 and 8 weeks old.

embryonic disk Thickened cell mass from which a baby develops.

embryonic stage Second stage of pregnancy (two to eight weeks); characterized by rapid growth and differentiation of body parts and systems.

encopresis Soiling with fecal matter.

enuresis Bed-wetting.

experimental study Study that manipulates one or more variables (independent variables) and examines effect of the manipulations on other variables (dependent variables). Experimental studies have highly controlled procedures and, therefore, can be replicated by the same or other researchers.

expressive jargon Type of prelinguistic speech that develops during the second year; characterized by a string of meaningless gibberish that contains pauses, inflections, and sentencelike rhythms.

fallopian tube Tube that conveys eggs from ovary to uterus; fertilization occurs here.

family therapy A therapeutic technique in which the whole family is seen together and viewed as the patient.

fetal alcohol syndrome Symptoms affecting the offspring of some women who drank heavily during pregnancy.

fetal stage Final stage of pregnancy (eight weeks to birth); rapid growth of organism occurs.

fetoscopy Used with ultrasound, this method allows for direct visual inspection of part of the fetus while still in the uterus. Detects some abnormal conditions.

fetus Conceptus between eight weeks and birth.

fluid intelligence A type of intelligence proposed by Cattell and Horn involving the ability to solve novel problems. Influenced by neurological development.

fontanels Soft spots on head of neonate.

formal operations stage According to Piaget, the final stage of cognition, which is characterized by the ability to think abstractly.

functional play Simple, repetitive play.

g-factor General intelligence influencing all-around performance.

gamete Sex cell (sperm or ovum).

gene Tiny segment, carried on chromosome, that determines hereditary characteristics.

generativity versus stagnation According to Eriksonian theory, the seventh critical alternative of personality development, characterizing midlife. The mature adult is concerned with establishing and guiding the next generation or else feels stagnation (personal impoverishment).

genetic counseling Analysis and communication of a couple's chances of producing a child with birth defects.

genital stage Freudian term for the psychosexual stage of mature sexuality; occurs during adolescence.

genotype Actual genetic composition of an individual; may differ from *phenotype* because of possession of recessive genes.

geriatrics Branch of medicine concerned with aging and the elderly.

germinal stage First stage of pregnancy (fertilization to two weeks); characterized by rapid cell division and increasing complexity.

gerontology Study of the elderly and of the process of aging.

gynosperm X-carrying sperm.

habituation Simple learning that involves becoming accustomed to a sound, sight, or other stimulus.

holophrases One-word sentences that occur at about age 1.

horizontal decalage Piagetian term for the child's inability to transfer what he or she has learned about one type of conservation to other types. Results in the child passing different types of conservation tasks for the first time at different ages (e.g., mass before weight before volume).

human development Study of quantitative and qualitative changes that an individual undergoes with age.

humanistic perspective A model of development that views the individual as able to take care of his or her life and foster his or her own development.

id According to Freudian theory, the aspect of personality that is present at birth; operates on the pleasure principle and is characterized by desire for immediate gratification. (See also *ego* and *superego*.)

identification Process by which an individual acquires the characteristics of a model.

identity versus role confusion According to Eriksonian theory, the fifth critical alternative of personality development, in which an adolescent must determine his or her own sense of self (identity).

imprinting Innate, instinctual, rapid form of early learning that occurs during a critical period in an organism's development.

induced abortion Deliberate termination of a pregnancy.

industry versus inferiority According to Eriksonian theory, the fourth critical alternative of personality development, which occurs during middle childhood. Children must learn the skills of their culture or face feelings of inferiority.

initiative versus guilt According to Eriksonian theory, the third critical alternative of personality development, which characterizes children from 3 to 6 years. Children develop initiative when they try out new things and are not overwhelmed by failure.

intellectualization Adolescent defense mechanism, described by Anna Freud, which is characterized by abstract intellectual discussions; related to adolescents' need to find identity and values.

intelligence Constantly active interaction between inherited ability and environmental experience, which results in an individual's being able to acquire, remember, and use knowledge; to understand both concrete and abstract concepts; to understand the relationships among objects, events, and ideas and to apply this understanding; and to use all the above in daily functioning.

intelligence quotient (IQ) Mathematical score computed by dividing an individual's mental age by chronological age and multiplying by 100: $IQ = MA/CA \times 100$.

intimacy versus isolation According to Eriksonian theory, the sixth critical alternative of personality development, which occurs during young adulthood. Young adults want to make commitments to others; and, if not, they may suffer from a sense of isolation and consequent self-absorption.

introjection Psychoanalytic term for identification with parent of same sex.

invention of new means through mental combinations Sixth substage of sensorimotor stage described by Piaget; characterized by problem solving that involves rudimentary foresight rather than trial and error.

karyotype A chart in which photographs of chromosomes are cut out and arranged according to size and structure. Demonstrates chromosomal abnormalities.

lallation Stage of prelinguistic speech that occurs in second half of first year; characterized by imperfect imitation.

language acquisition Process by which a child learns the grammatical rules of language.

language acquisition device (LAD) Inborn mental structure that enables children to build a system of language rules.

lanugo Fuzzy prenatal hair.

latency period According to Freud, a period of relative sexual quiescence that occurs after the Oedipus complex is resolved, during middle childhood.

long-term memory Type of memory that involves long-term storage of material; appears to hold up well with advanced age.

longitudinal study Study in which the same individual or group is measured on more than one occasion.

male menopause Imprecise term for male climacteric syndrome; refers to hormonal/physical and psychological changes in middle-aged men.

mechanistic model View of humanity that equates people with machines which react but do not initiate; sees change as quantitative, and development as continuous. (See also *organismic model*.)

meconium Fetal waste matter.

menarche First menstruation; does not necessarily indicate fertility.

menopause Cessation of menstrual cycle and ability to bear children. Median age in America is 49.2, with much individual difference.

midlife crisis Turmoil precipitated by the review and reevaluation of one's past, typically occurring in the early to middle forties. Reason for the review is, most likely, the awareness of one's own mortality, which occurs in midlife; this is followed by a period of stabilization.

monozygotic twins (identical twins) Twins that

result from the division of the zygote after conception.

multifactorial inheritance Pattern of inheritance in which a trait is carried either by a combination of several genes or through the interaction of genes with environmental factors.

mutation Change in a gene or chromosome.

naturalistic study Study that observes individuals in their natural habitats, without manipulating the environment.

neonate Newborn infant up to 2 to 4 weeks of age.

neurosis A morbidly anxious reaction to stress. This reaction interferes with a person's adjustment in society.

neurotic-depressive conditions Reactions to real or perceived emotional stresses in which the person is sad and depressed and loses interest in people and activities.

nocturnal emission Ejaculation of semen during sleep.

object permanence Awareness that an object or person does not cease to exist when out of sight

obsessive-compulsive neuroses Situations in which the person is consumed with unreasonable thoughts and ideas (obsessions) which he or she is driven to act out.

Oedipus complex Phenomenon described by Freud in which a male child in the phallic stage feels sexual attraction for the opposite-sex parent and rivalry toward the parent of the same sex.

operant conditioning Learning in which a response continues to be made because it has been reinforced.

operations Piagetian term for mental activities.

oral stage According to Freudian theory, the psychosexual stage of infancy (first year) that is characterized by reception of gratification in the oral region; feeding is the major situation in which gratification occurs.

organismic model View of humanity that sees people as active agents of their own development; focuses on qualitative changes and sees development as discontinuous. (See also *mechanistic model*.)

ovary   Female reproductive gland.

ovulation   Expulsion of ovum from ovary, which occurs once about every twenty-eight days from puberty to menopause.

ovum (plural, **ova**)   Egg, female sex cell.

penis envy   Freudian concept that female envies penis and wants one of her own.

phallic stage   Stage of psychosexual development described by Freud in which the preschool child receives gratification in genital area.

phenotype   Observable characteristics of a person; may vary from *genotype*.

phobia   Unreasonable fear of particular objects or situations.

placenta   Organ that conveys food and oxygen to conceptus and carries its body wastes away.

postconventional stage of moral development   According to Kohlberg, the third and most advanced level of moral development; involves attainment of self-accepted moral principles rather than the principles of others.

preconventional stage of moral development   According to Kohlberg, the first level of moral development; involves observation of standards of others to avoid punishments or gain rewards.

premature, or preterm, baby   Baby born before the thirty-seventh week of pregnancy, dated from the mother's last menstrual period.

prepared childbirth   Method of childbirth in which the woman is prepared for delivery by knowledge about the physiological processes involved and by learning a series of exercises that make the delivery easier.

primary circular response   Second substage of sensorimotor period described by Piaget; characterized by an active effort to reproduce an activity that was first produced by chance.

projection   According to Freud, a defense mechanism characterized by attributing one's own unacceptable thoughts and motives to another.

prosocial behavior   Behavior intended to help others, without external reward for the helper.

proximodistal principle   Principle that development proceeds in a near-to-far direction; parts of the body near the center develop before the extremities do.

psychosexual development   Essence of the Freudian theory which claims that human personality develops through a sequence of stages whereby gratification (pleasure) shifts from one bodily zone to another (oral, anal, genital), accompanied by a shift in the agent of gratification.

psychosis   A severe emotional disturbance which is characterized by loss of contact with reality.

psychosocial development   Theory of personality (ego) development that stresses cultural and societal influences; essence of Eriksonian theory.

psychotherapy   A therapeutic technique in which the patient generally gains insights into his or her personality and relationships with others by a therapist who helps him or her to interpret feelings and behaviors.

puberty   Point at which an individual is sexually mature and able to reproduce.

pubescence   Time of life span characterized by rapid physiological growth, maturation of reproductive functioning, and appearance of primary and secondary sex characteristics.

reaction formation   According to Freud, defense mechanism characterized by the replacement of an anxiety-producing feeling by its opposite.

realism   Piagetian term for the confusion of psychological events with objective reality.

referential communication   Ability to transmit information to a listener.

reflex   Involuntary reaction to stimulation. First substage of sensorimotor period described by Piaget; characterized by behavior that is based on reflexes.

regression   According to Freud, a defense mechanism characterized by behaviors of earlier ages.

reliability   A test is said to have good reliability when an individual or group receives similar scores each time the test is taken.

repression   According to Freud, a defense mechanism characterized by unconscious rejection of anxiety-producing situations.

restricted code   Type of speech pattern identified by Bernstein (1964) that is characterized by short, simple sentences and little detail; used by lower social classes. (See also *elaborated code*.)

reversibility Piagetian term for the awareness that an operation can be reversed to bring back the original situation (for example, a clay ball can be rolled into a sausage that can be rolled back into a ball).

s-factor Specific intelligence influence performance on different tasks.

schema (plural, schemata) Basic cognitive unit; generally named after the behavior involved.

secondary circular reaction Third substage of sensorimotor period described by Piaget; characterized by intentional action and a new interest in the results of actions.

secular trend in maturation Tendency toward earlier development and maturity in this generation compared with previous generations.

semen Fluid, produced by testes, that contains sperm and is ejaculated during sexual climax.

senescence Period of the life span accompanied by decrements in bodily functioning; begins at different ages for different people.

sensorimotor stage First of Piaget's stages of cognitive development characterizing the infant (birth to 2 years). During this stage children actively engage in contact with their environment and, thus, gain information about their world.

seriation Ability to order stimuli according to characteristics (for example, from shortest to longest).

sex chromosomes The one pair of chromosomes that determines the sex of the organism. (XX is female; XY is male.)

sex-linked inheritance Pattern of inheritance in which characteristics are carried on X chromosome. They are transmitted by the female and are expressed in the male.

sex typing Process by which children acquire attitudes and behaviors deemed by their culture to be appropriate for members of their sex.

short-term memory Type of memory involved with initial reception of material; process seems to be more efficient in younger than in older adults.

SIDS (Sudden Infant Death Syndrome) Major cause of death for American infants between 1 week and 1 year of age. The cause of SIDS is not known with certainty, although it probably has to do with an abnormality of the central nervous system.

sign Piagetian term for arbitrary but socially agreed-upon representation.

significates Piagetian term for the object or event represented by a signifier. (See also *symbolic function*.)

small-for-date baby Baby whose birthweight is below the tenth percentile for gestational age.

social cognition An area of study which examines how children come to understand the viewpoints and emotions of others.

socialized speech Speech that is intended to communicate.

sociolinguistics Study of the relationship between language and social setting.

sperm (spermatozoon; plural, spermatozoa) Male sex cell.

spontaneous abortion Expulsion from the uterus of a conceptus that cannot survive outside the womb; also called *miscarriage*.

state Periodic variation in an infant's cycles of wakefulness, sleep, and activity.

stranger anxiety Phenomenon that often occurs during second half of first year, when infants express fear of strange people and places and protest separation from parents.

structure of intellect Model of intelligence proposed by Guilford. Intelligence is the result of the interaction of *operations* (the ways we think), *contents* (what we think about), and *products* (the result of the application of a certain operation to a certain content, or our thinking a certain way about a certain issue.

stuttering Stammering. Repetitive speech.

sublimation According to Freud, a defense mechanism characterized by rechanneling of uncomfortable feelings (for example, sexual anxiety) into acceptable activities (such as schoolwork).

superego According to Freud, the aspect of personality known as conscience; results from Oedipus/Electra complex and incorporates the ethics and morals of society.

symbolic function Manifest in language, *symbolic play*, and *deferred imitation*; indicates presence of a representational system, allowing child to represent stimuli using symbols; develops between ages 2 and 4.

symbolic play Piagetian concept to describe play in which child makes something stand for something else.

temperament An individual's style of approaching people and situations.

tertiary circular reaction Fifth substage of sensori-motor stage described by Piaget; characterized by trial-and-error activity that seeks new solutions to problems.

testis (plural, *testes*) Male reproductive gland; also known as *testicle*.

theory A set of interrelated statements about data. The goal of a theory is to integrate data, explain behavior, and predict behavior.

tic Involuntary, repetitive muscular movement.

time-sampling Research technique in which a certain behavior is observed throughout a given time period.

trimester The first, second, or third 3-month period of pregnancy.

ultrasound Method of scanning the womb for detection of fetal outline to determine whether the pregnancy is progressing normally.

umbilical cord Cord attaching placenta to conceptus.

uterus Pear-shaped muscular organ in which fertilized egg develops until birth; also known as *womb*.

validity Characteristic of a test which measures what it is supposed to measure.

vernix caseosa Oily covering of neonate.

zygote One-celled organism resulting from the union of sperm and egg.

Abroms, K., & Bennett, J. Paternal contributions to Down's syndrome dispel maternal myths. *ERIC*, 1979.

Abt Associates. *Children at the center (Vol. I): Summary findings and policy implications of the National Day Care Study*. Washington, DC: U.S. Department of Health, Education, and Welfare, 1978.

ACOG (American College of Obstetricians and Gynecologists). *Newsletter*, May 1979, I; 7.

Ad Hoc Committee on Ethical Standards in Psychological Research. *Ethical principles in the conduct of research with human participants*. Washington, DC: American Psychological Association, 1973.

Adams, M. The single woman in today's society: A reappraisal. *American Journal of Orthopsychiatry*, 1971, **41**(5), 776–786.

Adelson, J. Adolescence and the generation gap. *Psychology Today*, 1979, **12**(9), 33–37.

Ahammer, I. Social learning theory as a framework for the study of adult personality development. In P. B. Baltes & K. W. Schaie (Eds.), *Life-span developmental psychology: Personality and socialization*. New York: Academic Press, 1973, pp. 253–284.

Ainsworth, M.D.S. Patterns of attachment behavior shown by the infant in interaction with his mother. *The Merrill-Palmer Quarterly of Behavior and Development*, 1964, **10**, 51–58.

Ainsworth, M. D. S. Object relations, dependency, and attachment: A theoretical review of the infant-mother relationship. *Child Development*, 1969, **40**, 969–1025.

Ainsworth, M.D.S., & Bell, S. Attachment, exploration, and separation: Illustration by the behavior of one-year-olds in a strange situation. *Child Development*, 1970, **41**, 49–67.

Akers, R. L. Teenage drinking and drug use. In E. D. Evans (Ed.), *Adolescents: Readings in behavior and development*. Hinsdale, IL: Dryden Press, 1970, pp. 267–288.

Allport, G. The fruits of eclecticism—bitter or sweet? *Psychologia*, 1964, **7**, 1–14.

Almy, M. *The early childhood educator at work*. New York: McGraw-Hill, 1975.

Almy, M., Chittenden, E., & Miller, P. *Young children's thinking: Some aspects of Piaget's theory*. New York: Teachers College, 1966.

Alper, M. The safety of obstetric anesthesia for the newborn. *Drug Therapy*, Oct. 1977, pp. 29–33.

Altman, L. K. Evacuation: Youngsters and the pregnant go first. *The New York Times*, April 2, 1979, p. A15.

Ambrose, L. Misinforming pregnant teenagers. *Family Planning Perspectives*, 1978, **10**(1), 51–57.

American Academy of Pediatrics. Juice in ready-to-use bottles and nursing bottle caries. *News & Comment*, 1978, **29**, 1.

American Academy of Pediatrics Committee Statement. The ten-state nutrition survey: A pediatric perspective. *Pediatrics*, 1973, **51**(6), 1095–1099.

American Academy of Pediatrics, Committee on Adolescence, Pregnancy and abortion counseling. *Pediatrics*, 1979, **63**(6), 920–921.

American Academy of Pediatrics, Committee on Drugs. Effects of medication during labor and delivery on infant outcome. *Pediatrics*, 1978, **62**(3), 402–403.

American Academy of Pediatrics, Committee on Nutrition, & Canadian Paediatric Society, Nutrition Committee. Nutritional needs of low-birth-weight infants. *Pediatrics*, 1977, **60**(4), 519–530.

American Cancer Society. *1976 cancer facts & figures*. New York: 1975.

The American family: Can it survive today's shocks? *U.S. News & World Report*, Oct. 27, 1975, pp. 30–46.

American Heritage Dictionary of the English Language [W. Morris (Ed.)]. Boston: Houghton Mifflin, 1971.

Ames, L. B., & Learned, J. Imaginary companions and related phenomena. *Journal of Genetic Psychology*, 1946, **69**, 147–167.

Anastasi, A. Heredity, environment, and the question "how?"? *Psychological Review*, 1958, **65**(4), 197–208.

Anastasi, A. *Psychological testing* (4th ed.). New York: Macmillan, 1976.

Anders, T. R., Fozard, J. L., & Lillyquist, T. D. Effects of age upon retrieval from short-term memory. *Developmental Psychology*, 1972, **6**(2), 214–217.

A

Anderson, J. N. Attachment behavior out of doors. In N. Blurton Jones (Ed.), *Ethological studies of child behavior.* London: Cambridge, 1972.

Anderson, L. D. The predictive value of infant tests in relation to intelligence at five years. *Child Development*, 1939, **10**, 202–212.

Anderson, R. Cardiac defects in children of mothers receiving anticonvulsant therapy during pregnancy. *Journal of Pediatrics*, 1976, **89**(2), 318–319.

Annett, M. The classification of instances of four common class concepts by children and adults. *British Journal of Educational Psychology*, 1959, **29**, 223–236.

Anthony S. The child's idea of death. In T. Talbot (Ed.), *The world of the child.* New York: Anchor Books, 1968.

Apgar, V. A proposal for a new method of evaluation of the newborn infant. *Current Researches in Anesthesia and Analgesia*, 1953, **32**, 260–267.

Arbeiter, S. Profile of the adult learner. *College Board Review*, Winter 1976, pp. 20–27.

Arbuthnot, J. Modification of moral judgment through role-playing. *Developmental Psychology*, 1975, **11**(3), 319–324.

Arena, J. Contamination of the ideal food. *Nutrition Today*, Winter 1970, pp. 2–8.

Aries, P. *Centuries of childhood.* New York: Vintage, 1962.

Arnon, S., Midura, T., Damus, K., Wood. R., & Chin, J. Intestinal infection and toxin production by *Clostridium botulinum* as one cause of SIDS. *Lancet,* June 17, 1978, 1273–1276.

Ash, P., Vennart, J., & Carter, C. The incidence of hereditary disease in man. *Lancet*, April 1977, 849–851.

Asher, S. Children's peer relations. In M. Lamb (Ed.), *Social and personality development.* New York: Holt, 1978, pp. 91–113.

Athanasiou, R., & Sarkin, R. *Archives of Sexual Behavior*, 1974, **3**(3), 207–224.

Athanasiou, R., & Yoshioka, G. A. The spatial character of friendship formation. *Environment and Behavior*, 1973, **5**, 143–165.

B

Bachtold, L., & Werner, E. Personality profiles of women psychologists. *Developmental Psychology*, 1971, **5**, 273–278.

Back, K. W. The ambiguity of retirement. In E. Busse & E. Pfeiffer (Eds.), *Behavioral adaptation to later life.* New York: Mosby, 1966, pp. 93–114.

Bakwin, H. Sleep-walking in twins. *Lancet*, Aug. 29, 1970, pp. 446–447.

Bakwin, H. Car-sickness in twins. *Developmental Medicine and Child Neurology*, 1971a, **13**, 310–312.

Bakwin, H. Constipation in twins. *Journal of Diseases of Children*, 1971b, **121**, 179–181.

Bakwin, H. Nail-biting in twins. *Developmental Medicine and Child Neurology*, 1971c, **13**, 304–307.

Bakwin, H. Enuresis in twins. *American Journal of Diseases of Children*, 1971d, **121**, 222–225.

Bakwin, H., & McLaughlin, S. M. Secular increase in height: Is the end in sight? *Lancet*, Dec. 5, 1964, pp. 1195–1196.

Baldwin, A. *Theories of child development.* New York: Wiley, 1968.

Baltes, P., & Goulet, L. Status and issues of a life-span developmental psychology. In L. Goulet & P. Baltes (Eds.), *Life-span developmental psychology.* New York: Academic, 1970.

Baltes, P., & Schaie, K. Aging and IQ: The myth of the twilight years. *Psychology Today*, 1974, **7**(10), 35–38.

Bandura, A. The stormy decade: Fact or fiction? *Psychology in the School*, 1964, **1**, 224–231.

Bandura, A., Gruser, J. E., & Menlove, F. L. Vicarious extinction of avoidance behavior *Journal of Personality and Social Psychology*, 1967, **5**, 16–23.

Bandura, A., Ross, D., & Ross, S. A. Transmission of aggression through imitation of aggressive models. *Journal of Abnormal and Social Psychology*, 1961, **63**, 575–582.

Bandura, A., Ross, D., & Ross, S. A. Imitation of film-mediated aggressive models. *Journal of Abnormal and Social Psychology*, 1963, **66**(1), 3–11.

Bandura, A., & Walters, R. H. *Adolescent aggression.* New York: Ronald Press, 1959.

Banta, D. & Thacker, S. Electronic fetal monitoring: Is it a benefit? *Birth and the Family Journal,* 1979, **6**(4), 237-249.

Banta, H., & Thacker, S. *Costs and benefits of electronic fetal monitoring: A review of the literature.* Washington, DC: U.S. Department of Health, Education, and Welfare, 1979.

Barber, B. The ethics of experimentation with human subjects. *Scientific American,* 1976, **234**(2), 25–31.

Bardwick, J. Psychological conflict and the reproductive system. In J. Bardwick, E. Douvan, M. Horner, & D. Gutman (Eds.), *Feminine personality and conflict.* Belmont, CA: Brooks/Cole, 1970.

Bardwick, J. M., Douvan, E., Horner, M., & Gutman, D. *Feminine personality and conflict.* Monterey, CA: Brooks/Cole, 1970.

Barker, P. *Basic child psychiatry* (3d ed). Baltimore: University Park Press, 1979.

Barnes, A., Colton, T., Gunderson, J., Noller, K., Tilley, B., Strama, T., Townsend, D., Hatab, P. and O'Brien, P. Fertility and outcome of pregnancy in women exposed in utero to diethystilbestrol, *New England Journal of Medicine,* 1980, **302** (11), 609–613.

Barnes, K. E. Preschool play norms: A replication. *Developmental Psychology,* 1971, **5**(1), 99–103.

Barnett, C. R., Leiderman, P. H., Grobstein, R., & Klaus, M. Neonatal separation: The maternal side of interactional deprivation. *Pediatrics,* 1970, **45**(2), 197–205.

Barry, W. A. Marriage research and conflict an integrative review. *Psychological Bulletin,* 1970, **73**(1), 41–54.

Battle, H. Relations between personal values and scholastic achievement. *Journal of Experimental Education,* 1957, **26**, 27–41.

Bauer, D. An exploratory study of developmental changes in children's fears. *Journal of Child Psychology and Psychiatry,* 1976, **17**, 69–74.

Baughman, E. E. *Black Americans.* New York: Academic Press, 1971.

Baum, J. Nutritional value of human milk. *Obstetrics and Gynecology,* 1971, **37**, 126–136.

Baumrind, D. Child care practices anteceding three patterns of preschool behavior. *Genetic Psychology Monographs,* 1967, **75**, 43–88.

Baumrind, D. Harmonious parents and their preschool children. *Developmental Psychology,* 1971, **4**(1) 99–102.

Baumrind, D., & Black, A. E. Socialization practices associated with dimensions of competence in preschool boys and girls. *Child Development,* 1967, **38**(2), 291–327.

Bayer, L. M., & Snyder, M. M. Illness experience of a group of normal children. *Child Development,* 1950, **21**(93), 120.

Bayley, N. Mental growth during the first three years. *Genetic Psychology Monographs,* 1933, **14**, 1–93.

Bayley, N. The development of motor abilities during the first three years. *Monographs of the Society for Research in Child Development,* 1935, **1**(1).

Bayley, N. Consistency and variability in the growth of intelligence from birth to 18 years. *Journal of Genetic Psychology,* 1949, **75**, 165–196.

Bayley, N. Comparisons of mental and motor test scores for age 1–15 months by sex, birth order, race, geographic location, and education of parents. *Child Development,* 1965, **36**, 379–411.

Bayley, N. Research in child development: A longitudinal perspective, *Merrill-Palmer Quarterly of Behavior and Development,* 1965, **11**, 184–190.

Bayley, N., & Oden, M. The maintenance of intellectual ability in gifted adults. *Journal of Gerontology,* 1955, **10**, 91–107.

Bayley, N., & Schaefer, E. Correlations of maternal and child behaviors with the development of mental abilities: Data from the Berkeley growth study. *Monographs of the Society for Research in Child Development,* 1964, **29**(6), 1–80.

Bealer, R., Willits, P., & Maida, P. The rebellious youth subculture: A myth. *Children,* 1964, **11**, 43–48.

Beard, R. J. The menopause. *British Journal of Hospital Medicine,* 1975, **12**, 631–637.

Beard, R. M. *An outline of Piaget's developmental psychology for students and teachers.* New York: Basic Books, 1969.

Beckwith, L. Relationships between infants' social behaviors and their mothers' behavior. *Child Development,* 1972, **43**(2), 397–411.

Behrman, R., Babson, G., & Lessel, R. Fetal and neonatal mortality in white middle-class infants: Mortality risks by gestational age and weight. *American Journal of the Diseases of Children,* 1971, **121**, 486–489.

Belbin, E., & Belbin, R. *New careers in middle age*. Proceedings of the 7th International Congress of Gerontology. Vienna: Verlag der Wiener Medizinischen Akademie, 1966, pp. 71–82.

Belbin, R. M. Middle age: What happens to ability? In R. Owen (Ed.), *Middle age*. London: BBC, 1967.

Bell, B., Wolf, E., & Bernholz, C. Depth perception as a function of age. *Human Development*, 1972, **3**, 77–82.

Bell, G. D. Processes in the formation of adolescents' aspirations. *Social Forces*, 1963, **42**, 179–195.

Bell, R. R. Parent-child conflict in sexual values. *Journal of Social Issues*, 1966, **22**, 34–44.

Bell, R. R. *Premarital sex in a changing society*. Englewood Cliffs, NJ: Prentice-Hall, 1966.

Belloc, N. B., & Breslow, L. Relationship of physical health status and health practices. *Preventive Medicine*, 1972, **1**(3), 409–421.

Belmont, L. Birth order, intellectual competence, and psychiatric status. *Journal of Individual Psychology*, 1977, **33**, 97–103.

Belmont, L., & Marolla, A. F. Birth order, family size, and intelligence. *Science*, 1973, **182**, 1096–1101.

Benedek, T., & Rubinstein, B. *The sexual cycle in women: The relation between ovarian function and psychodynamic processes*. Washington, DC: National Research Council, 1942.

Benedict, H. The role of repetition in early language comprehension. Paper presented at the annual meeting of the Society for Research in Child Development, Denver, 1975.

Bengston, V. *The social psychology of aging*. Indianapolis: Bobbs-Merrill, 1973.

Bengston, V., Cuellar, J. A., & Ragan, P. Group contrasts in attitudes toward death: Variation by race, age, occupational status and sex. Paper presented at the annual meeting of the Gerontological Society, Louisville, KY, Oct. 29, 1975.

Bensman, J., & Lilienfeld, R. Friendship and alienation. *Psychology Today*, 1979, **13**(4), 56–66; 114.

Berenda, R. W. *The influence of the group on the judgments of children*. New York: King's Crown Press, 1950.

Berg, A. The economics of breast-feeding. *Saturday Review of the Sciences*, 1973, **1**(4), 29–32.

Berger, M. J. & Goldstein, D. P. Impaired reproductive performance in DES-exposed women. *Obstetrics and Gynecology*, 1980, **55**(1), 25–27.

Bergman, A., & Weisner, L. Relationship of passive cigarette smoking to sudden infant death syndrome. *Pediatrics*, 1976, **58**(5), 665–668.

Berlin, C. Effects of LSD taken by pregnant women on chromosomal abnormalities of offspring. *Pediatric Herald*, January–February, 1969, **1**.

Bernard, J. *The future of marriage*. New York: World, 1973.

Bernstein, B. Social class and linguistic development: A theory of social learning. In A. H. Halsey, J. Floud, & C. A. Anderson (Eds.), *Education, economy, and society*. New York: Free Press, 1961.

Bernstein, B. Elaborated and restricted codes: Their social origin and some consequences. *American Anthropologist*, 1964, **66**(6), 55–69.

Berscheid, E., Walster, E., & Bohrnstedt, G. The happy American body, a survey report. *Psychology Today*, 1973, **7**(6), 119–131.

Bettelheim, B. *The empty fortress*. New York: Free Press, 1967.

Bettelheim, B. *The children of the dream*. New York: Macmillian, 1969.

Bibbo, M., Gill, W., Azizi, F., Blough, R., Fang, V., Rosenfield, R., Schumacher, G., Sleeper, K., Sonek, M., & Wied, G. Follow-up study of male and female offspring of DES-exposed mothers. *Obstetrics and Gynecology*, 1977, **49**(1), 1–8.

Bielby, D. Factors affecting career commitment of female college graduates. Unpublished doctoral dissertation, University of Wisconsin, Madison, 1975.

Bielby, D., & Papalia, D. Moral development and perceptual role-taking egocentrism: Their development and interrelationship across the life span. *International Journal of Aging and Human Development*, 1975, **6**(4), 293–308.

Biller, H. B. Father absence, maternal encouragement, and sex role development in kindergarten-age boys. *Child Development*, 1960, **40**, 539–546.

Biller, H. B., & Bahm, R. Father absences, perceived maternal behavior, and masculinity of self-concept among junior high school boys. *Development Psychology*, 1971, **4**, 178–181.

Biller, H. B. Father absence and the personality

development of the male child. *Developmental Psychology*, 1970, **2**, 181–201.

Bing, E. Effects of child-rearing practices on development of differential cognitive abilities. *Child Development*, 1963, **34**, 631–648.

Bingham-Newman, A., & Hooper, F. Classification and seriation instruction and logical task performance in the preschool. *American Educational Research Journal,* 1974, **11**(4), 379–393.

Bird, C. *The case against college.* New York: McKay, 1975.

Birns, B. The emergence and socialization of sex differences in the earliest years. *Merrill-Palmer Quarterly*, 1976, **22**, 229–254.

Birren, J. E. Translations in gerontology—from lab to life: Psychophysiology and speed of response. *American Psychologist,* 1974, **29**(11), 808–815.

Bishop, E. H., Israel, S. L., & Briscoe, C. C. Obstetric influences on premature infant's first year of development: A report from the collaborative study of cerebral palsy. *Journal of Obstetrics and Gynecology*, 1965, **26**, 628–635.

Bizen, P. When a youth takes his life. *Boston Globe* (Living Section), Jan. 6, 1973, p. 9.

Bjorksten, J. Crosslinkage and the aging process. In M. Rockstein, M. Sussman, & J. Chesley (Eds.), *Theoretical aspects of aging.* New York: Academic Press, 1974.

Blake, J. Is zero preferred? American attitudes toward childlessness in the 1970s. *Journal of Marriage and the Family*, 1979, **41**(2), 245–257.

Blank, M., & Solomon, F. A tutorial language program to develop abstract thinking in socially disadvantaged preschool children. *Child Development*, 1968, **39**, 379–389.

Blau, Z. S. Structural constraints on friendship in old age. *American Sociological Review*, 1961, **26**, 429–439.

Blau, Z. S. *Old age in a changing society.* New York: New Viewpoints, A Division of Franklin Watts, Inc., 1973.

Blauvelt, H. Dynamics of the mother-newborn relationship in goats. In B. Schaffner (Ed.), *Group processes.* New York: Macy Foundation, 1955.

Bledsoe, J. C. Self-concepts of children and their intelligence, achievement, interests, and anxiety. *Journal of Individual Psychology*, 1964, **20**, 55–58.

Blenkner, M. Social work and family relationships in later life with some thoughts on filial maturity. In

E. Shanas & G. F. Streib (Eds.), *Social structure and the family.* Englewood Cliffs, NJ: Prentice-Hall, 1965.

Bluebond-Langner, M. *Awareness and communication in terminally ill children: Pattern, process, and pretense.* Unpublished doctoral dissertation, University of Illinois, 1975.

Bluebond-Langner, M. Meanings of death to children. In H. Feifel (Ed.), *New meanings of death.* New York: McGraw-Hill, 1977, pp. 47–66.

Blum, J. E., & Jarvik, L. F. Intellectual performance of octogenarians as a function of education and initial ability. *Human Development*, 1974, **17**, 364–375.

Blum, S. Children who starve themselves. *The New York Times Magazine,* Nov. 10, 1974, pp. 63 ff.

Bogatz, G., & Ball, S. *The second year of Sesame Street: A continuing evaluation.* New Jersey: Educational Testing Service, 1971.

Bogue, D. J. *The population of the United States.* New York: Free Press, 1959.

Bohannan, P. The sex stations of divorce. In P. Bohannan (Ed.), *Divorce and after.* New York: Anchor, 1971.

Bongiovanni, A., DeGeorge, A., & Grumback, M. Masculinization of the female infant associated with estrogenic therapy alone during gestation. *Journal of Clinical Endocrinology and Metabolism*, 1959, **19**, 1004–1011.

Borders, W. British "Right to Die" group plans to publish a manual on suicide. *The New York Times*, Mar. 7, 1980, p. A18.

Bornstein, M., Kessen, W., & Weiskopf, S. The categories of hue in infancy. *Science*, 1976, **191**, 201–202.

Boston Children's Medical Center. *Pregnancy, birth, and the newborn baby.* Boston: Delacorte, 1972.

Boswell, D., & Williams, J. Correlates of race and color bias among preschool children. *Psychological Reports*, 1975, **36**, 147–154.

Botwinick, J. Cautiousness in advanced age. *Journal of Gerontology*, 1966, **21**, 347–353.

Botwinick, J., West, R. & Storandt, M. Predicting death from behavioral test performance. *Journal of Gerontology*, 1978, **33**(5), 755–762.

Bower, T. G. R. Repetitive processes in child

development. *Scientific American*, 1976, **235**(5), 38–47.

Bower, T. G. R.   *Primer of infant development*. San Francisco: Freeman, 1977.

Bowlby, J.   The nature of the child's tie to his mother. *International Journal of Psychoanalysis*, 1953, **39**, 350–373.

Bowlby, J.   Separation anxiety. *International Journal of Psychoanalysis*, 1960, **41**, 89–113.

Boyle, R. P.   The effects of the high school on students' aspirations. *American Journal of Sociology*, 1966, **71**, 628–639.

Brackbill, Y.   Extinction of the smiling response in infants as a function of reinforcement schedule. *Child Development*, 1958, **29**, 115–124.

Brackbill, Y.   The role of the cortex: Orienting reflex in an anencephalic human infant. *Developmental Psychology*, 1971, **5**, 193–201.

Brackbill, Y., & Broman, S. H.   Obstetrical medication and development in the first year of life. Unpublished manuscript, Jan. 15, 1979.

Bradley, R., & Caldwell, B.   Early home environment and changes in mental test performance in children from 6 to 36 months. *Developmental Psychology*, 1976, **12**(2), 93–97.

Brazelton, T. B.   Effects of prenatal drugs on the behavior of the neonate. *American Journal of Psychiatry*, 1970, **126**(9), 95–100.

Brazelton, T. B.   *Neonatal behavioral assessment scale*. Philadelphia: Lippincott, 1973.

Brecher, E., & the Editors of Consumer Reports.   *Licit & illicit drugs*. Mount Vernon, NY: Consumers Union, 1972.

Breland, H.   Birth order, family configuration, and verbal achievement. *Child Development*, 1974, **45**, 1011–1019.

Bridges, K. M. B.   Emotional development in early infancy. *Child Development*, 1932, **3**, 324–341.

Brim, O. G.   Theories of the male mid-life crisis. In N. Schlossberg & A. Entine (Eds.), *Counseling adults*. Monterey, CA: Brooks/Cole, 1977.

Brim, O. G.   Adult socialization. In J. Clausen (Ed.), *Socialization and society*. Boston: Little, Brown, 1968.

Brim, O. G.   Family structure and sex role learning by children: A further analysis of Helen Koch's data. *Sociometry*, 1958, **21**, 1–16.

Brittain, C.   Adolescent choices and parent-peer cross-pressures. *American Sociological Review*, 1963, **28**, 385–391.

Brock, D., Barron, L., Jelen, P., Watt, M., & Scrimgeour, J.   Maternal serum–alphafetoprotein measurements as an early indicator of low birthweight. *Lancet*, Aug. 6, 1977, pp. 267–270.

Brockman, L. M., & Riccuiti, H. N.   Severe protein calorie malnutrition and cognitive development in infancy and early childhood. *Developmental Psychology*, 1971, **4**(3), 312–319.

Brodbeck, A. J., & Irwin, O. C.   The speech behavior of infants without families. *Child Development*, 1946, **17**, 145–156.

Broderick, C. B., & Fowler, S. E.   New patterns of relationships between the sexes among preadolescents. *Marriage and Family Living*, 1961, **23**, 27–36.

Brody, E. B., & Brody, N.   *Intelligence*. New York: Academic, 1976.

Brody, J. E.   Most pregnant women found taking excess drugs. *The New York Times*, Mar. 18, 1973.

Brody, J. E.   Deaths of women linked to smoking. *The New York Times*, May 20, 1973.

Brodzinsky, D.   The role of conceptual tempo and stimulus characteristics in children's humor development. *Developmental Psychology*, 1975, **11**(6), 843–850.

Bromley, D. B.   *The psychology of human ageing* (2d ed.). Middlesex, England: Penguin, 1974.

Bronfenbrenner, U.   Freudian theories of identification and their derivatives. *Child Development*, 1960, **31**, 15–40.

Bronfenbrenner, U.   Response to pressure from peers versus adults among Soviet and American school children. *International Journal of Psychology*, 1967, **2**, 199–207.

Bronfenbrenner, U., Belsky, J., & Steinberg, L.   Daycare in context: An ecological perspective on research and public policy. Review prepared for Office of the Assistant Secretary for Planning and Evaluation, Department of Health, Education, and Welfare, 1977.

Bronfenbrenner, U.   *Two worlds of childhood: U.S. and U.S.S.R.* New York: Russell Sage, 1970.

Bronson, F. H., & Desjardins, C.   Agressive behavior and seminal vesicle function in mice: Differential sensitivity to androgen given neonatally. *Endocrinology*, 1969, **85**, 871–975.

Bronstein, A., & Petrova, E.   An investigation of the auditory analyzer in neonates and young infants. *Zh. vyssh. nerv. Deiatel.* 1952, **2**, 333–343.

Brooks, J., & Lewis, M.   Attachment behavior in

thirteen-month-old opposite sex twins. *Child Development*, 1974, **45**, 243–247.

Brooks, J., & Lewis, M. Infants' responses to strangers: Midget, adult, child. *Child Development*, 1976, **47**. 323–332.

Brooks, J., & Weinraub, M. A history of infant intelligence tests. In M. Lewis (Ed.), *Origins of intelligence*. New York: Plenum, 1976. pp. 19–58.

Brophy, J. E., & Good, T. L. Feminization of American elementary schools. *Phi Delta Kappan*, 1973, **54**, 564–566.

Brophy, J. E., & Good, T. L. *Teacher-student relationships*. New York: Holt, 1974.

Brotman, H. B. *Facts and figures on older Americans, no. 2. The older population revisited.* Washington, DC: U.S. Department of Health, Education, and Welfare, Administration on Aging, 1972.

Brotman, H. B. *Facts and figures on older Americans, no. 5. An overview.* Washington, DC: U.S. Department of Health, Education, and Welfare, Administration on Aging, 1972.

Brown, P., & Elliott, R. Control of aggression in a nursery school class. *Journal of Experimental Child Psychology*, 1965, **2**, 103–107.

Bruck, H. *The golden cage: The enigma of anorexia nervosa.* Cambridge: Harvard, 1978.

Brutten, M., Richarson, S., & Mangel, C. *Something's wrong with my child: A parent's book about children with learning disabilities.* New York: Harcourt Brace Jovanovich, 1973.

Bühler, C. *Der menschliche, Lebenslauf al pschologishes Problem.* Leipzig: Verlag von S. Herzel, 1933.

Bühler, C. Old age and fulfillment of life with considerations of the use of time in old age. *Acta Psychologica*, 1961, **19**, 126–148.

Bühler, C. The course of human life as a psychological problem. *Human Development*, 1968, **11**, 184–200.

Bühler, C. The development structure of goal setting in group and individual studies. In C. Bühler & F. Massarek (Eds.), *The course of human life*. New York: Spinger, 1968.

Bühler, C., & Allen, M. *Introduction to humanistic psychology.* Monterey, CA: Brooks/Cole, 1972.

Burger, G., Lamp, R., & Rogers, D. Developmental trends in childrens' perceptions of parental child-rearing behaviors. *Developmental Psychology*, 1975, **11**(3), 391.

Burgess, E. W., & Wallin, P. *Engagement and marriage.* Philadephia: Lippincott, 1953.

Burke, B. S., Beal, V. A., Kirkwood, S. B., & Stuart,

H.C. Nutrition studies during pregnancy. *American Journal of Obstetrics and Gynecology*, 1943, **46**, 38–52.

Burke, R., & Weir, T. Some personality differences between members of one-career and two-career families. *Journal of Marriage and the Family*, 1976, **38**(3), 453–459.

Burr, W. Satisfaction with various aspects of marriage over the life cycle. *Journal of Marriage and the Family*, 1970, **32**(1), 29–37.

Burt, C. The genetic determination of differences in intelligence: A study of monozygotic twins reared together and apart. *British Journal of Psychology*, 1966, **57**(1&2), 137–153.

Busse, E. Theories of aging. In E. Busse & E. Pfeiffer (Eds.), *Behavior and adaptation in late life*. Boston: Little, Brown, 1969.

Butler, F. "Over the garden wall/I let the baby fall." *The New York Times Magazine*, Dec. 16, 1973, pp. 90–95.

Butler, R. Re-awakening interests. *Nursing Homes: Journal of American Nursing Home Association*, 1961, **10**, 8–19.

Butler, R. The life review: An interpretation of reminiscence in the aged. In B. Neugarten (Ed.), *Middle age and aging*. Chicago: University of Chicago Press, 1968.

Butler, R. *Why survive? Being old in America.* New York: Harper & Row, 1975.

Butler, R., & Lewis, M. *Aging and mental health.* (2d ed.) St. Louis: Mosby, 1977.

Butler, R. N., Goldstein, H., & Ross, E. M. Cigarette smoking in pregnancy: Its influence on birth weight and perinatal mortality. *British Medical Journal*, 1972, **2**, 127–130.

Butterfield, E., & Siperstein, G. Influence of contingent auditory stimulation upon non-nutritional suckle. In J. Bosma (Ed.), *Oral sensation and perception: The mouth of the infant*. Springfield, IL: Charles C Thomas, 1972.

C

Cadoret, R., Cunningham, L., Loftus, R., & Edwards, J. Studies of adoptees from psychiatrically disturbed biologic parents. *Journal of Pediatrics*, 1975, **87**(2), 301–306.

California Department of Highway Patrol. *Annual*

Statistical Report. Sacramento: The Department, 1958, p. 108.

Cameron, J., Livson, N., & Bayley, N. Infant socializations and their relationship to mature intelligence. *Science*, 1967, **157**, 331–333.

Campbell, A. The American way of mating: Marriage si; children only maybe. *Psychology Today*, 1975, **8**(12), 37–43.

Campbell, A., Converse, P. E., & Rodgers, W. L. The Quality of American Life: Perceptions, evaluations, and satisfactions. New York: Russell-Sage, 1976.

Campbell, J. D. Peer relations in childhood. In M. Hoffman & L. Hoffman (Eds.), *Review of child development research.* New York: Russell Sage, 1964.

Campos, J. J., Langer, A., & Krowitz, A. Cardiac responses on the visual cliff in prelocomotor human infants. *Science*, 1970, **170**, 196–197.

Candee, D. The moral psychology of Watergate. *Journal of Social Issues*, 1975, **31**(2), 183–192.

Cantor, P. Suicide and attempted suicide among students: Problem, prediction and prevention. In P. Cantor (Ed.), *Understanding a child's world.* New York: McGraw-Hill, 1977.

Caputo, D. V., & Mandell, W. Consequences of low birth weight. *Developmental Psychology*, 1970, **3**, 363–383.

Carey, G. Sex differences in problem-solving performance as a function of attitude differences. *Journal of Abnormal and Social Psychology*, 1958, **56**, 156–160.

Carlson, C., Arnold, C., Becker, W., & Madsen, C. The elimination of tantrum behavior of a child in an elementary classroom. *Behavior Research and Therapy*, 1968, **6**, 117–119.

Carr, D. H. Chromosome studies in selected spontaneous abortions: 1, Conception after oral contraceptives. *Canadian Medical Association Journal*, 1970, **103**, 343–348.

Carson, A. S., & Raybin, A. I. Verbal comprehension and communication in negro and white children. *Journal of Educational Psychology*, 1960, **51**, 47–51.

Carter, H., & Glick, P. *Marriage and divorce: A social and economic study.* Cambridge: Harvard, 1970.

Catell, P. *The measurement of intelligence of infants and young children*, New York: The Psychological Corporation, 1947.

Cattell, R. B. *The scientific analysis of personality.* Baltimore: Penguin Books, 1965.

Catz, C. S. Drugs and breast milk. *Pediatric Clinics of North America*, February 1972.

Cavan, R., & Ferdinand, T. *Juvenile Delinquency* (3d ed.). Philadelphia: Lippincott, 1975.

Cazden, C. B. Three sociolinguistic views of the language and speech of lower-class children—with special attention to the work of Basil Bernstein. *Developmental Medicine and Child Neurology*, 1968, **10**, 600–612.

Cazden, C. B. Suggestions from studies of early language acquisition. In R. H. Anderson & H. G. Shane (Eds.), *As the twig is bent: Readings in early childhood education.* Boston: Houghton Mifflin, 1971.

Census finds adults wed later, divorce sooner. *The New York Times*, Jan. 8, 1976.

Cervantes, L. F. Family background, primary relationships, and the high school dropout. *Journal of Marriage and the family,* 1965, **5**, 218–223.

Chambers, M. Radical changes urged in dealing with youth crime. *The New York Times*. Nov. 30, 1975, pp. 1; 58.

Chandler, M. Egocentrism and antisocial behavior: The assessment and training of social perspective-taking skills. *Developmental Psychology*, 1973, **9**, 326–332.

Chandler, M., Greenspan, S., & Barenboim, C. Assessment and training of role-taking and referential communication skills in institutionalized emotionally disturbed children. *Developmental Psychology*, 1974, **10**(4), 546–553.

Charles, D. Historical antecedents of life-span developmental psychology. In L. Goulet & P. Baltes (Eds.), New York: Academic, 1970.

Check, W. Antenatal diagnosis: What is "standard"? *Journal of the American Medical Association*, 1979, **241**(16), 1666 ff.

Chess, S. Temperament and learning ability of school children. *American Journal of Public Health,* 1968, **58**(12), 2230–2239.

Chomsky, C.S. *The acquisition of syntax in children from five to ten.* Cambridge, MA: M.I.T., 1969.

Chomsky, N. *Language and mind* (2d ed.). New York: Harcourt Brace Jovanovich, 1972.

Chown, S. The effect of flexibility-rigidity and age

on adaptability in job performance. *Industrial Gerontology*, 1972, **13**, 105–121.

Church, J. *Three babies*. New York: Random House, 1966.

Clark, M., & Anderson, B. *Culture and aging*. Springfield, IL: Charles C Thomas, 1967.

Clark, T. Diagnoses of Tay-Sachs disease on blood obtained at fetoscopy. *Lancet*, May 5, 1979, pp. 972–973.

Clarke-Stewart, A. *Child care in the family: A review of research and some propositions for policy*. New York: Academic, 1977.

Clarren, S., & Smith, D. The fetal alcohol syndrome. *New England Journal of Medicine*, 1978, **298**(19), 1063–1067.

Clausen, J. A. Adolescent antecedents of cigarette smoking: Data from the Oakland growth study. *Social Science and Medicine*, 1968, **1**, 357–382.

Clayton, R. & Voss, H. Shacking up: Cohabitation in the 1970's. *Journal of Marriage and the Family*, 1977, **39**(3), 273–283.

Clayton, V., & Overton, W. The role of formal operational thought in the aging process. Paper presented at the annual meeting of the Gerontological Society, Miami, 1973.

Clemente, F. & Sauer, W. Life satisfaction in the United States. *Social Forces*, 1976, **54**(3), 621–631.

Clifton, C. Language acquisition. In T. D. Spencer & N. Kass (Eds.), *Perspectives in child psychology*. New York: McGraw-Hill, 1970.

Cobrinick, P., Hood, R., & Chused, E. Effects of maternal narcotic addiction on the newborn infant. *Pediatrics*, 1959, **24**, 288–290.

Cohen, L., & Campos, J. Father, mother, and stranger as elicitors of attachment behaviors in infancy. *Developmental Psychology*, 1974, **10**(1), 146–154.

Cohen, S., & Beckwith, L. Maternal language in infancy. *Developmental Psychology*, 1976, **12**(4), 371–372.

Cohn, V. New method of delivering babies cuts down "torture of the innocent." *Capital Times*, Nov. 5, 1975.

Combs, J., & Cooley, W. Dropouts: In high school and after school. *American Educational Research Journal*, 1968, **5**, 343–363.

Condry, J. & Condry, S. The development of sex differences: A study of the eye of the beholder. Unpublished manuscript. Cornell University, 1974.

Condry, J. C., Jr., Siman, M. L., & Bronfenbrenner, U. Characteristics of peer- and adult-oriented children. Unpublished manuscript, Department of Child Development, Cornell University, 1968.

Conger, J. J. *Adolescence and youth: Psychological development in a changing world*. New York: Harper & Row, 1973.

Conger, J. J. Adolescence, a time for becoming. In M. E. Lamb (Ed.), *Social and personality development*. New York: Holt, 1978, pp. 131–154.

Conger, J. J., Miller, W. C., & Walsmith, C. R. Antecedents of delinquency: Personality, social class, and intelligence. In P. H. Mussen, J. J. Conger, & J. Kagan (Eds.), *Readings in child development and personality. New York: Harper & Row, 1965.*

Conklin, E. S. *Principles of adolescent psychology*, New York: Holt, 1933.

Consumer Reports. The mystery of sudden infant death. June 1975, pp. 363–365.

Conway, D., & Lytton, H. Language differences between twins and singletons—biological, environmental, or both? Paper presented at the annual meeting of the Society for Research in Child Development, Denver, 1975.

Conway, E., & Brackbill, Y. Delivery medication and infant outcome: An empirical study. *Monographs of the Society for Research in Child Development*, 1970, **35**(4), 24–34.

Coopersmith, S. *The antecedents of self-esteem*. San Francisco:Freeman, 1967.

Cope, R., & Hannah, W. *Revolving college doors: The causes and consequences of dropping out, stopping out and transferring. New York: Wiley, 1975.*

Corah, N. L., Anthony, E. J., Painter, P., Stern, J. A., & Thurstan, D. Effects of prenatal anoxia after seven years. *Psychology Monographs*, 1965, **79** (Whole No. 596).

Corbin, C. *A textbook of motor development*. Dubuque, IA: W. C. Brown, 1973.

Corman, H. H., & Escalona, S. K. Stages of sensorimotor development: A replication. *Merrill-Palmer Quarterly*, 1969, **15**, 351–361.

Corrigan, G. The fetal alcohol syndrome. *Texas Medicine*, 1976, **72**, 72–74.

Corso, J. F. Sensory processes and age effects in normal adults. *Journal of Gerontology*, 1971, **26**(1), 90–105.

Corter, C. M. The nature of the mother's absence and the infant's response to brief separation. *Developmental Psychology*, 1976, **12**(5), 428–434.

Corter, C. M., Rheingold, H. L., & Eckerman, C.O. Toys delay the infant's following of his mother. *Developmental Psychology*, 1972, **6**, 138–145.

Costanzo, P. R., & Shaw, M. E. Conformity as a function of age level. *Child Development*, 1966, **37**, 967–975.

Cox, C. M. *Genetic studies of geniuses* (Vol. II). *The early mental traits of three hundred geniuses*. Stanford, CA: Stanford, 1926.

Crandall, V. J., Preston, A., & Rabson, A. Maternal reactions and the development of independence and achievement behavior in young children. *Child Development*, 1960, **31**, 243–251.

Cratty, B. *Perceptual and motor development in infants and children*. Englewood Cliffs, NJ: Prentice-Hall, 1979.

Croake. J. W. Fears of children. *Human Development*, 1969, **12**, 239–247.

Croake, J. W. The changing nature of children's fears. *Child Study Journal*, 1973, **3**(2), 91–105.

Crovitz, E. Reversing a learning deficit in the aged. *Journal of Gerontology*, 1966, **21**, 236–238.

Crow, L. D., Murray, W. I., & Smythe, H. H. *Educating the culturally disadvantaged child*. New York: McKay, 1966.

Crowell, D., Blurton, L., Kobayashi, L., MacFarland, J., & Yang, R. Studies in early infant learning: Classical conditioning of the neonatal heart rate. *Developmental Psychology*, 1976, **12**(4), 373–397.

Cuber, J., & Harroff, P. Five type of marriage. In A. Skolnick & J. Skolnick (Eds.), *Intimacy, family, and society*. Boston: Little, Brown, 1974.

Cumming, E., & Henry, W. *Growing old*. New York: Basic Books, 1961.

Cunningham, A. Morbidity in breast-fed and artificially fed infants. *Journal of Pediatrics*, 1977, **90**(59), 726–729.

Curtis, H. J., & Miller, K. Chromosome aberrations in liver cells of guinea pigs. *Journal of Gerontology*, 1971, **26**, 292–294.

Curzon, M. E. J. Dental implications of thumb-sucking. *Pediatrics*, 1974, **60**(5), 196–200.

D

Dalton, K. *The premenstrual syndrome*. Springfield, IL: Charles C Thomas, 1964.

Daniels, N. The smart white man's burden. *Harper's*, 1973, **247**(1481), 24–40.

Dantchakoff, V. Sur le mechanisme des déviations sexuelles dans une femelle génétique à la suite: a. de testosterinisation; b. du free-martinisme; c. des tumeurs de la surrénale (virilisme). *Comptes Rendus Hebdomadaries des Séances de l'Academie des Sciences,* 1938, **206**, 1411–1413.

Death fears: Black, brown, and white. *Human Behavior*, April 1976, p. 71.

DeFrain, J., & Ernst, L. The psychological effects of sudden infant death syndrome on surviving family members. *Journal of Family Practice*, 1978, **6**(5), 985–989.

Delatiner, B. Retirees studying "emotional backlash." *The New York Times*, Jan. 27, 1980, p. 8 L.I.

Denney, N. W., & Lennon, M. L. Classification: A comparison of middle and old age. *Developmental Psychology*, 1972, **7**(2), 210–213.

Dennis, W. A bibliography of baby biographies. *Child Development*, 1936, **7**, 71–73.

Dennis, W. Causes of retardation among institutional children: Iran. *Journal of Genetic Psychology*, 1960, **96**, 47–59.

Dennis, W. Creative production between the ages of 20 and 80. *Journal of Gerontology*, 1966, **21**(1), p. 8.

Deutscher, I. The quality of postparental life. *Journal of Marriage and the Family, 1964,* **26**(1).

Dickson, W. P. Referential communication performance from age 4 to 8: Effects of referent type, context, and target position. *Developmental Psychology*, 1979, **15**(4), 470–471.

Digest of Educational Statistics, 1979 Ed. National Center for Educational Statistics, U.S. Department of Health, Education, and Welfare.

Dine, M., Gartside, P., Glueck, C., Rheines, L., Greene, G., & Khoury, P. Where do the heaviest children come from? A prospective study of white children from birth to 5 years of age. *Pediatrics*, 1979, **63**(1), 1–6.

Dipboye, W. J., & Anderson, W. F. Occupational

stereotypes and manifest needs of high school students. *Journal of Counseling Psychology*, 1961, **8**, 296–304.

Doering, S., & Entwistle, D. Preparation during pregnancy and ability to cope with labor and delivery. *American Journal of Orthopsychiarty*, 1975, **45**(2), 825–837.

Doppelt, J. E., & Wallace, W. L. Standardization of the Wechsler Adult Intelligence Scale for older persons. *Journal of Abnormal and Social Psychology*, 1955, **51**, 312–330.

Dorfman, D. D. The Cyril Burt question: New findings, *Science*, 1978. **201**(4362), 1177–1186.

Doyle, N. C. Marijuana and the lungs. *American Lung Association Bulletin*, 1979, **65**(9), 2–7.

Drage, J. S., Kennedy, C., Berendes, H., Schwartz, B. K., & Weiss, W. Apgar score as index of infant morbidity: A report from collaborative study of cerebral palsy. *Developmental Medicine and Child Neurology*, 1966, **8**, 141–148.

Drillien, C. M. The incidence of mental and physical handicaps in school-age children of very low birth weights. *Pediatrics*, 1961, **27**, 452–464.

Duffy, M. Calling the doctor: Women complain about illness more often than men. *New York Daily News*, Feb. 8, 1979.

Dumars, K. Parental drug usage: Effect upon chromosomes of progeny. *Pediatrics*, 1971, **47**(6), 1037–1041.

Dunn, P. M. Some perinatal observations on twins. *Developmental Medicine and Child Neurology*, 1965, **7**, 121.

DuPont, R. Just what *can* you tell your patients about marihuana? *Resident and Staff Physician*, 1977, **23**(1), 103–110.

Durlak, J. A. Relationship between attitudes toward life and death among elderly women. *Developmental Psychology*, 1973, **8**(1), 146.

Dyer, E. Parenthood as crisis: A re-study. *Marriage and family Living*. 1963, **25**, 196–201.

Dytrych, Z., Matejcek, Z., Schuller, V., David, H. P., & Friedman, H. L. Children born to women denied abortion. *Family Planning Perspectives*, 1975, **7**(4), 165–171.

E

Eckerman, C., & Whatley, J. Toys and social interaction between infant peers. *Child Development*, 1977, **48**, 1645–1656.

Edwards, A., & Wine, D. Personality changes with age: Their dependency on concomitant intellectual decline. *Journal of Gerontology, 1963*, **18**, 182–184.

Ehrhardt, A. A., & Baker, S. W. Hormonal aberrations and their implications for the understanding of normal sex differentiation. Paper presented at the Society for Research in Child Development, Philadelphia, Mar. 31, 1973.

Ehrhardt, A. A., & Money, J. Progestin induced hermaphroditism: I.Q. and psychosocial identity. *Journal of Sexual Research*, 1967, **3**, 83–100.

Einstein, A. *Out of my later years*. Westport, CT: Greenwood, 1950.

Einstein, E. Stepfamily lives. *Human Behavior*, April 1979, pp. 63–68.

Eisenson, J., Auer, J. J., & Irwin, J. V. *The psychology of communication*. New York. Appleton-Century-Crofts, 1963.

Elardo, R., Bradley, R., & Caldwell, B. The relation of infants' home environments to mental test performance from six to thirty-six months: A longitudinal analysis. *Child Development*, 1975, **46**, 71–76.

Elkind, D. Quantity concepts in college students. *Journal of Social Psychology*, 1962, **57**, 459–465.

Elkind, D. Cognition in infancy and early childhood. In Y. Brackbill (Ed.), *Infancy and early childhood*. New York: Free Press, 1967.

Elkind, D. Egocentrism in adolescence. *Child Development*, 1967, **38**, 1025–1034.

Elkind, D., & Bowen, R. Imaginary audience behavior in children and adolescents. *Developmental Psychology*, 1979, **15**(1), 38–44.

Elliott, J. Risk of cancer, dysplasia for DES daughters found "very low." *Journal of the American Medical Association*, 1979, **241**(15), 1555.

Elmer, E., & Gregg, G. Developmental characteristics of abused children. *Pediatrics*, 1967, **40**, 596–602.

Emanuel, I., Sever, L., Milham, S., & Thuline, H. Accelerating aging in young mothers of children with Down's syndrome. *Lancet*, 1972, **2**, 361–363.

Emmerich, H. The influence of parents and peers on choices made by adolescents. *Journal of Youth and Adolescence*, 1978, **7**(2), 175–180.

Endsley, R., Odom, A., Gardner, A., & Martin M. Interrelationships among selected maternal behaviors, attitudes, and young children's curiosity. Paper presented at the annual meeting of the Society for Research in Child Development, Denver, 1975.

Englander-Golden, P., Willis, K. A., & Dienstbier, R. A. Stability of perceived tension as a function of the menstrual cycle. *Journal of Human Stress*, 1977, **3**(2), 14–21.

Entine, A. *Americans in middle years: Career options and educational opportunities.* California: Ethel Percy Andrus Gerontological Center, 1974.

Erb, L., & Andresen, B. The fetal alcohol syndrome (FAS): A review of the impact of chronic maternal alcoholism on the developing fetus. *Clinical Pediatrics*, 1978, **17**(8), 644–649.

Erikson, E. H. *Childhood and society.* New York: Norton, 1950.

Erikson, E. H. Youth: Fidelity and diversity. In E. Erikson (Ed.), *The challenge of youth.* New York: Anchor, 1965.

Erikson, E. H. *Childhood and society. New York: Norton, 1963.*

Erikson, E. H. Identity: Youth and crisis. New York: Norton, 1968.

Erikson, E. H. (Ed.) *The challenge of youth.* New York: Anchor, 1965.

Espenschade, A. Motor development. In W. R. Johnson (Ed.), *Science and Medicine of Exercise and Sports.* New York: Harper & Row, 1960.

Espenshade, T. J. *The value and cost of children. Population Bulletin* Vol. **32**(1). Washington, DC: Population Reference Bureau, 1977.

Espenshade, T. J. The economic consequences of divorce. *Journal of Marriage and the Family*, 1979, **41**(3), 615–625.

Estes, C. L. *The aging enterprise: A critical examination of social policies and services for the aged.* San Francisco: Jossey-Bass, 1979.

Estes, E. H. Health experience in the elderly. In E. Busse and E. Pfeiffer (Eds.), *Behavior and adaptation in late life.* Boston: Little, Brown, 1969.

Etaugh, C. Effects of maternal employment upon children: A review of recent research. Paper presented at the biennial meeting of the Society for Research in Child Development, Philadelphia, 1973.

Etaugh, C., & Harlow, H. School attitudes and performances of elementary school children as related to teacher's sex and behavior. Paper presented at the annual meeting of the Society for Research in Child Development, Philadelphia, March 1973.

Etzioni, A. Safeguarding the rights of human subjects. *Human Behavior*, 1978, **7**(11), 14.

Evans, E. D. *Contemporary influences in early childhood education* (2d ed.). New York: Holt, 1975.

Evans, G. The older the sperm. . . . *Ms. Magazine*, 1976, **4**(7), 48–49.

Evans, O. For the elderly, exploring some alternatives to the nursing homes. *The New York Times*, June 5, 1979, p. C12.

Eysenck, H. J., & Prell, D. B. The inheritance of neuroticism: An experimental study. *Journal of Mental Science*, 1951, **97**, 441–466.

F

Fagen, J. F., Fantz, R. L., & Miranda, S. B. Infants attention to novel stimuli as a function of post-natal and conceptual age. Paper presented at the meeting of the Society for Research in Child Development, Minneapolis, 1971.

Family trends now taking shape. *U.S. News and World Report*, Oct. 27, 1975, p. 32.

Fantz, R. Pattern vision in newborn infants. *Science*, 1963, **140**, 246–297.

FBI Uniform Crime Reports. Crime in the U.S., 1978 (U.S. Department of Justice). Washington DC: U.S. Government Printing Office, 1979.

Feifel, H. *New meanings of death.* New York: McGraw-Hill, 1977.

Feinberg, M., Smith, M., & Schmidt, R. An analysis of expressions used by adolescents at varying economic levels to describe accepted and rejected peers. *Journal of Genetic Psychology*, 1958, **93**, 133–148.

Feingold, B. B. *Introduction to clinical allergy.* Springfield, IL: Charles C Thomas, 1973.

Feldman, H. *Development of the husband-wife relationship.* Preliminary report. Cornell University, 1964.

Feldman, H. The effects of children on the family. In Michel, A. (Ed.), *Family issues of employed women in Europe and America.* Lieden, The Netherlands: E. F. Brill, 1971.

Feldman, H., & Feldman, M. Effect of parenthood at three points in marriage. Unpublished manuscript, 1976–77.

Ferguson-Smith, M., Rawlinson, H., May, H., Tait, H., Vince, J., Gibson, A., Robinson, H. & Ratcliffe,

J. Avoidance of anencephalic and spina bifida births by maternal serum-alphafetoprotein screening. *Lancet*, June 24, 1978, pp. 1330–1333.

Fielding, J. Adolescent pregnancy revisited. *New England Journal of Medicine*, 1978, **299**(16), 893–896.

Finke, W. D., & Ziei, H. K. Increased risk of endometrial carcinoma among users of conjugated estrogens. *New England Journal of Medicine*, 1975, **293**(23), 1167–1170.

Finkelstein, M., Dent, A., Gallacher, K., Ramey, C. Social behavior of infants and toddlers. *Developmental Psychology*, 1978, **14**(3), 257–262.

Fisch, R., Bilek, M., Deinard, A., & Chang, P. Growth, behavior and psychological measures of adopted children: The influence of genetic and socioeconomic factors in a prospective study. *Journal of Pediatrics*, 1976, **89**(3), 494–500.

Fischer, D. H. Putting our heads to the "problem" of old age. *The New York Times*, May 10, 1977, p. 33.

Fitzgerald, H., & Brackbill, Y. Classical conditioning in infancy: Development and constraints. *Psychological Bulletin*, 1976, **83**(3), 353–376.

Flaste, R. Helping handicapped into education's mainstream. *The New York Times*, May 19, 1974, p. E7.

Flaste, R. Career ambitions: Keeping the options open. *The New York Times*, Feb. 27, 1976, p. 15.

Flaste, R. In youngsters' books, the stereotype of old age. *The New York Times*, Jan. 7, 1977, p. A12.

Flavell, J. H. *The developmental psychology of Jean Piaget*. New York: Van Nostrand, 1963.

Flavell, J. H. Role-taking and communication skills in children. *Young Children*, 1966, **21**(3), 164–177.

Fleming, T. J., & Fleming, A. *Develop your child's creativity*, New York: Associated Press, 1970.

Fomon, S. J. A pediatrician looks at early nutrition. *Bulletin of the New York Academy of Medicine*, 1971, **47**, 569–578.

Fomon, S. J., Filer, L. J., Jr., Anderson, T. A., & Ziegler, E. E. Recommendations for feeding normal infants. *Pediatrics*, 1979, **63**(1), p.

Fontana, V. J. *Somewhere a child is crying*. New York: Mentor, 1976.

Fontana, V. J., & Robison, E. A multidisciplinary approach to the treatment of child abuse. *Pediatrics*, 1976, **57**(5), 760–764.

Forfar, J., & Arneil, G. (Eds.). *Textbook of paediatrics*. Edinburgh: Churchill Livingstone, 1973.

Frankl, V. *The doctor and the soul*. New York: Knopf, 1965.

Frasier, S. D., & Rallison, M. L. Growth retardation and emotional deprivation: Relative resistance to treatment with human growth hormone. *Journal of Pediatrics*, 1972, **80**, 603.

Freud, A. *The ego and the mechanism of defense*. New York: International Universities Press, 1946.

Freud, S. *A general introduction to psychoanalysis*. London: Boni and Liveright, 1924.

Freud, S. *A general introduction to psychoanalysis*. (J. Riviere, Trans.) New York: Permabooks, 1953.

Friedrich, L. K., & Stein, A. H. Aggressive and prosocial television programs and the natural behavior of preschool children. *Monographs of the Society for Research in Child Development*, 1973, **38**(4, Serial No. 151).

Frisch, H. Sex stereotypes in adult-infant play. *Child Development*, 1977, **48**, 1671–1675.

Frisch, R. E. Weight at menarche: Similarity for well-nourished and undernourished girls at differing ages, and evidence for historical constancy. *Pediatrics*, 1972, **50**(3), 445–450.

Frueh, T., & McGhee, P. Traditional sex role development and amount of time spent watching television. *Developmental Psychology*, 1975, **11**(1), 109.

Fuchs, V. R. *Who shall live? Health, economics and social choice*. New York: Basic Books, 1974.

Fuqua, R., Bartsch, T., & Phye, G. An investigation of the relationship between cognitive tempo and creativity in preschool age children. *Child Development*, 1975, **46**, 779–782.

Furry, C. A., & Baltes P. B. The effect of age differences in ability-extraneous performance variables on the assessment of intelligence in children, adults, and the elderly. *Journal of Gerontology*, 1973, **28**(1), 73–80.

Furstenberg, F. F., Jr. The social consequences of teenage parenthood. *Family Planning Perspectives*, July–August 1976, **8**(4), 148–164.

Furth, H. G., & Wachs, H. *Thinking goes to*

school: Piaget's theory in practice. New York: Oxford, 1975.

G

Galdston, K.   The effects of the cardiac pacemaker in adolescence. In E. M. Pattison (Ed.), *The experience of dying.* Englewood Cliffs, NJ: Prentice-Hall, 1977.

Gamer, E., Thomas, J., & Kendall, D. Determinants of friendship across the life span. In M. F. Rebelsky (Ed.) *Life: The continuous process.* New York: Knopf, 1975.

Garai, J. E., & Scheinfeld, A.   Sex differences in mental and behavioral traits. *Genetic Psychology Monographs*, 1968, **77**, 169–299.

Gardner, H.   Exploring the mystery of creativity. *The New York Times*, March 29, 1979, pp. C1; C17.

Garfield, C.   (Ed.). *Psychosocial care of the dying patient.* New York: McGraw-Hill, 1978.

Garfield, C., & Clark, R.   The SHANTI project; A community model of psychosocial support for patients and families facing life-threatening illness. In C. Garfield (Ed.), *Psychosocial care of the dying patient.* New York: McGraw-Hill, 1978, pp. 355–364.

Garn, S. M.   Growth and development. In E. Ginzberg (Ed.), *The nation's children.* New York: Columbia University Press, 1966, pp. 24–42.

Garn, S. M., & Clark, D. C.   Trends in fatness and the origins of obesity, *Pediatrics*, 1976, **57**(4), 443–456.

Garvey, C., & Hogan, R.   Social speech and social interaction: Egocentrism revisited. *Child Development*, 1973, **44**, 562–568.

Geber, M.   Development psychomoteur de l'enfant Africain. *Courier*, 1956, **6**, 17–29.

Geber, M.   The psycho-motor development of African children in the first year and the influences of maternal behavior. *Journal of Social Psychology*, 1958, **47**, 185–186; 194–195.

Geber, M.   Longitudinal study and psychomotor development among Baganda children. *Proceedings of the XIV International Congress of Applied Psychology*, 1962, **3**, 50–60.

Geber, M., & Dean, R. F. A.   The state develop-ment of newborn African children. *Lancet*, 1957, **1**, 1216–1219.

Gedda, L.   *Twins in history and science.* Springfield, IL: Charles C Thomas, 1961.

George, C. & Main, M.   Social interactions of young abused children. Approach, avoidance, and aggression. *Child Development*, 1979, **50**(2), 306–318.

Gesell, A.   Maturation and infant behavior patterns. *Psychological Review*, 1929, **36**, 307–319.

Gesell, A., & Amatruda, C. S.   *Developmental diagnosis* (2d ed.). New York: Hoeber-Harper, 1947.

Gewirtz, H. B., & Gewirtz, J. L.   Caretaking settings, background events, and behavior differences in four Israeli child-rearing environments: Some preliminary trends. In. B. M. Foss (Ed.), *Determinants of infant behavior, IV.* London: Methuen, 1968.

Gil, D.   *Violence against children.* Cambridge, MA: Harvard, 1970.

Gilligan, C.   In a different voice: Women's conceptions of self and of morality. *Harvard Educational Review*, 1977, **47**(4), 481–517.

Gilmore, J. B.   The role of anxiety and cognitive factors in children's play behavior. *Child Development*, 1966, **37**, 397–416.

Ginott, H.   *Between parent and child.* New York: Macmillan, 1965.

Ginsberg, H., & Opper, S.   *Piaget's theory of intellectual development* (2d ed.). Englewood Cliffs, NJ: Prentice-Hall, 1979.

Glass, D., Neulinger, J., & Brim, O.   Birth order, verbal intelligence and educational aspirations. *Child Development*, 1974, **45**(3), 807–811.

Glueck, S., & Glueck, E.   *Unraveling juvenile delinquency.* New York: Commonwealth Fund, 1950.

Goertzel, V., & Goertzel, M. G.   *Cradles of eminence.* Boston: Little, Brown, 1962.

Golbus, M., Loughman, W. Epstein, C., Halbasch, G., Stephens, J., & Hall, B.   Prenatal genetic diagnosis in 3000 amniocenteses. *New England Journal of Medicine*, 1979, **300**(4), 157–163.

Goldberg, S., & Lewis, M.   Play behavior in the year-old infant: Early sex differences. *Child Development*, 1969, **40**, 21–31.

Golden, M., & Birns, B.   Social class and cognitive development in infancy. *Merrill-Palmer Quarterly of Behavior and Development*, 1968, **14**, 139–149.

Golden, M., Birns, B., & Bridger, W.   Review and overview: Social class and cognitive development. Paper presented at the biennial meeting of the Society for Research in Child Development, Philadelphia, 1973.

Goldschmid, M. L., & Bentler, P. M. The dimensions and measurement of conservation. *Child Development*, 1968, **39**, 787–815.

Golub, S. The effect of premenstrual anxiety and depression on cognitive functioning. Paper presented at the annual meeting of the American Psychological Association, Chicago, 1975.

Goodenough, F. L. *Mental testing: Its history, principles, and applications*. New York: Rinehart, 1949.

Gordon, D., & Young, R. School phobia: A discussion of etiology, treatment, and evaluation. *Psychological Bulletin*, 1976, **39**, 783–804.

Gordon, J. Nutritional individuality. *American Journal of Diseases of Children*, 1975, **129**(4), 422–424.

Gordon, S. *The sexual adolescent*. North Scituate, MA: Duxbury Press, 1973.

Gordon, T. *P.E.T., parent effectiveness training*. New York: Wyden, 1970.

Gottesman, I. I. Differential inheritance of the psychoneuroses. *Eugenics Quarterly*, 1962, **9**, 223–227.

Gottesman, I. I. Heritability of personality. A demonstration. *Psychology Monographs*, 1963, **77**(9, Whole No. 572).

Gottesman, I. I. Personality and natural selection. In S. G. Vandenberg (Ed.), *Methods and goals in human behavior genetics*. New York: Academic Press, 1965, pp. 63–80.

Gottesman, I. I., & Shields, J. Schizophrenia in twins: 16 years consecutive admission to a psychiatric clinic. *British Journal of Psychiatry*, 1966, **112**, 809–818.

Gottfried, A., & Brody, N. Interrelationships between and correlates of psychometric and Piagetian scales of sensorimotor intelligence. *Developmental Psychology*, 1975, **11**(3), 379–387.

Gould, R. The phases of adult life: A study in developmental psychology. *American Journal of Psychiatry*, 1972, **129**(5), 521–531.

Gould, R. E. What we don't know about homosexuality. *The New York Times Magazine*, Feb. 24, 1974, pp. 13 ff.

Govatos, L. A. Relationships and age differences in growth measures and motor skills. *Child Development*, 1959, **30**, 333–340.

Government of Israel, Central Bureau of Statistics. *Statistical Abstract of Israel*, 1973, No. 24.

Graham, F. G., Matarazzo, R. G., & Caldwell, B. G. Behavioral differences between normal and traumatized newborns. *Psychology Monographs*, 1956, **70**(5), 427–438.

Graham, V. Suicide rate skyrockets among nation's teenagers. Madison (Wl.) *Capital Times*, July 21, 1978, p. 12.

Gratch, G., & Landers, W. F. Stage IV of Piaget's theory of infants' object concepts: A longitudinal study. *Child Development*, 1971, **42**, 359–372.

Gray, J. A., Lean, J., & Keynes, A. Infant androgen treatment and adult open-field behavior: Direct effects and effects of injections of siblings. *Physiology and Behavior*, 1969, **4**(2), 177–181.

Greenberg, M., & Morris, N. Engrossment: The newborn's impact upon the father. *American Journal of Orthopsychiatry*, 1974, **44**(4), 520–531.

Greenberg, S. B. Attides toward increased social, economic and political participation by women as reported by elementary and secondary students. Paper presented to AERA Convention, Chicago, 1972.

Greenberg, S. B., & Peck, L. Hofstra University, personal communication, 1974.

Griffiths, R. *The abilities of babies*. New York: Exposition, 1954.

Grimwade, J. D., Walker, D. W., & Word, D. Sensory stimulation of the human fetus. *Australian Journal of Mental Retardation*, 1970, **1**, 63–64.

Grinder, R., & Spector, J. C. Sex differences in adolescents' perceptions of parental resource control. *Journal of Genetic Psychology*, 1965, **106**, 337–344.

Gross, R. T., & Duke, P. The effect of early versus late physical maturation on adolescent behavior. In I. Litt (Ed.), Symposium on Adolescent Medicine. *The Pediatric Clinics of North America*, 1980, **27**(1), 71–78.

Grossmann, B., & Wrighter, J. The relationship between selection-rejection and intelligence, social status, and personality among sixth grade girls. *Sociometry*, 1948, **11**, 346–355.

Grotevant, H., Scarr, S., & Weinberg, R. Intellectual development in family constellations with adopted and natural children: A test of the

Zajonc and Markus model. *Child Development*, 1977, **48**, 1699–1703.

Group for the Advancement of Psychiatry. *The joys and sorrows of parenthood*. New York: Scribner's, 1973.

Grumbach, M. M., & Ducharme, J. R. The effects of androgens on fetal sexual development. *Fertility and Sterility*, 1960, **11**, 157–180.

Gubrium, F. F. Being single in old age. *International Journal of Aging and Human Development*, 1975, **6**(1), 29–41.

Guilford, J. P. Three faces of intellect. *American Psychologist*, 1959, **14**, 469–479.

Guilford, J. P. *The nature of human intelligence*. New York: McGraw-Hill, 1967.

Gutteridge, M. A study of motor achievement of young children. *Archives of Psychology*, 1939, **244**.

Guttmacher, A. F. *Pregnancy and birth*. New York: Signet, 1962.

H

Haggerty, R. J. Changing lifestyles to improve health. *Preventive Medicine*, 1977, **6**, 276–289.

Hagman, R. R. A study of fears of children of preschool age. *Journal of Experimental Education*, 1932, **1**, 110–130.

Haire, D. The cultural warping of childbirth. *International Childbirth Education Association News*, 1972, p. 35.

Heald, J. Mid-life career influence. *Vocational Guidance Quarterly*, 1977, **25**(4), 309–312.

Hall, G. S. *Adolescence*. New York: Appleton, 1916.

Hall, G. S. *Senescence: The last half of life*. New York: Appleton, 1922.

Halverson, H. M. An experimental study of prehension in infants by means of systematic cinema record. *Genetic Psychology Monographs*, 1932, **10**, 107–286.

Hanson, J., Streissguth, A., & Smith, D. The effects of moderate fetal alcohol consumption during pregnancy on fetal growth and morphogenesis. *Journal of Pediatrics*, 1978, **92**(3), 457–460.

Harkins, E. Effects of empty nest transition on self-report of psychological and physical well-being. *Journal of Marriage and the Family*, 1978, **40**(3), 549–556.

Harley, J. P., Matthews, C. G., & Eichman, P. Synthetic food colors and hyperactivity in children: A double-blind challenge experiment. *Pediatrics*, 1978, **62**(6), 975–983.

Harlow, H. F., & Harlow, M. K. The effect of rearing conditions on behavior. *Bulletin of the Menninger Clinic*, 1962, **26**, 213–224.

Harlow, H. F., & Zimmerman, R. R. Affectional responses in the infant monkey. *Science*, 1959, **130**, 421–432.

Harmin, M., & Simon, S. B. Values. In S. B. Simon & H. Kirschenbaum (Eds.), *Readings in values clarification*. Minneapolis: Holt, Rinehart, & Winston, 1973.

Harrell, R. F., Woodyard, E., & Gates, A. The effect of mothers' diets on the intelligence of the offspring. New York: Bureau of Publications, Teacher's College, 1955.

Hartley, R. E. Sex-role pressures and the socialization of the male child. *Psychological Reports*, 1959, **5**, 457–468.

Hartshorne, H., & May, M. A. *Studies in the nature of character: Vol. I, Studies in deceit; Vol. II, Studies in self-control; Vol. III, Studies in the organization of character*. New York: Macmillan, 1928–1930.

Hartup, W. H. Peer relations. In T. D. Spencer & N. Kass (Eds.), *Perspectives in child psychology: Research and review*. New York: McGraw-Hill, 1970.

Hartup, W. H. The origins of friendship. In M. Lewis & L. Rosenblum (Ed.). *Friendship and peer relations*. New York: Wiley, 1975, pp. 11–26.

Haryett, R. D., Hansen, R. C., & Davidson, P. O. Chronic thumbsucking: A second report on treatment and its physiological effects. *American Journal of Orthodontics*, 1970, **57**, 164.

Hass, A. *Teenage sexuality: A survey of teenage sexual behavior*. New York: Macmillan, 1979.

Hawke, S., & Knox, D. The one-child family: A new life-style. *The Family Coordinator*, 1978, **27**(3), 215–219.

Hayden, A., & Haring, N. Early intervention for high risk infants and young children. Programs for Down's syndrome children. In T. D. Tjossem (Ed.), *Intervention strategies for high risk infants and young children*. Baltimore: University Park Press, 1976, pp. 573–607.

Hayflick, L. The strategy of senescence. *The Gerontologist*, 1974, **14**(1), 37–45.

Haynes, H., White, B. L., & Held, R. Visual accommodation in human infants. *Science*, 1965, **148**, 528–530.

Haynes, S., McMichael, A., & Kuppers, L. Mortality around retirement: The rubber industry case. Paper presented at the annual meeting of the Gerontological Society, Portland, Ore., 1974.

Heald, J. Mid-life career influences. *Vocational Guidance Quarterly*, 1977, **25**(4), 309–312.

Healy, W., & Bronner, A. *New light on delinquency and its treatment.* New Haven: Yale University Press, 1936.

Hechinger, F. M. What can be done about dropouts? *The New York Times*, Oct. 23, 1979, p. C1; C4.

Heinonen, D., Slone, D., Monson, R., Hook, E., & Shapiro, S. Cardiovascular birth defects and antenatal exposure to female sex hormones. *New England Journal of Medicine*, 1977, **296**(2), 67–70.

Heisel, J., Ream, S., Raitz, R., Rappaport, M., & Coddington, R. The significance of life events as contributing factors in the diseases of children. III: A study of pediatric patients. *Journal of Pediatrics*, 1973, **83**(1), 119–123.

Helfer, R. M. The etiology of child abuse. *Pediatrics*, 1973, **51**(4), 777–779.

Helmreich, R. Birth order effects. *Naval Research Reviews*, 1968, **21**.

Hendry, L., & Gillies, P. Body type, body esteem, school, and leisure: A study of overweight, average, and underweight adolescents. *Journal of Youth and Adolescence*, 1978, **7**(2), 181–196.

Henig, R. M. Exposing the myth of senility. *The New York Times Magazine*, Dec. 3, 1978, pp. 158 ff.

Henig, R. M. Ageism's angry critic. *Human Behavior*, 1979, **8**(1), 43–46.

Henly, W. L., & Fitch, B. R. Newborn narcotic withdrawal associated with regional enteritis in pregnancy. *New York Journal of Medicine*, 1966, **66**, 2565–2567.

Henze, L., & Hudson, J. Personal and family characteristics of cohabiting and noncohabitating college students. *Journal of Marriage and the family*, 1974, **36**(4), 722–727.

Herbst, A. L., Kurman, R. J., Scully, R. E., & Poskanzer, D. D. Clear-cell adenocarcinoma of the genital tract in young females. *New England Journal of Medicine*, 1972, **287**(25), 1259–1264.

Herbst, A. L., Ulfelder, H., & Poskanzer, D. C. Adenocarcinoma of the vagina. *New England Journal of Medicine*, 1971, **284**(16), 878–881.

Herzog, E., & Sudia, C. E. Fatherless homes: A review of research. *Children*, 1968, **15**, 177–182.

Hess, B. *Amicability.* Unpublished doctoral dissertation, Rutgers University, 1971.

Hess, J. L. The scandal of care for the old. *The New York Times*, Jan. 12, 1975.

Hess, R. D., & Shipman, V. C. Early experiences and the socialization of cognitive modes in children. *Child Development.* 1965, **36**, 869–886.

Heston, L. L. Psychiatric disorders in foster-home-reared children of schizophrenic mothers. *British Journal of Psychiatry*, 1966, **112**, 819–825.

Hetherington, E. M. *Sex typing, dependency and aggression. In T. D. Spencer & N. Kass (Eds.), Perspectives in child psychology: Research review.* New York: McGraw-Hill, 1970.

Hetherington, E. M., Cox. M., & Cox, R. Beyond father absence: Conceptualization of effects of divorce. Paper presented at the annual meeting of the Society for Research in Child Development, Denver, 1975.

Hetherington, E. M., & Parke, R. *Child psychology: A contemporary viewpoint*(2d ed.). New York: McGraw-Hill, 1979.

Hexachlorophene—Interim caution regarding use during pregnancy. *FDA Drug Bulletin,* 1978, **8**(4), 26–27.

Hey, E. N. Thermal regulation in the newborn. *British Journal of Hospital Medicine*, 1972, pp. 51–64.

Hickey, T., Hickey, L., & Kalish, R. Children's perceptions of the elderly. *Journal of Genetic Psychology*, 1968, **112**, 227–235.

Hickey, T., & Kalish, R. Young peoples' perceptions of adults. *Journal of Gerontology*, 1968, **23**, 215–219.

Hiernaux, J. Ethnic differences in growth and development. *Eugenics Quarterly*, 1968, **15**, 12–21.

Hill, R. Decision making and the family life cycle.

In E. Shanas & G. Streib (Eds.), *Social structure and the family: Generational relations.* Englewood Cliffs, NJ: Prentice-Hall, 1965.

Hill, R. B. A profile of black aged. In *Minority aged in America.* Ann Arbor, MI: University of Michigan/Wayne State University, Institute of Gerontology, 1971.

Hirsch, J. Can we modify the number of adipose cells? *Postgraduate Medicine,* 1972, **51**(5), 83–86.

Hobbs, D., & Cole, S. Transition to parenthood: a decade replication. *Journal of Marriage and the Family,* 1976, **38**(4), 723–731.

Hobbs, D., & Wimbish, J. Transition to parenthood by black couples. *Journal of Marriage and the Family,* 1977, **39**(4), 677–689.

Hochschild, A. Disengagement theory: A critique and proposal. *American Sociological Review,* 1975, **40**, 553–569.

Hodes, H. Colostrum: A valuable source of antibodies. *Obstetrics-Gynecology Observer,* 1964, **3**, 7.

Hoffman, L. W. Effects of maternal employment on the child—A review of the research. *Developmental Psychology,* 1974, **10**(2), 204–228.

Hoffman, L. W., & Manis, J. The value of children in the United States: A new approach to the study of fertility. *Journal of Marriage and the Family,* 1979, **41**(3), 583–596.

Hoffman, L. W., & Nye, F. I. *Working mothers.* San Francisco: Jossey-Bass, 1974.

Hoffman, M. L. Moral development. In P. H. Mussen (Ed.), *Carmichael's manual of child psychology.* New York: Wiley, 1970.

Hogan, R., & Emler, N. Moral development. In M. E. Lamb (Ed.), *Social and personality development.* New York: Holt, 1978, pp. 200–223.

Holden, C. TV violence: Government study yields more evidence; no verdict. *Science,* 1972, **175**, 608–611.

Holland, J. L. Explorations of a theory of vocational choice: Part 1. Vocational images and choice, *Vocational Guidance Quarterly,* 1963, **11**(4), 232–239.

Holland, J. L. Explorations of a theory of vocational choice: Part II. Self-descriptions and vocational preferences. *Vocational Guidance Quarterly,* 1963, **12**(1), 17–24.

Hollingshead, A. *Elmstown's youth: The impact of social classes on youth.* New York: Wiley, 1949.

Holmes, F. An experimental investigation of a method of overcoming children's fears. *Child Development,* 1936, **7**, 6–30.

Holmes, L. Genetic counseling for the older pregnant women: New data and questions. *New England Journal of Medicine,* 1978, **298**(25), 1419–1421.

Holmes, T. H., & Masuda, M. Psychosomatic syndrome. *Psychology Today,* 1972, **106**, 71–72.

Holmes, T. H., & Rahe, R. H. The social readjustment rating scale. *Journal of Psychosomatic Research,* 1976, **11**, 213.

Honzik, M. P. Value and limitations of infant tests: An overview. In M. Lewis (Ed.), *Origins of intelligence.* New York: Plenum, 1976, pp. 59–96.

Honzik, M. P., Macfarlane, J. W., & Allen, L. The stability of mental test performance between two and 18 years. *Journal of Experimental Education,* 1948, **17**, 309–323.

Hooper, F. H., Fitzgerald, J., & Papalia, D. Piagetian theory and the aging process: Extensions and speculations. *Aging and Human Development,* 1971, **2**, 3–20.

Hoover, R., Gray, L., & Fraumeni, J. Stilboestrol (diethylstilbestrol) and the risk of ovarian cancer. *Lancet,* Sept. 10, 1977, pp. 533–534.

Horn, J. L. Intelligence—Why it grows, why it declines. *Transaction,* 1967, **5**(1), 23–31.

Horn, J. L. Organization of abilities and the development of intelligence. *Psychological Review,* 1968, **75**, 242–259.

Horn, J. L. Organization of data on life-span development of human abilities. In L. R. Goulet & P. B. Baltes (Eds.), *Life-span developmental psychology: Theory and research.* New York: Academic Press, 1970.

Horn, J. L., & Cattell, R. B. Age differences in primary mental ability factors. *Journal of Gerontology,* 1966, **21**, 210–220.

Hornblum, W., & Overton, W. Area and volume conservation among the elderly: Assessment and training. *Developmental Psychology,* 1976, **12**, 68–74.

Horner, M. The motive to avoid success and changing aspirations of college women. Edited by *Change Magazine,* New Rochelle, N.Y. *Women on campus, 1970: A Symposium.* Ann

Arbor, MI: Center for the Continuing Education of Women, 1970.

Houseknecht, S. K. Reference group support for voluntary childlessness. Evidence for conformity. Journal of Marriage and the Family, 1977, **39**(2), 285–292.

Houseknecht, S. K. Childlessness and marital adjustment, *Journal of Marriage and the Family*, 1979, **41**(2), 259–266.

Houston, S. H. The study of language: Trends and positions. In J. Eliot (Ed.), *Human development and cognitive processes*. New York: Holt, 1971.

Howard, M. Adolescent sex activity. *Perinatal Care*, 1978, **2**(7), 8–12.

Howell, M. C. Employed mothers and their families. *Pediatrics*, 1973, **52**(2), 252–263.

Howell, M. C. Effects of maternal employment on the child. *Pediatrics*, 1973, **52**(3), 327–343.

Hsu, L., Crisp, A., & Harding, B. Outcome of anorexia nervosa. *Lancet*, Jan. 13, 1979, pp. 61–65.

Hultsch, D. F. Organization and memory in adulthood. *Human Development*, 1971, **14**, 16–29.

Hunt, B., & Hunt, M. *Prime time*. New York: Stein & Day, 1974.

Hunt, M. M. *Sexual behavior in the 1970's*. New York: Dell, 1974.

Hunt, M. M. *The world of the formerly married*. New York: McGraw-Hill, 1966.

Hurlock, E. B. *Developmental psychology* (3d ed.). New York: McGraw-Hill, 1968.

Hutt, C. *Males and females*. Middlesex, England: Penguin Books, 1972.

Hutt, S. J., Lenard, H. G., & Prechtl, H. E. R. Psychophysiology of the newborn. In L. P. Lipsitt & H. W. Reese (Eds.), *Advances in child development and behavior*. New York: Academic Press, 1969.

I

Infante, P., & Russell, A. An epidemiologic study of dental caries in preschool children in the United States by race and socioeconomic level. *Journal of Dental Research*, March–April 1974, **53**(2, Part 2), 393–396.

Inglis, J., Ankus, M. N., & Sykes, D. H. Age-related differences in learning and short-term-memory from childhood to the senium. *Human Development*, 1968, **11**, 42–52.

Inouye, E. Similar and dissimilar manifestations of obsessive-compulsive neuroses in monozygotic twins. *American Journal of Psychology*, 1965, **121**, 1171–1175.

Institute of Medicine. *Report of a study: Legalized abortion and the public health*. The Institute, May 1975.

Irwin, T. First child? Second child? Middle child? Last child? Only child? What's the Difference? *Today's Health*, October 1969, p. 26.

Ivey, M., & Bardwick, J. Patterns of affective fluctuation in the menstrual cycle. *Psychosomatic Medicine*, 1968, **30**(3), 336–345.

J

Jacobs, J., & Teicher, J. Broken homes and social isolation in attempted suicide of adolescence. *International Journal of Social Psychiatry*, 1967, **13**, 139–149.

Jacobson, C. B., & Berlin, C. M. Possible reproductive detriment in LSD users. *Journal of the American Medical Association*, 1972, **222**(11), 1367–1373.

Jacques, J. M., & Chason, K. J. Cohabitation: Its impact on marital success. *The Family Coordinator*, 1979, **28**(1), 35–39.

Janerick, D., & Jacobson, H. Seasonality in Down syndrome: An endocrinological explanation. *Lancet*, March 5, 1977, pp. 515–516.

Jaques, E. The mid-life crisis. In R. Owen (Ed.), *Middle Age*. London: BBC. 1967.

Jarvik, L. Biological differences in intellectual functioning. *Vita Humana*, 1962, **5**, 195–203.

Jarvik, L. F. Thoughts on the psychobiology of aging. *American Psychologist*, 1975, **30**(5), 576–583.

Jarvik, L. F., Falek, A., Kallman, F. J., & Lorge, I. Survival trends in a senescent twin population. *American Journal of Human Genetics*, 1960, **12**, 170–179.

Jarvik, L. F., Kallman, F., & Kalber, N. M. Changing intellectual functions in senescent twins. *Acta Genetic Statistica Medica*, 1957, **7**, 421–430.

Jaslow, P. Employment, retirement and morale among older women. *Journal of Gerontology*, 1976, **31**(2), 212–218.

Jelliffe, D., & Jelliffe, E.   The uniqueness of human milk: An overview. *American Journal of Clinical Nutrition*, 1971, **24**, 1013–1024.

Jelliffe, D., & Jelliffe, E.   *Fat babies: Prevalence, perils and prevention.* London: Incentive Press, 1974.

Jelliffe, D., & Jelliffe, E   "Breast is best": Modern meanings. *New England Journal of Medicine,* 1977, **297**(17), 912–915.

Jensen, A. R.   How much can we boost IQ and scholastic achievement? *Harvard Educational Review*, 1969, **39**, 1–123.

Jersild, A. T.   Characteristics of teachers who are "liked best" and "disliked most." *Journal of Experimental Education*, 1940, **9**, 139–151.

Jersild, A. T.   Emotional development. In L. Carmichael (Ed.), *Manual of child psychology.* New York: Wiley, 1946.

Jersild, A. T.   *In search of self.* New York: Columbia University Press, 1952.

Jersild, A. T.   *Child psychology* (6th ed.). Englewood Cliffs, NJ: Prentice-Hall, 1968.

Jersild, A. T., & Holmes, F.   Children's fears. *Child Development Monographs*, 1935, **6**(20).

Johnson, A.   Juvenile delinquency. In S. Arieti (Ed.), *American handbook of psychiatry.* New York: Basic Books, 1959.

Johnson, F., Roche, A., Schell, L., & Wettenhall, N.   Critical weight at menarche. *American Journal of the Diseases of Children*, 1975, **129**, 19–23.

Johnson, H. R., Myhre, S. A., Ruvalcaba, R. H. A., Thuline, H. C., & Kelley, V. C.   Effects of testosterone on body image and behavior in Klinefelter's syndrome: A pilot study. *Developmental Medicine and Child Neurology*, 1970, **12**, 454–460.

Johnson, J.   Relations of divergent thinking and intelligence test scores with social and nonsocial make-believe play of preschool children. *Child Development*, 1976, **47**(4), 1200–1203.

Johnson, J., & Roopnarine, J.   Situational differences in children's play adjustments to younger children during social play. Paper presented at the annual meeting of the Midwestern Psychological Association, Chicago, 1979.

Johnson, S.   For some new reasons, many "old marrieds" are splitting up. *The New York Times,* Aug. 26, 1977, p. B4.

Johnston, C.   Berkeley group offers pressure valve for troubled parents. *Healthnews*, 1973, **1**(6), 9.

Jones, E. T.   Needs of Negro youth. In G. D. Winter & E. M. Nuss (Eds.), *The young adult: Identity and awareness.* Glenview, IL: Scott, Foresman, 1969.

Jones, H., & Conrad, H.   The growth and decline of intelligence: A study of a homogeneous group between the ages of 10 and 60. *Genetic Psychology Monographs*, 1933, **13**, 223–298.

Jones, K. L., Smith, D. W., Ulleland, C., & Streissguth, A. P.   Pattern of malformation in offspring of chronic alcoholic mothers. *Lancet*, 1973, **1**(7815), 1267–1271.

Jones, M. C.   The later careers of boys who were early or late maturing. *Child Development*, 1957, **28**, 113–128.

Jones, M. C., & Mussen, P. H.   Self-conceptions, motivations, and interpersonal attitudes of early- and late-maturing girls. *Child Development*, 1958, **29**, 491–501.

Jonsen, A. R.   Research involving children: Recommendations of the National Commission for the Protection of Human Subjects of Biomedical and Behavioral Research. *Pediatrics*, 1978, **62**(2), 131–136.

Jost, H., & Sontag, L.   The genetic factor in autonomic nervous system function. *Psychosomatic Medicine*, 1944, **6**, 308–310.

Jung, C. G.   *Modern Man in Search of a Soul.* New York: Harcourt, Brace, 1933.

Jung, C. G.   *The Archetypes and the collective unconscious* (Bollingen Series XX; 2d ed.). Princeton: Princeton University Press, 1968.

K

Kagan, J.   The child's perception of the parent. *Journal of Abnormal and Social Psychology,* 1956, **53**, 257–258.

Kagan, J.   Impulsive and reflective children: Significance of conceptual tempo. In J. D. Krumboltz (Ed.), *Learning and the educational process.* Chicago: Rand McNally, 1965.

Kagan, J.   *Personality development.* New York: Harcourt Brace Jovanovich, 1971.

Kagan, J.   Overview: Perspectives on human infancy. In J. Osofsky (Ed.), *Handbook of infant development.* New York: Wiley, 1979.

Kagan, J., Hoskin, B., & Watson, S. Child's symbolic conceptualization of parents. *Child Development*, 1961, **32**, 625–636.

Kagan, J., Kearsley, R., & Zelazo, P. *Infancy: Its place in human development*. Cambridge: Harvard, 1978.

Kagan, J., & Kogan, N. Individual variation in cognitive processes. In P. H. Mussen (Ed.), *Carmichael's manual of child psychology*. New York: Wiley, 1970.

Kagan, J., & Lemkin, I. The child's differential perception of parental attributes. *Journal of Abnormal and Social Psychology*, 1960, **61**, 440–447.

Kagan, J., & Moss, H. A. The stability of passive and dependent behavior from childhood through adulthood. *Child Development*, 1960, **31**, 557–591.

Kahana, B., & Kahana, E. Grandparents from the perspective of the developing grandchild. *Developmental Psychology*, 1970, **3**(1), 98–105.

Kahana, E., & Coe, R. M. Perceptions of grandparenthood by community and institutional aged. *Proceedings of the Seventy-seventh Annual Convention of the American Psychological Association*, 1969, **4**, 735–736 (summary).

Kakvan, M., & Greenberg, S. D. Cigarette smoking and cancer of the lung: A review. *Rhode Island Medical Journal*, 1977, **60**(12), 588–591, 606.

Kalish, R. A. *Late adulthood: Perspectives on human development*. Monterey, CA: Brooks/Cole, 1975.

Kalish, R., & Yeun, S. Americans of East Asian ancestry: Aging and the aged. *Gerontologist*, 1971, **11**(1), 36–47.

Kallman, F. J. *Heredity in health and mental disorder*. New York: Norton, 1953.

Kallman, F. J. Twin data on the genetics of aging. In G. E. W. Wolstenholme and C. M. O'Connor (Eds.), *Methodology of the study of ageing*. London: J. A. Churchill, 1957, pp. 131–143.

Kallman, F. J., Aschner, B. M., & Falek, A. Comparative data on longevity, adjustment to aging, and causes of death in a senescent twin population. In L. Gedda (Eds.), *Novant Anni delle Legge Mendelian*. Rome Instituto Gregorio Mendel, 1956, pp. 330–339. (Also in Riley, et al., 1968.)

Kamin, L. *The science and politics of I.Q.* Washington, DC: Erlbaum, 1974.

Kangas, J., & Bradway, K. Intelligence at middle age: A thirty-eight-year follow-up. *Developmental Psychology*, 1971, **5**(2), 333–337.

Kaplan, E., & Kaplan, G. The prelinguistic child. In J. Eliot (Ed.), *Human development and cognitive processes*. New York: Holt, 1971.

Karmel, B. Z. The effects of age, complexity and amount of contour on pattern preferences in human infants. *Journal of Experimental Child Psychology*, 1972, **4**.

Karnes, M. B., Teska, J. A., Hodgins, A. S., & Badger, E. D. Educational intervention at home by mothers of disadvantaged infants. *Child Development*, 1970, **41**, 925–935.

Kastenbaum, R. Death and development through the life span. In H. Feifel (Ed.), *New meanings of death*. New York: McGraw-Hill, 1977, pp. 17–45.

Kastenbaum, R. *Death, society, and human experience*. St. Louis: Mosby, 1977.

Kastenbaum, R. The kingdom where nobody dies. In S. Zart (Ed.), *Readings in aging and death: Contemporary perspectives*, New York: Harper & Row, 1977. (Reprinted from *Saturday Review*, Dec. 1972.)

Kastenbaum, R., & Candy, S. The 4% fallacy: A methodological and empirical critique of extended care facilities population statistics. *Aging and Human Development*, 1973, **4**, 15–22.

Kastenbaum, R., & Durkee, N. Elderly people view old age. In R. Kastenbaum (Ed.), *New thoughts on old age*. New York: Springer, 1964.

Kastenbaum, R., & Durkee, N. Young people view old age. In R. Kastenbaum (Ed.), *New thoughts on old age*. New York: Springer, 1964.

Katchadourian, J., & Lunde, D. *Fundamentals of human sexuality* (2d ed.). New York: Holt, 1975.

Katz, P., & Zalk, S. Modification of children's racial attitudes. *Developmental Psychology*, 1978, **14**(5), 447–461.

Kawi, A., & Pasamanick, B. The association of factors of pregnancy with the development of reading disorders in childhood. *Journal of the American Medical Association*, 1958, **166**, 1420–1423.

Keasey, C. B. Social participation as a factor in the moral development of preadolescents. *Developmental Psychology*, 1971, **5**, 216–220.

Kelly, O. Living with a life-threatening illness. M.

C. Garfield (Ed.), *Psychosocial care of the dying patient*. New York: McGraw-Hill, 1978, pp. 59–66.

Kempe, C. H.   A practical approach to the protection of the abused child and rehabilitation of the abusing parent. *Pediatrics*. 1973, **51**(4), 804–808.

Kempe, C. H.   Sexual abuse, another hidden pediatric problem. The 1977 C. Anderson Aldrich lecture. *Pediatrics*, 1978, **62**(3), 382–389.

Kempe, C. H., et al.   The battered child syndrome. *Journal of the American Medical Association,* 1962, **181**(Part 1), 17–24.

Kempe, R., & Kempe, C. H.   *Child abuse*. Cambridge, MA: Harvard, 1978.

Keinston, K.   Social change and youth in America. In E. Erikson (Ed.), *The challenge of youth*. New York: Anchor, 1963.

Keniston, K.   *Young radicals*. New York: Harcourt Brace Jovanovich, 1967.

Keniston, K.   Heads and seekers: Drugs on campus, counter-cultures, and American society. *The American Scholar*, Winter, 1968–69, **38**(1).

Keniston, K.   Youth: A "new" stage of life. *The American Scholar*, Autumn 1970, **39**, 631–654.

Keniston, K.   Alienation and American society. In H. Silverstein (Ed.), *The sociology of youth*. New York: Macmillan, 1973.

Keniston, K., & The Carnegie Council on Children.   *All our children*: *The American family under pressure*. New York: Harcourt Brace Jovanovich, 1977.

Kennedy, W. A.   School phobia: Rapid treatment of 50 cases. *Journal of Abnormal Psychology*, 1965, **70**, 285–289.

Kennedy, W. A.   *Child psychology*. Englewood Cliffs, NJ: Prentice-Hall, 1971.

Kennell, J., Jerauld, R., Wolfe, H., Chesler, D., Kreger, N., McAlpine, W., Steffa, M., & Klaus, M.   Maternal behavior one year after early and extended post-partum contact. *Developmental Medicine & Child Neurology*, 1974, **16**(2), 172–179.

Kermis, M., Monge, R., & Dusek, J.   Human sexuality in the hierarchy of adolescent interests. Paper presented at the annual meeting of the Society for Research in Child Development, Denver, 1975.

Keshet, H., & Rosenthal, K.   Fathering after marital separation. *Social Work*, 1978, **37**, 11–18.

Keyserling, M. D.   *Windows on day care*. New York: National Council of Jewish Women, 1972.

Kieren, D., Henton, J., & Marotz, R.   *Hers and his*. Hinsdale, IL: Dryden, 1975.

Kimbel, G.   *Hilgard and Marques' conditioning and learning* (2d ed.). New York: Appleton-Century-Crofts, 1961.

Kimmel, D. C.   *Adulthood and aging*. New York: Wiley, 1974.

Kinch, R. A. H.   Some sociomedical aspects of the adolescent pregnancy. Paper presented to the Sixth World Congress of Gynecology and Obstetrics, New York, Apr. 14, 1970.

King, W.   Life in Beaufort, S.C. is bleak and, by U.S. standards, short. *The New York Times*, Mar. 17, 1974.

Kinsey, A., et al.   *Sexual behavior in the human male*. Philadelphia: Saunders, 1948.

Kinsey, A., et al.   *Sexual behavior in the female*. Philadelphia: Saunders, 1953.

Kistin, H., & Morris, R.   Alternatives to institutionalized care for the elderly and disabled. *Gerontologist*, 1972, **12**(2), 139–142.

Klein, C.   *The single parent experience*. New York: Walker, 1973.

Klein, P., Forbes, G., & Nader, P.   Effects of starvation in infancy (pyloric stenosis) on subsequent learning abilities. *Journal of Pediatrics*, 1975, **87**(1), 8–15.

Klein, R. P., & Durfee, J. T.   Infants' reactions to strangers versus mothers. Paper presented at the annual meeting of the Society for Research in Child Development, Denver, 1975.

Knobloch, H., & Pasamanick, B.   Predicting intellectual potential in infancy. *American Journal of the Diseases of Children*, 1963, **107**(1), 43–51.

Knobloch, H., & Pasamanick, B.   Some etiologic and prognostic factors in early infantile autism and psychosis. *Pediatrics*, 1975, **55**(2), 182–191.

Koch, H. L.   Sissiness and tomboyishness in relation to sibling characteristics. *Journal of Genetic Psychology*, 1956, **88**, 231–244.

Kohlberg, L.   Moral development and identification. In H. W. Stevenson (Ed.), *Child Psychology*. University of Chicago Press, 1963, pp. 277–332.

Kohlberg, L.   The development of moral character and moral ideology. In M. Hoffman & L. Hoffman (Eds.), *Review of child development research*, Vol. 1. New York: Russell Sage Foundation, 1964.

Kohlberg, L. The child as a moral philosopher. *Psychology Today*, 1968, **2**(4), 25–30.

Kohlberg, L. Continuities in childhood and adult moral development revisited. In P. Baltes and K. W. Schaie (Eds.), *Life-span developmental psychology: Personality and socialization.* New York: Academic Press, 1973.

Kohlberg, L., & Gilligan, C. The adolescent as a philosopher: The discovery of the self in a postconventional world. *Daedalus,* Fall 1971. p. 1051–1086.

Kohn, M., & Rosman, B. L. Relationship of preschool social-emotional functioning to later intellectual achievement. *Developmental Psychology*, 1973 **6**(3), 445–452.

Kompara, D. Difficulties in the socialization on process of step parenting. *Family Relations*, 1980, **29**(1), 69–73.

Kon, S. K., & Cowie, A. T. (Eds.). *Milk: The mammary gland and its secretion.* New York: Academic Press, 1961.

Konner, M. J. Newborn walking: Additional data. *Science*, 1973, **179**, 307.

Koocher, G. Childhood, death, and cognitive development. *Developmental Psychology*, 1973, **9**, 369–375.

Korner, A. Neonatal startles, smiles, erections and reflexes as related to state, sex and individuality. *Child Development*, 1969, **40**, 1039–1053.

Korner, A., Guilleminault, C., Vanden Hold, J., & Baldwin, R. Paper presented at the annual meeting of the American Psychological Association convention, 1977.

Kostick, A. A day care program for the physically and emotionally disabled. *Gerontologist*, 1972, **12**(2), 134–138.

Kotelchuck, M. The nature of the infant's tie to his father. Paper presented at the meeting of the Society for Research in Child Development, Philadelphia, Mar. 29–Apr. 1, 1973.

Kramer, C. A sure formula for raising a violent child: Start by hitting a lot. . . . *Philadelphia Inquirer*, June 10, 1973, p. 3F.

Kramer, J., Hill, K., & Cohen, L. Infants' development of object permanence: A refined methodology and new evidence for Piaget's hypothesized ordinality. *Child Development*, 1975, **46**, 149–155.

Kraus, R., & Glucksberg, S. Social and nonsocial speech. *Scientific American*, 1977, **263**(2), 100–105.

Krauss, I. Predictors of competence in the elderly. Paper presented at the annual meeting of the Western Psychological Association, Los Angeles, 1976.

Kravitz, H., & Scherz, R. The importance of the position of infants on the SIDS: A new hypothesis. *Clinical Pediatrics*, 1978, **17**(5), 403–408.

Kreutzer, M., & Charlesworth, W. R. Infant recognition of emotions. Paper presented at the biennial meeting of The Society for Research in Child Development, Philadelphia, 1973.

Kübler-Ross, E. *On death and dying.* New York: Macmillan, 1969.

Kübler-Ross, E. Facing up to death. In *1973–1975 Annual Editions of Readings in Human Development*. Guilford, CT: Dushkin, 1973, pp. 258–260.

Kurfiss, J. Sequentiality and structure in a cognitive model of college student development. *Developmental Psychology*, 1977, **13**(6), 565–57I.

Kuypers, J., & Benston, V. Competence and social breakdown: A social-psychological view of aging. *Human Development*, 1973, **16**(2), 37–49.

L

LaBarbera, J. D., Izard, C., Vietze, P., & Parisi, S. Four- and six-month-old infants' visual responses to joy, anger, and neutral expressions. *Child Development*, 1976, **47**, 535–538.

Lamb, M. E. The development of mother-infant and father-infant attachments in the second year of life. *Developmental Psychology*, 1977, **13**(6), 637–648.

Lamb, M. E. Influence of the child on marital quality and family interaction during the prenatal, perinatal, and infancy periods. In R. Lerner & G. Spainer (Eds.), *Child influences on marital and family interaction: A life-span perspective.* New York: Academic Press, 1978.

Lamb, M. E. Social interaction in infancy and the development of personality. In M. E. Lamb (Ed.), *Social and personality development.* New York: Holt, 1978.

Lamb, M. E., & Roopnarine, J. Peer influences on sex-role development in preschoolers. Unpublished paper, 1978.

Lamb, M. E., & Urberg, K. The development of gender role and gender identity. In M. E. Lamb (Ed.), *Social and personality development*. New York: Holt, 1978, pp. 178–199.

Lange, C. The real difference between the sexes: An interview by Cynthia Lange with Jerome Kagan, Ph.D. *Parents' Magazine*, 1973, **48**(9) 37–62, 66.

Langer, E., & Rodin, J. The effects of choice and enhanced personal responsibility in an institutional setting. *Journal of Personality and Social Psychology*, 1976, **34**(2), 191–198.

Langer, J. *Theories of development*. New York: Holt, 1969.

Lawton, M. P. Environmental influences on the quality of life of older people. Presented at the annual meeting of the American Association for the Advancement of Science, New York, 1975.

Lawton, M. P. *Social and medical services in housing for the elderly*. Philadelphia: Philadelphia Geriatric Center, 1975.

Layton, B., & Siegler, I. Mid-life: Must it be a crisis? Paper presented at the annual meeting of the Gerontological Society, Dallas, 1978.

Leaf, A. Everyday is a gift when you are over 100. *National Geographic*, 1973, **143**(1), 93–118.

Leahy, R. Development of preference and processes of visual scanning in the human infant during the first three months of life. *Developmental Psychology*, 1976, **12**(3), 250–254.

Leboyer, F. *Birth without violence*. New York: Random House, 1975.

Lechtig A., et al. Maternal nutrition and fetal growth in developing societies. *American Journal of Diseases of Children*, 1975, **129**(4), 434–437.

Ledger, M. Aging. *Pennsylvania Gazette*, June 1978, pp. 18–23.

Lee, G. Marriage and morale in later life. *Journal of Marriage and the Family*, 1978, **40**(1), 131–139.

Lee, R. V. What about the right to say "no"? *The New York Times Magazine*, Sept. 16, 1973.

Leefeldt, C., & Callenbach, E. *The art of friendship*. New York: Pantheon Books, 1979.

Lefley, H. P. *Effects of an Indian culture program and familial correlates of self-concept among Miccosukee and Seminole children*. Ann Arbor,

MI: University Microfilms, 1973, no. 73–16, p. 856.

Lefley, H. P. Social and familial correlates of self-esteem among American Indian children. *Child Development*, 1974, **45**, 829–833.

Lehman, H. C. *Age and achievement*. Princeton, NJ: Princeton University Press, 1953.

Lehtovaara, A., Saarinen, P., & Jarvinen, J. *Psychological studies of twins: I. GSR reactions*. Psychological Institute, University of Helsinki, 1965.

Leifer, A. D. Ledierman, P. H., Barnett, C. R., & Williams, J. A. Effects of mother-infant separation on maternal attachment behavior. *Child Development*, 1972, **43**, 1203–1218.

Leiter, M. A study of reciprocity in preschool play groups. *Child Development*, 1977, **48**, 1288–1295.

Leland, C. et al. Men and women learning together: Co-education in the 1980's. Findings presented at conference, *Men/Women/College, The Educational Implications of Sex Roles in Transition*. December 1–2, 1978, at Brown University. Report published by Ford Rockefeller, and Carnegie Foundations, 1979.

LeMasters, E. E. Parenthood as crisis. *Marriage and Family Living*, 1957, **19**, 352–355.

LeMaster, E. E. Parents without partners. In E. E. LeMaster (Ed.) *Parents in modern America*. Homewood, IL: Dorsey, 1970, pp. 157–174.

Lemon, B., Bengston, V., & Peterson, J. An exploration of the activity theory of aging: Activity types and life satisfaction among in-movers to a retirement community. *Journal of Gerontology*, 1972, **27**(4), 511–523.

Lennard, H. L., & Associates. *Mystification and drug misuse*. San Francisco: Jossey-Bass, 1971.

Lenneberg, E. H. *Biological functions of language*. New York: Wiley, 1967.

Lenz, W. Malformations caused by drugs in pregnancy. *American Journal of Diseases of Children*, 1966, **112**, 99–106.

Lerner, R., & Lerner, J. Effects of age, sex, and physical attractiveness on child-peer relations, academic performance, and elementary school adjustment. *Developmental Psychology*, 1977, **13**(6), 585–590.

Leven, M. *Older Americans: Special handling required*. Washington, DC: National Council on Aging. 1971.

Levine, J. A. Fathering books—a new generation. *Psychology Today*, 1978, **12**(7), pp. 152–161.

Levinger, G. Physical abuse among applicants

for divorce, 1966. In S. Steinmetz & M. Straus (Eds.), *Violence in the family*. New York: Dodd, Mead, 1974.

Levinson, D. The psychological development of men in early adulthood and the mid-life transition. Paper published by the University of Minnesota Press, 1974.

Levinson, D. The mid-life transition: A period in adult psychosocial development. *Psychiatry*, 1977, **40**, 99–112.

Levinson, D., Darrow, C., Klein, E. Levinson, M., & McKee, B. The psychosocial development of men in early adulthood and the mid-life tradition. In D. F. Ricks, A. Thomas, & M. Roff (Eds.), *Life history research in psychopathology*. Minneapolis: University of Minnesota Press, 1974.

Levy, D. M. *Maternal overprotection*. New York: Norton, 1966.

Lewak, N., Van den Berg, B., & Beckwith, B. Sudden infant death syndrome: Prospective data review. *Clinical Pediatrics*, 1979, **18**(7), 404–411.

Lewin, K., Lippit, R., & White, R. K. Patterns of aggressive behavior in experimentally created "social climates." *Journal of Social Psychology*, 1939, **10**, 271–299.

Lewis, C., & Lewis, M. The potential impact of sexual equality on health. *New England Journal of Medicine*, 1977, **297**(11), 863–869.

Lewis, M. Sex typing within the opening months of life: Mother-infant interaction. Washington, 1972.

Lewis, M., & Brooks-Gunn, J. Toward a theory of social cognition: The development of self. In I. Uzgiris (Ed.), *Social interaction and communication during infancy*. San Francisco: Jossey-Bass, 1974, pp. 7–20.

Lewis, M., & Rosenblum, L. (Eds.). *Friendship and peer relations*. New York: Wiley, 1975.

Lewis, M., Young, G., Brooks, J., & Michalson, L. The beginning of friendship. In M. Lewis & L. Rosenblum (Eds.), *Friendship and peer relations*. New York: Wiley, 1975, pp. 27–66.

Lickona, T. An experimental test of Piaget's theory of moral development. Paper presented at the meeting of the Society for Research in Child Development, Philadelphia, 1973.

Lieber, C. S. Alcoholic fatty liver: Its pathogenesis and precursor role for hepatitis and cirrhosis. *Panminerva Medica*, 1976, **18**(9–10), 346–358.

Lieberman, A. Preschoolers' competence with a peer: Relations with attachment and peer experience. *Child Development*, 1977, **48**, 1277–1287.

Lieberman, M., & Coplan, A. Distance from death

as a variable in the study of aging. *Developmental Psychology*, 1970, **2**(1), 71–84.

Lieberman Research, Inc. The teenager looks at cigarette smoking. American Cancer Society, September 1969.

Liebert, R. M. Television and social learning: Some relationships between viewing violence and behaving aggressively. In J. P. Murray, E. A. Rubinstein, & G. A. Comstock (Eds.), *Television and social behavior* (Vol. II). Washington, DC: U.S. Government Printing Office, 1972.

Liebert, R., M., & Poulos, R. W. Television as a moral teacher. In T. Lickona (Ed.), *Moral development and behavior*. New York: Holt, 1976, pp. 284–298.

Liebert, R. M., Poulos, R. W., & Strauss, G. *Developmental psychology*. Englewood Cliffs, NJ: Prentice-Hall, 1974.

Life. The new fathers. July 14, 1972, p. 68.

Lightwood, R., Brimblecombe, F., & Barltrop D. (Eds.), *Paterson's sick children*. London: Bailliere, Tindall, & Cassell, 1971.

Lilienfeld, A. M., & Pasamanick, B. Association of maternal and fetal factors with the development of epilepsy. I. Abnormalities in the prenatal and paranatal periods. *Journal of the American Medical Association*, 1954, **155**, 719.

Lilienfeld, A. M., & Pasamanick, B. The association of prenatal and parinatal factors with the development of cerebral palsy and epilepsy. *American Journal of Obstetrics and Gynecology*, 1955, **70**, 93.

Lindeman, B. *The twins who found each other*. New York: Morrow, 1969.

Lipsitt, L. P., Engen, T., & Kaye, H. Developmental changes in the olfactory threshold of the neonate. *Child Development*, 1963, **34**, 371–376.

Lipsitt, L. P., & Kaye, H. Conditioned sucking in the human newborn. *Psychonomic Science*, 1964, **1**, 20–30.

Lipsitt, L. P., & Levy, N. Electrotactual threshold in the neonate. *Child Development*, 1959, **30**, 547–554.

Lipton, E. L., Steinschneider, A., & Richmond, J. B. Auditory discrimination in the newborn infant. *Psychosomatic Medicine*, 1963, **25**, 490.

Livson, F. Sex differences in personality development in the middle adult years: A longitudinal study. Paper presented at the annual meeting of the Geronotological Society, Louisville, KY, 1975.

Lloyd-Still, J. (Ed.). *Malnutrition and intellectual development.* Lancaster, England: M.T.P. Press, Ltd., 1976.

Lloyd-Still, J., Hurwitz, I., Wolff, P., & Shwachmar, H. Intellectual development after severe malnutrition in infancy. *Pediatrics*, 1974, **54**(3), 306–311.

Locke, R. Preschool aggression linked to TV viewing. *Wisconsin State Journal*, Jan. 7, 1979, p. 2.

Looft, W. R. Children's judgment of age. *Child Development*, 1971, **42**, 1282–1284.

Looft, W. R. Toward a history of life-span developmental psychology. Unpublished manuscript, University of Wisconsin, Madison, 1971.

Looft, W. R. Egocentrism and social interaction across the lifespan. *Psychological Bulletin*, 1972, **78**(2), 73–92.

Looft, W. R., & Charles, D. C. Egocentrism and social interaction in young and old adults. *Aging and Human Development*, 1971, **2**, 21–28.

Lopata, H. Living through widowhood. *Psychology Today*, 1973, **7**(2), 87–98.

Lorenz, K. Comparative study of behavior. In C. H. Schiller (Ed.), *Instinctive behavior.* New York: International Press, 1957.

Lougee, M., Grueneich, R., & Hartup, W. Social interaction in same- and mixed-age dyads of preschool children. *Child Development*, 1977, **48**, 1353–1361.

Lowenthal, M., & Chiriboga, D. Transition to the empty nest: Crisis, challenge, or relief? *Archives of General Psychiatry*, 1972, **26**, 8–14.

Lowenthal, M., & Haven, C. Interaction and adaptation: Intimacy as a critical variable. In B. Neugarten (Ed.), *Middle age and aging.* Chicago: University of Chicago Press, 1968.

Luckey, E., & Nass, G. A comparison of sexual attitudes and behavior in an international sample. *Journal of Marriage and the Family*, 1969, **31**, 364–379.

Lyberger-Ficek, S., & Sternglanz, S. Innate sex differences in neonatal crying: Myth or reality. Paper presented at the annual meeting of the

Society for Research in Child Development, Denver, 1975.

Lyle, J. G. Certain antenatal, perinatal, and developmental variables and reading retardation in middle-class boys. *Child Development*, 1970, **41**, 481–491.

Lynn, D. *The father: His role in child development.* Monterey, CA: Brooks/Cole, 1974.

Lystad, M. Violence at home: A review of literature. *American Journal of Orthopsychiatry*, 1975, **45**(3) 328–345.

M

Maccoby, E. *The development of sex differences.* Stanford, CA: Stanford University Press, 1966.

Maccoby, E., & Jacklin, C. *The psychology of sex differences.* Stanford, CA: Stanford University Press, 1974.

Macklin, E. Heterosexual cohabitation among unmarried college students. *The Family Coordinator*, 1972, **12**, 463–471.

Macrae, J., & Herbert-Jackson, E. Are behavioral effects of infant day care programs specific? *Developmental Psychology*, 1976, **12**(3), 269–270.

Maddox, G. Persistance of life style among the elderly. In B. Neugarten (Ed.), *Middle age and aging.* Chicago: University of Chicago Press, 1968.

Madigan, F. C., & Vance, R. B. Differential sex mortality: A research design. *Social Forces*, 1957, **35**, 193–199.

Madison, P. *Personality development in college.* Reading, MA: Addison-Wesley, 1969.

Maier, H. W. *Three theories of child development.* New York: Harper & Row, 1969.

Malcolm A. . . . but a hearty longevity is the norm for Franklin, Nebraska. *The New York Times*, Mar. 17, 1974.

Manosevitz, M., Prentice, N. M., & Wilson, F. Individual and family correlates of imaginary companions in preschool children. *Developmental Psychology*, 1973, **8**(1), 72–79.

Maratsos, M. Nonegocentric communication abilities in preschool children. *Child Development*, 1973, **44**, 697–700.

Marcia, J. Development and validation of ego identity status. *Journal of Personality and Social Psychology*, 1966, **3**, 551–558.

Marcia, J. Identity six years after: A follow-up study. *Journal of Youth and Adolescence*, 1976, **5**(2), 145–160.

Markides, K., & Martin, H.   A causal model of life satisfaction among the elderly. *Journal of Gerontology*, 1979, **34**(1), 86–93.

Marquis, D. P.   Can conditioned responses be established in the newborn infant? *Journal of Genetic Psychology*, 1931, **39**(4), 479–492.

Maslow, A.   *Motivation and Personality*. New York: Harper & Row, 1954.

Mason, S.   Ross Laboratories, Columbus, Ohio, Mar. 28, 1973. Personal communication.

Masters, W. H., & Johnson, V. E.   *Human sexual response*. Boston: Little, Brown, 1966.

Maurer, D., & Salapatek, P.   Developmental changes in the scanning of faces by young children. *Child Development*, 1976, **47**, 523–527.

Maw, W. H., & Maw, E. W.   Self-concepts of high- and low-curiosity boys. *Child Development*, 1970, **41**, 123–129.

Mayer, J.   Fat babies grow into fat people. *Family Health*, 1973, **5**(3), 24–26.

Mazano, H.   Radiation debate: Ob-Gyns. vs. ACR on risk levels. *Hospital Tribune*, Jan. 24, 1977.

McAlister, A. L., Perry, C., & Maccoby, N.   Adolescent smoking: Onset and prevention. *Pediatrics*, 1979, **63**(4), 650–658.

McAnarney, E.   Adolescent pregnancy—A national priority. *American Journal of the Diseases of Children*, 1978, **132**, 125–126.

McCall, R.   Challenges to a science of developmental psychology. In S. Chess & A. Thomas (Eds.), *Annual progress in child psychiatry and child development*. New York: Brunner/Mazel, 1978, pp. 3–23. (Reprinted from *Child Development*, 1977, **48**, 333–344.)

McCallon, E. L.   Self-ideal discrepancy and the correlates sex and academic achievement. *Journal of Experimental Education,* 1967, **35**, 45–49.

McCall's.   How parents feel about their teenage children. Dec. 1973, p. 33.

McCary, J. L.   *Freedom and growth in marriage*. Santa Barbara, CA: Hamilton, 1975.

McCaskill, C. L., & Wellman, B. A.   A study of common motor achievements at the preschool ages. *Child Development*, 1938, **9**, 141–150.

McClelland, D., Constantian, C., Regalado, D., & Stone, C.   Making it to maturity. *Psychology Today*, 1978, **12**(1), 42–53; 114.

McDermott, J. F.   Divorce and its psychiatric sequelae in children. *Archives of General Psychiatry*, 1970, **23**(5), 421–427.

McDougall, W.   Drugs in pregnancy. *Update*, 1971, **3**(12), 1517–1522.

McFadden, R. D.   EPA, citing miscarriages, restricts 2 herbicides. *The New York Times*, Mar. 2, 1979, p. A10.

McFarland, R. A., Tune, G. B., & Welford, A.   On the driving of automobiles by older people. *Journal of Gerontology*, 1964, **19**, 190–197.

McGraw, M. B.   Neural maturation as exemplified in achievement of bladder control. *Journal of Pediatrics*, 1940, **16**, 580–589.

McKenry, P. C., Walters, L. H., & Johnson, C.   Adolescent pregnancy: a review of the literature. *The Family Coordinator*, 1979, **23**(1), 17–28.

McNeil, D. G., Jr.   100 Love Canal families are urged to leave area. *The New York Times*, Feb. 10, 1979, p. 21.

McPhee, R.   Personal communication, Nov. 15, 1966.

McTavish, D. G.   Perceptions of old people: A review of research methodologies and findings. *The Gerontologist*, 1971, **11**(4, Part 2), 90–101.

Mead, M.   *Sex and temperament in three primitive societies*. New York: Morrow, 1935.

Mead, M.   *Male and female*. New York: Morrow, 1949.

Mead, M.   *Coming of age in Samoa*. New York: Marrow, 1961.

Mead, M., & Newton, N.   Fatherhood. In S. A. Richardson & A. F. Guttmacher (Eds.), *Childbearing—Its social and psychological aspects*. Baltimore: Williams & Wilkins, 1967, pp. 189–192.

Medley, M.   Marital adjustment in the post-retirement years. *The Family Coordinator*, 1977, **26**(1), 5–11.

Mednick, B. R., Baker, R. L., & Sutton-Smith, B.   Teenage pregnancy and perinatal mortality, 1979. Unpublished paper reporting on a study supported by the National Institute of Child Health and Human Development of the U.S. Department of Health, Education, and Welfare, contract 1–117–82807.

Meichenbaum, D.   Self-instructional strategy training: A cognitive prosthesis for the aged. *Human Development*, 1974, **17**, 273–280.

Meisels, A., Bégin, R., & Schneider, V.   Dysplasias of uterine cervix. Epidemiological aspects: Role of age at first coitus and use of oral contraceptives. *Cancer*, 1977, **40**(6), 3076–3081.

Mendelson, M. A. *Tender loving greed*. New York: Knopf, 1974.

Mennuti, M. Prenatal genetic diagnosis: Current status. *New England Journal of Medicine*, 1977, **297**(18), 1004–1006.

Meredith, N. V. Body size of contemporary groups of eight-year-old children studied in different parts of the world. *Monographs of the Society for Research in Child Development*, 1969, **34**(1).

Mestyan, G., & Varga, F. Chemical thermoregulation of full-term and premature newborn infants. *Journal of Pediatrics*, 1960, **56**, 623–629.

Miles, C., & Miles, W. The correlation of intelligence scores and chronological age from early to late maturity. *American Journal of Psychology*, 1932, **44**, 44–78.

Milkovich, L., & Van den Berg, B. J. Effects of prenatal Meprobamate and Chlordiazycoxide on embryonic and fetal development. *New England Journal of Medicine*, 1974, **291**(24), 1268–1271.

Millar, T. P. The child who refuses to attend school. *The American Journal of Psychiatry*, 1961, **118**(5), 398–404.

Miller, B., & Gerard, D. Family influences on the development of creativity in children: An integrative review. *The Family Coordinator*, 1979, **28**(3), 295–312.

Miller, H., Hassanein, K., Chin, T., & Hensleigh, P. Socioenonomic factors in relation to fetal growth in white infants. *Journal of Pediatrics*, 1976, **84**(4), 638–643.

Miller, P., Smith, D., & Shepard, T. Maternal hyperthermia as a possible cause of anencephaly. *Lancet*, Mar. 11, 1978, 519–521.

Miller, S. M. Effects of maternal employment on sex-role perception, interests, and self-esteem in kindergarten girls. *Developmental Psychology*, 1975, **11**(3), 405–406.

Milman, D., & Su, W. Patterns of illicit drug and alcohol use among secondary school students. *Journal of Pediatrics*, 1973, **83**(2), 314–320.

Minuchin, P. Sex-role concepts and sex typing in childhood as a function of school and home environments. *Child Development*, 1965, **36**, 1031–1048.

Miranda, S., Hack, M., Fantz, R., Fanaroff, A., & Klaus, M. Neonatal pattern vision: Predictor of future mental performance? *Journal of Pediatrics*, 1977, **91**(4), 642–647.

Mitchell, P. *Act of love: The killing of George Zygmanik*. New York: Knopf, 1976.

Mittler, P. Psycholinguistic skills in four-year-old twins and singletons. Doctoral dissertation, University of London, 1969.

Mittler, P. Biological and social aspects of language development in twins. *Developmental Medicine and Child Neurology*, 1970, **12**, 741–757.

Mittler, P. *The study of twins*. Baltimore: Penguin, 1971.

Moir, D. J. Egocentrism and the emergence of conventional morality in preadolescent girls. *Child Development*, 1974, **45**, 299–304.

Money, J. Cytogenetic and psychosexual incongruities with a note on space-form blindness. *American Journal of Psychiatry*, 1963, **119**, 820–827.

Money, J., & Ehrhardt, A. *Man & woman, boy & girl*. Baltimore: Johns Hopkins, 1972.

Money, J., Ehrhard, A., & Masica, D. N. Fetal feminization induced by androgen insensitivity in the testicular feminizing syndrome: Effect on marriage and maternalism. *Johns Hopkins Medical Journal*, 1968, **123**, 105–114.

Money, J., & Pollitt, E. Cytogenetic and psychosexual ambiguity: Klinefelter's syndrome and transvestism compared. *Archives of General Psychiatry*, 1964, **11**, 589–595.

Montagu, A. *Life before birth*. New York: New American Library, 1964.

Montagu, A. *Touching: The human significance of the skin*. New York: Columbia University Press, 1971.

Moore, A. U. Studies on the formation of the mother-neonate bond in sheep and goats. Paper presented at the annual meeting of the American Psychological Association, 1960.

Moore, J. Mexican-Americans. *Gerontologist*, 1971, **11**(1), 30–35.

Moore, K., & Meltzoff, A. Neonate imitation: A test of existence and mechanism. Paper presented at the annual meeting of the Society for Research in Child Development, Denver, 1975.

Moore, M. The nature of aging. In M. Riley, et al.

(Eds.), *Aging and society*, Vol. I. New York: Russell Sage, 1968.

Morland, J. A comparison of race awareness in northern and southern children. *American Journal of Orthopsychiatry*, 1966, **36**, 22–31.

Morrison, J. R., & Stewart, M. A. The psychiatric status of the legal families of adopted hyperactive children. *Archives of General Psychiatry*, 1973, **28**, 888–891.

Moskowitz, B. A. The acquisition of language. *Scientific American*, 1978, **239**(5), 92–108.

Moss, F., & Halamandaris, V. *Too old, too sick, too bad*. Germantown, MD: Aspen Systems Corp., 1977.

Moss, H. A. Sex, age, and state as determinants of mother-infant interaction. *Merrill-Palmer Quarterly of Behavior and Development*, 1967, **13**(1), 19–36.

Moss, H. A. Early sex differences and mother-infant interaction. In R. C. Friedman, R. M. Richart, & R. L. VandeWeile (Eds.), *Sex differences in behavior*. New York: Wiley, 1974.

Moss, H. A., & Kagan, J. Maternal influences on early IQ score. *Psychological Reports*, 1958, **4**, 655–661.

Moss, H. A., Robson, K. S., & Pederson, F. Determinants of maternal stimulation of infants and consequences of treatment of later reactions to strangers. *Developmental Psychology*, 1969, **1**(3), 239–246.

Mothner, I. Teenage mothers USA. *RF Illustrated*, Rockefeller Foundation, May 1977, **3**(3), unpaged.

Mowrer, O. H. *Learning theory and the symbolic processes*. New York: Wiley, 1960.

Muller, E., & Luces, T. A developmental analysis of peer interaction among toddlers. In M. Lewis & L. Rosenblum (Eds.), *Friendship and peer relations*. New York: Wiley, 1975, pp. 223–258.

Mull, M. M. The tetracyclines. *American Journal of Diseases of Children*, 1966, **112**, 483–493.

Murchison, C., & Langer, S. Tiedemann's observations on the development of the mental facilities of children. *Journal of Genetic Psychology*, 1927, **34**, 205–230.

Murphy, C. M., & Bootzin, R. R. Active and passive participation in the contact desensitization of snake fear in children. *Behavior Therapy*, 1973, **4**, 203–211.

Murphy, D. P. The outcome of 625 pregnancies in women subjected to pelvic radium reontgen irradiation. *American Journal of Obstetrics and Gynecology*, 1929, **18**, 179–187.

Murphy, D. P. *Congenital malformation* (2d ed.). Philadelphia: University of Pennsylvania Press, 1947.

Mussen, P. H. Early sex-role development. In D. A. Goslin (Ed.), *Handbook of socialization theory and research*. Chicago: Rand McNally, 1969.

Mussen, P. H., Conger, J. J., & Kagen, J. *Child development and personality*. New York: Harper & Row, 1969.

Mussen, P., H., & Dister, L. Masculinity, identification and father-son relationships. *Journal of Abnormal and Social Psychology*, 1959, **59**, 350–356.

Mussen, P. H., & Eisenberg-Berg, N. *Roots of caring, sharing, and helping: The development of prosocial behavior in children*. San Francisco: Freeman, 1977.

Mussen, P. H., & Jones, M. C. Self-conceptions, motivations, and interpersonal attitudes of late- and early-maturing boys. *Child Development*, 1957, **28**, 243–256.

Muuss, R. E. Adolescent development and the secular trend. *Adolescent*, 1970, **5**, 267–284.

Muuss, R. E. Puberty rites in primitive and modern societies. *Adolescence*, 1970, **5**, 109–128.

Muuss, R. E. *Theories of adolescence* (3d ed.). New York: Random House, 1975.

N

Naeye, R. L., Blanc, W., & Paul, C. Effects of maternal nutrition on the human fetus. *Pediatrics*, 1973, **52**(4), 494–503.

Nagy, M. The child's theories concerning death. *Journal of Genetic Psychology*, 1948, **73**, 3–27.

National Clearinghouse for Smoking & Health. Patterns and prevalance of teenage cigarette smoking: 1968, 1970, and 1972. U.S. Department of Health, Education, and Welfare, Aug. 6, 1972.

National Council on Aging. *Fact book on aging: A profile of America's older population*. Washington, DC: NCOA, 1978.

National Council on the Aging. *Fact sheet: NCOA retirement planning program.* Washington, DC: NCOA, 1979.

National Foundation/March of Dimes. *Genetic counseling.* New York, 1973.

National Institute of Child Health and Human Development. Smoking in children and adolescents. *Pediatric Annals*, 1978, **7**(9), 130–131.

Neiswender, M., Birren, J., & Schaie, K. W. Age and the experience of love in adulthood. Paper presented at the annual meeting of the American Psychological Association, Chicago, 1975.

Nelson, N., Enkin, M., Saigal, S., Bennett, K., Milner, R., and Sackett, D. A randomized clinical trial of the Leboyer approach to childbirth. *New England Journal of Medicine*, 1980, **302**(12), 655–660.

Nelson, W., Vaughan, V., & McKay, R. J. *Textbook of pediatrics* (10th ed.). Phaldelphia: Saunders, 1975.

Nemy, E. Where disturbed parents find help. *The New York Times*, Mar. 15, 1972.

Neugarten, B. The awareness of middle age. In R. Owen (Ed.), *Middle age*. London: BBC, 1967.

Neugarten, B. Adult personality toward a psychology of the lifecycle. In B. Neugarten (Ed.), *Middle age and aging*. Chicago: University of Chicago, 1968.

Neugarten, B. The rise of the young-old. *The New York Times*, Jan. 18, 1975.

Neugarten, B. Personality and aging. In J. Birren & K. W. Schaie (Eds.), *Handbook of the psychology of aging*. Princeton, NJ: Van Nostrand, 1977, pp. 626–649.

Neugarten, B., Havighurst, R., & Tobin, S. Personality and patterns of aging. In B. Neugarten (Ed.), *Middle age and aging*. Chicago: University of Chicago Press, 1968.

Neugarten, B., & Moore, J. The changing age-status system. In B. Neugarten (Ed.), *Middle age and aging*. Chicago: University of Chicago Press, 1968, pp. 5–21.

Neugarten, B., Moore, J., & Lowe, J. Age norms, age constraints, and adult socialization. In B. Neugarten (Ed.), *Middle age and aging*. Chicago: University of Chicago Press, 1968.

Neugarten, B., & Weinstein, K. The changing American grandparent. *Journal of Marriage and the Family*, 1964, **26**, 199–205.

Neugarten, B., Wood, V., Kraines, R., & Loomis, B. Women's attitudes toward the menopause. *Vita Humana*, 1963, **6**, 140–151.

New York Times. Elderhostel: An intellectual summer tonic for both young and old. Aug. 13, 1976, p. B1.

New York Times. College women and self-esteem. Dec. 10, 1978, p. 85.

New York Times. Colleges drawing on retirees' experience. Apr. 22, 1979, p. 47.

New York Times. Survey shows campus drug use down slightly but still prevalent. May 14, 1979, p. D9.

Newman, H. H., Freeman, F. H., & Holzinger, K. J. *Twins: A study of heredity and environment.* Chicago: University of Chicago Press, 1937.

News CASE. Council for Advancement and Support of Education. June 1976.

Newsday. 1 million divorces in 1975. Jan. 22, 1976, p. 7A.

Newsday. The LI poll, directed by B. Bookbinder. May 29, 1977, pp. 4; 36.

Newton, N. *Maternal emotions.* New York: Paul B. Hoeber, Inc., Medical Book Department of Harper & Row, 1955.

Newton, N., & Newton, M. Psychologic aspects of lactation. *New England Journal of Medicine*, Nov. 30, 1967, **277**, 1179–1188.

NIH Consensus Development Conferences. Antenatal diagnosis. *Clinical Pediatrics*, 1979, **18**(7), 390–403.

Nobenini, M., & Neugarten, B. A follow-up study of adaptation in middle-aged women. Paper presented at the annual meeting of the Gerontological Society, Portland, 1975.

Nydegger, C. Middle age: Some early returns—a commentary. *International Journal of Aging and Human Development*, 1976, **7**(2), 137–141.

Nyquist, E. B., & Hawes, G. R. (Eds.). *Open education: A sourcebook for parents and teachers.* New York: Bantam, 1972.

O

O'Brien, P., Noller, K., Robboy, S., Barnes, A., Kaufman, R., Tilley, B., & Townsend, D. Vaginal epithelial changes in young women enrolled in the National Cooperative Diethylstilbestrol Adenosis (DESAD) Project. *Obstetrics and Gynecology*, 1979 **53**(3), 300–308.

O'Brien, T. Excretion of drugs in human milk. *American Journal of Hospital Pharmacology*, 1974, **31**, 844–854.

O'Connor, M. The nursery school environment. *Developmental Psychology*, 1975, **11**(5), 556–561.

Oelsner, L. More couples adopting victims of genetic defect. *The New York Times*, March 8, 1979, pp. A1; B14.

Offer, D. *The psychological world of the teenager: A study of normal adolescent boys*. New York: Basic Books, 1969.

Offer, D., & Offer, J. B. Normal adolescent males: The high school and college years. *Journal of the American College Health Association*, 1974, **22**, 209–215.

Offer, D., Ostrov, E., & Marohn, R. C. *The psychological world of the juvenile delinquent*. New York: Basic Books, 1972.

Olds, S. W. Menopause: Something to look forward to? *Today's Health*, May 1970, pp. 48 ff.

Olds, S. W. Why can't you stay in the hospital with your child? *McCall's*, May 1975.

Olds, S. W. Choosing your own relatives. *McCall's*, Oct. 1975, p. 38.

Olds, S. W. When homemakers lose their jobs. *McCall's*, Mar. 1976, p. 38.

Olds, S. W. A new look at the day-care controversy. *Redbook*, Nov. 1978, pp. 65–68.

Olds, S. W., & Eiger, M. S. *The complete book of breastfeeding*. New York: Bantam, 1973.

O'Leary, V., & Braun, J. Antecedents and correlates of professional careerism among women. Paper presented at the 82nd annual convention of the American Psychological Association, New Orleans, 1974.

Oppel, W. C., Harper, P. A., & Rider, R. V. The age of attaining bladder control. *Pediatrics*, 1968, **42**(4), 614–626.

Oppie, I., & Oppie, P. *The lore and language of the school child*. Oxford: Clarendon, 1959.

Orlofsky, J., Marcia, J., & Lesser, I. Ego identity status and the intimacy versus isolation crisis of young adulthood. *Journal of Personality and Social Psychology*, 1973, **27**(2), 211–219.

Ory, M. The decision to parent or not: Normative and structural components. *Journal of Marriage and the Family*, 1978, **40**(3), 531–539.

Ossofsky, J. A special analytical perspective by the National Council on Aging in *Retirement preparation: Growing corporate involvement*. New York: Ruder & Finn, 1979.

Oswald, P. F., & Peltzman, P. The cry of the human infant. *Scientific American*, 1974, **230**(3), 84–90.

Otto, H., & Healy, S. Adolescents' self-perception of personality strengths. *Journal of Human Relations*, 1966, **14**(3), 483–490.

Owens, W. A. Age and mental abilities: A second adult follow-up. *Journal of Educational Psychology*, 1966, **57**(6), 311–325.

P

Paige, K. Women learn to sing the menstrual blues. *Psychology Today*, 1973, **7**(4), 41–46.

Papalia, D. The status of several conservation abilities across the life-span. *Human Development*, 1972, **15**, 229–243.

Papalia, D., & Bielby, D. Cognitive functioning in middle and old age adults. A review of research on Piaget's theory. *Human Development*, 1974, **17**, 424–443.

Papalia, D., & Tennent, S. Vocational aspirations in preschoolers: A manifestation of early sex-role stereotyping. *Sex Roles*, 1975, **1**(2), 197–199.

Papalia-Finlay, D. The life concept in female college students: An exploratory analysis. *Journal of Youth and Adolescence*, 1978, **7**(2), 133–139.

Pape, K., Buncic, R., Ashby, S., & Fitzhardinge, P. The status at 2 years of low-birth-weight infants born in 1974 with birth-weights of less than 2,001 gm. *Journal of Pediatrics*, 1978, **92**(2), 253–260.

Papousek, H. A method of studying conditioned food reflexes in young children up to age six months. *Pavlovian Journal of Higher Nervous Activity*, 1959, **9**, 136–140.

Papousek, H. Conditioned motor alimentary reflexes in infants: 1. Experimental conditioned sucking reflex. *Ceskoslovenska Pediatrie*, 1960a, **15**, 861–872.

Papousek, H. Conditioned motor alimentary reflexes in infants: II. A new experimental method of investigation. *Ceskoslovenska Pediatrie*, 1960b, **15**, 981–988.

Papousek, H. Conditioned head rotation relexes in infants in the first months of life. *Acta Paediatrica*, 1961, **50**, 565–576.

Parlee, M. The premenstrual syndrome. *Psychological Bulletin*, 1973, **80**(4), 454–465.

Parlee, M. The rhythms in men's lives. *Psychology Today*, 1978, **11**(11), 82 ff.

Parten, M. Social play among preschool children. *Journal of Abnormal and Social Psychology*, 1932, **27**, 243–269.

Pascoe, E. J. New alternatives to old-age homes. *McCall's*, July 1976, p. 49.

Patten, B. *Human embryology*. New York: McGraw-Hill, 1968.

Patterson, G. R., Littman, R. A., & Bricker, W. Assertive behavior in children: A step toward a theory of aggression. *Monographs of the Society for Research in Child Development*, 1967, **32**(5, Serial No. 113).

Pattison, E. M. The experience of dying. In E. M. Pattison (Ed.), *The experience of dying*. Englewood Cliffs, NJ: Prentice-Hall/Spectrum, 1977.

Pauker, J. D. Fathers of children conceived out of wedlock: Prepregnancy, high school, psychological test results. *Developmental Psychology*, 1971, **4**(2), 215–218.

Pavlov, I. P. *Conditioned reflexes*. New York: Liveright, 1927.

Peck, R. Psychological development in the second half of life. In B. Neugarten (Ed.), *Middle age and aging*. Chicago: University of Chicago Press, 1968.

Pedersen, F., & Robson, K. Father participation in infancy. *American Journal of Orthopsychiatry*, 1969, **39**, 466–472.

Pedersen, F. A., Rubenstein, J., & Yarrow, L. J. Father absence in infancy. Paper presented at the meeting of the Society for Research in Child Development, Philadelphia, Mar. 29–Apr. 1, 1973.

Peel, E. A. *The psychological basis of education* (2d ed.). Edinburgh and London: Oliver and Boyd, 1967.

Perlman, R. Antisocial behavior of the minor in the United States. *Federal Probation*, 1964, **28**(4), 23–27.

Perry, T., Hechtman, P., & Chow, J. Diagnosis of Tay-Sachs disease on blood obtained at fetoscopy. *Lancet,* May 5, 1979, pp. 972–973.

Perry, W. G. *Forms of intellectual and ethical development in the college years*. New York: Holt, 1970.

Peterson, D. *The crisis of retirement finance: The views of older Americans*. Ann Arbor, MI: University of Michigan/Wayne State University, Insitute of Gerontology, no date.

Petri, E. Untersuchungen zur erbedingtheit der menarche. *Z. Morph. Anthr.*, 1934, **33**, 43–48.

Pettigrew, T. F. Negro American intelligence. In T. F. Pettigrew (Ed.), *Profile of the Negro American*. Princeton, NJ: Van Nostrand, 1964, pp. 100–135.

Pfeiffer, E. Sexual behavior in old age. In E. Busse & E. Pfeiffer (Eds.), *Behavior and adaptation in late life*. Boston: Little, Brown, 1969.

Phoenix, C., Goy, R., Gerall, A., & Young, W. C. Organizing action of prenatally administered testosterone propionate on the tissues mediating mating behavior in the female guinea pig. *Endocrinology*, 1959, **65**, 369–383.

Piaget, J. *Judgment and reasoning in the child*. New York: Harcourt Brace, 1926.

Piaget, J. *Play, dreams, and imitation* (C. Gattegno & F. M. Hodgson, Trans.) New York: Norton, 1951.

Piaget, J. *The child's conception of number*. London: Routledge & Kegan Paul, 1952.

Piaget, J. *The origins of intelligence in children*. New York: International Universities Press, 1952.

Piaget, J. *The child's construction of reality*. London: Routledge & Kegan Paul, 1955.

Piaget, J. *The moral judgment of the child*. New York: Macmillan, 1955.

Piaget, J. Comments on Vygotsky's critical remarks concerning *The language and thought of the child,* and *Judgment and reasoning in the child*. Attachment to L. S. Vygotsky, *Thought and language*. Cambridge, MA: M.I.T., 1962.

Piaget, J. Intellectual evolution from adolescence to adulthood. *Human Development*, 1972, **15**, 1–12.

Piaget, J., & Inhelder, B. *La Genèse des structures logiques élémentaires: Classifications et sériations*. Neuchâtel: Delachaux et Niestlé, 1959.

Piaget, J., & Inhelder, B. *The psychology of the child*. New York: Basic Books, 1969.

Pilpel, H. F., Zuckerman, R. J., & Ogg, E. *Abortion: Public issue, private decision*. New York: Public Affairs Committee, Inc., 1975.

Pineo, P. Disenchantment in the later years of marriage. *Marriage and Family Living*, 1961, **23**, 3–11.

Pines, M. Why some three-year-olds get A's—and some get C's. *The New York Times Magazine*, July 6, 1969.

Pines, M. Head Head Start. *The New York Times Magazine*, Oct. 26, 1975, p. 14.

Pines, M. St-st-st-st-st-st stuttering. *The New York Times Magazine*, Feb. 13, 1977, pp. 261 ff.

Pisacano, J., Lichter, H., Ritter, J., & Siegal, A. An attempt at prevention of obesity in infancy. *Pediatrics*, 1978, **61**(3), 360–364.

Plemons, J., Willis, S., & Baltes, P. Modifiability of fluid intelligence in aging: A short-term longitudinal training approach. *Journal of Gerontology*, 1978, **33**(2), 224–231.

Pogrebin, L. C. Sexism rampant. *The New York Times*, Mar. 19, 1976, p. 33.

Pollitt, E., Eichler, A., & Chan, C. Psychosocial development and behavior of mother of failure to thrive children. *American Journal of Orthopsychiatry*, 1975, **45**(4), 527–537.

Pomeroy, G. *Girls & sex*. New York: Dell, 1969.

Porter, S. The dying with dignity movement accelerates. *New York Daily News*, Oct. 15, 1979, p. 39.

Powell, G. F., Brasel, J. A., & Beizzard, R. M. Emotional deprivation and growth retardation simulating idiopathic hypopituitarism. *New England Journal of Medicine*, 1967, **276**, 1271–1278.

Powers, E., & Bultena, G. Sex differences in intimate friendships of old age. *Journal of Marriage and the Family*, 1976, **38**(4), 739–747.

Pratt, K. C., Nelson, A. K., & Sun, K. H. *The behavior of the newborn infant*. Columbus, OH: Ohio State University Press, 1930.

Prechil, H. F. R., & Beintema, D. J. *The neurological examination of the full-term newborn infant: Clinics in developmental medicine*, no. 12. London: Heinemann, 1964.

Prentice, N., & Fathman, R. Joking riddles: A developmental index of children's humor. *Proceedings of the 80th Annual Convention of the American Psychological Association,* 1972, **80**(7), 119–120.

President's Commission on Law Enforcement and Administration of Justice. The challenge of crime in a free society. Washington, DC: U.S. Government Printing Office, 1967.

Price-Bonham, S., & Skeen, P. A comparison of black and white fathers with implications for parent education. *The Family Coordinator,* 1979, **28**(1), 53–59.

Pulaski, M. A. S. *Understanding Piaget: An introduction to children's cognitive development.* New York: Harper & Row, 1971.

Q

Quinn, R. P., & Staines, G. L. *The 1977 quality of employment survey*. Ann Arbor, MI: Institute for Social Research, University of Michigan, 1978.

Quinn, R., Staines, G., & McCullough, M. *Job satisfaction: Is there a trend?* U.S. Department of Labor, Manpower Research Monograph No. 30. Washington, DC, 1974.

R

Rabban, M. Sex role identification in young children in two diverse social groups. *Genetic Psychology Monographs*, 1950, **42**, 81–158.

Rabushka, A., & Jacobs, B. Are old folks really poor? Herewith a look at some common views. *The New York Times*, Feb. 15, 1980, p. A29.

Rachal, J. V., Williams, J. R., Brehm, M. L., Cavanaugh, B., Moore, R. P., & Eckerman, W. C. *A national study of adolescent drinking behavior, attitudes, and correlates*. Research Triangle Institute Project No. 23U-891, Research Triangle Park, NC, 1975.

Radin, N. Maternal warmth, achievement motivation, and cognitive functioning in lower-class preschool children. *Child Development*, 1971, **42**, 1560–1565.

Radin, N. Father-child interaction and the intellectual functioning of four-year-old boys. *Developmental Psychology*, 1972, **6**(2), 353–361.

Radin, N. L., & Epstein, A. Observed paternal behavior and the intellectual functioning of preschool boys and girls. Paper presented at the annual meeting of the Society for Research in Child Development, Denver, 1975.

Rapoport, R., & Rapoport, R. The dual-career family: A variant pattern and social change. In A.

Skolnick & J. Skolnick (Eds.), *Intimacy, family and society*. Boston: Little, Brown, 1974.

Raths, L. E., Harmin, M., & Simon, S. B. *Values and teaching*. Columbus, OH: Merrill, 1966.

Read, M. S., Habicht, J-P., Lechtig, A., & Klein, R. E. Maternal malnutrition, birth weight, and child development. Paper presented before the International Symposium on Nutrition, Growth and Development, May 21–25, 1973, Valencia, Spain.

Rebelsky, F., & Hanks, C. Fathers' verbal interaction with infants in the first three months of life. *Child Development*, 1972, **42**, 63–68.

Rebenkoff, M. Study shows teen years are easiest for childbirth. *The New York Times*, Apr. 24, 1979, p. C5.

Rees, J., & Botwinick, J. Detection and decision factors in auditory behavior of the elderly. *Journal of Gerontology*, 1971, **26**, 133–136.

Rees, W., & Lutkins, S. Mortality of bereavement. *British Medical Journal*, 1967, **4**, 13–16.

Reese, H. Relationships between self-acceptance and sociometric choices. *Journal of Abnormal and Social Psychology*, 1961, **62**, 472–474.

Reese, H. W., & Lipsitt, L. P. *Experimental Child Psychology*. New York: Academic, 1970.

Reich, W. Ethical issues related to research involving elderly subjects. *Gerontologiest*, 1978, **18**(4), 326–337.

Reichard, S., Levson, F., & Peterson, P. *Aging and personality: A study of 87 older men*. New York: Wiley, 1962.

Reimanis, G., & Green, R. Imminence of death and intellectual decrement in the aging. *Developmental Psychology*, 1971, **5**(2), 270–272.

Reinhold, R. The early years are crucial. *The New York Times*, Oct. 21, 1973.

Reinhold, R. Trend to living alone brings economic and social change. *The New York Times*, Mar. 20, 1977, pp. 1; 59.

Reinhold, R. Census finds unmarried couples have doubled from 1970 to 1978. *The New York Times*, June 27, 1979, p. A1.

Renkonnen, K., & Makela, L. Factors affecting human sex ratio. *Nature*, 1962, **194**, 308–309.

Renwick, P., Lawler, E., & Psychology Today. What you really want from your job. *Psychology Today*, 1978, **11**(12), 53–65 ff.

Resnick, R. Piaget, preschoolers, and pediatrics. Paper presented at the meeting of the Jean Piaget Society, Philadelphia, 1975.

Rheingold, H. L. The modification of social responsiveness in institutionalized babies. *Monographs of the Society for Research in Child Development*, 1956, **21** (Whole No. 63), 5–48.

Rheingold, H. L., Gewirtz, J. L., & Ross, H. W. Social conditioning of vocalization in the infant. *Journal of Comparative and Physiological Psychology*, 1959, **52**, 68–73.

Rheingold, H. L., & Eckerman, C. O. The infant separates himself from his mother. *Science*, 1970, **168**, 78–83.

Rice, B. Brave new world of intelligence testing. *Psychology Today*, 1979, **13**(4), 27–41.

Richards, M. P. M. Social interaction in the first week of human life. *Psychiatria, Neurologia, Neurochirugia*, 1971, **74**, 35–42.

Richmond, J. Physician's advisory: Health effects of the pregnancy use of diethylstilbestrol. Oct. 4, 1978, U.S. Department of Health, Education, and Welfare.

Riegel, K. F., & Riegel, R. M. Development, drop, and death. *Developmental Psychology*, 1972, **6**(2), 306–319.

Rieser, J., Yonas, A., & Wilkner, K. Radial localization of odors by human newborns. *Child Development*, 1976, **47**, 856–859.

Riley, M., Foner, A., et al. *Aging and society. Vol. I: An inventory of research findings*. New York: Russel Sage, 1968.

Ringler, N., Kennell, J., Jarvella, R., Navojosky, B., & Klaus, M. Mother-to-child speech at two years—Effects of early postnatal contact. *Journal of Pediatrics*, 1975, **86**(1), 141–144.

Roberts, B. The middle years: Suggestions and solutions. In A. Entine (Ed.), *Americans in middle years: Career options and educational opportunities*. Los Angeles: USC, 1974.

Roberts, J., & Sutton-Smith, B. Child training and game involvement. *Ethnology*, 1962, **1**, 166–185.

Robinson, M. J., et al. In S. M. Gellis (Ed.), *The yearbook of pediatrics*. Chicago: Yearbook Medical Publishers, 1974.

Robinson, R. Low-birth-weight babies. In R. Robinson (Ed.), *Problems of the newborn*. London: British Medical Association, 1972.

Robson, K. S. The role of eye-to-eye contact in maternal-infant attachment. *Journal of Child Psychology and Psychiatry*, 1967, **8**, 13–25.

Robson, K. S., & Moss, H. A. Patterns and determinants of maternal attachment. *Journal of Pediatrics*, 1970, **77**(6), 976–85.

Roche, A. F., & Davila, G. H. Late adolescent growth in stature. *Pediatrics*, 1972. **50**(6), 874–880.

Rockstein, M., & Sussman, M. *Biology of aging.* Belmont, CA: Wadsworth, 1979.

Rodeck, C., & Campbell, S. Early prenatal diagnosis of neural-tube defects by ultasound-guided fetoscopy. *Lancet*, May 27, 1978, pp. 1128–1129.

Rodgers, R. R., Bronfenbrenner, U., & Devereux, E. C., Jr. Standards of social behavior among children in four cultures. *International Journal of Psychology*, 1968, **111**(1), 31–41.

Rodstein, M. Accidents among the aged: Incidence, causes and prevention. *Journal of Chronic Diseases*, 1964, **17**, 515–526.

Roe, K. Infants' mother-stranger discrimination at 3 months as a predictor of cognitive development at 3 and 5 years. *Developmental Psychology*, 1978, **14**(2), 191–192.

Roesler, T., & Deisher, R. Youthful male homosexuality. *Journal of the American Medical Association*, 1972, **219**(8), 1018–1023.

Rogers, C. R. *Client-centered therapy.* Boston: Houghton Mifflin, 1951.

Rogers, S. E. Elders share homes, lives aided by match-up service. *Moneysworth*, March 1980, p. 6.

Rohn, R., Sarles, R., Kenny, T., Reynolds, B., & Heald, F. Adolescents who attempt suicide. *Journal of Pediatrics,* 1977, **90**(4), 636–638.

Rollin, B. Motherhood: Who needs it? In A. Skolnick & J. Skolnick (Eds.), *Family in transition.* Boston: Little, Brown, 1971. (Reprinted from *Look*, Sept. 22, 1970, pp. 15–17.)

Rollins, B., & Galligan, R. The developing child and marital satisfaction of parents. In R. Lerner & G. Spanier (Eds.), *Child influences on marital and family interaction: A life-span perspective.* New York: Academic, 1978, pp. 71–105.

Roopnarine, J., & Johnson, J. Cross-age and same-age social play in a laboratory and a naturalistic setting. Unpublished manuscript, University of Wisconsin, 1978.

Rose, R. M., Gordon, T. P., & Bernstein, I. S. Plasma testosterone levels in the male rhesus: Influences of sexual and social stimuli. *Science*, 1972, **178**(4061), 643–645.

Rosen, B. C. Social class and the child's perception of the parent. *Child Development*, 1964, **35**, 1147–1153.

Rosen, C. The effects of sociodramatic play on problem-solving behavior among culturally disadvantaged preschool children. *Child Development*, 1975, **45**, 920–927.

Rosen, R., & Lightner, E. Phenotypic malformations associated with maternal trimethadione therapy. *Journal of Pediatrics*, 1978, **92**(2), 240–243.

Rosenblith, J. E. The modified Graham behavior test for neonates, test-retest reliability, normative data and hypotheses for future work. *Biologia Neonatorum*, 1961, **3**, 174–192.

Rosenthal, R., & Jacobson, L. *Pygmalion in the classroom.* New York: Holt, 1968.

Rosenthal, R., & Jacobson, L. Teacher expectations for the disadvantaged. *Scientific American*, 1968, **218**(4), 19–23.

Rosow, I. *Social integration of the aged.* New York: Free Press, 1967.

Rosow, I. Old people: Their friends and neighbors. *American Behavioral Scientist*, 1970, **14**, 59–69.

Ross, J. B., & McLaughlin, M. (Eds.). *A portable medieval reader.* New York: Viking, 1949.

Rothbart, M. K., & Maccoby, E. E. Parents' differential reactions to sons and daughters. *Journal of Personality and Social Psychology*, 1966, **4**(3), 237–243.

Rothman, K. J., Fyler, D. C., Goldblatt, A., & Kreidberg, M. B. Exogenous hormones and other drug exposures of children with congenital heart disease. *American Journal of Epidemiology*, 1979, **109**(4), 433–439.

Rothman, K. J., & Louik, C. Oral contraceptives and birth defects. *New England Journal of Medicine*, 1978, **299**(10), 522–524.

Rowe, N., Garn, S., Clark, D., & Guire, K. The effect of age, sex, race, and economic status on dental caries experience of the permanent dentition. *Pediatrics,* 1976, **57**(4), 457–461.

Rubin, A. Birth injuries. *Hospital Medicine*, Sept. 1977, pp. 114–130.

Rubin, J., Provenzano, P., & Luria, Z. The eye of the beholder: Parents view of sex of newborns. *American Journal of Orthopsychiatry*, 1974, **44**(4), 512–519.

Rubin, K. H., Attewell, P., Tierney, M., & Tumolo, P. Development of spatial egocentrism and conservation across the life span. *Developmental Psychology*, 1973, **9**(3), 432.

Rubin, K. H., Maioni, T., & Hornung, M. Free play behaviors in middle-class and lower-class preschoolers: Parten and Piaget revisited. *Child Development*, 1976, **47**, 414–419.

Rubin, K. H. Decentration skills in institutionalized and noninstitutionalized elderly. Paper presented at the annual meeting of the American Psychological Association, 1973.

Rubin, L. *Women of a certain age.* New York: Harper & Row, 1979.

Rubin, K., & Balow, B. Measure of infant development and socioeconomic status as predictors of later intelligence and school achievement. *Developmental Psychology*, 1979, **15**(2), 225–227.

Rubin, V., & Comitas, L. *Effects of chronic smoking of Cannabis in Jamaica.* Unpublished report by the Research Institute for the Study of Man to the Center for Studies of Narcotic and Drug Abuse, National Institute of Mental Health, Contract No. HSM-42-70-97.

Rugh, R., & Shettles, L. B., with Einhorn, R. N. *From conception to birth: The drama of life's beginnings.* New York: Harper & Row, 1971.

Runyan, W. Perceived determinants of highs and lows in life satisfaction. *Developmental Psychology*, 1979, **15**(3), 331–333.

Russell, A. Progesterone is harmful to male fetus. *Pediatrics News*, January 1969.

Russell, C. Transition to parenthood: Problems and gratifications. *Journal of Marriage and the Family*, 1974, **36**(2), 294–302.

Russell, L. B., & Russell, W. L. Radiation hazards to the embryo and fetus. *Radiology*, 1952, **58**(3), 369–376.

Rutter, M. Parent-child separation: Psychological effects on the children. *Journal of Child Psychology and Psychiatry,* 1971, **12**, 233–260.

Rutter, M. Separation experiences: A new look at an old topic. *Pediatrics*, 1979, **95**(1), 147–154.

Ryerson, A. J. Medical advice on child rearing, 1550–1900. *Harvard Educational Review*, 1961, **31**, 302–323.

S

Sagi, A., & Hoffman, M. Empathic distress in newborns. *Developmental Psychology*, 1976, **12**(2), 175–176.

Salapatek, P., & Kessen, W. Visual scanning of triangles by the human newborn. *Journal of Experimental Child Psychology*, 1966, **3**, 155–167.

Salber, E., & Feinlib, M. Breast-feeding in Boston. *Pediatrics*, 1966, **37**, 299–303.

Salthouse, T. Speed and age: Multiple rates of age decline. *Experimental Aging Research*, 1976, **2**, 349–359.

Saltz, E., Dixon, D., & Johnson, J. Training disadvantaged preschoolers on various fantasy activities. Effects on cognitive functioning and impulse control. *Child Development*, 1977, **48**, 367–380.

Saltz, E., Soller, E., & Sigel, I. The development of natural language concepts. *Child Development*, 1972, **43**, 1191–1202.

Saltz, R. Effects of part-time mothering on I.Q. and S.Q. of young institutionalized children. *Child Development*, 1973, **44**, 166–170.

Sameroff, A. The components of sucking in the human newborn. *Journal of Experimental Child Psychology*, 1968, **6**, 607–623.

Sameroff, A. Can conditioned responses be established in the newborn infant? *Developmental Psychology*, 1971, **5**, 1–12.

Sanders, S., Laurendeau, M., & Bergeron, J. Aging and the concept of space: The conservation of surfaces. *Journal of Gerontology*, 1966, **21**, 281–285.

Sandoz Pharmaceuticals. *Enquiry into aging: Answers to the questionnaire on retirement.* East Hanover, NJ: Sandoz, November 1976.

Sapir, E. *Language.* New York: Harcourt, 1921.

Saul, S. *Aging: An album of people growing old.* New York: Wiley, 1974.

Saunders, C. Dying they live: St. Christopher's Hospice. In H. Feifel (Ed.), *New meanings of death.* New York: McGraw-Hill, 1977, pp. 153–179.

Scales, P. Males and morals: Teenage contraceptive behavior amid the double standard. *The Family Coordinator*, 1977, **26**(3), 211–222.

Scarf, M. Husbands in crisis. *McCall's*, June 1972, pp. 76–77, 120–125.

Scarf, M. The more sorrowful sex. *Psychology Today*, 1979, **12**(1), 45 ff.

Scarr, S., & Weinberg, R. IQ performance of black children adopted by white families. *American Psychologist*, 1976, **31**(10), 726–739.

Scarr, S., & Weinberg, R. The influence of "family background" on intellectural attainment. *American Sociological Review*, 1978, **43**(5), 674–692.

Scarr-Salapatek, S., & Williams, M. L. The effects of early stimulation on low-birth-weight infants. *Child Development*, 1973, **44**, 94–101.

Schachter, S. *The psychology of affiliation*. Stanford, CA: Stanford University Press, 1959.

Schaefer, C. E. Imaginary companions and creative adolescents. *Developmental Psychology*. 1969, **1**, 747–749.

Schaeffer, D. L. *Sex differences in personality: Readings*. Belmont, CA: Brooks/Cole, 1971.

Schaffer, H. R., & Emerson, P. The development of social attachments in infancy. *Monographs of the Society for Research in Child Development*, 1964, **29**(3).

Schaie, K. W. Translations in gerontology—from lab to life: Intellectual functioning. *American Psychologist*, 1974, **29**(11), 802–807.

Schaie, K. W. External validity in the assessment of intellectual development in adulthood. Paper presented at the annual meeting of the American Psychological Association, Washington, DC, 1976.

Schaie, K. W., & Gribben, K. Adult development and aging. In M. Rosenzweig & L. Porter (Eds.), *Annual review of psychology*, Vol. 26. Palo Alto, CA: Annual Reviews, 1975.

Schaie, K. W., & Labouvie-Vief, G. Generational versus ontogenetic components of change in adult cognitive behavior: A fourteen-year cross-sequential study. *Developmental Psychology*, 1974, **10**(3), 305–320.

Schaie, K. W., & Strother, C. A cross-sequential study of age changes in cognitive behavior. *Psychological Bulletin*, 1968, **70**, 671–680.

Schanche, D. What really happens emotionally and physically when a man reaches 40? *Today's Health*, Mar. 1973, pp. 40–43; 60.

Schifrin, B., & Dame, Y. Fetal heart rate patterns: Predicting of Apgar scores. *Journal of the American Medical Association*, 1972, **219**(10), 1322–1355.

Schmeck, H. M., Jr. Trend in growth of children lags. *The New York Times*, June 10, 1976, p. 13.

Schmidt, R. S. Child abuse programming—What a community can do. Paper presented at the annual meeting of the American Home Economics Association, San Antonio, Texas, 1975.

Schmitt, M. H. Superiority of breast-feeding: Fact or fancy? *American Journal of Nursing*, July 1970, pp. 1488–1493.

Schneideman, E. The college student and death. In H. Feifel (Ed.), *New meanings of death*. New York: McGraw-Hill, 1977.

Schulz, R. *The psychology of death, dying, and bereavement*. Reading, MA: Addison-Wesley, 1978.

Schwartz, A. N. Self esteem: Linchpin of quality of life for the aged. Paper presented at the annual meeting of the American Association for the Advancement of Science, New York, Jan. 27–30, 1975.

Schwartz, M. A. Career strategies of the never married. Paper presented at the 71st annual meeting of the American Sociological Association, New York, Sept. 3, 1976.

Schwarz, J. C., Strickland, R., & Krolick, G. Infant day care: Behavioral effects at preschool age. *Developmental Psychology*, 1974, **10**(4), 502–506.

Scott, J. P. *Animal behavior*. Chicago: University of Chicago Press, 1958.

Scrimshaw, N. S. Malnutrition, learning and behavior. *American Journal of Clinical Nutrition*, 1967, **20**, 493–502.

Scully, C. Down's syndrome. *British Journal of Hospital Medicine*, July 1973, pp. 89–98.

Sears, P. Life satisfaction of Terman's gifted women: 1927–72: Comparison with the gifted men and with normative samples. Paper presented at the 5th annual conference, School of Education, University of Wisconsin, Madison, 1977.

Sears, R. R. Relation of early socialization experiences to self-concepts and gender role in middle childhood. *Child Development*, 1970, **41**, 267–289.

Sears, R. R., Maccoby, E. E., & Levin, H. *Patterns of child rearing*. New York: Harper & Row, 1957.

Seelbach, W. C., & Hansen, C. J. Satisfaction with

family relations among the elderly. *Family Relations*, 1980, **29**(1), 91–96.

Seiden, R. Campus tragedy: A study of student suicide. *Journal of Abnormal Psychology*, 1966, **71**, 389–399.

Seligman, M. Giving up on life. *Psychology Today*, 1974, **7**(12), 81–85.

Selman, R. L. A structural analysis of the ability to take another's social perspective: Stages in the development of role-taking ability. Paper presented at the meeting of the Society for Research in Child Development, 1973.

Selman, R. L., & Selman, A. P. Children's ideas about friendship: A new theory. *Psychology Today*, 1979, **13**(4), 71–80; 114.

Serbin, L. A., O'Leary, K. D., Kent, R. N., & Tonick, I. J. A comparison of teacher response to the preacademic and problem behavior of boys and girls. *Child Development*, 1973, **44**, 796–804.

Serunian, S., & Broman, S. Relationship of Apgar scores and Bayley mental and motor scores. *Child Development*, 1975, **46**, 696–700.

Shah, F., Zelnik, M., & Kantner, J. Unprotected intercourse among unwed teenagers. *Family Planning Perspectives*, 1975, **7**(1), 39–44.

Shainess, N. A re-evaluation of some aspects of femininity through a study of menstruation: A preliminary report. *Comprehensive Psychiatry*, 1961, **2**, 20–26.

Shaman, D. In old age, someone to share the hearth. *The New York Times*, Aug. 5, 1979, p. LI17.

Shanas, E. Family help patterns and social class in three countries. In B. Neugarten (Ed.), *Middle age and aging*. Chicago: University of Chicago Press, 1968. [Reprinted from *Journal of Marriage and the Family*, 1967, **29**(2).]

Shanas, E., Townsend, P., Wedderburn, D., Friis, H., Milhoj, P., & Stehouwer, J. (Eds.). *Old people in 3 industrial societies*. New York: Atherton, 1968.

Shannon, D., Kelly, D., & O'Connell, K. Abnormal regulation of ventilation in infants at risk for SIDS. *New England Journal of Medicine*, 1977, **297**, 747–750.

Shapiro, A. K., Shapiro, E., & Wayne, H. L. The symptomatology and diagnosis of Gilles de la Tourette's syndrome. *Journal of the American Academy of Child Psychiatry*, 1973, **12**(4), 702–723.

Shapiro, H. D. Do not go gently . . . *The New York Times Magazine*, Feb. 6, 1977, pp. 36 ff.

Sheehan, N., & Papalia, D. The nature of the life concept across the life-span. Paper presented at the Gerontological Society Meeting, Portland, OR, 1974.

Sheehy, G. Passages. New York: Dutton, 1976.

Sheehy, G. The happiness report. *Redbook*, 1979, **153**(3), 29; 64 ff.

Sheikh, A. A., & Beglis, J. F. Development of the self-concept on Negro and white children. Paper presented at the biennial meeting of the Society for Research in Child Development, Philadelphia, Mar. 29–Apr. 1, 1973.

Shenker, I. How do parents talk to their children? Two psychologists listened in . . . *The New York Times*, Oct. 10, 1971.

Sherman, A., Goldrath, M., Berlin, A., Vakhariya, V., Banoom, F., Michaels, W., Goodman, P., & Brown, S. Cervical-vaginal adenosis after in utero exposure to synthetic estrogen. *Obstetrics and Gynecology*, 1974, **44**(4), 531–545.

Sherman, M. The differentiation of emotional responses in infants. I. Judgments of emotional responses from motion picture views and from actual observations. *Journal of Comparative Psychology*, 1927, **7**, 265–284.

Sherrod, K., Vietze, P., & Friedman, S. *Infancy*. Belmont, CA: Brooks/Cole, 1978.

Shigaki, I., & Zorn, V. Leadership program in the care of infants and toddlers: A training model. National Institutes of Health, 1978.

Shinn, M. Father absence and children's cognitive development. *Psychological Reports*, 1978, **85**(2), 295–324.

Shipman, G. The psychodynamics of sex education. *Family Coordinator*, 1968, **17**, 3–12.

Shirley, M. M. The first two years: A study of twenty-five babies. Vol. II, *Intellectual development*. Minneapolis: University of Minnesota, 1933.

Shneidman, E. The college student and death. In H. Feifel (Ed.), *New meanings of death*. New York: McGraw-Hill, 1977, pp. 67–88.

Shore, M. F. Drugs can be dangerous during pregnancy and lactation. *Canadian Pharmaceutical Journal*, Dec. 1970, **103**(12), 358–367.

Sigman, M., Kopp, C., Parmelee, A., & Jeffrey, W. Visual attention and neurological organization in infants. *Child Development*, 1973, **44**, 461–466.

Silberman, C. E. *Crisis in the classroom: The remaking of American education.* New York: Random House, 1970.

Siman, M. Application for a new model of peer group influence to naturally existing adolescent friendship groups. *Child Development*, 1977, **48**, 270–274.

Simner, M. L. Newborn's response to the cry of another infant. *Developmental Psychology*, 1971, **5**(1), 136–150.

Simon, S. P., & Olds, S. W. *Helping your child learn right from wrong: A guide to values clarification.* New York: Simon & Schuster, 1976.

Singer, J. E., Westphal, M., & Niswander, K. R. Sex differences in the incidence of neonatal abnormalities and abnormal performance in early childhood. *Child Development*, 1968, **39**, 103–222.

Skard, A. G. Maternal deprivation: The research and its implications. *Journal of Marriage and the Family*, 1965, **27**, 333–343.

Skeels, H. M. Adult status of children with contrasting early life experiences. *Monographs of the Society for Research in Child Development,* 1966, **31**(Whole No. 3), 1–65.

Skeels, H. M., & Dye, H. B. A study of the effects of differential stimulation on mentally retarded children. *Program of the American Association of Mental Deficiency*, 1939, **44**, 114–136.

Skinner, B. F. *The behavior of organisms: An experimental approach.* New York: Appleton-Century, 1938.

Skolnick, A. *The intimate environment.* Boston: Little, Brown, 1973.

Skolnick, A., & Skolnick, J. (Eds.), *Family in transition.* Boston: Little, Brown, 1971.

Skolnick, A., & Skolnick, J. (Eds.). *Intimacy, family, and society.* Boston: Little, Brown, 1974.

Slade, M. "Empty nest": Empty myth. *Psychology Today*, 1978, **12**(7), 44–45.

Slater, E., with Shields, J. Psychotic and neurotic illnesses in twins. *Medical Research Council Special Report.* Series No. 278. London: HMSO, 1953.

Slater, P. Parental role differentiation. In R. L. Closer (Ed.), *The family: Its structure and functions.* New York: St. Martin's, 1958.

Smith, C. G. Age incidences of atrophy of olfactory nerves in man. *Journal of Comparative Neurology*, 1942, **61**, 477–508.

Smith, D., Clarren, S., & Harvey, M. Hyperthermia as a possible teratogenic agent. *Journal of Pediatrics*, 1978, **92**(6), 878–883.

Smith, D. C., Prentice, R., Thompson, D. J., & Herrmann, W. L. Association of exogenous estrogen and endometrial carcinoma. *New England Journal of Medicine*, 1975, **293**(23), 1164–1167.

Smith, D. W., & Wilson, A. A. *The child with Down's syndrome (mongolism).* Philadelphia: Saunders, 1973.

Smith, G. H. Sociometric study of best-liked and least-liked children. *Elementary School Journal*, 1950, **51**, 77–85.

Smith, M. B. Conflicting values affecting behavioral research with children. *Children*, 1967, **4**(5), 377–382.

Smith, P., & Green, M. Aggressive behavior in English nurseries and play groups: Sex differences and response of adults. *Child Development*, 1975, **46**, 211–214.

Smith, R. P. *"Where did you go?" "Out." "What did you do?" "Nothing."* New York: Pocket Books, 1959.

Smoking and intrauterine growth. *Lancet,* Mar. 10, 1979, pp. 536–537.

Soares, A. T., & Soares, L. M. Self-perceptions of culturally disadvantaged children. *American Educational Research Journal*, 1969, **6**, 31–45.

Soddy, K., & Kidson, M. *Men in middle life, cross-cultural studies in mental health.* Philadelphia: Lippincott, 1967.

Solkoff, N., Yaffe, & Weintraub, D. The effects of handling on the development of premature infants. Paper presented at the meeting of the Eastern Psychological Association Convention, Boston, 1967.

Solomon, T. History and demography of child abuse. *Pediatrics.* 1973, **51**(4), 773–776.

Solomons, H. The malleability of infant motor development. *Clinical Pediatrics*, 1978, **17**(11), 836–839.

Sontag, L., & Wallace, R. I. Preliminary report of the Fels fund: A study of fetal activity. *American Journal of Diseases of Children*, 1934, **48**, 1050–1057.

Sontag, L. W., & Wallace, R. I. The effect of

cigarette smoking during pregnancy upon the fetal heart rate. *American Journal of Obstetrics and Gynecology*, 1935, **29**, 3–8.

Sontag, L. W., & Wallace, R. I. Changes in the heart rate of the human fetal heart in response to vibratory stimuli. *American Journal of Diseases of Children*, 1936, **51**, 583–589.

Sontag, S. The double standard of aging. In *No longer young: The older woman in America*. Ann Arbor, MI: University of Michigan/Wayne State University, Institute of Gerontology, 1975.

Sorenson, R. C. *Adolescent sexuality in contemporary America*. New York: World, 1973.

Spearman, C. *The abilities of man*. New York: Macmillan, 1927.

Spiro, M. Is the family universal? *American Anthropologist*, 1954, **56**, 839–846.

Spiro, M. E. *Children of the kibbutz*. Cambridge, MA: Harvard University Press, 1958.

Spitz, R. A. Hospitalism: An inquiry into the genesis of psychiatric conditioning in early childhood. In D. Fenschel, et al. (Eds.), *Psychoanalytic studies of the child*, Vol. I. New York: International Universities Press, 1945, pp. 53–74.

Spitz, R. A. Hospitalism: A follow-up report. In D. Fenschel, et al. (Eds.), *Psychoanalytic studies of the child*, Vol. 2. New York: International Universities Press, 1964, pp. 113–117.

Spock, B. *Baby and child care*. New York: Pocket Books, 1976.

Spreitzer, E., & Riley, L. Factors associated with singlehood. *Journal of Marriage and the Family*, 1974, **36**(3), 533–542.

Sroufe, L. A. Socioemotional development. In J. Osofsky (Ed.), *Handbook of infant development*, New York: Wiley, 1979.

Sroufe, L. A., & Wunsch, J. The development of laughter in the first year of life. *Child Development*, 1972, **43**, 1326–1344.

Stacey, M., Dearden, R., Pill, R., & Robinson, D. *Hospitals, children and their families: The report of a pilot study*. London; Routledge & Kegan Paul, Ltd., 1970.

Staffieri, J. R. A study of social stereotype of body image in children. *Journal of Personality and Social Psychology*, 1967, **7**, 101–104.

Stamps, L. Temporal conditioning of heart rate responses in newborn infants. *Developmental Psychology*, 1977, **13**(6), 624–629.

Starfield, B. Enuresis: Focus on a challenging problem in primary care. *Pediatrics*, 1978, **62**(6), 1036–1037.

Stechler, G., Bradford, S., & Levy, H. Attention in the newborn: Effect on motility and skin potential. *Science*, 1966, **151**, 1246–1248.

Steele, B. F., & Pollack, C. B. A psychiatric study of parents who abuse infants and small children. In R. E. Helfer & C. H. Kempe (Eds.), *The battered child*. Chicago: University of Chicago Press, 1968.

Stein, A. Imitation of resistance to temptation. *Child Development*, 1967, **38**, 157–169.

Stein, A., & Friedrich, L. Impact of television on children and youth. In E. M. Hetherington (Ed.), *Review of Child Development Research*, Vol. 5. Chicago: University of Chicago Press, 1975.

Stein, M. I., & Heinze, S. J. *Creativity and the individual*. New York: Free Press, 1960.

Stein, P. J. Being single: Bucking the cultural imperative. Paper presented at the 71st annual meeting of the American Sociological Association, Sept. 3, 1976.

Stein, Z., & Susser, M. Prenatal nutrition and mental competence. In J. Lloyd-Still (Ed.), *Malnutrition and intellectual development*. England: M.T.P. Press, Ltd., 1976.

Stein, Z., Susser, M., Saenger, G., & Marolla, F. Nutrition and mental performance. *Science*, 1972, **173**, 708–712.

Stendler, C. B., & Young, N. Impact of first grade entrance upon the socialization of the child: Changes after 8 months of school. *Child Development*, 1951, **22**(2), 113–122.

Stennett, N., Carter, L., & Montgomery, J. Older persons' perceptions of their marriages. *Journal of Marriage and the Family*, 1972, **34**, 665–670.

Stephens, W. *Reflections on marriage*. New York: Thomas Y. Crowell, 1968.

Sternglanz, S., & Lyberger-Ficek, S. An analysis of sex differences in academic interactions in the college classroom. Paper presented at the bienniel meeting of the Society for Research in Child Development, Denver, 1975.

Stevenson, M., & Lamb, M. Effects of infant sociability and the caretaking environment on infant cognitive performance. *Child Development*, 1979, **50**, 340–349.

Stewart A., & Reynolds, E. Improved prognosis

for infants of very low birth-weight. *Pediatrics,* 1974, **54**(6), 724–735.

Stewart, M. M., Pitts, F., Craig, A., & Dieruf, W. The hyperactive child syndrome. *American Journal of Orthopsychiatry,* 1966, **36**, 861–867.

Stewart, M. A., & Olds, S. W. *Raising a hyperactive child.* New York: Harper & Row, 1973.

Stock, M. B., & Smythe, P. M. Does undernutrition during infancy inhibit brain growth and subsequent intellectual development? *Archives of the Diseases of Children,* 1963, **38**, 546–552.

Stocker, J. *Early childhood education: Current trends in school policies and programs.* Arlington, VA: National School Public Relations Association, 1973.

Stockmal, H. F., Jr. Career Education Coordinator, Fairfield, CN, Public Schools. Personal communication, Mar. 9, 1976.

Stolz, H. E., & Stolz, L. M. Adolescence related to somatic variation. In N. B. Henry (Ed.), *Adolescence: 43d Yearbook of the National Committee for the Study of Education.* Chicago: University of Chicago Press, 1944, pp. 80–99.

Stone, L. J., Smith, H. T., & Murphy, L. B. *The competent infant: Research and commentary.* New York: Basic Books, 1973.

Storr, A. A new life in middle age. In R. Owen (Ed.), *Middle age.* London: BBC, 1967.

Strain, B., & Vietze, P. Early dialogues: The structure of reciprocal infant-mother vocalization. Paper presented at the annual meeting of the Society for Research in Child Development, Denver, 1975.

Straus, M. A. Sexual inequality, cultural norms, and wife-beating. *Victimology,* 1976. **1**(1), 54–70.

Strauss, M., Lessen-Firestone, J., Starr, R., & Ostrea, E. Behavior of narcotics-addicted newborns. *Child Development,* 1975, **46**, 887–893.

Streib, G., & Thompson, W. Adjustment in retirement. *Journal of Social Issues,* 1958, **14**(21), 1–63.

Streissguth, A., Herman, C., & Smith, D. Intelligence, behavior, and dysmorphogenesis in the fetal alcohol syndrome: A report on 20 patients. *Journal of Pediatrics,* 1978, **92**(3), 363–367.

Strong, E. K., Jr. *Change of interests with age.* Stanford, CA: Stanford, 1959.

Stubblefield, H. Contributions of continuing education. *Vocational Guidance Quarterly,* 1977, **25**(4), 351–355.

Stunkard, A., d'Aquili, E., Fox, S., & Filion, R. Influences of social class on obesity and thinness in children. *Journal of American Medical Association,* 1972, **221**, 579–584.

Sugar, M. Children of divorce. *Pediatrics,* 1970, **46**(4), 588–595.

Sullivan, W. Very old people in the Andes are found to be merely old. *The New York Times,* Mar. 17, 1978, p. A8.

Szinovacz, M. Female retirement: Effects on spousal roles and marital adjustment: A pilot study. Paper presented at the meeting of the Society for the Study of Social Problems, San Francisco, 1978.

T

Talbot, T. *The world of the child.* New York: Anchor, 1968.

Tank, G. Relation of diet to variation of dental caries. *Journal of the American Dental Association,* 1965, **70**, 394–403.

Tanner, J. M. The adolescent growth-spurt and developmental age. In G. A. Harrison, J. S. Werner, J. M. Tannert, & N. A. Barnicot (Eds.), *Human biology: An introduction to human evolution, variation, and growth.* Oxford: Clarendon Press, 1964, pp. 321–339.

Tanner, J. M. Earlier maturation in man. *Scientific American,* 1968, **218**, 21–27.

Tanner, J. M. Growing up. *Scientific American,* 1973, **229**(3), 35–43.

Tanner, J. M. *Fetus into man: Physical growth from conception to maturity.* Cambridge, MA: Harvard, 1978.

Targ, D. B. Toward a reassessment of women's experience at middle-age. *The Family Coordinator,* 1979, **28**(3), 377–382.

Taub, H., Goldstein, K., & Caputo, D. Indices of neonatal prematurity as discriminators of development in middle childhood. *Child Development* 1977, **48**(3), 797–805.

Tautermannova, M. Smiling in infants. *Child Development,* 1973, **44**, 701–704.

Tec, N. Some aspects of high school status and differential involvement with marijuana. *Adolescence,* 1972, **6**, 1–28.

Teltsch, K. Young terminal patients to get loving

hospice. *The New York Times*, Apr. 10, 1980, p. B14.

Terman, L. M.   In symposium: Intelligence and its measurement. *Journal of Educational Psychology*, 1921, **12**, 127–133.

Terman, L. M.   Psychological approaches to the study of genius. *Papers on Eugenics*, 1947, **4**, 3–20.

Terman, L. M., & Oden, M. H.   *Genetic studies of genius, V. The gifted group at mid-life*. Stanford, CA: Stanford, 1959.

Thomas, A., Chess, S., & Birch, H. G.   *Temperament and behavior disorders in children*. New York: New York University Press, 1968.

Thomas, A., Chess, S., Birch, H. G., Hertzig, M. E., & Korn, S.   *Behavioral individuality in early childhood*. New York: New York University Press, 1963.

Thomas, J. P.   Injuries and diseases of the oral region. In S. S. Gellis & B. V. Kagan (Eds.), *Current pediatric therapy*. Philadelphia: Saunders, 1976.

Thomas, L.   Mid-career changes: Self-selected or externally mandated? *Vocational Guidance Quarterly*, 1977, **25**(4), 320–328.

Thomas, R.   *Comparing theories of child development*. Belmont, CA: Wadsworth, 1979.

Thompson, G.   Work vs. leisure roles: An investigation of morale among employed and retired men. *Journal of Gerontology*, 1973, **281**, 339–344.

Thompson, W., Streib, G., & Kosa, J.   The effect of retirement on personal adjustment: A panel analysis. *Journal of Gerontology*, 1960, **15**, 165–169.

Thorndike, E. L.   *Man and his works*. Cambridge, MA: Harvard University Press, 1943.

Thurstone, L. L., & Thurstone, T. G.   Factorial studies of intelligence. *Psychometric Monographs*, 1941, **2**.

Tietze, C., & Lewit, S.   Legal abortion. *Scientific American*, 1977, **236**(1), 21–27.

Timmons, F.   Freshman withdrawal from college: A positive step toward identity formation? A follow-up study. *Journal of Youth and Adolescence*, 1978, **7**(2), 159–173.

Timras, P. S.   *Developmental physiology and aging*. New York: Macmillan, 1972.

Tolstoy, L.   The death of Ivan Ilych. In L. Tolstoy, *The death of Ivan Ilych and other stories*. New York: New American Library, 1960.

Tomlinson-Keasey, C.   Formal operations in females from eleven to fifty-six years of age. *Developmental Psychology*, 1972, **6**(2), 364.

Tomlinson-Keasey, C., & Keasey, C.   The mediating role of cognitive development in moral judgment. *Child Development*, 1974, **45**, 291–298.

Torgersen, A. M., & Kringlen, E.   Genetic aspects of temperamental differences in infants: A study of same-sexed twins. *Journal of the American Academy of Child Psychiatry*, 1978, **17**, 433.

Traisman, A. S., & Traisman, H. S.   Thumb and finger sucking: A study of 2650 infants and children. *Journal of Pediatrics*, 1958, **53**, 566.

Troll, L.   The family of later life: A decade review. *Journal of Marriage and the Family*, 1971, **33**(2), 263–290.

Troll, L.   *Early and middle adulthood*. Belmont, CA: Wadsworth, 1975.

Troll, L., Miller, S., & Atchley, R.   *Families in later life*. Belmont, CA: Wadsworth, 1979.

Troll, L., & Smith, J.   Attachment through the life span. *Human Development*, 1976, **3**, 156–171.

Tronick, E., Koslowski, B., & Brazelton, T. B.   Neonatal behavior among urban Zambians and Americans. Paper presented at the biennial meeting of the Society for Research in Child Development, Minneapolis, Apr. 4, 1971.

Trotter, R.   East side, West side: Growing up in Manhattan. *Science News*, 1976, **109**, 315–318.

Trowbridge, H., & Trowbridge, L.   Self-concept and socio-economic status. *Child Study Journal*, 1972, **2**(3), 123–139.

Tuddenham, R. D.   Studies in reputation: III. Correlates of popularity among elementary school children. *Journal of Educational Psychology*, 1951, **42**, 257–276.

Tulkin, S., & Kagan, J.   Mother-child interaction in the first year of life. *Child Development*, 1972, **43**, 31–41.

Turner, J., & Helms, D.   *Contemporary adulthood*. Philadelphia: Saunders, 1979.

U

U.S. Bureau of the Census.   *Census of the population: 1970 final report occupational characteristics*. Washington, DC: 1973.

U.S. Bureau of the Census.   *Estimates of marital status of the population*. Population Estimates and Projections, Series P-25, No. 607, August 1975.

U.S. Bureau of the Census. *Household and family characteristics*. Current Population Reports, Special Studies, Series P-20, No. 291, March, 1975.

U.S. Bureau of the Census. *A statistical portrait of women in the U.S.* Current Population Reports, Special Studies, Series P-23, No. 58. 1976.

U.S. Bureau of the Census. *Demographic aspects of aging and the older population in the United States.* Current Population Reports, Special Studies, Series P-23, No. 59, May 1976.

U.S. Bureau of the Census. *Household and family characteristics*. Current Population Reports, Special Studies, Series P-20, No. 326, March 1977.

U.S. Department of Health, Education, and Welfare. *Vital Statistics of the U.S.*, 1960 (Vol. 3: Marriage and Divorce). Washington, DC, Public Health Service, 1964.

U.S. Department of Health, Education, and Welfare. *Vital Statistics of the U.S.* Washington, DC, Public Health Service, 1967, 1969.

U.S. Department of Health, Education, and Welfare. Summary report and selected papers from a research conference on Epidemiology of Aging, June 11–13, 1972.

U.S. Department of Health, Education, and Welfare. *Facts on older Americans.* Washington, DC, 1973. DHEW Pub. No (OHD) 78-20006.

U.S. Department of Health, Education, and Welfare. *The health consequences of smoking.* Washington, DC, 1973.

U.S. Department of Health, Education, and Welfare. Births, marriages, divorces, and deaths for 1975. *Monthly Vital Statistics Report*, Mar. 4, 1976, **24**(12).

U.S. Department of Health, Education, and Welfare. *Health, United States, 1975.* DHEW Pub. No. (HRA) 76-1232. Rockville, MD: National Center for Health Statistics, 1976.

U.S. Department of Health, Education, and Welfare. *National child care consumer study.* Washington, DC: 1976.

U.S. Department of Health, Education, and Welfare. Final divorce statistics, 1976. *Monthly Vital Statistics Report*, Aug. 16, 1978, **27**(5). DHEW Pub. No. (PHS) 78-1120.

U.S. Department of Health, Education, and Welfare. *Alzheimer's disease.* Bethesda, MD: National Institute of Health, 1979 (NIH Publ. No. 79-1646)

U.S. Department of Health, Education, and Welfare. Births, marriages, divorces, and deaths for 1978. *Monthly Vital Statistics Report, March 15, 1979,* **27**(12).

U.S. Department of Labor, Employment Standards Administration, Women's Bureau. *20 facts on women workers*. Washington, DC, August 1979.

U.S. Department of Labor, Employment Standards Administration, Women's Bureau. *1975 handbook on women workers* (Bulletin 297). Washington, DC, 1975.

U.S. Department of Labor, Employment Standards Administration, Women's Bureau. *The earnings gap between women and men.* Washington, DC, 1979.

U.S. National Commission for the Protection of Human Subjects of Biomedical and Behavioral Research. *Report and recommendations on research involving children.* DHEW Pub. No. (05) 77-0004. U.S. Department of Health, Education, and Welfare, 1977.

U.S. News & World Report. The American family: Can it survive today's shocks? Oct. 27, 1975, pp. 30–46.

Utech, D. A. Modeling, praise, and logical explanations for influencing the objective and subjective moral judgments of boys and girls. Paper presented at the annual meeting of the Midwestern Psychological Association, Cleveland, 1972.

Uzgiris, I. C. Patterns of vocal and gestural imitation in infants. Paper presented at the annual meeting of the International Society for the Study of Behavioral Development, University of Nijmegen, Netherlands, July 4–8, 1971.

Uzgiris, I. C., & Hunt, J. *Assessment in infancy.* Urbana: University of Illinois, 1975.

Uzgiris, I. C. Patterns of cognitive development in infancy. Merrill-Palmer Institute Conference on Infant Development, Detroit, Feb. 9–12, 1972.

V

Vahanian, T. Interview with S. W. Olds, Jan. 23, 1980.

Vaillant, G., & McArthur, C. Natural history of male psychologic health. I. The adult life cycle from 18–50. *Seminars in Psychiatry*, 1972, **4**(4), 415–427.

Vandenberg, S. G. The nature and nurture of intelligence. Paper presented at conference on

Biology and Behavior, Rockefeller University, New York, 1966.

Vandenberg, S. G. Hereditary factors in normal personality traits (as measured by inventories) (1965). In J. Wortes (Ed.), *Recent advances in biological psychiatry* (Vol. 9). New York: Plenum, 1967, pp. 65–104.

Veevers, J. Voluntary childless wives 1973. In A. Skolnick & J. Skolnick (Eds.), *Intimacy, family and society*. Boston: Little, Brown, 1974.

Verbrugge, L. M. Marital status and health. *Journal of Marriage and the Family*, 1979, **41**(2), 267–285.

Vincent, C. E. *Unmarried mothers*. New York: Free Press, 1961.

Vinick, B. Remarriage in old age. *The Family Coordinator*, 1978, **27**(4), 359–363.

Vore, D. H. Prenatal nutrition and post-natal intellectual development. Paper presented at the annual meeting of the Society for Research in Child Development, Minneapolis, April 1971.

Voss, H., Wendling, A., & Elliott, D. Some types of high-school dropouts. *Journal of Education Research*, 1966, **59**, 363–368.

Vulliamy, D. G. *The newborn child*. Edinburgh: Churchill Livingstone, 1973.

Vygotsky, L. S. *Thought and language*. Cambridge, MA: M.I.T., 1962.

W

Waber, D. Sex differences in mental abilities, hemispheric lateralization and rate of physical growth at adolescence. *Developmental Psychology*, 1977, **13**(1), 29–38.

Wachs, T. Relation of infants' performance on Piaget's scales between 12 and 24 months and their Stanford Binet performance at 31 months. *Child Development*, 1975, **46**, 929–935.

Wagner, N. N. Adolescent sexual behavior. In E. D. Evans (Ed.), *Adolescents: Readings in behavior and development*. Hinsdale, IL: Dryden Press, 1970, pp. 44–51.

Wake, S., & Sporakowski, M. An intergenerational comparison of attitudes toward supporting aged parents. *Journal of Marriage and the Family*, 1972, **34**(1), 42–48.

Waldfogel, S., Coolidge, J., & Hahn, P. The development, meaning, and management of school phobia. *American Journal of Orthopsychiatry*, 1957, **27**, 754–780.

Waldrop, M., & Halverson, C. Intensive and extensive peer behavior: Longitudinal and cross-sectional analyes. *Child Development*, 1975, **46**, 19–26.

Walk, R. D., & Gibson, E. J. A comparative and analytical study of visual depth perception. *Psychology Monographs*, 1961, **75**(15), 170.

Walker, W. J. Changing United States life-style and declining vascular mortality: Cause or coincidence? *New England Journal of Medicine*, 1977, **297**(3), 163–165.

Wall Street Journal. Enrollments surge in nursery school, Census Bureau finds. Feb. 22, 1978.

Wallace, C. Granny bashing. *New York Daily News*, Feb. 7, 1980, p. 58.

Wallach, M., & Kogan, N. *Modes of thinking in young children: A study of the creativity-intelligence distinction*. New York: Holt, 1965.

Wallach, M. A., & Kogan, N. Creativity and intelligence in children's thinking. *Transaction*, 1967, **4**(1), 38–43.

Wallach, L., & Sprott, R. Inducing number conservation in children. *Child Development*, 1964, **35**, 1057–1071.

Walster, E., & Walster, G. W. *A new look at love*. Cambridge, MA: Addison-Wesley, 1978.

Warren, M. Classification of offenders as an aid to efficient management and effective treatment. *Journal of Criminal Law, Criminology, and Police Science*, 1971, **62**, 239–258.

Warren, N. African infant precocity. *Psychological Bulletin*, 1972, **78**(5), 353–367.

Watson, J. B. *Psychology from the standpoint of a behaviorist*. Philadelphia: Lippincott, 1919.

Watson, J. B., & Rayner, R. Conditioned emotional reactions. *Journal of Experimental Psychology*, 1920, **3**, 1–14.

Watson, J. S., & Ramey, C. T. Reactions to response-contingent stimulation in early infancy. *Merrill-Palmer Quarterly of Behavior and Development*, 1972, **18**(3), 219–227.

Watson, P. Coping with grief. *The Sunday Times* (London), July 13, 1975, p. 9.

Wechsler, D. *The measurement of adult intelligence*. Baltimore: Williams & Wilkins, 1944.

Wegman, M. E. Annual summary of vital statistics—1978. *Pediatrics*. 1979, **64**(6), 835–842.

Weiffenback, J., & Thach, B. Taste receptors in the tongue of the newborn human: Behavioral evidence. Paper presented at the biennial meeting of the Society for Research in Child Development, Denver, 1975.

Weil, W. Current controversies in Childhood obesity. *Journal of Pediatrics*, 1977, **91**(2), 175–187.

Weinstock, E., Tietze, C., Jaffe, F. S., & Dryfoos, J. G. Abortion need and services in the United States, 1974–1975. *Family Planning Perspectives*, 1976, **8**(2), 58–69.

Weisberg, P. Social and nonsocial conditioning of infant vocalizations. *Child Development*, 1963, **34**, 377–388.

Weiss, L., & Lowenthal, M. Life-course perspectives on friendship. In M. Lowenthal, M. Thurner, & D. Chiriboga (Eds.), *Four stages of life*. San Francisco: Jossey-Bass, 1975.

Weitzman, L., Eifler, D., Hokada, E., & Ross, C. Sex-role socialization in picture books for preschool children. *Journal of Sociology*, 1972, **77**(6), 1125–1150.

Wellman, H., & Lampers, J. The naturalistic communicative abilities of two-year-olds. *Child Development*, 1977, **48**, 1052–1057.

Wender, E. H. Statement summarizing research findings on the issue of the relationship between food-additive-free diets and hyperkinesis in children. Paper delivered before the 46th annual meeting of the American Academy of Pediatrics, New York, Nov. 8, 1977.

Werner, E., Bierman, L., French, F. E., Simonian, K., Connor, A., Smith, R., & Campbell, M. Reproductive and environmental casualties: A report on the 10-year follow-up of the children of the Kauai pregnancy study. *Pediatrics*, 1968, **42**(1), 112–127.

Werner, E. E., Honzik, M. P., & Smith, R. S. Prediction of intelligence and achievement at ten years from twenty month pediatric and psychological examinations. *Child Development*, 1968, **39**, 1063–1075.

Werner, H., & Kaplan, B. *Symbol formation*. New York: Wiley, 1963.

Westinghouse Learning Corporation. *The impact of Head Start*. Athens, OH: Ohio University Press, 1969.

What the new retirement law says. *Changing Times*, Oct. 1978, pp. 15–16.

Whipple, D. V. *Dynamics of development: Euthenic pediatrics*. New York: McGraw-Hill, 1966.

Whisnant, L., & Zegans, L. A study of attitudes toward menarche in white middle class American adolescent girls. *American Journal of Psychiatry*, 1975, **132**(8), 809–814.

White, B. L. Fundamental early environmental influences on the development of competence. Paper presented at Third Western Symposium on Learning: Cognitive Learning. Western Washington State College, Bellingham, WA, Oct. 21–22, 1971.

White House Conference on Aging. *Aging and blindness*. Special Concerns Session Report. Washington, DC, 1971.

White House Conference on Children. *Profiles of children*. Washington, DC, 1970.

White House Conference on Children. *Report to the President*. Washington, DC, 1970.

Whorf, B. L. *Language, thought and reality*. Cambridge, MA: M.I.T., 1956.

Will, J. A. Neonatal cuddliness and maternal handling patterns in the first month of life. Paper presented at annual meeting of the Eastern Psychological Association, Philadelphia, 1979.

Willerman, L. Activity level and hyperactivity in twins. *Child Development*, 1973, **44**, 288–293.

Williams, J., Best, D., & Boswell, D. The measurement of children's racial attitudes in the early school years. *Child Development*, 1975, **46**, 494–500.

Williams, J., Boswell, D., & Best, D. Evaluative responses of preschool children to the colors white and black. *Child Development*, 1975, **46**, 501–508.

Williams, T. H. *Huey Long*, New York: Knopf, 1969.

Williams, T. M. *Summary and implications of review of literature related to adolescent smoking*. Bethesda, MD: U.S. Department of Health, Education, and Welfare, 1971.

Williamson, N. Boys or girls? Parents' preferences and sex control. *Population Bulletin*, 1978, **33**(1). Washington, DC: Population Reference Bureau.

Willoughby, R. R. Family similarities in mental test abilities (with a note on the growth and decline of these abilities). *Genetic Psychology Monographs*, 1927, **2**, 235–237.

Wilson, A. B. Residential segregation of social classes and aspirations of high school boys. *American Sociological Review,* 1959, **24**, 836–845.

Wilson, D. The programmed theory of aging. In M. Rockstein, M. Sussman, & J. Chesky (Eds.), *Theoretical aspects of aging.* New York: Academic, 1974.

Wilson, G., McCreary, R., Kean, J., & Baxter, J. The development of preschool children of heroin-addicted mothers: A controlled study. *Pediatrics,* 1979, **63**(1), 135–141.

Wilson, J. F., Lahey, M. E., & Heiner, D. C. Studies on iron metabolism. V. Further observations on cow's milk–induced gastrointestinal bleeding in infants with iron-deficiency anemia. *Journal of Pediatrics,* 1974, **84**(3), 335–344.

Wilson, R. S. Twins: Early mental development. *Science,* 1972, **175**(4024), 915–917.

Wilson, R. S., & Harpring, E. B. Mental and motor development in infant twins. *Developmental Psychology,* 1972, **7**(3), 277–287.

Wilson, S. R., & Wise, L. *The American citizen: 11 years after high school.* Palo Alto, CA: American Institutes for Research, 1975.

Winick, M. Malnutrition and brain development. *Journal of Pediatrics,* 1969, **74**, 667.

Winick, M., Brasel, J., & Rosso, P. Head circumference and cellular growth of the brain in normal and Marasmic children. *Journal of Pediatrics,* 1969, **74**, 774–778.

Winnick, M., & Nobel, A. Cellulan response with increased feeding in neonatal rats. *Journal of Nutrition,* 1966, **91**, 179–182.

Wisconsin State Journal. Marijuana use shows increase. May 13, 1974, p. 10.

Wolfenstein, M. *Children's humor.* New York: Free Press, 1954.

Wolff, P. H. Observations on the early development of smiling. In B. M. Foss (Ed.), *Determinants of infant behavior, II.* London: Methuen, 1963.

Wolff, P. H. The causes, controls, and organizations of behavior in the newborn. *Psychological Issues, 1966,* **5**(1 Whole No. 17), 1–105.

Wolff, P. H. The natural history of crying and other vocalizations in early infancy. In B. Foss (Ed.), *Determinants of infant behavior, IV.* London: Methuen, 1969.

Wood, B. (Ed.). *A pediatric vade-mecum* (8th ed.). London: Lloyd-Luke, 1974.

Woods, M. B. The unsupervised child of the working mother. *Developmental Psychology,* 1972, **6**(1), 14–25.

Woodson, R. Hospice care in terminal illness. In C. Garfield (Ed.), *Psychosocial care of the dying patient.* New York: McGraw-Hill, 1978, pp. 365–385.

Woodworth, R., & Schlosberg, H. *Experimental psychology.* New York, Holt, 1954.

Wortis, R. The acceptance of the concept of the maternal role by behavioral scientists: Its effect on women. *American Journal of Orthopsychiatry,* 1971, **41**(5), 733–746.

Y

Yancy, W. S., Nader, P. R., & Burnham, K. Drug use and attitudes of high school students. *Pediatrics,* 1972, **50**(5), 739–745.

Yang, R., Zweig, A., Douthelt, T., & Federman, E. Successive relationships between maternal attitudes during pregnancy, analgesic medication during labor and delivery, and newborn behavior. *Developmental Psychology,* 1976, **12**(1), 6–14.

Yarrow, Y. Emotional development. *American Psychologist,* 1979, **34**(10), 951–957.

Yarrow, M. R. Altruism in children. Paper presented at program, *Advances in Child Development Research,* New York Academy of Sciences, New York, Oct. 31, 1978.

Yarrow, M., et al. Child-rearing in families of working and non-working mothers. *Sociometry,* 1962, **25**, 122–140.

Yarrow, M., Blank, P., Quinn, O., Youmans, E., & Stein, J. Social psychological characteristics of old age. In *Human aging.* Washington, DC: U.S. Government Printing Office, Pub. No. (HSM) 71-9051, 1975.

Young-Browne, G., Rosenfield, H., & Horowitz, F. Infant discrimination of facial expressions. *Child Development,* 1977, **48**, 555–562.

Youniss, J., & Volpe, J. A relational analysis of children's friendship. In W. Damon (Ed.), *Social cognition.* San Francisco: Jossey-Bass, 1978, pp. 1–22.

Yudkin, S., & Holme, A. *Working mothers and their children.* London: Sphere Books, 1969.

Zabin, L. S., Kantner, J. F., & Zelnik, M. The risk of adolescent pregnancy in the first months of intercourse. *Family Planning Perspectives*, 1979, **11**(4), 215–222.

Zacharias, L., Rand, W. M., & Wurtman, R. J. A prospective study of sexual development and growth in American girls: The statistics of menarche. *Obstetrical and Gynecological Survey*, 1976, **31**(4), 323–337.

Zacharias, L., & Wurtman, R. J. Age at menarche. *New England Journal of Medicine*, 1969, **260**, 868–875.

Zajonc, R. B. Family configuration and intelligence. *Science*, 1976, **197**(4236), 227–236.

Zarin-Ackerman, J., Lewis, M., & Driscoll, J. Language competence of two-year-old normal and high-risk infants. Paper presented at the biennial meeting of the Society for Research in Child Development, Denver, 1975.

Zarit, S. (Ed.). *Readings in aging and death: Contemporary perspectives*. New York: Harper & Row, 1977.

Zegiob, L., & Forehand, R. Maternal interactive behavior as a function of race, socio-economic status and sex of child. *Child Development*, 1975, **46**, 564–568.

Zelazo, P. R., Zelazo, N. A., & Kolb, S. Walking in the newborn. *Science*, 1972, **176**(4032), 314–315.

Zelnik, M., & Kantner, J. Survey of female adolescent sexual behavior. Conducted for Commission of Population, Washington, DC, 1972.

Zelnik, M., & Kantner, J. F. Sexual and contraceptive experience of young women in the United States. *Family Planning Perspectives*, 1977, **9**(2), 55–71.

Zelnik, M., & Kantner, J. F. Contraceptive patterns and premarital pregnancy among women aged 15–19 in 1976. *Family Planning Perspectives*, 1978, **10**(3), 135–142.

Zelnik, M., Kim, Y. J., & Kantner, J. F. Probabilities of intercourse and conception among U.S. teenage women, 1971 and 1976. *Family Planning Perspectives*, 1979, **11**(3), 177–183.

Zigler, E., Levine, J., & Gould, L. Cognitive challenge as a factor in children's humor appreciation. *Journal of Personality and Social Psychology*, 1967, **6**, 332–336.

Zusman, J. Some explanations of the changing appearance of psychotic patients: Antecedents of the social breakdown syndrome concept. *The Millbank Memorial Fund Quarterly*, 1966, **64**(1), p. 20.

Zylman, R. Age is more important than alcohol in the collison involvement of young and old drivers. *Journal of Traffic Safety Education*, 1972, **20**(1), 7–8; 34.

ACKNOWLEDGMENTS

I Know Why the Caged Bird Sings by Maya Angelou. © 1969, Random House, Inc.

Marie Bashkirtseff: The Journal of a Young Artist, translated by Mary J. Serrano. copyright © 1919 by E. P. Dutton; renewal by Mr. Harold G. Villard. Reprinted by permission of the publishers, E. P. Dutton.

Small Voices by Josef and Dorothy Berger. Reprinted by permission of Paul S. Eriksson, Publisher.

The View in Winter by Ronald Blythe; © 1979, Harcourt Brace Jovanovich, Inc.

Our Bodies, Ourselves, The Boston Women's Health Book Collective. © 1976 Simon & Schuster, Inc.

A Life of One's Own (Farrar Strauss & Giroux, 1962, and Cambridge University Press, 1979) © 1962, Gerald Brenan. Reprinted by permission of the author and C & J Wolfers Ltd.

Le Journal de Marguerite by Mathilde von Buddenbroch, translated from the German by L. Louis-Filliol. A. Cherbuliez et Comp., Geneva, 1875. Translation from the French by Molly Prescott for Heart Songs: The Intimate Diaries of Young Girls, by Laurel Holliday, 1978.

Through the Flower: My Struggle as a Woman Artist by Judy Chicago. Copyright © 1975 by Judy Chicago. Reprinted by permission of Doubleday & Company, Inc.

Reprinted by permission of the publisher from Dorothy H. Cohen and Virginia Stern's Observing and Recording the Behavior of Young Children, 2d Edition. New York: Teachers College Press, Copyright © 1978 by Teachers College, Columbia University. All rights reserved.

Making It from 40 to 50 by Joel Davitz and Lois Davitz. 1976, Random House, Inc.

The Diary of a Young Girl by Anne Frank. © 1967, Doubleday & Company, Inc.

Nigger by Dick Gregory. © 1964, E. P. Dutton.

Kathie's Diary: Leaves from an Old, Old Diary by Kathie Gray, pseudonym, edited by Margaret W. Eggleston. copyright 1926 by George H. Doran Co.

Diary in Duo by Flora and Benoite Groult, translated from the French by Humphrey Hare, copyright 1965 by Les Editions Denoel, Paris.

Kotto by Lafcadio Hearn, Macmillan, New York, 1902.

These Rich Years: A Journal of Retirement, Copyright © 1969, Jean Hersey and Robert Hersey. Reprinted by permission of McIntosh and Otis, Inc.

Reprinted by permission of Dodd, Mead & Company, Inc. from The Diary of Alice James, edited by Leon Edel. Copyright © 1964 by Leon Edel. Originally published in 1934 as Alice James, Her Brothers, Her Journal, edited by Anna R. Burr.

Jeannette Rankin: First Lady of Congress by Hannah Josephson, copyright © 1974 by Hannah Josephson, reprinted by permission of the publisher, The Bobbs-Merrill Company, Inc.

Excerpt from It Takes a Long Time to Become Young by Garson Kanin. Copyright © 1978 by T. F. T. Corporation. Reprinted by Permission of Doubleday & Company, Inc.

Listen to Us! © 1978 by Dorriet Kavanaugh. Reprinted by permission of the Workman Publishing Co., Inc., New York.

Excerpt from Times to Remember by Rose Fitzgerald Kennedy. Copyright © 1974 by The Joseph P. Kennedy, Jr. Foundation. Reprinted by permission of Doubleday & Company, Inc.

Arrow in the Blue By Arthur Koestler. (New York: Macmillan Publishing Co., Inc.) © Arthur Koestler 1952, 1969. Reprinted by A.D. Peters & Co. Ltd., London.

The Diaries and Letters of Käthe Kollwitz, Chicago, 1955. Originally published as Käthe Kollwitz: Ich Wirke in Dieser Zeit, Gebrüder Mann Verlag, Berlin, 1952.

Revelations: Diaries of Woman by Mary Jane Moffat and Charlotte Painter, editors. Vintage Books, Random House, Inc., 1975.

"Middle Age Needn't Be Like Dark Ages," © 1973/80 by The New York Times Company. Reprinted by permission.

Toni Martinazzi, quoted in "5,000 on Coast Hail Cross-Country Hikers." © 1980 by The New York Times Company. Reprinted by permission.

Memoirs of Richard Nixon by Richard M. Nixon. Published by Grosset & Dunlap, Inc., 1978.

The Book of Maggie Owen, copyright 1941 by The Bobbs-Merrill Company, Inc. Reprinted by permission of the publishers.

Excerpts from Maybe I'll Pitch Forever by Satchel Paige as told to David Lipman. Copyright © 1962 by David Lipman. Copyright © 1961 by Curtis Publishing Company. Reprinted by permission of Doubleday & Company, Inc.

The Diary of Nelly Ptaschkina, edited by M. Jacques Povolotsky. Jonathan Cape Ltd., London, 1923.

"Choosing a Dream: Italians in Hell's Kitchen" by Mario Puzo in **The Immigrant Experience** by Thomas Wheeler, 1971, The Dial Press.

The Autobiography of Bertrand Russell, 1872– 1914. © 1967 by George Allen & Unwin, Ltd.

The Autobiography of Bertrand Russell, 1944– 1969. Reprinted by permission of Simon & Schuster and George Allen & Unwin, Ltd.

Joshua, First Born by Frances Karlen Santamaria. Copyright © 1970 by Frances Karlen Santamaria. Reprinted by permission of The Dial Press.

Nobody Speaks for Me! Self-Portraits of American Working Class Women by Nancy Seifer, Simon & Schuster, 1976.

ACKNOWLEDGMENTS

651

Bubbles: A Self-Portrait by Beverly Sills. Copyright © 1976 by Beverly Sills, reprinted by permission of the publisher, The Bobbs-Merrill Company, Inc.

Changing by Liv Ullman. Alfred A. Knopf, 1978.

The Autobiography of William Allen White (Copyright 1946 by Macmillan Publishing Co., Inc., renewed 1974 by Macmillan Publishing Co., Inc. and W. L. White.)

INDEX